Prevention in
Health Psychology

Primary Prevention of Psychopathology
George W. Albee and Justin M. Joffe, *General Editors*

Prevention in Health Psychology

James C. Rosen and
Laura J. Solomon, editors

Published for the Vermont Conference on
the Primary Prevention of Psychopathology
by University Press of New England
Hanover and London, 1985

University Press of New England

Brandeis University

Brown University

Clark University

University of Connecticut

Dartmouth College

University of New Hampshire

University of Rhode Island

Tufts University

University of Vermont

Printed in the United States of America

LIBRARY OF CONGRESS CATALOGING IN PUBLICATION DATA

Vermont Conference on the Primary Prevention of
   Psychopathology (8th : 1983 : University of
   Vermont)
   Prevention in health psychology.

   (Primary prevention of psychopathology ; 8)
   Outgrowth of the 8th Vermont Conference on the Primary
Prevention of Psychopathology, held in 1983 at the
University of Vermont.
   1. Medicine and psychology—Congresses.   2. Health
behavior—Congresses.   3. Medicine, Preventive—
Congresses.   4. Adjustment (Psychology)—Congresses.
5. Mental illness—Prevention—Congresses.   1. Rosen,
James C., 1949-   .   11. Solomon, Laura J.
111. University of Vermont.   IV. Title.   V. Series:
Vermont Conference on the Primary Prevention of
Psychopathology. Primary prevention of psychopathology ;
8. [DNLM: 1. Adaptation, Psychological—congresses.
2. Attitude to Health—congresses.   3. Mental
Disorders—prevention & control—congresses.
4. Psychopathology—congresses.
w3 PR945CK v.8 / WM 100 V527 1983p]
RC454.V46   1977 vol. 8   616.89'05 s   84-40594
[R726.5]   [610'.1'9]
ISBN 0-87451-320-0

Contents

Preface

This volume on prevention in health psychology is the eighth book in the only series of publications exclusively focused on the prevention of psychopathology and promotion of mental and physical well-being. Its roots can be traced back to 1975 when George Albee organized the first Vermont Conference on the Primary Prevention of Psychopathology. The purpose of that conference and the seven subsequent Vermont Conferences has been to stimulate research and interventions directed toward promoting mental and physical well-being through prevention rather than through treatment of existing problems. These conferences have dealt with basic issues in the prevention of psychopathology, promoting social competence and coping in children and in adults, facilitating infant development, prevention through political action and social change, and promoting positive sexuality. Each conference has resulted in a published volume. The contributors to this volume participated in the workshop on "Preventing Health Risk Behaviors and Promoting Coping with Illness," hosted by the Vermont Conference and held on the campus of the University of Vermont in the summer of 1983.

The present topic encompasses the two ends of the health care continuum: prevention and modification of early risk factors for disease and development of coping strategies necessary for psychological adaptation to chronic illness. Both ends of the health care continuum require a prevention perspective. The value of preventive activities in the first case is obvious, since reduction in health risk behaviors can lead to a reduction in illness onset. However, prevention activities are also necessary at the other end of the continuum with respect to avoiding the psychopathological reactions that may follow chronic illness.

The topic of the eighth Vermont Conference was selected with three considerations in mind. First, most of the major causes of premature death and morbidity in the United States have behavioral antecedents. For example, smoking is a significant independent risk factor for cardiovascular disease and several forms of cancer; abusive drinking patterns contribute to enormous numbers of accidents, homicides, and cases of cirrhosis of the liver each year. Because these risk factors are behaviorally based, psychologists and other behavioral scientists may have much to offer in the prevention of physical illness.

Second, over the past decade we have seen a dramatic and continuing escalation in medical care costs. Although it is true that there have been major advances in medicine to improve treatment outcome, many of these advances are costly procedures performed within the hospital setting when the disease process is quite advanced. As long as the number of new cases of major diseases remains high, the high costs in dollars and in human suffering will continue. Prevention activities offer the greatest hope for a decline in incidence rates and a concomitant improvement in the general health of our population. We have seen much evidence of the success of this strategy in the field of public health. For example, we have observed the virtual elimination of smallpox and polio through vaccinations and have witnessed a reduction in dental caries following the fluoridation of water. Large-scale, preventive programs are vitally needed to reduce the onset of cardiovascular disease, cancer, and the other major causes of premature death in this country. Such activities suggest possible solutions to the problem of rising health care costs.

Finally, the focus on physical health at the Vermont Conference was inspired by increasing evidence of the relationship between ways of coping with illness and psychological functioning. Serious physical illness, especially illness involving painful and disabling conditions, is a major life stress for most individuals. Considering that such illness and disability burdens the individual with threats to self-esteem and to normal functioning in social, familial, and vocational spheres, it is not surprising that psychopathology is a common outcome in illness situations. It is within the "preventionists'" realm to consider strategies to assist chronically ill individuals to adjust to the stress of physical disease. With that in mind, we chose to address during this conference on primary prevention both the prevention of physical illness and the prevention of psychopathology as a consequence of illness.

From a public health perspective, primary prevention refers to the reduction of new cases of a disease and the promotion of health. Primary prevention activities are directed to individuals or groups of individuals who currently do not have evidence of the disease of interest. Thus prevention initiatives are designed to prevent illness onset in healthy persons. Within this context, both the prevention and the modification of health risk behaviors such as smoking, sedentary lifestyle, coronary-prone behavior pattern, and alcohol abuse may constitute primary prevention activities. Smoking cessation programs for nondiseased adults and smoking prevention programs for young children are both examples of primary prevention efforts. Both forms of primary prevention will be addressed in the chapters included in Part I, where the focus is on the reduction of health risk behaviors associated with physical illness.

In contrast to the first part of this book, which deals with the behavioral antecedents of disease, the second part concerns the behavioral consequences of physical illness. The purpose of primary prevention activities in mental health is to lower the incidence of psychological disorder and to promote mental health. In health psychology, primary prevention would involve the application of mental health interventions with physically ill individuals or their families prior to the onset of psychological disorder which might otherwise occur as a result of illness induced stress. Examples of interventions to prevent psychopathology in medical populations include psychological preparation for stressful medical procedures, the use of social support networks to facilitate coping with illness, and communication skills training in health care providers. These approaches differ from other interventions by health psychologists such as psychotherapy, which are designed to minimize or overcome established psychopathology.

As for all of our conferences and publications, the present work resulted from the efforts of a small group of people in the Department of Psychology of the University of Vermont. We are especially grateful to George Albee and Justin Joffe, who as members of the Vermont Conference planning committee and as general editors of the series on Primary Prevention of Psychopathology generously assisted us during all phases of this project. We also benefitted from the conference coordination talents of Barbara York, who each year has facilitated an educational and pleasurable experience for the conference attendees. In addition to the Vermont Conference, several other organizations provided financial support to this project. We wish to thank Stephen Goldston, director of the Office of Prevention at the National Institute of Mental Health, who facilitated a contract to fund the original meeting of the contributors to this volume. Additional contributions came from Perrier, Transamerica Occidental Life Insurance Company, and UpJohn Company.

J. C. R.
L. J. S.

Preventing Health Risk Behaviors

Introductory Notes

Part I of this volume focuses on the prevention and modification of specific behaviors and behavior patterns causally linked to illness. Five of the chapters in this section (Evans, Nathan, Striegel-Moore and Rodin, Haskell, and Chesney et al.) discuss a single health risk factor; however, this organizational format does not imply that prevention activities need be independently pursued. Nor does our selection of certain health risk behaviors reflect a belief that these are all of the risk factors worth discussing in a volume such as this. The identified behaviors (e.g., smoking, alcohol abuse, dietary excesses, sedentary lifestyle, and coronary-prone behavior pattern) represent widely practiced personal habits that contribute in substantial ways to disease incidence. However, the prevention and modification of these behavioral excesses involves far more than individual behavior change. Successful modification requires careful consideration of the individual, social, economic, and environmental contingencies that encourage and maintain the behaviors. Four of the chapters in this section (Mechanic, Stunkard et al., Leventhal et al., and Warner and Murt) specifically address the complex, interacting influences that shape and perpetuate health risk behaviors. Several of these authors present strategies designed to promote large-scale behavior change.

This section begins with an overview chapter by David Mechanic, University Professor and Dean of the College of Arts and Sciences at Rutgers University. Drawing on epidemiological studies, Mechanic describes the relationship between disease and several social variables including education, marital status, religious participation, social integration, employment status, and stress. He suggests that these broad-based variables predict health behavior to a greater degree than do more specific factors such as an underlying trait of responsibility for health. Mechanic notes that health behavior is the product of overall living pattern which is influenced by social values, psychological well-being, and the degree to which one is integrated into a dominant cultural mode. Possible factors mediating the experience of psychological distress are also explored. Mechanic proposes that introceptiveness, or the tendency to attend to internal sensations, is predictive of distress and common physical symptoms. However, he concludes that the most powerful way to promote positive health behavior is to weave desirable patterns with the culture of natural support groups.

The second chapter is by Richard Evans, professor of psychology and director of the Social Psychology/Behavioral Medicine Research and Graduate Training Group at the University of Houston. Evans discusses several general issues relevant to community prevention activities for cardiovascular risk factors as a backdrop for his smoking prevention program. By outlining such considerations as the relative role of fear arousal messages in promoting health behavior change, Evans develops a clear rationale for a social learning model for the prevention of smoking. The model depicts the social and intrapersonal influences that interact to determine adolescent decision making regarding smoking. Combining a social learning perspective with principles from the communication-persuasion literature, Evans and his colleagues developed a series of films designed to help young adolescents resist social influences to smoke. This smoking inoculation intervention was delivered to adolescents in the schools in a 10-week pilot study with favorable results. Evans presents these findings and suggests the need for long-term follow-up of such programs.

Chapter 3 addresses the prevention of alcoholism. The author, Peter Nathan, is professor of psychology and director of the Alcohol Behavior Research Lab at Rutgers University. In his paper, Nathan presents an overview of the alcohol prevention programs designed to influence the host (individuals at risk for alcoholism), the agent (availability of alcohol), and the environment (drinking context). He notes that prevention of alcoholism has been a low priority as measured by funding allocations. Even in industry where a favorable cost-benefit ratio should provide an impetus for alcohol prevention activities, such activities are not often part of employee assistance programs. Nathan reports that prevention efforts directed to high alcohol risk populations (e.g., women, youth, minorities, and the elderly) have not been successful in reducing drinking rates. Furthermore, even though drunk driving and fetal alcohol syndrome are recognized public health problems, prevention activities have not yet substantially impacted these areas.

In chapter 4, Ruth Striegel-Moore and Judith Rodin, both in the Department of Psychology at Yale University, discuss the long-term factors impacting weight regulation and specifically contributing to obesity. These etiological variables are presented from a developmental perspective and include: genetic input, prenatal influences, feeding practices during infancy, childhood learning, adolescent learning, and physical activity. The authors note that much of the obesity research with human infants has examined the role of overfeeding and dietary content as they contribute to overweight. Contrary to popular assumptions, Striegel-Moore and Rodin point out that overweight parents do not differ in their infant feeding behavior from normal weight parents; however, they suggest that breast-feeding and the delayed presentation of solid foods may help prevent obesity in high-risk infants. Throughout the chapter the authors identify prevention activities for the onset of obesity, and they highlight specific research questions requiring further investigation. Because of the enormous emphasis placed on weight by our society, the authors stress the value of sensible, relatively easy modifications in eating habits and caution against excessive prevention recommendations that might further fuel overconcern about weight.

The fifth chapter is authored by William Haskell, an exercise physiologist at the Stanford University School of Medicine. Haskell is co-director of the Stanford Cardiac Rehabilitation Program and is actively involved with the Stanford Heart Disease Prevention Project. In his paper Haskell reviews the current findings on the health benefits of physical activity in terms of lower risk of coronary heart disease, normalization of carbohydrate metabolism, maintenance of optimal body composition, retention of bone mineral with age, and improved psychological status. In considering the type and quantity of exercise needed to induce benefits, he describes a dose-related effect with the most beneficial impact occurring when sedentary people begin light physical activity (e.g., walking, gardening). Large muscle, dynamic exercise performed at moderate intensity contributes to improved health status, and dose-related exercise effects have been found in regard to several psychological variables including generalized hostility and depression. Issues of adherence are discussed, and factors contributing to adherence problems and solutions are highlighted.

Margaret Chesney is a senior health psychologist at SRI International. She and her colleagues discuss the characteristics of coronary-prone behavior pattern in their chapter entitled "Modification of Type A Behavior." Particular emphasis is placed on time-urgency, joyless striving, and hostility as characteristics most associated with coronary heart disease. Chesney et al. note that primary prevention studies find that behavioral interventions result in a reduction in self-report of Type A behavior, but little change in the behavior itself. Secondary prevention studies now underway, however, reveal reduced rates of recurrent myocardial infarctions among heart attack patients who receive behavioral interventions. The authors provide several suggestions for the modification of Type A behavior. These suggestions involve changing one or more of three interacting factors: environmental demands, the person's responses to the environmental demands, and physiological concomitants of Type A behavior.

In an unusually descriptive paper, Albert Stunkard and his colleagues in the Department of Psychiatry at the University of Pennsylvania document the process involved in developing and implementing the County Health Improvement Program of Pennsylvania (CHIP). Now in its third year of operation, CHIP is a large-scale, community-based program designed to reduce cardiovascular risk factors in a cost-effective manner in order to decrease mortality and morbidity due to cardiovascular disease. In their description of the program, Stunkard et al. highlight the five channels through which the health promotion activities were directed. These channels include: mass media, work sites, the health sector, schools, and voluntary community organizations. For each channel, the authors present objectives and specific activities designed to stimulate health behavior change. Of particular interest is the success of CHIP's work site weight loss contest, where several companies competed against each other to promote weight loss among overweight employees. Preliminary data on weight loss and dropout rates are presented. Stunkard et al. give us an opportunity to examine the process of community intervention, and they conclude with an example of the way in which the multichannel approach elicits changes in the community to support changes in the health behavior of individuals.

Howard Leventhal and his colleagues in the Department of Psychology at the University of Wisconsin at Madison present a life-span perspective on health behavior. They begin their chapter with a historical overview of prevention in medicine. They note that prevention activities are not new; however, the challenge lies in the development of an experimental science for prevention rather than in the creation and application of new technologies. The authors pose three basic questions regarding health and risk behaviors which must be addressed if we are to reduce disease and disability by altering lifestyle. First, are lifestyle behaviors homogeneous or heterogeneous? Second, what are the psychological mechanisms underlying the development and regulation of health and risk behaviors? Third, does age change health and illness behavior? Data from recent studies are presented to shed light on these questions. Results indicate there are only weak relationships among health behaviors. In response to the second question, Leventhal et al. describe four mechanisms for controlling health and risk behaviors (i.e., social control, affective-stress control, symptom-based control, and conceptual control), and they note that one cannot link any specific health behavior with any one mechanism. Finally, the authors present data to suggest that health and risk behaviors and beliefs change with age. Leventhal et al. argue that interventions must take into account the developmental history of health and risk behavior to be effective.

In the final chapter of this section, Kenneth Warner, a health economist, and his associates in the Department of Health Planning and Administration at the University of Michigan discuss the impact of economic incentives on health behavior. Warner et al. present a matrix of four types of economic incentives and two places of application: inside and outside the employment setting. In the work place, monetary incentives for positive health behavior are just emerging; preliminary evidence supports the idea that economic incentives can promote favorable changes in health behavior. Insurance incentives include reduced premiums for lower risk ratings (there are no empirical studies to demonstrate effects on behavior) and variable co-payments for medical utilization (utilization decreases as a function of increased co-payment; preventive medical services are more often used with lower co-payments). Warner et al. point out that income tax deductions for medical expenses encourage utilization; however, the absence of the tax deductibility of certain health-related costs (e.g., smoking cessation and weight reduction programs) make them less appealing. Thus, income tax policy has little effect on positive health behavior. In contrast, excise taxes do affect consumption patterns, particularly in the case of cigarette consumption. Therefore, economic disincentives to consume certain substances may be an avenue for future prevention work.

I
Health and Behavior
Perspectives on Risk Prevention

David Mechanic

It is commonly recognized that the vast resources our nation invests in health care come too late in most instances to do more than ameliorate the course of disease and disability. Much energy and money are spent on halfway technologies that save and extend lives but involve large economic, social, and psychological costs for the community, the patient, and the family. Prevention is, of course, a better strategy in every sense, but if it is to be more than an empty slogan, it must be built on a strong infrastructure of basic research in the biological and behavioral sciences that directs intervention in meaningful ways.

Those working in the curative health arena not uncommonly express impatience with the advocates of prevention. In their view, there is not much we know how to prevent beyond current efforts. In most circumstances involving death and disability—as in the case of heart disease, cancer, and mental disorder—basic scientific knowledge of etiology is inadequate and interventions remain problematic. Where identifiable risk factors can be controlled, the barriers in doing so often relate to the difficulty of altering cultural patterns and individual behavior, and on resolving conflicts with important social, economic, and political agendas. While there is much we can still do in smoking and hypertension control, immunization, prenatal and child care efforts, and other selected areas where interventions can make a difference, the barriers typically are not in our knowledge but rather in our politics. It is unlikely that we would ignore any technical intervention that prevented or clearly limited disease. The gap is mainly in how we respond to indirect evidence of risk factors, particularly when such responses involve economic or political costs for powerful interest groups.

The recognition that patterns of disease and mortality substantially depend on our environment and social structure is now commonplace. While medicine has brought many achievements, and has contributed immeasurably to disease management and a sense of personal security, it contributes within narrow constraints set by economic and cultural patterns, values, and the general state of technology. Despite these constraints, progress in promoting health has been impressive. In this century longevity has increased substantially in all developed countries and in many underdeveloped ones, in large part due to improved food production, standards of nutrition, and economic circumstances. In the first half of the century, progress was most notable in the control of infectious disease and infant death, but in many countries dramatic changes occurred as well in chances of survival at older ages. In the United States, life expectancy remained relatively constant after 1955 for a number of years, but in more recent years considerable gains have been achieved in expected survival throughout the life span. Age-specific mortality for most causes, including cardiovascular disease, has decreased reflecting a wide range of factors associated with standards of living, medical progress, and changes in behavior. The precise contributors remain unclear.

A Framework for Understanding Risk Factors and Prevention

Much of our understanding of risk factors derives from epidemiological studies that provide leads for more focused investigations and experimental and clinical research. Ultimately, the value of an intervention must be assessed through controlled investigations, preferably using random assignment. But even a favorable result in a randomized controlled trial, while enhancing prevention, does not establish understanding. Knowledge of disease processes is firm when we understand basic processes and can demonstrate such understanding experimentally.

Epidemiology views disease and disorder through time and space, working against the parochialism of short-term study of selected, and frequently biased, samples. The approach makes clear the necessity to differentiate factors contributing initially to illness (incidence) from those that affect the course of disorder (prevalence). Moreover, it facilitates differentiation between the character of disorders and processes of seeking and utilizing help. Thus it is a useful way of examining etiological factors, those factors that affect prognosis, and the processes of acquiring medical and other types of care.

In preventing disease, ideally we want to proceed on the basis of specific understanding of disease mechanisms, but indirect evidence is often useful. In the classic cases of Snow's investigation of cholera and Goldberger's study of pellagra, it was possible to prevent the occurrence of disease through water control and dietary measures, respectively, despite the fact that the specific agents remained unidentified. More contemporary examples include smoking, weight control, diet, and exercise. But these examples illustrate the weaknesses as well as the utility of indirect knowledge. Advice on dietary precautions has changed over time, is inconsistent from one disease to another, and in the aggregate is often confusing. The advantages of precise knowledge in targeting more effective interventions should be clear.

In examining trends in morbidity and longevity, general characteristics of populations are often better predictors than biological or psychological markers other than sex and age. The frequency of disease and mortality increases over the life span, and women retain an advantage in longevity of approximately eight years. A remarkable number of studies also show disease and mortality linked with schooling, poverty, marital status, social and community integration, employment availability, and stable living conditions. The measures vary from one study to another, controls are often absent or inadequate, and cause and effect confused or unclear; but the consistency of results across populations, theoretical perspectives, methods, and measures suggest that these indirect associations are worthy of our attention.

Schooling, one of the best predictors of good health, longevity, and use of preventive and other health services, is an instructive example. Schooling is substantially correlated with income, but invariably has effects on health beyond income. Education is associated with life changes and many other attributes associated with health, including habits, coping capacities, and self-esteem. While it is plausible that intervening variables would explain the education effects, no study yet has been successful in doing so. It has been suggested that perhaps the most effective way of promoting health is to increase levels of education and income, but the costs and inefficiencies are high and political barriers are considerable, relative to identifying specific influential causative factors.

One of the most neglected, but important, predictors of health is marital status, comparable in effect to that of a person's sex. While marriage favors men more than women, both gain appreciably relative to the unmarried, particularly relative to divorced persons. Some of the outcomes result from the alienation and distress accompanying divorce, exemplified by excessive drinking, accidents, and violence. But the marriage effect is nonspecific, affecting disease rates and mortality more extensively. Marriage, of course, is a powerful social institution, and it not only typically provides established routines in respect to nutrition, sleep, and other matters, but also involves strong expectations, personal commitments, and goals beyond one's own interests.

The marital status variable is a complex one and illustrates the risks of focusing on broad associations in contrast to specific etiologic agents. Marital status and marital stability involve strong social selection factors, and the meaning of marriage changes in varying age cohorts with historical shifts. It would seem premature to argue that maintaining marriage is a positive goal for health maintenance, but such claims are made by even relatively sophisticated advocates (Lynch, 1977). This advocacy is not unlike that for changing behavior types (Friedman & Rosenman, 1974), an uncertain endeavor deriving from the growing literature linking Type A behavior pattern to coronary heart disease.

Findings in respect to religious participation, psychological well-being, and social integration all probably share a common core. There is no particular reason why persons attending church should live longer than those who do not, although churchgoing is probably related to greater conventionality and thus more regularity in lifestyles. Moreover, religious participation may be associated with positive health behavior in respect to smoking, drinking, and other risks, consequences clearly apparent among Mormons, Seventh Day Adventists, and other religious groups. Religious participation also implies a commitment, a sense of belonging, and a network of social relationships many studies show to be important in dealing with adversities and in maintaining health. Recent sophisticated studies demonstrate that intimacy and social networks not only protect against the occurrence of depression (Brown & Harris, 1978) and other morbid conditions, but also promote longevity (House, Robbins, & Metzner, 1982).

Integration into larger social networks of associations not only provides an arena for personal and social commitment, but also may offer an established and health-promoting routine, social support, and tangible assistance when needed. Group association may serve as a basis for personal gratification and self-esteem as well. While the concept of social integration implies a variety of causal interpretations, studies more specifically focused on psychological distress demonstrate clearly that personal distress is always associated with a range of bodily symptoms.

Poor health and mortality also are associated with involuntary disruptions in people's adaptations to their environment, including such events as unemployment, forced retirement, and involuntary relocations. Employment, of course, is related to economic as well as psychological factors, but for many—if not a majority of—people, work provides a sense of meaning, participation, and involvement with others central to one's life. The causal sequence is complex, since unemployment or retirement may be accompanied by a significant reduction in income and a change in lifestyle, and aging, which brings more health problems, need to be taken into account. Retirement as defined in our society, by itself, does not appear to be a risk factor if aging effects and prior health status are controlled (Ekerdt, Baden, Bossé, & Dibbs, 1983).

The significance of "meaning" affecting biological events is illustrated in an intriguing study of "death dips" prior to events of important cultural significance (Phillips & Feldman, 1973). A "death dip" is the occurrence of fewer deaths than expected. Studies of various groups of famous people show that they are more likely to die following a birthday than before, and the more famous the individuals, the larger the death dip. Birthdays of famous people are more likely to be publicly celebrated, or to be associated with tokens of respect and admiration. A death dip prior to presidential elections, and for Jewish populations prior to the Jewish Day of Atonement, have also been demonstrated. Although the biological mechanism remains unclear, people can postpone their deaths, an observation commonly made by clinicians working with critically ill patients. That death can be very much accelerated through psychological processes has long been recognized, dating back to Walter Cannon's discussion of voodoo death.

Finally, there are abundant historical data tracing patterns of disease and mortality following forced relocations of populations, the movement of populations from rural to urban living, and the movement of elderly patients from one institution to another. While these data tend to be sketchy, they depict populations experiencing disorientation with rapid social change in their surroundings. Such periods appear to be characterized by high rates of disease and mortality until the population adjusts to its new surroundings. Elderly persons moved from one institution to another die beyond usual expectations, as do persons losing a spouse. John Cassel, an eminent epidemiologist who devoted many years to such questions (Cassel, 1970), suggested that rapid social change has undermined the adaptive capacities of populations that have evolved over long periods of time, and the effects of changes such as movement from rural to urban factory life have been evident even for the offspring of those initially affected (Cassel & Tyroler, 1961).

At a more manageable level for rigorous research, there has evolved a vast body of evidence linking life change events with the occurrence of illness (Dohrenwend & Dohrenwend, 1974, 1981). An important underlying hypothesis is that major changes require adjustments that strain the biological system and result in adverse health outcomes. While the debate continues on the types of events that most dramatically affect health and the causal processes involved, the literature supports the assumption that major discontinuity in living conditions increases vulnerability to ill health.

Examining Intervening Processes: Some Examples

The types of broad relationships I have described only take us partway in identifying risk factors that can be efficiently modified. Much of the challenge remains in identifying intervening processes and how biolog-ical propensities interact with personal traits and sociocultural and situa-tional influences. Here I turn to some of our own efforts to understand personal appraisals of health status, factors encouraging sensitivity to symptoms and psychological distress, and determinants of health behav-ior.

In 1961, I selected a sample of mother-child pairs from the population of Madison, Wisconsin, and independent data were obtained from mothers, children, teachers, and official school records. In addition, 198 mothers completed daily illness diaries for themselves and their children for 15 days following their interviews. The sample included all fourth-grade children in five schools and half of the eighth-grade students, chosen randomly, from the three middle schools in the city. The socio-economic distributions of the fourth- and eighth-grade populations were substantially the same. The sample of 350 mother-child pairs constituted 93% of the eligible sample population. Mothers were interviewed at home, whereas information from the children was obtained in school (Mechanic, 1964).

The 1961 study provided a variety of interesting findings (Mechanic, 1964, 1968; Mechanic & Newton, 1965). Perhaps most impressive was the difficulty in demonstrating the transmission of the content of health behavior from mother to child. Whereas we found many such relation-ships, the amount of variance accounted for was small and the pattern of results was not fully consistent. The best predictors of the children's illness behaviors were age and sex. As in other studies, we found that mothers' reports about themselves and their children were often cor-related; mothers under stress, for example, reported not only more symptoms for themselves but also for their children, and they were more likely to phone the doctor concerning their children's health. However, there were fewer and smaller associations when data were independently obtained from mothers, children, teachers, and official records, subse-quently found to be true in many areas of study. These initial findings alerted us to the importance of respondent effects, particularly when people report not only for themselves but also for others, and in our subsequent studies of medical care we have tried to obtain data for inde-pendent and dependent variables from separate sources. In 1977, we located 333 of the original 350 children (95%). Of the remaining 17, 6 had died and 11 could not be found. Of those located, 302 (91%) com-pleted detailed questionnaires.

Neither our data nor other studies find much support for the view that various types of health behavior reflect an underlying dimension of re-sponsibility for health maintenance. However, one approach to the study of positive health behavior is to score respondents on the extent to which they adhere to behavior believed to be consistent with health status (Bel-loc & Breslow, 1972). Thus, we constructed an index based on eight measures of health response, including smoking, drinking, seat belt use, exercise, physical activity, risk taking, preventive medical behavior, and preparation for emergencies (Mechanic & Cleary, 1980). Men had lower scores on this index, reflecting more drinking and risk taking, and less preventive medical behavior. Other predictors of high scores on positive health behavior included education, concern with health, and a conventional behavioral orientation. Perhaps most interesting was the fact that both psychological well-being and subjective assessments of excellent physical health were associated with high scores on positive health behavior. Whereas a selection hypothesis is plausible in that physical stamina may be associated with exercise and physical activity, it is more difficult to explain why poorer subjective health status should result in smoking, failure to use seat belts, or less preventive medical care.

Our analyses lead us to speculate that patterns of health behavior tend to be part of lifestyles related to the ability to anticipate problems, to mobilize to meet them, and to cope actively. A measure of psychological distress (symptoms indicating anxiety and depression), for example, is significantly related to five components of the behavior index: drinking (.21); smoking (.25); failure to use seat belts (.16); lower physical activity (−.23); and less exercise (−.23). Behaviors like smoking and drinking may, in part, be efforts to alleviate distress, whereas others, like physical inactivity and failure to use seat belts, may reflect poor anticipation and inertia. Persons with poorer health behavior also appear to be less integrated into the conventional culture.

These data are consistent with the more global description I presented earlier. The significance is not, as some believe, that there is an easily modifiable, underlying trait of responsibility for health. More important, I think, the data emphasize the extent to which behavior derives from an overall living pattern, reflecting social values, psychological well-being, and integration into a dominant cultural mode. To the extent to which there is a personal orientation to good health practices, all evidence to date suggests that this orientation is at best loosely organized, with each particular behavior sequence having relatively unique determinants. Different health behaviors are not only usually modestly correlated but are, in some instances, negatively associated. Persons, for example, who are physically active—a commendable goal for encouraging positive health—also take more risks involving danger.

Vulnerability to Psychological and Physical Distress

We have been engaged for many years in studies of illness behavior and the individual's use of medical and psychiatric services. These studies, and the literature more generally, indicate that a relatively limited proportion of the population makes a large and disproportionate demand for services, and that such patients constitute not only the very ill in a medical sense but also many who complain of physical and psychological distress but have no demonstrable clinical illness. Our follow-up study of children allowed us to examine such states of distress in a developmental context.

We used two measures of distress: the first, an index of psychological distress with seven items depicting anxiety and depression; the second, a summary measure of 15 common physical complaints. These two measures are correlated .42, and neither is associated with sex in this sample. Since the results are similar for the two dependent variables, I focus on psychological distress, but will later briefly note some differences in determinants of the two types of complaints.

These dependent variables, typical of measures used in psychiatric epidemiology, do not measure illness as such, but there is considerable disagreement as to what they actually represent. It has been suggested that they reflect demoralization, self-dissatisfaction, or a quasi-neurosis, and may either accompany or be independent of tangible illness. High scores on these measures appear to tap the diffuse neuroses that have been of particular interest to psychodynamically oriented ego psychologists and psychiatrists. The index used in our study had an average correlation of .56 with five other variables denoting low psychological well-being: self-description of unhappiness (.46), description of low spirits ($-.44$), degree of worry about eight specified life problems (.56), high neuroticism on the Eysenck scale (.77), and low self-esteem ($-.59$). Our index was also correlated .41 with respondents' reports in 1977 that they had emotional problems, nervous trouble, or chronic "nerves."

The theoretical hypothesis used in the analysis was that the sense of distress measured by our index was shaped by three aspects: (1) body sensations, symptoms, or feelings different from those ordinarily experienced; (2) social stress; and (3) cognitions appraising what a person is feeling (Mechanic, 1972). Changes in body sensations, I argue, increase self-awareness, and stress contributes to body arousal and psychological disorientation further motivating attention to inner feelings. The regression analyses are consistent with the conclusion that factors focusing the child's attention on internal states and teaching a pattern of internal monitoring contribute to a distress syndrome. Respondents with such syndromes were more likely to come from families in which the mother was more upset and symptomatic, the child had more common physical symptoms such as colds and sore throats, and attention was directed to such symptoms by keeping the child home from school. Moreover, the data do not support the hypothesis that adulthood distress syndromes are simply a continuous pattern of illness from childhood to young adulthood. Although learned internal monitoring appears to be an important aspect of distress, it is only a vulnerability factor. The regression model based on the four most influential 1961 predictors of distress, childhood physical symptoms, school absence, and two maternal measures, explains only 9% of the variance. Whether a distress syndrome will develop depends on many additional influences, such as the degree of psychological and bodily dysfunction, adverse life experience, and influences that reinforce a focus on internal feeling states.

There is increasing experimental evidence that simply drawing a subject's attention to some aspect of bodily functioning results in an increased prevalence of symptom reporting (Pennebaker & Skelton, 1978), and experimentally induced self-awareness most commonly results in negative evaluation (Wicklund, 1975). Thus, it is plausible that persons who focus on feelings and bodily changes will be more likely to experience disturbing states. In an earlier epidemiological study of Wisconsin students, Greenley and Mechanic (1976) found that respondents high on a scale of identification with introspective others not only reported more psychological symptoms, but also were more likely to use medical, counseling, and other formal helping services. In the child follow-up study, introspectiveness was measured by a scale in which respondents indicated the degree to which they were "sensitive and introspective," "worried about meaning in life," and were "interested in psychology." Scores on this scale are correlated .47 with the distress measure despite the fact that the items do not directly measure symptoms and describe everyday concerns. The effect is approximately the same for each item in the scale. When added to various regression models of distress, introspectiveness retains its strength as a predictor, overshadowing all other predictors.

As one might anticipate, the introspectiveness score is related to parental variables similar to those predicting adult distress, particularly measures of parental negative behavior toward the child. Conceivably, such a pattern of concern with self and self-scrutiny results when familial patterns are disrupted, and such self-appraisal usually culminates in negative self-evaluation.

As noted earlier, our scales of psychological distress and of reporting common physical symptoms are substantially correlated, have many similar predictors, and are amenable to a common theoretical interpretation. Two possible important determinants that differentiate persons who favor psychological and those who favor physical complaining are actual adult experience with symptoms and illness on the one hand, and cultural influences on the definition of illness on the other. Whereas reporting physical symptoms is culturally more neutral, reporting psychological symptoms is more dependent on social acceptability. Social desirability response bias was significantly associated with reporting psychological symptoms ($-.18$), but was not significantly associated with reporting physical symptoms ($-.06$). In contrast, reports of chronic illness, bed disability days, and tendency to get sick were more highly correlated with physical symptoms than with psychological reports. We believe that the types of perceptual and definitional processes that have been described filter objective physical experience and cultural influences.

Reinforcing Factors

I have concentrated thus far on internal factors that either reinforce or distract attention from bodily concerns, but external reinforcements are equally important. The literature on behavior change attests to the ease of achieving short-term modifications of behavior, but rarely do these effects persist for long periods with significant proportions of the population. Evidently frequent and repeated external reinforcement is an essential aspect of desired behavioral continuity (Haggerty, 1977). Such reinforcement may come through family settings, peer relations, the work place, and a variety of other life contexts—a fact generally appreciated. It is less commonplace to understand the extent to which effective reinforcements, or their obverse, are implicit in the social and cultural systems we take for granted, and they may be far more powerful, in part, because they are not intended to bring about behavior consistent with a public agenda. Good health practices that occur not because they are good for health, but because they are consistent with how people choose to live, are more significant than any efforts we can reasonably make to change behavior. Promoting health is, thus, in large part an effort in social and cultural change and, most fundamentally, involves the conscious and unconscious designs for living that people follow. These conclusions in no way denigrate the importance of smoking control, treatment of obesity, or whatever; but they alert us to the limitations of our own efforts. We can anticipate major difficulties in preventive efforts if we fail to take account of the degree to which behaviors we wish to promote or change are embedded in routine habits and social patterns. The most powerful facilitation of positive health behavior is to integrate successfully desired patterns with the culture of natural supportive groups. Behaviors routinely reinforced by the social context are more robust than those requiring special programs.

In many instances the promotion of health is more likely to be successful through technological or regulatory means than through behavior change. If we wish to reduce accidents and deaths among teenagers—an extremely high-risk group for auto deaths—we do better by delaying the legal age for driving than by driver's education (Robertson, 1983). Even the most elaborate campaigns for seat belt use achieve only modest use. Automatic safety devices and environmental controls frequently offer greater benefits at less cost. In practice, we typically end up with some mix of education, technology, and regulation. Whatever the issue, an aggregate strategy calling upon a number of methods simultaneously offers the best possibilities, particularly when the noxious behavior is personally and socially rewarding in some way. Clearly, we also do better to prevent noxious behaviors initially. Targeting high-risk groups is a sensible priority.

While it is commonplace to give lip service to the role people have in their own health and the importance of health promotion, efforts to understand the causal process affecting these behaviors or to evaluate the impact of varying strategies in preventing or changing such patterns still receive little public support. A model of health promotion based on sound principles of intervention offers as much potential for health maintenance as any curative medical technology. Ironically, there is very little relationship between publicly stated aspirations and rhetoric, and the willingness to finance development of the necessary knowledge and programming for future efforts.

References

Belloc, N. B., & Breslow, L. Relationship of physical health status and health practice. *Preventive Medicine*, 1972, *1*, 409–421.

Brown, G. W., & Harris, T. *Social origins of depression: A study of psychiatric disorder in women*. New York: The Free Press, 1978.

Cassel, J. Physical illness in response to stress. In S. Levine and N. A. Scotch (Eds.), *Social stress*. Chicago: Aldine, 1970, pp. 189–209.

Cassel, J., & Tyroler, H. A. Epidemiological studies of social change: Health status and recency of industrialization. *Archives of Environmental Health*, 1961, *3*, 25–33.

Dohrenwend, B. S., & Dohrenwend, B. P. (Eds.). *Stressful life events*. New York: John Wiley & Sons, 1974.

Dohrenwend, B. S., & Dohrenwend, B. P. *Stressful life events and their contexts*. New Brunswick, N.J.: Rutgers University Press, 1981.

Ekerdt, D. J., Baden, L., Bossé, R., & Dibbs, E. The effect of retirement on physical health. *American Journal of Public Health*, 1983, *73*, 779–783.

Friedman, M., & Rosenman, R. H. *Type A behavior and your heart*. New York: Knopf, 1974.

Greenley, J. R., & Mechanic, D. Social selection in seeking help for psychological problems. *Journal of Health and Social Behavior*, 1976, *17*, 249–262.

Haggerty, R. J. Changing life styles to improve health. *Preventive Medicine,* 1977, *6,* 276–289.

House, J., Robbins, C., & Metzner, H. L. The association of social relationship and activities with mortality: Prospective evidence from the Tecumseh community health study. *American Journal of Epidemiology,* 1982, *116,* 123–140.

Lynch, J. J. *The broken heart: The medical consequences of loneliness.* New York: Basic Books, 1977.

Mechanic, D. The influence of mothers on their children's health attitudes and behavior. *Pediatrics,* 1964, *33,* 444–453.

Mechanic, D. *Medical sociology: A selective view.* New York: The Free Press, 1968.

Mechanic, D. Social psychologic factors affecting the presentation of bodily complaints. *New England Journal of Medicine,* 1972, *286,* 1132–1139.

Mechanic, D., & Cleary, P. Factors associated with the maintenance of positive health behavior. *Preventive Medicine,* 1980, *9,* 805–814.

Mechanic, D., & Newton, M. Some problems in the analysis of morbidity data. *Journal of Chronic Disease,* 1965, *18,* 569–580.

Pennebaker, J. W., & Skelton, J. A. Psychological parameters of physical symptoms. *Personality and Social Psychology Bulletin,* 1978, *4,* 524–530.

Phillips, D., & Feldman, K. A dip in deaths before ceremonial occasions: Some new relationships between social integration and mortality. *American Sociology Review,* 1973, *38,* 678–696.

Robertson, L. S. Injury epidemiology and the reduction of harm. In D. Mechanic (Ed.), *Handbook of health, health care, and the health professions.* New York: The Free Press, 1983.

Wicklund, R. Objective self-awareness. In L. Berkowitz (Ed.), *Advances in experimental social psychology* (Vol. 8). New York: Academic Press, 1975, pp. 233–275.

2

Psychologists in Health Promotion Research

General Concerns and Adolescent Smoking Prevention

Richard I. Evans

I am particularly pleased to participate in the Vermont Conference on the Primary Prevention of Psychopathology. Its emphasis on the relationship between lifestyle and morbidity and mortality reflects a critical, emerging focus for psychologists. For example, if conceptualization and research from psychologists can be employed in developing, evaluating, and implementing programs to modify lifestyle, contributing to the prevention of cancer and cardiovascular disease, this accomplishment could become the most important contribution of the behavioral sciences in the latter part of the twentieth century. However, as the field of health psychology develops, there are a number of concerns. This presentation within the context of these concerns will recount the development of the author's own research activities as a social psychologist as they relate to disease prevention and health promotion, with emphasis on the prevention of cigarette smoking in adolescents.

First, to the concerns. As the psychologist enters the field of disease prevention, is there a danger that more might be promised than can be truly delivered? This concern is in part related to the problem of territoriality. Although entering the field of preventive health behavior may seem to be fairly recent for most psychologists, it is a field that already has been pursued by a number of other professional specialties. In addition to various subspecialties of medicine such as community medicine, preventive medicine, pediatrics, oncology, and cardiology, the fields of dentistry, public health, health education, nursing, social work, medical sociology, and medical anthropology are among those that have been

The research reported in this chapter was supported by the National Heart, Lung & Blood Institute (Grant #17269) and the National Cancer Institute (Contract #N01-CN-95469).

actively concerned with disease prevention for many years. These areas
have often employed conceptualization and methodology from psychology in their disease prevention and health promotion activities, not to
mention the special skills and knowledge from their own fields. A fundamental question that must be asked is, what can psychologists offer as
individuals or in collaboration with individuals in these various specialties and subspecialties that is in itself a unique and worthwhile contribution to this field?

Another concern in the field of disease prevention relates to philosoph-
ical and ethical considerations. For example, psychologists might employ their knowledge and skill to assist physicians in what many of them
consider a major problem: getting patients to comply with their recommendations in the course of treatment, such as taking prescribed drugs.
What responsibility does the psychologist have for assessing the cost-
benefit of the physician's prescription, that is, the possible adverse effects
to the patient as against possible benefits?

Another ethical consideration, in more broad-based terms, might be
related to health promotion activities in which the psychologist may be
designing persuasive strategies to influence the public's health lifestyle
based on biomedical research of which the results may be equivocal. An
illustration of this point is the tremendous influence on public health
practices of the Framingham Heart Disease Study (e.g., Haynes, Levine,
Scotch, Feinleib, & Kannel, 1978). As a result of this major prospective
investigation, the risk factor concept in cardiology appeared to be so well
documented that it has become almost a cliché to recommend to the
public not to smoke, to modify dramatically its diet so as to reduce intake
of animal fats and/or maintain a normal weight, to detect and treat
hypertension, to exercise, to manage stress, etc. Yet, there remain concerns about the scientific validity of some of these recommendations.
How certain can we be, in terms of at least some conflicting evidence,
that for the well-being of the public we should be presenting massive
health promotion efforts aimed at reducing all of these risk factors collectively or individually? For example, in the area of diet and its relationship
to cardiovascular disease, there may be some questions concerning the
mechanisms of this process (e.g., Mann, 1977; Rosenman, 1983) that
raise questions concerning the validity of the recommendation that diets
be significantly altered. As pointed out by another speaker at this conference, Richard Lazarus (1985), there may also be some question on what
we really know about another risk factor area, stress and stress management, not to mention the fact that in biomedical terms it may be even less
clear how stress is related to disease (Gulius & Cottier, 1983; Herd, 1983;
Schneiderman, 1983).

One of the dangers that may ultimately reduce the credibility of psychologists and their contributions to the area of disease prevention is that they fall victim to a "health promotion ideology" that seems to have seriously jeopardized the objectivity of many health professionals both in and out of medicine. It may be becoming more fashionable to espouse a personal health (Risk Factor Reduction) ideology than an anti-environmental pollution ideology.

Even in an area like smoking control, which deals with one of the best established risk factors, we may be contributing to a type of mass hypochondriasis resulting in increasingly diminishing freedom in human lifestyle. Already we seem to have produced a small percentage of the population who may have developed a health-threatening preoccupation with jogging. To an increasing number, the idea of sitting down and eating a meal has become more of a threat than a pleasure because of fear of harm from eating certain foods. A balance must be struck in health promotion between modifying truly destructive, health-threatening behaviors and reducing considerable freedom and spontaneity in the lifestyle of the individual. This balancing act is not unlike the problem we are facing with the increasing paranoia concerning crime in our communities, which may have already seriously reduced some of our freedom to locomote in a natural and necessary manner.

Still another concern centers around the responsibilities of psychologists in addressing a community problem such as health promotion. Researchers may become involved in a health promotion program directed at the community, but too often may lack the necessary community support to do more than complete an initial evaluation. Such programs too rarely include concerns with their continuation by the community, if warranted by the evaluation data, following the involvement by the psychologist-researcher.

The balance of this presentation will illustrate one example of a community primary prevention program in disease prevention. It will trace the process though which our research became involved with one risk factor, cigarette smoking. We have possibly avoided some of the above-mentioned concerns in the area of disease prevention because of the area we have chosen, prevention of cigarette smoking in adolescents, but it is unlikely we have avoided all of them. Some concerns in the area of prevention of smoking in adolescents, therefore, will also be discussed.

When we first became interested in health promotion research, an examination of the effects of fear arousal on health behavior became a focus of our social psychology/behavioral medicine research group. We decided to conduct a series of experiments to learn more about why fear arousal appeared to be relatively ineffective as a means of motivating an alteration of lifestyle to protect health. First, we searched for a health area where the general public was still relatively uninformed of the relationship between certain behaviors and health maintenance. Preventive dentistry appeared to be such an area. It seems well known to dental scientists but not to society-at-large that, by merely brushing and flossing teeth properly, it is possible to eliminate virtually all tooth decay and gum disease (Arnim, 1963). Here was significant information concerning disease prevention behaviors of which most people were unaware, unlike widely held knowledge such as the relationship between smoking and cancer or cardiovascular disease. This situation would, therefore, be ideal for setting up experimental situations allowing us to learn at a grassroots level more about why simply being made aware of the dangers of a disease (fear arousal) does not motivate individuals to do what is necessary to prevent that disease. Reviews of the fear arousal literature (Higbee, 1969; Sutton, 1982) and an assessment of this field by Janis (Evans, 1980) indicate that no blanket statement can be made concerning the value of fear as a motivator of health behavior. An earlier exploration of this problem was made by Janis and Feshbach (1953), who reported in a now classic study that a minimal fear appeal with general toothbrushing instructions was more effective in increasing the incidence of toothbrushing than a *strong* fear appeal. However, this study had to rely on subjects' *reports* of toothbrushing. No more adequate estimate of actual toothbrushing behavior was involved. Furthermore, this study focused only on fear arousal as a "motivator." Also of importance, and not considered by Janis and Feshbach, is the question of whether a positive appeal, one that emphasizes a good, favorable result to the individual, may not be more powerful as a motivator than fear. Subsequently, Leventhal, Singer, and Jones (1965) not only challenged the importance of fear arousal as a "motivator" to change behavior, but found in their research (involving persuasion to encourage tetanus inoculations) that highly *specific* instructions, even without fear, might be the most effective way of motivating individuals to engage in a preventive health behavior. The author's social psychology research group further pursued this problem of the relative effectiveness of fear arousal in two basic studies in preventive dentistry (Evans, Rozelle, Lasater, Dembroski, & Allen, 1968, 1970).

Very briefly, these studies involved as subjects junior high school students. They included a "pretest" of these students which involved: (1) photographing their pink-stained teeth to determine the cleanliness of their teeth before oral hygiene instructions were given; (2) obtaining reports of their brushing behavior; and (3) administering certain behavioral tests.

One week after the pretesting, students in one experimental group were subjected to general oral hygiene instructions plus a very *high* fear message, such as was used by Janis and Feshbach. Another group, in addition to the general oral hygiene instructions, received a positive appeal, providing information that stressed many of the favorable effects of brushing. A third group received elaborated, more specific instructions with no accompanying fear or positive appeals. A last group served as the control. The students were retested after five days, two weeks, and six weeks.

The results clearly indicated that reported oral hygiene behavior differed significantly from actual behavior, as determined from the photographs of the students' teeth, suggesting that studies relying on *reported* behavior as a criterion of change may be misleading. Perhaps of greater interest was the fact that merely exposing the students on only *one* occasion to elaborated, specific instructions without using emotional appeals (fear or positive) produced sufficiently heightened oral hygiene behavior, resulting in significantly cleaner teeth than was evident in the pretest. Furthermore, the general oral hygiene instructions coupled with a positive appeal were nearly as effective. Effective, but significantly less so, were the fear appeals when coupled with general oral hygiene instructions. When this type of investigation was extended to longer periods of time (Evans, Rozelle, Noblitt, & Williams, 1975), it was discovered that behavior changes were maintained and that simply testing the subjects (possibly perceived as monitoring) at irregular intervals was almost as effective in increasing brushing behavior as various persuasive messages including those using fear arousal.

Skinner (Evans, 1968) and Rogers (Evans, 1975) have independently concluded that failures in our educational system may be partly due to depending too much on motivating students through fear of punishment for failure rather than stressing individual satisfaction in learning. Difficulties in child rearing in general may result from too much emphasis on fear of punishment as a motivational device. Perhaps we should not be too surprised, therefore, by the limitations of primarily stressing fear arousal as a motivational device in health education as well.

Of course, even as Janis and Feshbach (1953) originally suggested, fear probably does have some impact on us, at least in effecting short-term changes in our health behavior. For example, right after a heart attack individuals may change their lifestyles to prevent a recurrence; but, many patients will return to their previous risk-taking lifestyles (Marston, 1970). Even under conditions of intense fear of the consequences of behavior, such as experienced by postcoronary patients, therefore, *permanent* changes in health habits may not occur. In fact, when a habit such as smoking cigarettes has become especially well integrated into a lifestyle, health professionals are rarely able to alter permanently that behavior using fear arousal or, for that matter, any other approach (Evans, Henderson, Hill, & Raines, 1979b; Lichtenstein & Mermelstein, in press).

Because smoking cessation may, in fact, present a more clinical than social psychological problem, we decided to focus on prevention of smoking in adolescents. The complex, multidimensional nature of smoking, incorporating biological, social, and social psychological variables, has become widely documented (e.g., Evans et al., 1979a, 1979b; Evans & Raines, 1982; Leventhal & Cleary, 1980; Lichtenstein & Mermelstein, in press; Reeder, 1977). Identifying and coping with the factors involved in the initiation of smoking among adolescents is an endeavor that may require the utilization of diverse conceptualizations and strategies (Evans, 1982). Various conceptions in social and developmental psychology would appear to be useful in generating hypotheses to account for the initiation of smoking and in providing conceptual bases for prevention programs. The section which follows presents the specific rationale for what might be described as our social inoculation approach, and summarizes some of our prospective investigations utilizing this intervention strategy.

In order to apply any concept or rationale to the problem of smoking prevention, it should be noted that smoking occurs in an upward trend from the elementary grades, but begins most significantly in junior high school and into high school (Johnson, Backman, & O'Malley, 1979a, 1979b; NIH, 1976). This trend has been reported consistently in the literature (Cresswell, Huffman, & Stone, 1970; Evans et al., 1979b; Thompson, 1978). Because of this estimate of smoking frequency, it was determined that the most effective way to attack the problem would be to influence entering junior high school students not to initiate smoking.

A survey of junior high school programs dealing with smoking prevention (Evans & Raines, 1982) revealed that more traditional efforts, (1) generally were focused perhaps too intensely on fear arousal; (2) largely emphasized the future consequences of smoking such as heart disease or cancer, failing to recognize that teenagers may tend to be more concerned with the present than the future; (3) when utilizing films and other media of communication, failed to use previous research on the effective use of media; and (4) evoked responses that may even be counterproductive. In light of these findings, we decided to undertake a long-term study addressing some of these limitations in the Houston Independent School District (Evans, 1976; Evans, Rozelle, Maxwell, Raines, Dill, Guthrie, Henderson, & Hill, 1981; Evans, Rozelle, Mittelmark, Hansen, Bane, & Havis, 1978), perhaps one of the largest school districts in the United States.

Interviews conducted before both a pilot study (Evans, 1976) and a three-year study (Evans et al., 1978) with a large population of seventh graders suggested that peer pressure, models of smoking parents, and smoking models or messages in the mass media such as cigarette advertising may individually or collectively outweigh the belief of adolescents that smoking is dangerous. Some of them, when between the ages of four and eleven, had even spent time trying to persuade their parents to give up smoking. As they grew older, social pressures to smoke became superimposed on the fear of this behavior, and the fear and knowledge of the dangers of smoking became insufficient to prevent its onset.

From among the various available conceptions in psychology which generally might have related to our intervention strategy, Bandura's (1977) social learning theory offered particularly relevant insights. As applied to the initiation of smoking (Evans, Smith, & Raines, in press), this theory suggested that through observation children acquire expectations and learned behaviors with regard to smoking. For example, children can learn vicariously that cigarette smoking relieves tension or anxiety. Thus, they might come to expect that smoking will have a relaxing effect. In addition, when a model engages in an apparently enjoyable behavior that the observer expects to be socially prohibited, but negative consequences do not follow, disinhibition results. That is, the child's learned expectation of negative consequences is weakened, possibly to the point where the child will engage in the same behavior as the model. Vicariously learned expectations, then, of the positive and negative consequences of cigarette smoking would appear to be important factors in the ultimate decision regarding smoking. Figure 2.1 reflects the array of possible influences to smoke.

This model, which emerged from our investigations, postulates that both the social environmental and "personality" determinants contribute to the complex of psychological predispositions related to smoking. These psychological predispositions tend to produce an intention either to smoke or not to smoke. Nevertheless, the actual decision to smoke (or not to smoke) on a particular occasion may depend on the impact of situational social influences. Teaching adolescents to cope with such influences might decrease the probability that they would initiate smoking. Also, such an approach could logically be incorporated within existing school health education programs. After examining the other components of smoking initiation as reflected in Figure 2.1, we felt that within the constraints in the school system with which we would be working we would not be able to design significant interventions modifying the social environment. Likewise, although other investigators (e.g., Botvin, Eng, & Williams, 1980; Hurd, Johnson, Pechacek, Bast, Jacobs, & Leupker, 1980) subsequently developed interventions directed toward altering some of the intrapersonal determinants of smoking, we felt that within the constraints of the institutions with which we would be working such an alteration attempt would require too complex an array of commitments. Inoculation against social influences to smoke, therefore, became the primary focus of our intervention.

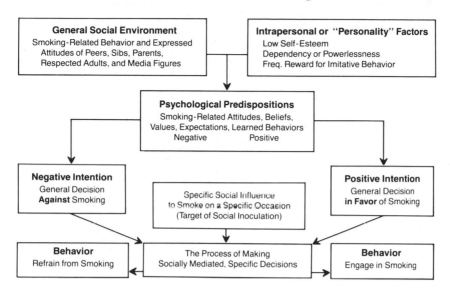

Figure 2.1. A Model of Smoking-Related Social Psychological Processes Impacting Behavior

To guide the development of our interventions, we found McGuire's (1968) communication–persuasion model both relevant and provocative. It analyzes the impact of communications according to five components: attention, comprehension, yielding, retention, and action. Obviously, to be effective, a communication must hold the person's attention and be understandable. In addition, the communication must elicit yielding (or agreement) on the part of the person exposed to the message. Induced agreement must be maintained (retention) over time in order for it to be translated into action in appropriate situations.

Various elements of the filmed messages we produced address the problems of attention, comprehension, and yielding (Evans et al., in press). First, instead of adults, adolescent narrators selected for their poise and appearance take the role of information brokers. Using language specifically geared to the audience's level of comprehension, the narrators present scientific information. However, in keeping with their role as information brokers, these student narrators make no claim to scientific expertise of their own. Thus, phrases such as "the researchers asked me to tell you . . ." and "the researchers found that . . ." are included at appropriate points.

Second, much of the content of the films and discussions dealing with psychosocial influences to smoke and with strategies for coping with these influences is based on data obtained from students similar to those in the audience. For example, most of the footage in the films shows students acting out situations their peers have described to us in pre-intervention surveys and focused group interviews. Our process evaluation suggests that these scenes and situations are perceived by the student audience as realistic.

Third, the messages in the films and discussions are presented in a manner directed toward reinforcing self-attributions, or the ability of the members of the audience to self-determine their decision whether or not to smoke. The student narrators repeatedly tell the audience "you can decide for yourself" and "knowing these facts might help you to decide" and "here's something you might want to think about." Process evaluations have indicated that the student audiences are favorably impressed by this self-attributional aspect of the films and discussions.

In addition to tailoring our intervention to the model, as suggested earlier, we also employ a behavioral variation of McGuire's (1961) "inoculation" approach to attitude change. McGuire suggests that existing attitudes may be strengthened by inoculating individuals against counterarguments to which they might be exposed. By explicating the nature of various social influences to smoke, our intervention program attempts to inoculate the audience against these influences. Further, we suggest to the students specific strategies they might use to cope with these social influences when they are encountered.

To increase the probable impact of the social inoculation interventions, information is presented to motivate the student to develop a negative smoking intention, an intention *not* to smoke. Information presented includes the immediate health effects of smoking, negative social consequences of smoking, and the cost of smoking. A film depicting immediate health effects includes statements of commonly held beliefs about smoking followed by demonstrations that either confirm or refute the accuracy of these beliefs. Another message attempts to increase students' awareness of the dangers of experimental smoking.

Prior to the presentation of the social inoculation messages, various messages familiarized the students with various social influences to smoke. Three social influences were defined in our pilot study (Evans et al., 1978)—modeling, peer pressure, and cigarette advertising—and scenes representing examples of each of these influences were presented. Our current investigation has incorporated adult nagging, since responses in a pre-intervention survey cited this factor more frequently as an effect in smoking than had previously been apparent. In the case of cigarette advertising, content analyses of ads are used to reveal to students the techniques employed by advertisers. When students subsequently encounter a situation where a social influence to smoke is present, they will be better able to recognize consciously that social

influence and to understand how it operates. This recognition and understanding might well enable the student to make a specific decision based
more on personal intention than on the demands of the particular situation. As indicated earlier, in the various filmed messages and group
discussions the student is encouraged to make a *conscious* decision about
smoking, rather than to be pressured by external influences without
being sufficiently vigilant concerning the effects of such influences.

The social inoculation content consists of the presentation of strategies
and skills for coping with social influences to smoke which may be
encountered in the future. For example, various films depict specific
strategies the nonsmoking students themselves indicate they use for coping with peer pressure to smoke. During discussions following the films,
students are given the opportunity to role-play peer pressure situations
they might encounter, and to rehearse coping with them.

As we proceeded to evaluate this social inoculation strategy, as suggested earlier, we concluded that school systems appeared to be the most
promising agencies for the delivery of such smoking prevention programs to large groups of adolescents. There is no other agency in our
culture with the school's capability to reach adolescents from all racial,
ethnic, religious, and socioeconomic groups. But within the context of
the educational institution the developer of an intervention program
must consider the following constraints:

(1) the amount of class time the school is willing to allocate to smoking prevention; and

(2) the amount of time required for school personnel to be trained
adequately to implement the program.

Guided by these considerations, we decided to develop a system for
delivering interventions requiring a minimum of class time, necessitating
no prior training of school personnel or students, and relatively immune
to the unique characteristics of the presenter. This delivery system involves four interrelated modes. First, a set of films or videotapes present
a number of messages. Second, discussions and role plays are used to
reinforce, clarify, and personalize these messages. Third, posters assist
students in retaining information. Fourth, feedback is provided concerning retention of knowledge and frequency of smoking as the intervention
program progresses.

The timing of each intervention session and the frequency of intervention, of course, are negotiated with the school system officials. The
central core of our intervention is designed to require one class period on
each of four occasions. Apparently there is a point of diminishing returns
in the amount of classroom time devoted to the intervention because of
possible habituation or "nag" effects.

Although in the pilot study the sequence of presentation of the intervention components was more concentrated, the essence of the intervention procedure remained essentially the same. Films presented on the first day included information about the dangers of smoking to health and, most prominently, a section describing and illustrating peer pressure and its effect on smoking behavior. Other films recapped the first film and presented information about parental influence on smoking behavior, including a depiction of parental pressure to smoke and not to smoke and children's modeling of parents' smoking behavior. Still other films recapped the first two films and presented information dealing with mass media pressure to smoke. These films included a pictorial analysis of advertising techniques such as artistically hiding the Surgeon General's warning on cigarette packages and appeals based on implied sexual attractiveness and popularity. The final films were a general recap of earlier films. The various treatment films of the pilot were either presented in their entirety (all four films presented) or absent (no treatment presented) in various experimental and control groups.

Following the films, students were asked for written and oral responses to questions. The experimenter distributed brief questionnaires for subjects' written responses. Four sets of questions were prepared and presented in conjunction with each film. The questions, which incorporated a quasi-role-playing device of allowing the respondent to make decisions concerning whether or not to respond to social pressure to smoke, were formulated in such a way as to attribute motivation to resist pressures to smoke to persons who have seen the film, and attributed ability to decide whether or not to smoke to persons subjected to smoking pressure.

Each film presentation was followed by a discussion designed to reinforce the messages in the films. Also to reinforce these messages, posters representing scenes from the films were displayed in the classrooms. These posters thus served as continuous reminders of the film messages.

The five dependent measures include smoking information, smoking attitudes, intention to smoke, and reported smoking behavior, as well as the nicotine-in-saliva analysis of Horning and his collaborators (1973), used as an objective measure of the presence or absence of smoking. In the earlier investigations, the Horning test determined the amount of nicotine present in the saliva samples by a mass spectrometric analysis. In later investigations, thiocyanate analyses were employed. These analyses provided the basis for inferences about the degree of smoking behavior of the subjects. Cost of these chemical analyses precluded analysis for each subject on each occasion, so a sampling of saliva specimens from each group was analyzed both as an indicator of smoking frequency and as part of a technique to increase the validity of self-reports of smoking. Earlier studies (e.g., Evans, Hansen, & Mittelmark, 1977) had found that when subjects learned from a short film that in some instances their saliva would be analyzed to determine smoking behavior and how this analysis was done, self-reports of smoking frequency increased.

In a ten-week pilot study (Evans et al., 1978), rates of onset of smoking in the treatment schools were significantly lower than the onset rates in the pretest and single posttest control groups. More than 18% of the control groups had begun smoking, while less than 10% in the experimental groups had begun smoking. (The small number of subjects already smoking in the various experimental groups precluded a statistical comparison of onset rates among the experimental groups and the control group.) In a follow-up, three-year study (Evans et al., 1981) involving 13 junior high schools utilizing a complex, multiple experimental-control group design, results indicate that those who gained information from films were smoking less than those who did not gain information. Using the criterion of smoking two cigarettes a day or more, 7% fewer students in the treatment schools were smoking this frequently than in the control schools. Using the criterion of still not smoking at all, there were 8% fewer students in the control schools than in the treatment schools; these differences were both statistically significant. Furthermore, significant interactions were found among information presented in the films and discussions, intention to smoke, and smoking. These results indicate that such interventions may prove more useful in deterring smoking among junior high school students than merely instructing them in more traditional health education programs. Perhaps of most importance, these findings suggest that various kinds of interventions may be effective if they have a reasonable social psychological conceptual base framed in terms of data from the target audience about its perceptions of the influences to smoke and how to cope with them (Evans et al., 1979a, 1979b; Evans & Raines, 1982). Other investigators (e.g., Hurd et al., 1980; McAlister, Perry, & Maccoby, 1979) using variations of our conceptual and developmental approaches have also reported promising results, appearing to support this contention.

In conclusion, a word of caution might be introduced regarding some of the concerns related to the psychologist in health promotion discussed earlier in this paper. Surely the results of our social psychologically derived primary prevention program, this social inoculation strategy to deter smoking, do demonstrate some promise. Similar programs have also appeared to be promising (e.g., Botvin et al., 1980; Hurd et al., 1980; McAlister et al., 1979). Yet, it must be remembered that the bottom line for prevention of smoking is not demonstrated in a program's relatively short-termed effectiveness, that is, reducing smoking through the early adolescent years. Rather, as these adolescents move through high school, will such a strategy actually reduce the incidence of addictive smoking? This fact cannot be determined until individuals reach the end of their high school years, since very little cigarette smoking is initiated after the individual leaves high school and the incidence of smoking addiction among high school seniors approaches the level of the general adult population (Evans & Raines, 1982). It is therefore important to continue evaluating such interventions and their impact, or to introduce additional interventions through later adolescent years. A similar caution must be considered in evaluating any program directed at the primary prevention of disease that involves children and/or adolescents, particularly when the endpoints of such programs involve not only influencing a behavior (as in the case of our social inoculation approach) but ultimately influencing the incidence of morbidity and mortality.

A final concern is that too few research psychologists are sufficiently sophisticated in community organizational processes. These processes include competency in working with other disciplines in the health promotion area as well as identifying and working with the indigenous community leaders that need to be involved, not only to initiate and evaluate a program, but to assure its continuation. Disease prevention or health promotion programs too often are introduced only to carry out a relatively short-term evaluation research program concerning the efficacy of an intervention. But have the social-political and even economic mechanisms been introduced to insure that the intervention will be continued (should it prove to be effective) *after* the behavioral research group is no longer involved? This continuation calls for intricate cooperative preplanning to insure this critical commitment. The present author's social psychology/behavioral medicine research group has recently received federal funding to attempt to analyze and blueprint such a community organizational process accompanying an adolescent health promotion intervention program. Hopefully, other psychologists in this area will be able to proceed with similar projects in the future.

References

Arnim, S. S. The use of disclosing agents for measuring tooth cleanliness. *Journal of Periodontology*, 1963, *34*, 227–245.
Bandura, A. *Social learning theory*. Englewood Cliffs, N.J.: Prentice-Hall, Inc., 1977.
Botvin, G. J., Eng, A., & Williams, C. L. Preventing the onset of cigarette smoking through life skills training. *Preventive Medicine*, 1980, *9*(1), 135–143.
Cresswell, W. H., Huffman, W. J., & Stone, D. B. *Youth smoking behavior characteristics and their educational implications*. A report of the University of Illinois Anti-Smoking Education Study. Champaign, University of Illinois, June 30, 1970.
Evans, R. I. *B. F. Skinner: The man and his ideas*. New York: E. P. Dutton, 1968.

Evans, R. I. *Carl Rogers: The man and his ideas.* New York: E. P. Dutton, 1975.

Evans, R. I. Smoking in children: Developing a social psychological strategy of deterrence. *Journal of Preventive Medicine,* 1976, 5(1), 122–127.

Evans, R. I. *The making of social psychology: Discussions with creative contributors.* New York: Gardner Press, 1980.

Evans, R. I. Modifying health lifestyles in children and adolescents: Development and evaluation of a social psychological intervention. In A. Baum & J. E. Singer (Eds.), *Handbook of psychology and health: Issues in child health and adolescent health* (Vol. 2). Hillsdale, N.J.: Lawrence Erlbaum Associates, 1982.

Evans, R. I., Hansen, W. E., & Mittelmark, M. B. Increasing the validity of self-reports of smoking behavior in children. *Journal of Applied Psychology,* 1977, 62(4), 521–523.

Evans, R. I., Henderson, A. H., Hill, P. C., & Raines, B. E. Current psychological, social and educational programs in control and prevention of smoking: A critical methodological review In A. M. Gotto & R. Paoletti (Eds.), *Atherosclerosis reviews* (Vol. 6). New York: Raven Press, 1979. (a)

Evans, R. I., Henderson, A. H., Hill, P. C., & Raines, B. E. Smoking in children and adolescents—Psychosocial determinants and prevention strategies. In *Smoking and health: A report of the surgeon general* (DHEW Publication No. [PHS] 79-50066). Washington, D.C.: U.S. Government Printing Office, 1979. (b)

Evans, R. I., & Raines, B. E. Control and prevention of smoking in adolescents: A psychosocial perspective. In T. Coates & C. Perry (Eds.), *Promoting adolescent health: A dialogue on research and practice.* New York: Academic Press, 1982.

Evans, R. I., Rozelle, R. M., Lasater, T. M., Dembroski, T. M., & Allen, B. P. New measures of effects of persuasive communications: A chemical indicator of toothbrushing behavior. *Psychological Reports,* 1968, 23(2), 731–736.

Evans, R. I., Rozelle, R. M., Lasater, T. M., Dembroski, T. M., & Allen, B. P. Fear arousal, persuasion and actual versus implied behavior change: New perspective utilizing a real-life dental hygiene program. *Journal of Personality and Social Psychology,* 1970, 16(2), 220–227.

Evans, R. I., Rozelle, R. M., Maxwell, S. E., Raines, B. E., Dill, C. A., Guthrie, T. J., Henderson, A. H., & Hill, P. C. Social modeling films to deter smoking in adolescents: Results of a three-year field investigation. *Journal of Applied Psychology,* 1981, 66(4), 399–414.

Evans, R. I., Rozelle, R. M., Mittelmark, M. B., Hansen, W. B., Bane, A. L., & Havis, J. Deterring the onset of smoking in children: Knowledge of immediate physiological effects and coping with peer pressures, media pressure, and parent modeling. *Journal of Applied Social Psychology,* 1978, 8, 126–135.

Evans, R. I., Rozelle, R. M., Noblitt, R., & Williams, D. L. Explicit and implicit persuasive communications over time to initiate and maintain behavior change: A new perspective utilizing a real-life dental hygiene program. *Journal of Applied Social Psychology,* 1975, 5(2), 150–156.

Evans, R. I., Smith, C. K., & Raines, B. E. Deterring cigarette smoking in adolescents: A psycho-social-behavioral analysis of an intervention strategy. In A. Baum, J. Singer, & S. Taylor (Eds.), *Social psychological aspects of health.* Hillsdale, N.J.: Lawrence Erlbaum, in press.

Gulius, S., & Cottier, C. Behavior and hypertension. In T. M. Dembroski, T. H. Schmidt, & G. Vlumpzherv (Eds.), *Biobehavioral bases of coronary heart disease.* New York: Karger, 1983.

Haynes, S. G., Levine, S., Scotch, N. A., Feinleib, M., & Kannel, W. B. The relationship of psychosocial factors to coronary heart disease in the Framingham study. *American Journal of Epidemiology*, 1978, 107, 362–383.

Herd, J. A. Physiological bases for behavioral influences in arteriosclerosis. In T. M. Dembroski, T. H. Schmidt, & G. Vlumpzherv (Eds.), *Biobehavioral bases of coronary heart disease*. New York: Karger, 1983.

Higbee, K. C. Fifteen years of fear arousal: Research on threat appeals, 1953–1968. *Psychological Bulletin*, 1969, 72, 426–444.

Horning, E. C., Horning, M. G., Carrol, D. I., Stilwell, R. N., & Dzidic, I. Nicotine in smokers, non-smokers and room air. *Life Science*, 1973, 13(10), 1331–1346.

Hurd, P. D., Johnson, C. A., Pechacek, T., Bast, L. P., Jacobs, D. R., & Leupker, R. V. Prevention of cigarette smoking in seventh grade students. *Journal of Behavioral Medicine*, 1980, 3(1), 15–28.

Janis, I. L., & Feshbach, S. Effects of fear-arousing communications. *Journal of Abnormal and Social Psychology*, 1953, 48, 78–92.

Johnson, L. D., Backman, J. G., & O'Malley, P. M. *Drugs and the class of '78. Behaviors, attitudes and recent national trends* (U.S. DHEW Public Health Service Publication No. [ADM] 79-877). Washington, D.C.: U.S. Government Printing Office, 1979. (a)

Johnson, L. D., Backman, J. G., & O'Malley, P. M. *1979 Highlights: Drug and the nation's high school students. Five-year national trends* (U.S. DHEW Public Health Service Publication No. [ADM] 80-930). Washington, D.C.: U.S. Government Printing Office, 1979. (b)

Lazarus, R. The trivialization of distress. In J. C. Rosen & L. J. Solomon (Eds.), *Prevention in health psychology*. Hanover, N. H.: University Press of New England, 1985.

Leventhal, H., & Cleary, P. D. The smoking problem: A review of the research and theory in behavioral risk modification. *Psychological Bulletin*, 1980, 88(2), 370–405.

Leventhal, H., Singer, R., & Jones, S. Effects of fear and specificity of recommendations upon attitudes and behaviors. *Journal of Personality and Social Psychology*, 1965, 2, 20–29.

Lichtenstein, E., & Mermelstein, R. Review of approaches to smoking treatment strategies: Behavior modification strategies. In N. E. Miller, J. D. Matarazzo, S. M. Weiss, J. A. Herd, & S. M. Weiss (Eds.), *Handbook of Behavioral Health*. Chichester: John Wiley and Sons, Inc., in press.

Mann, G. V. Diet-heart: End of an era. *New England Journal of Medicine*, 1977, 297, 644–650.

Marston, M. V. Compliance with medical regimes: A review of the literature. *Nursing Research*, 1970, 19, 312–323.

McAlister, A. L., Perry, C., & Maccoby, N. Adolescent smoking: Onset and prevention, *Pediatrics*, 1979, 63, 650–658.

McGuire, W. J. The effectiveness or supportive refutational defenses in immunizing and restoring beliefs against persuasion. *Sociometry*, 1961, 24, 184–197.

McGuire, W. J. The nature of attitudes and attitude change. In G. Lindzey & E. Aronson (Eds.), *Handbook of social psychology* (Vol. 3): *The individual in a social context*. Reading, Mass.: Addison-Wesley, 1968.

National Institutes of Health. *Teenage smoking: National patterns of cigarette smoking, ages 12 through 18, in 1972 and 1974* (U.S. Department of Health, Education and Welfare Public Health Service Publication No. [NIH] 76–391). Washington, D.C.: U.S. Government Printing Office, 1976.

Reeder, L. G. Sociocultural factors in the etiology of smoking behavior: An assessment. In M. E. Jarvik, J. W. Cullen, E. R. Gritz, T. M. Magt, & L. J. West (Eds.), *Research and smoking behavior* (NIDA Research Monograph No. 17, U.S. DHEW, PHS, ADA/MHA, NIDA, DHEW Publication No. [ADM] 78–581). Washington, D.C.: U.S. Government Printing Office, December 1977, 186–201.

Rosenman, R. H. Current state of risk factors in Type A behavior pattern in the pathogenesis of ischemic heart disease. In T. M. Dembroski, T. H. Schmidt, & G. Vlumpzherv (Eds.), *Biobehavioral bases of coronary heart disease*. New York: Karger, 1983.

Schneiderman, N. Behavior, autonomic function and animal models of cardiovascular pathology. In T. M. Dembroski, T. H. Schmidt, & G. Vlumpzherv (Eds.), *Biobehavioral bases of coronary heart disease*. New York: Karger, 1983.

Sutton, S. R. Fear-arousing communications. A critical examination of theory and research. In J. F. Eiser (Ed.), *Social psychology and behavioral medicine*. Chichester: John Wiley and Sons, 1982.

Thompson, E. I. Smoking education programs 1960–1976. *American Journal of Public Health*, 1978, *68*, 250–257.

3
Prevention of Alcoholism
A History of Failure

Peter E. Nathan

This chapter reviews recent efforts to prevent alcoholism and its consequences. We define prevention as did the National Academy of Sciences,
Institute of Medicine, in *Alcoholism and Related Problems: Opportunities for
Research* (1980): Prevention includes "actions designed to keep from happening, to forestall, or to diminish the detrimental effects of alcohol."
The reach of this review, then, includes both efforts to prevent development of alcoholism and problem drinking and, when those efforts
have not succeeded, to prevent as many of the malignant consequences of
alcohol as possible.

Perspectives on Prevention

Models of Prevention

Three models of prevention, the Sociocultural/Environmental Model,
the Distribution of Consumption Model, and the Public Health Model,
have lent structure to both theoretical and empirical studies of prevention
through the years.

Sociocultural/Environmental Model.
The Sociocultural/Environmental Model of prevention (Blane, 1976)
stresses the crucial role societal drinking norms and attitudes about alcohol play in abusive drinking. As a consequence, this prevention model
emphasizes the importance of consistent and effective efforts to alter
prevailing social norms and attitudes surrounding alcohol use and abuse
as means to prevent alcoholism and problem drinking.

Distribution of Consumption Model.
The Distribution of Consumption Model (Bruun, Edwards, Lumio,
Makela, Pan, Popham, Room, Schmidt, Skog, Sulkunen, & Osterberg,

This chapter is based on a previous article by this author entitled "Failures in Prevention:
Why We Can't Prevent the Devastating Effect of Alcoholism and Drug Abuse" which
appeared in *American Psychologist*, April 1983.

1975; Ledermann, 1956) is based on the assumption of a strong relationship between per capita consumption of alcohol and heavy or abusive use of alcohol by some members of society. Accordingly, the Distribution of Consumption Model of prevention stresses efforts to reduce per capita consumption of alcohol, on the assumption that this reduction will yield a corresponding decrease in incidence of problem drinking and alcoholism.

Public Health Model.

The Public Health Model of prevention (Plaut, 1967) derives from epidemiological studies of communicable diseases indicating that proper treatment planning requires knowledge of host, agent, and environment. The host is the individual susceptible to the disease; the agent is the disease-causing substance or the pathogen; the environment is the physical setting of the disease. Hence, the Public Health Model of alcoholism prevention directs simultaneous attention to *host* (individuals at high risk to develop alcoholism ought to be primary targets of prevention efforts), *agent* (modifications in the availability of alcohol can reduce incidence and prevalence of alcoholism), and *environment* (systematic modification of the setting or context within which drinking occurs affects the drinking itself).

Criticisms of Prevention Models.

All three prevention models have been criticized; none has met universal acceptance. The Sociocultural Model has been criticized on measurement grounds; reliable measurement of drinking norms, for example, is notoriously difficult, as is generalization of these norms from one social or cultural grouping to another (Frankel & Whitehead, 1981). The Distribution of Consumption Model has been vigorously opposed by those who question one or more of its most basic assumptions: that a change in average or per capita consumption of alcohol will be accompanied by a similar change in proportion of heavy drinkers, that per capita consumption is causally linked to the physical and social damage that results from abusive drinking, and that prevention or control measures that affect overall consumption will also affect incidence of alcohol problems (Pittman, 1980; Schmidt & Popham, 1978).

The Public Health Model has been attacked by some who see in it a neo-prohibitionistic stance on prevention: Control of the agent by high taxation, to reduce availability, will reduce incidence of alcoholism (Lieber, 1982). Other critics of this model have faulted it for failing to consider social or psychological factors in planning prevention efforts (Conrad & Schneider, 1980). Lieber (1982) suggested recently a modification of this prevention model which he labelled "Disease Control." The method is to rely on "early detection of alcoholism (utilizing, in part, biochemical markers of heavy drinking), screening among heavy consumers for signs of medical complications . . . and reducing the task of treatment to a manageable size by focusing major therapeutic efforts on susceptible subgroups" (p. 175).

Controversy among proponents of one or another of these models of prevention has impeded implementation of a consistent and effective national prevention policy by inhibiting cooperation among agencies and individuals involved in prevention activities.

Prevention and Public Policy

Failure to agree on a single prevention model has not been the only barrier to effective public policy in guiding prevention activities. For instance, a recent study of the effects on consumption of alcoholic-beverage-control laws, a basic prevention/control strategy in all 50 states, identified the following impediments to effective prevention ("Effects of Alcoholic-Beverage-Control Laws," 1979): (1) the necessary caution that must be exercised in moving from research findings to social policy implementation; (2) the power of those with vested economic power to impede or direct change; and (3) the absence of an effective influence group to advocate a position other than the status quo.

Others have concluded that ineffective methods, more than conflicting models or shifting public policy, are responsible for disappointing outcomes. Support for this view comes from the findings of many of the projects reviewed elsewhere in this review, as well as from the results of the California Prevention Demonstration Program (Wallack & Barrows, 1981). Implemented in 1977 with substantial funding at two experimental sites in the San Francisco Bay area and a comparison site some distance away, the program energetically disseminated moderation-in-drinking messages through the mass media and by community organization and development activities. Despite an ambitious program, ample funding, enthusiastic cooperation from policymakers and a state-of-the-art advertising campaign, program effects were limited. While an increase in awareness of alcohol problems was observed, degree of concern about those problems did not change; and, while information about alcohol and alcoholism was increased moderately in some study sites, corresponding attitude or behavior changes were not found. Most important, the frequency of episodes of drinking to intoxication did not change.

Etiologic Models and Prevention Strategies

Implicit in the effort to develop prevention models is recognition of the complexity of alcoholism etiology and other influences on drinking patterns, and their importance in planning and implementing prevention strategies. The most adequate models of alcoholism ought to reflect the fact that patterns of alcohol consumption, including alcoholic patterns, in individuals as well as societies are multiply determined and multiply expressed.

Influences on drinking, including alcohol drinking, include genetic and prenatal factors, interpersonal and environmental factors, psychological, psychiatric, and behavioral factors, and sociocultural and ethnic factors. These influences on drinking, in turn, can operate at societal, institutional, community, family, peer group, and individual levels; influences on drinking, moreover, derive from social norms, social controls, access and availability of beverage alcohol in the society in question, the drinker's personal dispositions and behavior patterns, etc. As a consequence, both intervention and prevention efforts can be set in time (e.g., shortly after birth, during childhood, during adolescence, in adulthood, in old age) and implemented via diverse technologies and modes of prevention (e.g., via legal restrictions, alcohol education programs, use of mass media, etc.) Given the complexity of factors impinging on drinking behavior of individual drinking patterns, and of intervention and prevention approaches to problem drinking, the effort to model intervention or prevention unidimensionally (for example, according to the parameters of a single prevention model) is doomed to provide an essentially unrealistic view of the phenomena that must be confronted.

To take one example: Given (1) that interpersonal and environmental factors influence both social and abusive drinking, and (2) that peer group influences are a key environmental/interpersonal factor; how is one to choose (1) the "proper" time-focus for prevention efforts (e.g., is the peer group most influential during adolescence, childhood, or early adulthood?), as well as (2) the "best" technology for prevention (e.g., will the peer group be reached and influenced best via mass media efforts within a small-group discussion format, at school or after school, or elsewhere?). The absence of a formal theory permitting choice among these prevention foci, and the fact that a multitude of prevention efforts have, nonetheless, failed to yield a single approach to prevention with quantitative or qualitative superiority lead us to extreme modesty in our discussions of what is known to be most effective in preventing alcoholism.

Plan of the Chapter

The chapter is organized around the Public Health Prevention Model because that model extends prevention efforts to host, agent, and environment rather than to but one. In its purview, the Public Health Model recognizes more adequately than other alcoholism prevention models the importance of a multifaceted attack on the multifaceted problem of alcoholism.

It is important to note that, while this chapter concerns itself with a variety of efforts to prevent alcoholism, it is almost impossible to separate those efforts from efforts to prevent other kinds of drug abuse. More and more persons are being diagnosed and treated as polydrug abusers; many of the most successful efforts to treat and to prevent drug abuse also impact positively on alcoholism. Hence, the reader should understand that our review of efforts to prevent alcoholism by focusing on host, agent, and environment includes many projects which impacted, either directly or indirectly, either by design or otherwise, both alcohol and other drug abuse.

Prevention in the Host

Although most prevention activities are directed to a generic host and do not target prevention efforts, an effort has been made in recent years to focus on groups of individuals who have not before been targets of prevention efforts, who remain at special risk, or both. This section reviews efforts to convey prevention messages and program prevention activities to these groups, which include women, youth of both sexes, members of minority groups, and the elderly. Generic, untargeted prevention efforts are reviewed elsewhere through the chapter.

Prevention Among Women

Reported rates of alcoholism among women have been on the rise during much of the 20th century (Shaw, 1980), although this rise seems either to have stopped (Bower, 1980) or slowed sharply (Braiker, 1982). Though some have claimed that this rate increase simply reflects a greater willingness on the part of women to acknowledge and seek help for existing alcohol problems, the implications of the rise are important for treatment and for prevention regardless of its cause.

Alcohol and alcoholism produces important behavioral and biological effects that differ in men and women (Hill, 1982; Knupfer, 1982); these differences also affect focus of prevention efforts. To this end, recent evidence from Scandinavian, Canadian, and American studies suggests strongly that morbidity and mortality (e.g., successful suicide, death from accidents, and death from liver cirrhosis) associated with alcoholism and alcohol-related problems are significantly greater among women than men alcoholics. Women may also be more likely than men to develop drinking-related cancers, cardiovascular disorders, brain damage, and other complications at the same level of alcohol dependency, though data on sex differences in the prevalence of these alcohol-related disorders are less complete. Possibly related to these apparent sex differences may be differences in genetic predisposition to alcoholism; though genetic predisposition is essentially confirmed for both men (Goodwin, Schulsinger, Knop, Mednick, & Guze, 1977) and women (Bohman, Sigvardsson, & Cloninger, 1981), it may well be at different creditability levels. To this time, few other plausible explanations for the apparently greater susceptibility of women to alcohol-related morbidity and mortality have been posited. Some have speculated that these differences derive from the toxic effects of alcohol on the hypothalamic-pituitary-gonadal axis in women, basing these speculations in part on clinical observations of excessive rates of infertility, miscarriage, hysterectomy, and sexual dysfunction among women with alcohol-related problems (Hill, 1982). The significance of these findings for accelerated prevention efforts in women seems clear: The cost to society of comparable alcoholism levels in men and women appears even greater for women than men.

It is fortunate that women, apparently, drink less than men and that, accordingly, the overall severity of alcoholism in the average woman is less than that in the average man (Knupfer, 1982). One reason for this significant difference in consumption rates may be social norms, which tolerate heavy drinking in women less than in men. Interesting in this context are studies that identify those women with highest rates of heavy drinking: young women with small children, women with alcoholic husbands, and employed women, especially those in stressful occupations. Prevention efforts directed at these groups would seem to hold great promise.

These data on prevalence, drinking patterns, morbidity, and mortality, available only recently, are particularly valuable since, to this time, virtually all alcohol education or alcoholism prevention efforts have either focused exclusively on men and boys or been directed to both sexes. This single-minded prevention focus is all the more surprising in view of the designation of women, as far back as 1975, as one of five high-priority submarkets by the distilled spirits industry (Gavin-Jobson Associates, 1975). As well, magazines and comic books read by women and girls have recently begun to treat alcohol use more sympathetically (De Foe & Breed, 1980); prime-time television shows, though, still portray drinking as more acceptable for men than for women (Breed & De Foe, 1981).

Prevention approaches designed specifically for women, as noted above, have been few. Recently implemented are programs based on the view that alcohol problems may result from deficits in assertiveness, self-esteem, and ability to handle stress; prevention efforts that provide behavioral training in assertiveness, encourage enhancement of self-esteem (with exercise and physical fitness programs and womens' support groups), and offer stress management seminars have been developed on these assumptions (Irwin, 1976; Sandmaier, 1976). Additional prevention programs for women that assume that self-perceived interpersonal or social inadequacy might contribute to alcohol problems have sponsored training in communication skills, interpersonal conflict resolution, problem-solving techniques, and career and life planning. Unfortunately, these programs are based on etiologic views of alcoholism that have never been confirmed empirically; as unhappily, to this time, empirical data on the programs' effectiveness have not been reported.

Alcohol education programs designed specifically for women have become more numerous in recent years. Notable among them is the National Center for Alcohol Education (1977) course, "Reflections in a Glass," designed to provide information and learning experiences for women without current alcohol problems, enabling them to determine rationally the role alcohol plays in their lives and the role they wish it to play in years to come. Unfortunately, while empirical assessment of the program indicated significant gains in knowledge by participants, it did not include an assessment of its effects on drinking.

The Alcoholism Center for Women, Los Angeles County, has recently developed a systematic community approach to identification and delivery of prevention activities to adult women at high risk for alcoholism, following an extensive needs assessment. Notable was the special attention paid to development of a methodology to target populations of high-risk women, to identify psychological and sociological predisposition to alcohol abuse within this population, and to implement an effective prevention strategy that is multimedia and multimodal.

Another sign that prevention programs for women have assumed higher priority is that the NIAAA's own National Clearinghouse for Alcohol Information Women's Program has begun gathering data on alcohol consumption by women and on the special problems women who drink heavily experience, both in support of an alcohol education program of special relevance and appeal to women (National Clearinghouse for Alcohol Information, 1981).

Efforts to prevent alcoholism among women by controlling the agent—by restricting the availability of alcohol—rather than by decreasing the host's desire to seek out and consume alcohol are thought by some probably to be ineffective since a smaller proportion of women than men drink heavily; as a result, reducing per capita consumption within the general population would likely affect consumption by women less than men (Wilsnack, 1982). Conversely, raising the minimum drinking age may have a relatively greater impact on the drinking behavior of young women (who are somewhat more likely to be law-abiding) than young men (Whitehead & Ferrance, 1977).

Prevention strategies that set out to alter the environment and the drinking context are buttressed by data pointing to the impact of social environmental factors on heavy drinking by women. For example, there is evidence that women drink more in the company of men, particularly in large, mixed-sex groups, than they do when alone with other women (Rosenbluth, Nathan, & Lawson, 1978; Harford, Wechsler, & Rohman, 1980), that heavy- and problem-drinking women are more likely than others to be married to or living with a heavy- or problem-drinking man (Morrissey & Schuckit, 1979), that social drinking norms for women are more inconsistent than for men (Wilsnack & Wilsnack, 1978), and that women drinkers who drink heavily may experience fewer social consequences than their male counterparts (Donovan & Jessor, 1978; Wilsnack, 1982). With the exception of social support and consciousness-raising groups designed to address the sex-role problems for women posed by our society, programs designed to prevent alcoholism by altering the context of drinking for women have been virtually nonexistent.

Prevention Among Youth

Alcohol education programs for youth 18 years of age and younger have focused on both unselected youth populations and special populations at risk for alcohol problems (Hewitt, 1982). Alcohol education programs for the former have ranged from those delivering only alcohol-related information to those with little or no alcohol-related content, designed to foster the personal development of participants to reduce the likelihood of later alcohol problems. Programs aimed at high-risk groups of youth have been developed for youth from alcoholic families, disadvantaged youth, and delinquents, dropouts, and troubled youth. Unfortunately, attempts to evaluate the effectiveness of "targeted" alcohol education programs have been few, with the result that the cost-effectiveness of special programs for special groups remains uncertain.

Educational efforts have also been directed at groups of adults who interact with young people and are in a position to influence their drinking choices (Hewitt, 1982). Programs for parents and other family members and for teachers and other community professionals and lay people have been developed, on the assumption that providing these key "gatekeepers" with information on alcohol and alcoholism may well impact the youth for whom they are responsible.

The relatively few evaluations of alcohol education programs for youth (and their elders) that have been reported reveal (1) that significant increases in knowledge about alcohol are often observed (e.g., Fullerton, 1979; Staulcup, Kenward, & Frigo, 1979), (2) that less dramatic but nonetheless real changes in attitudes toward alcohol or toward self and others also occur, especially when attitude change is an explicit goal of the program (e.g., Evans, Steer, & Fine, 1979; Weisheit, Kearney, Hopkins, & Mauss, 1979), and (3) that modest or no changes in actual drinking behavior typically result from these programs (though many fewer evaluations set out to measure behavioral change than change in attitudes toward or knowledge about alcohol [e.g., Fullerton, 1979; Staulcup et al., 1979]). This important omission notwithstanding, it is encouraging that more program directors appear to recognize the need to evaluate what they do (Hewitt, 1982).

Elementary Age Children.
This group of children has recently been the focus of increased prevention activities. Bartlett's (1981) recent analysis of failures of alcohol education programs to impact elementary and high school age youth faults health educators for overemphasizing cognitive learning and lecture-oriented teaching methods, failing properly to assess students' receptivity to the material and to appreciate the problems caused by the "captive population" syndrome, and ignoring the importance of coordinating alcohol education programs with related community resources. Non-traditional programs that involve students more often in curriculum design and interactive learning are most successful.

Two recent reports of targeted elementary age prevention programs, albeit as yet unproven, propose promising models. The first describes a Napa (California) program designed to evaluate substance abuse prevention strategies for elementary and junior high school students as well as to study etiologic factors (NIDA, 1980). Although possible etiologic factors were identified and sensible prevention strategies were employed, robust evaluation indices were not elicited, making it impossible to judge the worth of the program. Unfortunately, the same must be said of an innovative prevention approach to grade school children—the Alpha Center Prevention Model—in place in two Florida counties (Pringle, Gregory, Ginkel, & Cheek, 1981). The Alpha Centers assume that alcohol abuse, like other behavioral problems, derives from early developmental problems. Hence, students aged 8 to 12 who display maladaptive behaviors at home and school attend special classes to improve both social and academic skills. Their teachers learn classroom behavior management techniques and interpersonal communication skills; a counselor focuses on working with parents at home. The Alpha Center concept, representing a "total push" approach to a group of high-risk youngsters, remains essentially unproven but promising.

Adolescents.
Adolescence is when most youth begin to drink. It is also when youth are most often involved in the most troubling of the behavioral consequences of problem drinking and intoxication—including, above all, drunken driving and its consequences. As a result, adolescents have received more attention from the developers of prevention programs than any other group.

Among recent findings on adolescent alcohol abuse of relevance to prevention efforts are that (1) alcohol is the most widely used drug by youth between the ages of 12 and 17 (making this group an obvious prevention target), (2) problem drinking increases sharply with advancing age during adolescence, (3) adolescent problem drinkers use illicit drugs much more often than nondrinkers, (4) heavy drinking during adolescence is typically accompanied by other antisocial behaviors, (5) both parental and peer influences strongly impact problem drinking, and (6) adolescent problem drinkers differ from nonproblem-drinking adolescents—they are less religious, more tolerant of deviance, less successful in school, and more enamored of independence than of academic success (Braucht, 1982). These data add to the complexity of prevention programs for adolescents, especially for groups at risk for alcoholism. They also suggest that existing prevention models are probably not sufficiently attuned to the special characteristics of the adolescent problem drinker to be effective.

Traffic accidents, many alcohol related, constitute the most frequent cause of death and disability for American youth (Douglass, 1982). While 16- to 24-year-old youths are exposed to more alcohol-related driving than older adults, their rates of accidents are disproportionate even to these higher levels. In other words, exposure to drinking and driving alone does not account for their extraordinarily high rates of involvement in accidents involving alcohol. One possible explanation comes from Braucht (1982), who observes that antisocial, acting-out-behavior typically accompanies heavy drinking by adolescents. One assumes, accordingly, that it is the heavy-drinking adolescent, by virtue of his greater exposure to drinking and driving and his greater tendency toward antisocial behavior, who is most likely to cause or be involved in a crash associated with alcohol.

In this context, it is worth remembering that lowering legal drinking ages, thereby making beverage alcohol more available to more youth, increases alcohol-related traffic accidents and alcoholic-related crashes, at least in the short run (Douglass, 1982). Unfortunately, design and methodology problems with these studies prevent reliable assessment of the long-term effects of this change.

Recently reports have appeared describing innovative programs with a focus on adolescent drinking: (1) An intensive alcohol problem training program has been developed for the staff of the Partners Program, a nonprofit volunteer organization designed to provide services to youths in trouble with the law in Denver (Resource Alternatives Corp., 1982). Notable in the report is an evaluation study design that provides for three control groups, all enrolled in the program before the alcohol education/prevention component was offered staff. Results of the evaluation revealed that youths' perceptions of the negative consequences of drug and alcohol use increased after their counselors had been exposed to alcohol education; but no change in actual alcohol or drug use followed counselor training. (2) A diverse group of state prevention programs for adolescents has appeared (Williams & Vejnoska, 1981), ranging from alcohol education efforts alone, to more ambitious health promotion projects that encourage development of health-conscious lifestyles incompatible with problem drinking, and to legislative and other means to reduce the accessibility of alcohol to adolescents. Unfortunately, few of these efforts have been evaluated or assessed for changes in consumption levels. (3) A program focusing on prevention of drunken driving, by identifying primary alcoholics from among drunken adolescents who come to the St. Mary's (Ohio) General Hospital has also been described ("Inpatient Care," 1980). Following identification, these patients and their families are shifted to therapy units where drinking and driving are a focus of treatment. (4) An ambitious project has been conducted jointly by the American Medical Association and the American Association of Motor Vehicle Administrators (Hames & Petrucelli, 1980). On the assumption that teenagers in the process of getting their driver's license are maximally motivated to cooperate with an alcohol education program attached to that process, the program required teenagers applying for a license in New York, Wisconsin, and Oklahoma to view an alcohol education film in high school driver education classes. Students were then tested for knowledge increase and retention. Results indicated the information was retained, at least for a short time. Unfortunately, the impact of the program on subsequent rates of drunken driving was not assessed. (5) Also recently described was one of the most thorough studies of the impact of alcohol education on adolescents (Stuart, 1980). Lectures were given to almost 1000 junior and senior high school students on the physiology and pharmacology of drugs including alcohol and the legal, social, and psychological ramifications of their use. While information levels increased, drug and alcohol use also increased, in some instances, suggesting again that alcohol and drug education sometimes produces better-informed drug and alcohol users, not abstainers. (6) By contrast, a study by Goodstadt, Sheppard, and Chan (1982) found that educating 7th- to 10th-grade students on myths about alcohol, beverage advertising, reasons for drinking, and effects of alcohol on the family, driving, sports, fitness, and sexuality improved their knowledge but had mixed effects on their attitudes on alcohol, led to predictions of less future alcohol use, and, in fact, yielded decreases in current alcohol usage. One of the few adolescent alcohol education projects that both assessed behavior change and found it, Goodstadt's study clearly deserves careful scrutiny and possible replication.

Another innovative approach to prevention among junior high school students (McAlister, Perry, Killen, Slinkard, & Maccoby, 1980) involved intensive training of several teams of five to seven high school students, followed by their placement in one of two California junior high schools where they led six classroom sessions of instruction during the first school year and two further 45-minute sessions in the second year. The objective of the sessions was to increase students' commitment not to start smoking and to "inoculate" them psychologically against pressures to smoke. Several of the later sessions also included similar activities aimed at deterring use of alcohol and other drugs. When the experimental and control schools were compared following 21-months of longitudinal observation, the experimental school's students were smoking and drinking significantly less than students in the control school, who had received an intensive course of health education but no peer-group sessions with high school students.

College Age Youth.
NIAAA has made a major effort to develop prevention programs at the college level in recognition of both the paucity of such programs to this time and the differences in approach and strategy required for effective intervention with this population (Bryan, 1982; Dean, 1982).

Among the most interesting approaches to prevention with this key "host" group are the following: (1) A survey of 457 Memphis State University students and 30 mental health professionals working in the university setting revealed that the students considered substance abuse problems to be the most serious of 24 mental health problems experienced by students. By contrast, the professionals rated other problems as more serious (Henggeler, Sallis, & Cooper, 1980). (2) Evaluations of alcohol education programs at the University of Virginia (Portnoy, 1980) and Saint Mary's College (Leavy, 1980) both demonstrated the apparent ease with which information bases on alcohol knowledge can be changed, and the real difficulty with which actual drinking behavior changes. The same lesson was learned at Brown University by a "Sons and Daughters of Alcoholics" group, designed as a prevention strategy at this Ivy League university (Donovan, 1980).

Between 1975 and 1980, a comprehensive alcohol education program for college students was developed, implemented, and evaluated at the University of Massachusetts (Kraft, 1982). In 1978, a systematic replication and extension of this project was begun at the University of North Carolina (McCarty, Poore, Mills, & Morrison, in press; Mills, McCarty, Ward, Minuto, & Patzynski, in press). These two projects were among the most carefully evaluated of all large-scale prevention projects directed at this population of young drinkers. The University of Massachusetts project was multifaceted in methodology. It programmed mass media appeals to raise awareness of drinking and driving, accidental injuries, and the alcoholic content of various beverages; group discussions, lectures, and special courses to enable small groups of students to explore various topics more intensively; community development techniques to influence ways in which alcohol was consumed by target groups; and, efforts to influence institutional norms and practices involving alcohol to modify alcohol consumption at campus parties. As a result of these efforts, 69% of the students recalled at least one message produced by the project, while 5% attended one or more workshops. Environmental changes on campus were also observed. Further, knowledge and attitude change took place. Unhappily, actual behavioral changes in drinking did not accompany the other observed positive changes (Kraft, 1982).

Among the innovative approaches to prevention sponsored by the North Carolina program was a university residence hall tavern, operated by undergraduates enrolled in an alcohol education course. The tavern was established in order to improve student participation in alcohol abuse prevention activities. Baseline and follow-up studies of tavern use indicated that the tavern promoted an increase in the consumption of nonalcoholic beverages, altered for the better students' attitudes towards heavy drinking and drinking and driving, and improved decorum during residence hall parties. Beer, wine, and liquor consumption on campus did not change, however, nor did self-reports of problems derived from alcohol consumption, including hangover, drinking and driving, noise, and litter (Mills et al., in press). The North Carolina program also tested a direct mail campaign to increase student participation in the program and their knowledge about alcohol and its effects, and to reduce drinking and driving. While 93% of the students receiving the information by mail read and learned from it, their drinking-related behavior did not change.

Prevention Among Minorities

For many years, accurate data on the nature and extent of alcoholism among ethnic and racial minorities without this country were unavailable, making the task of targeting prevention efforts within and between these groups impossible. Now, however, better data are available on alcoholism and problem drinking among black, Asian, Hispanic, and native Americans.

An important issue preventing a full understanding of variations among ethnic groups in use of alcohol and incidence of alcohol problems has been whether these variations derive more from sociocultural or biophysiological differences. Current data attribute more responsibility for these differences to the former rather than to the latter explanation (Schaefer, 1982), although a final answer to the question awaits more sensitive bio-assay methods and more adequate sociocultural survey designs.

The problem and consequences of alcoholism among blacks seem to be growing worse and worse. Little in the way of targeted treatment of documented efficacy or targeted prevention of proven worth has been reported (King, 1982). One explanation is that the black community itself apparently has not recognized as threatening the problem of alcoholism among blacks, so that social norms in that community continue to promote rather than deter heavy alcohol use. Some see the failure of society at large to accord high priority to prevention and treatment of alcoholism among blacks a reflection of its willingness to maintain blacks in an inferior socioeconomic position (King, 1982), though this hypothesis has thus far defied empirical confirmation. The drinking behavior of youth and the elderly in the black community remains largely undocumented; this gap in data is particularly unfortunate since these two groups may well represent potent foci for prevention efforts (Payton, 1981; Scott, 1981).

A few prevention programs focused on black youth (Crisp, 1980; Miranda, 1981) and black women (Gaines, 1976) have been reported. None has been studied in depth and none appears to have been proven effective on empirical grounds. Why has the black community failed to benefit from prevention or treatment efforts? Some have blamed the problem on an ideological rather than pragmatic emphasis in program planning within the black community (Holliday, 1981), others have attributed it to minority inexperience in grant writing and fund raising (Monroe-Scott & Miranda, 1981), while still others have pointed to the cultural and economic bias of nonminority professionals who would otherwise be expected to provide prevention and treatment services (Crisp, 1980).

Studies of drinking by Asian Americans tend to confirm the prevailing folklore that they drink less than the average non-Asian American, though there are considerable variations in drinking pattern among the 20 nationalities covered by the term Asian American. While Asians do metabolize ethanol more quickly than non-Asians, causing discomfort and the "flushing reflex," the relationship between sensitivity to ethanol and consumption patterns remains uncertain. Perhaps because alcohol is usually not a problem for them, perhaps because they feel unwelcome, perhaps because they believe they must "take care of their own," Asian Americans rarely use treatment facilities or involve themselves in prevention activities. Though many have predicted a rise in Asian American rates of alcohol consumption with acculturation, that rise has not yet been documented, so an enhanced need for treatment and prevention programs for Asian Americans has not yet been established (Kitano, 1982).

By contrast, rates of alcoholism among Hispanic Americans appear to be higher than the national average (Garza, 1979). Among the variables put forth to explain these rates of alcohol abuse are sociocultural norms and values that encourage heavy drinking, especially by men, minority group status and the problems of acculturation and their associated stresses, and possible biophysiological factors; a causal relationship between these factors, singly or together, and alcoholism in either given individuals or groups of individuals has to this time only been inferred. Hispanic Americans, like other minority groups, underutilize treatment and rehabilitation resources; prevention programs designed for this sociocultural group have been very few (Alcocer, 1982).

One of these programs was an NIAAA-funded, Clinical Alcoholism Project of the School of Social Work at San Jose (California) State University (Arevalo & Minor, 1981). Its goal was to develop a Hispanic-oriented curriculum on alcohol abuse for social workers. The project revealed the special difficulties of planning for the needs of the Hispanic community, especially the needs of Chicanas, whose role in the culture and, consequently, predisposition to develop alcoholism is particularly problematic. Others (Herrell & Herrell, 1979; Regalado, 1981); have also speculated on the special pressures on Chicanas that may lead to alcoholism, and on the importance of recognizing their need for prevention efforts.

A review of what is known about alcoholism among native Americans reveals many assumptions, opinions, and undocumented beliefs, but few empirically derived findings (Merker, 1981). What is known is that rates of alcoholism among American Indians and native Alaskans are high, and that effective treatment and prevention programs for them have not been developed (Lewis, 1982). Before their alcohol problems can be addressed, many believe, the social problems experienced by these people must be solved. And as bad as rates of alcoholism among American Indians on the reservation are, they are that much worse when American Indians enter the world of urban America (Weibel, 1982). Even more torn from cultural and family ties, even less able to merit a positive sense of self-esteem, the urban American Indian has the highest rates of alcoholism, benefits least from available treatment resources, and is unreached by prevention messages.

Alcoholism has only recently been recognized as a particular problem within the gay community. Some (e.g., Schwartz, 1980) have estimated rates of alcoholism among lesbians and gay men to be between 20 to 32%, with most reports concluding that men and women are affected equally. Given these figures, clearly treatment and prevention programs must be developed for this large group of Americans, although the formidable problems of training workers sensitive to the normative and cultural differences between lesbians and gay men and heterosexuals have only recently been addressed (Mongeon & Ziebold, 1980).

Prevention Among the Elderly

There is strong evidence that the percentage of drinkers declines at and beyond age 50, while the percentage of heavy drinkers drops as well. At age 60 to 65, the percentage of heavy drinkers among males drops even more sharply. Unhappily, during the same time period (from age 50 on), a certain number of older people who have been lifelong abstainers or moderate social drinkers become problem drinkers (Brody, 1982; NASADAD, 1981). Three groups of elderly problem drinkers, natural targets for prevention efforts, have been identified. They include: (1) the aging, long-term alcoholic; (2) the elderly problem drinker whose problem is of recent onset; and (3) the elderly problem drinker who has been an intermittent problem drinker in the past. Differences between middle-aged and older male problem drinkers have also recently been identified; in general, the older the person, the more destructive his alcoholism is in his life. For this reason, because of the heterogeneity of older alcoholics, and because of the negative attitudes of many mental health professionals towards older persons seeking help, the prevention and treatment of alcoholism in the elderly has proven very difficult. One solution may be support for self-help groups—older persons helping those in need—as well as a greater emphasis on preretirement planning to anticipate the emotional consequences of retirement on use—and abuse—of alcohol (Gomberg, 1982).

An assessment model to help plan treatment and prevention services for the elderly has been proposed (Kola & Kosberg, 1981). Designed to consider the special needs of the elderly for prevention and treatment services, the model nonetheless recognizes the importance of integrating these services into existing community treatment and prevention resources. A program effectively integrated into its community is the Eagleville Hospital and Rehabilitation Center. The Eagleville Center began drug and alcohol prevention services for the elderly in the county in which it operates (Montgomery County, Pennsylvania) in 1978, following a countywide survey. The focus of prevention is a group of older adults, operating from a local senior adult center and constituting a self-help group called ALERT (Leigh, 1980).

Section Summary and Conclusions

Data on rates of alcoholism and alcohol problems among youth, women, members of minority groups, and the elderly have been gathered more carefully in recent years. As a consequence, recognition has grown that alcoholism problems within several of these groups are serious, to this time underattended, and overdue for focus. Hypotheses on etiologic factors associated with alcoholism within these groups have also been generated with enthusiasm; few of these theories, however, have been accompanied by empirical findings in confirmation. Hence, it can be said that prevention based on hypotheses about etiology (e.g., focusing on loneliness among the elderly on the assumption of a causal relationship between it and alcohol abuse) are on less firm ground than prevention depending largely on data on demography and prevalence.

Despite the increased attention the alcohol problems of these groups have received and despite the moderate increases in treatment resources these groups have experienced, prevention resources for these groups, with a single exception, have been few and without consistent documented behavioral effectiveness. The exception is the strong focus on youth, drinking, and driving that has recently become a focus of prevention activities by the federal government (Mayer, 1982).

Research Needs

Previous *Reports to Congress* have stressed the need for accurate data on rates of alcoholism among these subgroups at risk. These needs now appear to have been met, in large part. As a consequence, policymakers can now allocate resources for prevention services to groups in great need and at high risk (e.g., youth, young women). The paucity of prevention efforts directed at minority groups seems to indicate, however, that not all at-risk groups are receiving their due share of prevention resources.

Happily, data on outcome are now being reported much more systematically and thoroughly than before. Most often, simultaneous asessment of changes in information level and attitude is reported; less often are data on behavioral change gathered. Prevention efforts—when directed to the host, most often in the form of alcohol education—frequently yield attitude changes and increases in alcohol information. Unhappily, these positive changes are almost never associated with behavior change—change in consumption—even though it is, after all, the ultimate goal of prevention. In fact, behavior change is much less often assessed than information or attitudes, perhaps because it is much more risky to determine change in consumption from self-reports than change in information level or attitudes toward consumption.

We suggest that explicit efforts be made by funding and evaluation groups to ensure (1) that evaluation be a part of every prevention effort; (2) that evaluation of behavior change as well as other changes be a part of every evaluation; and (3) that more attention be paid to prevention programs for minority groups, especially blacks and Hispanics.

Prevention of Consequences in the Host

Prevention of the Fetal Alcohol Syndrome

The effects of alcohol on the developing human fetus can be quite severe. In both animals (Randall, 1982; Riley, 1982) and humans (Landesman-Dwyer, 1982), the fetal alcohol syndrome (FAS) manifests itself as an abnormal pattern of growth and development found more frequently in the offspring of heavy-drinking mothers than in those of nondrinkers or occasional drinkers. Major mental and motor retardation may occur in these cases. While the exact number of FAS children affected by maternal alcoholism is unknown, estimates are that 1 in every 750 to 1000 live births may show the FAS. In addition, moderate- and heavy-drinking women, compared to abstainers and light-drinking women, more often bear children who show reduced physical growth, increased rates of spontaneous abortion, stillbirth, and damage to the central nervous system.

Now that the existence of the FAS is common knowledge and the dimensions of the problem are generally recognized, attention is also being paid to FAS prevention programs. Some recent data are of value to those planning FAS prevention programs: (1) Infants born with alcohol-related birth defects in New York State during a single year will cost the state's economy at least $155,000,000 in lifetime care; consequently, preventive efforts will have clear cost-effectiveness (Blume, 1981). (2) A mail survey of women who gave live birth in Los Angeles County during a three-month period in 1979 revealed that 96% had been exposed to mass media messages about FAS. Despite this exposure, 20% reported risky drinking practices during their most recent pregnancy. Women who did not discuss their drinking with their doctors or nurses were 1.5 times more likely to have risky drinking practices, suggesting that future FAS prevention efforts ought to focus on interactions between pregnant women and their health care providers (Minor & Van Dort, 1982).

One of the best documented FAS prevention programs is the Fetal Alcohol Syndrome Demonstration Program, University of Washington School of Medicine (Little, Streissguth, & Guzinski, 1980; McIntyre, 1980). This program aims to provide model public and professional education on the FAS, clinical services for pregnant women, assessment services for FAS children, and on-going evaluation of these activities. A recent report (Lowman, 1982) from the program's evaluation unit documented a decrease in reported alcohol use among Seattle's pregnant women, corresponding to an increase in overall public knowledge about the risk to normal fetal development posed by maternal alcohol use. The 3000 women included in the sample (1500 sampled before and 1500 sampled after the Surgeon General's advisory on drinking by pregnant women) make this study one of the largest of this kind.

Prevention of Drunk Driving

Drunk driving, a factor in as many as 25,000 deaths and 75,000 injuries each year in the United States, is also one of the leading causes of death among the nation's young people. Important recent prevention efforts affecting drunk driving include the recent appointment of the Presidential Commission on Drunk Driving, new prevention initiatives recently launched by the National Highway Safety Administration, and the Health and Human Services Secretary's teen-age drinker initiative. As well, legislative approaches currently under consideration or in the process of enactment—to set new laws mandating stringent minimum penalties for drunk driving offenders, raising minimum drinking ages, and supporting more intensive enforcement of drunk driving laws—promise to establish new limits on driving and drinking and to decrease the incidence of drunk driving.

A recent "new look" at drunk driving prevention (Borkenstein, 1981) suggests that the role of alcohol in traffic accidents can be curtailed by (1) reducing per capita alcohol consumption (by increasing price or raising drinking age); (2) constructing streets and highways that place fewer demands on drivers so the effects of alcohol are not as severe; and (3) increasing enforcement to bring about general deterrence of drinking and driving. On the same issue, Gusfield (1981) reviews the grassroot movement for legislation to control drunk driving (e.g., by MADD—Mothers Against Drunk Drivers). He concludes that the costs of more determined enforcement of drinking and driving laws may be more than society wishes to bear—either in terms of money or the curtailment of civil liberties. Gusfield suggests that safer autombiles and streets may be necessary before citizens will accept the other costs of successsful prevention efforts.

Unequivocal data on the impact of lowering or raising the legal drinking age on drinking and drunk driving do not exist. The experience in Michigan, which lowered the legal drinking age from 21 to 18 in 1972 and then raised it again to 21 in 1978, illustrates the problems with such data. Alcohol-related motor vehicle crashes increased between 15 to 25% following the 1972 reduction (Douglass, 1980; Wagenaar, 1980). A sophisticated time series statistical analysis of crash data before and after the 1978 increase in drinking age suggested, in turn, that raising the legal drinking age from 18 to 21 caused a significant crash reduction among drivers aged 18 to 20. *However,* correlated increases in alcoholic beverage availability and consumption between 1972 and 1978 (Wagenaar, 1982a, 1982b), less driving due to the energy crisis, and an increase in the price of bottled and canned beer in 1979 may have interacted with the changes in legal drinking age to obscure their direct effects. This possibility notwithstanding, officials of the New York State Division of Alcoholism and Alcohol Abuse, Bureau of Alcohol and Highway Safety, following a survey of the effects of increases in minimum purchase age for alcohol in other states (Lillis, Williams, Chupka, & Williford, 1982), conclude that it is a viable means of reducing alcohol-related crashes among young drivers and, accordingly, that legislation raising the purchase age should be part of a comprehensive drunk driving prevention strategy.

The other accepted approach to prevention of drunk driving is more consistent and intensive enforcement of drunk driving laws. In this regard, the development and impact of 35 Alcohol Safety Action Projects (ASAPs) located throughout the United States was recently discussed (DOT, 1979). All were designed to (1) streamline the efficiency of the enforcement process and increase the number of arrests for driving while intoxicated (DWI); (2) develop more rapid and efficient procedures for processing DWIs; (3) create a system to refer DWIs to alcohol education rehabilitation programs; (4) develop mass media public education programs to call public attention to the DWI problem; and (5) evaluate the overall impact of the programs. Date on reductions in DWIs following implementation of the ASAPs have not been reported, in part because of the difficulty of segmenting their impact on drunk driving from other factors that influence it.

Two other recent prevention programs focus on DWI countermeasures. (1) The Responsible Driving Program, San Mateo County, California, reported six-month data (Giguiere, 1981) indicating that requiring a DWI to maintain total abstinence, attend alcohol education programs, be counseled for alcohol abuse, and maintain frequent contact with an enforcement officer lowered drunk driving recidivism. (2) The AAA Counterattack Program (Yaksich, 1980) is among the most comprehensive of DWI prevention programs. The program focuses on DWIs, but also includes high school DWI mini-courses, junior high and elementary school alcohol education and traffic safety courses, and senior citizens alcohol mini-programs. The unfortunate absence of an evaluation design prevents comparison of outcome data from this comprehensive program with data from other programs that differ in focus and content.

The international literature on "Scandinavian-type" laws, which stress drunk driving prevention by enactment and rigid enforcement of laws on drunk driving, has also recently been surveyed (Ross, 1981). It suggests that adoption and enforcement of such laws nearly always produce a deterrent effect on drunk driving in the short run, although the long-term deterrent effects are lessened a great deal when the realistic probability of apprehension for drunk driving is low (as it so often is).

Section Summary and Conclusions

FAS prevention efforts, especially those aimed at reducing alcohol consumption by pregnant women, have increased markedly in recent years. What has not yet been documented is the ability of these efforts to reduce alcohol consumption by pregnant women with the heaviest drinking problems who arc, hcncc, most likely to be associated with the FAS. An increase in attempts to reach health care providers with the FAS message so that they will intensify their efforts to curb heavy drinking by the pregnant women under their care also seems appropriate at this time.

Although increasing the legal drinking age and more consistently and rigidly enforcing laws against drunk driving are associated with short-term decreases in drunk driving and accidents associated with alcohol, the long-term effects of these two prime control measures is less certain, in part because research designs do not permit control of all relevant factors contributing to alcohol consumption and accidents. The recent multifaceted attack on drunk driving by federal and state authorities provides an excellent opportunity for careful assessment of the effects of legislative and judicial remedies for the drunk driving problem.

Research Needs

(1) While seemingly clear that a disproportionate number of automobile accidents and fatalities are caused by drunken adolescents and, hence, that this group of drinkers is a most appropriate target for primary prevention, it is unclear which subgroups of adolescent drinkers ought to be targeted for energetic prevention efforts. Should adolescent drinkers with concomitant drug problems, those who are adjudged juvenile delinquents, those with a history of familial alcoholism, lower socioeconomic status adolescent drinkers, or other subgroups be targeted for primary prevention? The same can be said of FAS prevention: What subgroup or subgroups of pregnant drinkers should be targeted for FAS prevention?

(2) Continued research on the continuum of the FAS is indicated. While seemingly likely that heavy or alcoholic drinking is causally linked to the syndrome, it is not so clear that social or infrequent drinking yields significant decrements in physical and intellectual status of the drinker's offspring. The question is an important one. If *no* drinking by pregnant women is to be the goal of prevention efforts, because *any* alcohol is associated with enhanced risk of FAS, then prevention is much more difficult and targeting virtually impossible. If only heaviest drinkers are to be reached, however, at least the problem of targets for intensive primary prevention is made a good deal easier.

(3) As discussed below, the linkage between per capita consumption and consumption by alcoholic drinkers remains a subject of debate. If

availability is decreased in order to decrease the likelihood of FAS and drunk driving, both apparently largely the responsibility of our society's heaviest drinkers, then it must be shown that per capita consumption *does* yield decreases in drinking by alcoholics.

Prevention in the Agent

Impact of Price on Consumption

The basis for the belief that the pricing of alcoholic beverages affects both consumption and problems associated with consumption is based on the work of Ledermann (1956). He proposed that the distribution of alcohol consumption is lognormal in all populations, that there is a constant relationship between consumption and the prevalence of heavy drinking, and that the incidence of alcohol problems can be reduced by lowering per capita consumption through limiting the availability of alcoholic beverages. Although many of the assumptions underlying Ledermann's theory and the data put forth to support it have been widely criticized (e.g., Parker & Harman, 1978; Pittman, 1980; Sulkunen, 1978), the view persists that increasing the price of alcoholic beverages reduces both consumption and problems associated with heavy consumption (e.g., Plymat, 1979; Schmidt & Popham, 1978). That view colors prevention efforts that focus on control of consumption by control of price.

On balance, the weight of opinion appears to be that consumption *is* affected by price. Few of those taking this position and offering data in its support, however, can add the all-important, additional data to the effect that reduction in overall consumption affects consumption by the heaviest segment of drinkers.

A review of the literature linking price and consumption in the United States, Canada, and several European countries (Ornstein, 1980) found beer to be price inelastic (i.e., an increase in price does not significantly lower demand), distilled spirits to be price elastic in the United States and inelastic in Europe, and wine to be variable in price elasticity. Ornstein concludes that the disagreement between those who would and those who would not use price as a control measure cannot be resolved by these data. Another review on the same topic (Cook, 1981) concludes, a bit differently, that "available evidence on the price elasticity of demand for alcohol . . . tends to support the view that liquor consumption is moderately responsive to price in the United States." Cook believes, accordingly, that increases in the tax rate of spirits will reduce both the auto fatality rate and the cirrhosis rate. Smith (1981) draws the same conclusion. A review of these relationships worldwide by WHO, the Finnish Foundation for Alcohol Studies, and the Addiction Research Foundation of Ontario, Canada (WHO, 1979) concludes with still another view: that while alcoholic beverages behave like other market commodities (in that consumption is affected by price), there are also complicated interactions between the availability of alcohol and the density of the distribution network, on the one hand, and the pricing of alcohol on the other. The same conclusion is drawn by Colon (1980).

Despite the controversy over the impact of price on consumption—and the failure by researchers to link higher price and lower consumption to a meaningful reduction in rates of alcoholism, problem drinking, and their sequelae—most countries have tended toward the view that increasing the price of alcoholic beverages is a viable control strategy. Sweden (Somervuori, 1977), Finland (Koski, 1977), Australia (Luey, 1979), Poland (Malec, 1980), and some but not all the European Economic Community countries (Sulkunen, 1978) employ some form of price policy as a consumption control.

Impact of Drinking Age on Consumption

We have reviewed data, above, which suggests that an increase in legal drinking age leads to a reduction in auto accidents in the short run, although the long-term effects of this deterrent remains uncertain. This section addresses, briefly, the intervening variable in the equation: increase in drinking age → decrease in consumption by adolescent drinkers → decrease in auto accidents. Does increasing the legal drinking age lead to a decrease in drinking by youthful drinkers?

A time series analysis of beverage alcohol distribution in Michigan from 1969 through 1980 (Wagenaar, 1982b), used to estimate changes in alcohol consumption associated with decreasing the legal drinking age, then raising it while a mandatory beverage container deposit law was implemented, provides the most recent empirical answer to this question. Wagenaar reports that a statistically significant, but temporary, increase in aggregate draft beer sales in Michigan followed the reduction in legal minimum drinking age from 21 to 18 in 1972; no concomitant changes in total beer, package beer, or wine sales were associated with the lowered drinking age. Significant decreases in total beer and package beer distribution and large increases in draft beer distribution occurred in 1979–1980, after the legal drinking age was raised from 18 to 21 and a mandatory beverage container deposit law was implemented; no concomitant change in wine distribution was observed. Although aspects of these changes provide "some support for the availability theory," the simultaneous change in several variables affecting availability (legal drinking age, beverage container deposit law, and a major economic recession in Michigan during 1979–1980) makes a causal interpretation of either data set impossible. The impossibility of developing a research design to permit separate analysis of each of the influences on consump-

tion makes a definitive judgment about the relationship between availability and consumption impossible.

Section Summary and Conclusions

Most policymakers worldwide—as well as in the United States—accept
the view that reducing availability of alcoholic beverages, by increasing
price or the legal drinking age, or both: (1) reduces consumption,
(2) reduces consumption by heavy drinkers, and (3) reduces the incidence
of phenomena associated with heavy drinking, including liver cirrhosis
and auto fatality and accident rate. The acceptance of this view has led to
efforts, apparently now accelerating, to increase the legal drinking age.

While the empirical data available on these issues provide modest support for the first of these presumed relationships (between availability
and overall consumption), the relationships identified have been, for the
most part, modest, and those reporting them have also pointed to crucial
design and methodology problems that proscribe an uncritical acceptance of the relationship. As important, almost no studies have linked
decreased availability with decreased drinking by the heaviest segment of
drinkers in any society and to concomitant decreases in the sequelae of
heavy drinking. The relationship, then, between availability and drinking by alcoholics and problem drinkers, assumed and acted upon by
many policymakers, appears essentially unproven.

Research Needs

Two major research needs readily present themselves:

(1) A research design that would permit an unencumbered view of the
relationship between availability and overall consumption is required.
This design would permit what are now simply correlational data to be
interpreted causally, by factoring out or controlling for concomitant
environmental events affecting availability, consumption, or both. A
laboratory model linking availability and consumption might be a suitable starting point for the development of this model. While some clinical researchers have attempted such a laboratory model, most of their
efforts involved alcoholics whose drinking is almost certainly not governed by the same rules that govern social drinkers.

(2) Determination of the relationship between per capita consumption
and consumption by the heaviest segment of the drinking population is
also required in order to determine whether the assumptions implicit in
the Ledermann model are valid. While much public discussion of these
assumptions and this linkage has taken place, the question remains, essentially, unresolved. Until it is resolved, a final assessment of the viability of the availability model of control is impossible.

Prevention in the Environment

Education

Many of the focused prevention activities described above have depended heavily on education components. Education efforts bulk especially large in prevention programs for youth; they are also important elements in programs for women, minorities, and the elderly, as well as untargeted programs for all citizens. As well, education programs have been influential in addressing the fetal alcohol syndrome and drunk driving problems.

A recent critical review of education strategies for alcohol prevention (Hochheimer, 1981) concludes that behavior change can be induced by alcohol education methods, but only when they inform about not only some of the problems associated with alcohol abuse, but also about how behaviors associated with alcohol consumption can be changed. Hochheimer's review of a number of mass education campaigns that failed suggests to her, not that this approach is not viable, but that insufficient attention to some of the crucial principles of mass persuasion and social learning theory prevented the messages from being maximally effective. Hochheimer recommends a simultaneous focus on knowledge, attitudes, and behavior; prior education efforts have focused only on the first or, less often, the second or third. Hochheimer believes that knowledge and attitudes *can* be influenced by mass media information programs, while a combination of mediated and interpersonal persuasion works best in carrying change through all three levels.

Milgram (1980) has evaluated a large number of alcohol education materials published between 1973 and 1979; she has then compared them to an earlier review of materials published between 1950 and 1973. Current (1973–1979) materials included 854 titles (425 books and 429 pamphlets and leaflets): 29% were created for the general public, 23% for professionals, 18% for educators, 9% for counselors, and 21% for youth at ages ranging from elementary school to college. An objective rating system established that the strongest materials were directed at professionals, educators, and counselors; weakest were materials prepared for the general public; materials for youth fell in between in quality. Compared with alcohol education materials published between 1950 and 1973, the quantity and quality of the newer material were judged by Milgram to be improving.

One of the more promising innovations in alcohol education is the Career Teacher Grant Program, an alcohol and drug abuse education program for health professionals, sponsored by NIAAA and NIDA. Initial preparations, curriculum development, implementation, and evaluation are described in a recent report (Labs, 1981). Designed to educate the trainers of the next generation's health professionals, this program trains health educators in the "interpersonal persuasion" strategies that Hochheimer's detailed analysis of alcohol education efforts suggested works best.

Mass Media

Recent discussions of the use of mass media for prevention and to advertise alcoholic beverages reveal how little is known for certain about the impact of this medium for either purpose. Commenting on a survey of alcohol prevention messages conveyed via mass media, Wallack (1980) concludes that relatively little is known about their effects on the general public. One special problem is that most evaluations have measured changes in individual behavior, attitudes, or knowledge, even though the message is conveyed to the group. Hence, alternative evaluation approaches focusing on group consensus and group decision making, to reflect changes in group attitudes and behavior, are suggested.

More attention has been paid to mass media advertising than to mass media prevention. The one recent—albeit brief—consideration of the two in juxtaposition (Orr, 1981) suggests that counteradvertising—preventive advertising—adopt some of the advertising techniques used successfully by industry to encourage alcohol consumption, in order to deglamorize alcohol use. Unfortunately, no examples are given.

Two empirical explorations of alcohol advertising of relevance to prevention have also recently been published. The first (Atkin & Block, 1980) examined the content and effects of beer, wine, and liquor advertisements in magazines, newspapers, and television. It focused on features and content that affected (1) levels of response to message exposure, (2) awareness and knowledge, (3) images, attitudes, and preferences, and (4) changes in drinking behavior. The relevance to prevention of this very thorough study lies in the value of such a sophisticated methodology for analysis of mass media prevention messages, in order that they might more effectively compete with messages urging consumption of alcoholic beverages.

A recent comprehensive review of the effects of advertising and other "controllable marketing factors" (e.g., relative price, taxation level, number of distribution outlets, legal drinking age, introduction of breath testing) on alcohol consumption in all 10 Canadian provinces between 1951 and 1974 (Bourgeois & Barnes, 1979) indicated that while per capita consumption of beverage alcohol almost doubled during this period (from 1.28 to 2.3 gallons), consumption was not significantly related to total print or broadcast advertising, relative beverages prices, or number of outlets. Consumption was, however, negatively related to taxes (increases in taxes were associated with decreases in consumption) and positively related to the lowering of the drinking age and introduction of breath testing. Bourgeois and Barnes conclude that advertisements and other "controllable marketing factors" influence alcohol consumption less than uncontrollable factors like employment status, ethnicity, etc.

Governmental Policies and Efforts

Worldwide Efforts.

While alcoholism continues to be a major problem around the world, prevention efforts vary tremendously among countries. Worldwide prevention strategies largely involve limiting the supply of and reducing the demand for alcoholic beverages (Madeley, 1981). In an effort to promote more international cooperation in formulation and implementation of prevention policies, strategies, and plans of action, the World Health Organization (1980) has induced more than 80 countries to share information on the extent and nature of their alcohol problems, each nation's preventive possibilities, and the relevant prevention policies and programs embarked upon by each. Notable is the heavy emphasis, worldwide, on untargeted, mass media alcohol education campaigns, and the apparent willingness of most governmental agencies to sponsor prevention programs that do not evaluate their successes.

United States Governmental Efforts.

The latest *Report to the United States Congress on Federal Activities on Alcohol Abuse and Alcoholism, FY 1980* (NIAAA, 1982) reveals that, of a total of $584.1 million in federal funds expended on alcohol-related actions (including research, interventions, treatment and rehabilitation, resource development, general program support and administration, and prevention), $24.4 million of those funds, or 4%, were allocated to prevention. Federal agencies sponsoring a substantial number of prevention research or demonstration projects were NIAAA, the Department of Defense, and the National Highway Traffic Safety Administration. The federal government was responsible for 63.5% ($24.4 million of $38.4 million) of all public funds expended for the purposes of alcoholism prevention; viewed this way, the level of federal involvement in prevention is impressive and substantial. Viewed another way, that only 4% ($24.4 million of $584.1 million) of federal funds for alcohol-related activities went to prevention activities, the prevention fraction appears scandalously low given the potential of primary prevention activities to return their costs many times over.

Beyond the specific roles of ADAMHA (1981) and NIAAA (Mayer, 1982a, 1982b; Steinhauer, 1982) in developing innovative prevention demonstration programs and in sponsoring evaluation research on those programs, the military has expended substantial funds, on a relative basis, to provide prevention programs to its personnel. The Navy (Bunn, 1982) and the Air Force (Armor, Orvis, Carpenter-Huffman, &

Polich, 1981; Orvis, Armor, Williams, Barras, & Schwarzbach, 1981) have been especially active in this regard.

A recent study of Air Force prevention activities illustrates the scope of the alcoholism problem in that branch of the military, the nature of prevention activities brought to bear on the problem, and the results of those prevention efforts. In the report (Carpenter-Huffman, Orvis, Armor, & Burkholz, 1981), the Social Actions Seminar Program, designed to educate Air Force personnel about drug and alcohol abuse, is evaluated. The program includes two, four-hour seminars, one for lower-grade enlisted personnel, the other for higher-grade enlisted personnel and officers. Every Air Force enlisted person or officer attends one or the other of these seminars every three years on average. The programs are designed: (1) to promote responsible and informed use of alcohol, and (2) to acquaint attendees with Air Force policies and programs relating to alcohol abuse. The total Alcohol Abuse Control Program cost about $6.5 million in FY 1977; the seminar program accounted for about one-tenth of this total. Considerable variation in seminar implementation, thrust, and focus was noted from one airbase to another. Seminar effectiveness was evaluated by means of a controlled field study conducted at 13 bases representing 8 largest Air Force commands worldwide.

The evaluation revealed no seminar effects on alcohol-related behaviors, including rates of excessive drinking, alcohol dependence symptoms, and work impairment. Similarly, no effects were found on referrals of persons with alcohol problems, either by self-identification or by supervisors' actions. While the seminars did have some immediate effects according to several attitudinal and informational measures, in almost all cases these effects were not large and were short-lived. Carpenter-Huffman and her colleagues conclude the seminar program "is not the most effective approach for preventing alcohol abuse." They suggest, instead, that attempts to change attitudes and behavior, by noninformaton means, be reserved for special groups at risk or persons responsible for identification.

The value of this report lies not only in its documentation of the ineffectiveness of this costly prevention activity and in its suggestions for improving behavior change potential, but also in its evaluation methodology, which required random assignment of persons to the seminar program and their subsequent, intensive follow-up. Individual rather than group evaluation designs and very intensive follow-up provided data of which policymakers could make maximal use.

Prevention in the Work Place

In a recent contribution to a volume on alcoholism prevention, Nathan (1983) drew the following conclusions about alcoholism prevention in the work place:

Alcoholism prevention efforts in the workplace are still modest, imperfect, and variable in quality. Many or most corporations have moved no farther than recognition that the alcoholism problems of their employees may be costing them money; some have progressed a bit farther, to the point where Employee Assistance Programs of one sort or another have been funded. But treatment, despite its problems, still seems far more cost-effective than prevention to most managers. In other words, to this time, industry has failed to recognize the dollars and cents value of alcoholism prevention; as a consequence, when prevention efforts are undertaken, they are usually a small, ineffective afterthought grafted onto a treatment program. It is clear that data on the cost-effectiveness of prevention *per se* are essential before hard-headed managers will heed our appeals to heighten efforts at prevention of alcoholism. (pp. 403, 404)

Despite both the conceptual (Kelsey, 1982; Trice, 1981; Watkins, 1981) and practical (McLatchie, Grey, Johns, & Lomp 1981; Plant, 1981) advantages of primary prevention of alcoholism in the work place, prevention is rarely accorded high priority in industrial alcoholism programs. Roman (1981), in fact, concludes that "programs for alcoholic employees have shifted their emphases from prevention and constructive confrontation to self-referrals, through 'employee assistance programs,' for counseling and treatment" (p. 244). Why has this unfortunate shift away from prevention taken place? Roman implicates management's desire to move away from "constructive confrontation" with employees over deficits in job performance, often caused by alcoholism, in favor of self-referral for treatment outside the work environment; the latter is clearly a "safer" management strategy. He also sees as partially responsible for this development the shift away from alcohol-focused programs to more generic programs—more concerned with non-alcohol-related personal and familial problems. Ironically, this apparent decline in emphasizing prevention in worksite alcoholism programs comes at a time when, apparently, these alcoholism programs have become much more widely accepted as cost-effective (Roman, 1981; Rundell, Jones, & Gregory, 1981; Schramm, 1980).

Wellness programs offer additional opportunities for alcoholism prevention at the worksite. Wellness programs—positive lifestyle change programs—offer healthy employees the opportunity to modify lifestyles that might, at a future date, cause health problems. Smoking cessation, exercise, stress management, weight control, and nutrition programs are typically offered in the effort to promote healthier lifestyles, improve quality of life at present, and to reduce health risks in the future. A number of large corporations, including Johnson & Johnson and Control Data, have put wellness programs into place. While these programs do not typically provide alcoholism components, relying instead on existing Employee Assistance Programs to reach employees with alcohol problems, the existence of comprehensive positive lifestyle change programs may impact drinking practices and general awareness of healthy life-styles, in that way preventing the development of alcohol problems in some individuals. Of course, empirical studies of the impact of these programs on alcohol problems are necessary before their role in prevention can be accepted.

Section Summary and Conclusions

The heterogeneous group of issues considered in this section—the impact of alcohol education, mass media prevention programs, and governmental policies and efforts on prevention worldwide, in this country, and in the work place—defies a summary or coherent conclusions. Virtually the only meaningful generalization that can be drawn is that alcohol education, the most common prevention method, and the mass media, the most frequent choice of a means to convey the prevention message, have in recent years been fully employed by local, state, federal, and foreign policymakers and implementers for the purposes of alcoholism prevention. Prevention efforts have clearly blossomed worldwide. Evaluation of these efforts, moreover, provides encouragement by suggesting the power of alcohol education in enhancing alcohol information levels; as well, attitudes towards alcohol and alcoholism change in positive directions in the face of effective prevention messages. What has been harder to achieve, geography, message, and medium notwithstanding, is behavior change—meaningful reduction in consumption.

Research Needs

The number one research need, no matter whether one views data on prevention outcomes from the viewpoint of host, agent, or environment, is a developmental effort designed to create prevention packages, approaches, or methods that will lead to behavior change as well as to information and attitude change. A "boot-strap" approach may be required, by which data on those (few) prevention programs that do generate behavior change are brought together and reanalyzed for their elements. Those elements, some of which, presumably, could account for the behavior change, could then be integrated into new prevention programs which would, then, be evaluated specifically for their capacity to induce more robust behavior change. In other words, in the absence of measured changes in consumption after a prevention program, it is difficult to be sure the program has succeeded in its major purpose, no matter how robust changes may seem to be in information on alcohol and alcoholism or in attitudes towards drunkenness, drunk driving, or alcohol use.

References

ADAMHA. *ADAMHA prevention policy and programs 1979–1982*. Rockville, Md.: ADAMHA, 1981.

Alcocer, A. Alcohol use and abuse among the Hispanic American population. In *Alcohol and Health Monograph No. 4: Special Population Issues*. Rockville, Md.: NIAAA, 1982, pp. 361–382.

Arevalo, R., & Minor, M. (Eds.). *Chicanas and alcoholism: A socio-cultural perspective of women*. Monograph from San Jose State University School of Social Work, 1981.

Armor, D. J., Orvis, B. R., Carpenter-Huffman, P., & Polich, J. M. *The control of alcohol problems in the US Air Force*. Santa Monica, Calif.: The Rand Corporation, December 1981. (R-2867-AF)

Atkin, C., & Block, M. *Content and effects of alcohol advertising*. East Lansing, Mich.: Michigan State University, 1980.

Bartlett, E. E. Contribution of school health educators to community health promotion: What can we reasonably expect? *American Journal of Public Health*, 1981, *71*, 1384–1391.

Blane, H. T. Education and the prevention of alcoholism. In B. Kissin & H. Begleiter (Eds.), *Biology of alcoholism* (Vol. 4). New York: Plenum, 1976, pp. 519–578.

Blume, S. B. Drinking and pregnancy: Preventing fetal alcohol syndrome. *New York State Journal of Medicine*, 1981, *81*, 95–98.

Bohman, M., Sigvardsson, S., & Cloninger, C. R. Maternal inheritance of alcohol abuse: Cross-fostering analysis of adopted women. *Archives of General Psychiatry*, 1981, *38*, 965–969.

Bonnie, R. J. Discouraging unhealthy personal choices through government regulation: Some thoughts about the minimum drinking age. In H. Wechsler (Ed.), *Minimum-drinking-age laws*. Lexington, Mass.: Lexington Books, 1980.

Borkenstein, R. F. Problems of enforcement. In L. Goldberg (Ed.), *Alcohol, drugs and traffic safety*. Stockholm: Almqvist & Wiksell International, 1981, pp. 818–837.

Bourgeois, J. C., & Barnes, J. G. Does advertising increase alcohol consumption? *Journal of Advertising Research*, 1979, *19*, 19–29.

Bower, S. Tools for change: Issues, strategies, and resources: Prevention of alcohol-related problems. *Journal of Addictions and Health*, 1980, *1*, 242–249.

Braiker, H. The diagnosis and treatment of alcoholism in women. In *Alcohol and Health Monograph No. 4: Special Population Issues*. Rockville, Md.: NIAAA, 1982, 111–139.

Braucht, G. Problem drinking among adolescents: A review and analysis of psychosocial research. In *Alcohol and Health Monograph No. 4: Special Population Issues*. Rockville, Md.: NIAAA, 1982, pp. 143–164.

Breed, W., & De Foe, J. R. The portrayal of the drinking process on primetime television. *Journal of Communication*, 1981, *31*, 58–67.

Brody, J. A. Aging and alcohol abuse. *Journal of the American Geriatrics Society*, 1982, *30*, 123–126.

Bruun, K., Edwards, G., Lumio, M., Makela, K., Pan, L., Popham, R. E., Room, R., Schmidt, W., Skog, O. J., Sulkunen, P., & Osterberg, E. *Alcohol control policies in public health perspectives*. Finnish Foundation for Alcohol Studies (Vol. 25). New Brunswick, N.J.: Center of Alcohol Studies, 1975.

Bryan, W. A. Administering a campus alcohol program. In J. C. Dean & W. A.

Bryan (Eds.), *Alcohol programming for higher education*. Carbondale, Ill.: ACPA Media, 1982, pp. 44–57.

Bunn, G. A. *Continuum of care: Treatment, training, prevention.* Paper presented at the International Conference on Alcoholism, Oxford, 1982.

Carpenter-Huffman, P., Orvis, B. R., Armor, D. J., & Burkholz, G. M. *The effectiveness of Air Force Alcohol Education Seminars.* Santa Monica, Calif.: The Rand Corporation, September 1981. (R-2727-AF)

Colon, I. *Alcohol control, policies and their relation to alcohol consumption and alcoholism.* Unpublished doctoral dissertation, Brandeis University, 1980.

Conrad, P., & Schneider, J. W. *Deviance and medicalization.* St. Louis: C. V. Mosby, 1980.

Cook, P. Effect of liquor taxes on drinking, cirrhosis, and auto accidents. In M. H. Moor & D. R. Gerstein (Eds.), *Alcohol and public policy.* Washington, D.C.: National Academy Press, 1981.

Crisp, A. D. Making substance abuse prevention relevant to low-income black neighborhoods. II. Research findings. *Journal of Psychedelic Drugs,* 1980, *12,* 139–156.

Dean, J. C. Alcohol programming: A conceptual model. In J. C. Dean & W. A. Bryan (Eds.), *Alcohol programming for higher education.* Carbondale, Ill.: ACPA Media, 1982, pp. 15–29.

De Foe, J. R., & Breed, W. The mass media and alcohol education: A new direction. *Journal of Alcohol and Drug Education,* 1980, *25,* 48–58.

Donovan, B. *Collegiate group for the sons and daughters of alcoholics.* Paper presented at the NADC Conference, Washington, 1980.

Donovan, J. E., & Jessor, R. Adolescent problem drinking: Psychosocial correlates in a national sample study. *Journal of Studies on Alcohol,* 1978, *39,* 1506–1524.

DOT. *Summary of national Alcohol Safety Action Projects.* Washington, D.C.: National Highway Safety Administration, Department of Transportation, 1979.

Douglass, R. L. Legal drinking age and traffic casualties: A special case of changing alcohol availability in a public health context. *Alcohol and Health Research World,* 1980, *4,* 18–25.

Douglass, R. L. Youth, alcohol, and traffic accidents. In *Alcohol and Health Monograph No. 4: Special Population Issues.* Rockville, Md.: NIAAA, 1982, pp. 197–223.

Effects of alcoholic-beverage control laws. *Medicine in the public interest* (Vol. 8). Washington, D.C., 1979.

Evans, G. B., Steer, R. A., & Fine, E. W. Alcohol value clarification in sixth graders: A filmmaking project. *Journal of Alcohol and Drug Education,* 1979, *24,* 1–10.

Frankel, B. G., & Whitehead, P. C. *Drinking and damage: Theoretical advances and implications for prevention.* New Brunswick, N.J.: Rutgers Center of Alcohol Studies, 1981.

Fullerton, M. A. A program in alcohol education designed for rural youth. *Journal of Alcohol and Drug Education,* 1979, *24,* 58–62.

Gaines, J. J. Alcohol and the black woman. In F. D. Harper (Ed.), *Alcohol abuse and black America.* Alexandria, Va.: Douglass Publishers, 1976, pp. 153–162.

Garza, R. El alcoholico. *Impact,* 1979, *9,* 4–5.

Gavin-Jobson Associates. *The liquor handbook.* New York: Gavin-Jobson Associates, 1975.

Giguiere, W. *Program designed to test the effectiveness of frequent contact, abstinence,*

and chemical testing on repeat DWI offenders in San Mateo County, California.
Redwood City, Calif.: Hall of Justice and Records, County of San Mateo,
1981.

Gomberg, E. Alcohol use and problems among the elderly. In *Alcohol and Health
Monograph No. 4: Special Population Issues.* Rockville, Md.: NIAAA, 1982,
pp. 263–290.

Goodstadt, M. S., Sheppard, M. A., & Chan, G. C. An evaluation of two
schoolbased alcohol education programs. *Journal of Studies on Alcohol,* 1982, *43,*
352–369.

Goodwin, D. W., Schulsinger, F., Knop, J., Mednick, S., & Guze, S. B. Alcoholism and depression in adopted-out daughters of alcoholics. *Archives of
General Psychiatry,* 1977, *34,* 751–755.

Gusfield, J. R. Grass-root movement against drinking-driving. *Abstracts & Reviews in Alcohol & Driving,* 1981, *2,* 8–9.

Hames, L. N., & Petrucelli, E. Plan for influencing teenage drinking drivers.
American Association for Automotive Medicine, October 1980, 17–21.

Harford, T. C., Wechsler, H., & Rohman, M. *Contextual drinking patterns of
college students: The relationship between typical companion status and consumption
level.* Paper presented at the National Council on Alcoholism Annual Meeting,
Seattle, 1980.

Healy, P. Pregnant pause campaign: An explanation and an outline. *Focus on
Women,* 1980, *1,* 204–213.

Henggeler, S. W., Sallis, J. F., & Cooper, P. F. Comparison of university mental
health needs priorities identified by professionals and students. *Journal of Counseling Psychology,* 1980, *27,* 217–219.

Herrell, L. I., & Herrell, J. M. *Puerto Rican woman: Her role in substance abuse
prevention.* Paper presented at the Bicultural Women's Forum, Center for Mul-
ticultural Awareness Conference, Washington, 1979.

Hewitt, L. Current status of alcohol education programs for youth. In *Alcohol
and Health Monograph No. 4: Special Population Issues.* Rockville, Md.: NIAAA,
1982, pp. 227–260.

Hill, S. Biological consequences of alcoholism and alcohol-related problems
among women. In *Alcohol and Health Monograph No. 4: Special Population
Issues.* Rockville, Md.: NIAAA, 1982, pp. 43–73.

Hochheimer, J. L. Reducing alcohol abuse: A critical review of educational
strategies. In M. H. Moore & D. R. Gerstein (Eds.), *Alcohol and public policy.*
Washington, D.C.: National Academy Press, 1981, pp. 286–335.

Holliday, B. G. *Making the best of a bad situation: Pragmatic planning strategies for
black alcohol prevention efforts in the 1980s.* Paper presented at the NIAAA Skills
Development Workshop, Agenda for Black Alcoholism Programs, Jackson,
Mississippi, 1981.

Inpatient care can rescue many alcoholic teenagers. *Medical World News,* May 12,
1980, pp. 46–47.

Irwin, K. D. *Women, alcohol, and drugs: A feminist course focusing on causes and
prevention of abuse.* Paper presented at the American Public Health Association
Annual Meeting, Miami, 1976.

Kelsey, J. E. Practical approach to prevention. *Labor-Management Alcoholism Journal,* 1982, *11,* 142–143.

King, L. Alcoholism: Studies regarding black Americans. In *Alcohol and Health
Monograph No. 4: Special Population Issues.* Rockville, Md.: NIAAA, 1982,
pp. 385–407.

Kitano, H. Alcohol drinking patterns: The Asian Americans. In *Alcohol and Health Monograph No. 4: Special Population Issues.* Rockville, Md.: NIAAA, 1982, pp. 411–430.

Knupfer, G. Problems associated with drunkenness in women. In *Alcohol and Health Monograph No. 4: Special Population Issues.* Rockville, Md.: NIAAA, 1982, pp. 3–39.

Kola, L. A., & Kosberg, J. I. Model to assess community services for the elderly alcoholic. *Public Health Reports,* 1981, *96,* 458–463.

Koski, H. Labor market and alcohol prices. *Alkoholpolitik,* 1977, *40,* 37–38.

Kraft, D. P. *A program to prevent alcohol problems among college students: Successes and failures.* Paper presented at the American Psychological Association Annual Meeting, Washington, 1982.

Labs, S. M. Career teacher grant program: Alcohol and drug abuse education for the health professions. *Journal of Medical Education,* 1981, *56,* 202–204.

Landesman-Dwyer, S. Drinking during pregnancy: Effects on human development. In *Alcohol and Health Monograph No. 2: Biomedical Processes and Consequences of Alcohol Use.* Rockville, Md.: NIAAA, 1982, pp. 335–358.

Leavy, R. L. First steps in campus prevention programs. *CAFC News,* July–August 1980.

Ledermann, S. *Alcool, alcoolisme, alcoolisation.* (Donnees scientifiques de caractere physiologique, economique et social. Institut d'Etudes Demographiques, Cahier No. 29.) Paris: Press Universitaire, 1956.

Leigh, D. H. *Prevention work among the elderly: A workable model.* Paper presented at the National Alcoholism Forum, Seattle, 1980.

Lewis, R. Alcoholism and the native Americans—A review of the literature. In *Alcohol and Health Monograph No. 4: Special Population Issues.* Rockville, Md.: NIAAA, 1982, pp. 315–328.

Lieber, C. S. A public health approach for the control of the disease of alcoholism. *Alcoholism: Clinical and Experimental Research,* 1982, *6,* 171–177.

Lillis, R. P., Williams, T. P. Chupka, J. Q., & Williford, W. R. *Highway safety considerations in raising the minimum legal age for purchase of alcoholic beverages to nineteen in New York State.* Albany, N.Y.: New York State Division of Alcoholism and Alcohol Abuse, 1982.

Little, R. E., Streissguth, A. P., & Guzinski, G. M. Prevention of fetal alcohol syndrome: A model program. *Alcoholism: Clinical and Experimental Research,* 1980, *4,* 185–189.

Lowman, C. FAS researchers studying increased public knowledge. *NIAAA Information and Feature Service,* August 30, 1982, p. 5.

Luey, P. Can alcohol taxes reduce consumption? *Australian Journal of Alcoholism and Drug Dependence,* 1979, *6,* 119–122.

Madeley, J. Cost of a drink. *World Health,* August 1981, 5–7.

Malec, J. Methods of reducing alcohol consumption. *Problemy Alkoholizmu,* 1980, *27,* 3–4.

Mayer, W. *Letter outlining a national Secretarial initiative to combat teenage alcohol abuse.* Washington, D.C.: Alcohol, Drug Abuse, and Mental Health Administration, October 29, 1982. (a)

Mayer, W. *Statement on alcohol and drug prevention before the US Senate Subcommittee on Alcoholism and Drug Abuse* (Committee on Labor and Human Resources), 1982. (b)

McAlister, A., Perry, C., Killen, J., Slinkard, L. A., & Maccoby, N. Pilot study of smoking, alcohol and drug abuse prevention. *American Journal of Public Health,* 1980, *70,* 719–721.

McCarty, D., Poore, M., Mills, K. C., & Morrison, S. Direct mail techniques and the prevention of alcohol-related problems among college students. *Journal of Studies on Alcohol,* in press.

McIntyre, C. E. *Evaluating prevention and education: Fetal alcohol syndrome.* Paper presented at the National Council on Alcoholism Annual Meeting, Seattle, 1980.

McLatchie, B. H., Grey, P. M., Johns, Y., & Lomp, K. G. Component analysis of an alcohol and drug program: Employee education. *Journal of Occupational Medicine,* 1981, *23,* 477–480.

Merker, J. F. *Indians of the Great Plains: Issues in counseling and family therapy.* Paper presented at the National Council on Alcoholism Annual Meeting, New Orleans, 1981.

Milgram, G. G. Descriptive analysis of alcohol education materials, 1973–1979. *Journal of Studies on Alcohol,* 1980, *41,* 1209–1216.

Mills, K. C., McCarty, D., Ward, J., Minuto, L., & Patzynski, J. A. residence hall tavern as a collegiate alcohol abuse prevention activity. *Addictive Behaviors,* in press.

Minor, M. J., & Van Dort, B. Prevention research on the teratogenic effects of alcohol. *Preventive Medicine,* 1982, *11,* 346–359.

Miranda, V. L. *Agenda for black alcoholism programs.* Paper presented at the NIAAA Skills Development Workshop, Jackson, Mississippi, 1981.

Mongeon, J. E., & Ziebold, T. O. *Preventing alcohol abuse in the gay community: Towards a theory and model.* Paper presented at the National Council on Alcoholism Annual Meeting, Seattle, 1980.

Monroe-Scott, B., & Miranda, V. *Guidebook for planning alcohol prevention programs with black youth.* Rockville, Md.: National Clearinghouse for Alcohol Information, 1981.

Morrissey, E. R., & Schuckit, M. A. *Drinking patterns and alcohol-related problems in a population of alcoholic detoxification patients: Comparison of males and females.* Paper presented at the National Council on Alcoholism Annual Meeting, Washington, D.C., 1979.

NASADAD. Alcohol and drug abuse among the elderly: Out of sight, out of mind? *NASADAD alcohol and drug abuse report,* 1981.

Nathan, P. E. Alcoholism prevention in the workplace: Three examples. In P. M. Miller & T. D. Nirenberg (Eds.), *Prevention of alcohol abuse.* New York: Plenum Publishing Corporation, 1983.

National Academy of Sciences, Institute of Medicine. *Alcoholism and related problems: Opportunities for research.* Washington, D.C., July 1980. (IOM 80-04)

National Center for Alcohol Education. *Program overviews of the decisions and drinking series.* Arlington, Va., 1977.

National Clearinghouse for Alcohol Information. *Spectrum: Alcohol problem prevention for women by women.* DHHS Pub. No. (ADM) 81-1036, 1981.

NIAAA. *Report to the United States Congress on federal activities on alcohol abuse and alcoholism, FY 1980.* Rockville, Md.: NIAAA, 1982.

NIDA. *Napa Project.* Rockville, Md.: NIDA, 1980.

Ornstein, S. I. The control of alcohol consumption through price increases. *Journal of Studies on Alcohol,* 1980, *41,* 807–818.

Orr, B. Counteradvertising against the current: The unselling of alcohol. *Alcoholism: The National Magazine,* 1981, *2,* 36–38.

Orvis, B. R., Armor, D. J., Williams, C. E., Barras, A. J., & Schwarzbach, D. S. *Effectiveness and cost of alcohol rehabilitation in the United States Air Force.* Santa Monica, Calif.: The Rand Corporation, December 1981. (R-2813-AF)

Parker, D. A., & Harman, M. S. Distribution of consumption model of prevention of alcohol problems: A critical assessment. *Journal of Studies on Alcohol*, 1978, *39*, 377–399.

Payton, C. R. Substance abuse and mental health: Special prevention strategies needed for ethnics of color. *Public Health Reports*, 1981, *96*, 20–25.

Pittman, D. J. *Primary prevention of alcohol abuse and alcoholism: An evaluation of the control of consumption policy*. St. Louis, Mo.: Social Science Institute, Washington University, 1980.

Plant, T. D. Education and prevention through employee assistance programs. *Labor-Management Alcoholism Journal*, 1981, *10*, 167–177.

Plaut, T. A. *Alcohol problems: A report to the nation*. New York: Oxford University Press, 1967.

Plymat, W. N. *Economic strategies for prevention*. Paper presented at the Third World Congress for the Prevention of Alcoholism and Drug Dependency, Acapulco, 1979.

Portnoy, B. Effects of a controlled-usage alcohol education program based on the Health Belief Model. *Journal of Drug Education*, 1980, *10*, 181–195.

Pringle, H., Gregory, J., Ginkel, K., & Cheek, C. Alpha Centers: A viable prevention model for substance abuse agencies and public schools. In A. J. Schecter (Ed.), *Drug dependence and alcoholism* (Vol. 2). New York: Plenum Press, 1981, pp. 183–189.

Randall, C. Alcohol as a teratogen in animals. In *Alcohol and Health Monograph No. 2: Biomedical Processes and Consequences of Alcohol Use*. Rockville, Md.: NIAAA, 1982, 291–307.

Reed, D. S. Reducing the costs of drinking and driving. In M. H. Moore & D. R. Gerstein (Eds.), *Alcohol and public policy*. Washington, D.C.: National Academy Press, 1981, pp. 336–387.

Regalado, R. New approaches for prevention and education of alcoholism among Hispanic women. In R. Arevalo & M. Minor (Eds.), *Chicanas and alcoholism: A socio-cultural perspective of women*. Monograph from San Jose State University School of Social Work, 1981.

Resource Alternatives Corp. *Prevention of alcohol abuse among pre-delinquent youth: An overview of the evaluation results*. Washington, D.C.: Resource Alternatives Corp., 1982.

Riley, E. Ethanol as a behavioral teratogen: Animal models. In *Alcohol and Health Monograph No. 2: Biomedical Processes and Consequences of Alcohol Use*. Rockville, Md.: NIAAA, 1982, 311–332.

Roman, P. M. From employee alcoholism to employee assistance: Deemphases on prevention and alcohol problems in work-based programs. *Journal of Studies on Alcohol*, 1981, *42*, 244–272.

Rosenbluth, J., Nathan, P. E., & Lawson, D. M. Environmental influences on drinking by college students in a college pub: Behavioral observations in the natural environment. *Addictive Behaviors*, 1978, *3*, 117–121.

Rosett, H. L., & Weiner, L. Identifying and treating pregnant patients at risk from alcohol. *Canadian Medical Association Journal*, 1981, *15*, 149–154.

Ross, H. L. *Deterrence of the drinking driver: An international survey*. Washington, D.C.: National Highway Safety Administration, Department of Transportation, 1981.

Rundell, O. H., Jones, R. K., & Gregory, D. Practical benefit-cost analysis for alcoholism programs. *Alcoholism: Clinical and Experimental Research*, 1981, *5*, 497–508.

Sandmaier, M. *Women and alcohol abuse: A strategy for prevention.* Paper presented at the American Public Health Association Annual Meeting, Miami, 1976.

Schaefer, J. Ethnic and racial variations in alcohol use and abuse. In *Alcohol and Health Monograph No. 4: Special Population Issues.* Rockville, Md.: NIAAA, 1982, pp. 293–311.

Schmidt, W., & Popham, R. E. Single distribution theory of alcohol consumption: A rejoinder to the critique of Parker and Harman. *Journal of Studies on Alcohol,* 1978, *39,* 400–419.

Schramm, C. J. Evaluating industrial alcoholism programs: A human-capital approach. *Journal of Studies on Alcohol,* 1980, *41,* 702–713.

Schwartz, L. R. *Alcoholism among lesbian/gay men: A critical problem in critical proportions.* Phoenix, Arizona: Do It Now Foundation, 1980.

Scott, B. M. *Alcohol prevention for black communities.* Paper presented at the Alcoholism in the Black Community Seminar, Newark, N.J., 1981.

Shaw, S. The causes of increasing drinking problems amongst women: A general etiological theory. In *Women and alcohol.* New York: Tavistock Publications, 1980, pp. 1–40.

Smith, R. Relation between consumption and damage. *British Medical Journal,* 1981, *283,* 895–898.

Somervuori, A. Pricing as an instrument of alcohol policy. *Alkoholpolitik,* 1977, *40,* 85–93.

Staulcup, H., Kenward, K., & Frigo, D. A review of federal primary alcoholism prevention projects. *Journal of Studies on Alcohol,* 1979, *40,* 943–968.

Steinhauer, G. L. *Statement by a representative of the National Council on Alcoholism before the US Senate Subcommittee on Alcoholism and Drug Abuse* (Committee on Labor and Human Resources), 1982.

Stuart, R. B. Teaching facts about drugs: Pushing or preventing? In D. A. Ward (Ed.), *Alcoholism: Introduction to theory and treatment.* Dubuque, Iowa: Kendall/ Hunt, 1980, pp. 211–225.

Sulkunen, P. *Developments in the availability of alcoholic beverages in the EEC countries.* Helsinki: Social Research Institute of Alcohol Studies, 1978.

Trice, H. M. Two basic ways of looking at primary prevention. In *Preventing alcoholism: Primary prevention* (Rev. ed.). Mill Neck, N.Y., 1981, pp. 74–75.

Wagenaar, A. C. *Raised legal drinking age and motor vehicle accidents in Michigan.* Paper presented at the American Public Health Association Annual Meeting, Detroit, 1980.

Wagenaar, A. C. Aggregate beer and wine consumption. Effects of changes in the minimum legal drinking age and a mandatory beverage container deposit law in Michigan. *Journal of Studies on Alcohol,* 1982, *43,* 469–487. (a)

Wagenaar, A. C. Raised legal drinking age and automobile crashes: A review of the literature. *Abstracts and Reviews in Alcohol and Driving,* 1982, *3,* 3–8. (b)

Wallack, L. M. Assessing effects of mass media campaigns: An alternative perspective. *Alcohol Health and Research World,* 1980, *5,* 17–29.

Wallack, L. M., & Barrows, D. C. *Preventing alcohol problems in California: Evaluation of the three year "Winners" program.* Berkeley, Calif.: University of California, School of Public Health, Social Research Group, 1981.

Watkins, G. T. In-house. *EAP Digest,* 1981, *1,* 5.

Weibel, J. American Indians, urbanization and alcohol: A developing urban Indian drinking ethos. In *Alcohol and Health Monograph No. 4: Special Population Issues.* Rockville, Md.: NIAAA, 1982, pp. 331–358.

Weisheit, R. A., Kearney, K. A., Hopkins, R. H., & Mauss, A. L. *Evaluation of a model alcohol education project for the public schools: Phase II, an overview of the first year's activities and results.* Pullman, Wash.: Washington State University, 1979.

Whitehead, P. C., & Ferrance, R. G. Liberated drinking: New hazard for women. *Addictions,* 1977, *24,*36–53.

Williams, M., & Vejnoska, J. Alcohol and youth: State prevention approaches. *Alcohol Health and Research World,* 1981, *6,* 2–13.

Wilsnack, R. W., & Wilsnack, S. C. Sex roles in drinking among adolescent girls. *Journal of Studies on Alcohol,* 1978, *39,* 1855–1874.

Wilsnack, S. C. Prevention of alcohol problems in women. In *Alcohol and Health Monograph No. 4: Special Population Issues.* Rockville, Md.: NIAAA, 1982, pp. 77–108.

World Health Organization. Alcohol control policies. In D. Robinson (Ed.), *Alcohol problems.* New York: Holmes & Meier Publishers, 1979.

World Health Organization. *Prevention of alcohol-related problems: An international review of preventive measures, policies, and programs.* Toronto, Ontario: Alcoholism and Drug Addiction Research Foundation, 1980.

Yaksich, S. AAA DWI counterattack—From rehabilitation to prevention. *Abstracts in Alcohol & Driving,* 1980, *9,* 13–16.

4
Prevention of Obesity

Ruth Striegel-Moore and Judith Rodin

Defining the Problem

Obesity has been recognized as a major health problem of modern times. According to a health examination survey conducted in the early 1970s, 14% of all males and almost 24% of all females between 20 and 74 years of age deviated by at least 20% from desirable weight (Health, United States, 1978). Approximately 25% of all children are overweight (Forbes, 1975), many of whom can be expected to remain overweight throughout their lives (Abraham & Nordsieck, 1960; Charney, Goodman, McBride, Lyon, & Pratt, 1975). Dieting and excessive worrying about one's physical appearance are so common, especially among women, that they can be described as a national obsession (Rodin, Silberstein, & Striegel-Moore, in press).

Obesity poses risks for both physical and psychological health. Obesity has been well documented as a primary contributing factor in the development of adult-onset diabetes, hypertension, myocardial hypertrophy, arthritis, gout, menstrual abnormalities, and reproductive problems. Obesity is considered a secondary contributing factor in the development of endometrial cancer and, finally, obesity is correlated with artherosclerotic disease, gall-bladder disease, and death, though these relationships are not causal. For men, these risk factors increase dramatically and in almost linear fashion with degree of overweight greater than 30 to 40% above average. For women, apparently even greater extremes of overweight are permissable before there is a strong association between health and overweight (Keys, 1980).

In addition to the numerous potential medical problems caused by or correlated with obesity, the overweight person typically faces psychological and social risks. Society has a strong, negative bias toward obesity (Allon, 1975; Harris, 1983; Wooley, Wooley, & Dyrenforth, 1979). Negative attitudes toward fat people are already found in children as young as six years of age (Staffieri, 1967), and social pressures for thinness are particularly powerful for women (Ananth, 1982; Dyrenforth, Wooley, & Wooley, 1980; Harris, 1983; Rodin et al., in press).

These grim data on the physical and psychological costs of obesity have prompted researchers and clinicians over and over again to call for preventive interventions aimed at reducing the incidence and prevalence of obesity in our society. However, thus far the vast majority of all medical and psychological interventions have been therapeutic rather than preventive.

Ideally, prevention programs should be developed on sound knowledge of the etiology of the target problem. However, as Caplan (1976) emphasized, instead of waiting until full etiological knowledge is obtained, more can be gained by taking action based on partial knowledge, provided that intervention efforts are evaluated rigorously so that reasons for success or failure can be determined. Etiological research in obesity is a fascinating area, requiring the cooperation of widely diverse disciplines. The search for the causes of obesity takes place in settings ranging from the microbiology laboratory to anthropological field studies, and we have yet to unravel the intricate interrelationships among the many etiological variables identified thus far.

Though many different etiological factors have been suggested, we are unlikely to find a specific causal explanation for a particular individual's obese condition. The term obesity stands for a group of heterogenous disorders, each of which most likely is multiply determined. However, all "obesities" share in common the fact that the afflicted individual has an excess of body fat due to an imbalance between energy input and energy expenditure (Van Itallie, 1984; Vasselli, Cleary, & Van Itallie, 1983). Moreover, the correlation between etiology and prevention is not perfect. It is possible for a specific variable to figure importantly in the etiology of obesity (e.g., an overly anxious mother regarding the infant's food intake), and yet the opposite pole (a less anxious mother) may not be an effective prevention intervention. Or a factor may be crucial to prevention (e.g., exercise), and yet its opposite (inactivity) may not be a major factor in the etiology of obesity. In still other instances, prevention and etiology may bear a good relationship (e.g., breast- vs. bottle-feeding).

We do not attempt in this paper to describe every possible etiological factor and prevention strategy. Rather we have elected to focus on developmental factors whose impact on weight regulation have been shown to extend for long periods of time and where prevention efforts may make a major difference. We will suggest which factors seem best candidates for prevention and the types of prevention strategies that might be tested.

Basic Considerations in the Conceptualization of Obesity Prevention

Obesity is conceptualized in a multifactorial model (Rodin, 1981b), including genetic, physiological, psychological, and sociocultural variables. As depicted in Figure 4.1, obesity is mediated by biological changes that in turn have been induced by a combination of long-term and short-term factors. Short-term factors include variables that exert a time-limited influence, for example the sight and smell of tasty food, whereas long-term factors encompass all those variables that persist over long periods of time (i.e., months, years, or, as in the case of genetic variables, even a lifetime), for example eating habits established during one's childhood years.

Importantly, the processes underlying the dynamic phase of obesity (i.e., the period during which weight is gained) differ from those underlying the static phase of obesity (i.e., weight maintenance). For example, while in most instances overeating can be identified in the dynamic stage, it is not always present during weight maintenance when metabolic changes due to changes in endocrine levels and/or fat cell mass may serve to maintain overweight without frank overeating. In short, obesity itself is associated with a wide range of consequences that promote maintenance of the elevated body weight (Rodin, 1981a). Factors maintaining obesity in the static phase are relevant in treatment efforts, yet for our discussion of prevention of obesity only factors influencing the dynamic phase of weight gain will be considered here.

Genetic factors are of great importance to the likelihood of weight gain and the development of obesity. The evidence is quite convincing that genetic variables are important as determinants of fat cell number, body size, and fat deposition sites, and/or of metabolic profiles (Bray, 1981). The present paper will review these data only briefly, however, since genetic variables cannot be targeted directly in primary prevention efforts. They are, however, important as cues for the identification of high-risk groups and thus for secondary prevention, and studies relevant to this purpose will be included in our discussion.

Most research on the development of human obesity has focused on short-term factors of obesity, and the majority of these experiments have measured the influence of these factors on one meal only or on regulation from one meal to the next. What is missing in most of these studies is a sufficiently long follow-up period to determine if the effect of short-term factors (e.g., overeating in response to the plentiful availability of tasty food) overrides other social or cognitive factors that influence food intake (e.g., self-control of eating behavior due to a desire to stay slim). Because these factors have been well discussed elsewhere (Spitzer & Rodin, 1981)

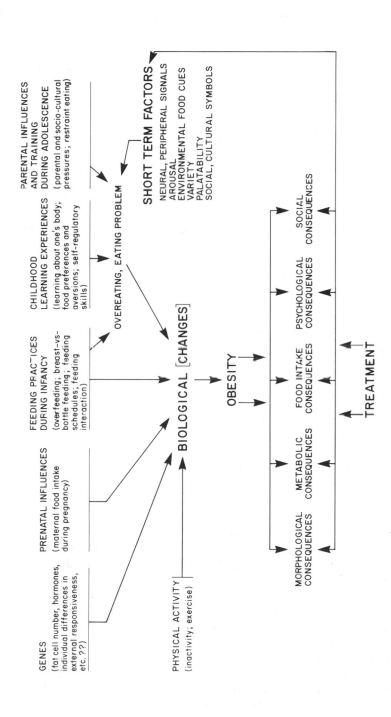

Figure 4.1. A comprehensive model of the development, maintenance, and change of obesity (adapted from Rodin, 1981b).

and because prevention efforts towards long-term factors may be more important in long-term weight regulation, this chapter will focus on long-term factors implicated in the development of obesity. These will be discussed according to the developmental stage during which they appear to emerge. Very little work has been done so far on health habits relevant to weight control (for example, eating habits and physical activity) from a life-span perspective. Therefore, our categories are necessarily tentative and open to revision. For most factors listed in Figure 4.1, we cannot answer questions such as how persistent a particular variable's influence is, if and when it changes, and if it has greater importance during certain stages and then fades into the background. Certain characteristics of taste perception, for example, have been found to change over time. Though absolute taste thresholds appear to remain relatively constant across the life cycle, intensity of taste perception reportedly decreases with age (Bartoshuk, 1978). Developmental research on nutrition and behavior is clearly needed (Stellar, Henning, Rodin, Rozin, & Wilson, 1980). For each developmental stage, a variety of preventive interventions is suggested.

Long-term Factors in the Development of Obesity

The etiological variables reviewed in this paper fall into one of six global categories: genetic potential, prenatal influences, feeding practices during infancy, childhood learning (including learning about one's own body, the acquisition of food preferences, and learning of self-control skills), learning in adolescence, and physical activity.

(1) Genetic Potential

Regardless of the *degree* to which genes contribute to obesity, an issue on which there is some disagreement, most investigators concur that people do differ genetically in their obesity potential (i.e., there are likely to be polygenic determinants underlying metabolic, endocrine, or neural processes and fat cell morphology that can increase or decrease a person's likelihood of becoming overweight). Reviewing studies on inheritance of obesity, Bray (1981) concluded that genetic factors undoubtedly play a role in the development of obesity. Children of overweight parents are clearly at risk to develop obesity themselves. A thorough analysis of parent/child interrelationships showed that children with two heavy parents had fatness levels three times as high as children with two lean parents (Garn & Clark, 1976). In addition to genetic factors, environmental factors also contribute to the risk that children with overweight parents will develop obesity. In fact, research has shown that parents' weight status is related to their childrern's weight, even if the children have been adopted (Garn, Cole, & Bailey, 1976).

Aside from anatomical and physiological differences, large behavioral differences between babies are observable even on the first day of birth. Newborns are quite different from one another in temperament (Thomas, Chess, & Birch, 1968; Thomas, Chess, Birch, Hertzig, & Korn, 1963), in their response to touch (Ainsworth & Bell, 1969), and in their responsiveness to visual and taste stimuli (Desor, Maller, & Turner, 1973; Engen, Lipsitt, & Peck, 1974; Engen, Lipsitt, & Robinson, 1978; Grinker, 1978; Milstein, 1980; Nisbett & Gurwitz, 1970). Investigators interested in obesity have, for obvious reasons, been most persistent in their attempts to understand the differences in response to taste. The results of studies considering the relation between birth weight and response to sweet taste are confusing and inconsistent, probably because most used *amount* consumed as their measure of preference, thus potentially confounding the effects of postingestional factors. Furthermore, using intake as the *measure* of taste responsiveness prevents us from assessing the relationship *between* taste responsiveness and ingestion. Using a better approach than the earlier studies, Milstein (1980) assessed taste responsiveness by a sucking measure (pressure with respect to time), and kept constant the amount ingested for all subjects. Sucking rate can be taken as an index of the relative avidity with which the infant responds to the fluid.

Milstein found that both skinfold thickness and body mass index were significantly related to preference for increasing concentrations of glucose, suggesting that differential preference is related to fatness, or rather thinness, of the infant at birth. Babies who were medium or greater in fatness preferred the highest concentrations of glucose, but the thin babies seemed to find the highest concentrations of sugar aversive. Milstein argued that it is more appropriate to think in terms of thinness rather than fatness of the infant as an effect on taste. In other words, he suggested there may be a protective effect from being thin at birth in the form of reduced responsiveness to higher sugar concentrations.

The Milstein study is also impressive because he measured visual responsiveness as well as taste responsiveness, the first time that both noneating and eating-related measures were taken in the same set of newborn infants concurrently. The noneating measure was a visual perception test (Salapatek & Kessen, 1966), revised by Milstein to be an analogue for infants to Rodin's (1973) measure of distractability in externally responsive adults. Interestingly, Milstein found that none of the measures of fatness or thinness of the infants predicted visual responsiveness to different intensities in the visual stimuli presented. Instead, weight of the parents seemed to be the critical determinant of infant responsiveness on this measure. Babies of overweight parents were more distractable (i.e., hyperresponsive) than babies of normal weight parents.

The scanning patterns of the babies of the overweight parents did not appear to be random or eccentric, but were influenced by the actual stimulus intensities. The children of overweight and normal parents did not differ in birth weight or gestational age, factors that might have artifactually influenced these findings. Thus, it is possible at birth to identify differences among newborns in their responsiveness to visual cues in the environment seemingly related to the weight of their parents, and to uncover differences in their preference for sweet taste apparently related to their own birth weight.

Here, then, is at least one testable hypothesis about two psychological factors present at birth that can influence the relative risk of an infant overeating and gaining excess weight. Thin babies of normal weight parents may be at least risk, given their relative aversion to high concentrations of glucose and the fact that they may actually be less responsive to environmental food cues. Babies of moderate or of greater adiposity at birth, whose parents are overweight, are at greatest risk because they bring heightened responsiveness to external cues and a preference for higher concentrations of sugar to an environment that may be likely to abound in food cues.

All available infants in the Milstein study are being followed prospectively. As Table 4.1 shows, a regression analysis to predict weight at age 3 suggests that, aside from family history of obesity, the best predictors at birth of early childhood obesity were responsiveness to visual cues and sweet taste. Prospective studies using larger samples are needed to allow a more confident interpretation of these results.

(2) Prenatal Influences

Effects of maternal health and nutrition on infant birth weight have been widely studied (e.g., Antonov, 1947; Blackwell, Chow, & Chinn, 1973; Metcoff, 1981; Ravelli, Stein, & Susser, 1976; Stein, Susser, & Rush, 1978). Much attention has focused on maternal undernutrition as it is related to low infant birth weight and poor health (Metcoff, Costiloe,

TABLE 4.1.
Regression Results for Weight Percentile on Tanner Norms

Variable	Beta	F	P
Family history of obesity	.3454	15.33	<.001
Visual responsiveness at birth	.2106	4.96	<.05
Responsiveness to sweet taste at birth	.2048	4.16	<.05
BMI at birth	.0844		ns
Schedule vs demand feeding	.0634		ns
Breast vs formula feeding	.0020		ns
Interaction of schedule/demand feeding and taste responsiveness	.1830	3.97	<.10

Crosby, Bentle, Seschachalam, Sandstead, Bodwell, Weaver, & Mc-Clain, 1981; Rosso, 1981; Susser, 1981), but it also appears recipro-cally that maternal weight and perhaps overnutrition, both prior to and during pregnancy, may be related to fatter infants (Udall, Harrison, Vaucher, Walson, & Morrow, 1978). The relationship between high birth weight and the later development of obesity is not yet clear (Fish, Singer, & Benjamin, 1975; Harrison & Udall, 1978;), but it may be that factors other than birth weight, deriving from genetic factors, maternal weight, or maternal behavior prior to or during pregnancy, are highly predictive of later childhood obesity.

Women differ in their dietary habits before and during pregnancy, and the hormonal changes resulting from pregnancy may induce certain cravings or aversions in pregnant women. Although common in folk-lore, changes in dietary habits have not been systematically investigated in women (Hook, 1978), but a prospective study is currently underway to fill this gap (Rodin, unpublished manuscript).

It may well be that maternal nutrition and hormonal changes during pregnancy influence fetal taste responsiveness by altering the composi-tion of the amniotic fluid. Apparently, the human fetus has structurally mature taste buds at 13 to 15 weeks of gestation (Bradley, 1972; Bradley & Stern, 1967) and begins to swallow regularly at about that time. Thus, for a considerable length of time the fetus is exposed to a wide range of chemicals present in the amniotic fluid, and the fetus's sensory experi-ences in the intrauterine environment may influence the formation of neural connections in the taste system (Mistretta & Bradley, 1977).

Prevention.
At present, more research is needed before we can determine whether maternal nutrition during pregnancy should be targeted as a variable in preventing obesity in her offspring. Specific issues to be addressed in prospective studies include the relative importance of maternal caloric intake and dietary composition both prior to and during pregnancy as predictors of birth weight. Another interesting question, for example, is whether adhering to a low-sugar diet during pregnancy will result in reduced responsiveness to sweet taste in the infant. Such prospective studies on maternal eating habits are quite laborious and expensive and clearly can only be realized if considerable financial resources are avail-able. Governmental and private funding agencies should assign high-priority status to this area of research.

(3) Feeding Practices During Infancy

Amount of Food Provided.
Our ethnic and cultural stereotypes are full of jokes about mothers mak-ing babies plump by pushing food into their mouths to show love and

affection or to ward off distress. But, surprisingly, very little empirical data exists either identifying clear circumstances in which overfeeding is likely to occur or showing a definite link between overfeeding and childhood obesity. Wooley, Dyrenforth, and Jaffe (1979) surveyed mothers of newborns to assess their own weight history and dieting tendencies, their preferences for a series of baby pictures with the babies varying in weight from fat to thin, and their feeding practices. They found that when weight of the mother and tendency to diet were separated statistically, being overweight per se was associated with a preference for thinner babies and a clear unwillingness to feed their own infants much food. A mother's tendency to diet and dissatisfaction with her own weight, however, was correlated with overinterpretation of the baby's hunger, preference for a fatter baby, and a greater willingness to provide food. According to Wooley and Wooley (1979), these findings suggest that overweight mothers may experience conflicting impulses around feeding their infants. Based on these data it remains unresolved whether or not overweight mothers actually overfeed their infants. In direct observations of mother feeding their newborns, Grinker (1980) reported that overweight mothers did not differ from average weight mothers.

Studies with preweanling rats have demonstrated the powerful influence of early nutritional experience on adult body size and weight. Weight differences between animals reared in small litters (where the offspring has optimal access to food) and in large litters (where one mother has to nurse many pups) increase with age, even when both groups are permitted free access to food after weaning (Sclafani, 1978). Rats from small litters develop more and larger adipocytes, which predisposes them to develop obesity (Johnson, Stern, Greenwood, Zucker, & Hirsch, 1973; Knittle & Hirsch, 1968; Lemonnier, Suquet, Aubert, & Rosselini, 1973). Correlational studies in humans have investigated the relationship between the dietary intake of babies (as it is controlled by both the mother and the infant) and body weight indices at various stages in the infants' development. Most of the research thus far has focused on the mode of feeding, namely breast-feeding versus bottle-feeding, and its potential impact on obesity.

Breast- versus Bottle-feeding.
There has been a continuing debate over the role of bottle-feeding in the development of childhood obesity. In general, pediatricians recommend breast-feeding because of the nutritional value of breast milk, and because breast-fed children are assumedly less prone to develop obesity (American Academy of Pediatrics, 1980; American Medical Association, 1979; Fomon, 1971). Bottle-fed infants have been found consistently to show greater gains in weight and length than do breast-fed infants (Hooper & Alexander, 1971; Neumann & Alpaugh, 1976). In an un-

precedented study, Fomon and his colleagues tracked weight indices of almost 470 children born between 1966 and 1971 (Fomon, Rogers, Ziegler, Nelson, & Thomas, unpublished manuscript). The first follow-up of these infants, performed at age 112 days, showed an accelerated growth rate in bottle-fed babies, an effect most pronounced when comparing a subgroup of fastest-growing, bottle-fed infants with fastest-growing, breast-fed infants (Fomon, 1971). However, when these children were measured at 8 years of age, the rate of gain in weight from 8 to 112 days of age demonstrated only a relatively low correlation with weight indices at age 8 years (Fomon et al., unpublished manuscript). Though this result suggests that fatness in infancy bears little predictive value with regard to weight status in childhood, Fomon and his colleagues (unpublished manuscript) point out that the effects of weight status in infancy may only become apparent when growth has been completed.

At least two competing hypotheses may explain this result. One suggests that body weight indices are primarily determined by genetic factors, and that the dietary differences experienced by the babies in this study affect body weight parameters only temporarily. Once solid food replaces breast- and bottle-feeding, the influence of mode of feeding vanishes. An alternative explanation is that as the infant grows older, the number of variables determining weight gain increases dramatically, thus making it more and more difficult to establish a direct relationship between a single variable (in this case mode of feeding during infancy) and body weight indices. Fomon and colleagues (unpublished manuscript) propose yet a third hypothesis, arguing that the effects of early nutritional experiences may only become apparent when growth has been completed. In order to evaluate this hypothesis, Fomon and his coworkers are planning to examine their cohort at age 18 (Ziegler, 1983).

Of the many variables differentiating breast-feeding from bottle-feeding, three deserve further attention in our discussion: the amount of food consumed, the composition of the dietary intake, and the relative control the infant has in the feeding situation. Comparing bottle-fed and breast-fed infants' intake poses methodological problems for the breast-fed infants in that measuring the amount of liquid consumed during a feeding is either imprecise or necessitates elaborate and quite intrusive technology. Test weighing the baby after a feeding may be inaccurate if the baby is too restless to permit an accurate reading (Houston, Howe, & McNeily, 1983). One alternative method developed by Woolridge and coworkers involves interposing an ultrasound transducer located in a latex nipple shield between the mother and the baby, a method which may not be acceptable to mothers if they have to use it over an extended period of time (Woolridge, How, Drewett, Rolfe, & Baum, 1982). In spite of the methodological problems, detailed analysis of the mother-child interaction during feeding, including the amount of food ingested over a period of time, could provide invaluable information on the variables determining the dietary experience of infants. At present, however, we do not have any empirical data to confirm the hypothesis that bottle-fed infants receive a food regimen of higher caloric content than breast-fed infants.

A second variable that has been proposed to explain weight differences between bottle-fed and breast-fed babies is the qualitative difference between breast milk and bottle milk (formula or cow milk). Formulas are relatively homogeneous in composition, while breast milk becomes increasingly higher in fat content during the course of a feeding. Although there is no evidence that milk intake is influenced by fat concentration in very young babies (less than 9 days old) (Nysenbaum & Smart, 1982; Woolridge, Baum, & Drewett, 1980), it may be that breast-fed babies learn to use milk fat concentration as an auxiliary cue for regulating intake (Hall, 1975).

An interesting aspect in the debate over breast-feeding versus bottle-feeding is the question of who controls the amount of milk ingested. When breast-feeding, it is difficult for the mother to tell how much her baby has ingested. In the absence of visual cues, readily available in bottle-feeding, the mother may be more attentive to the infant's behavioral signals of satiety. When babies cease to suck and swallow, mothers assume they are satisfied. The bottle-fed baby, on the other hand, may be encouraged to continue drinking until the bottle is empty. This encouragement may override the baby's signals and introduce an artificial endpoint to the feeding process (Fomon, 1971).

Another controversial issue in infant feeding is the question of when to introduce beikost (i.e., foods other than breast milk, milk, or formula). Most infants today are introduced to fruit juices and solid foods at a very early age. In the Bogalusa Heart Study, which followed 440 infants from their day of birth, it was found that at age 1 month already 89% of the infants received at least one type of beikost. Dry cereal, strained fruit, and fruit juices are among the most common foods given to very young infants, and the range of foods added to the babies' diets expands rapidly within the first 6 months of age (Frank, Webber, & Berenson, 1982). This practice has been attributed to aggressive marketing strategies by the baby food industry, and to the belief that feeding "solid food" will help the baby sleep through the night (Fomon, Filer, Anderson, & Ziegler, 1979). Criticisms against the introduction of beikost at this early age are based on two arguments. First, young babies are not developed enough motorally to be able to communicate satiety (for example, by leaning back or turning their heads away from the food). Second, while the impact of meal frequency has not been investigated in human infants, animal studies and research with human adults have shown consistently that frequency of meals is inversely related to accumulation of excess body fat (Fabry, 1967; Sclafani, 1978).

Schedules of Feeding.
Animal studies suggest that the feeding schedule imposed on newborn animals plays an important part in the development of external responsiveness to environmental stimuli. Gross (1968) created three groups of experimental animals immediately after weaning. One group was allowed to eat freely, the second group was placed on a deprivation schedule in which they were fed once every 22 hours, and the third group was placed on a random deprivation schedule in which they were fed on the average every 22 hours, with the time deprivation ranging from 8 to 48 hours. All animals were kept on these schedules for 100 days. Gross found that rats maintained under conditions of randomly varied deprivation were highly responsive to variations in the taste and caloric density of their diets. This finding was interpreted as an increase in external control in the randomly deprived animals as compared to rats having regularly available food. After 100 days, the animals were allowed to feed when they chose, but, even under these conditions of abundance, the randomly deprived rats continued to exhibit externally oriented responses to dietary variations.

Most interestingly, the randomly deprived rats also demonstrated a pattern of external control in a measure of external responsiveness to food cues that did not involve eating. Gross tested this hypothesis by recording the amount of time the rats remained in contact with food in an open field, although they were not allowed to eat the food. This result is reminiscent of the observations on nonconsummatory, food-relevant activity reported by Nisbett and Kanouse (1969), who showed that the supermarket shopping of obese human beings was unrelated to their internal state of depletion or satiety. Like these human shoppers, the randomly deprived rats in Gross' experiment exhibited an interest in food independent of their internal states of deprivation. The animals seemed to have "hungry eyes."

The implications of Gross' (1968) study are that, even when controlling for heredity, imposing irregular feedings with periods of scarcity can facilitate the development of external control of eating. Given the uncertainty of such a schedule, it would be best to eat whenever possible, regardless of one's internal state of deprivation. Although most babies in our society do not live in an environment of scarcity, many may live in a very unpredictable food environment and thus may learn to be externally responsive. Thus, Gross' results suggest that externality does not only have its origin in genetic or prenatal factors (as Milstein's study implied), but can also be an acquired trait. Other studies with human subjects have shown that externality is a fairly stable characteristic (Rodin, Slochower, & Fleming, 1977) that may be found in some obese but also in some normal weight persons (Levitz, 1975; Rodin, 1975; Ross, Pliner, Nesbitt, & Schachter, 1971). Given that human food intake is determined by a multitude of variables, it comes as no surprise that externality is not strongly correlated with current weight status; rather, it is one of many risk factors. Studies are needed comparing externally responsive individuals of varying current weight status and weight history in order to identify variables that counterbalance the influence of externality.

Adjunctive Responses.
Even the schedules used by mothers to minister to the nonfood needs of their infants may have effects on feeding behavior through the development of adjunctive responses. Adjunctive behaviors are those that develop in association with the satisfaction of another set of behaviors and drive states. They are based on schedules of reward that have certain fixed properties regarding the time between reinforcements. Falk (1961, 1969, 1977) has shown, for example, that when periodic food pellets are presented to hungry rats under certain schedules, they also come to drink excessive amounts of water, totalling as much as half their body weight in three hours. One can also produce schedule-induced hyperphagia in both rats and humans as a result of comparable experimental procedures. Thus, overeating can be learned and maintained without deprivation-induced drive states, simply as a result of certain specifiable arrangements of environmental contingencies.

Our discussion of risk factors in infancy for developing childhood obesity has been limited thus far to nutritional factors, including meal type (e.g., breast milk versus formula), meal size, and feeding schedules. However, we strongly avoid a simplistic conclusion that there is a direct relationship between early overfeeding and body weight or relative weight gain in childhood. Svegar and his colleagues (Svegar, Lindberg, Weibull, & Ollson, 1975), for example, found very slight differences in mean caloric intake between groups of normal and rapidly gaining obese infants, replicating the findings of Rose and Mayer (1968). While other investigations on overfeeding are clearly needed, we also need to direct our attention to other features of the mother–infant interaction which may affect overeating and the development of obesity.

Learning from the Feeding Interaction.
Psychologists have long asserted that it is in the early feeding interactions that children learn their first important lesson regarding trust, warmth, and tenderness and that a variety of important developmental processes are begun (Ainsworth, 1979). There are also data suggesting that here, also, learning about hunger and satiety undoubtedly takes place. Bruch (1973) has argued that childhood-onset obesity, at least, may stem from

faulty learning in infancy. Bruch has suggested that some mothers have failed to differentiate their child's need for food from their signals regarding other aversive states, and therefore feed the child indiscriminately. She suggests that as a result of this learning process the infant comes to confuse hunger with other internal, unpleasant sensations—a confusion that persists into adulthood and accounts for maladaptive eating habits and obesity.

While one may agree or disagree with Bruch's contention, many have come to suggest, in recent years, that hunger has a large, learned component (Blundell, 1979; Booth, 1981b; Robbins & Fray, 1980). These assertions challenge earlier views that hunger is simply the psychological experience of an innate, biological drive state. Therefore, it is entirely plausible that mislearning or a failure to learn about hunger can occur, and probably occurs quite early in the mother-child feeding interaction.

Support for the importance of learning in labeling hunger in infancy and its relation to food intake comes from a series of fascinating case studies reported by Dowling (1977). He studied infants with an esophageal atresia who could not receive nutrition by mouth because their esophagus was not fully formed. Such infants obtain their nutrition through a tube going directly into the stomach. To prevent aspiration, another fistula is placed in an opening made from the upper segment of the esophagus to the side of the neck, where saliva and ingested materials can pass out.

What is significant for our purpose is that these infants experience complete severance of oral activity with nutritional intake, from birth until surgical correction. Further, a state of hunger is in no way required for the ingestion of food, which is simply injected into the stomach with a syringe. Nor is satiation necessarily a signal for termination of feeding. Thus, nutritional repletion may not be associated with the infant's oral activity or its state of hunger or satiety.

Dowling studied several infants fed in a variety of ways. He reports that following surgical correction, normal responses to food occurred just in those infants fed into their gastric tube only when they showed some signs of hunger, and for whom feeding was discontinued when they evidenced signs of satiety. Also crucial was the coupling of oral feeding, which spilled out from the esophageal fistula, with the gastric feeding. Unless gastric feeding was given in response to infant-initiated cues and oral ingestion was simultaneously permitted, very disordered development often occurred, including problematic feeding behavior. These case studies point strongly, albeit extremely, to the important role of learning in the development of the complete experience of hunger and its relation to normal feeding behavior.

We still do not know exactly how hunger is learned in normal infants and how various aspects of the mother-child feeding interaction impact upon this learning experience. We can, however, glean some hypotheses from earlier studies not specifically concerned with the relationship between feeding and obesity.

Alberts, Kalverboer, and Hopkins (1983) observed two feeding interactions of each of seven mother-infant pairs. A first observation was obtained at the second feeding after birth and the second occurred at the sixth to ninth feeding. For all mothers (including four primaparae), the authors reported a close relationship between the mothers' tactile behaviors (stroking, jiggling) and the infants' sucking. Specifically, tactile behavior occurred primarily during the sucking pauses. At the second feeding it appeared that during a pause the infants would postpone the resumption of sucking until the mothers ended their tactile stimulation. Mothers reported that they used tactile stimulation both as a means of encouraging the infant to resume sucking, and as a way of communicating love and affection to their babies. The literature on biosocial risk factors during early development suggests that lack of contingencies between the behavior of the infant and that of the social environment may lead to an increased risk for psychopathology (Sawin, Hawkins, Walker, & Penticuff, 1980; Thoman, 1980). It is possible that a lack of contingencies during early feedings may contribute to eating pathology, but larger samples of mother-infant dyads are needed to support this speculation.

Ainsworth and Bell (1969) followed a sample of 26 babies of white, middle-class, American parents as these babies interacted with their mothers during feeding, from birth to age 3 months. Twenty-two of these infants were bottle-fed. For each mother-infant dyad observed during home feedings, interactions were classified on the following dimensions: (1) type of feeding—breast versus bottle; (2) timing of the feedings by the mother; (3) who determined the amount of food and the end of the feeding; (4) the mother's handling of the baby's preferences for different kinds of foods; (5) the pacing of the baby's intake; and (6) problems related to feeding. This qualitative scoring procedure allowed determination of how the typical responses between mother and infant determined meal frequency and size.

Examination of the individual data of the 26 babies reveals some fascinating patterns. For example, two of the mother-infant dyads were characterized as showing excessive demand feeding, where the mothers appeared to treat too broad a spectrum of their infants' signals as hunger. These mothers also coaxed their infants to eat in a given feeding, and to have frequent meals. These two babies both became overweight and remained so. Interestingly, the mothers were not themselves obese. In two other mother-infant dyads, characterized by scheduled feeding with overfeeding to gratify the baby, the mothers woke the infants to feed them, at which point they coaxed their infants to overeat. In this case, the mothers appeared to respond inappropriately to their infants' cues, since the infants were fed although they failed to show hunger signals. Here, despite the overfeeding, no obesity developed. These data point first to the suggestion, once again, that overfeeding does not result in infant obesity in all cases, and, second, to the hypothesis that differences in the mothers' responses merit further consideration. For example, S. Wooley et al. (1979) suggest that mothers experiencing conflict about food and their own weight, regardless of what they actually weigh, may engage in inconsistent, emotionally charged feeding practices that could lead to eating and weight problems in the child.

Prevention.

Most of the obesity research with human infants has focused on the role of overfeeding and dietary composition (breast vs. bottle milk; beikost) in the etiology of obesity. Pediatricians recommend breast-feeding and a delay in introducing solid foods. This advice may be especially important for infants at risk to become obese, namely those with one or two over-weight parents. However, the protective value of such practices still needs to be established empirically in a more extensive way. Even though longitudinal, prospective studies on the long-term effects of various feeding practices (e.g., breast-feeding vs. bottle-feeding) are difficult to conduct, Fomon et al. (unpublished manuscript) have demonstrated that such studies are possible. Thus far, research has almost exclusively focused on *overfeeding* as an etiological factor during infancy, possibly leading to the false assumption that excessive food intake is the primary or only cause of obesity. Also, let us be careful not to perpetuate the myth that overweight parents overfeed their children. We have few empirical data to suggest that overweight parents differ in their feeding behavior from normal weight parents.

Animal research on feeding schedules shows the dramatic effects various schedules can have on body weight. Comparable longitudinal studies with human infants are needed to determine the relative usefulness of one feeding schedule over another. For example, in a prospective study, infants whose mothers feed them upon demand should be compared with infants who are fed according to a fixed schedule. Animal studies suggest that more but smaller feedings result in lower levels of body fat. Furthermore, feedings should follow a predictable and reliable pattern in order to avoid learned externality.

While the literature on eating disorders has postulated that the early mother-infant interactions, especially during feedings, are of great importance for a child's psychological well-being, empirical studies on feeding interactions between infants and their primary caretakers are rare. In focusing on the *mother* (or any other primary caretaker), we should be careful not to assume that she is to blame if her infant's eating pattern is disturbed. Studies such as Alberts et al.'s (1983) clearly document that the infant's behavior serves as a powerful stimulus for the mother's behavior.

During infancy, the major focus of prevention efforts is on those individuals directly involved in feeding the infant (e.g., parents, day-care personnel). Currently, educational material on infant nutrition is provided mainly by pediatricians, by the baby food industry, and by the media (e.g., parent magazines) and, to a lesser extent, in childbirth preparation classes. We were unable to find any studies evaluating the usefulness of these educational efforts. These materials primarily address questions regarding the amount of food and the types of foods to be given to the infant, and the feeding schedules to be chosen. Often, pediatricians' informal advice to mothers is to "be relaxed" about feeding her infant. This advice is related to the findings reported by S. Wooley et al. (1979), where mothers concerned about their own weight may have engaged in inconsistent and emotionally charged feeding practices. This contention needs to be verified in a larger sample. If fact, we have no good empirical data yet on how mothers' and fathers' attitudes toward weight and food affect their feeding behavior toward their infants and, later on, their children.

Clearly a wide array of variables influence food intake during infancy. Studies are needed in which more than just one variable (e.g., breast- vs. bottle-feeding) are investigated and where their relative contribution to the variance in body weight can be computed.

(4) Childhood Learning Experiences

Beyond infancy, many learning experiences may impact the development of obesity, but the present discussion will focus on three in particular because of their special psychological importance: learning about one's own body, learning food preferences and aversions, and learning self-control skills.

Learning About One's Own Body.
Childhood is the major time for learning about oneself. Piaget (1955) has described child development as increasing differentiation of thought and body perception regarding one's self. It has generally been shown that feelings about one's body are correlated with feelings about the self (Mendelson and White, 1982; Rosen and Ross, 1968). For girls, in particular, physical appearance may be a major determinant of definitions of self and feelings of self-worth. Thus far, this relationship has been studied mainly in adolescents or in college students. Though we know little about children's body image and their sense of self-esteem as related

to physical appearance, there is a large body of data confirming a negative stereotype toward obesity not only in adults, but also in children.

Numerous studies have demonstrated that, at an early age, children of both sexes develop clear preferences for lean bodies and concomittant aversions to chubby builds (Brownell & Stunkard, 1980; Goodman, Dornbusch, Richardson, & Hastorf, 1963; Lenow & Gellert, 1969; Richardson, Hastorf, Goodman, & Dornbusch, 1961). In a study of 6- to 10-year-old male children, for example, Staffieri (1967) found that boys of all body types attributed positive traits to silhouettes of mesomorphic male children (e.g., happy, healthy, honest, smart) and uniformly unfavorable traits to endomorphic silhouettes (e.g., cheats, dirty, argues, lazy, sloppy, mean, stupid). Girls (Staffieri, 1972) attributed an even greater number of negative characteristics to the obese body build than did the boys (worries, fights, naughty, sad, and lonely), suggesting that girls perceive an even greater cost to being overweight, largely in terms of increased social isolation.

There is some evidence that these negative messages affect children's self-esteem. Obese children were found to have lower self-esteem than their normal weight peers (Felker & Kay, 1971). Mendelson and White (1982) reported a significant correlation between self-esteem and body-esteem (i.e., ratings of how much one's own body is valued by oneself and by others) in elementary schoolchildren. These studies were based on small samples, and further exploration is needed to gain a better understanding of how children develop a concept of their physical self and how that understanding, in turn, influences general self-esteem.

We thus have a striking picture before us. Children learn at an early age that there is something dreadful about being overweight. As Wooley, Wooley, & Dyrenforth (1979) pointed out, not only is the impact of this hatred on the overweight child probably irreversible, but the anti-fat attitudes learned in childhood most likely become the basis for self-loathing among those who later become overweight. While these studies clearly show the psychological consequences of obesity, they do not tell us what impact the strong negative stereotype has on children's eating behavior and on their parents' feeding practices.

Acquisition of Food Preferences and Food Aversions.
During the childhood years, children acquire the food habits prevalent in their culture and ethnic group. Children are exposed to the culture's particular 'cuisine' (Rozin, 1982)—its staple foods, processing methods, and added flavorings. Children also learn about the sequencing of foods in meals (Douglas and Nicod, 1974), as well as the etiquette and significance of eating. Of particular interest to our discussion of prevention of obesity is the development of taste preferences and aversions.

Infants are born with the ability to discriminate tastes, and they show an innate preference for sweet substances (Crook, 1978; Desor et al., 1973) and an aversion to bitter substances (Rozin and Fallon, 1980). These taste biases presumably have their adaptive basis in the fact that sweet taste usually is associated with an energy source and bitter taste with a poisonous substance (Shallenberger & Acree, 1971). Both animals and humans also may have an innate preference for high-fat foods (Sclafani & Springer, 1976), an adaptive bias in environments where food supplies are irregular and difficult to obtain, characteristics that, for the most part, no longer apply to our society.

Through experience, the intensity of innate preferences and aversions can be changed or, as in the case of some bitter (e.g., coffee) or irritant and spicy (e.g., chili peppers) foods, even reversed, and new aversions and preferences can be learned (Rozin, 1984). Regarding the function of learning in liking or disliking food, LeMagnen (1978) suggested that the body possesses some mechanism for anticipating the metabolic consequences of food, and that the mechanism operates on the basis of the food's flavor and odor. Booth and his coworkers (Booth, 1978; Booth, Lee, & McAleavey, 1976; Booth, Mather, & Fuller, 1982) have shown persuasively that rather rapid learning occurs during which both food odors and tastes come to predict the metabolic consequences of ingesting a particular food. This knowledge leads the organism to take anticipatory action to adjust the amount consumed. Booth et al. (1982) were able to demonstrate that starch eaten while hungry resulted in a relative preference for the food flavor associated with the starch. When the same starch was ingested in a state of repletion, the rated pleasantness of its flavor decreased significantly.

Booth (1981a) and Fuller (1980) have speculated that individual differences in reactivity to salient cues may impact the way individuals learn about the metabolic consequences of food. They found that overreactivity to the most obvious sensory characteristics of a food can distract or overwhelm attention from its presumably less-obvious postingestional effects, and therefore interfere with learning the predictive cues (e.g., flavor or texture) of a food and its postingestional effects. Perhaps eating problems would then be more likely to develop in these individuals.

In addition to the classical conditioning process outlined above, three other mechanisms are apparently relevant in the acquisition of food preferences and aversions: mere exposure, instrumental conditioning, and, for humans, modeling.

Several studies have reported exposure effects in children (Beauchamp & Moran, 1982; Birch & Marlin, 1982; Pliner, 1982). Exposure is said to extinguish neophobia (the fear of eating) of novel foods. Neophobia of unknown foodstuff is of adaptive value because it reduces the risk of ingesting poisonous substances. Neophobia can readily be observed in young children. In Birch and Marlin's (1982) experiment on the effect of exposure on liking, many of the 2-year-old subjects spat out the novel foods during the initial exposure trial, yet they all developed a liking for these foods provided exposure was repeated several times. Our food preferences are formed during the childhood years and, once established, may be difficult to change. An unexplored question is whether there are developmental phases during which neophobia is less pronounced and new foods could be introduced with relative ease. Controlled studies on the development or change of taste preferences in adults as a consequence of mere exposure are scarce. Pliner (1982) demonstrated that exposure increased college students' liking of fruit juices, but this effect could not be maintained at a one-week follow-up.

Exposure is only one of many variables determining food preferences in children. Presenting food in a pleasant social context or giving a food item as a reward increases children's liking of that particular food item (Birch, Zimmerman, & Hind, 1981). If, however, food has to be eaten in order to gain access to a reward (i.e., instrumental eating), preference ratings for that particular food may decrease (Birch, Birch, Marlin, & Kramer, 1982). In a carefully designed experiment, Birch, Marlin, and Rotter (in press) investigated the effect of instrumental eating more closely and in a naturalistic context in order to secure maximum generalizability of their results. They compared children's responses to two types of contingency conditions. One involved an explicitly stated means–end contingency ("if you drink this cup of juice, you will be allowed to see a movie"). The second involved a temporal contingency (after the children had drunk a glass of juice, they were shown a movie). The temporal contingency by itself was not sufficient to affect the preference ratings, while the means–end contingency induced a negative shift in preference. These results clearly suggest that presenting foods as rewards or within a rewarding context increases liking, while using consumption of a certain food as the instrumental component of a means–end contingency decreases liking.

These results are fascinating because of their immediate relevance to child-rearing practices related to teaching healthy eating habits. In a survey of 2000 households with preschool children, 60% of the mothers reported using food as rewards—most commonly sweet foods—and withholding sweets as punishment (Eppright, Fox, Fryer, Lamkin, Vivian, & Fuller, 1972). We have no empirical data on the frequency with which parents institute instrumental eating ("you can have dessert if you eat your vegetables"), but more than likely parents try to teach their children to eat nutritious but nonpreferred foods in an instrumental paradigm, an effort that defeats its own purpose according to the findings of Birch and her colleagues.

Modeling is another powerful variable influencing children's food preference. Observing a peer consume a nonpreferred food increases the observing child's liking of this food (Birch, 1980). Television advertisements capitalize on modeling effects, and American children are exposed to the food industry's relentless efforts to shape their food preferences. Nearly half of the $1.2 billion spent annually on food advertisement goes toward commercials targeting children as the audience. The average American child spends nearly 4 hours a day watching television, which, over the course of a year, adds up to more time in front of the television set than in the classroom (Federal Trade Commission, 1978). During this time, children are exposed to approximately 10,000 food commercials. During the Saturday and Sunday daytime hours, cereals are the most often promoted foods, making up 51% of all ads aimed at children, followed by ads for candy and gum (22%), and cookies and crackers 11%) (Choate, 1977).

In their review of the literature, Wadden and Brownell (in press) concluded that efforts by the food industry do not remain unrewarded: surveys and behavioral observations of parents' shopping behavior found consistently that children are well able to influence their parents' selection of sugared foods (Atkin, 1975; Gussow, 1972; Reilly Group, 1973; Ward & Wackman, 1972).

In a study of 400 infants and young children, sweetened, carbonated beverages were identified as the most common snacks for 3-year-olds (Berenson, Blonde, Farris, Foster, Frank, Srinivasan, Voors, & Webber, 1979). These findings clearly indicate that any form of preventive effort toward promoting nutritious foods at the expense of non-nutritious foods will have to address the question of how to change or combat the food industry's aggressive marketing of sugared foods.

Self-Regulatory Skills.
The Freudian notion of human development portrays the infant as an impulse-driven, uncontrolled savage upon whom development and socialization must impose ever thicker layers of control (Freud, 1961). Regardless of whether or not infants really are driven by these primal impulses, quite clearly a large part of childhood socialization does involve issues of self-control. Children receive early training in self-regulation, since part of childhood socialization involves instruction for, and reinforcement of, self-controlling responses, especially those involved in resisting temptation (Aronfreed, 1968; Mischel, 1974).

The skills of self-regulation depend on the ability to identify and maintain cues that can help in controlling one's own behavior (Kanfer, 1970; Kanfer & Karoly, 1972). Those cues can either be in the environment or in one's thoughts, feelings, or internal states (Rodin, Maloff, & Becker, 1983). Successful learning of self-regulation skills requires the combination of explicit instruction and a gradual weakening of external controls. To take an example possibly important for the development of obesity, suppose parents attempt to constrain and control their child's intake of food. If eating behavior is too greatly controlled, the child may fail to experience and develop intrinsic and self-mediated controls over the eating process. In the absence of external obstacles to eating, the typically constrained child may then overeat whenever food is attractive, salient, and available. This speculation is consistent with psychological theory (Lepper & Greene, 1975), which proposes that strong external rewards or punishments undermine a child's utilization of *self*-control.

Dyrenforth, Wooley, and Wooley (1980) report data, based on patients who have come to their clinic for eating disorders with histories of chronic overweight and severe problems of underweight, that also support the importance of learning about control. They indicate that almost independent of initial body weight, the presenting profiles of these patients contained a common theme: distress over apparent lack of control. Subjects express difficulty in asserting themselves at home, at work, or in the community, since they feel they are disenfranchised by their own real or perceived lack of self-regulation skills. Food and their own struggle to control eating have assumed a central role in their daily lives, usurping energy and time from other pursuits.

Not surprisingly, given this line of reasoning, it has recently been reported that maintenance of weight loss among children, as opposed to regain, is directly related to the amount of *self*-regulation of food intake and weight management utilized (Cohen, Gelfand, Dodd, Jensen, & Turner, 1980). Regaining, on the other hand, was correlated with more parental regulation of weight management. Effective psychological treatments for weight loss have often been those that explicitly teach self-regulation skills (Mahoney & Mahoney, 1976; Rodin, 1977, 1983a, 1983b). Understanding the processes involved in learning self-control and outlining how external and internal cues participate in the self-regulation of behavior may provide an important insight regarding one more psychological determinant of overeating and obesity: strengthening self-control of behavior may be a major preventive strategy. Interestingly, lacking a sense of self-control, one component in the multidimensional concept of locus of control (Reid & Ware, 1973, 1974), has also been implicated in the development of anorexia nervosa and bulimia (Allerdissen, Florin, & Rost, 1981; Hood, Moore, & Garner, 1982; Rost, Neuhaus, & Florin, 1982).

Prevention.
We know little about the role of parents, peers, and the media in the development of children's body images. Our clinical experiences suggest that clients with weight or eating problems often express strong affect

regarding parental attitudes toward the clients' physical appearance. How do parents' concerns over their children's weight translate into specific behaviors? And how do certain parental behaviors (e.g., rigid control of the child's intake) affect the children's image of themselves and their bodies, and their food intake? Stunkard (personal communication, 1984) has suggested a study of families with one normal weight and one obese child during a meal and during a non-eating situation, to gain insight into possible differences in the parents' behavior toward the obese child. Observing family lunches has been a common strategy of family therapists working with anorexic patients (Roseman, Minuchin, & Liebman, 1975), but systematic observational records are needed in order to verify the hypothesis of differential parental behavior toward a child with an eating disorder.

The research on food preferences clearly shows that children and animals show neophagia (i.e., the refusal of novel foods). In their efforts to motivate children to eat healthy foods (e.g., vegetables), parents should be advised not to reinforce their children for eating these foods. Rather, parents should present these foods early in a meal, when the child is more hungry and thus more likely to eat. Also, rather than presenting these less preferred foods *together* with more preferred foods on the same plate, sequencing food items will make it impossible for the child to fill up on the more preferred food items first. Finally, exposure and modelling are potent strategies to increase liking. Children should be asked to try a few bites of the less preferred (or rejected) food items, and parents should model their consumption.

As we have pointed out, the media play a major role in shaping children's preferences. Public and private agencies could use the media to shape children's food preferences toward more healthy foods. The government should offer tax incentives to the food industry for promoting healthier foods for children, such as cereals low in sugar content.

Several educational programs have been implemented with the goal of influencing children's and adolescents' dietary habits by improving their knowledge of nutrition and exercise. Three reviews of the literature (Levy, Iverson, & Walberg, 1980; Saylor, Coates, Killen, & Slinkard, 1982; Wadden & Brownell, in press) concluded that better methodological approaches should be used in evaluating their effectiveness. Most of the studies including an evaluation focus on the acquisition of information alone, and neglect possible attitudinal and behavioral changes. A better approach was implemented by Coates, Jeffery, and Slinkard (1981). Seventy-two fourth graders and 89 fifth graders underwent a nutritional education program that occupied three 45-minute class periods for two weeks. The program focused on (1) using fruits and vegetables for snacks; (2) eating "heart-healthy" meals (low in cholesterol, saturated fat, salt, and sugar); (3) reading food labels; and (4) training in physical exercise. At baseline, the children's lunch boxes were examined to determine the number of "heart-healthy" foods they contained. Trash cans were assessed to find out how much and what types of foods were thrown away. After the two-week program, the fourth and fifth graders' lunch boxes contained 39 and 38% more "heart-healthy" foods, respectively, and the percent of "heart-healthy" foods thrown away decreased approximately 6% in both groups. At a four-month follow-up, students were still consuming a significantly greater number of "heart-healthy" foods. This study demonstrates that children's eating habits can be influenced successfully and that the effect of a nutrition education program can be maintained for a considerable period of time. The reviews cited earlier (Levy et al., 1980; Saylor et al., 1982; Wadden & Brownell, in press) also suggest that interventions are most successful if they implement a wide variety of teaching methods, if they elicit social support from parents, and if they incorporate various sectors of the school system (e.g., cafeteria service, physical education teachers).

We have emphasized the importance of self-control in the development of obesity. It may well be that self-control over one's own impulses in general (and not just regarding food), as well as perceived control over one's environment, is crucial in developing healthy eating habits. Intrinsic motivation and self-directed behavior can be encouraged both in the family and at school, though some have criticized our public school system for interfering with such learning. The relative contribution of training in self-control skills to the prevention of obesity has yet to be investigated.

The community-wide prevention programs that have been developed for adults (for a review see Wadden & Brownell, in press), in which the family, the school system, supermarkets, restaurants, and the media (Stunkard, 1979) are targets of intervention efforts, should expand their focus to include children. An interesting research question is how parents' behavior changes, due to such a community-wide effort, affect their children's behaviors.

The question of how to change health habits is also of considerable theoretical interest and has stimulated social-psychological research regarding the relative importance of knowledge, attitudes, and behavior in the formation, maintenance, and change of health behaviors (Janis & Rodin, 1979). Anyone interested in mounting a behavioral change program to improve health habits will find this literature informative and useful (Allard & Mongeon, 1982; Brinberg & Durand, 1983; Flay, Di-Tecco, & Schlegel, 1980).

(5) Parental Influence and Training in Adolescence

Puberty is associated with important biological changes, including pro-liferation of fat cells, especially for females. It is also a period of major psychological changes in which there are shifts in body image, in reference groups from family to peers, and in one's perceived identity. There is an increasing understanding of the relationship between food intake, energy output, and body weight (Wellman & Johnson, 1982), and an increasing self-determination regarding food intake. At the same time, adolescents become increasingly aware of cultural norms regarding weight, and, with the growing concern about peer approval in general and heterosexual relationships in particular, being attractive becomes more and more important (Rodin et al., in press).

Beginning in early childhood and extending throughout adolescence, already overweight children, girls especially, may experience considerable parental pressure to restrict their food intake. Woody and Constanzo (1982) described significant differences in how parents responded to overweight sons and daughters. Parents of an overweight son were unlikely to blame their son for his weight status. Woody and Constanzo (1982) explain this finding with the fact that parents of overweight sons described their sons as exhibiting average levels of activity and as being easy to manage. These descriptions differ from how parents of normal weight sons describe their sons (i.e., "excitable," "extremely active"). Parents of overweight sons may be generally pleased with their sons' compliant behavior and thus be less likely to attribute their obesity to the sons' behavior.

For obese girls, however, Woody and Constanzo (1982) found a very different result. Parents saw their daughters as liable to eat in response to both negative and positive moods. Parents conceptualized their daughters' obesity in terms of problematic eating behavior and, consequently, were more inclined to take an active role in restraining food intake in the obese girls than in the obese boys. Usually parents tried to instill control by applying parental restrictions on eating, thus minimizing options for learning the self-control skills discussed earlier.

These parental concerns and behaviors may be the origins of the feelings of the need for restraint that Herman and his colleagues have identified in many young women (Herman & Mack, 1975). Such learning experiences may also explain why, for weight conscious females (but not for males), the presence of other people becomes a signal for not eating (Conger, Conger, Constanzo, Wright, & Matter, 1980) or for eating smaller portions (Chaiken, Mori, & Pliner, 1983), reflecting relatively low internalized self-control and relatively high dependence on agents of external control.

In summary, parental influence and training may be quite different after the onset of obesity than before its start, especially for females, and may serve to make females' eating behaviors more disregulated than males. Apparently some of the behavioral characteristics associated with an obese person in adulthood arrive from the manner in which middle-class parents and socializers attempt to save the child from the negative social consequences of being fat. Restraint appears to be an important aspect of the heavier child's socialization, especially for females. If restraint is taught in response to obesity or fear of weight problems, the consequences would undoubtedly be an increased sense of the importance of food and probably a hyperresponsiveness to external food cues.

Although restraint in eating has been documented in overweight individuals, and though restraint scores have reportedly correlated with age of onset of obesity (O'Neil, Paine, Riddle, Currey, Malcolm, & Sexauer, 1981), restraint is also fairly common among women of normal body weight. In fact, a restrained eater is defined as an individual who, *regardless of actual under- or overweight,* is continually concerned with controlling food intake and body weight (Herman & Mack, 1975).

In simplest terms, the cognitive processes involved in the regulation of body weight originate from a comparison between one's actual body weight and a desirable weight. If the actual weight exceeds the desirable weight, the most common response is to diet. These dieting attempts, induced by cultural or social pressures, begin a process of biological, cognitive, and behavioral disregulation whose ultimate consequence may be overweight (Rodin, 1983a; Wooley & Wooley, 1973). Dieting results in a lowered basal metabolic rate, meaning that the essential functions of life can be carried out with less energy expenditure. This effect reportedly increases every time an individual goes on a diet. The metabolic rate does not immediately increase once the dieting is ended. Furthermore, subsequent to a period of starvation, hormonal changes occur that promote fat storage (Even & Nicolaidis, 1981; Garrow, 1978a, 1978b; Rodin, 1977). The physiological changes induced by dieting, such as plateaus in the process of weight loss, or cravings and binges due to a severely restrictive diet, contribute to the development of increasingly compulsive strategies in the pursuit of the ideal weight. Data on the physiological and psychological effect of severely restrictive diets suggest that dieting, the very mechanism by which the majority of all Americans try to achieve the slim ideal, may cause overweight. Given this assumption, it is particularly distressing to know that many females begin to diet before they reach maturity. From animal studies we know that dietary manipulations are especially powerful and have long-lasting effects on the organism if they occur before growth has been completed. Unfortunately, we know very little about the actual eating habits of adolescents, and prospective, longitudinal studies are needed to provide further data on both normative and pathological processes during this important developmental stage.

Prevention.

In addition to the wide range of preventive efforts outlined for children, during adolescence considerable efforts need to be made to help adolescents accept the normal physical changes that accompany adolescence. Great stress should be placed on the ill effects of dieting to control body weight. Community-level changes are necessary to implement successfully prevention efforts aimed at reducing the effects of social pressure for thinness. For example, a wider range of the female beauty ideal is needed, and the media in particular could have a critical role in this change. Becoming heavier is one aspect of growing into an adult that is particularly difficult for girls to accept. The sociocultural pressures to maintain a sylphlike body motivate thousands of girls to follow unhealthy diets that may upset their biological balance and thus contribute to later obesity, and that also may result in major eating disorders such as anorexia nervosa and bulimia.

(6) Physical Activity

Physical activity has been linked with the development of obesity in two ways. First, inactivity has been postulated as an etiological variable of obesity and, second, physical exercise has been reported as an effective strategy in preventing fat cell development. The actual period in the human life span when physical activity begins to exert its influence on obesity remains unclear. We speculate that both inactivity and physical exercise are influential throughout the life span. To avoid repetitions in the sections on infancy, childhood, and adolescence, we will discuss the research on physical activity separately.

Inactivity.

Epidemiological data suggest a positive relationship between inactivity and obesity. Despite a 10% reduction in caloric consumption since 1900, the prevalence of obesity in the United States has approximately doubled since then (Van Itallie, 1977). A British study investigated the food intake of 14-year-old boys in 1964 and in 1971. Over a period of seven consecutive days, the 14-year-olds in the 1971 sample ate 185 calories less per day, but had a higher percentage of body fat (18.4% compared to 16.3%), while height and weight were similar in both samples (Durnin, Lonergan, Good, & Ewan, 1974). These cohort differences have been related to advancements in technology, which allow us to curtail physical activity. For example, Stern (1984) reported that, based on an estimate by the Illinois Bell Telephone Company, an extension phone saves an individual approximately 70 miles of walking in the course of a year.

Additional evidence regarding the etiological significance of inactivity comes from the observation that body fat and weight increase with age (Forbes & Reina, 1970; Montoye, Epstein, & Kjelsberg, 1965; Parizkowa, 1977), whereas activity decreases with age (deVries, 1974; Wessel & Van Huss, 1969).

Despite the intuitive attractiveness of the hypothesis that inactivity leads to obesity, empirical evidence of such a direct etiological relationship has not yet been clearly established (Brownell, 1982; Garrow, 1978a; Rodin, 1977, 1981b). Usually, the role of inactivity in the development of obesity has been studied by comparing activity levels of obese individuals and normal weight individuals. In their extensive review of the literature, Thompson, Jarvie, Lahey, and Cureton (1982) documented the conflicting results that characterize this area of research. While some studies found significantly lower activity levels in obese infants (Rose & Mayer, 1968), children and adolescents (Bullen, Reed, & Mayer, 1964; Corbin & Pletcher, 1968; Johnson, Burke, & Mayer, 1956), and adults (Chirico & Stunkard, 1960; Rand & Stunkard, 1974), others have found no significant differences (Bradfield, Paulos, & Grossman, 1971; Lincoln, 1972; Mayfield & Koniski, 1966; Stunkard & Pestka, 1962; Wilkinson, Parkin, Pearlson, Strong, & Sykes, 1977). The discrepant results may be due in part to the fact that quite diverse methods have been used for collecting the activity data (e.g., self-report, behavioral observation, mechanical devices). Furthermore, as Garrow (1978a) has argued, the emphasis on differences in energy expenditure during athletic activity poorly estimates general activity expenditure during the day for all but elite class athletes, who spend most of each day in physical training. Moreover, the estimated differences do not subtract the energy the person would have expended at rest, leading to gross overestimates. For example, a person who exercises may spend 320 calories while the person at rest spends 200, leaving a net gain of only 120 calories, not the 320 usually used as the data point.

Although it is not clear that inactivity alone can cause obesity, it is likely to be involved in maintaining the overweight state. Further, exercise is often related to weight loss, presumably mediated by physiological changes induced by exercise. Exercise decreases insulin levels, decreasing the likelihood that available energy will be stored as fat. In addition to the increased energy expenditure produced by activity itself, several studies have further demonstrated an increase in metabolic rate that outlasted the activity, if that activity was aerobic (deVries & Gray, 1963). Finally, depending on the type of exercise performed, exercise can change the body composition toward a lower percentage of fat and a higher percentage of muscle cells (Bjorntorp, 1981; Gwinup, 1975; Leon, Conrad, Hunninghake, & Serfass, 1979; Parizkowa, 1977).

Exercise.

Important to our discussion of the prevention of obesity are a number of animal studies demonstrating that physical exercise helped retard the development of fat cells in animals still growing (Kutch & McArdle, 1977; Oscai, Spirakis, & Wolff, 1972). In more recent work, two groups of animals were fed identical high-fat, high-calorie diets, but only one group was encouraged to exercise. The exercised group showed none of the endocrine or fat cell alterations associated with overconsumption of high-fat diets, nor did they gain weight (Stern, 1983). Although these data strongly support a role for exercise in the prevention of obesity, an additional condition suggests that the exercise regimen must be maintained to continue its beneficial effects. Animals in the exercise group were taken off the exercise regimen after several weeks. Half the animals were continued on the high-fat, high-calorie diet and half were changed to standard lab chow. Exercised animals fed high-fat diets, when taken off exercise, began to show worse endocrine and fat cell profiles than animals on the high-fat diets that had never exercised at all. Only animals on low-fat, standard lab chow maintained the benefits of the prior exercise period.

Conclusions

We have described a wide range of long-term variables, each of which may contribute to a set of biological outcomes and changes that, in turn, may lead to overweight or obesity. These long-term factors are innate or acquired during early development, and their impact most likely lasts throughout the life span.

Throughout this paper we have tried to indicate the kinds of prevention strategies best suited to the various possible etiological factors relevant to obesity. Intervention trials are greatly needed, especially those using longitudinal designs and component analyses of the efficacy of multiple intervention procedures. For example, while most prevention programs effectively use a variety of different procedures in a single intervention, they do not test which aspects of the intervention are crucial and which are superfluous. Adding conditions where one or another of the components is missing allows this type of determination.

Other questions arise about the best age of a target population for prevention programs. The present review suggests the individual's mother during pregnancy may be the appropriate place to start; certainly the periods of infancy and early childhood are not too early. Nonetheless, in making these recommendations we must note our concern that an emphasis on early intervention is a double-edged sword.

We have elsewhere reviewed the causes and consequences of the extraordinary emphasis placed on weight by our society, which we believe is at the root of the enormous increase in eating disorders among subcultures most affected by this weight obsession (e.g., women, dancers, wrestlers, jockeys, gymnasts) (Rodin et al., in press). We do not wish to heighten the fervor of public concern and activity about overweight with a long list of early prevention recommendations. Having voiced this caveat, however, we do see the need for sensible, relatively easy adjustments in public behavior and food habits that could increase the health and well-being of numerous people currently fighting excess weight. Carefully controlled trials will be needed to assess the full efficacy of this approach.

References

Abraham, S., & Nordsieck, M. Relationship of excess weight in children and adults. *Public Health Report*, 1960, *75*, 263–273.

Ainsworth, M. Infant-mother attachment. *American Psychologist*, 1979, *34*, 932–937.

Ainsworth, M., & Bell, S. Some contemporary patterns of mother-infant interaction in the feeding situation. In A. Ambrose (Ed.), *Stimulation in early infancy*. London: Academic Press, 1969.

Alberts, E., Kalverboer, A. F., & Hopkins, B. Mother-infant dialogue in the first day of life: An observational study during breast-feeding. *Journal of Child Psychology and Psychiatry*, 1983, *24*, 145–161.

Allard, R., & Mongeon, M. Associations between nutritional knowledge, attitude, and behaviors in a junior college population. *Canadian Journal of Public Health*, 1982, *73*, 416–419

Allerdissen, R., Florin, I., & Rost, W. Psychological characteristics of women with bulimia nervosa. *Behavioral Analysis and Modification*, 1981, *4*, 314–318.

Allon, N. The stigma of overweight in everyday life. In G. A. Bray (Ed.), *Obesity in perspective*. Washington, D.C.: U.S. Government Printing Office, 1975.

American Academy of Pediatrics. Encouraging breast-feeding. *Pediatrics*, 1980, *65*, 657–658.

American Medical Association. Concepts of nutrition and health. *Journal of the American Medical Association*, 1979, *242*, 2335–2338.

Ananth, J. Psychological aspects of obesity. *Child Psychiatry Quarterly*, 1982, *15*, 75–82.

Antonov, A. N. Children born during siege of Leningrad in 1942. *Journal of Pediatrics*, 1947, *30*, 250.

Aronfreed, J. *Conduct and conscience: The socialization of internalized control over behavior*. New York: Academic Press, 1968.

Atkin, A. *Effect of television advertising on children: Parent-child communication in supermarket breakfast cereal selection* (Report #7). Unpublished manuscript, Michigan State University, 1975.

Bartoshuk, L. M. The psychophysics of taste. *American Journal of Clinical Nutrition*, 1978, *31*, 1068–1077.

Beauchamp, G. K., & Moran, M. Dietary experience and sweet taste preference in human infants. *Appetite*, 1982, *3*, 139–152.

Berenson, G. S., Blonde, C. U., Farris, R. P., Foster, T. A., Frank, G. C.,

Srinivasan, S. R., Voors, A. W., & Webber, L. S. Cardiovascular disease risk factor variables during the first year of life. *American Journal of Diseases in Children*, 1979, *133*, 1049–1057.

Birch, L. L. Effects of peer models' food choices and eating behaviors on preschoolers' food preferences. *Child Development*, 1980, *51*, 489–496.

Birch, D., Birch, L. L., Marlin, D. W., & Kramer, L. Effects of instrumental consumption on children's food preferences. *Appetite*, 1982, *3*, 125–134.

Birch, L. L., & Marlin, D. W. I don't like it; I never tried it: effects of exposure on two-year-old children's food preferences. *Appetite*, 1982, *3*, 353–360.

Birch, L. L., Marlin, D. W., & Rotter, J. Eating as the "means" activity in a contingency: Effects on young children's food preference. *Child Development*, in press.

Birch, L. L., Zimmerman, S., & Hind, H. The influence of social-affective context on the formation of children's food preferences. *Child Development*, 1981, *51*, 856–861.

Bjorntorp, P. Adipocyte precursor cells. In P. Bjorntorp, M. Cairella, & A. N. Howard (Eds.), *Recent advances in obesity research: III*. London: John Libbey, 1981.

Blackwell, R. Q., Chow, B. F., Chinn, K. S. K. et al. Prospective material nutrition study in Taiwan: Rationale, study design, feasibility, and preliminary findings. *Nutrition Reports International*, 1973, *7*, 522.

Blundell, J. Hunger, appetite and satiety: Constructs in search of identities. In M. Turner (Ed.), *Nutrition and lifestyles*. London: Applied Science Publishing, Ltd., 1979.

Booth, D. A. Satiety and appetite are conditioned reactions. *Psychosomatic Medicine*, 1977, *39*, 76–81.

Booth, D. A. Acquired behavior controlling energy intake and output. *Psychiatric Clinics of North America*, 1978, *1*, 547–579.

Booth, D. A. The physiology of appetite. *British Medical Bulletin*, 1981, *37*, 117–119. (a)

Booth, D. A. Hunger and satiety as conditioned reflexes. In H. Weiner, M. Hofer, & A. J. Stunkard (Eds.), *Brain, behavior, and bodily disease*. New York: Raven Press, 1981. (b)

Booth, D. A., Lee, M., & McAleavey, C. Acquired sensory control of satiation in man. *British Journal of Psychology*. 1976, *67*, 137–147.

Booth, D. A., Mather, P., & Fuller, J. Starch content of ordinary foods associatively conditions human appetite and satiation, indexed by intake and eating pleasantness of starch-paired flavours. *Appetite*, 1982, *3*, 163–184.

Bradfield, R. B., Paulos, J., & Grossman, L. Energy expenditure and heart rate of obese high school girls. *American Journal of Clinical Nutrition*, 1971, *24*, 1482–1488.

Bradley, R. M. Development of the taste bud and gustatory papillae in human fetuses. In J. F. Bosma (Ed.), *The third symposium on oral sensation and perception: The mouth of the infant*. Springfield: Thomas, 1972.

Bradley, R. M., & Stern, I. B. The development of the human taste bud during the fetal period. *Journal of Anatomy*, 1967, *101*, 743–752.

Bray, G. A. The inheritance of corpulance. In L. A. Cioffi, W. P. T. James, & T. B. Van Itallie (Eds.), *The body weight regulatory system: Normal and disturbed mechanisms*. New York: Raven Press, 1981.

Brinberg, D., & Durand, J. Eating at fast-food restaurants: An analysis using two behavioral intention models. *Journal of Applied Social Psychology*, 1983, *13*, 459–472.

Brownell, K. B. Obesity: Understanding and treating a serious, prevalent, and refractory disorder. *Journal of Consulting and Clinical Psychology*, 1982, *50*, 820–840.

Brownell, K. D., & Stunkard, A. J. Physical activity in the development and control of obesity. In A. J. Stunkard (Ed.), *Obesity*. Philadelphia: Saunders, 1980.

Bruch, H. *Eating disorders: Obesity, anorexia nervosa and the person within*. New York: Basic Books, 1973.

Bullen, B. A., Reed, R. B., & Mayer, J. Physical activity of obese and nonobese adolescent girls, appraised by motion picture sampling. *American Journal of Clinical Nutrition*, 1964, *14*, 211–223.

Caplan, G. *The theory and practice of mental health consultation*. New York: Basic Books, 1976.

Chaiken, S., Mori, D., & Pliner, P. *Eating "lightly" and the self-presentation of femininity*. Manuscript in preparation, Vanderbilt University, Nashville, Tennessee, 1983.

Charney, E., Goodman, H. C., McBride, M., Lyon, B., & Pratt, R. Childhood antecedents of adult obesity: Do chubby infants become obese adults? *New England Journal of Medicine*, 1975, *295*, 6.

Chirico, A., & Stunkard, A. J. Physical activity and human obesity. *New England Journal of Medicine*, 1960, *263*, 935–940.

Choate, R. B. *Edible television, your child, and food commercials*. Washington, D.C.: Federal Trade Commission, U.S. Government Printing Office, 1977.

Coates, T. J., Jeffery, R. W., & Slinkard, L. A. Heart healthy eating and exercise: Introducing and maintaining changes in health behaviors. *American Journal of Public Health*, 1981, *71*, 15–23.

Cohen, E., Gelfand, D., Dodd, D., Jensen, J., & Turner, C. Self-control practices associated with weight loss maintenance in children and adolescents. *Behavior Therapy*, 1980, *11*, 26 37.

Conger, J. C., Conger, A. J., Constanzo, P. R., Wright, K. L., & Matter, J. A. The effects of social cues on the eating behavior of obese and normal subjects. *Journal of Personality*, 1980, *48*, 258–271.

Corbin, C. B., & Pletcher, P. Diet and physical activity patterns of obese and nonobese elementary school children. *Research Quarterly*, 1968, *39*, 922–928.

Crook, C. K. Taste perception in the newborn infant. *Infant Behavioral Development*, 1978, *1*, 52–69.

Desor, J. A., Maller, O., & Turner, R. Taste in acceptance of sugars by human infants. *Journal of Comparative Physiological Psychology*, 1973, *58*, 63–67.

deVries, H. A. *Physiology of exercise*. Dubuque, Iowa: William C. Brown, 1974.

deVries, H. A., & Gray, D. E. After-effects of exercise upon resting metabolism rate. *Research Quarterly*, 1963, *34*, 314–321.

Douglas, M., & Nicod, M. Taking the biscuit: The structure of British meals. *New Society*, 1974, *19*, 744–747.

Dowling, S. Seven infants with esophageal atresia. *Psychoanalytical Study of the Child*, 1977, *32*, 215–256.

Durnin, J. O. G. A., Lonergan, M. E., Good, J., & Ewan, A. A cross-sectional nutritional and anthropometric study with an interval of 7 years on 611 young adolescent school children. *British Journal of Nutrition*, 1974, *32*, 169–179.

Dyrenforth, S. R., Wooley, O., & Wooley, S. A woman's body in a man's world. A review of findings on body image and weight control. In R. Kaplan (Ed.), *The special relationship between women and food*. Englewood Cliffs, N.J.: Prentice-Hall Inc., 1980.

Engen, T., Lipsitt, L. P., & Peck, M. E. Ability of newborn infants to discriminate sapid substances. *Developmental Psychology*, 1974, *10*, 741–744.

Engen, T., Lipsitt, L. P. & Robinson, D. O. The human newborn's sucking behavior for sweet fluids as a function of birthweight and maternal weight. *Infant Behavior and Development*, 1978, *1*, 118–121.

Eppright, E. S., Fox, H. M., Fryer, B. H., Lamkin, G. H., Vivian, V. M., & Fuller, E. S. Nutrition of infants and preschool children in the north central region of the United States of America. *World Review of Nutrition and Dietetics*, 1972, *14*, 269–332.

Even, P., & Nicolaidis, S. Changes in efficiency of ingestants are a major factor of regulation of energy balance. In L. A. Cioffi, W. P. T. James, & T. B. Van Itallie (Eds.), *The body weight regulatory system: Normal and disturbed mechanism.* New York: Raven Press, 1981.

Fabry, P. Metabolic consequences of the pattern of food intake. In C. F. Code (Ed.), *Handbook of physiology* (Vol. 1). Washington, D.C.: American Physiological Society, 1967.

Falk, J. L. Production of polydipsia in normal rats by an intermittant food schedule. *Science*, 1961, *133*, 569–593.

Falk, J. L. Conditions producing psychogenic polydipsia in animals. *Annals of the New York Academy of Science.* 1969, *157*, 569–593.

Falk, J. L. The origin and functions of adjunctive behavior. *Animal Learning and Behavior*, 1977, *5*, 325–335.

Federal Trade Commission. *FTC staff report on television advertising to children.* Washington, D.C.: Federal Trade Commission, 1978.

Felker, D. W., & Kay, R. S. Self-concept, sports interests, sports participation and body-type of seventh- and eighth-grade boys. *Journal of Psychology*, 1971, *78*, 223.

Fish, S. T., Singer, I., & Benjamin, W. B. Insulin-induced adenosine 3 double-bond 5-cyclic monophosphate-independent phosphorylation of a fat-cell protein-effect of starving and refeeding. *Biochemical Society Transactions*, 1975, *2*, 920–922.

Flay, B. R., DiTecco, D., & Schlegel, R. P. Mass media in health promotion: an analysis using an extended information-processing model. *Health Education Quarterly*, 1980, *7*, 127–147.

Fomon, S. J. A pediatrician looks at early nutrition. *Bulletin of New York Academic Medicine*, 1971, *47*, 567–578.

Fomon, S. J., Filer, L. J., Anderson, T. A., & Ziegler, E. Recommendations for feeding normal infants. *Pediatrics*, 1979, *63*, 52–59.

Fomon, S. J., Rogers, R. R., Ziegler, E. E., Nelson, S. E., & Thomas, L. N. *Indices of fatness and serum cholesterol at age eight years in relation to feeding and growth during early infancy.* Unpublished manuscript, Department of Pediatrics, University of Iowa Hospital, Iowa City, Iowa.

Forbes, G. B. Prevalence of obesity in childhood. In G. A. Bray (Ed.), *Obesity in perspective* (Vol. 2). Washington, D.C.: U.S. Department of Health, Education and Welfare, 1975.

Forbes, G., & Reina, J. C. Adult lean body mass declines with age: Some longitudinal observations. *Metabolism*, 1970, *19*, 653–663.

Frank, G. C., Webber, L. S., & Berenson, G. S. Health-risk eating behavior dietary studies of infants and children—the Bogalusa Heart Study. In T. J. Coates (Ed.), *Crossing the barriers—Adolescent health promotion.* New York: Academic Press, 1982.

Freud, S. *A general introduction to psychoanalysis* (3rd ed.). New York: Washington Square Press, 1961.

Fuller, J. *Caloric learning in human appetite.* Unpublished doctoral dissertation, University of Birmingham, 1980.

G. Reilly Group, Inc. Meals and snacking: The child and what he eats. *The Child*, 1973, *2*, 98–106.

Garn, S. M., & Clark, D. C. Trends in fatness and the origins of obesity. *Pediatrics*, 1976, *57*, 433–456.

Garn, S. M., Cole, P. E., & Bailey, S. N. Effect of parental fatness level on the fatness of biologic and adoptive children. *Ecology, Food and Nutrition*, 1976, *6*, 1–3.

Garrow, J. S. *Energy balance and obesity in man.* Amsterdam: Elsevier/North-Holland Biomedical Press, 1978.(a)

Garrow, J. S. The regulation of energy expenditure in man. In G. A. Bray (Ed.), *Recent advances in obesity research II.* London: Newman Publishing, 1978.(b)

Goodman, N., Dornbusch, S. M., Richardson, S. A., & Hastorf, A. H. Variant reactions to physical disabilities. *American Sociological Review*, 1963, *28*, 429–435.

Grinker, J. A. Infant taste responses are correlated with birthweight and unrelated to indices of obesity. *Pediatrics Research*, 1978, *12*, 371.

Grinker, J. A. *Development of the sensory system.* Paper presented at the Satellite Symposium to the 3rd International Congress on Obesity, Anacapri, Italy, 1980.

Gross, L. *The effects of early feeding experience on external responsiveness.* Unpublished doctoral dissertation, Columbia University, 1968.

Gussow, J. Counternutritional messages of TV ads aimed at children. *Journal of Nutritional Education*, 1972, *8*, 52–57.

Gwinup, G. Effects of exercise alone on the weight of obese women. *Archives of Internal Medicine*, 1975, *135*, 676–680.

Hall, B. Changing composition of human milk and early development of an appetite control. *Lancet*, 1975, *1*, 779–781.

Harris, M. B. Eating habits, restraint, knowledge and attitudes toward obesity. *International Journal of Obesity*, 1983, *7*, 271–288.

Harrison, G. G., & Udall, J. N. Effect of maternal obesity on fetal growth. *American Journal of Physical Anthropology*, 1978, *48*, 403.

Health, United States. *Third annual report on the health status of the nation* (DHEW Publication No. [PHS] 78-1232). Hyattsville, Md.: U.S. Government Printing Office, 1978.

Herman, C. P., & Mack, D. Restrained and unrestrained eating. *Journal of Personality*, 1975, *43*, 647–660.

Hood, J., Moore, T. E., & Garner, D. M. Locus of control as a measure of ineffectiveness in anorexia nervosa. *Journal of Consulting and Clinical Psychology*, 1982, *50*, 3–13.

Hook, E. B. Dietary cravings and aversions during pregnancy. *The American Journal of Clinical Nutrition*, 1978, *31*, 1355–1362.

Hooper, P. D., & Alexander, E. L. Infant morbidity and obesity. A survey of 151 infants from general practice. *Practitioner*, 1971, *207*, 221.

Houston, M. J., Howe, P. W., & McNeily, A. S. Factors affecting the duration of breast feeding: 1. Measurement of breast milk intake in the first week of life. *Early Human Development*, 1983, *8*, 49–54.

Janis, I. L., & Rodin, J. Attribution, control, and decision making: social psychology and health care. In G. C. Stone, F. Cohen, & N. E. Adler (Eds.), *Health psychology*. San Francisco: Jossey-Bass, 1979.

Johnson, M. L., Burke, B. S., & Mayer, J. Relative importance of inactivity and overeating in the energy balance of obese high school girls. *American Journal of Clinical Nutrition*, 1956, *4*, 37–44.

Johnson, P. R., Stern, J. S., Greenwood, M. R. C., Zucker, L. M., & Hirsch, J. Effect of early nutrition on adipose cellularity and pancreatic insulin release in the Zucker rat. *Journal of Nutrition*, 1973, *103*, 738.

Kanfer, F. H. Self-regulation: Research issues and speculation. In C. Neuringer & J. Michael (Eds.), *Behavioral modification in clinical psychology*. New York: Appleton-Century-Crofts, 1970.

Kanfer, F. H., & Karoly, P. Self-control: A behavioristic excursion into the lion's den. *Behavior Therapy*, 1972, *3*, 398–416.

Keys, A. Overweight, obesity, coronary heart disease and mortality. *Nutrition Review*, 1980, *38*, 297–307.

Knittle, J. L., & Hirsch, J. Effects of early nutrition on the development of rat epididyman fat pads: Cellularity and metabolism. *Journal of Clinical Investigation*, 1968, *47*, 2091.

Kutch, F. J., & McArdle, W. D. *Nutrition, weight control and exercise*. Boston: Houghton Mifflin, 1977.

LeMagnen, J. Metabolically driven and learned feeding responses in man. In G. A. Bray (Ed.), *Recent advances in obesity research: II*. London: Newman Publishing, 1978.

Lemonnier, D., Suquet, J. D., Aubert, R., & Rosselini, G. Long-term effect of mouse neonate food intake on adult body composition, insulin and glucose serum levels. *Hormone and Metabolic Research*, 1973, *5*, 223.

Lenow, R. M., & Gellert, F. Body build identification, preference, and aversion in children. *Developmental Psychology*, 1969, *5*, 256–462.

Leon, A. S., Conrad, J., Hunninghake, D. B., & Serfass, R. Effects of a vigorous walking program on body composition and carbohydrate and lipid mechanism of obese young men. *American Journal of Clinical Nutrition*, 1979, *32*, 1776–1787.

Lepper, M. R., & Greene, D. Turning play into work: Effects of adult surveillance and extrinsic rewards on children's intrinsic motivation. *Journal of Personality and Social Psychology*, 1975, *31*, 479–486.

Levitz, L. S. The susceptibility of human feeding behavior to external cues. In G. A. Bray (Ed.), *Obesity in perspective*. Washington, D.C.: U.S. Government Printing Office, 1975.

Levy, S. R., Iverson, B. K., & Walberg, H. J. Nutrition education research: An interdisciplinary evaluation and review. *Health Education Quarterly*, 1980, *7*, 107–126.

Lincoln, J. E. Caloric intake, obesity, and physical activity. *American Journal of Clinical Nutrition*, 1972, *25*, 390–394.

Mahoney, M. J., & Mahoney, K. *Permanent weight control*. New York: Norton, 1976.

Mayfield, E., & Koniski, F. Patterns of food intake and physical activity in obesity. *Journal of the American Dietetic Association*, 1966, *49*, 406–408.

Mendelson, B. K., & White, D. R. Relationship between body-esteem and self-esteem of obese and normal children. *Perceptual and Motor Skills*, 1982, *54*, 899–905.

Metcoff, J. Association between fetal growth and maternal nutrition. In *Nutrition* in *Health and Disease and International Development*. Symposia from the XII International Congress on Nutrition, 1981.

Metcoff, J., Costiloe, J. P., Crosby, W., Bentle, L., Seschachalam, D., Sandstead, H. H., Bodwell, C. E., Weaver, F., & McClain, P. Maternal nutrition and fetal outcome. *American Journal of Clinical Nutrition*, 1981,*34*, 708–721.

Milstein, R. M. Responsiveness in newborn infants of overweight and normal weight parents. *Appetite*, 1980, *1*, 65–74.

Mischel, W. Processes in delay of gratification. In L. Berkowitz (Ed.), *Advances in experimental social psychology* (Vol. 7). New York: Academic Press, 1974.

Mistretta, C. M., & Bradley, R. M. Taste in utero: Theoretical considerations. In J. E. Weiffenbach (Ed.), *Taste and development*. Bethesda, Md.: U.S. Department of Health, Education & Welfare, 1977.

Montoye, H. J., Epstein, F. H., & Kjelsberg, M. O. The measurement of body fatness: A study in a total community. *American Journal of Clinical Nutrition*, 1965, *16*, 417–427.

Neumann, C. G., & Alpaugh, M. Birth-weight doubling time: A fresh look. *Pediatrics*, 1976, *57*, 469–473.

Nisbett, R. E., & Gurwitz, S. B. Weight, sex, and the eating behavior of human newborns. *Journal of Comparative Physiological Psychology*, 1970, *73*, 245–253.

Nisbett, R. E., & Kanouse, L. E. Obesity, food deprivation, and supermarket shopping behavior. *Journal of Personality and Social Psychology*, 1969, *12*, 289–295.

Nysenbaum, A. N., & Smart, J. L. Sucking behavior and milk intake of neonates in relation to milk fat content. *Early Human Development*, 1982, *6*, 205–213.

O'Neil, P. M., Paine, P. M., Riddle, F. E., Currey, H. S., Malcolm, R., & Sexauer, J. D. Restraint and age at onset of obesity. *Addictive Behavior*, 1981, *6*, 135–138.

Oscai, L. B., Spirakis, C. N., & Wolff, C. A. Effects of exercise and of food restriction on adipose tissue cellularity. *Journal of Lipid Research*, 1972, *13*, 588–592.

Parizkowa, J. *Body fat and physical fitness*. The Hague, The Netherlands: Martinus Nijhoff, 1977.

Piaget, J. *The construction of reality in the child*. London: Routledge and Kegan Paul, 1955.

Pliner, P. The effects of mere exposure on liking edible substances. *Appetite*, 1982, *3*, 203–290.

Rand, C., and Stunkard, A. J. Obesity and psychoanalysis. *American Journal of Psychiatry*, 1974, *135*, 547–551.

Ravelli, G. P., Stein, Z. A., & Susser, M. W. Obesity in young men after famine exposure in utero and early infancy. *New England Journal of Medicine*, 1976, *295*, 349.

Reid, D. W., & Ware, E. E. Multidimensionality of internal-external control. Implications for past and future research. *Canadian Journal of Behavioral Science*, 1973, *5*, 264–271.

Reid, D. W., & Ware, E. E. Multidimensionality of internal versus external control: Addition of a third dimension and non-distinction of self versus others. *Canadian Journal of Behavioral Science*, 1974, *6*, 131–142.

Richardson, S. A., Hastorf, A. H., Goodman, N., & Dornbusch, S. M. Cultural uniformity in reaction to physical disabilities. *American Social Review*, 1961, *26*, 241–247.

Robbins, T. W., & Fray, P. J. Stress-induced eating: Fact, fiction or misunderstanding? *Appetite*, 1980, *1*, 103–133.

Rodin, J. Effects of distraction on the performance of obese and normal subjects. *Journal of Comparative Physiological Psychology*, 1973, *83*, 68–75.

Rodin, J. The effects of obesity and set point on taste responsiveness and intake in humans. *Journal of Comparative Physiological Psychology*, 1975, *89*, 1001–1009.

Rodin, J. Obesity: Why the losing battle? *Master Lecture Series.* Washington, D. C.: American Psychological Association, 1977.

Rodin, J. The current status of the internal-external obesity hypothesis: What went wrong? *American Psychologist*, 1981, *36*, 361–372. (a)

Rodin, J. Psychological factors in obesity. In P. Bjorntorp (Ed.), *Recent advances in obesity*. London: Libbey, 1981. (b)

Rodin, J. *Controlling your weight.* Toronto: John Wiley & Sons, 1983. (a)

Rodin, J. *Exploding the weight myths.* London: Multimedia Press, 1983. (b)

Rodin, J. *Gravid food behavior, infant responsiveness and weight gain* (Research project in progress). Unpublished manuscript, Yale University, New Haven, Conn.

Rodin, J., Maloff, D., & Becker, H. Self-control: the role of environmental and self-generated stimuli. In P. Levison (Ed.), *Substance abuse: Habitual behavior and self-control.* Boulder, Colo.: Westview/Praeger, 1983.

Rodin, J., Silberstein L., & Striegel-Moore, R. Overweight: A woman's shame. In T. B. Sonderegger (Ed.), *Nebraska Symposium of Motivation, 1983: Gender and Psychology.* Lincoln, Nebr.: University of Nebraska Press, in press.

Rodin, J., Slochower, J., & Fleming, B. The effects of degree of obesity, age of onset, and energy deficit on external responsiveness. *Journal of Comparative Physiological Psychology*, 1977, *91*, 586–597.

Rose, H., & Mayer, J. Activity, calorie intake, and the energy balance of infants. *Pediatrics*, 1968, *41*, 18–29.

Roseman, B., Minuchin, S., & Liebman, R. The family session: An introduction to family therapy in anorexia nervosa. *American Journal of Orthopsychiatry*, 1975, *45*, 846–853.

Rosen, G. M., & Ross, A. D. Relationship of body image to self-concept. *Journal of Consulting and Clinical Psychology*, 1968, *32*, 100.

Ross, L. D., Pliner, P., Nesbitt, P., & Schachter, S. Patterns of externality and internality in eating behavior of obese and normal college students. In S. Schachter (Ed.), *Emotion, obesity and crime.* New York: Academic Press, 1971.

Rosso, P. Nutrition and maternal-fetal exchange. *American Journal of Clinical Nutrition*, 1981, *34*, 744–755.

Rost, W., Neuhaus, M., & Florin, I. Bulimia nervosa: Sex role attitude, sex role behavior, and sex role related locus of control in bulimiarexic women. *Journal of Psychosomatic Research*, 1982, *26*, 403–408.

Rozin, E. The structure of cuisine. In L. Barker (Ed.), *The psychobiology of human food selection.* Westport, Conn.: AVI Publishing Co., Inc. 1982.

Rozin, P. The acquisition of food habits and preferences. In F. Weiss (Ed.), *Handbook of behavioral health.* New York: John Wiley & Sons, 1984.

Rozin, P., & Fallon, A. Psychological categorization of foods and nonfoods: A preliminary taxonomy of food rejections. *Appetite*, 1980, *1*, 193–201.

Salapatek, P. H., & Kessen, W. Visual scanning of triangles by the human newborn. *Journal of Experimental Child Psychology*, 1966, *3*, 115–167.

Sawin, D. B., Hawkins, R. C., Walker, L. O., & Penticuff, J. H. (Eds.). *Exceptional infant: Psychosocial risks in infant-environment transactions* (Vol. 4). New York: Brunner/Mazel, 1980.

Saylor, K., Coates, T., Killen, J., & Slinkard, L. Nutrition education research: Fast or famine? In T. J. Coates (Ed.), *Crossing the barriers—Adolescent health promotion*. New York: Academic Press, 1982.

Sclafani, A. Dietary obesity. In G. A. Bray (Ed.), *Recent advances in research*. London: Newman Publishing, 1978.

Sclafani, A., & Springer, D. Dietary obesity in adult rats: Similarities to lympothalamic and human obesity and syndromes. *Physiology and Behavior*, 1976, *17*, 461–471.

Shallenberger, R., & Acree, T. E. Chemical structures of compounds and their sweet and bitter tastes. In L. Biedler (Ed.), *Handbook of sensory physiology, IV: Chemical sense, 2: Taste*. New York: Springer, 1971.

Spitzer, L., & Rodin, J. Human eating behavior: A critical review of studies in normal weight and overweight individuals. *Appetite*, 1981, *2*, 293–329.

Staffieri, J. R. A study of social stereotype of body image in children. *Journal of Personality and Social Psychology*, 1967, *7*, 101–104.

Staffieri, J. R. Body build and behavioral expectancies in young females. *Developmental Psychology*, 1972, *6*, 125–127.

Stein, Z., Susser, M., & Rush, D. Prenatal nutrition and birth weight: Experiments and quasi-experiments in the past decade. *Journal of Reproductive Medicine*, 1978, *21*, 287.

Stellar, E., Henning, S. J., Rodin, J., Rozin, P., & Wilson, G. T. Nutrition, behavior and the life cycle. *Appetite*, 1980, *1*, 321–331.

Stern, J. S. Is obesity a disease of inactivity? In A. J. Stunkard & E. Stellar (Eds.), *Eating and its disorders*. New York: Raven Press, 1983.

Stunkard, A. J. Obesity and the social environment: Current status, future prospects. In G. A. Bray (Ed.), *Obesity in America* (NIH Publication No. 79-359). Washington, D.C.: U.S. Department of Health, Education, and Welfare, 1979.

Stunkard, A. J. Personal communication. September, 1984.

Stunkard, A. J., & Pestka, J. The physical activity of obese girls. *American Journal of Diseases of Childhood*, 1962, *103*, 812–817.

Susser, M. Prenatal nutrition, birthweight, and psychological development: An overview of experiments, quasi-experiments, and natural experiments in the past decade. *American Journal of Clinical Nutrition*, 1981, *34*, 1.

Svegar, T., Lindberg, T., Weibull, B., & Ollson, V. Nutrition, over-nutrition, and obesity in the first year of life in Malmo, Sweden. *Acta Paediatrica Scandinavica*, 1975, *64*, 635.

Thoman, E. B. Disruption and asynchrony in early parent-infant interaction. In D. B. Sawin, R. C. Hawkins, L. O. Walker, and J. H. Penticuff (Eds.), *Exceptional infant: Psychosocial risks in infant-environment transactions* (Vol. 4). New York: Brunner/Mazel, 1980.

Thomas, A., Chess, S., & Birch, H. G. *Temperament and behavior disorders in children*. New York: New York University Press, 1968.

Thomas, A., Chess, S., Birch, H. G., Hertzig, M. E., & Korn, S. *Behavior individuality in early childhood*. New York: New York University Press, 1963.

Thompson, J. K., Jarvie, G. L., Lahey, B. B., & Cureton, K. J. Exercise and obesity: Etiology, physiology, and intervention. *Psychological Bulletin*, 1982, *91*, 55–79.

Udall, J. N., Harrison, G. G., Vaucher, Y., Walson, P. D., & Morrow, O. Interaction of maternal and neonatal obesity. *Pediatrics*, 1978, *62*, 17–21.

Van Itallie, T. B. *Testimony before the Senate Select Committee on Nutrition and Human Needs*. Washington, D.C.: U.S. Government Printing Office, 1977.

Van Itallie, T. B. The enduring storage capacity for fat: Implications for treatment of obesity. In A. J. Stunkard & E. Stellar (Eds.), *Eating and its disorders.* New York: Raven Press, 1984.

Vasselli, J. R., Cleary, M. P., & Van Itallie, T. B. Modern concepts of obesity. *Nutrition Reviews,* 1983, *41,* 361–373.

Wadden, T. A., & Brownell, K. D. The development and modification of dietary practices in individuals, groups, and large populations. In J. D. Matarazzo, N. E. Miller, S. M. Weiss, J. A. Herd, & S. M. Weiss (Eds.), *Behavioral health: A handbook of health enhancement and disease prevention.* New York: Wiley, in press.

Ward, B., & Wackman, K. Children's purchase influence attempts and parental yielding. *Journal of Marketing Research,* 1972, *9,* 316–319.

Wellman, H. M., & Johnson, C. M. Children's understanding of food and its functions: A preliminary study of the development of concepts of nutrition. *Journal of Applied Developmental Psychology,* 1982, *3,* 135–148.

Wessel, J. A., & Van Huss, W. D. The influence of physical activity and age on exercise adaptation of women 20–69 years. *Journal of Sports Medicine and Physical Fitness,* 1969, *9,* 173–179.

Wilkinson, P. W., Parkin, J. M., Pearlson, G., Strong, H., & Sykes, P. Energy intake and physical activity in obese children. *British Medical Journal,* 1977, *1,* 756.

Woody, E., & Constanzo, P. The socialization of obesity prone behavior. In S. Brehm, S. Kassin, & R. Gibbons (Eds.), *Developmental social psychology,* London: Oxford Press, 1982.

Wooley, O. W., & Wooley, S. C. Salivation to sight and thought of food. *Psychosomatic Medicine,* 1973, *35,* 136.

Wooley, O. W., Wooley, S. C., & Dyrenforth, S. R. Obesity and women, II: A neglected feminist topic. *Women's Studies International Quarterly,* 1979, *2,* 81–92.

Wooley, S. C., Dyrenforth, S., & Jaffe, A. Cited in S. C. Wooley & O. W. Wooley, Obesity and women, I: A closer look at the facts. *Women's Studies International Quarterly,* 1979, *2,* 69–79.

Wooley, S. C., & Wooley, O. W. Obesity and women, I. A closer look at the facts. *Women's Studies International Quarterly,* 1979, *2,* 69–79.

Woolridge, M. W., Baum, J. D., & Drewett, R. F. Effect of a traditional and of a new nipple shield on sucking patterns and milk flow. *Early Human Development,* 1980, *4,* 357–364.

Woolridge, M. W., How, T. U., Drewett, R. F., Rolfe, P., & Baum, J. D. The continuous measurement of milk intake at a feed in breast-fed babies. *Early Human Development,* 1982, *6,* 365–373.

Ziegler, E. E. *Fatness and plasma lipics of adults: Relation to infant feeding.* Unpublished grant proposal, Department of Pediatrics, University of Iowa, June 1983.

5
Exercise Programs for Health Promotion

William L. Haskell

Participation in physical activity on a regular basis has become a health habit frequently promoted by professionals and organizations interested in chronic disease prevention or general health and performance improvement (U.S. Department of Health, Education and Welfare, 1979). Based upon the results of several national surveys, such promotion appears to have had a major impact on the beliefs held by the general public regarding the potential health benefits of exercise: an overwhelming proportion of American and Canadian adults state that exercise is important for maintaining good health (Harris, L., & Associates, 1979; White, 1983). However, careful analysis of survey data on reported exercise habits indicates that while the percentage who report performing some type of exercise is quite high, usually exceeding 80% of those surveyed, many individuals actually exercise quite infrequently, or the type of exercise performed is not considered to provide significant health benefits (Harris, L., & Associates, 1979). This low rate of regular participation in more vigorous exercise is especially true in men and women over age 45. Fewer than 10% of women aged 45 to 65 years report any vigorous exercise during leisure time. If there is such a broad-based and strong belief in the health benefits of exercise, then why has it been so difficult to achieve sustained adherence to so many of the health-oriented exercise programs evaluated to date (Oldridge, 1982)?

The major objectives of this paper are to review the scientific basis for the major health benefits of physical activity, the characteristics of physical activity likely to be health promoting, and some of the factors apparently related to the initiation or maintenance of participation in exercise for health reasons. The secondary purpose is to provide the information needed by health counselors to design individualized, health-oriented exercise programs for clients and to assist them in the successful implementation of these programs.

Health Benefits of Exercise

The biological and psychological benefits ascribed to exercise are extremely diverse and vary substantially with regard to scientific documentation of a causal relationship. Some of the benefits have been established definitely and are achievable by anyone who exercises appropriately. Other benefits, frequently promoted by exercise advocates, usually do not occur and, at times, inappropriate advice has placed individuals at undue risk for exercise-caused morbidity or mortality. As with many other areas of health promotion, enthusiasm to help others by encouraging them to exercise can easily outstrip the scientific rationale for such actions.

Most of the health-related benefits of exercise result from the increase in metabolism required to provide the energy needed for skeletal muscle contraction. This increase in demand for energy triggers a number of changes enhancing the efficiency and capacity of the skeletal muscle to perform work and to minimize fatigue. Changes also occur in those systems that support the increased energy requirements of the skeletal muscles, including the nervous, endocrine, cardiovascular, respiratory, and skeletal systems.

Of the various claims regarding the health benefits of exercise, those with the greatest scientific basis are the prevention of coronary heart disease, the maintenance of optimal body weight or composition, and the normalization of fat and carbohydrate metabolism. Other likely benefits, but for which definitive data are not yet available, include the prevention of elevated blood pressure or hypertension, the maintenance of bone density (the loss of which occurs with aging and results in osteoporosis), improved psychological status, and the prevention of the low back pain syndrome. There are a number of other areas where patients with an established disease who exercise show clinical improvement, but there is no evidence that exercise prevents these disorders. Diseases in this category include Type I diabetes, chronic obstructive lung disease (emphysema or bronchitis), renal failure, Type II hyperlipidemia, and arthritis. There are little, if any, data supporting the notion that exercise prevents infectious disease nor that physically active people have greater morbidity and mortality rates from accidents than would be expected if they remained sedentary.

Physical Fitness versus Health

Increases in physical working capacity often are equated inappropriately with improvements in health status or disease prevention. This distinction is important and often difficult to make: that while a very high level of physical fitness usually requires good health, an improvement in fitness does not ensure an increase in resistance to disease. For example, patients with disorders such as emphysema, diabetes, or hypertension can increase significantly their working capacity through exercise without necessarily changing the severity of their disease or their medical prognosis. Becoming more physically fit and improving health status are interrelated, but not synonymous.

The most effective method of achieving an increase in physical working capacity or "physical fitness" is through a systematic increase in habitual exercise (exercise training). This increase in capacity is an adaptive response by the body to the stress placed on various tissues and biologic functions by the increased metabolic or physical demands of the exercise. If the appropriate type of exercise is performed at the proper intensity, duration, and frequency, sedentary individuals of all ages will achieve significant improvements in physical working capacity. After training, they will be able to exercise at a greater intensity and for a longer duration. Also, at the same submaximal exercise intensity, they will experience less fatigue. This increase in functional capacity is due to enhanced metabolic capacity of skeletal muscle, increased capacity for substrate and oxygen delivery to the muscle, and changes in autonomic nervous system regulation during exercise.

Prevention of Coronary Heart Disease

Men who select a physically active lifestyle generally demonstrate fewer clinical manifestations of coronary heart disease (CHD) than do their sedentary counterparts, and when coronary events do occur they tend to be less severe and appear at an older age (Paffenbarger, Wing, & Hyde, 1978). A recent report from Finland provides evidence of a similar relationship for women (Salonen, Puska, & Tuomilehto, 1982). A majority of the published studies tend to support this conclusion with some reporting significantly lower disease rates for the more active, some showing only a favorable trend, and some finding no difference (Froelicher & Oberman, 1972). It is important to point out that no study has found that more active individuals have a significantly *higher* rate of CHD. These results demonstrate an association between level of exercise and a reduced risk of CHD, but do not establish a cause and effect relationship. To date there has been no adequately designed, randomized clinical trial establishing a causal relationship.

The amount (both intensity and duration) of activity associated with a decrease in CHD varies substantially among the various studies. In some studies, the greatest difference in risk is achieved between those people who do almost nothing and those exercising moderately on a regular basis (Shapiro, Weinblatt, Frank, & Sager, 1969). Much smaller differentials in risk are observed when moderately active individuals are compared to the most active participants. This relationship appears to be true for both job- and nonjob-related activity, and only for recent activity as compared to activity performed in years past. However, the results of other studies indicate that a "threshold" of higher intensity or amount of activity is needed in order to obtain a cardiovascular benefit (Paffenbarger et al., 1978; Cassel, Heyden, Bartel et al., 1971).

The types of activity performed by the more active groups frequently include brisk walking on the level or upstairs, the lifting and carrying of light objects, the lifting of heavy objects, the operation of machinery or appliances, light and heavy gardening, home maintenance or repairs, and the participation in active games and sports. Participation in "physical fitness" or "athletic conditioning" programs contributes very little to the more active classification in most population studies.

The amount of energy expended per day (above that expended by the least active group) associated with a decreased risk of CHD is in the range of 100 to 500 kilocalories per day for nonjob activity and 300 to 800 for job-related activity. This difference for nonjob or leisure-time activity, which averages around 300 kilocalories per day, is an amount of activity achievable by most healthy adults within 30 to 60 minutes of moderate intensity exercise. This level of energy expenditure (5 to 12 kilocalories per minute) can be achieved most easily by performing large muscle, dynamic exercise and is one of the scientific cornerstones on which the exercise prescription for improving health is based.

How Exercise Protects Against Heart Disease

A variety of biologic mechanisms have been proposed to explain how physical activity might prevent the development of CHD. Most of these mechanisms act in some way to decrease the likelihood that the oxygen demands of the myocardium will exceed the oxygen delivery capacity of the coronary arteries and prevent the development of myocardial ischemia. Thus, mechanisms can be classified as either those that contribute to the maintenance or increase of oxygen supply to the myocardium or those that contribute to a decrease in myocardial work and oxygen demands. Most preventive and therapeutic measures for reducing clinical manifestations of CHD are considered to operate through these very same mechanisms.

Because the primary cause of symptoms resulting from coronary atherosclerosis is a reduction in the supply of oxygen to the myocardium, the most direct beneficial effect of physical training might be to maintain or increase myocardial oxygen delivery. Enhanced oxygen availability to the myocardium could be achieved by the delayed progression of coronary atherosclerosis, by an increase in lumen diameter of major coronary arteries, or by coronary collateral vascularization. A major factor limiting our ability to directly collect information about these possibilities is the difficulty of obtaining the necessary invasive measurement of coronary artery status before and after training in both exercise training groups and comparable control groups.

Delay of Atherosclerosis.
Two ways that exercise training could maintain or enhance myocardial oxygen supply would be by retarding the progression of coronary atherosclerosis or by stimulating regression of existing plaques. The concept of coronary atherosclerosis prevention or reversibility as observed in primates (Kramsch, Aspen, Abramowitz, Kreimendahl, & Hood, 1981) is very attractive, but only limited human experimental data are available to support the isolated animal and epidemiologic observations that lend support to such a possibility. No study has been reported in which the progression of coronary atherosclerosis in relation to exercise status has been measured in asymptomatic individuals, and only a few studies have reported any such data on cardiac patients (Selvester, Camp, & Sanmarco, 1977).

Indirect evidence that vigorous exercise might retard the rate of atherosclerosis is suggested by the relationship of exercise to several established CHD risk factors. In healthy adults exercise training alters the blood lipoprotein profile in a direction thought to be less atherogenic: high density lipoprotein cholesterol (HDL-C) is increased, while low density lipoprotein cholesterol (LDL-C), very low density lipoprotein cholesterol (VLDL-C), total cholesterol, and triglycerides are sometimes decreased (Wood, Haskell, Blair et al., 1983). Of particular interest recently is the apparent antiatherogenic effect of increased HDL-C, and the elevating effect both endurance exercise and weight loss have on it.

Coronary Collateral Vascularization.
The intriguing hypothesis that exercise training might be an adequate stimulus for the development of coronary collateral vessels was supported by some early animal studies (Eckstein, 1957). Such encouraging results, however, have not been obtained systematically in any human study using coronary arteriography (Ferguson, Petitclerc, Choquette et al., 1974), nor has there been any evidence of an increase in coronary blood flow as a result of exercise training by cardiac patients (Ferguson, Cote, Gauthier, & Bourassa, 1978). This discrepancy is probably due to a species difference, although the insensitivity of the measurement technique in detecting small changes in coronary anatomy and coronary blood flow should not be overlooked.

Decreases in Myocardial Oxygen Demand.
A reduction in the clinical manifestations of CHD may occur with physical training as a result of a decrease in myocardial oxygen requirement at rest and during exercise. Following exercise training, a substantial per-

centage of angina patients increase the exercise intensity necessary to provoke ischemia, and, in some patients, exertional ischemia is eliminated altogether (Eshani, Health, Hagberg, Sobel, & Holloszy, 1981). The primary reason for this increase in ischemia-free working capacity is a decrease in myocardial oxygen demand due to a decrease in exercise heart rate with less of a reduction in systolic blood pressure. The precise mechanism by which training produces exercise bradycardia is still not fully understood. It currently appears that the training-induced decrease in exercise heart rate is due to changes in the skeletal muscle used for training and to some other more central changes, such as increased blood volume or altered central nervous system regulation.

Exercise Effects on Carbohydrate Metabolism

It has been recognized repeatedly throughout recent medical history that exercise decreases the symptoms of hyperglycemia in many diabetic patients. Allen, Stillman, and Fritz (1919) demonstrated many years ago that the role of glucose uptake from the blood in diabetic patients increased significantly during exercise. Such results generally were ignored, with little attention given to the potential role of exercise in the prevention or treatment of adult onset of Type II diabetes. The idea that exercise had little if any role in normalizing glucose metabolism was due, at least in part, to the lack of consistent difference in the fasting plasma glucose levels between healthy sedentary and active adults.

The difference in glucose metabolism becomes apparent when the rate of glucose uptake from the blood and plasma insulin levels are measured in response to an oral glucose challenge (Leon, Conrad, Hunninghake, & Serfass, 1979) or during infusion of glucose into the blood stream. Under these situations, the rate of glucose removal tends to be more rapid in physically active individuals, and the amount of insulin required during this enhanced glucose uptake is significantly less (Soman, Veikko, Deibert, Felig, & DeFronzo, 1979). In the physically active state, the sensitivity of insulin receptors in skeletal muscle and adipose tissue increases, with a lower insulin production being required for the body to use a given amount of glucose.

Carbohydrate metabolism improves with endurance exercise of moderate intensity or duration, and even greater changes occur with more vigorous exercise. Rate of glucose uptake from the plasma is enhanced in sedentary adults undertaking a 30- to 40-minute per day, 3 day per week exercise program for 6 weeks (Soman et al., 1979), while reduced insulin levels during an oral glucose tolerance test were observed in sedentary obese male college students following 16 weeks of vigorous walking (3.2 mph at 10%), 90 minutes per day, 5 days per week (>1100 kilocalories per session) (Leon et al., 1979). In men with impaired glucose tolerance, an exercise training program (2 times per week for 45 minutes) at 60 to 90% of maximal oxygen uptake and lasting 6 months significantly increased glucose uptake during a glucose tolerance test with no further improvements at 12 and 18 months of training (Saltin, Lindgarde, Houston et al., 1979). Thus, the regular performance of endurance-type exercise, especially when coupled with maintenance of optimal body composition, significantly contributes to the normalization of carbohydrate metabolism and may reduce the frequency of or delay the onset of Type II diabetes.

Exercise and Optimal Body Composition

During the past decade, health professionals have developed a much better understanding of the contribution of exercise to the maintenance of optimal body composition. The value of exercise becomes especially important for long-term weight control for optimal health in a culture that encourages people to be inactive as a result of automation and makes high-density calorie foods readily available at a relatively low cost. Also, it is now more frequently recognized that, within a highly industrialized culture, those individuals consuming the greatest number of calories tend to be the leanest, while the more overweight individuals consume fewer calories (Yano, Rhoads, Kagan, & Tillotson, 1978). This difference is especially evident when the caloric intake of highly active adults, like regular joggers or tennis players, is compared to their sedentary counterparts. The more active men and women are significantly leaner yet consume up to 25% more calories per day (Blair, Ellsworth, Haskell et al., 1981). Along with these calories come more essential nutrients, reducing the likelihood of any nutritional deficiency (possibly an important consideration for people with poor eating habits who are trying to stay slim).

Exercise can potentially influence body composition (the amount of fat in relation to lean tissue or body weight) by several different mechanisms. Although exercise cannot be used to achieve rapidly a large decrease in body fat, the actual increase in calories expended during exercise can have a significant effect over the long term. Moderate intensity exercise performed for 30 minutes can result in an increase in energy expenditure of 300 kilocalories during the activity (American College of Sports Medicine, 1978). In addition, there is some evidence that following exercise of moderate to vigorous intensity the metabolic rate remains elevated for some hours, thus further increasing the contribution of exercise to weight loss (deVries & Gray, 1963).

It is unlikely that the resting or basal metabolic rate (BMR) of a cell that does not change in size as a result of exercise is increased. Thus, if exercise training does not increase muscle mass, it is unlikely that basal metabolic rate is increased. However, because exercise can help retain or increase muscle mass (more often in men than in women and more with strength-type rather than endurance-type exercise), the potential does exist for exercise to influence BMR. There are two situations where this effect may be important: first, in retaining lean body mass as we grow older, and, second, in combining exercise with caloric restriction during a period of weight loss, lean body mass is retained, causing a greater proportion of the weight loss to be fat tissue (Zuti & Golding, 1976).

Some health professionals suggest that exercise may reset the appetite control center or "appestat" so that a better balance exists between caloric intake and need (Woo, Garrow, & Pi-Sunyer, 1982). When activity decreases to a certain level, appetite and caloric intake do not decrease proportionately and adiposity increases. The level at which increased energy expenditure brings no further increase in appetite is not known. Very active people consume more calories than sedentary individuals, yet the former have a more optimal body composition (Blair et al., 1981). When individuals are sufficiently active, it is likely they can respond to social pressures to eat, consume the readily available, high caloric density foods, and still not achieve a state of positive calorie balance. Under these conditions, appetite once again may be "allowed" to regulate calorie intake.

Exercise and Hypertension Control

Exercise should not be considered a first line therapy for the control of high blood pressure, even though as a general preventive measure an active lifestyle probably is of some benefit. It is well established that individuals can have a high level of physical fitness and be hypertensive, yet, in the general population, more active individuals tend to have lower systolic and diastolic pressures (Cooper, Pollock, Martin et al., 1976). Several studies have found that endurance-type exercise training by mild hypertensives results in a lower blood pressure, with the decline usually greater in systolic than diastolic pressure (Choquette & Ferguson, 1973). The results of many such studies are difficult to interpret, as nonexercising control groups were not included and some of the blood pressure reduction could be attributed to increased familiarization with the research personnel and environment or to regression towards the mean in studies of hypertensive patients.

Aging, Exercise, and Bone Strength

Bone strength decreases in older adults due to a decrease in bone mineral content. This loss of minerals usually begins in men around age 50 and progresses quite slowly. In women it can start as early as age 30 to 35 and progress much more rapidly, especially during the first decade after menopause. By age 70 some women may have lost up to 70% of their bone mineral mass. The clinical term for this bone loss is osteoporosis, and it is the primary cause of the increased frequency of bone fractures in older adults. The exact mechanism that produces this demineralization of the bone has not been established, but contributing factors include hormonal changes, nutritional factors, and mechanical forces consisting of gravity and the action of muscles.

Exercise will not prevent all the bone mineral loss associated with aging, but there is increasing evidence that bone mineral content varies significantly with chronic changes in gravitational or muscular forces acting on the bone. Extended periods of weightlessness experienced during space flight also produce significant bone mineral loss (Mack, La-Chance, Vose et al., 1967). The opposite effect has been shown as well: with vigorous exercise the mineral content and cross-sectional area of bones in the exercising limb are substantially increased.

Moderate exercise, well within the capacity of many older adults, appears to increase total body calcium and maintain or increase bone mineral content. When Smith and colleagues (Smith, Reddan, & Smith, 1981) had elderly women exercise 30 minutes per session, 3 days a week for 3 years, they observed an increase in bone mineral content of the radius of 2.29%. Twelve women remaining sedentary during this time showed a decrease of 3.28% (p<.005).

These data suggest that arrangements should be made (1) to prevent unnecessary bed rest or immobilization of older adults, and (2) to develop appropriate exercise programs for the elderly. Walking, daily home care activities, or gardening-type exercises, as well as formal conditioning programs, are apparently of benefit and could easily be implemented.

Psychological Benefits of Exercise

When regular exercisers are asked about the psychological benefits of exercise, the most likely response is one of enthusiasm. They tend to report that exercise makes them "feel better," that they can "handle stress better," or that they "feel more energetic." These are the successes, but what about the many exercise failures who either intend to start exercising and never do or who have started and stopped once or many times? Do they experience similar positive effects or is exercise basically a psychological "turn-off" for them? Physical activity is a socially acceptable means of separating mind and body from the many stress-producing circumstances at home or at work. It is very difficult to concentrate on physical tasks like hitting or kicking a ball, skiing a steep slope, or running a "personal best" and still have other problems on your mind. It is not known to what extent or how frequently there are psychological benefits in exercise. Nor is it known if there is a biological basis to the positive psychological reports. These issues require further investigation.

Comparisons of active versus inactive individuals usually result in the active persons reporting a more positive psychological profile, including greater self-confidence (Jasnoski, Holmes, Olomon, & Agular, 1981), less anxiety (Young, 1979), and less depression (Greist, Klein, Eischens et al., 1979). However, these studies have a major problem with self-selection: it may be that more confident individuals who are less anxious and less depressed choose to become regular exercisers. There have been very few adequately designed studies examining the psychological benefits of exercise among previously sedentary adults. The results of several controlled studies are encouraging, where men randomized to aerobic-type exercise training for one year and jogging more than 8 to 10 miles per week showed a decrease in anxiety, depression, and hostility compared to sedentary controls (Graham, Ho, Wood et al., 1981). Also, there is a tendency for men demonstrating the Type A behavior pattern to show a reduction in these characteristics as a result of exercise training.

Some of the stress-reducing benefits of exercise may have a biological basis. Circulating catecholamines at rest and submaximal exercise are reduced in some people following aerobic-type conditioning (Cousineau, Ferguson, de Champlain et al., 1977). Whether or not these changes enable an individual to manage psychological stress with fewer negative health consequences has not been established. The increase in beta-endorphines has received a lot of attention and has been cited as the possible mechanism for producing an "exercise high." These compounds do increase in the blood with exercise (Carr, Bullen, Skrinar et al., 1981); however, their role in brain functioning and their relationship to the psychological state of exercisers are not understood.

Designing an Activity Plan for Health

The results of many of the studies cited in the first section of this chapter have two common themes: (1) more active individuals tend to be healthier than more sedentary persons, and (2) the amount of exercise required to attain many health benefits is achievable by most adults. The type, intensity, and amount of exercise (duration times frequency) are well within the capacity of most healthy people at any age. Because the health benefits are diverse, and because substantial variations exist among adults regarding their exercise capacity, interests, skills, and accessability, an individualized activity plan or exercise prescription must be developed to maximize the likelihood of a successful outcome.

Many of the concepts and procedures used to prepare athletes for competition have been applied to activity plans for health improvement.

While some of these ideas and methods are transferable, others are not only inappropriate but may be misleading or contraindicated. For example, while the idea of "no pain, no gain" may be needed to achieve peak athletic performance, such an approach is not needed and may be detrimental in exercise activities to maintain health or prevent disease.

Principles of Exercise Training

Knowledge of three scientific principles or concepts can be extremely valuable in helping clients understand how the health benefits of exercise are achieved. These principles form the scientific basis for developing an individualized exercise plan.

Overload.
The principle of overload is the key to nearly all the benefits of exercise. Overload means that the body responds to an increase in exercise by a combination or series of adaptations. Even a slight increase in the amount or intensity of exercise will make new demands on various tissues or systems in the body, and they will respond to this demand by enhancing their capacity or efficiency. Thus, exercise training effects are nothing more than the body's attempts to adjust to new demands or stresses. The characteristics of the body's adaptation to a new exercise demand will depend on the type of exercise and its intensity.

Progression.
The principle of progression simply means that in order for a person to continue experiencing improvement as a result of exercise, the increased exercise demand (overload) needs to be applied in small increments. After a few days or weeks of exercising at a set amount and intensity, the body will adapt to those demands and new adaptations will occur only when exercise is increased by a small amount. As long as an individual does not try to progress too quickly, the adaptations the body makes to the increased demands will be positive. However, if one attempts to progress too rapidly, there is enhanced likelihood of fatigue, soreness, and tissue injury or damage. It is important to note that everyone will not progress at the same rate. Some people will progress more slowly. This slow pace may be due to their basic constitution or heredity, how active they have been in the past, and their current health status. For example, being substantially overweight or a heavy cigarette smoker usually requires a slower rate of progression.

Specificity.
The concept of specificity implies that adaptations will occur only in those tissues or body systems that experience increased demands or overload during exercise. For example, if the goal is to increase stamina, then exercises are required that put demands on the oxygen transport and

metabolic functions of the body, since these limit stamina. If the goal is to increase the strength of leg muscles, then it is necessary to perform resistive exercises with those muscles. Lifting weights will not increase endurance capacity, nor will jogging increase the muscle tone of arms. Thus, specificity not only applies to parts of the body, but also to the types of changes (endurance, strength, flexibility, weight loss, etc.) desired from the exercise program. It is necessary to select the right exercises to meet the specific goals of the program; as the goals change, the combination of required exercises must also change. Specificity means that the many effects of different types of exercise are not interchangeable.

The Characteristics of Exercise to Promote Health

An individualized exercise plan can be described by the type, intensity, duration, and frequency of the exercise to be performed. The specifics for each of these characteristics depend on the individual's goals, exercise capacity, interests, skills, and exercise opportunities (schedule, facilities, equipment, partners, competitions, etc.). Characteristics of the plan should vary depending upon increases in exercise capacity, development of new skills or interests, and changes in opportunities (change of season, new facilities, etc.). For individuals without any recent exercise experience, participation for several months in a supervised program conducted by a knowledgeable exercise leader or specialist can be of substantial value in setting proper exercise intensity and in developing proper technique or skills.

Exercise Type.
The type of exercise providing the greatest health benefits and permitting the greatest increase in energy expenditure with the least fatigue consists of rhythmically contracting large muscles, moving the body over a distance or against gravity. This exercise activity is referred to as endurance or "aerobic" exercise, because most resynthesis of high energy compounds in the muscle occurs in the presence of oxygen. Examples of this type of exercise include walking, hiking, jogging or running, cycling, cross-country skiing, swimming, active games and sports, selected calisthenics, and vigorous at-home chores. While very specific activities may be required when training for athletic competition, for health purposes aerobic exercise seems to be of benefit if performed frequently enough at the proper intensity.

Exercise Intensity.
The exercise-induced changes that contribute to health are achieved when the exercise **intensity** is somewhat greater than that usually performed by the individual. This increased intensity or overload causes adaptations that allow the metabolic needs of the muscles during exercise

to be met more readily. Though even slight increases in exercise intensity will produce changes, the usual recommendation for optimizing health is that exercise be performed at 50 to 75% of the individual's oxygen transport (aerobic) capacity, or at 60 to 85% of maximum achievable heart rate. Using these guidelines, exercise training heart rates for individuals 30 years of age would range from 114 to 162 beats per minute, whereas at age 60 the range would be from 96 to 137 beats per minute. For most people this recommendation produces a substantial intensity overload, since individuals usually do not exercise at more than about 45% of their aerobic capacity during everyday activities.

Exercise Amount.
The recommended exercise **duration** will depend on the person's health or fitness goals and exercise capacity, as well as on the type of exercise performed. One interpretation of the data available on exercise and health is that people who exercise even a little bit on a regular basis are better off than those who do almost nothing. A reasonable goal seems to be an energy expenditure over usual activities of approximately 300 kilocalories per session with a **frequency** of at least every other day. Most clinically healthy adults have the capacity to expend from 400 to 700 kilocalories per hour while performing activity of moderate intensity; thus, they can expend 300 kilocalories in 25 to 45 minutes. Activities meeting this goal include walking or jogging 4 kilometers, cycling or swimming for 30 minutes, or playing several sets of singles tennis lasting for 45 minutes. Lower-intensity exercise such as walking or gardening generally will not produce a large increase in exercise capacity; however, if these exercises are performed for longer periods of time or more frequently, they provide many of the health benefits derived from more vigorous exercise (i.e., weight control, bone mineral retention, etc.).

In addition to aerobic or endurance exercise, some exercises to maintain or develop muscle strength and flexibility of joints should be included as part of an exercise session. These activities promote a retention of lean body mass, help protect joints against injury, and contribute to the prevention of low back pain. Only a few minutes per day are required to obtain significant increases in strength and flexibility (Wilmore, 1982). These exercises can be performed before or after the endurance exercise or at a separate time.

Factors Influencing Exercise Adherence

Compared to the extensive research that has been conducted evaluating determinants of adherence to other health behavior changes such as smoking cessation, alcohol reduction, and weight loss by diet, there has been very limited systematic investigation of the barriers and facilitators of participation in health-oriented exercise. A majority of adults who successfully initiated exercise programs during the past decade have done so on their own and not as participants in formal group programs. Research results and clinical observations have identified various personal experiences or characteristics apparently related to initiation or maintenance of exercise by healthy adults or patients.

Past Experiences.

Individuals rating their early exercise experiences as favorable, especially during elementary school, tend to demonstrate greater exercise adherence as adults (Harris, 1970; Foss & Reuschlein, 1980). However, post-elementary experiences do not seem to predict adherence. Learning exercise skills at a young age may be an important element of this relationship, as many adults are hesitant to learn new athletic skills. Sonstroem (1978) suggests that self-perception of physical ability significantly affects self-esteem, which, in turn, determines participation. It is possible that skill deficiencies manifested at an early age are translated into perceived deficiencies in physical abilities, causing the avoidance of exercise in order to preserve self-esteem.

Socioeconomic Status.

Adults with higher levels of education participate in more health-oriented exercise programs than do less-educated adults (Harris, L., & Associates, 1979). It is not known whether this participation level is the result of increased opportunities due to more available time, increased income, different childhood experiences, or increased health awareness. In general, there is a strong negative relationship between level of education and many major chronic disease risk factors: the higher the level of education, the lower the risk factor. Additionally, among patient populations blue-collar workers, compared to their white-collar counterparts, have poorer adherence to exercise programs (Oldridge, 1982).

Long-Term Goals.

Individuals with specific, long-term, health-related goals tend to demonstrate better exercise program adherence (Heinzelmann & Bagley, 1970). Such long-term goals as reduced illness, improved psychological state, and reduced risk of heart attack appear to be more predictive of good exercise adherence than are short-term goals such as losing weight or learning how to become more physically fit. This observation contradicts the emphasis frequently found in behavior therapy regarding the development of short-term goals. Keefe and Blumenthal (1980) reported that over time the intrinsically rewarding aspects of exercise take on greater importance than external reinforcers.

Self-Predicted Behaviors and Psychological Status.

As with other health-related behaviors, one of the better predictors of adherence to exercise is the participant's own estimation of his/her adherence capabilities (Haynes, 1976). Individuals who firmly believe they will adhere to the program even if they are not meeting all of their expectations have better adherence in supervised exercise programs than do those expressing doubt about their continued participation under such conditions.

Preliminary data indicate that even within the clinically healthy population, elevations in depression or hostility are associated with reduced participation in a jogging program (Graham et al., 1981). Others have shown that such exercise actually decreases depression and anxiety (Greist, Klein, Eischens, Faris, Gurman, & Morgan, 1978). Thus, those who might obtain the greatest psychological benefit from exercise could present the greatest challenge with regard to adherence. Whether or not psychological characteristics predict adherence to other types of physical activities, such as competitive sports, has not been established.

Program Characteristics.
A number of features within the exercise program itself may influence adherence; however, few of these features have been evaluated systematically. In supervised programs, the quality of the leadership and the convenience of the program both contribute to adherence (Durbeck, Heinzelmann, Schachter, Haskell, Payne, Moxley, Nemiroff, Limoncelli, Arnoldi, & Fox, 1972). Important leadership characteristics include a good knowledge of exercise, experience at providing instruction and leading a class, a fit-looking and attractive appearance, friendliness, and enthusiasm (Oldridge, 1982). Convenience factors include location, time of day, and transportation or parking availability. Program cost is a consideration, but the role of financial commitment as an incentive for enhancing adherence has not been established. Women, more than men, prefer group exercise programs, and women, especially those under age 45, have been the primary participants in rhythm-oriented exercise such as aerobic dance.

Exercise Safety

When recommending exercise for health promotion, one does battle with the proverbial two-edged sword. Inappropriate exercise literally can pose dangers to limbs and life. The most commonly encountered problem is musculoskeletal discomfort or injury due to trauma or overuse. Of more severe consequence, but much less frequent, is the precipitation of a major cardiac event, usually ventricular fibrillation. However, the likelihood is remote that exercise will cause a cardiac arrest in individuals free of cardiac disease.

There are other health risks related to exercise; however, these usually are limited to individuals with established disease (e.g., diabetes, asthma, or renal failure) or occur after very extensive physical activity. The most important of these risks is the development of severe heat injury. Total prevention of these injuries is unlikely to be achieved if adults are to increase their exercise, but the risks can be reduced by proper medical evaluation, individualized exercise recommendations, and improved public education.

Orthopedic injuries occur most often during jogging, running, and racket sports from the added weight-bearing stress on feet, ankles, legs, knees, and lower back. Most of these injuries are due to irritations of bones, tendons, ligaments, and muscles. There is a wide range of susceptibility to such injuries, and it is difficult to predict who will have problems and who will not as the intensity and amount of exercise increases. Risk becomes greater with advancing age, history of previous injury, overexertion, and substantial obesity. Preventive procedures include engaging in nonweight-bearing activities such as swimming, riding a stationary cycle or rowing machine, and substituting brisk walking or hiking in the hills for jogging. If possible, exercise should be performed on soft surfaces. Well-constructed athletic or running shoes with thick, shock-absorbing soles, raised heels, and arch supports are valuable. It is important to begin a new program of exercise very slowly to allow the body's support structures to accommodate to the new stress being placed on them. When problems do develop, one can relieve the stress by decreasing the amount or intensity of activity, switching to an alternate exercise, or resting and applying appropriate therapy.

Most cardiac events can be prevented if individuals remain under good general medical care (periodic evaluations and appropriate treatment when needed), control major cardiac risk factors, learn the proper skills for health-oriented exercise, use this knowledge in carrying out a program of regular exercise, and take heed of body signals that indicate the exercise plan should be modified or medical attention sought. Proper medical clearance, individualized program planning and implementation, and personal monitoring are the keys to safe exericse.

Conclusions

Documentation has shown that appropriate exercise can make a substantial contribution to a comprehensive program of health improvement. Exercise can help delay the onset and reduce the rate of progression of several major chronic degenerative diseases common in Western industrialized culture. Exercise may be of particular benefit in the prevention and rehabilitation of coronary heart disease, the normalization of fat and carbohydrate metabolism, weight control, the reduction of bone mineral loss with aging, and the enhancement of psychological status.

The level of exercise required to achieve many of the health benefits is well within the capacity of most healthy adults. Large muscle, dynamic exercise performed at moderate intensity appears to contribute the most to health status, with the major stimulus for improvement being a sustained increase in energy expenditure. Initial goals should include increasing activity levels to produce a 150 to 200 kilocalorie increase in energy expenditure. The longer-term goal of an exercise program might involve expending 300 to 400 kilocalories at a moderate intensity at least every other day.

The greatest success in maintaining health-oriented exercise is obtained with individually designed programs that consider personal interests, skills, and exercise opportunities as well as program goals and exercise capacity. The exercise selected should be convenient, enjoyable, and appropriate to the person's general lifestyle. Exercise adherence is increased when exercisers have knowledge of what to do and why, confidence that they can be successful, and the patience to wait for the benefits to accrue.

References

Allen, F. M., Stillman, E., & Fritz, R. *Total dietary regulation in the treatment of diabetes.* In *Exercise* (Chap. 5). New York: Rockefeller Institute of Medical Research, 1919 (Monograph #11), 486–491.

American College of Sports Medicine. Position statement on the recommended quantity and quality of exercise for developing and maintaining fitness in healthy adults. *Medicine and Science in Sports,* 1978, *10,* vii–x.

Blair, S. N., Ellsworth, N. M., Haskell, W. L., et al. Comparison of nutrient intake in middle-aged men and women runners and controls. *Medicine and Science in Sports and Exercise,* 1981, *13,* 310–315.

Carr, D. B., Bullen, B. A., Skrinar, G. S., et al. Physical conditioning facilitates the exercise-induced secretion of beta-endorphin in beta-lipotropin in women. *New England Journal of Medicine,* 1981, *305,* 560–563.

Cassel, J., Heyden, S., Bartel, A., et al. Occupation and physical activity and coronary heart disease. *Archives of Internal Medicine,* 1971, *128,* 920–928.

Choquette, G., & Ferguson, R. J. Blood pressure reduction in "borderline" hypertensives following physical training. *Canadian Medical Journal,* 1973, *108,* 697–703.

Cooper, K. H., Pollock, M., Martin, R., et al. Physical fitness levels vs. selected coronary risk factors. *Journal of the American Medical Association,* 1976, *236,* 116–169.

Cousineau, D., Ferguson, R., de Champlain, J., et al. Catecholamines in coronary sinus during exercise in man before and after training. *Journal of Applied Physiology,* 1977, *43,* 801–806.

deVries, H. A., & Gray, D. E. After-effects of exercise upon resting metabolic rate. *Research Quarterly,* 1963, *34,* 314–321.

Durbeck, D. C., Heinzelmann, F., Schachter, J., Haskell, W. L., Payne, G. H., Moxley, R. T., Nemiroff, M., Limoncelli, D. D., Arnoldi, L. B., & Fox,

S. M. The National Aeronautics and Space Administration—U.S. Public Health Service Health Evaluation and Enhancement Program: Summary of results. *American Journal of Cardiology*, 1972, *36*, 784–790.

Eckstein, R. W. Effect of exercise and coronary artery narrowing on coronary collateral circulation. *Circulation Research*, 1957, *5*, 230–235.

Eshani, A., Health, G., Hagberg, J., Sobel, B., & Holloszy, J. Effects of 12 months of intense exercise training on ischemic ST-segment depression in patients with coronary artery disease. *Circulation*, 1981, *64*, 1116–1124.

Ferguson, R. J., Cote, P., Gauthier, P., & Bourassa, M. G. Changes in exercise coronary sinus blood flow with training in patients with angina pectoris. *Circulation*, 1978, *58*, 41–47.

Ferguson, R. J., Petitclerc, R., Choquette, G., et al. Effect of physical training on treadmill exercise capacity, collateral circulation, and progression of coronary disease. *American Journal of Cardiology*, 1974, *34*, 764–769.

Foss, P., & Reuschlein, P. Factors governing urban adults female participation in physical activity programs. *Medicine and Science in Sports and Exercise*, 1980, *12*, 99.

Froelicher, V. F., & Oberman, A. Analysis of epidemiologic studies of physical inactivity as a risk factor for coronary artery disease. *Progress in Cardiovascular Disease*, 1972, *15*, 209–227.

Graham, L., Ho, P., Wood, P. D., et al. Exercise and psychological/behavioral characteristics: A one-year randomized controlled trial. *CVD Epidemiology Newsletter*, 1981, *30*, 48.

Greist, J. H., Klein, M. H., Eischens, R. R., Faris, J., Gurman, A. S., & Morgan, W. P. Running through your mind. *Journal of Psychosomatic Research*, 1978, *22*, 259–294.

Greist, J. H., Klein, M. H., Eischens, R. R., et al. Running as treatment for depression. *Comprehensive Psychiatry*, 1979, *20*, 41–54.

Harris, D. V. Physical activity history and attitudes of middle-aged men. *Medicine and Science in Sports*, 1970, *2*, 203–208.

Harris, L., & Associates. *The Perrier study: Fitness in America.* Greenwich, Conn.: Perrier—Great Waters of France, Inc., 1979.

Haynes, R. B. A critical review of the "determinants" of patient compliance with therapeutic regimens. In D. L. Sackett & R. B. Haynes (Eds.), *Compliance with therapeutic regimens*. Baltimore: Johns Hopkins University Press, 1976, 26–39.

Heinzelmann, F., & Bagley, R. W. Response to physical activity programs and their effects on health behavior. *Public Health Reports*, 1970, *85*, 905–911.

Jasnoski, M., Holmes, D., Olomon, S., & Agular, C. Exercise, changes in aerobic capacity and changes in self perception: An experimental investigation. *Journal of Research in Personality*, 1981, *15*, 460–466.

Keefe, F. J., & Blumenthal, J. A. The life fitness program: A behavioral approach to making exercise a habit. *Journal of Behavior Therapy and Experimental Psychiatry*, 1980, *11*, 31–34.

Kramsch, D. M., Aspen, A., Abramowitz, B., Kreimendahl, T., & Hood, W. B. Reduction of coronary atherosclerosis by moderate conditioning exercise in monkeys on an atherogenic diet. *New England Journal of Medicine*, 1981, *305*, 1483–1489.

Leon, A., Conrad, J., Hunninghake, D., & Serfass, R. Effects of a vigorous walking program on body composition, and carbohydrate and lipid metabolism of obese young men. *American Journal of Clinical Nutrition*, 1979, *32*, 1776–1787.

Mack, P. B., LaChance, P. A. Vose, G. P., et al. Bone demineralization of foot and hand of Gemini-Titan IV, V and VII astronauts during orbital flight. *American Journal of Roentgenology*, 1967, *100*, 503–511.

Oldridge, N. B. Compliance and exercise in primary and secondary prevention of coronary heart disease: A review. *Preventive Medicine*, 1982, *11*, 56–70.

Paffenbarger, R. S., Wing, A. L., & Hyde, R. T. Physical activity as an index of heart attack in college alumni. *American Journal of Epidemiology*, 1978, *108*, 161–175.

Salonen, J. T., Puska, R., & Tuomilehto, J. Physical activity and risk of myocardial infarction, cerebral stroke and death: A longitudinal study in Eastern Finland. *American Journal of Epidemiology*, 1982, *115*, 526–537.

Saltin, B., Lindgarde, F., Houston, M., et al. Physical training and glucose tolerance in middle-aged men with chemical diabetes. *Diabetes*, 1979, *28* (suppl. 1), 30–32.

Selvester, R., Camp, J., & Sanmarco, M. Effects of exercise training on progression of documented coronary atherosclerosis. In P. Milvey (Ed.), *The marathon: Physiological, medical, epidemiological, and psychological studies.* New York: New York Academy of Sciences, 1977, 495–508.

Shapiro, S., Weinblatt, E., Frank, C., & Sager, R. V. Incidence of coronary heart disease in a population insured for medical care (HIP). *American Journal of Public Health*, 1969, *59*, 1–101.

Smith, E. L. Reddan, W., & Smith, P. E. Physical activity and calcium modalities for bone mineral increase in aged women. *Medicine and Science in Sports and Exercise*, 1981, *13*, 60–64.

Soman, V. R., Veikko, A. K., Deibert, D., Felig, P., & DeFronzo, R. A. Increased insulin sensitivity and insulin binding to monocytes after physical training, *New England Journal of Medicine*, 1979, *301*, 200–204.

Sonstroem, R. J. Physical estimation and attraction scales: Rationale and research. *Medicine and Science in Sports*, 1978, *10*, 97–102.

United States Department of Health, Education and Welfare. *Healthy people: The Surgeon General's Department on Health Promotion and Disease Prevention* (U.S. Public Health Service Publication No. 79-55071). Washington, D.C.: U.S. Government Printing Office, 1979, 132–135.

White, F. M. M. The Canadian fitness survey: Implications for health research and public health practice. *Canadian Journal of Public Health*, 1983, *74*, 91–95.

Wilmore, J. H. *Training for sports and activity* (2nd ed.). Boston, Mass.: Allyn and Bacon, Inc., 1982.

Woo, R., Garrow, J. S., & Pi-Sunyer, F. X. Effect of exercise on spontaneous calorie intake in obesity. *American Journal of Clinical Nutrition*, 1982, *36*, 470–477.

Wood, P. D., Haskell, W. L., Blair, S., et al. Increased exercise level and plasma lipoprotein concentrations: A one-year randomized, controlled study in sedentary, middle-aged men. *Metabolism*, 1983, *32*, 31–39.

Yano, R., Rhoads, G., Kagan, A., & Tillotson, J. Dietary intake and the risk of coronary heart disease in Japanese men living in Hawaii. *American Journal of Clinical Nutrition*, 1978, *31*, 1270–1279.

Young, R. J. The effect of regular exercise on cognitive functioning and personality. *British Journal of Sports Medicine*, 1979, *13*, 110–117.

Zuti, W. B., & Golding, L. B. Comparing diet and exercise as weight reduction tools. *Physician and Sports Medicine*, 1976, *4*, 49–57.

6
Modifying Type A Behavior

Margaret A. Chesney, Nanette M. Frautschi, and Ray H. Rosenman

Coronary heart disease (CHD) is the leading cause of death and disability in the United States. Each year 600,000 people die from this disease, with 35% of these deaths being premature (i.e., among persons under age 65). High levels of the disease have stimulated medical research regarding causal factors. Elevated blood pressure and serum cholesterol, cigarette smoking, diabetes, and obesity have been established as risk factors, and attempts at primary and secondary prevention traditionally have focused on changing these risk factors through medical intervention or lifestyle change. However, taken together, these factors are unable to explain historical changes or geographic differences in CHD prevalence. Therefore, while attention was directed to further delineating the role of these important risk factors in CHD, the search continued for additional CHD risk factors and led to the recognition of Type A behavior's role in heart disease risk.

The Type A behavior pattern (TABP) was defined in the 1950s by two cardiologists; however, in retrospect, certain commonalities in the behavior of CHD patients were already noted in earlier medical literature. In 1892, Sir William Osler strongly implicated stress and hard-driving behavior, describing the coronary disease patient as a "keen and ambitious man, who has his engine set at full speed ahead" (Osler, 1910). Indeed, early characterizations of heart attack victims as hostile, aggressive, impatient persons overinvolved in their work have become part of our medical lore. The definition of TABP and demonstration of its role as a CHD risk factor in subsequent, prospective studies confirmed these earlier observations.

Persons with the TABP are engaged in a relatively chronic struggle to do and achieve more and more in less time, often in competition with their own standards, other persons, or opposing forces in the environment. The TABP most often emerges in response to environmental challenge or stress. Individuals without Type A behavior are classified "Type B" and exhibit a different style of coping in response to similar stresses and challenges. The first evidence of the causal relationship between TABP and CHD was provided by the Western Collaborative Group Study (Rosenman, Brand, Jenkins, Friedman, Straus, & Wurm, 1975). In this study, subjects identified as having the TABP later suffered twice the CHD rate experienced by Type B individuals. Other prospective studies in Belgium and at Framingham confirmed this two-fold risk (Haynes, Feinleib, & Kannel, 1980; Kornitzer, Magotteau, Degre, Kittel, Struyven, & van Thiel, 1982). Furthermore, since the initial study, TABP has been correlated with severity of coronary atherosclerosis observed at autopsy (Friedman, Rosenman, Straus, Wurm, & Kositchek, 1968), as well as in angiographic studies (Blumenthal, Williams, Kong, Schanberg, & Thompson, 1978; Frank, Heller, Kornfeld, Sporn, & Weiss, 1978; Zyzanski, Jenkins, Ryan, Flessas, & Everist, 1976).

After consideration of the growing body of research confirming the risk associated with TABP, a critical review panel convened by the National Heart, Lung, and Blood Institute recognized Type A behavior as an independent risk factor for coronary heart disease (The Review Panel on Coronary-prone Behavior and Coronary Heart Disease, 1981). Moreover, this review concluded that the increased risk associated with Type A behavior is "over and above that imposed by age, blood pressure, serum cholesterol, and smoking, and appears to be of the same order of magnitude as the relative risk associated with any of these factors." Given the high personal and social costs of CHD, there is considerable interest in methods of modifying TABP. In this chapter, a detailed description of TABP will be given, and recommendations for changing certain Type A behaviors will be presented.

Type A Behavior Pattern

The TABP is characterized by a constellation of behaviors particularly exhibited in response to salient environmental stress. Individuals with TABP exhibit enhanced aggressiveness, competitiveness, and impatience both in their work and leisure activities, and an ambitiousness and deep involvement in their work. Among these characteristics, there were several singled out early in Type A research as particularly coronary prone, namely time urgency, joyless striving, and hostility (Rosenman, 1978a, 1979; Rosenman & Friedman, 1977). Recent research appears to confirm the importance of these factors in coronary-prone behavior (Dembroski, MacDougall, Shields, Petitto, & Lushene, 1978; Diamond, 1982; Matthews, Glass, Rosenman, & Bortner, 1977).

Time Urgency

Type A's are hard-driving and achievement-oriented individuals who, in an attempt to accomplish more, struggle against the clock, thereby giving rise to a sense of time urgency. As a result, Type A's are often engaged in "polyphasic activity" (i.e., doing more than one thing at a time). For example, it is not unusual for such persons to read mail while talking on the telephone, to read newspapers or professional journals while eating a meal or watching television, and to carry reading material to occasions where they anticipate feeling bored or having to wait.

Feeling time pressured, Type A individuals often schedule commitments too tightly and underestimate the time needed to complete tasks. As a result, they often struggle to "catch up" with the schedules they set. This fact should not imply that Type A's are disorganized. Indeed, commonly they are admired for their compulsive organization and memory for details. With today's bureaucratic, complex, interwoven world, even the most efficient Type A individual frequently encounters obstacles to well-laid plans and often falls behind schedule. For example, an automobile trip begun at the designated time may be thrown off schedule by the passage of a long freight train at a railroad crossing. Such barriers and interferences often engender the time-urgency and impatient hostility components of the TABP. Thus, the irritability and potential for hostility are triggered when time-urgent Type A's are blocked in achieving their plans.

Joyless Striving

The joyless striving characteristic of the TABP is associated with excessive achievement orientation and competition, major Type A attributes. Type A's are often very self-critical, competing with very high personal standards that are repeatedly adjusted upward. Thus, while being praised by some, they conduct a private "post-mortem," chastising themselves for minor errors and demanding greater heights of achievement. Friedman and Rosenman (1974) conjectured that the constant struggle to seek recognition and reward may be a means of allaying underlying fears of inadequacy and insecurity. In this way, the TABP may be similar to the "manic" defense against depression observed in psychiatric patients. Indeed, there is evidence that emotional exhaustion and feelings of despair, hopelessness, and depression belong to the predromata of myocardial infarction and sudden death (Appels, 1983; Elliott & Eisdorfer, 1982; Nixon, 1976). Thus, it may be that Type A's joyless striving culminates in feelings of resignation and malaise. Loss of prestige and loss of employment have also been implicated as risk factors for myocardial infarction (Kavanagh & Shepard, 1973; Parkes, Benjamin, & Fitzgerald, 1969). Positive associations also have been reported between depression and coronary atherosclerosis (Jenkins, Zyzanski, Ryan, Flessas, & Tannerbaum, 1977). In sum, the pattern of chronic striving may be an attempt on the part of Type A individuals to overcome underlying feelings of depression, an emotional state associated with manifest CHD.

Hostility

Type A individuals often possess an enhanced "potential for hostility." Short of expressed anger, this "potential" is manifested as an edginess or irritability. Indeed, Type A's are ever "on guard" or suspiciously alert to possible challenges interfering with their progress. The potential for hostility is habitual and may be easily provoked by even minor circumstances. Such provoked feelings of anger may or may not be expressed. When expressed, this anger may be displaced onto inanimate objects or others not directly involved in the provocation. For example, while driving in heavy traffic, some Type A's are quick to flash their lights or honk their horn when provoked by another driver. Others mutter to themselves or speak sharply to the open space or to a companion.

Intervention

There is increasing interest in modification of TABP, both for primary and secondary prevention. A number of relatively small, comparative studies have examined serum lipid and blood pressure levels following such interventions. A comprehensive review of these studies is provided by Suinn (1982) and indicates that, in general, these studies have reported reductions in self-report of Type A behaviors following behavioral interventions. Changes in risk factor levels have been less consistent with a number of studies reporting reductions (Lobitz & Brammell, 1981; Roskies, Kearney, Spevack, Surkis, Cohen, & Gilman, 1979; Roskies, Spevack, Surkis, Cohen, & Gilman, 1978) and others reporting increased risk factor levels or mixed findings (Jenni & Wollersheim, 1979; Levenkron, Cohen, Mueller, & Fisher, 1982; Suinn, 1975; Suinn & Bloom, 1978). These studies assessed the effects of intervention with primarily healthy individuals. One major clinical trial is underway at this writing assessing the effects of Type A intervention on the rate of recurring coronary events (Thoresen, Friedman, Gill, & Ulmer, 1982). Preliminary reports from this trial indicate that recurrence rates are lower for patients receiving both Type A behavior modification and standard medical advice than for patients receiving medical advice alone. Though the results of those intervention studies assessing changes in CHD risk factors in healthy individuals are mixed and underscore the need for further research in this area, the findings of the clinical trial are very promising and suggest an important role for Type A intervention in secondary prevention.

Recommendations

Interventions to modify TABP should be directed toward changing one or more of three interacting factors: environmental demands, the individual's responses to the environment (both behavioral and cognitive), and physiological concomitants of TABP such as enhanced adrenergic arousal.

Changing Environmental Demands

Western industrial society provides an environment that elicits and systematically reinforces Type A behaviors. The environment is a collage of highways, bureaucracies, densely populated cities, and interdependent individuals and activities with interlocking deadlines. Performance demands and time pressures abound, with socioeconomic status frequently dependent upon meeting these demands. In short, the environment often "triggers" TABP.

There are a number of alternative strategies to counteract environmental demands or triggers. Primarily, these strategies involve placing limits on the amount of time spent in environments that are stressful and that evoke Type A behavior. For example, Type A's might limit the time they devote to work and the time spent in settings where work occurs. In some cases, the restriction of effort devoted to work may require negotiating with an employer regarding project deadlines and rescheduling deadlines that require prolonged periods of overtime. When it is not possible to reduce or limit a heavy workload, its salience may be reduced by eliminating unnecessary clutter from desk tops and keeping only needed materials in view. Another way to reduce environmental triggers of Type A behavior involves interruptions, a frequently cited source of stress at work and elsewhere. It may be possible for Type A's to arrange for time without such interruptions by changing the environment, for example, by using telephone answering machines to reduce unwanted telephone interruptions and to increase the time available to accomplish high-priority tasks.

Changing the Individual's Response to the Environment

Although the environment obviously places demands on people, unfortunately only rarely can the environment be significantly altered to reduce stress. Therefore, in addition to changing the environment, it is frequently necessary to alter the characteristic manner in which Type A persons respond to these demands. This process involves two basic methods of behavior change, self-observation and self-contracting, that may be applied to both behavior and cognitions of Type A individuals.

Self-observation.

To modify Type A behaviors, Type A's must develop the capacity to witness their own actions in daily living and relate these actions to their environmental cues. While Type A's are keen observers of the behavior of others, some are relatively unaware of their own reactions. Many Type A's are adept at identifying the shortest line or the most efficient clerk at the post office. Such observational skills can be used to identify Type A behaviors as potential targets for change and to record information regarding the frequency of these behaviors and the circumstances under which they occur (i.e., who, what, where, and when). Recorded diaries can be reviewed to select target behaviors for modification and can be used to document change.

Self-contracting.

After observing and recording maladaptive behavior, many Type A's continue to respond to environmental demands with excessive competitiveness, time urgency, and hostility. Self-contracting may be used to facilitate change in Type A behaviors subsequent to self-observation. This process involves the selection of a target—either overt behavior or covert thoughts—to be changed, setting a goal, and designating a plan to achieve the goal. For example, a Type A might choose to alter irritable and impatient behavior while waiting in lines. The goal in this instance might be to maintain a relaxed stance and watching or chatting with passersby, rather than becoming angry or attempting to use the time for work-related or otherwise "constructive" activities. The plan to achieve this goal might involve going to the post office once a week at noon and substituting more relaxed behavior, such as engaging in pleasant imagery, while waiting in line. Small changes in everyday activities such as this are of great importance in modifying the TABP. Type A behavior is ubiquitous, requiring an intervention focused on altering which might appear to be superficial habits rather than an individual's reactions to unique or infrequent events. Additionally, because Type A's tend to establish unrealistically high goals for themselves and therefore demand of themselves immediate changes in lifestyle, it is critical that established goals and plans be realistic and that criteria for judgment of whether a goal has been achieved be clearly specified.

Maintenance of the plan can be enhanced by discussing it with others, such as spouses, utilizing reminders, such as notes on the calendar, and providing self-rewards if the plan is successfully implemented and the goal met. Taking such steps can greatly reduce the likelihood of good intentions falling by the wayside. Self-contracting provides Type A's with an opportunity to take advantage of their ogranizational skills and make their Type A behavior work for, rather than against, them. However, Type A behaviors are learned slowly over many years and it similarly requires time to alter these well-ingrained habits, particularly the time-urgency and competitive hostility that characterize TABP.

Time Urgency.
Type A's are involved in an ongoing battle to achieve more and more in less and less time. As a result, they become overextended and may experience chronic feelings of time urgency. Because adding hours to the day is impossible, the solution to this problem is to drop less important activities. The daily sense of time urgency may be greatly reduced by periodic "purges," that is, times when commitments are reviewed and less important tasks are eliminated or delegated to others. However, this plan typically proves to be a difficult strategy for Type A's to implement. The difficulty lies in their inability to set *priorities*. Rather than establish priorities when approaching multiple tasks, Type A's often increase their speed or attempt to accomplish tasks simultaneously, frequently switching to begin a second or third activity before completing the first. Moreover Type A's often have difficulty assigning work to others, following the axiom, "If it's worth doing, it's worth doing right and if you want it done right, you do it yourself." These difficulties result in Type A's frequently "making time" for additional work—increasing their polyphasic activity and taking time from family, friends, and sleep.

Recommendations.
Spouses, family, and coworkers can assist in setting priorities, sometimes evaluating the importance of tasks with greater objectivity than those directly involved with the work. Such reevaluation usually makes clear that many events previously considered critical are of less importance and may be assigned to others or even dismissed. However, Type A's must recognize that when they delegate work, it may not be done according to their standards. By challenging their internal demands for high standards and by allowing for some degree of human error, Type A's are more able to give up responsibility for less important chores and free themselves for more critical work.

In addition to "purging" their schedules of less important commitments, Type A's should be trained to reschedule commitments more realistically. Type A's habitually underestimate both the time required by assignments and the probability of obstacles such as inclement weather, long freight trains, and roads under construction. By decreasing the number of commitments scheduled within a particular time frame, Type A's are better able to accommodate unexpected events, as well as to enjoy interactions with coworkers. Opportunities to engage in pleasant conversation and to incorporate humor and affection in interpersonal contacts are diminished when schedules are too tight.

Joyless Striving.

As described earlier in this chapter, joyless striving is a feature frequently observed in Type A's and is thought to be related to an overinvolvement with their work. Often, time with friends and family are sacrificed for the more tangible rewards of career. As a result, Type A's become isolated from those who could be supportive and feel alone. This isolation is reinforced by hostility that can further estrange Type A's from others. Some have argued that Type A's emphasis on competitive achievement and work causes them to lose their ability to enjoy leisure-time activities that are not goal directed, such as art, music, and literature. Despite the attention and value placed on work, the goal of accomplishing a task appears to take precedence over the enjoyment of the process, and traditional or usual solutions to problems are favored over creative innovation.

Recommendations.

As in the modification of all facets of TABP, changing the pattern of joyless striving also requires practice. A "contract" to explore new hobbies or sports or recultivate old ones may greatly enrich life. Similarly, the renewal of relationships may provide an increased awareness of social support. "Purges" of unnecessary or unimportant tasks from their schedules allow type A's more time to enjoy leisure-time activities, but care must be taken that these new activities are not pursued with the same competitive style that characterized work. Tasks should be undertaken for their own sake rather than as a means of demonstrating expertise, and critical self-evaluation must be avoided.

Perhaps of greater importance than the incorporation of particular hobbies or leisure-time activities is modifying the style with which everyday activities are performed. Placing greater importance on the *process* whereby activities are performed rather than simply the end product may increase the sense of fulfillment and enjoyment in both work and leisure activities. Avoiding routinization of lifestyle and introducing creativity or novelty into even mundane chores enriches everyday experiences.

Hostility.

Hostility, an important behavior within the Type A constellation, is often selected as a target for change. Although there are situations where it is appropriate to experience and express anger, Type A's become irritated or even angry too frequently and for extended periods of time, even in response to mild provocations. Minor disruptions tend to provoke Type A hostility throughout the day, for example, file cabinets that stick and televisions that malfunction may trigger angry outbursts. Other Type A's may become angry when they experience obstacles in meeting their goals. Unfortunately, because the western social milieu often involves situations characterized by "hurry-up and wait," meeting obstacles is an extremely common source of hostility in Type A's. Basically, Type A's become angry when something, even of relatively minor importance, is not going as they think it can and should. There are a multitude of situations that may trigger the Type A's potential for hostility, ranging from a subordinate's failure to meet deadlines to the failure of store clerks to mark the price of a merchandise item. This hostility can be observed even during leisure activities. For example, a Type A hotel clerk on vacation may become irritated in response to a delay in his or her hotel reservation and criticize the hotel's operations, either privately to a companion or to the hotel staff. The Type A's potential for hostility is commonly viewed by others as "taking things too seriously," a further consequence of not setting priorities. If discriminations or priorities are not set on a situation's importance, then all situations tend to be taken seriously and are capable of eliciting irritation and hostility.

Recommendations.
The most effective strategy for reducing the extent of Type A hostility is avoiding provocative or frustrating situations that elicit irritating responses. Creating environments that minimize time urgency, interruptions, overcrowding, distractions, and equipment failures will reduce the frequency of irritation and hostility.

Though it may not always be possible to eliminate or avoid frustrating circumstances, changes usually can be made to reduce their potential to trigger irritation. For example, for Type A persons who become irritated while driving, pleasant back roads may be chosen as an alternative to congested highways, or mass transit and car-pooling may be used as less provocative commuting strategies. If stressful tasks are unavoidable, perhaps these commitments can be scheduled at times when Type A's are feeling rested and relaxed rather than fatigued and quarrelsome. Simply choosing an attractive location to work on unpleasant tasks may make them seem less burdensome.

Another alternative involves evaluating whether a situation needs to be taken so seriously. The way an event is experienced is largely determined by the meaning assigned to it, rather than by any objective quality of the event itself. Type A's tend to assign critical importance to all their responsibilities and challenges in the environment, responding with heightened performance and arousal even to tasks others might designate as being of relatively minor significance. To assist Type A's in assigning appropriate importance to situations, they should be taught the cardiovascular consequences of anger and hostility including clinically significant elevations in catecholamines, heart rate, and blood pressure. After Type A's are aware of these physiologic responses, they should be encouraged to decide whether anger-provoking situations warrant the health risks associated with them.

A final strategy for reducing Type A hostility involves practicing new responses in situations typically eliciting irritation. Specifically, Type A's are instructed to place themselves in those situations that typically elicit hostile responses and to practice coping with the situation without becoming irritated. Strategies for positive coping include keeping the situation in perspective, observing other people's behavior, and substituting generosity for anger. With these approaches, more cooperative behavior may be elicited from others as well, leading to less competitive and less frustrating interchanges in the future.

In changing hostile behavior, it is again important to select only one target behavior on which to focus at a time. For example, the route taken while commuting to work might be changed first, without making changes in the routes taken while making social visits. More importantly, new responses must be practiced on a regular basis. Once a new behavior is established, an emphasis is placed on maintaining this new behavior while initiating the modification of additional Type A behaviors. This practice may seem trivial; however, Type A behavior is developed over time and it takes time to learn to respond to environmental challenges without Type A behaviors.

Changing Physiological Concomitants of Type A Behavior

Three major avenues for changing Type A behaviors were outlined earlier in this chapter. The first involved changing the environment and the second stressed changing behavioral responses to the environment. Recently, with increased knowledge about the adrenergic hyperresponsivity of many Type A's, there is interest in a third approach—reducing the enhanced physiologic response to stress many Type A's exhibit. This approach is most often suggested as an adjunct to changing the environment or behavior.

To date, physiologic interventions have emphasized training Type A's in the use of progressive relaxation and biofeedback. The rationale is that, once trained in these procedures, Type A's can reduce or manage their physiological hyperresponsiveness to stress. Initial findings indicate that Type A's do show reduced cardiovascular arousal while practicing relaxation and biofeedback exercises and that these effects *may* be sustained in the natural environment (Roskies et al., 1979; Suinn, 1975). However, not all Type A's feel comfortable relaxing, being far more accustomed to heightened arousal, and care must be taken to insure an adequate fit between person and treatment modality.

Most recently, there has been increased interest in the possibility that pharmacologic approaches, such as the prescription of beta-blockers, might be used to control the hyperresponsivity found in the Type A's apparently at high risk (Krantz & Durel, 1983; Rosenman, 1978b, 1982). Though the prescription of beta-blockers may not be the treatment choice for a large number of Type A's, it may be an alternative intervention for individuals unresponsive to behavioral interventions and may shed light on the physiological events underlying various aspects of TABP.

Conclusion

In this chapter, the TABP and several of its important components, time urgency, joyless striving, and hostility, were described. Recommendations for modification of Type A behaviors were made and involved changing one or more of three interacting factors: environmental demands, the individual's responses to the environment, and physiological concomitants of the TABP. Relevant research examining the outcome of Type A intervention was briefly summarized. Mixed findings regarding the physiological effects of Type A intervention in healthy individuals indicate a need for further research in this area. Alternately, preliminary results of a large, clinical trial assessing the effects of intervention on the rate of recurring coronary events are highly promising and suggest an important role for Type A intervention in secondary prevention of CHD and, potentially, in primary prevention as well.

References

Appels, A. The year before myocardial infarction. In T. M. Dembroski, T. H. Schmidt, & G. Blümchen (Eds.), *Biobehavioral bases of coronary heart disease.* New York: Karger, 1983.

Blumenthal, J. A., Williams, R., Kong, Y., Schanberg, S. M., & Thompson, L. W. Type A behavior and angiographically documented coronary disease. *Circulation,* 1978, *58,* 634–639.

Dembroski, T. M., MacDougall, J. M., Shields, J. L., Petitto, J., & Lushene, R. Components of the Type A coronary-prone behavior pattern and cardiovascular responses to psychomotor challenge. *Journal of Behavioral Medicine,* 1978, *1,* 159–176.

Diamond, E. L. The role of anger and hostility in essential hypertension and coronary heart disease. *Psychological Bulletin,* 1982, *92*(2), 410–433.

Elliott, G. R., & Eisdorfer, C. *Stress and human health: Analysis and implications of research.* New York: Springer Publishing Co., 1982.

Frank, K. A., Heller, S. S., Kornfeld, D. S., Sporn, A. A., & Weiss, M. B. Type A behavior pattern and coronary angiographic findings. *Journal of the American Medical Association,* 1978, *240*(8), 761–763.

Friedman, M., & Rosenman, R. H. *Type A behavior and your heart.* New York: Alfred A. Knopf, 1974.

Friedman, M., Rosenman, R. H., Straus, R., Wurm, M., & Kositcheck, R. The relationship of behavior pattern A to the state of coronary vasculature. *American Journal of Medicine*, 1968, *44*, 525–537.

Haynes, S. G., Feinleib, M., & Kannel, W. B. The relationship of psychosocial factors to coronary heart disease in the Framingham study. III. Eight-year incidence of coronary heart disease. *American Journal of Epidemiology*, 1980, *3*, 37–58.

Jenkins, C. D., Zyzanski, S., Ryan, T., Flessas, A., & Tannerbaum, S. Social insecurity and coronary prone Type A responses as identifiers of severe atherosclerosis. *Journal of Consulting and Clinical Psychology*, 1977, *45*, 1060–1067.

Jenni, M., & Wollersheim, J. Cognitive therapy, stress management training and Type A behavior pattern. *Cognitive Therapy and Research*, 1979, *3*, 61–73.

Kavanagh, T., & Shepard, R. J. The immediate antecedents of myocardial infarction in active men. *Canadian Medical Association*, 1973, *109*, 19–22.

Kornitzer, M., Magotteau, V., Degre, C., Kittel, F., Struyven, J., & van Thiel, E. Angiographic findings and the Type A pattern assessed by means of the Bortner scale. *Journal of Behavioral Medicine*, 1982, *5*, 313–320.

Krantz, D. S., & Durel, L. A. *The possible role of adrenergic blocking drugs in reducing behavioral concomitants of anger*. Paper presented at the NIMH Conference on Assessment and Intervention for Disabling Anger, SRI International, Palo Alto, California, January 1983.

Levenkron, J., Cohen, J., Mueller, H., & Fisher, E. *Modifying the Type A coronary-prone behavior pattern*. Unpublished manuscript, 1982.

Lobitz, W., & Brammell, H. *Anxiety management training versus aerobic conditioning for cardiac stress management*. Paper presented at the annual meeting of the American Psychological Association, Los Angeles, August 1981.

Matthews, K. A., Glass, D. C., Rosenman, R. H., & Bortner, R. W. Competitive drive, Pattern A, and coronary heart disease: A further analysis of some data from the Western Collaborative Group Study. *Journal of Chronic Disease*, 1977, *30*, 489–498.

Nixon, P. G. F. The human function curve with special reference to cardiovascular disorders: Part 1. *The Practitioner*, 1976, *217*, 765–770.

Osler, W. The Lumlenian Lectures on angina pectoris. *Lancet*, 1910, *1*, 389–844.

Parkes, C. M., Benjamin, B., & Fitzgerald, R. G. Broken heart: A statistical study of increased mortality among widowers. *British Medical Journal*, 1969, *1*, 740–743.

The Review Panel on Coronary-prone Behavior and Coronary Heart Disease. Coronary-prone behavior and coronary heart disease: A critical review. *Circulation*, 1981, *63*(6), 1199–1215.

Rosenman, R. H. Role of Type A behavior pattern in the pathogenesis of ischemic heart disease, and modification for prevention. *Advances in Cardiology*, 1978, *25*, 35–46. (a)

Rosenman, R. H. The role of the Type A behavior pattern in ischemic heart disease: Modification of its effects by beta-blocking agents. *British Journal of Clinical Practice*, 1978, *32*, 58–66. (b)

Rosenman, R. H. The heart you save may be your own. In G. K. Chacko (Ed.), *Health handbook*. Amsterdam, The Netherlands: North-Holland Publishing Co., 1979.

Rosenman, R. H. Coronary-prone behaviour pattern and coronary heart disease: Implications for the use of beta-blockers in primary prevention. In R. H. Rosenman (Ed.), *Psychosomatic risk factors and coronary heart disease: Indications for specific preventive therapy*. Vienna: Hans Huber Publishers, 1982.

Rosenman, R. H., Brand, R. J., Jenkins, D., Friedman, M., Straus, R., & Wurm, M. Coronary heart disease in the Western Collaborative Group Study: Final follow-up experience of 8½ years. *Journal of the American Medical Association,* 1975, *233,* 872–877.

Rosenman, R. H., & Friedman, M. Modifying Type A behaviour pattern. *Journal of Psychosomatic Research,* 1977, *21,* 323–331.

Roskies, E., Kearney, H., Spevack, M., Surkis, A., Cohen, C., & Gilman, S. Generalizability and durability of treatment effects in an intervention program for coronary-prone (Type A) managers. *Journal of Behavioral Medicine,* 1979, *2,* 195–207.

Roskies, E., Spevack, M., Surkis, A., Cohen, C., & Gilman, S. Changing the coronary-prone (Type A) behavior pattern in a nonclinical population. *Journal of Behavioral Medicine,* 1978, *1,* 201–216.

Suinn, R. The cardiac stress management program for Type A patients. *Cardiac Rehabilitation,* 1975, *5*(4), 13–15.

Suinn, R. Intervention with Type A behavior. *Journal of Consulting and Clinical Psychology,* 1982, *50,* 933–949.

Suinn, R., & Bloom, L. Anxiety management training for Pattern A behavior. *Journal of Behavioral Medicine,* 1978, *1,* 25–35.

Thoresen, C. E., Friedman, M., Gill, J. J., & Ulmer, D. The recurrent coronary prevention project: Some preliminary findings. *Acta Medica Scandinavica,* 1982, Supplement 660, 172–192.

Zyzanski, S. J., Jenkins, C. D., Ryan, T. J., Flessas, A., & Everist, M. Psychological correlates of coronary angiographic findings. *Archives of Internal Medicine,* 1976, *136,* 1234–1237.

7
Mobilizing a Community to Promote Health
The Pennsylvania County Health Improvement Program (CHIP)

Albert J. Stunkard, Michael R. J. Felix, and Rita Yopp Cohen

This chapter describes the development of an important new form of social organization: the mobilization of an entire community to improve its health. This development is illustrated by a specific program, the Pennsylvania County Health Improvement Program (CHIP). CHIP is a community-based, multiple risk factor intervention trial designed to decrease mortality and morbidity from cardiovascular disease in a county of 118,000 persons in north central Pennsylvania. Efforts are directed towards reduction of five risk factors: smoking, hypertension, elevated levels of serum cholesterol, obesity, and physical inactivity. CHIP is a cooperative program currently involving the University of Pennsylvania, Lycoming College, and, notably, the community of Lycoming County. Important contributions in the past have been made by the Pennsylvania Department of Health, which played a key role in initiating the program, the Pennsylvania State University, and the social marketing firm of Porter, Novelli, and Associates.

CHIP is one of the small number of large-scale, community health promotion programs that derived their inspiration from two pioneering ventures of the early 1970s—the Stanford Three-Community Study (Farquhar, Maccoby, Wood et al., 1977; Meyer, Nash, McAlister, Maccoby, & Farquhar, 1980) and the North Karelia Project in Finland (Puska, 1981)—described below. Three large community cardiovascular disease prevention programs were subsequently initiated by the National Heart, Lung, and Blood Institute at Stanford University, the University of Minnesota, and the Pawtucket Hospital in Rhode Island. CHIP is similar to these programs in some ways and different from them in other ways. It similarities lie in the *evaluation*, which has been carefully standardized with the other programs to ensure comparability of results. In research where the community is the experimental unit and the number of experimental units is thus extremely limited, each additional experimental-control pair is unusually important.

The differences of CHIP from the other three community programs lie in the *interventions*. These differences arise first from the nature of the funding. Since the beginning of their planning, the other three programs have been supported by the National Institutes of Health at a relatively high level. CHIP's budget, by contrast, has been considerably less than 20% of that of the other programs. As a result, it has involved community participation from the outset, has utilized existing resources and facilities, and was designed to be a permanent community program, owned by the community. Out of necessity, but, increasingly, also out of conviction, strenuous efforts have been made to keep costs sufficiently low so that CHIP can be widely replicated. These efforts have apparently succeeded, and the present report is offered as a description of the development of a cost-effective, community health promotion program.

The Concept of Coronary Risk Factors

Efforts to prevent coronary heart disease have an advantage over other efforts at disease prevention and health promotion. This advantage is derived from more than 30 years of epidemiological research on the predictors of coronary heart disease. This research has elucidated many of the factors that predict coronary disease by establishing: (1) their strong relationship, both individually and in combination, to coronary heart disease, (2) the consistency of this relationship in many studies in many different cultures, (3) the great frequency of their occurrence in middle-aged men in industrialized societies with high rates of coronary disease, and (4) the converging evidence of the role of these factors from laboratory, clinic, and population studies. These studies have achieved a level of prediction unequalled for any other major disease. The history of cardiovascular disease prevention can well serve as a model for efforts to prevent other diseases. To appreciate this history, let us review briefly how predictors of coronary heart disease were discovered; for, this discovery led directly to the change from a passive contemplation of predictors to the active search for methods to control these predictors, now called "risk factors."

Over a number of years, it was established that six factors make a major contribution to premature coronary heart disease—heart disease occurring in persons under the age of 60. The evidence supporting the importance of three of these risk factors is overwhelming. This evidence has been primarily epidemiological for two of them: *smoking* (Aravanis,

1983; Doll & Peto, 1976; Feinleib & Williams, 1975; Keys, 1980; Pooling Project, 1978; U.S. DHEW 1964, 1979a; 1979b) and *elevated serum cholesterol* (Aravanis, 1983; Frantz, Dawson, Kuba et al., 1975; Hjermann, 1983; Keys, 1980; Miettinen, Turpeinen, Karvonen et al., 1972; Pooling Project, 1978; Robertson, Kato, Gordon et al., 1977; Shekelle, Shyrock, Paul, Lepper, & Stamler, 1981; Stamler, 1978; Stamler, Berkson, & Lindberg, 1972). A very recent therapeutic study, however, has provided strong additional evidence for the importance of elevated serum cholesterol (Lipid Research Clinics Program, 1984 a or b), and therapeutic studies provide the primary evidence for the role of *hypertension* (Aravanis, 1983; HDFP, 1979a, 1979b, 1982; Keys, 1980; Pooling Project, 1978; VA Cooperative Study Group, 1967, 1970).

There is strong and growing evidence that an independent contribution to coronary disease is made by three other risk factors: *physical inactivity* (Koplan, Powell, Sikes, Shirley, & Campbell, 1982; Leon & Blackburn, 1977; Morris, Chave, Adam et al., 1974; Paffenberger, Hale, Brand et al., 1977; U.S. DHEW, 1979a), *Type A or coronary-prone behavior* (Brand, Rosenman, Sholtz, & Friedman, 1976; Haynes, Feinleib, & Kannel, 1980; Review Panel on Coronary-prone Behavior and Coronary Heart Disease, 1981), and *obesity* (Hubert, Feinleib, McNamara, & Castelli, 1983; Pooling Project, 1978). Finally, obesity is an important *secondary* risk factor for cardiovascular disease by promoting hypertension, diabetes, and elevated serum cholesterol (Berchtold, Jorgens, Finke, & Berger, 1981; Chiang, Perlman, & Epstein, 1969; U.S. DHEW, 1979a).

Risk factors occur not only singly, but also in combination; and, just as the increasing severity of a single risk factor increases the risk of coronary heart disease, so does an increase in the number of risk factors. Indeed, an increase in the number of risk factors produces a striking increase in risk. This phenomenon is well illustrated by results of the Framingham study shown in Figure 7.1. The combination of three risk factors, even though each is only modestly elevated, gives rise to a fivefold increase in risk for a 45-year-old man. Whether the effect of such combinations is multiplicative or only additive, it is sufficiently powerful to be a key consideration in any program of risk factor reduction.

The Rationale for a Multiple Risk Factor, Multiple Channel Intervention

After these six risk factors were identified, efforts to control them were intensified. Early efforts were confined to single risk factor intervention trials. Many of them were successful, particularly the several studies of hypertension control conducted by the Veterans Administration and by the Hypertension Detection and Follow-up Program (HDFP, 1979a,

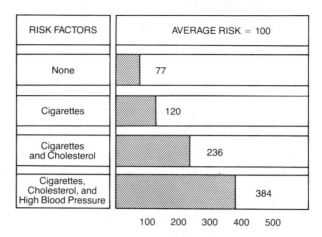

RISK FACTORS	AVERAGE RISK = 100
None	77
Cigarettes	120
Cigarettes and Cholesterol	236
Cigarettes, Cholesterol, and High Blood Pressure	384

100   200   300   400   500

Figure 7.1. The dangers of heart attack increase with the number of risk factors present. This chart shows how a combination of three major risk factors can increase the likelihood of heart attack. For purposes of illustration, this chart uses an abnormal blood pressure level of 180 systolic and a cholesterol level of 310 in a 45-year-old man.

Source: McGee, D. The probability of developing certain cardiovascular diseases in eight years at specified values of some characteristics. In W. B. Kannel & T. Gordon (Eds.), *The Framingham study: An epidemiological investigation of cardiovascular diseases.* National Heart, Lung, and Blood Institute, Bethesda, Md., 1973.

1979b, 1982; VA Cooperative Study Group, 1967, 1970). These studies revealed that the control of hypertension could produce major reductions in mortality and morbidity.

As effective as single risk factor interventions have been, multiple risk factor intervention may be even more promising. There are two reasons for this surmise. One is the deleterious effects of multiple risk factors. The second arises from the nature of interventions to control risk factors.

Most of the interventions to control risk factors require changes in personal habits and lifestyles. Such changes are difficult to make, but, when one health behavior is changed, sometimes only a modest additional effort must be made to change others. Indeed, change in one health behavior almost inevitably leads to changes in others. Whether or not the untoward effects of risk factors interact, efforts to modify these risk factors do. Figure 7.2 shows how attempts to change only one health behavior influence other health behaviors. Reduction of fat in the diet will lower not only serum cholesterol but also blood pressure and body weight. Weight reduction programs not only reduce weight but also serum cholesterol and blood pressure, and they usually increase physical activity. Programs of physical activity may have a relatively modest effect via physical activity as an independent risk factor, but a relatively large impact via the other four risk factors. A striking example of such

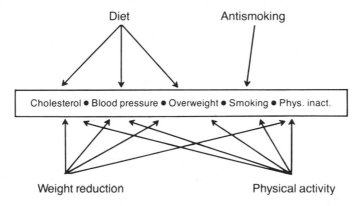

Figure 7.2. Indirect effects of risk factor reduction programs. Although programs of smoking cessation affect only smoking, others affect other risk factors. Programs of physical activity affect all five risk factors.

indirect effects was revealed by a survey of recreational runners. Eighty-one percent of the men and 75% of the women who had been smokers when they began running subsequently stopped smoking (Koplan et al., 1982).

Another rationale for multiple risk factor reduction is the distribution of the various risk factors within the population. Table 7.1 from Blackburn (1972) shows that 10% of middle-aged men have three or more elevated risk factors. Their probability of contracting coronary disease is far higher than that of persons with only one elevated risk factor. A multiple risk factor intervention thus has two advantages over a single risk factor approach: it addresses the smaller percentage of persons at high risk as well as the larger percentage of persons at lower risk. They contribute, however, no more than 20% of cases of coronary heart disease, a relatively small contribution to the overall burden of disease. At the other end of the spectrum, the 80% of middle-aged men with at least one elevated risk factor contribute 90% of cases of coronary heart dis-

TABLE 7.1.
Number of Risk Factors and Incidence of Coronary Heart Disease

Number of elevated risk factors	Percent of middle-aged men at each risk level	Percent of coronary disease cases in middle-aged men resulting at each risk level
3	10	20
2 or more	40	60
1 or more	80	90

ease. Between these extremes, the 40% of the population with two risk factors contribute about 60% of new cases. Although the majority of the cases of coronary heart disease results from a single risk factor, each individual risk factor contributes substantially to the incidence rate. A multiple risk factor intervention should provide a more favorable cost-effectiveness ratio than single factor interventions. A multiple risk factor intervention thus has two advantages over a single risk factor approach: It addresses the smaller percentage of persons at high risk as well as the larger percentage of persons at lower risk.

Clearly there are persuasive reasons for multiple risk factor interventions (as opposed to single factor approaches). These reasons gave rise to the large-scale, Multiple Risk Factor Intervention Trial sponsored by the National Heart, Lung, and Blood Institute. This trial attempted to lower levels of smoking, blood pressure, and serum cholesterol in a sample of 20,000 men at high risk for coronary disease by a stepped program of advice and counseling carried out in the offices of participating physicians (Multiple Risk Factor Intervention Trial Research Group, 1982). The results were equivocal, which is perhaps not surprising. Medical auspices may not be the most effective ones for changing behaviors as firmly established as smoking, eating, and exercise. Occasional visits to a doctor's office constitute a pitifully small effort against a social environment expending billions of dollars a year to maintain these behaviors.

Instead of battling the social environment, why not try to change it? Health behavior changes may require extensive social supports of a kind best provided by the cooperative efforts of many persons and many agencies within a community. The first two, large, community-based programs achieved results suggesting that this multifaceted approach is best. They were the Stanford Three-Community Study and the North Karelia Project in Finland.

The Stanford Three-Community Study was an innovative, broad-scale program for reducing coronary risk factors in two towns, each with populations of 14,000 (Farquhar et al., 1977). The major intervention was an intensive and sophisticated mass media campaign that each year included 50 television and 100 radio messages, several hours of more extensive television and radio programs, newspaper columns, posters and billboards, and direct mail. In one of the towns, the media campaign was supplemented by a face-to-face instruction campaign directed at two-thirds of the persons in the top quartile of risk for coronary disease.

The results of the Stanford Study were encouraging. The two-year campaign reduced the risk of coronary disease by 17% in the treatment towns, compared to an *increase* of 6% in the control town. The populations were so small, however, that the program had no measurable impact upon mortality or morbidity.

A measurable impact upon both morbidity and mortality *was* reported in North Karelia with its population of 180,000 (Puska et al., 1983a; Puska et al., 1983b). Over the 10 years of the North Karelia Project, the incidence of cardiovascular disease mortality decreased from 24% compared to a national decrease of 11% and a decrease in the control county of 12%. The differences between counties is statistically significant.

The North Karelia Project included a mass media program similar to that of the Stanford Study, but it also included greater involvement of community organizations. The first step in the North Karelia Project, for example, was a "community diagnosis" of all aspects of the province and how community institutions and leaders might be mobilized for health promotion. Several of the groups identified by this diagnosis played key roles in the project: the local heart associations were prominent in health education, the physicians and local health stations in hypertension control, the Finnish housewives' organizations in nutrition education, and a variety of institutions in smoking control (Puska et al., 1981).

The four, second-generation community studies in the United States have drawn extensively from these early pioneering programs. We provide here a first description of a second-generation study.

The Goals of CHIP

The goal of CHIP is to reduce mortality and morbidity from cardiovascular disease in Lycoming County by means of a cost-effective, multiple risk factor intervention program. The research asks five questions:

1. Can a community be mobilized to improve its health practices?

2. Can improvement in these practices produce sustained change in individual health behavior?

3. Can changes in individual health behavior affect risk factors for coronary heart disease and stroke?

4. Can reduction in risk factors reduce mortality and morbidity from these diseases?

5. Can these results be achieved by cost-effective means?

Lycoming County

An understanding of CHIP is helped by some knowledge of its site of action. Lycoming County, the site of CHIP, is located in north central Pennsylvania where the Appalachian mountains and the Susquehanna River turn east. Most of the population is located in a relatively limited section in the southern part of the county around the river, reflecting the historical economic base of the county. For many years, Williamsport, the county seat, was a major lumbering center, milling timber that was floated down the river from both Pennsylvania and New York. During the mid-19th century, the area was quite prosperous and descendants of the old "lumber barons" are still among the prominent families. Since then, the area has shared in the economic decline of Appalachia, and it was hit particularly hard by the Great Depression of the 1930s. Despite widespread diversification of the light industry that provides the economic base of the county, the recession of 1981 again caused major problems, with the unemployment rate reaching 20%.

Lycoming is one of the largest counties in Pennsylvania. Its 1,216 square miles, most of which is forest and farmland, makes it 2 square miles larger than the state of Rhode Island. The population of the county at the 1980 census was 118,000, an increase of 4.5% over 1970. Williamsport, the county seat, is the largest city, with a population of 33,000, two excellent hospitals, two colleges, and an enlightened civic leadership. The next two largest towns have populations of only 10,700 and 6,500, and most of the population resides in very small towns or rural areas. The ethnic background is primarily old American and only 2% is nonwhite; in- and out-migration is very low. Per capita income was $7,235 in 1980. The age-adjusted death rate per 100,000 population is high—450.

The level of cardiovascular risk factors in Lycoming County is similar to the national level and is also high (Norman & Stolley, 1982b). Thus, 24% of the adult population was hypertensive, and only 38% of hypertensives were under adequate control. Of those not under control, 36% were aware they were hypertensive and 26% were undetected prior to the CHIP risk factor survey. Thirty-three percent of adults were currently smoking cigarettes, 25% had stopped, and 42% had never smoked. The average total serum cholesterol level was 199.5 mg/dl, with 28% of the population having levels greater than 220 mg/dl. Only the values for obesity exceeded national averages: 26% of men and 28% of women were more than 20% overweight.

History of CHIP

A history of the six years of CHIP is helpful in understanding this type of exploratory, pioneering venture for which there are few precedents or models. There is good reason to believe that communities can be mobilized for all manner of altruistic purposes, including health promotion, but we are far from understanding the principles underlying such processes. A careful description, a natural history, is perhaps the most useful contribution to our current level of understanding.

CHIP arose out of a meeting in April of 1977 between Dr. Leonard

Bachman, then secretary of health of the Commonwealth of Pennsylvania, and Dr. Stunkard, who had visited him to report on the favorable progress of a commonwealth-sponsored, obesity control project in Lycoming County. Dr. Bachman, who had been favorably impressed with the North Karelia Project, wished to involve the Department of Health in an innovative program of preventive medicine. Dr. Stunkard, who had been associated with the Stanford Three-Community Study, proposed that the Department of Health sponsor a community coronary prevention trial based upon the experience of the earlier programs. Soon thereafter, Dr. Bachman convened a meeting in the state capital attended by leaders in the fields of epidemiology, cardiology, and community studies, who enthusiastically endorsed the idea. As a result, early in 1978 Dr. Bachman established a coordinating center in the Department of Health, with Ms. Carol Schechter as director and Dr. Katherine Marconi as research associate. Planning for evaluation of the program was begun soon thereafter by Drs. Paul Stolley and Sandra Norman and Ms. Joan Davies of the Department of Research Medicine of the University of Pennsylvania. They were subsequently joined by Drs. Charles Crawford and Samuel Leadley of the Pennsylvania State University, who coordinated the base-line risk factor survey in 1980.

In the autumn of 1978, a steering committee of community leaders was appointed by the CHIP staff. The Steering Committee, with strong support from the Coordinating Center, made two important appointments: Mr. Felix as executive director of CHIP, and the social marketing firm of Porter, Novelli, and Associates to direct mass media activities. On July 11, 1980, after three years of planning, CHIP began active programs in Lycoming County.

Much of the subsequent history of CHIP is described in accounts of the different programs. It should be noted, however, that, as the scope of these programs increased, Mr. Felix was joined in program development at the Field Office by Ms. Nancy Cooley, Ms. Sherry Hessert, and Ms. Mary Fleming and at the University of Pennsylvania by Dr. Kelly Brownell.

At the beginning of the third year in the field, in July of 1982, changes in funding sources led to changes in the structure of CHIP. The Coordinating Center of the Department of Health and the summative evaluation activities at the University of Pennsylvania were discontinued, and programmatic evaluation was begun at the University of Pennsylvania under the direction of Dr. Rita Cohen.

To summarize, the programs described below were carried out with a field staff that never numbered more than four persons, none with an advanced degree, assisted by one and a half professional equivalents at the University of Pennsylvania. Clearly the costs of these programs have been contained.

Selection of Risk Factors

In early planning for CHIP, five risk factors were chosen as the focus of intervention and ranked according to their relative importance: (1) smoking, (2) hyptertension, (3) cholesterol, (4) obesity, and (5) inactivity. The choice of risk factors and the ranking of their importance were determined by expected costs and benefits. Smoking and hypertension headed the list. Cigarette smoking is considered the greatest preventable cause of disease in the United States, and reduction in smoking would have a major impact upon the rate of cardiovascular disease, as well as of lung cancer. Hypertension, likewise, has serious cardiovascular consequences. The major benefits to be achieved from the control of smoking and of hypertension and the availability of (admittedly only modestly effective) measures for this control led to their choice as the two major targets of intervention by CHIP.

Although elevated total serum cholesterol is a well-established risk factor, the weakness of measures for lowering it led to the decision to place a lower priority on dietary interventions. Since both obesity and physical inactivity have a less powerful impact upon cardiovascular risk than do the other three risk factors, and since community-based efforts had enjoyed only limited success in these areas, these two risk factors were accorded the lowest priority in initial planning. As soon as CHIP entered the field, however, experience altered these priorities. Programs of exercise and weight control turned out to be more popular than the others and far more suitable as a means of gaining access to new organizations. As a result, they received a higher priority than was warranted by their value in risk reduction.

Two risk factors were not included in CHIP programs—Type A behavior and salt restriction. This decision was not based upon doubts as to their contribution to cardiovascular disease but rather on perceived problems in mounting cost-effective programs. The problem with Type A behavior was that, at the time of initial CHIP planning, there was no evidence either that an intervention could reduce Type A behavior or that reducing Type A behavior could reduce the risk of cardiovascular disease. Accordingly, it seemed improvident to invest the limited CHIP resources in an effort with such uncertain results. The other three community programs, which were not subject to comparable limitations in resources, *did* mount programs of stress reduction. The purpose of these programs, however, was to help gain access to a community or work site rather than to reduce cardiovascular risk. CHIP was forced to pursue other, more direct, means to such access.

The decision not to mount programs encouraging salt restriction was based upon other cost-benefit considerations. Although the benefits to some salt-sensitive hypertensives might be significant, the number of such persons was unknown and possibly quite limited. The costs, on the other hand, of being perceived as taking something from the community seemed to outweigh these benefits. An intermediate strategy, which we are considering, is to limit programs of salt restriction to the more restricted population of identified hypertensives.

Research on Type A behavior and salt restriction is being monitored by CHIP staff, and, whenever the cost-benefit ratio seems to warrant it, programs to reduce these risks will be introduced.

Evaluation

There are few precedents for community-based efforts to change health behavior and even fewer precedents for evaluating them. Traditionally, preventive medicine has required no more than passive participation on the part of subject populations. Draining swamps, constructing sewage systems, even administering programs of immunization have required little more than acquiescence on the part of those benefiting from them. Prevention of cardiovascular disease and stroke, on the other hand, requires active participation of individuals of a kind without precedent in the history of public health: they must make major changes in their lifestyles and personal habits.

This need for vastly increased participation of individuals means that the traditional, randomized clinical trial is not adequate to assess outcome. The randomized trial assumes only minimal cooperation on the part of participants. But when active participation is a key feature of the program, such an assumption is no longer adequate, for extensive health behavior change may require community support and such support precludes randomizing individuals within the community. As a consequence, the community becomes the unit of measurement and the number of experimental units becomes extremely limited.

This limitation influenced the evaluation plans of CHIP. Wherever possible, measurements were designed to be compatible with those of the other three community cardiovascular disease prevention programs. Since random assignment of communities was not possible, evaluation of these programs is conducted by a quasi-experimental design, in which changes in variables over time in experimental communities are compared with those in reference communities. Franklin County in southern Pennsylvania was selected as the reference community for Lycoming County. Its demographic and occupational characteristics closely match those of Lycoming County, as do its morbidity and mortality profiles (Norman & Stolley, 1982a). Accordingly, the effectiveness of CHIP is being measured by comparing changes in five health-relevant indices in the two counties: (1) mortality, (2) morbidity, (3) risk factors, (4) community resource inventory, and (5) cost-effectiveness.

The first outcome measure is mortality, obtained at minimal cost from the annual report on *Natality and Mortality Statistics* of the Pennsylvania Department of Health. Differences between Lycoming County and the reference county in mortality rates that develop during the CHIP program will provide valid data as to its effectiveness.

The second outcome measure is morbidity from myocardial infarction and stroke, obtained also from the annual reports. The quality of these data, however, may be insufficient to warrant their use for research purposes. Should this insufficiency be the case, research-quality data can be obtained from local hospitals and health agencies. Recent advances in hospital data management systems should make it possible to carry out rapid ascertainment of probable episodes of cardiovascular disease, which can then be subjected to a more rigorous diagnosis.

The third outcome measure is a survey, the Community Resource Inventory. This inventory serves two purposes—research and program management. For the former, the inventory compares change in health activities of the institutions in Lycoming County with those in the reference county. For the latter, it provides information for planning intervention strategies. In this capacity it functions as did the "community diagnosis" of the North Karelia Project, to which much of the success of that project was attributed. The first step in establishing the Community Resource Inventory was identifying any institution of at least 100 members that might conceivably be mobilized for health promotion purposes—a total of 157 in Lycoming and 142 in the reference county. Table 7.2 lists the types of institutions contacted by telephone to ascertain their health promotion activities.

The fourth outcome measure is a risk factor survey. Although reduction in mortality and morbidity is the ultimate goal of CHIP, reliance on these measures alone would seriously limit what can be learned. In the event of a negative outcome, exclusive reliance on these measures could make the results very difficult to interpret. It would be unclear whether the outcome was due to a failure to reduce risk factors or a failure of reduced risk factors to reduce risk. Knowledge of risk factor reduction could help make this critical distinction and might indicate how close the program had come to success. In the event of a favorable outcome, knowledge of risk factor reduction would be even more important, for it could give an indication of the relative contribution of the serious risk factors. Quite possibly some relatively economical intervention (such as hypertension detection and control) exerts a stronger influence than some more costly ones (such as nutrition programs). This kind of information would be invaluable in planning future programs.

Knowledge of changes in risk factors could also help monitor progress of the project and indicate how long it should continue to achieve reduc-

TABLE 7.2.
Community Resource Inventory

1. Health Organizations	5. Business and Industry
2. Government (Federal, State, and County)	6. Unions
	7. Schools and Colleges
3. Social Service Organizations	8. Religious Organizations
4. Civic, Service, and Fraternal Organizations	9. Professional and Trade Organizations

tions in mortality and morbidity. A base-line risk factor assessment was carried out in the spring of 1980 shortly before the initiation of CHIP programs. It has provided valuable data about the status of cardiovascular risk factors in Lycoming County (and in the reference county). Funding for the planned repeat assessments has not yet been obtained, but a more modest telephone survey during the summer of 1982 provided information about the first two years of CHIP programs (Greenberg, Wagner, & Norman, 1983). Conducted by Porter, Novelli, and Associates, this survey reached over 400 persons each in Lycoming and in the reference county with a response rate of more than 70%.

The fifth outcome measure is a cost-effectiveness evaluation. The costs of CHIP have been modest—no more than $150,000 a year devoted to program efforts (the costs of evaluation, similarly modest, have varied greatly depending upon the projects being undertaken). By contrast, direct and indirect costs of cardiovascular disease in Lycoming County for 1984 were estimated at $33.04 million. A reduction in coronary heart disease of no more than 10%—half that achieved in North Karelia— would realize savings of $3.3 million in direct and indirect costs. A larger reduction in coronary heart disease, and the reduction in stroke, would lead to even more favorable cost-effectiveness ratios.

Program Evaluation.

A problem in evaluating the overall outcome of a broad-scale, community program is how to disentangle the effects of the various programs and to determine which program produced which results. Such information would be of value in understanding community programs and in planning more effective ones. Possibly this information simply cannot be obtained. In a program that places major emphasis on the interaction of organizations and people within the community, any effects may well be interactive ones, and some of the most important effects may be the most interactive. The "Get Squeezed" hypertension detection program described below is a prime example of such interactions and of the impossibility, in this case at least, of determining the influence of any individual contribution. For this reason, efforts have been made to carry out carefully focused evaluations of those programs lending themselves best to

such efforts, particularly those at the work sites. These program evaluations are of considerable value apart from the summative evaluation of
the entire CHIP programs. In addition, they may make it possible to
compare the relative impact of each channel on the overall outcome of
CHIP.

The Planning Process

Two major tools in the planning process were the base-line Risk Factor
Survey, which identified key targets for intervention, and the Community Resource Inventory, which identified key agencies to undertake the
intervention. Another development with important implications for the
future was the appointment of a CHIP steering committee.

The introduction of a major activity such as CHIP into a community
requires the active support of key opinion leaders, and, at the outset of a
program, these opinion leaders are not known to the program staff.
Identification of these leaders is a critical early step.

This step was begun in collaboration with one of the persons with
whom CHIP staff was familiar, the director of planning for the Williamsport Hospital, the largest in the county. His position had put him in
contact with a wide variety of influential local persons, and his good
judgement enabled him to make an educated guess regarding persons
who could effectively introduce CHIP to the community. Accordingly,
his choices were given a high priority in the first list of invitations to join
a CHIP steering committee in 1978. Many of these choices were excellent, and four of the original members of the Steering Committee have
remained with it to the present time. By the end of the first year of
Steering Committee operations, it was functioning effectively and leaders had begun to emerge. They, in turn, proposed new members and less
interested ones dropped out, refining the Steering Committee into a
group of committed and dedicated community leaders. The list of their
occupations (Table 7.3) conveys a little of the scope of these leaders and
of the institutions they were able to enlist in the CHIP enterprise.

CHIP followed five principles of community organization: (1) community analysis, (2) joint professional/local planning, (3) consensus-
building in networks, (4) use of existing community resources, and
(5) use of a change agent. The first principle, *community analysis,* is illustrated by the Community Resource Inventory. The second principle,
joint professional/local planning, was implemented from the start. A search
for opinion leaders constituted the first step; establishing and refining the
Steering Committee was the second. Other large, preventive medicine
trials have been directed by health professionals and heavily staffed by
them. Limitations of funding precluded this course in CHIP, where it

TABLE 7.3.
Steering Committee Member Profile

1. Newspaper Editor	8. Community Spokeswoman
2. College President	9. Cardiologist
3. Bank President	10. Thoracic Surgeon
4. Personnel Manager, Industry	11. General Practitioner
5. Representative of Junior League	12. Chief of Hospital Medical Staff
6. General Manager, Industry	13. Attorney
7. Bank Vice-president	14. Attorney

was found, surprisingly, that the purely professional contributions, although essential, were less important than had been expected. The major professional contributions at CHIP's beginnings were to make decisions such as choosing risk factors and ordering their priorities. The rationale for these decisions was easily grasped by local nonprofessional planners and readily accepted.

A key element, *consensus building in community networks,* involved the networks of the Steering Committee members. An instructive example arose during problems over the location of CHIP headquarters. Much of the early planning had been carried out at the Williamsport Hospital, and the expectation had been that CHIP would be headquartered there. When competition between the local hospitals made this location unfeasible and other locations presented problems, a network of Steering Committee members succeeded in relocating CHIP to the neutral territory of Lycoming College. An example of a large-scale community network is the "Get Squeezed" hypertension screening program, while smaller scale networks are represented by the Heart Health Committees established at the work sites.

Existing community resources were used in all aspects of CHIP, as illustrated below. Finally, the appointment of Mr. Felix as executive director introduced an experienced and knowledgeable *local change agent* into the direction of CHIP programs. Mr. Felix's five years of experience directing the County Drug and Alcohol Program enabled him to move promptly into cardiovascular disease prevention.

An important decision in the initial planning process was in selecting the channels through which CHIP programs would operate: (1) the mass media, (2) work sites, (3) the health sector, (4) voluntary organizations, and (5) schools. The channels are of two general types: diffuse channels designed to reach large numbers of persons as individuals, and focused channels designed to deliver programs through specific institutions. The prime example of a diffuse channel is the mass media, although the voluntary organization channel is also rather diffuse. The three focused channels consist of work sites, health organizations, and schools.

Clearly, there are interactions between the channels, as described below, and the mass media channel profoundly influenced activities in the other four channels.

Channel 1: Mass Media

The first channel to be activated was the mass media. This decision, made early in the planning process, was based upon both practical and theoretical reasons. The practical reasons involved the success of the mass media in both the Stanford Heart Disease Prevention Program (Farquhar et al., 1977) and the North Karelia Project (Puska, 1981). The theoretical reasons were based upon the view that, as the primary means by which the American public acquires new information and new perceptions, the mass media set the public agenda. Lazarsfeld and Merton (1971) note that the media "tell us what is right, what is important and what really matters." The importance of mass media messages is reinforced through opinion leaders, whose reliance on media messages is usually greater than that of the population at large (Rogers & Shoemaker, 1971). Furthermore, Haines and Ward (1981) indicate that the mass media are second only to the personal physician as a source of information about health matters.

A rigorous selection process, aided by the leadership of the Stanford Heart Disease Prevention Program, resulted in the choice of Porter and Novelli, a social marketing firm in Washington, D.C., for directing the media program. This firm, the only professional component of CHIP, had had extensive experience in the field of health promotion, including major roles in the National High Blood Pressure Education Program and the President's Council on Physical Fitness and Sports. It began in a professional manner by establishing a set of objectives.

Objectives of the Media Program

1. To introduce CHIP to the community and to help establish its credibility.

2. To increase knowledge about heart disease risk reduction and to alter favorably health attitudes and behaviors.

3. To provide information about CHIP activities.

The role of mass media in CHIP changed markedly during the course of the program. Initially, as defined by the objectives, it played a vital and pervasive role in introducing CHIP. For a period of time thereafter, much of the direct CHIP activities were carried out through the mass media in efforts to change knowledge, attitudes, and behavior regarding health. Over time, the mass media were increasingly involved in providing information about other CHIP activities, and the dominant role of the mass media receded as interpersonally mediated channels assumed a larger and larger role.

The Planning Process

An intensive planning effort was carried out the year before CHIP entered the field (Greenberg & Saffitz, 1982). Much of this time was devoted to establishing the objectives noted above, to defining the target audiences and their characteristics, and to developing communication strategies. National data and the CHIP risk factor survey were used for this purpose. As one example, the risk factor survey showed that among the group at highest risk of premature cardiovascular disease—middle-aged men—only 11.5% of smokers had tried to quit during the previous year. Accordingly, strategies were developed to increase the motivation of smokers to quit, deferring until later efforts to teach the skills necessary for quitting.

Considerable effort was directed towards identification and selection of the appropriate media channels. It was learned that Lycoming County was primarily a radio market and that efforts to make extensive use of television were unlikely to succeed. A survey of the nine major local radio stations defined the characteristics of their audiences and of the kinds of programs they preferred (for example, either 30-second public service announcements, 2-minute health messages, or talk shows). The print media consist largely of one daily newspaper with a circulation of 35,000 and a weekly newspaper with a circulation of 40,000. Newspapers were widely read but they conveyed little health information. Accordingly, a biweekly health column, "Ask CHIP," was developed, which has continued with considerable success to the present time. Because of the goal of making CHIP a cost-effective program easily replicable, an early decision was made that no media time or space would be purchased. Instead, efforts were made to obtain coverage in both radio and print by news, health features, and other programs. This strategy provided far greater depth and frequency of exposure than is possible solely through public service or advertising messages.

The development of messages and materials was also guided by the goal of rigorous cost containment. As a result, as many messages and materials as possible were imported from other programs. This effort was highly successful and large numbers of messages were obtained from organizations that have devoted themselves to such preparation—the National High Blood Pressure Education Program, the President's Council on Physical Fitness and Sports, the Office of Smoking and Health, the American Health Association, the American Lung Association, and other national, regional, and local agencies. The major efforts these organizations had devoted to pre-testing and evaluating their materials meant that CHIP could rely on them to be personally relevant, believable, and informative. Despite this assurance, however, many of the messages were pre-tested in the county with the aid of small focus groups. These pre-tests helped choose materials appropriate to the county, rejecting, for example, certain smoking messages as too hortatory and guilt provoking. The pre-tests also helped design an attractive CHIP logo of a red heart superimposed upon a blue map of Lycoming County, with the white letters CHIP within the heart.

The final media planning stage was coordinating the program with key members of the Steering Committee and being introduced by them to media leaders.

The First Wave

Media activities were initiated with a special seminar for 35 media leaders shortly before CHIP entered the field. After a presentation of plans for the overall media program, the role each medium was to play was discussed. This seminar had two purposes: to involve media gatekeepers more deeply in the program and to test the ability of such an activity to generate news coverage. Extensive coverage was generated, and this favorable experience encouraged the extensive use of this method of gaining access to the media in the years that followed.

The first use of this method was at the inaugural ceremony introducing CHIP to the community. This ceremony, on July 11, 1980, was addressed by the secretary of health of the state and was attended by 250 persons, including many of the most influential members of the community.

The ceremony initiated the first wave of media activity, designed to promote awareness of CHIP and to establish its credibility. To this end, for four months extensive news coverage of the introduction of CHIP was provided through both broadcast and print media, followed closely by the release of a large number of radio public service announcements. These announcements included many by celebrity doctors such as the Surgeon General of the United States, the director of the National Heart Institute, and Art Ulene of the "Today" show, as well as others by well-known, local physicians. In addition, there was widespread use of billboards and posters and the introduction of pamphlet holders to over 100 sites, including retail outlets and doctors' offices. This media campaign set the stage for over 200 personal presentations to 4,000 persons by the executive director, introducing CHIP to the channels (Table 7.4).

Four months after the introduction of CHIP to the community, the first risk factor campaign was introduced—four months focused upon the control of high blood pressure. The campaign had two parts: a

TABLE 7.4.

Introducing Chip to the Channels

Channel	Number of Meetings During First Year
Mass Media	28
Work Sites	58
Health Sector	45
Community Organizations	76
Schools	30

screening program to detect unaware hypertensives and a monitoring program to improve blood pressure control among hypertensives already in treatment. Five waves of radio messages and two waves of television messages were distributed to all the appropriate outlets, and extensive news coverage was given to the visits of cardiovascular disease experts, including Dr. Pekka Puska, the director of the North Karelia Project. Posters were distributed throughout the county, pamphlets on hypertension were inserted into all the pamphlet holders, and the availability of these products was publicized both in media messages as well as in the "Ask CHIP" column, devoted to hypertension control throughout the campaign. The extent of media coverage during this campaign is illustrated in Table 7.5.

The hypertension campaign served as a model for subsequent CHIP efforts. Every four months the major focus of CHIP media efforts rotated among three risk factors—hypertension, smoking, and nutrition. During the campaign directed towards one risk factor, most media activities focused upon this risk factor, although a low, background level of activity continued to reinforce messages from the previous campaigns.

The first hypertension campaign introduced the first community action program—the high blood pressure screening campaign called "Go Get Squeezed"—which will be described below. Only four months after the introduction of CHIP, the media channel was thus already interacting with other channels in risk factor reduction campaigns.

TABLE 7.5.

Media Output in One Month

Media	Messages	Exposures
Radio	900	113,000
Television	23	45,000
Newspapers	4.5	110,000
Billboards	5.0	470,000
Pamphlet Holders	190	
Pamphlets	16,500	33,000

The second major campaign was directed to smoking cessation. As noted above, the base-line survey indicated that only 11.5% of Lycoming County smoking residents had made efforts to stop smoking in the past year. This information led the first campaign to focus on motivating people to quit smoking, including help with the weight gain problem that follows smoking cessation, a problem that had discouraged many smokers. Coordination insured that all the media channels presented compatible messages. These channels included billboards, many radio spots and a well-publicized program in which a local radio personality quit smoking on the air, the "Ask CHIP" column, and distribution of the American Cancer Society's "Helping Smokers Quit" to all physicians and dentists in the county. Important interactions among these efforts included frequent references in the broadcast media and in the "Ask CHIP" column to the availability of the more extensive information provided by the "Quit Kits."

During the second year of the program, when the desire to quit smoking had increased, an ambitious program to teach skills for quitting was developed for radio, using as a model a television program from the North Karelia Project. This program, entitled "Quit with the Q," provided five carefully edited, half-hour segments for prime time during which six Williamsport residents, including its leading news announcer, quit smoking "on the air." In the first session, they discussed with Dr. Brownell, the moderator, their reasons for quitting, and on successive evenings they described their reactions to quitting and how they coped with the craving to smoke. Local industry bought space in the newspaper to advertise the program and to print monitoring sheets for individuals to use in their attempts to quit smoking.

The third major campaign was devoted to diet and exercise. By the time this campaign was mounted, there were already extensive health promotion programs under way at work sites. Undoubtedly, the weight loss competitions that began to be featured so prominently in the work site programs were greatly stimulated by the extensive media campaign that preceded them.

During the second year of the program, the emphasis of the mass media changed from its earlier focus upon introducing CHIP and providing information. Skills training played a progressively larger role in media activities, and these efforts were combined with skills training programs carried out through the other channels. Increasingly, mass media activities involved coordinating programs within and between the channels and in publicizing CHIP events.

At the end of the second year, when specific funding for mass media activities expired and, therefore, Porter and Novelli activities terminated, these activities were transferred without interruption to the

CHIP field staff and local institutions. A major goal of CHIP has been ultimately to transfer its activities to local institutions. The first such transfer, in the mass media channel, was accomplished with surprising success, a testimony to the effective working relationships that had been developed by CHIP staff with the local mass media.

Evaluation of the mass media channel was undertaken by surveys, which revealed awareness of CHIP by 58% of county residents at the end of the first year, rising to 76% at the end of the second year. During the first two weeks of the extensive mass media program, formative evaluation went hand in hand with summative evaluation, and the two types of research were not easily disentangled. Indeed, the experience with the mass media channel brought into awareness a major problem in all community studies: the difficulty in disentangling the influence of the various components. In fact, as the example of "Go Get Squeezed" will make clear, it may be unreasonable to hope that these components can be disentangled. If the various elements of a community study work, they probably work together and their greatest efficacy may well arise from their interaction. The media greatly changed Lycoming County in ways difficult to measure and in ways that set the tone for much of what followed. The relative ease with which some programs in the other channels were able to develop, for example, is probably due in part to the influence of the mass media channel.

Channel 2: Work Sites

The second CHIP channel to be activated, and the most highly developed one—in large part because of generous funding from the W. K. Kellogg Foundation—is the work site channel. Work site programs are among the most rapidly growing health promotion activities in America, and they have captured the imagination of many of the most progressive industries in the country. The reasons are clear. Changing health behavior is difficult at best and is particularly difficult when attempted in isolation, without the social supports that sustain a person's daily activities (Stunkard & Brownell, 1980). CHIP seeks to provide this kind of support through the geographical community. But geographical communities are not the only communities in which people participate. Everyone is a member of various and overlapping communities, and, among them, the community at the work site may well be the most promising for health behavior change. People may spend more of their time at work than at any other waking activity. The work site provides access to large numbers of persons who can be provided environmental and social support as well as skills training at a relatively low cost. (McGill, 1979). Kristein (1980) has suggested how work site programs might favorably influence productivity, absenteeism, fire risk, work-men's compensation, and other accident losses.

Work site health promotion has played a key part in CHIP planning, guided by the findings of the Community Resource Inventory. When CHIP began, few work sites had health promotion activities, and it was possible to plan what may well be the first, integrated program between work sites within a geographical area. During the first three years of CHIP, a total of 58 different health promotion programs were started at 12 different work sites employing 3800 persons. One fruit of these en-deavors was the development of a process for establishing health promo-tion programs at the work site, a process important to the success of these programs (Felix, Stunkard, Cohen, & Cooley, in press).

The Fourteen-Step Work Site Program Process

1. *Introduction of the program to management.* The CHIP executive direc-tor sends a letter to the company's management, followed shortly by a personal presentation of the proposed program to the management.

2. *Announcement of the program to the employees.* This announcement is made by the chief executive officer, either through the company news-letter or, even better, by a personal letter to the employees' homes.

3. *Recruitment and organization of a "Heart Health Committee."* A key element is the inclusion of a broad cross-section of both labor and man-agement on the committee.

4. *In-house communication planning.* Communication within the indus-try was carried out by company newsletters at two-thirds of the sites and, at the remainder, by newly formed CHIP newsletters.

5. *Employee interest and risk factor surveys.* The committee takes respon-sibility for two types of surveys. The first is an Employee Interest Survey to assess the extent of employee interest in various health promotion activities, as an aid in program planning. The second is a Risk Factor Survey conducted at no cost by the State Department of Health.

6. *Formation of risk factor subcommittees.* The original Heart Health Committee has from 6 to as many as 20 members. If the process is on schedule, the need for specialized activities mandates the formation of subcommittees for each of the five risk factors—smoking, hypertension, elevated serum cholesterol, obesity, and physical inactivity.

7. *Exploration of community risk factor reduction programs.* The newly formed subcommittees explore existing community resources for risk factor reduction and assess the costs and effectiveness of the various programs. If resources in an area are found inadequate, the subcommit-tees may attempt to develop them, encouraging the expansion of existing programs or the establishment of new ones.

8. *Committee review and program selection.* Subcommittee explorations are reviewed with the parent Heart Health Committee and initial selection of programs is made.

9. *Development of a program proposal.* The Heart Health Committee develops a proposal to serve as a blueprint for future development and as a basis for discussion with management.

10. *Discussion of the proposal with management.* In this discussion, management contribution to the selected programs is negotiated, the extent of this contribution providing an important index of management support. These contributions range from released time to modest financial assistance, as, for example, partial payment for smoking cessation programs.

11. *Promotion of programs and recruitment of employees.* The Heart Health Committee promotes the programs that have been selected and recruits participants.

12. *Sched.:ling of programs.* The Heart Health Committee schedules programs on the basis of its Employee Interest Survey.

13. *Program implementation.* If planning has proceeded as described, implementation follows as a matter of course.

14. *Evaluation and feedback.* The results of evaluation of the programs are fed back to the committee and subcommittees to promote program revision and ongoing discussion with management. Further programs are developed following the sequence from step 8 above.

Selection of Programs

An important goal of CHIP was to select programs that would accommodate as many people as possible and that would generate enthusiasm for CHIP. At least three factors guided this selection. First was the level of interest on the part of employees, as assessed by the Employee Interest Survey. Second was the availability of programs in the community, as determined by the Community Resource Inventory and by subcommittee explorations. Third was the ease with which programs could be offered at the work site. Most of the programs selected met all three criteria.

Problems at the Work Site

Surprisingly few problems were encountered in CHIP work site programs. The most serious problem was the very limited record keeping by employers, even of such vital information as utilization of health and disability insurance, employee productivity, and absenteeism. A second problem, deriving from the economic recession, was the extensive layoffs of employees. The effect of layoffs on employee morale was always serious: when layoffs reached 80% of the work force, as in one instance, the work site program collapsed. The third problem was inadequate support by top management, which permitted middle management personnel to interfere with health promotion programs, particularly if it seemed the programs might threaten production goals. A major surprise was the fact that confidentiality of employee records was not a problem and posed no impediment to the program.

Ownership and Economy

A distinctive result of the CHIP process is the feeling of program ownership that arises among employees. Active participation in the development of health promotion programs fosters a psychological investment often lacking in programs developed at the initiative of management. A second strength of the CHIP program is the modesty of its costs. This modesty has made the programs particularly attractive to industry in the current, economically depressed circumstances of Lycoming County, and small companies with limited work forces have been particularly appreciative. Traditional health promotion activities, with special facilities and expensive programs, are far beyond the means of these small companies in Lycoming County, and probably in most other parts of the country as well. A program that makes use of existing facilities permits these companies to take full advantage of the benefits of health promotion at the work site.

Creativity at the Work Site: Weight Loss Competitions

The work site process, which elicited a sense of ownership on the part of employees, also resulted in highly creative and imaginative programs. One example of this creativity is the development of competitions among employees for risk factor reduction. Although most of the competitions to date have involved weight loss, competitions involving other risk factors have been explored and will play an increasingly important part in future CHIP work site programs. The weight loss competitions developed because of a disappointing record of weight loss at the work site, the subject of four reports, including one by one of the authors of this paper (Abrahms & Follick, 1983; Brownell, Stunkard, & McKeon, unpublished manuscript; Fisher, Lowe, Levenkron, & Newman, 1982; Foreyt, Scott, & Gotto, 1980; Sangor & Bichanich, 1977).

The initial work site competition was *between* industries—three commercial banks. All employees were invited to participate, and weight loss goals were kept modest to discourage crash dieting. Each participant paid $5.00 to enter the program, and the pool was awarded to the winning industry. A large bulletin board, similar to the United Way thermometer, was placed in a prominent location in each work place to show the weekly progress of each team. Weigh-ins occurred weekly in a central location in each industry, accompanied by considerable publicity and a high level of employee interest. At each weigh-in, employees were given an installment of a behavioral weight reduction manual (Brownell, 1979). Professional time allocated to the program was confined to planning and preparing the first program at the bank. Subsequent programs have required only minimal assistance by nonprofessional personnel.

The results of the weight loss competition at the three banks were striking and without precedent among weight loss programs at the work site. They are summarized in Table 7.6, in which the results of the bank competition are contrasted with those of the largest previous program of weight reduction at the work site. The bank program, adapted from a clinical model, was conducted over a period of three years by Brownell, Stunkard, and McKeon (unpublished manuscript). Note the remarkably low dropout rate of 0.5%, unusual even in the finest clinical programs. Furthermore, the bank program (with its weight loss of 13 pounds) lasted only 12 weeks, in contrast to the 16-week program in the Storeworkers Union that produced only a 7.8 pound weight loss. These large weight losses were paralleled by marked improvement in a number of psychological parameters, for example, employee morale and energy level.

A number of subsequent competitions have taken place within different industries. Although these competitions were initiated by individual Heart Health Committees, they could not have been better planned for research purposes. Thus, competitions have been carried out among different divisions of a single industry and, also, among employees of a single industry, randomly assigned to different teams. The results of these programs suggest that competition *among* industries is more effective than is competition *within* industries. This result suggested that competition alone was not the critical element but, rather, competition on behalf of an in-group. To test this hypothesis, a program was carried out in which individuals competed against each other. The results fully confirmed the hypothesis: dropout numbers were even higher and weight losses even lower than in traditional programs of weight loss at

TABLE 7.6.
Results of Two Programs of Weight Control at the Work Site

	Storeworkers	Banks
Number of participants	172	175
Dropouts	34%	0.5%
Weight loss (pounds)	7.3	13.0

the work site. Cooperation within the competitive unit is the key to the effectiveness of competition.

Another competition assessed the effects upon women as compared to men. Men not only lost more weight, as might be expected from their greater weight, but also lost a greater percentage of overweight. Further study supporting the suggestion that competitions are effective with men would be of great importance in view of the limited appeal to men of traditional programs. Finally, weight loss competitions seem to be a useful means of involving blue-collar workers in health promotion programs. Health promotion programs have traditionally held little attraction for blue-collar workers. If competition can be utilized to involve them, it may have important, unexpected benefits. An attempt to involve blue-collar workers at one of the work sites is currently under way through a competition among their wives.

Evaluation of Work Site Programs.

Each CHIP channel is being evaluated in a manner consistent with its overall goals. The most careful evaluation has been carried out in the work site channel; accordingly, this evaluation will be described in some detail. Since CHIP is a unique program of community organization, particular attention is being paid to careful documentation.

The first research question is whether work sites can be mobilized to improve health practices; clearly the answer is yes. Two methods are used to document this process—a check list and a staff log. The check list is based on the steps of the work site process described above. For each work site, the date on which each step was implemented is recorded and any deviation from the process is noted. The goal is to delineate which of the 14 steps are crucial to the successful implementation of a work site program. Accompanying the check list is a staff log in which is recorded each contact at a work site, the length of the contact, and the topics discussed. A comparison of the speed of implementation over time shows a rapid acceleration. The first industry required three times more contact hours than did later industries, a finding consistent with the literature on the diffusion of innovation.

The second research question is whether the health promotion programs change health behaviors and maintain these changes. To answer this question, base-line surveys are conducted at work sites before programs begin to determine health status, health beliefs, and health practices. Subsequent records include figures on attendance, responses to questionnaires, and assessment of each risk factor—changes in smoking, blood pressure, and weight, for example. The response rate to these surveys is remarkably high, averaging about 75%, a fact probably due to the manner in which the surveys are conducted. Each member of the Heart

Health Committee personally gives each questionnaire to about 20 persons, explaining the importance of the survey and urging that the questionnaire be completed. An envelope accompanies all questionnaires so the employee can send them directly to the CHIP office, ensuring confidentiality.

The high response rate is all the more remarkable in that employees are asked to sign all survey instruments. This procedure makes it possible to carry out more sophisticated analyses than are customary in work site programs. Such programs usually collect only anonymous questionnaires, forcing analyses to use aggregate data that combine participants and nonparticipants. By differentiating participants from nonparticipants, CHIP can take the first step in determining if changes among employees are actually due to the programs in which they participated.

The third research question is whether changes in health behavior affect mortality and morbidity from cardiovascular disease. Information on absenteeism, insurance utilization, and cardiovascular disease-related hospitalizations is being obtained from the records of each of the industries as well as from the Prudential Insurance Company and Blue Cross/ Blue Shield. The records for the two years before implementation of the program are being compared with those for each year of the program. This comparison should reveal the extent of the impact of the program (if any) on absenteeism in the near future, and on cardiovascular disease at a later time.

The fourth research question deals with the cost-effectiveness in each industry and in each program. Information is being obtained on the number of hours of volunteer and professional efforts, direct costs of the programs, and indirect costs such as released time for program participation. Plans include a cost estimate related to the outcome for each individual program. For example, analyses have already determined the cost per pound of weight lost in the different weight reduction programs.

The fifth research question is the extent and nature of work site programs and their impact on the community. As noted above, during the first three years of CHIP, 58 health promotion programs were established at 12 different work sites employing 3800 persons. These programs were heavily weighted towards physical inactivity and hypertension. Table 7.7 shows that 39 of the programs were designed to increase physical activity and improve blood pressure control. Nutrition programs were underrepresented. Distribution of programs across industries was also skewed. Two industries mounted 12 programs each during this time, while another four mounted four to eight. Six industries, primarily those recruited most recently, provided from one to three programs.

The telephone survey conducted by Porter, Novelli, and Associates indicated that CHIP had already made an impact by 1982 (Greenberg et

TABLE 7.7.

Risk Factor Reduction Programs 1980–1983

Exercise Classes and Walking Programs	21
Blood Pressure (Screening and Monitoring)	18
Weight Loss	10
Smoking Cessation	7
Nutrition	2
	58

al., 1983). Thus, of persons who had participated in a work site program in Lycoming County, 48% reported that it had been a heart disease-related program, compared to 17% of such persons in the reference county. This difference was mirrored by responses from the general population. Of the respondents in Lycoming County, 6% had participated in a heart disease-related program at the work site, compared to no more than 2% in the reference county, a highly significant difference.

The Future

CHIP's active program of work site health promotion shows what can be done in a prepared community. As such, CHIP is probably testing the limits of effectiveness of work site health promotion. It would be surprising if similarly favorable results could be obtained in work site programs in communities that had not undergone the sensitization and education provided by CHIP programs in the other channels.

A major concern of CHIP from the beginning has been the institutionalization of its programs so they will continue after active CHIP intervention is ended. Towards this end, CHIP has encouraged interaction among the managers at the different work sites, and informal communication channels have been established among them, as is so natural in a small, well-integrated community. Plans for formal institutionalization of CHIP work site health promotion programs are now under way. They include the establishment of a health subcommittee, a permanent subcommittee of the Lycoming County Chamber of Commerce. The Chamber of Commerce is one of the most important local institutions, and establishment of this subcommittee as a permanent part of its structure will go far towards the institutionalization of work site health promotion in Lycoming County.

Channel 3: The Health Sector

One might expect that the health sector would play an important part in health promotion. The reputed lack of physician interest in health, as opposed to illness, however, raises questions about this expectation. It is, therefore, important to review the potential contribution to health promotion of the health sector, and particularly of physicians.

Physicians have many opportunities to contribute to health promotion. They are widely viewed as the most credible source of information about health and illness, and they have widespread access to people worried about their health. The average American adult, for example, makes four visits a year to a physician, and 85% make at least one visit a year. The potential impact of the physician is well illustrated by a recent report. When a physician simply suggested that a smoker stop smoking, the one-year quit rate rose from a base line of 0.3% to 3.3%, and adding no more than a short instructional pamphlet increased it further, to 5.1% (Russell, Wilson, Taylor, & Baker, 1979). If every physician in England carried out this simple procedure, the result would be the equivalent of 10,000 smoking control clinics.

Physicians are similarly important in controlling hypertension. Once the diagnosis has been made, the success of treatment depends largely upon the skill of the physician in helping patients adhere to effective regimens. This success has been modest at best. Caldwell and coworkers (1970) found that no more than 26% of hypertensives continued in a clinic for five years, and Engelland, Alderman, and Powell (1979) reported that half the hypertensives in the practice of a New York City internist were not in treatment a year later. There have, of course, been more impressive results. One aggressive follow-up program resulted in blood pressure control of 80% of hypertensives (Wilber & Barrow, 1969). Furthermore, despite the importance of community blood pressure screening, most hypertensives are diagnosed in the physician's office.

Although dentists have traditionally been less involved in risk factor reduction than have been physicians, their credibility and access to patients provides opportunities every bit as favorable as those of physicians. Finally, state departments of health and public health nurses have long had a major commitment to health promotion.

Health Professionals in Lycoming County

There are 136 physicians in active practice in Lycoming County, of whom 50 are involved in primary care. In addition, there are 56 dentists, 20 dental hygienists, and 44 office nurses, together with 24 community pharmacies.

The first approach to the health sector occurred early in CHIP planning with a presentation to the County Medical Society. The response was something less than enthusiastic, therefore, the energetic advocacy of CHIP by physicians on the Steering Committee was most welcome. Thereafter, CHIP went forward with the tolerance of organized medicine, which gradually developed into acceptance. Even before CHIP entered the field, the journal of the county Medical Society published an article on the rationale and plans for CHIP (Stunkard, Schechter, Taylor, Marconi, Norman, & Stolley, 1979), and the Continuing Medical Education Program of the Williamsport Hospital incorporated programs on the control of smoking and obesity. The major medical support for CHIP, however, came primarily from individual physicians, several of whom participated in the campaigns to control hypertension and smoking.

Hypertension: Control

The health sector plays a key part in hypertension screening in Lycoming County (as described below in the section on "Go Get Squeezed"). In addition, the health sector is involved in a controlled trial of hypertension monitoring.

Although hypertensive medication can control the blood pressure of most hypertensives, poor adherence severely limits the effectiveness of treatment. In an effort to improve adherence to antihypertensive regimens, CHIP has developed a program for monitoring hypertensive patients in the doctor's office. It is based upon the idea that a major cause of poor adherence is missed appointments and failure of the physician to follow up these missed appointments (Engelland et al., 1979). The monitoring system consists of a 3×5 file box with monthly dividers and a tabbed file card for each patient listing name, address, phone number, and appointments kept and missed. Each time a patient is scheduled to return for an office visit, the file card is pulled and a note is made as to whether the appointment was kept or missed. If the patient has kept the appointment, the date of the next scheduled appointment is noted and the card is filed under the appropirate month. If the appointment is broken, the patient is contacted by phone as soon as possible to arrange another appointment. If three attempts to reach the patient by phone are unsuccessful, an appointment is sent by post card and the date is recorded on the patient's card.

To evaluate this system, tracking programs have been set up in the offices of 10 physicians with 281 hypertensive patients whose blood pressures have been measured under standardized conditions under CHIP auspices. The tracking system has been activated in four doctors' offices with a total of 150 patients, while the other six doctors' offices with 131 patients serve as controls. The experimental period of one year will be completed shortly and the effectiveness of the monitoring system will be ascertained.

Smoking Control

The health sector has participated in a more modest manner in programs of smoking control. This participation occurs during the four-month media campaigns devoted to smoking cessation, when the media urge smokers to contact their doctors for help. At these times, CHIP mails these help materials to physicians and dentists. The materials include reprints of the paper by Russell et al. (1979) on the effectiveness of physician recommendations, together with copies of the American Cancer Society's pamphlet, "Helping Smokers Quit," and pamphlet holders to display them in the office. In addition, as noted above, CHIP contributes to the Continuing Medical Education programs of the Williamsport Hospital devoted to risk factor reduction and smoking cessation. Finally, CHIP has stayed in close touch with the manufacturers of nicotine chewing gum and plans a vigorous new smoking cessation campaign as soon as the Food and Drug Administration approves this agent.

Channel 4: The Schools

The school channel was the last of the five channels to be activated. The reasons for this delay help in understanding how priorities were set in CHIP, for school programs were integral parts of the other three, large, community cardiovascular prevention programs from the outset, and with good reason. A program that seeks to organize an entire community can ill afford to neglect the large and vital constituency of the young, and school programs clearly facilitated organization of the community.

The reason for CHIP's delay in activating the school channel was the limitation of resources. This limitation argued against programs that did not have a direct effect upon risk reduction, and school programs gave little promise of directly reducing cardiovascular disease in the short-term years. However useful in organizing the community, a traditional school program meant diverting resources from programs that could directly reduce cardiovascular risk.

The delay in activating the school channel had its advantages. It provided time for CHIP and its executive director to achieve credibility, engender trust, and prepare the ground. When an innovative, new school program was conceived and funded, it was thus far easier to implement than it otherwise would have been. The innovative aspect of the CHIP school program is that it seeks not only to change the health behavior of children, but also to teach children to change the health behavior of their parents. This new aspect of the program helps justify, on cost-effectiveness grounds, the inclusion of a school channel as an integral part of a community cardiovascular disease prevention program. It is a mea-

sure of the acceptance of CHIP in the community that this proposal was
warmly welcomed by the school community.

The Health Behavior of Children

Although the health behavior of children has little or no immediate
impact upon cardiovascular disease, recent research has revealed major
health problems among children stemming from their behavior and has
discovered major opportunities for coping with these problems. Smoking is the largest of these problems. From 1968 to 1974, when there was a
major decrease in smoking among adults (from 42% to 33%), the percentage of regular smokers among all teenagers increased dramatically
(from 11.5% to 15.6%) (U.S. Department of Health and Human Services, 1980). Although this increase has been arrested and a decline has
begun, 20% of 18-year olds still smoke, and ominous implications remain that they will persist in this strong addictive habit.

Family and peer pressures are the important determinants of teenage
smoking. Teenagers whose parents smoke are twice as likely to smoke as
are teenagers whose parents are nonsmokers, and this figure rises to four
times the rate of nonsmokers when a sibling also smokes (U.S. Department of Health, Education and Welfare, 1979b). The immediate stimulus
for starting smoking, however, is peer pressure (Newman, 1970). These
facts formed the bases for the newer approaches to the prevention of
smoking among adolescents. Disregarding earlier scare tactics, Evans
(1976) developed a curriculum for junior high schools based upon social
psychological principles: children were "inoculated" with a small dose of
the disease (social pressure to smoke) and then received an effective
"antidote" of social skills training. This curriculum has been further
developed by McAlister, Perry, and Maccoby (1979), who used high
school peer counselors to provide intensive training in behavioral measures designed to help students resist peer pressures to smoke. Controlled studies show that the program is effective. Two years after
administration of this "CLASP" (Counseling Leadership About Smoking Pressure) program, only 5.2% of students were smoking, compared
to 15.2% in a comparison school. CLASP has been chosen as the basis
for the CHIP smoking prevention program described below.

Using children to help their parents change health behaviors may well
be without precedent. Using parents to help their children change their
health behaviors is almost as rare. Yet, such efforts should be useful, and
two studies suggest they are. Both Brownell, Kelman, and Stunkard
(1983), and Epstein, Wing, Koeske, Andraski, and Ossip (1981) reported
improvement in weight loss programs for children when their parents
were also involved.

The CHIP school program reflects the overall CHIP program in its search to reduce more than one risk factor. There has been only one previous such attempt with children. A two-year program of the North Karelia Project reduced the number of 13-year olds who started smoking and improved their nutrition. It did not, however, reduce their blood pressure (Puska, Vartiainen, Pallonen, Salonen, Poyhia, Koskela, & McAlister, 1982).

The Schools in Lycoming County

Lycoming County has seven independent school districts with 45 schools and 23,328 children. The Williamsport Consolidated School District is by far the largest in the county, containing five elementary schools with 3,000 students, three junior high schools with 2,800 students, and one high school with 2,200 students. Because of their size and the ease of access to these schools, the program will be conducted in Williamsport.

Preliminary Programs

Three preliminary programs have laid the basis for the large-scale school program to begin shortly. The first was the *Peer Helper Program,* conducted by Mr. Felix when he was director of the Drug and Alcohol Program in the county. The second was a weight reduction program conducted by Dr. Brownell in elementary schools in Williamsport. The third and most relevant of the preliminary programs was a test of the modified CLASP smoking prevention program developed by Dr. Cohen. Carried out among seventh graders in three junior high schools, the test compared the standard health education program of the school district with the modified CLASP program conducted by peer helpers from the high schools. The basic format of the program involved three, consecutive, daily classroom exercises of 45 minutes, and three follow-up exercises at three-week intervals. During these exercises, slide-tape shows and discussions conveyed basic information about smoking, including the role of peer pressure in initiating it. The largest part of the program, however, was devoted to behavioral exercises led by the peer helpers, who made extensive use of role-playing. They modeled appropriate behaviors for the students, who then practiced them and received feedback on their performance. Great importance was placed on learning to be assertive in resisting pressures to smoke. Finally, the program tested the new measures for helping children influence their parents' behavior. The same behavioral methods used to help students resist peer pressure were used to help them learn how to talk to parents who smoke. At the same time, parents received messages especially tailored for this program.

The effects on smoking by the students may, as in other programs, take some time to become evident, but the effects on the parents are already clear. A base-line telephone survey of all 780 families of children to be involved in the program was undertaken as a public service by the Williamsport Junior League. No resistance was encountered and a striking response rate of 93% was obtained. The survey revealed that 352 families (32%) contained at least one member who smoked. When the parents who smoked were resurveyed six months after the program, 83% of the fathers and 67% of the mothers of children in the experimental program reported that discussions with their children had led them to seriously consider stopping smoking. The comparable figure among parents in the control program was 27% of the fathers and 31% of the mothers.

The Proposed Programs

The final version of the revised CLASP program builds upon the experience gained in the pilot project. The number of peer helpers will be reduced from the CLASP-recommended nine per classroom to three, and the six follow-up exercises shortened to three. But the major effort has been devoted to formulating protocols for training children to talk to their parents and developing the materials to be sent to the parents.

The school channel will also include programs to control hypertension and improve nutrition. As in the smoking program, these efforts will include training children to change the health behavior of their parents. The basic programs are ones whose efficacy has been well established: the "School High Blood Pressure Education Program" of the Georgia Heart Association (1979) and the "Heart Healthy Eating Program" (Coates, Jeffrey, & Slinkard, 1981). In the hypertension program, sixth-grade students learn to measure blood pressure and then measure the blood pressure of their parents and siblings in the home. The program provides a superb opportunity to screen parents for hypertension and to encourage hypertensive parents to adhere to their treatment regimens, and children will be taught to take full advantage of this opportunity. Coates and Perry (1980) have reported considerable success with the basic nutrition program for fifth graders, to which will be added the methods for influencing parental behavior.

Evaluation

Programs for each individual risk factor will be evaluated separately for children and for parents. Measures include those at base line, at the end of the program, and at a two-year follow-up. Additional evaluation efforts will determine the relative effectiveness (and costs) of multiple versus single risk factor interventions. Evaluation will involve not only changes in risk factors but also changes in health attitudes and behaviors, such as are measured by the Health Locus of Control Scale (Wallston, Wallston, & DeVellis, 1978).

Since children cannot be randomly assigned to treatment and control groups, a quasi-experimental design will use schools as the unit of assignment (Campbell & Stanley, 1963). Schools will be used as their own controls and, in a cross-over design, as controls for each other. The large number of classes and of students permit extensive analysis of results. Thus, five classes of 500 fifth graders will receive the nutrition program, five classes of 500 sixth graders will receive the hypertension program, and three classes of 750 junior high school students will receive the smoking program. Repeating the program the second year permits assessment of the effects of a second intervention on children who had been in the fifth and sixth grades during the first year. The very low outmigration from Lycoming County provides the opportunity for one of the first long-term follow-ups of any school program.

Channel 5: Voluntary Organizations

Voluntary organizations are critical to the success of a community program, and they constitute the fifth channel of the CHIP program. These organizations, which include social, civic, religious, voluntary-health, and fraternal groups, are important elements of a community (U.S. Department of Health, Education and Welfare, 1979b), and great emphasis was placed upon their development in the planning for CHIP. Voluntary organizations are ideal vehicles for reaching large numbers of people, for changing their health behaviors, and for helping them maintain these changed behaviors. They thereby become the means for diffusing innovations and for incorporating them into community norms and values (Rogers & Shoemaker, 1971).

These organizations are called intermediaries in the social marketing literature, where they are viewed as particularly valuable in providing direct access to target populations (Kotler, 1975). In addition, they help create a more receptive environment for programs such as CHIP, since they are seen as credible and influential sources of information. Intermediaries provide one of the most cost-effective methods of bringing about community-wide change, and they have been utilized extensively in the Stanford Heart Disease Prevention Program. This economy of effort made them particularly appealing to CHIP, with its limited resources and outsized ambitions. Accordingly, from the outset, serious efforts were made to work with intermediaries, helping them achieve their own goals (Andreasen, 1981) and, in the process, helping them join and support other groups in their efforts.

The Number of Voluntary Organizations

The Community Resource Inventory provided important background information for planning voluntary organization activities, as it did in so many other areas. The inventory indicated the presence of a number of voluntary organizations with more than 100 members in Lycoming County, including 37 social and civic clubs, 22 social services organizations, 16 health organizations, and 7 religious organizations (other than churches). A few, such as the County Heart Association and County Lung Association, had specific health interests that could potentially be mobilized, but, otherwise, there was little health promotion activity in the county. The first step in increasing this activity was to establish a series of program objectives, based upon a review of the literature.

Program Objectives

1. To utilize existing channels of communication within voluntary organizations for increasing knowledge about heart health risk factors.

2. To motivate behavior change through special events and activities sponsored and implemented by voluntary organizations.

3. To institute mechanisms for maintaining heart health behavior change by creating and expanding social support networks among voluntary organizations.

4. To utilize the resources of community organizations, particularly their volunteer forces, in carrying out community-wide, heart health events and in creating environmental changes in the community.

The literature review led CHIP planners to expect that programs in the voluntary organizations channel would develop much as had those in the work site, health sector, and school channels. Actually, however, they did not. The reasons expectations were not met are instructive, for voluntary organizations possess many potential strengths.

Voluntary organizations should be easier to mobilize for health promotion than organizations in other channels. Unlike the latter, voluntary organizations do not need to be formed or activated; they are already active. They need only be given new direction. Furthermore, they are structured to give service rather than to receive it, as do the other channels. Programs in the other channels have specific functions and are designed to achieve specific aims that may conflict with programs of health promotion. Voluntary organizations, by contrast, with more open-ended goals, are well suited to move in new directions and to provide social support for programs in other channels. The contributions of voluntary organizations were of precisely this type—enhancing cooperation and facilitating programs in other channels. Finally, members of voluntary organizations were viewed as opinion leaders and helped define expected and appropriate behavior in health as in other areas.

Despite these advantages of voluntary organizations, they had serious drawbacks. The focus of the voluntary organizations channel was more diffuse than that of other channels, and its programs did not have the same kind of specific functions as those of the other channels. To a far greater degree than in the other four channels, attendance and even membership in voluntary organizations are intermittent, and it is difficult to define a fixed group with which to work. This more casual nature is reflected also in the fact that the ties binding members are voluntary and facilitative rather than the necessary ones that bind people to their work. Curiously, although voluntary organizations could involve members in promotion of their own health, they do not. These drawbacks, and perhaps others, prevented the voluntary organizations from playing as large a role as had been anticipated. Nevertheless, many of them were quite active in CHIP.

Very early in CHIP, voluntary organizations were instrumental in organizing the first health promotion campaign, the large-scale, hypertension screening program known as "Go Get Squeezed," described in greater detail below. Other less ambitious programs of voluntary organizations have involved other risk factors. The groups helped introduce the "Eat Hearty" nutrition program of the American Heart Association, designed to assist restaurants in providing tasty, low-calorie food. Similarly, the "Safe Slimming" weight loss program of the Extension Office of the Pennsylvania State University was promoted by voluntary organizations.

Another type of activity by the voluntary organizations was the survey of smoking undertaken by the Junior League as part of the school program. A local voluntary organization is ideally suited to assist in research involving the collection of sensitive information. The 93% response rate achieved by the Junior League is probably higher than could have been achieved by a commercial firm, particularly in a small, well-integrated community like Williamsport. CHIP, however, could not afford to pay such a firm. The potential of voluntary organizations for assisting in research has certainly been underestimated.

Interactions Among the Channels—The Example of "Go Get Squeezed"

A key element of CHIP is the interaction between programs, both within channels and between channels. Figure 1 showed the extraordinary degree to which attempts to change one health behavior influence other health behaviors. In a similar manner, programs within one channel exert powerful influences upon programs in other channels. Some of the most impressive effects of CHIP have been the result of such interactions between channels. An instructive example is the high blood pressure screening program, "Go Get Squeezed."

"Go Get Squeezed" was initiated within four months of the start of CHIP as part of the very first risk factor reduction campaign—hypertension control. There were various motives for this program. One was to mount a program that would promptly secure media coverage for the fledgling CHIP organization. A second motive was to allay the concern of the voluntary health organizations that CHIP might be a competitor. In a series of carefully planned meetings, the executive director was able to present CHIP, instead, as a facilitator of their activities, helping them to cooperate in the first, large-scale blood pressure screening program in the county. The County Heart Association was thus helped to fulfill its mandate, while it provided CHIP with the expertise and resources to further programs of mutual interest, such as "Go Get Squeezed."

It was not the Heart Association, however, that provided the largest initial thrust for "Go Get Squeezed," but rather the Rotary Clubs of the county. The executive director met with the six Rotary Clubs and proposed that they engage in a competition to see which one could screen the largest number of persons for high blood pressure. The Rotary Clubs eagerly accepted this challenge and proceeded, with the guidance of the Steering Committee and the executive director, to institute the competition. They selected the sites for the screenings and negotiated for their use with the various responsible parties, played a major part in managing the sites, and were active in promoting the program. The Heart Association, of course, was active in the recruitment of volunteers and their placement at the different sites, and was joined in this activity by the Red Cross and a number of voluntary organizations.

An even larger number of voluntary organizations took part in "Go Get Squeezed" in later years, a total of 18 such groups taking part in the 1982 program. Although this enterprise was initiated by voluntary organizations, all five CHIP channels took part in it. Figure 7.3 depicts the participants in "Go Get Squeezed" and the interactions between them. The names of participants representing channels are denoted by titles surrounded by rectangles, other participants are denoted by ovals.

The *mass media* were recruited for service in "Go Get Squeezed" by the voluntary organizations working with the executive director. The many contacts leaders of the voluntary organizations had with leaders of the mass media greatly facilitated this recruitment, by helping to legitimize participation in "Go Get Squeezed" and by precept and example. As indicated by the arrows in Figure 7.3, which are pointing in each direc-

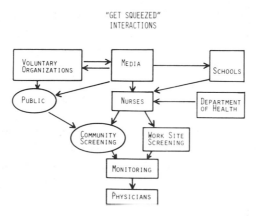

Figure 7.3. Interactions in the "Go Get Squeezed" Program. All five CHIP channels (indicated by rectangles) are involved in the program, as well as other agencies, indicated by ovals. Some of the interactions, as, for example, between the voluntary ogranizations and the schools, are not shown because the contact among them is less direct than those depicted.

tion, the relation between the voluntary organizations and the mass media was an interactive one. Not only did the voluntary organizations recruit the mass media into the program, but the promotion of "Go Get Squeezed" by the mass media helped recruit other voluntary organizations.

Much of the mass media participation in the first "Go Get Squeezed" campaign reflected its primary activities in the early phases of CHIP—providing general information about hypertension (particularly its asymptomatic nature), about the value of a screening program, and about the part being played by CHIP. Even in these early days, however, the mass media conducted activities more characteristic of its later phase—providing specific information as to the location of the screening sites and the times they were open.

Work sites played an increasingly important part in "Go Get Squeezed." Although the initial plans for the campaign had placed major emphasis on community screenings, the rapid development of the work site programs made it natural to include them. Furthermore, several plant managers specifically asked that their plants be included in the program, in part as a result of their personal relationships with members of the voluntary organizations. In fact, memberships in the work site and voluntary organization channels often overlapped. There were many advantages to this increased participation of work sites in "Go Get Squeezed." The excellent organization at the work sites rendered screening more efficient than at community sites and resulted in a large percentage of suspected hypertensives receiving medical attention. At the same time, the widespread publicity about "Go Get Squeezed" enlisted far more persons at the work sites than would have occurred under ordinary circumstances. The success of the work site screenings in "Go Get Squeezed" led them to play a larger and larger part in subsequent campaigns, even as the community screenings decreased in importance.

The *school channel* was well represented in "Go Get Squeezed" by the contribution of student nurses of the Williamsport Area Community College. A total of 150 of them volunteered to take blood pressures at the screening sites, contributing greatly to the large number of persons it was possible to screen. These nurses were recruited in part by the mass media, as shown in Figure 7.3, but also in part by the voluntary organizations, not shown in the Figure.

The *health sector,* as might be expected, was one of the most important elements in "Go Get Squeezed," serving in four capacities. First, about 25 nurses in the community volunteered to take blood pressures, supplementing the activities of the student nurses. Second, the State Department of Health instructed the nurses in standardized blood pressure measurement.

Third, the State Department of Health developed a program for the referral of persons with elevated blood pressures. This program, carried out by the public health nurse at the Lycoming County Health Center, was modeled after that of the North Karelia Project (Puska, 1981) and was initiated with the help of Dr. Aulikki Nissinen of the North Karelia Project. It began with an exit interview following the screening, at which time persons with elevated blood pressures were counseled as to the need for medical follow-up. Subsequent action depended upon the level of blood pressure:

140/88 to 158/94—advice to recheck blood pressure within a month.

160/95 to 188/118—advice to make an appointment with a physician within a month. The nurse calls within a week to verify the appointment.

190/120 and above—immediate referral to a physician.

As noted in Figure 7.4, the public health nurse calls clients two days after the screening in the case of severe hypertensives and one week after the screening in milder cases to find out if they made the appointment. If they have not, she continues to call for two weeks. If, at the end of this time, patients have made appointments with their physicians but have not kept them, the medical director of the Central District of the Department of Health so informs these physicians.

The fourth capacity in which the health sector participated in "Go Get Squeezed" was via physicians. Great emphasis was placed upon inform-

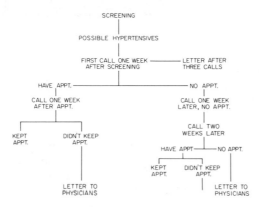

Figure 7.4. Diagram of the referral process for persons found to have elevated blood pressures in the "Go Get Squeezed" program.

ing physicians about the program and involving them in it. All members of the county Medical Society received a direct mailing that described goals and objectives of the program and prepared them for referrals. Surveys had indicated that older physicians in the county tended not to treat persons with blood pressures lower than 160/95. Accordingly, special efforts were made to provide them with educational materials, including two reports from the National High Blood Pressure Education Program—"Five-Year Findings of the Hypertension Detection and Education Program" and "Management of Hypertension in the Elderly."

As is so often the case in blood pressure screenings, evaluation of the program has been difficult. "Go Get Squeezed" reached large numbers of people—1500 in 1980 and twice that number in the subsequent two years. The percentage of persons with elevated blood pressure readings at screening has remained constant during this period, about 33%, proving no evidence that the program has had an effect. The percentage of persons with markedly elevated blood pressure, however, has declined significantly at screening sites (all of which are work sites) where it has been possible to compare results. Thus, the percentage of persons with diastolic blood pressures greater than 120 mm Hg fell from 7.5% in 1981 to 4% in 1982. Although alternative explanations are possible, these results suggest that "Go Get Squeezed" may have had a measurable impact upon those persons most likely to benefit from it.

This impression is supported by the results of the 1982 telephone survey (Greenberg et al, 1982). It showed that 29% of the men in Lycoming County reported having been told they had high blood pressure, up from 21% found in the 1980 Risk Factor Survey. There was no difference between the rates in 1980 and 1982 in the reference county. Furthermore, 34% of the male hypertensives in Lycoming County, compared to 21% in the reference county, reported that they had been told they had high blood pressure in the previous two years.

Changes in the Community

CHIP was designed as a true community study rather than as "a study of individuals conducted in a community," as an earlier program has been characterized (Leventhal, Safer, Cleary, & Gutmann, 1980). As such, it sought to elicit changes in the community that would support changes in health behavior of individuals. Such changes are prone to relapse, and many of them did relapse in an earlier program that relied primarily upon mass media (Meyer et al., 1980). CHIP's use of a multichannel approach seems to offer more hope of changing the community and, thus, of sustaining change in the health behavior of individuals. Did CHIP change the community?

The Community Resource Inventory was designed to answer this question by assessing the change in health promotion activities by organizations within the county. These results constitute one of the first outcome measures of the effectiveness of the second generation of community cardiovascular disease prevention programs.

The Community Resource Inventory was performed in both Lycoming County and in the reference county just prior to the entry of CHIP into the field in 1980. At that time, health promotion activities in the two counties were quite similar. As shown in Table 7.8, in Lycoming County 42% of the 157 organizations had at least one health promotion program, nearly half of which were relatively extensive. In the reference county, the percentages were somewhat smaller. The Community Resource Inventory was administered again in 1983 to those organizations that had been surveyed in 1980. The changes in these three years were striking.

The number of organizations offering health promotion programs in the reference county fell by 42%, quite possibly because of the severely depressed economic climate in this section of the country. By contrast, in this same depressed climate, the number of programs in Lycoming County doubled!

Summary

The Pennsylvania County Health Improvement Program (CHIP) is a community-based, multiple risk factor intervention trial designed to decrease mortality and morbidity from cardiovascular disease in a county (Lycoming) of 118,000 persons in north central Pennsylvania. It seeks this end through reduction of five risk factors: smoking, hypertension, elevated levels of serum cholesterol, obesity, and physical inactivity.

TABLE 7.8.

Summary of the Results of the Community Resource Inventory
In Lycoming and The Reference County in 1980 and 1983

	1980	1983
Lycoming County		
Organizations with blood pressure screening	29	52
Organizations with more extensive programs	21	50
Total organizations with health promotion programs	66	68
Total organizations in county	157	154
Reference County		
Organizations with blood pressure screening	29	22
Organizations with more extensive programs	12	13
Total organizations with health promotion programs	56	32
Total organizations in county	142	126

Programs are delivered through five "channels": the mass media, work sites, the health sector, the schools, and voluntary agencies. Evaluation of the program compares the effects in Lycoming County with those in a reference county on mortality and morbidity from cardiovascular disease, on coronary risk factors, and on health promotion activities, and estimates the costs of these outcomes. After three years of planning, CHIP entered the field in July of 1980. This report describes this planning and the first three years of operations. The first outcome measures are favorable—a doubling of health promotion activities in Lycoming County in the face of a 42% decrease in the reference county.

References

Abrahms, D. B., & Follick, M. J. Behavioral weight loss intervention at the work site: feasibility and maintenance. *Journal of Consulting and Clinical Psychology*, 1983, *51*, 226–233.

American Heart Association. *Heart facts*. Dallas, Texas, 1984.

Andreasen, A. R. *"Power potential" channel strategies in social marketing* (Faculty Working Paper No. 743, College of Commerce and Business Administration). University of Illinois at Urbana-Champaign, February, 1981.

Aravanis, C. The classic risk factors for coronary heart disease: Experience in Europe. *Preventive Medicine*, 1983, *12*, 16–19.

Berchtold, P., Jorgens, V., Finke, C., & Berger, M. Epidemiology of obesity and hypertension. *International Journal of Obesity*, 1981, 5 (Suppl. 1), 1–7.

Blackburn, H. Multifactor preventive trials (MPT) in coronary heart disease. In G. T. Stewart (Ed.), *Trends in epidemiology: Application to health services research and training*. Springfield: Charles C. Thomas, 1972, 212–230.

Brand, R. J., Rosenman, R. H., Sholtz, R. I., & Friedman, M. Multivariate prediction of coronary heart disease in the Western Collaborative Group Study. *Circulation*, 1976, *53*, 348–355.

Brownell, K. D. *Behavior therapy for obesity: A treatment manual*. Unpublished manuscript, University of Pennsylvania, 1979.

Brownell, K. D., Cohen, R. Y., Stunkard, A. J., Felix, M. R. J., & Cooley, N. B. Weight loss competitions at the work site: Impact on weight, morale and cost effectiveness. *Journal of the American Medical Association,* in press.

Brownell, K. D., Kelman, J. H., & Stunkard, A. J. Treatment of obese children with and without their mothers: Changes in weight and blood pressure. *Pediatrics,* 1983, *71,* 515–523.

Brownell, K. D., Stunkard, A. J., & McKeon, P. M. *Weight reduction at the work site: a promise partially fulfilled.* Manuscript submitted for publication.

Caldwell, J. R., Cobb, S., Dowling, M. D., & deSongh, D. The dropout problem in antihypertensive treatment: A pilot study of social and emotional factors influencing a patient's ability to follow antihypertensive treatment. *Journal of Chronic Diseases,* 1970, *22,* 579.

Campbell, D. T., & Stanley, J. C. *Experimental and quasi-experimental designs for research.* Chicago: Rand McNally College Publishing Co, 1963.

Chiang, B. N., Perlman, L. V., & Epstein, F. H. Overweight and hypertension. A review. *Circulation,* 1969, *39,* 403–421.

Coates, T. J., Jeffrey, R. W., & Slinkard, L. A. Heart healthy eating and exercise: Introducing and maintaining changes in health behaviors. *American Journal of Public Health,* 1981, *71,* 15–23.

Coates, T. J., & Perry, C. Multifactor risk reduction with children and adolescents: Taking care of the heart in behavioral group therapy. In D. Upper & S. Ross (Eds.), *Behavioral group therapy.* Champaign, Ill.: Research Press, 1980.

Doll, R., & Peto, R. Mortality in relation to smoking: 20 years observation in male British doctors. *British Medical Journal,* 1976, *2,* 1525–1536.

Engelland, A. L., Alderman, M. H., & Powell, H. B. Blood pressure control in private practice: A case report. *American Journal of Public Health,* 1979, *69,* 25–29.

Epstein, L. H., Wing, R. R., Koeske, R., Andrasik, F., & Ossip, D. J. Child and parent weight loss in family-based behavior modification programs. *Journal of Consulting and Clinical Psychology,* 1981, *49,* 674–685.

Evans, R. I. Developing a social psychological strategy of deterrence. *Preventive Medicine,* 1976, *5,* 122–127.

Farquhar, J. W., Maccoby, N., Wood, P. D., et al. Community education for cardiovascular disease. *Lancet,* 1977, *1,* 1192–1195.

Feinleib, M., & Williams, R. R. Relative risks of myocardial infarction, cardiovascular disease and peripheral vascular disease by type of smoking. In *Proceedings of the Third World Conference on Smoking and Health* (Vol. 1). DHEW Publication (NIH 76-1221), 1975, 245–256.

Felix, M. R. J., Stunkard, A. J., Cohen, R. Y., & Cooley, N. B. A process for establishing health promotion programs at the work site. *Journal of Occupational Medicine,* in press.

Fisher, E. B., Jr., Lowe, M. R., Levenkron, J. C., & Newman, A. Reinforcement and structural support of maintained risk reduction. In R. B. Stewart (Ed.), *Adherence, compliance and generalization in behavioral medicine.* New York: Bruner-Mazel, 1982.

Foreyt, J. P., Scott, L. W., & Gotto, A. M. Weight control and nutrition education programs in occupational settings. *Public Health Reports,* 1980, *95,* 127–139.

Frantz, I. D., Jr., Dawson, E. A., Kuba, K., et al. The Minnesota Coronary Survey: Effect of diet on cardiovascular events and deaths. *Circulation,* 1975, *51,* (Suppl. 2:II-4).

Georgia Heart Association. *Today it's the 3 R's plus HBP: A description of the Heart Association's High Blood Pressure Education Program for the Schools.* Atlanta, Ga.: Georgia Heart Association, 1979.

Greenberg, R., & Saffitz, G. Developing mass education for community health programs: A social marketing approach. *Health Education,* 1982, *21,* 6–9.

Greenberg, R., Wagner, U., & Norman, S. *Program evaluation report: County Health Improvement Program (CHIP).* Prepared by Porter, Novelli, & Associates for the Pennsylvania Department of Health, January 1983.

Haines, C. M., & Ward, G. W. Recent trends in public knowledge, attitudes and reported behavior: High blood pressure. *Public Health Reports,* 1981, *96,* 514–522.

Haynes, S. G., Feinleib, M., & Kannel, W. B. The relationship of psycho-social factors to coronary heart disease in the Framingham Study III. Eight year incidence of coronary heart disease. *American Journal of Epidemiology,* 1980, *3,* 37–58.

Hjermann, I. A randomized primary prevention trial in coronary heart disease: The Oslo Study. *Preventive Medicine,* 1983, *12,* 181–184.

Hubert, H. B., Feinleib, M., McNamara, P. M., & Castelli, W. P. Obesity as an independent risk factor for a cardiovascular disease: A 26-year follow-up of participants in the Framingham Heart Study. *Circulation,* 1983, *67,* 968–977.

Hypertension Detection and Follow-up Program Cooperative Group. Five-year findings of the hypertension detection and follow-up program. I. Reduction in mortality of persons with high blood pressure, including mild hypertension. *Journal of the American Medical Association,* 1979, *242,* 2562–2571. (a)

Hypertension Detection and Follow-up Program Cooperative Group. Five-year findings of the hypertension detection and follow-up program. II. Mortality by race, sex and age. *Journal of the American Medical Association,* 1979, *242,* 2572–2577. (b)

Hypertension Detection and Follow-up Program Cooperative Group. Effects of treatment on mortality of mild hypertension. Five-year findings of the hypertension detection and follow-up program. *New England Journal of Medicine,* 1982, *307,* 976–980.

Keys, A. *Seven countries. A multivariate analysis of death and coronary heart disease.* Cambridge: Harvard University Press, 1980.

Koplan, J. P., Powell, K. E., Sikes, R. K., Shirley, R. W., & Campbell, C. C. An epidemiological study of the benefits and risks of running. *Journal of the American Medical Association,* 1982, *248,* 3118–3121.

Kotler, P. *Marketing for non-profit organizations.* Englewood Cliffs: Prentice-Hall, 1975.

Kristein, M. *Smoking and the work place.* Paper presented at the National Interagency Council on Smoking and Health: National Conference. Chicago, Illinois, January 9, 1980.

Lazarsfeld, P., & Merton, R. Mass communication, popular taste and organized social action. In W. Schramm & D. Roberts (Eds.), *The process and effects of mass communication* (2nd ed.). Urbana: University of Illinois, 1971.

Leon, A. S., & Blackburn, H. The relationship of physical activity to coronary heart disease and life expectancy. *Annals of the New York Academy of Sciences,* 1977, *301,* 561–578.

Leventhal, H., Safer, M. A., Cleary, P. D., & Gutmann, M. Cardiovascular risk modification by community-based programs for life-style change: Comments on the Stanford Study. *Journal of Consulting and Clinical Psychology,* 1980, *48,* 150–158.

Lipid Research Clinics Program. The Lipid Research Clinics Coronary Primary Prevention Trial results. I. Reduction in incidence of coronary heart disease. *Journal of the American Medical Association,* 1984, *251,* 351–364. (a)

Lipid Research Clinics Program. The Lipid Research Clinics Coronary Primary Prevention Trial results. II. The relationship of reduction in incidence of coronary heart disease to cholesterol lowering. *Journal of the American Medical Association,* 1984, *251,* 365–374. (b)

McAlister, A. L., Perry, C., & Maccoby, N. Adolescent smoking: Onset and prevention. *Pediatrics,* 1979, *63,* 650–658.

McGill, A. *Proceedings of the National Conference on Health Promotion Programs in Occupational Settings, January 17–19, 1979.* Washington, D.C.: U.S. Government Printing Office, 1979.

Meyer, A. J., Nash, J. D., McAlister, A. L., Maccoby, N., & Farquhar, J. W. Skills training in a cardiovascular health education campaign. *Journal of Consulting and Clinical Psychology,* 1980, *48,* 129–142.

Miettinen, M., Turpeinen, O., Karvonen, M. J., et al. Effect of cholesterol-lowering diet on mortality from coronary heart disease and other causes: A twelve-year clinical trial in men and women. *Lancet,* 1972, *2,* 835–838.

Morris, J. N., Chave, S. P. W., Adam, C., et al. Vigorous exercise in leisure time and incidence of coronary heart disease. *Lancet,* 1973, *1,* 333–339.

Multiple Risk Factor Intervention Trial Research Group, Multiple Risk Factor Intervention Trial. Risk factor changes and mortality results. *Journal of the American Medical Association,* 1982, *248,* 1465–1477.

Newman, I. M. Peer pressure hypothesis for adolescent cigarette smoking. *School Health Review,* 1970, *1,* 15–20.

Norman, S. A., & Stolley, P. D. Results of the 1980 County Health Improvement Program (CHIP) survey of risk factors for heart disease and stroke: Franklin County. Report submitted to the Pennsylvania Department of Health, October, 1982. (a)

Norman, S. A., & Stolley, P. D. Results of the 1980 County Health Improvement Program (CHIP) survey of risk factors for heart disease and stroke: Lycoming County. Report submitted to the Pennsylvania Department of Health, October, 1982. (b)

Paffenberger, R. S., Jr., Hale, W. E., Brand, R. J., et al. Work-energy level, personal characteristics, and fatal heart attack: A birth-cohort effect. *American Journal of Epidemiology,* 1977, *103,* 200–213.

Pooling Project Research Group. Relationship of blood pressure, serum cholesterol, smoking habit, relative weight and ECG abnormalities to incidence of major coronary events: Final report of the Pooling Project. *Journal of Chronic Diseases,* 1978, *31,* 201–306.

Puska, P. The North Karelia Project: Health promotion in action. In L. K. Y. Ng & D. L. Daws (Eds.), *Strategies for public health: Promoting health and preventing disease.* New York: Van Nostrand Reinhold, 1981, 317–335.

Puska, P., Nissinen, A., Salonen, J. T., & Tuomilehto, J. Ten years of the North Karelia project; results with community based prevention of coronary heart disease. *Scandinavian Journal of Social Medicine,* 1983, *11,* 65–68. (a)

Puska, P., Salonen, J. T., Nissinen, A., Tuomilehto, J., Vartiainen, E., Korhonen, H., Tanskanen, A., Ronnquist, P., Koskela, K., & Huttinen, J. Change in risk factors for coronary disease during 10 years of a community intervention programme (North Karelia Project). *British Medical Journal,* 1983, *287,* 1840–1844. (b)

Puska, P., Neittaanmaki, L., & Tuomilehto, J. A survey of local health personnel and decision makers concerning the North Karelia Project: A community program for control of cardiovascular diseases. *Preventive Medicine*, 1981, *10*, 564–576.

Puska, P., Vartiainen, E., Pallonen, U., Salonen, J. T., Poyhia, P., Koskela, K., & McAlister, A. L. *The North Karelia Project: Evaluation of two years intervention on health behavior and cardiovascular risk factors among 13 to 15 year old children.* Unpublished manuscript, 1982.

Review Panel on Coronary-prone Behavior and Coronary Heart Disease. Coronary-prone behavior and coronary heart disease: A critical review. *Circulation*, 1981, *63*, 1199–1215.

Robertson, T. L., Kato, H., Gordon, T., et al. Epidemiologic studies of coronary heart disease and stroke in Japanese men living in Japan, Hawaii and California. Incidence of myocardial infarction. *American Journal of Cardiology*, 1977, *39*, 233–243.

Rogers, E. M., & Shoemaker, F. F. *Communication of innovations.* New York: MacMillan, 1971.

Russell, M. A. H., Wilson, C., Taylor, C., & Baker, C. D. Effect of general practitioners' advice against smoking. *British Medical Journal*, 1979, *2*, 231–235.

Sangor, M. R., & Bichanich, P. Weight reducing program for hospital employees. *Journal of the American Dietetic Association*, 1977, *71*, 531–536.

Shekelle, R. B., Shyrock, A. M., Paul, O., Lepper, M., Stamler, J., et al. Diet, serum cholesterol, and death from coronary heart disease—The Western Electric Study. *New England Journal of Medicine*, 1981, *304*, 65–70.

Stamler, J. Lifestyles, major risk factors, proof and public policy. *Circulation*, 1978, *58*, 3–19.

Stamler, J., Berkson, D. M., & Lindberg, H. A. Risk factors: Their roles in the etiology and pathogenesis of the atherosclerotic diseases. In R. W. Wissler & J. C. Gerr (Eds.), *The pathogenesis of atherosclerosis.* Baltimore: Williams and Wilkins, 1972, 41–119.

Stunkard, A. J., & Brownell, K. D. Worksite treatment for obesity. *American Journal of Psychiatry*, 1980, *137*, 252–254.

Stunkard, A. J., Schechter, C., Taylor, A., Marconi, K., Norman, S., & Stolley, P. D. The Pennsylvania Community Health Intervention Project (CHIP). *Lycoming Medicine*, 1979, *68*, 205–213.

U.S. Department of Health, Education and Welfare, Public Health Service. *Smoking and health: A report of the Advisory Committee to the Surgeon General of the Public Health Service* (PHS Publication No. 1103). Washington, D.C.: U.S. Government Printing Office, 1964.

U.S. Department of Health, Education and Welfare. *Healthy People. The Surgeon General's report on health promotion and disease prevention.* (DHEW Publication No. 79-55071). Washington, D.C.: U.S. Government Printing Office, 1979. (a)

U.S. Department of Health, Education and Welfare, Public Health Service. *Smoking and health: A report of the Surgeon General* (DHEW Publication No. 79-50066). Washington, D.C.: U.S. Government Printing Office, 1979. (b)

U.S. Department of Health and Human Services. National Institutes of Health. National Cancer Institute. *Smoking programs for youth* (NIH Publication No. 80-2156). Washington, D.C.: U.S. Government Printing Office, 1980.

Veterans Administration Cooperative Study Group on Antihypertensive Agents. Effects of treatment on morbidity in hypertension. Results in patients with diastolic blood pressures averaging 115 through 129. *Journal of the American Medical Association*, 1967, *202*, 116–122.

Veterans Administration Cooperative Study Group on Antihypertensive Agents. Effects of treatment on morbidity in hypertension. II. Results in patients with diastolic blood pressure averaging 90 through 114. *Journal of the American Medical Association*, 1970, *213*, 1143–1152.

Wallston, K. A., Wallston, B. S., & DeVellis, R. Development of the multidimensional health locus of control scales. *Health Education Monographs*, 1978, *6*, 160–170.

Wilber, J. A., & Barrow, J. G. Reducing elevated blood pressure. Experience found in a community. *Minnesota Medicine*, 1969, *52*, 1303.

8
Preventive Health Behavior Across the Life Span

Howard Leventhal, Thomas R. Prohaska, and Robert S. Hirschman

Prevention, we are told, is "an idea whose time has come" (Richmond, 1979). Conferences and books abound, and excitement runs high among behavioral scientists and health professionals. Yet, while much is done in the name of prevention, the concept of preventive health itself has borne relatively little scrutiny. As with other concepts, prevention holds different meanings and is perceived in various ways by different people. Previously, we have documented how the meaning of prevention differs according to an individual's profession (Leventhal & Hirschman, 1982). For example, physicians are likely to hold a biomedical view of prevention and to look for technological interventions (e.g., inoculations) to block disease agents and processes. In contrast, public health professionals emphasize environmental means to block exposure and to minimize the spread of disease, and behavioral scientists focus on altering risk behaviors. Concepts of prevention differ according to one's response styles or habits (e.g., athletes versus sitters) and according to one's current and past state of health. Concepts of prevention also vary according to one's stage of development, from childhood through young and middle adulthood to old age. These changes reflect changes in the types of health problems one faces, alterations across the life span, and the diseases to which one is susceptible. Finally, one's view of prevention depends upon one's age cohort, that is, upon where one falls in the life course of the culture. As we shall see, these historical, contextual factors are powerful determinants of both the types of diseases plaguing humanity and our views of prevention.

This chapter has several goals. The first is to review briefly the justifications for a theoretically based behavioral science of prevention in light of the fact that theoretically based investigations have received little encouragement by adherents of the dominant, biomedical perspective. The second goal is to discuss the perceptual and cognitive mechanisms that regulate health and risk behaviors in order to anticipate some of the problems we will face if we try to prevent disease by behavioral interventions. While these interventions have been plagued by the weak-to-moderate intercorrelations among preventive health behaviors, we hope to demonstrate that a perceptual-cognitive control model can enhance our understanding of the relations among these behaviors and, thereby, to suggest more efficacious interventions. The third goal is to examine data on how the factors that control preventive health behaviors change over the life course. We will consider the implications of these models and life-course changes for the practice and science of prevention. We believe that movement toward these goals will help set realistic expectations for the practice of prevention and alert us to the varied challenges of developing a science of prevention.

The Contemporary and Historical Views of Prevention

Our reading of the literature of prevention and our exchanges with biomedical and public health officials suggest that the biomedical view of prevention dominates the research in this area, and that the biomedical scientist's view of the behavioral aspects of prevention is different from that of the behavioral scientist. In fact, it may be that the biomedical view is interfering with the development of a complete science of prevention. To make this point, we will present the biomedical perspective on prevention and compare it to the quite different view of prevention that motivated a flurry of successful prevention activity in the 19th and 20th centuries.

The Biomedical View

Biomedicine is concerned with disturbances in physiological processes that lead to disease. A specific agent, such as a type of bacteria, virus, carcinogen, or hormone, distorts normal physiological processes. This distortion may lead to early symptoms, eventually cause a distinct change in these processes, and generate a set of symptoms or signs that can be given a disease label. This model identifies three types of prevention: *primary,* the goal of which is either to destroy or to inoculate against the agent so as to render it harmless and prevent disruption of normal physiological processes; *secondary* the goal of which is to detect physiological changes very early in the sequence, destroy the agent, and either cure or prevent the further spread of the disease; and *tertiary,* which aims to contain and limit the damage caused by an established disease process (see Fielding, 1978).

For biomedicine, the key to prevention is similar to that for cure: the development of specific medical interventions to destroy or inoculate against a known disease agent. Biomedical research seeks to discover the agents and physiological processes that permit the development of "magic bullets" or interventions to block disease-producing changes. It appears to be widely accepted that ever greater numbers of technological advances will insure us a longer, healthier, and better life at lower financial and psychological cost.

The biomedical view of prevention developed during the last half of the 19th and the first half of the 20th centuries. This period saw rapid and major biomedical progress with advances including Pasteur's germ theory in the 1860s and the development of powerful antibacterial agents from 1940 onward. These advances have been credited with the enormous success in the control of infectious disease. For example, acute infections such as tuberculosis and influenza, which had been top killers in 1900, are now all but eliminated (Dingle, 1973). Substantial decreases in infant mortality rates have also occurred (Braudel, 1979). Insuring early survival for more and more people has produced a major change in the make-up of our population. The proportion of older to younger people has steadily increased; and, as the number of aged has risen, society has had to face new problems, including that of a steady increase in the number of people facing disability and death due to long-term, chronic illness such as cancer and heart disease (Fries, 1980). The biomedical goal for chronic disease has remained unchanged from that for acute illnesses: find the magic bullet to cure and prevent traditional disease. The success of this approach, however, is only partial, and it has failed to provide specific, complete, and inexpensive technologies to cure chronic illnesses. Its contributions to "tertiary prevention" are at best "halfway" or ameliorative (Bennett, 1977). Moreover, these halfway technologies are expensive. Magazines and newspapers are filled with articles on the increasing cost of medical care, which rose from $10 billion in 1950 to $130 billion in the mid-1970s and is projected to exceed $250 billion in the 1980s (Thomas, 1977).

We believe that acceptance of the biomedical approach to chronic illness has led investigators to a limited and dead-end view of the behavioral aspects of prevention. The search for magic bullets focuses prevention research on the problem of compliance. Their view is that when biomedicine discovers how to prevent cancer, the problem for behavioral researchers will be to get people to comply with the prescribed prevention (Leventhal, Zimmerman, & Gutmann, in press). Two types of data make clear the limitations of this approach. First, many people do not avail themselves of remedies even when they are available. Thus, despite the availability of highly effective inoculants, the risk of infectious disease epidemic is rising (Mortimer, 1978; Saward & Sorensen,

1978). Second where sound epidemiological research has identified the multiple risks associated with specific behaviors—including cigarette smoking (Doll & Peto, 1976; Hammond, 1966; U.S. Dept. of Health, Education, and Welfare, 1964; Vogt, 1982), elevated blood pressure and blood lipids (Dawber, Meadors, & Moore, 1951; Truett, Cornfield, & Kannel, 1967), and Type A behavior pattern (Matthews, 1982)—there is a far from universal acceptance that these behaviors are dangerous and only limited public adoption of healthful alternatives. Moreover, medically oriented prevention research has focused most heavily on only one aspect of prevention: does change in a risk factor reduce morbidity and mortality? A second set of questions—how do people come to believe they are personally at risk and how do they go about altering their health and risk behaviors—is often ignored.

The truth of the above assertions can be seen by an examination of preventive studies. For example, VA studies (1967, 1970) have shown that chemotherapy can reduce blood pressure and lead to significant reductions in heart attacks and strokes, even in the case of relatively mild elevations of pressure (VA Cooperative Study Group, 1970). Also several massive programs such as the Multiple Risk Factor Intervention Trial (MRFIT, 1982) and the community-wide interventions in Finland (Puska, Tuomilehto, Salonen, Neittaanmaki, Maki, Virtamo, Nissinen, Koskela, & Takalo, 1979), Belgium (Kornitzer, DeBacker, Dramaix, & Thilly, 1980), and Scotland (McKennell, 1968) have been designed to demonstrate that reductions in risk factors lower morbidity and mortality. Some of these studies were experimental, with high-risk participants randomly assigned to intervention and standard treatment "controls." Unfortunately, there are few instances in which behavioral scientists and behavioral theory have had an important influence on the design or evaluation of these interventions. At best, behavioral science has provided the technologies (e.g., approaches to mass media and behavioral therapies) used to produce behavioral change, while the assessments have focused on the benefits of reduced risk factors on morbidity and mortality. There has seldom been any assessment of how the behavioral technology worked, and the investigations have ignored questions regarding the processes of change, such as: "Were people exposed to the program's messages?" "Did they remember and believe them?" "How did the messages fit prior knowledge and expectations?" "Did people act when persuaded?" "Did they discuss the material with others?" "Did recall, acceptance, or action depend upon discussion with others or membership in groups that supported the prevention program?" When the behavioral role is viewed as simply that of compliance, how compliance is achieved is of little consequence (see Leventhal, Safer, Cleary, & Gutmann, 1980). One consequence of this bias, for example, was the set of results in the

MRFIT (1982) study, in which the amount of behavioral change was inadequate to test the link between risk reduction and morbidity and mortality, leaving the investigators with little data on why they did not create the behavioral change needed to test their biomedical hypothesis.

The Early Reformer's View

It is doubtful whether we can develop a comprehensive science of primary prevention if research is dominated by the biomedical model and if no attention is given to the scientific side of the social psychology of prevention. The history of the conquest of infectious disease illustrates this point. As we said earlier, the impression is that biomedical miracles were responsible for the sharp decline in infectious disease. However, Dubos (1959), McKeown and his collaborators (McKeown, 1976; McKeown, Record, & Turner, 1975), and the McKinlays (McKinlay & McKinlay, 1981) have shown that biomedicine had little to do with the large-scale reductions in morbidity and mortality that have occurred over the last 100 years. For example, the sharp reductions in the incidence of a variety of infectious diseases during the 20th century were achieved *prior* to the development of specific biomedical interventions. The vaccine for measles appeared well after the major drop in its incidence; izoniazid appeared in the 1940s, when tuberculosis had nearly reached its lowest point; sulphonomide appeared in the late 1930s, when the death rate for pneumonia was approaching its low point; and the same was true for influenza, diphtheria, typhoid, and other infectious ills (McKinlay & McKinlay, 1981).

The factors that led to the decline appear to be economic change, social change, and public health measures. Though we may question their precise contribution, there is little doubt that many of these changes were spearheaded by evangelical health reformers of the 19th and early 20th centuries such as Sylvester Graham, the advocate of natural foods, and William Alcott, who advocated moderation in diet, sexual behavior, and dress (Whorton, 1982). Martin Holbrook tried to create an ethical capitalism that would expunge unfitness by means of hygiene rather than by a ruthless natural selection. Lucy Gaston summoned sufficient zeal to lead 14 states to prohibit cigarette smoking (Wallack, 1981), while Horace Fletcher, who at 40 years of age carried 217 pounds on a 5'7" frame, lost enormous amounts of weight and found renewed vigor through careful and thorough mastication of food. Fletcher urged Americans to chew their food to a watery consistency and to monitor their health by assessing the odor, ashlike consistency, and quantity of their stools. Strange and exaggerated though these practices and beliefs may seem, they formed the backbone and public thrust for the founding of a federal-level cabinet position on health, were responsible for the

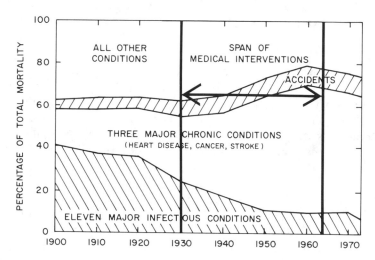

Figure 8.1. Pictorial Representation of the Changing Contribution of Chronic and Infectious Conditions to Total Mortality, with Year Span in which Medical Interventions for 9 Major Infectious Conditions were Introduced.

major downward revision of protein requirements, and led to the formation of organizations that united physicians, physiologists, other scientists, and ministers.

An examination of the work of these health reformers shows that their practices were often partially correlated with regimens that made "physiological" sense and that could lead to substantial reductions in morbidity and mortality. Yet, they failed to make a lasting contribution to the public or biomedical consciousness respecting primary prevention. Indeed, biomedical advances were mistakenly credited for the gains achieved, in large part, by these health reformers and the public health measures they advocated.

The socioeconomic and hygienic changes stimulated by the health reformers represented a major change in the ecology that, in interaction with human biology, led to vast changes in the illness experiences and likely time of death for different cohorts. Life-course changes of this magnitude have undoubtedly altered the conception of life, of aging, of the role of the aged, and of health and illness behaviors by preventing early death and by maintaining a healthy life. The increase in the number of elderly is by itself sufficient to alter attitudes toward the nature and process of aging (Kiesler, 1981). But, though social and demographic changes may be critical determinants of both the biology and the social norms defining the process of aging (Featherman, 1983), the emphasis on media in our culture is also likely to have caused altered conceptions of aging and health. The growth of the mass media has resulted in a broader sharing of ideas about age, illness, the worth of various preventive health behaviors, and the risks of behaviors such as smoking than was shared during the 19th century, when the value of many health promotion ideas was likely to have been restricted to a narrower group of social and religious reformers. In sum, we can see how change in life expectancy and age distribution brought about by the health reformers and changes in the culture interact with each other and influence social conceptions of the aging process and of health.

A Science of Prevention

We need to question whether future generations of prevention activists will ignore our activities as we have ignored those of Graham, Alcott, and Fletcher. The health reformers wrote and cajoled, but did not produce a systematic, theoretical view of the process of behavioral change, of the development of processes of behavioral change through the life span, or of the processes by which change in the environment and behavior can lead to the reduction of morbidity and mortality. These flaws may explain why their work is no longer cited, though their notions have been rediscovered and restated regularly by the health reformers of the 1970s and 1980s.

If we allow epidemiology and biomedicine to define the problems, and if we permit behavioral scientists to function only as technicians, applying ill-tested technologies without evaluating how or why the methods work, then current prevention research and activity will also be short-lived (Leventhal & Cleary, 1979). Indeed, Kirscht (1983) describes current intervention research based on this weak foundation as "more art form than application of scientifically based knowledge" (p. 293).

Preventive Health Behaviors and Lifestyles

If we are to reduce disease and disability by changing lifestyle behaviors, our first step is to define what types of behaviors we wish to change. What are lifestyle behaviors? Are they a coherent class or are they relatively independent of one another? If lifestyle behaviors are highly interrelated, then changes in certain health behaviors may be simply a function of altering other behaviors. If they are largely independent, we may have to consider the arduous task of changing each separately and of focusing on those behaviors most likely to reduce the incidence of chronic illness.

Belloc and Breslow (1972) offer one starting point. In a study of 5,958 Alameda County residents, they found that sleeping 7 to 8 hours nightly, eating breakfast daily, not eating between meals, not smoking, taking no more than one or two alcoholic drinks daily, being physically active, and being no more than 10% overweight resulted in less chronic disease, less disability, and higher energy levels. We would classify some of these behaviors, including eating breakfast daily and sleeping 7 to 8 hours a night, as health promotive; others, such as not smoking and limiting alcohol intake to two drinks daily, we would classify as risk avoidant (see Leventhal & Hirschman, 1982). This division is one possible common-sense classification, but there is also an empirical question about whether we would find two such classes and whether the responses we would classify a priori in each would actually relate to one another. There is also an empirical question regarding exactly which behaviors would be included in each class. For example, might one classify monitoring energy expenditure and feelings of stress a health-promotive behavior (see Mullen & Suls, 1982)? The questions regarding classification of preventive behaviors can be numerous and may, in the long run, contribute little to an understanding of preventive behaviors, particularly from a life-course perspective.

Consistency Among Health and Risk Behaviors

What evidence do we have regarding how preventive health behaviors cluster together and whether there is any consistency among them? Langlie (1977, 1979) assessed 11 different types of health and risk behaviors. In a 14-page questionnaire mailed to 617 randomly sampled adult respondents in Rockford, Illinois, from which she obtained 383 responses, she distinguished between direct and indirect risks. Four of these behaviors—driving behavior (signals to turn, doesn't speed, etc.), pedestrian behavior, smoking, and personal hygiene (washes hands before touching food, etc.)—she labelled *direct risk*-producing behaviors. Seven others—use of seat belts, medical checkups, dental care, immunization, screening exams, exercise, and nutrition—she labelled *indirect risks,* since performing or not performing them can leave one susceptible to harm but does not directly result in danger. The individual scales were interrelated: 60% of the correlations were significant, and the two factors we described above emerged from a factor analysis. But none of the intercorrelations between the scales was of great magnitude: the highest positive correlation was .44, the lowest negative one, −.22. The majority of the significant correlations were about .20, and smoking was weakly correlated with the other scales.

Another search for consistency in health-protective behaviors was conducted by Harris and Guten (1979). They asked 842 respondents about 30 different health behaviors and found that 18 of these behaviors clustered in five groups: personal health practices, safety practices, preventive health care, environmental hazard avoidance, and harmful substance avoidance. The magnitude of relationship among these variables was slight, and only 41 of the 435 phi coefficients they computed exceeded .20.

Recent data from our laboratory show a similar picture. Zimmerman (1983) computed Pearson coefficients for scales of eating habits, salts, exercise, and weight; the respondents were 674 insurance company employees. Coefficient alphas for the scales were substantial (.61 to .75), but the interscale correlations never exceeded .23 (good eating habits with low salt use). Low levels of exercise were related both to use of salt (.08) and being overweight (.19). The three behaviors (exercise, reduced salt use, and proper eating habits) had been recommended to these respondents in a hypertension screening program conducted nine months earlier, so one might have expected somewhat stronger associations between them.

In another large-scale study of hypertensives, Steele, Gutmann, Leventhal, and Easterling (1983) assessed 11 different health practices recommended to 250 patients to control their high blood pressure. When we computed the relationships between these behaviors (eating special foods, quitting smoking, getting more sleep, avoiding some types of food and drink, exercising, relaxing, cutting out salt, and taking antihypertensive medications as prescribed), none of the phi coefficients exceeded .30. Though the majority of the coefficients were positive, statistically significant, and stronger than most of the relationships found in the previously mentioned studies, they were still modest.

The above studies, as others like them (e.g., Steele & McBroom, 1972; Williams & Wechsler, 1972), suggest there are real but small associations between health and risk behaviors. However, the magnitude of these associations may be higher in some subgroups, for example, for respondents pressured to engage in risk reduction (see also Langlie, 1979), although the associations are still only modest in size. These studies also indicate that health and risk behaviors form clusters that can be interpreted as harm-avoidant behaviors (Langlie, 1977) and as risk or deviant behaviors (Jessor & Jessor, 1977). The clusters may also reflect the social pressures felt by specific subgroups of the population. These groupings fit what we would call "common-sense" notions about people and illness: that is, there are people who are risktakers, people who are sensible and abstain from smoke and drink, people who are "health nuts," and people who have a hypochondriacal interest in health. Finally, the intercorrelations between health-protective behaviors apparently remain low throughout the adult life span. In a small-scale survey conducted at various community health fairs, Prohaska, Keller, E. Leventhal, and H. Leventhal (1983) found low intercorrelations for 20 health behaviors in three age ranges: young adults (20–34 years of age, N = 130), middle-aged adults (35–49 years, N = 130), and older adults (50 years and older, N = 130).

What does the low consistency mean? Should we conclude that our measures are poor (Kirscht, 1983)? Would we find substantially more robust associations if we developed better scales or used direct observation of behavior? We doubt there is a problem with our measurements and believe, instead, that the low relationships reflect the true state of the world. Health-promotive and risk behaviors are poorly intercorrelated. Indeed, when we examine the social, psychological, and biological mechanisms controlling health and risk behaviors we will see that weak associations are to be expected. The regularities or order sought by behavioral scientists will be found in the mechanisms controlling health behaviors and not in the surface associations of the behaviors themselves. Furthermore, we may expect little temporal consistency within behaviors across the life span (e.g., Mechanic, 1979), since the mechanisms controlling these behaviors are likely to change with age.

The Mechanisms Determining Health and Risk Behaviors

Are health and risk (lifestyle) behaviors caused by the same factors? Can we identify the factors controlling these behaviors? There are six reasons why it will not be easy to identify these mechanisms:

1. It is likely that different factors control different health and risk behaviors.

2. It is possible that different factors control the same health or risk behavior for different people.

3. The factors controlling a specific health or risk behavior may change over the natural history of the behavior.

4. The factors controlling a specific health or risk behavior may change across the life span of the individual.

5. The natural history of a specific health or risk behavior may differ from one individual to another.

6. Factors and the cultural context change.

In addressing these issues, we will attempt to identify a number of models that underlie the initiation, maintenance, and change of illness behavior. The factors that determine how people decide if they are ill, what they see as the cause and consequences of illness, and how long they believe it takes for illness to develop and be cured are likely to play an important role in determining their adoption of health-promotive acts and elimination of risk behaviors. Moreover, different health and risk behaviors may be related to or controlled by different factors at different points in time for both the culture and the person.

Our developmental view, therefore, is concerned with the processes influencing health and risk behavior with respect to the history of the *acts* themselves, the person, and the social context. Specific examples of this developmental process are the "burnout" or cessation of smoking (Caplan, Cobb, & French, 1975), drinking (Bailey, Haberman, & Alksne, 1965), and narcotics use (Winnick, 1962) with age. These examples suggest that age-related changes are occurring in control mechanisms. We also need to consider how historically determined cohort differences, such as those stimulated by earlier health reform movements, interact with health behavior changes across individuals' life spans.

The basic question facing us is whether we can identify the mechanisms that control health and risk behaviors. This issue is important for two reasons. First, if we can find the determinants of health behaviors, we may be able to encourage and help people develop behaviors that are helpful and eliminate harmful behaviors. Second, we will develop a deeper understanding of human behavior in general and see why health actions are so poorly interrelated.

If the factors controlling behavior are themselves organized, regulatory mechanisms, we can expect to find a limited number of systems involved in the initiation, development, and maintenance of health and risk actions. While the identification of these mechanisms will take time, progress is being made in many laboratories, and we will sketch a few of the findings coming from our group.

Mechanisms Controlling Health Behaviors

It is useful to review briefly the major components of our general-systems model (Leventhal, 1982; Leventhal & Nerenz, 1983) before identifying the mechanisms that control health and illness behavior. This review will provide a framework for understanding our current research perspective in preventive health behaviors across the life span.

The general-systems model that has guided our studies of the ways in which people respond to illness threats can be depicted as a series of steps or stages: (1) the *representation* stage, or how people perceive and think about the disease; (2) the *coping* stage, or what individuals plan and do about the problem; and (3) the *appraisal* stage, or how they evaluate coping outcomes. The *representation* is constructed by combining situational information with memories of both the concrete and abstract features of prior illness episodes. We describe the representation by four attributes: (1) the sensory properties (symptoms) and their label or identification of the illness, (2) the perceived causes of the illness, (3) the potential consequences, and (4) the expected duration of illness. The representation defines the framework for planning and action that we label *coping* and sets the criteria for *appraisal* or evaluation of the coping response, the representation, oneself, or one's resources.

Our findings on patients in chemotherapy treatment for cancer illustrate how the model operates. First, the patients identify cancer both abstractly (they know they have cancer) and concretely (they may be able to feel the tumors or see them in x-rays). Second, the patients know that to cope with the disease and survive, they must stay in treatment for an average of 9 months. In many cases, however, the patient's palpable tumors disappear a few weeks after the start of treatment, leading to an inconsistency between perception (the tumor is gone and I'm cured) and conception (I may still have cancer, and coping [treatment] must continue). These patients become highly distressed because of this inconsistency and may wish to quit treatment (Nerenz, Leventhal, & Love, 1982). Thus, both concrete symptoms and abstract knowledge represent the identity of the disease, and each defines a different time-course for treatment.

This example illustrates the control of distress and illness behavior (coping with treatment) by a cognitive-symptom model of cancer. Clearly, such representations control coping behavior. What is not clear is how these representations develop and change across the life span. To explore this problem, we will present data on four different types of control (behavior regulation) mechanisms apparently operating throughout the life span from early childhood. These mechanisms are: (1) social control, (2) affective-stress control, (3) symptom-based control, and (4) abstract decisional, or what we call conceptual control. We will then examine some specific, age-related changes in the control mechanisms affecting preventive health behaviors.

Social Control.
Studies of health and risk behaviors frequently focus on social or interpersonal determinants. Langlie (1977) found that social class (of family and neighborhood) and social network variables, such as frequency of interaction with friends (rather than relatives) and amount of integration in a social network, accounted for 26% of the variance in her indirect risk behaviors (visiting the doctor, seat belt use, nutrition, etc.) and only 7% of the variance in her direct risk health behaviors (driving carefully, good hygiene, not smoking, and walking carefully). Slesinger (1976) also found a relationship between social integration and preventive action. In addition, Harris and Guten (1979) found that education and income were related to several of their health practice variables. Relationships between socioeconomic status and health practices have been thought to be mediated by learned norms from childhood (Coburn & Pope, 1974) or by social isolation (Bullough, 1972).

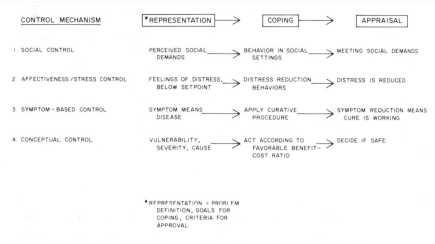

Figure 8.2. Self-Regulation Process for Different Control Mechanisms.

Variables such as education, income, and social networks affect the informational environment and the base of knowledge from which people construct their representations of health threats and develop their alternatives for coping. Thus, the better-educated persons in a supportive social network may perceive Langlie's indirect risk behaviors as effective ways of detecting and preventing known health dangers. Being part of a supportive network can also foster a sense of interdependence, so that one sees one's own self-preservation as important for the ongoing needs of other people.

Studies of the development of smoking behavior also have shown that social factors play a key role in the development of risk behavior (Bewley, Bland, & Harris, 1974). In the first of three studies conducted by our group, individual interviews were conducted with 386 youngsters. We compared those who had smoked a cigarette with those who never smoked and found that those who had tried a cigarette were more likely to have parents and friends who smoked (Hirschman, Leventhal, & Glynn, 1983). Our systems model led us to examine precisely how social factors were represented at the time smoking began. We found that the first cigarette is typically smoked in the company of peers and is often "borrowed" from a parent or older sibling. In some instances, peers made offers and "requests" to try smoking, though very few of the youngsters identified these requests as "pressure." We can see, therefore, that social factors determined the availability of the cigarette and that the pressure to smoke was seen primarily as an act of friendly sharing. Youngsters whose parents and siblings smoked also may have adapted to the sensory properties of the cigarette and, therefore, experienced fewer noxious symptoms in their first try. Having parents and peers who smoked also appeared to erode antismoking attitudes, quite strong in youngsters during the years prior to first tries at smoking.

In a recent study of more than 1,000 youngsters in the third through eighth grades of a rural school system, Mosbach (1983) has found that young people who smoke are likely to do so while drinking coffee with friends: both acts are tightly linked to social behaviors. Therefore, early converts to smoking represent the act as a social behavior and are likely to participate in other social behaviors that might mark them as "prematurely" adult.

Affective-Stress Control.
In addition to examining the social mechanisms that generated the representation or experience of the first cigarette, we also looked at the next steps in the development of the behavior and the types of factors affecting it. We found that only 30% of those who tried one cigarette had tried another, but among youngsters who tried two cigarettes, 77% tried a third. When we examined the time span over which these steps occurred, we found that somewhat over half of the youngsters who tried a second cigarette waited a week to a year or more before doing so, while 43% tried a second within a week, and often within the same day, of the first try.

To see why there were such differences in time between the first and second cigarettes, we ran two regression models: the first compared those who tried a second cigarette within a week to those who did not try a second; the second compared those who did not try a second to those who tried another a week to a year or more after the first. The two models differed with respect to two types of factors: social pressures and the emotional needs of the individual. Those who made a rapid transition were affected by stress: they reported a sense of hopelesness, that is, failing to meet and giving up on trying to meet goals set by parents, teachers, or peers. Removing social factors from the regression for these rapid transition smokers resulted in less reduction of the total amount of variance than removing the stress variable. Just the opposite pattern held for the slow transition smokers: the removal of social factors substantially reduced the explained variance, while removing the stress variables did not.

Apparently, therefore, at least two different pathways exist for the transition from nonsmoker to smoker: a social process and a stress- or anxiety-regulating process. The pathways are not sharply demarcated, since social and stress factors can operate in both, but there is reason to believe they are somewhat distinct. Differences of this sort also appear when adult smokers complete the Reasons-for-Smoking Schedule developed by Ikard, Green, and Horn (1969), and when we look at the conditions that stimulate smoking in regular smokers: some respondents smoke when anxious (Ikard & Tomkins, 1973), others through boredom or when stimulated by the smells and taste of tobacco (Leventhal & Avis, 1976).

The relationship of distress to other types of health and illness behavior was also uncovered in this sample of youngsters. Glynn (1983) developed a six-item scale of illness behaviors (getting upset when in pain or when sick; frequency of sickness, of stuffy nose, and of coughs), which she used together with two items on self-reported health status and an eight-item, health behavior scale (eating breakfast; eating three meals per day; frequency of use of coffee; frequency of use of alcohol; smoking; tooth brushing; regular bedtime; regular exercise). Scores on the illness behavior scale declined with increasing age for male subjects, dropping most sharply at about the sixth grade, but were stable for females. The means on the health behavior scale declined with age for both sexes and, especially, for females. The two scales were also negatively correlated. Both scales were related to indices of distress. The higher the distress (dissatisfaction with goal attainment, conflict with peers, nervous habits, etc.), the higher the level of illness behavior ($r = .30$ in males and $.28$ in females), and the lower the level of health behavior ($-.19$ in males, $-.09$ in females, $-.23$ in whites, and $-.07$ in nonwhites).

Both analyses, of smoking and of illness and health behaviors, suggest that a particular pattern of environmental perceptions, coping, and appraisals (e.g., change of environment, loss of hope about ability to meet important life demands, and conflict with others) arouses distress that disrupts positive health behaviors. There are several ways, however, to look at the association of health and risk behaviors with the regulation of emotion. First, one might speculate that developmental changes lead to increases in distress that youngsters learn to control by using specific behaviors, such as smoking. A somewhat different thesis would argue that the levels of distress are more or less stable and that the change observed in health and risk behaviors represents age-related changes in the behaviors used to regulate distress. For example, youngsters who smoked to cope with distress in the sixth through the tenth grades may have regulated distress by eating candy or drinking cola beverages when younger.

Symptom-Based Control.
Health and risk behaviors appear to be regulated by a third type of mechanism, one in which bodily sensations or symptoms are monitored and interpreted as signs of illness threats. In this model, the processing or combining of bodily sensations with perceptual and conceptual memo-

ries generates feelings and thoughts (representations) of illness threats, and the various attributes of the representation stimulate coping and set criteria for its appraisal.

The study of cancer patients conducted by Nerenz, Leventhal, and Love (1982) illustrates this approach. An example much closer to the topic of prevention is the study of hypertension conducted by Meyer (1981). Hypertensives are at risk for stroke and a variety of cardiac and kidney complications if their disorder is not controlled. Control can be achieved with medications and, in some cases, by improved health habits such as reducing salt intake, weight loss, smoking cessation, etc. When Meyer asked respondents in his actively treated group (people in uninterrupted treatment for 3 months to 15 years) if they believed that, "People can't tell when their blood pressure is elevated," 80% of the respondents agreed that people could not. However, 88% of these respondents also believed that they themselves "could tell." The majority believed they could monitor their own blood pressure by signs such as headache (23%), warmth or a flushing face (21%), dizziness (19%), and nervousness (13%), with a variety of other signs mentioned by the remaining 12% who monitored their own pressure. The numbers were similar for the 65 re-entry patients (people who had returned to treatment after at least a 3-month dropout), but significantly lower for the 65 patients who were new to treatment: 71% of this last group believed they could tell, but that figure rose to 92% at a 6-month follow-up interview.

The participants in this study not only believed they could tell when their blood pressure was elevated, but also altered their treatment on the basis of these beliefs. Thus, there was significantly less compliance with medication and significantly poorer control of blood pressure in actively treated patients who felt the treatment did not benefit them or affect their symptoms. Among the newly treated, the percentage of patients dropping out of treatment was higher for those who were symptomatic (43%) than for those who were not (21%), and the difference was greater yet between those who mentioned symptoms to their practitioner on the first visit and those who did not (61% versus 24%). Having symptoms and reporting them to the doctor appear to influence dropping out of treatment.

It is not surprising that people pay attention to symptoms and stay or leave treatment depending on whether treatment makes them feel better or worse. Yet, there is virtually no evidence that symptoms such as headache or a flushed face are related to variation in blood pressure. Meyer reported a correlation of less than .10 between symptoms and blood pressure in his actively treated group. Baumann (1982) took 20 blood pressures, 2 per day for 10 days, of 44 insurance company employees. She measured moods and symptoms and asked subjects to predict whether their blood pressures were low, normal, or high at each blood pressure measurement. Looking at the subjects over time, she found no evidence that people could predict variations in systolic pressure and no evidence that variations in systolic pressure were related to symptoms or mood states. Moods and symptoms, however, did relate to predictions. When people felt symptomatic or in ill humor they assumed their pressure was elevated, even though there was little evidence to support this assumption.

Symptom monitoring in one area may affect preventive health behaviors in other areas. If we feel well, we may worry less about health threats and, therefore, be less vigilant about eating properly, getting enough sleep, or not smoking. When we are symptomatic, however, we may rush to the doctor or attempt to make changes in our lifestyles (Berkanovic, Telesky, & Reeder, 1981). We are then likely to revert to our old ways if the symptoms clear up.

Symptom monitoring may have various effects on different health actions. For example, in a study of 250 hypertensives (Steele et al., 1983), preliminary analyses show that symptom monitoring is related both to missing medication and to trying and successfully quitting smoking. We do not know if these individuals are "compensating" for their missing medication by more rigorous regulation of smoking and other risk behaviors, or whether they notice symptoms when smoking and hence regulate that behavior more tightly than they regulate medication usage. The point is that the very same mechanism may have different effects on two different health actions because the feedback differs for each.

We have also seen evidence that the rules for interpreting symptoms change with age. For example, while it is well known that older individuals *report* more symptoms than younger people (NCHS, 1970), it has not been demonstrated that this greater number of symptoms are actually *associated* with particular illnesses that increase with age, or that this increased reporting of symptoms leads to increased health action among older people. Indeed, Cockerham, Sharp, and Wilcox (1983) found that despite the tendency with age to report symptoms, perceived health status becomes significantly more positive with age, especially for people 60 and over.

Conceptual Control.
The fourth type of control mechanism, control by concepts, represents those cases where commitments to specific beliefs, in contrast to observations of concrete symptoms, feelings of fear, or observations of social demands, control health and risk behaviors. The Health Belief Model is the basis of most research on this type of mechanism. According to this model, people will take protective action if they believe they are vulnerable to a serious health threat, and they will select a protective action they

perceive to be both beneficial (effective in preventing disease) and low in cost (not painful or harmful). In an early and classic study, Hochbaum (1958) found that people who believed they could contract tuberculosis without knowing it or that tuberculosis could be asymptomatic were likely to take a preventive screening x-ray. In a subsequent study of 400 families (200 in each of two cities), Leventhal, Rosenstock, and Hochbaum (1960) found that respondents who believed they were vulnerable to Asian flu were more likely to get a flu shot in the weeks following their initial interview than subjects not holding such beliefs. Other respondents who obtained shots did so because someone they knew was ill with flu.

The above data suggest that abstract health beliefs can promote preventive health behavior. They also show that abstract beliefs are important in the absence of symptomatic control of behavior. In addition, Harris and Guten (1979) found that beliefs in vulnerability to illness predicted preventive health behaviors, but the phi coefficient, while statistically significant, was very small (.01). Langlie's (1977) data are more robust, the health belief variables accounting for 34% of the variance in direct risk behaviors (careless driving, etc.) and 22% of the variance in indirect risk behaviors among "consistent" responders. The important predictors were the low cost of the action, favorable attitudes, and the belief that one can control health outcomes, the last being the single best predictor in the complete and reduced regression equation.

Reviews of studies on the Health Belief Model (Becker & Maiman, 1975; Rosenstock & Kirscht, 1979) reveal that factors concerning health beliefs account for at least some portion of the variance in health behaviors. However, the model apparently works only when the preventive behaviors being studied are voluntary and there is an occasion for action (Kirscht, 1983). Furthermore, the portion of explained variance is usually small and apparently independent of the variation accounted for by symptomatic and social factors. In fact, in a recent, large-scale study, Berkanovic et al. (1981) accounted for far more variance in the decision to seek medical care with symptom-related factors (e.g., disability from symptoms, perceived seriousness of symptoms, and perceived efficacy of care in dealing with the specific symptom) than with social or health belief factors. This finding is consistent with our information-processing model of fear communication and self-regulation, in which concrete sensory and perceptual information has more immediate control over automatized behaviors such as health actions than does abstract conceptual information (see Leventhal, 1970, 1982; Leventhal, Meyer, & Nerenz, 1980).

The belief that one can control health outcomes was a significant determinant of preventive health actions in Langlie's data and has been related to health behaviors in other studies (see Wallston & Wallston, 1982). It is doubtful that general measures of perceived control will do as well in predicting particular health actions as do beliefs specific to the behaviors (see Ajzen & Fishbein, 1977). This latter approach was clearly of value in an analysis of data on hypertensive patients conducted by Steele, Gutmann, Leventhal, and Easterling (1983). We found that patients who believed their blood pressure was elevated because they smoked, were overweight, and had poor diets were much more likely to try to alter these behaviors and were also less likely to miss medication. Believing they could control the cause of the disorder led them to believe they could also control its cure (see also Lau & Hartman, 1983).

A great variety of abstract health beliefs may play a role in the control of health behaviors. (One would hope, however, that the number is finite.) Moreover, one might expect the beliefs to be arranged in some hierarchical order with the most abstract beliefs, such as belief in one's ability to control one's fate and one's health outcomes, acting in conjunction with more specific beliefs about causes of and vulnerability to specific health threats.

Age-Related Changes in Health and Risk Behaviors

Humanity has made steady strides in controlling the environment and in expanding our numbers over the past 700 years (Braudel, 1979). We also have adopted an increasingly rational and scientific view of illness, as seen in the gradual spread of the germ theory of disease (Lilienfeld & Lilienfeld, 1980). We can trace the evolution of these changes, including their advances and setbacks, in our cultural history. Can we also detect changing themes within the individual life span, and can we separate them from those of history? In other words, can we detect age-related changes separate from differences between age groups that reflect the time at which the individuals were born and raised (cohort differences) (Riley, 1979)?

Earlier we mentioned that historical changes may influence health beliefs and health and risk behaviors, and may have lifelong consequences for individuals in a specific cohort. We also mentioned that the factors initiating health and risk behaviors may be different from those that maintain them. The confounding of historical, developmental, and contextual influences poses substantial barriers to understanding changes in health behaviors across the life span using simple longitudinal and cross-sectional methods. If normative, individual change is the focus of study, then sequential strategies designed to disentangle time-of-measurement, cohort, and age effects are the appropriate methodologies for such investigations (Baltes, Reese, & Nesselroade, 1977; Schaie, 1965; Schaie & Baltes, 1975).

We are using two strategies for exploring life-span effects on health and risk behaviors: (1) the examination of changes in health and risk behaviors with age, and (2) the examination of changes in the factors controlling health and risk behaviors with age. Both approaches can be carried out in cross-sectional, longitudinal, or sequential designs. Most of the available data are cross-sectional, and we will have to protect ourselves against false inferences by trying to assess whether differences associated with age are truly reflective of life-span change or, rather, of historical cohort effects.

Little is known about changes in specific health and risk behaviors over a broad portion of the life span, and the available data are not very informative. Fortunately, several investigators have examined differences by age for the seven health and risk behaviors studied by Belloc and Breslow (1972). Although the questions used to assess these behaviors differ from one study to another, we can outline some of the changes that apparently occur between about 8 to 70 years of age.

We begin our discussion with the development of health behaviors in younger children. Glynn (1983) has examined the health and illness behaviors in second to tenth graders in the Milwaukee school system and plans to extend this analysis to twelfth graders in the Milwaukee schools and to 1,000 third through eighth graders in a rural Wisconsin school system. As we mentioned earlier, we have found a gradual and consistent decline in health behaviors from second to tenth grades, the drop being somewhat steeper for females than for males. Much of the change reflects decreased regularity in sleeping and eating patterns, although cigarette smoking as well as consumption of alcoholic beverages and a decline in regular physical activity also contribute to the change.

When we examine adults from 20 to 64 years of age, the pattern is less clear, since few studies find change in these behaviors with advancing age. For example, Wilson and Elinson (1981) analyzed data from the National Survey of Personal Health Practices and Consequences and found, "Age differences in favorable health practices existed, but with no consistent pattern, except for the variable 'eats breakfast almost every day.' There is a marked increase with age for this practice" (p. 220). While Belloc and Breslow (1972) found that more older than younger individuals adopted their seven health habits, this result may have been due less to increased concern with health habits with advancing age than to the increased rate of survival of the individuals who practiced these habits. Longitudinal data by Palmore (1970) support this hypothesis.

In a series of small-scale surveys carried out both in shopping centers and homes, Prohaska, Keller, E. Leventhal, and H. Leventhal (1983) asked their respondents if they were practicing each of 20 health behaviors. We divided our sample of 390 respondents into three age groups—

20 to 34, 35 to 49, and 50 and over—that were first compared on self-rated frequency (1 = never to 5 = always) of performing these behaviors. Nine items showed significant differences, with subjects over 50 years of age claiming they more frequently avoided harmful health habits, tried to breathe clean air and drink pure water, avoided excessive physical exertion, got enough sleep, ate a balanced diet, ate bran or high-fiber foods, avoided salt, and had regular medical check-ups. They were, however, less likely to engage in regular strenuous exercise. These differences were all significant at the .01 level or better but were small in magnitude. Only medical check-ups and strenuous exercise reflected large magnitude differences between age groups.

In the study just described we wanted to see if age differences in the belief that performing these behaviors would prevent particular diseases would account for the age differences found in the health behaviors. We therefore asked the respondents to rate the efficacy of each of the 20 behaviors for preventing one of the following diseases: high blood pressure, heart attack, cold, colon-rectal cancer, lung cancer, and senility. There were virtually no age differences in the perceived effectiveness of the responses, showing that perceived effectiveness does not account for age differences among behaviors. One exception was that, in comparison to younger subjects, respondents over 50 saw regular aerobic or strenuous exercise (an action they were less likely to do) as less effective.

While there were no age differences for perceived effectiveness, there were significant differences by disease. Both old and young repondents saw specific relationships between particular behaviors and the prevention of specific diseases. We defined effectiveness as a rating of 3.5 or higher on a scale of 1 to 5 where 1 meant the individual strongly disagreed that the behavior is effective, and 5 meant the individual strongly agreed. The nine health practices in which we had found age differences in behaviors were seen as effective in preventing the six tested diseases in 44% (23 of 54) of the possible instances (nine items by six diseases). For example, cardiovascular disease (high blood pressure and heart attack) was seen to be preventable by avoiding harmful health habits and avoiding salt. Colon-rectal cancer, on the other hand, was viewed as preventable by eating a bran or a high-fiber diet. Having good health habits was considered effective in general, while no specific health behavior was seen as effective in preventing colds or senility. These relationships appear logical when we consider common-sense representations of diseases and how they might be prevented.

In sum, while older people reported engaging somewhat more often in a variety of health actions, they did not, relative to younger respondents, perceive these actions to be especially effective for the prevention of high blood pressure, heart attack, colds, colon-rectal cancer, lung cancer, and senility. All subjects seemed to link a few particular practices to the prevention of a few specific illnesses, and these associations appeared to reflect culturally accepted biomedical beliefs. To cite some examples, eating a balanced diet was believed to be efficacious in preventing five of the six diseases, with lung cancer being the exception. Respondents viewed having regular medical check-ups as valuable against all diseases with the exception of colds and senility. Lastly, respondents frequently believed that avoiding salt was very effective in preventing high blood pressure and heart attacks. Many of the other ratings were near the neutral point (i.e., in most instances, the respondents did not believe these remaining practices were particularly effective in disease prevention).

We were not disappointed in these results since we had little reason to expect large age differences in healthful behaviors or in the perception that behaviors are effective in preventing specific diseases. What we wanted to see was whether the relationships between beliefs and behavior make sense from a lay point of view. If we define rationality as adherence to commonly accepted cultural practices, we would have to conclude that our respondents were rational. The notions that avoiding salt prevents hypertension and eating fiber prevents colon-rectal cancer are clearly prevalent in the popular literature.

Now that we have discussed age and disease differences among observable health behaviors, we will examine age patterns among emotional-cognitive strategies to cope with stress and illness threats. In the study just described (Prohaska et al., 1983), we also found statistically significant age differences on four items tapping what we would call emotional-cognitive control strategies. Compared to younger respondents, older persons were more likely to say they frequently attempted to avoid anger, anxiety, depression, and emotional stress, and to take things as they came. The mean response for older people was about 3.5 on a scale from 1 (never do) to 5 (always do) for reported action, reflecting a considerable degree of commitment to strategies by the 50 + age group. Scores for the two younger age groups were about a half scale unit lower. Older people also reported more frequently trying to stay alert and active, though this latter effect was small.

Although these emotional and cognitive strategies were not seen as effective ways of preventing colds or lung or colon-rectal cancer, they—particularly avoiding stress, anger, anxiety, and depression—were judged effective in preventing the two cardiovascular diseases (high blood pressure and heart attack) and in avoiding senility. In this latter case, only respondents over 50 years of age judged the three emotional control strategies (avoiding anger, anxiety, and depression; avoiding stress; taking things as they come) effective preventives for senility. Staying alert and active was seen as the most useful measure, but was judged equally so by both older and younger groups.

Controlling emotional states and staying mentally active were believed to be important preventive actions, and these beliefs were significantly more prevalent among our over-50-year-old population. Perceived effectiveness and performance are most closely age-linked, therefore, in this area. These practices focus primarily on cardiovascular illness and senility and were not seen as significant for colds and cancer. Since stress is viewed as an important part of cardiovascular illness (perceived to be more common in older people), our respondents agreed that stress control was effective, and older persons were more likely to try to control it. A similar consensus holds for specific practices such as eating high-fiber foods to prevent colon-rectal cancer and avoiding harmful health habits and salt to prevent cardiovascular disease. Older persons, probably more vulnerable, are also more likely to engage in these actions. We also found that older people placed more value on control of their emotions as a means of avoiding senility, while younger people place more value on vigorous exercise as an effective form of prevention for all diseases with the exception of senility.

We doubt that stronger age differences would have emerged had we used a different set of health and risk behaviors or a different set of illnesses other than the six listed. First, the list of health and risk behaviors was extensive. Second, five of the six illnesses—high blood pressure, heart attack, cold, colon-rectal cancer, and senility—were chosen from a longer list of 20 illnesses, rated on a variety of scales that yielded two factors when analyzed: (1) age-related, serious, incurable, and uncontrollable, and (2) preventable and related to bad health habits. The five varied in preventability (in the order listed above). Senility, heart attack, and colon-rectal cancer were high on the age-related factor, high blood pressure at its zero point. Cold was on the negative side of this factor. In sum, the five were selected to give fair representation to the distribution of diseases along their perceived dimensions. The sixth illness, lung cancer, was added to compensate for subjects' possible lack of familiarity with colon-rectal cancer.

Summary of Age Changes.
From this review of changes in health behaviors, we can see some small but clearly discernible trends. We have seen a decline in health behaviors, particularly decreased regularity in eating and sleeping, but also an increase in new risk behaviors such as smoking and drinking in the youngest children aged 8 to 15, especially in females (Glynn, 1983). At some point during young adulthood, however, this pattern reverses itself, and we can detect small, gradual improvements in some health behaviors. For example, Belloc and Breslow (1972), Prohaska et al.

(1983), and Wilson and Elison (1981) have all found that reported eating habits improve with age. The latter two investigations found that other health behaviors—with the exception of physical exertion—also increase with age. This exception is unfortunate in light of Palmore's (1970) evidence that, of the health behaviors investigated, lack of exercise showed the highest level of association to illness and mortality in the aged. We also noted that cognitive control strategies increase with age.

Age and Mechanisms.

Though we appear to have found some important age-related differences in health and risk behaviors among adults, these differences do not tell us whether different mechanisms (e.g., social, emotional, cognitive-symptom, and cognitive-conceptual ones) are contributing in different degrees to the health and risk behaviors of younger and older respondents. How might the mechanisms controlling health and illness behavior change with age? One possibility is that these changes in the controlling mechanisms are global. For example, emotions and their control may become more important to older people than cognitive controls. Alternatively, there may be changes occurring in more specific components of the behavioral control system, such as in the way illnesses are represented (their perceived causes, consequences, duration, and means of identification), in the ways they are coped with, or in the means of appraisal (see Figure 8.3).

The data already reviewed suggest there is no decline in the use by older persons of a wide range of relevant coping tactics; in most areas, older people appear as or more active than younger persons. One area where older persons seemed to differ from younger persons was in the greater use of control over anger, anxiety, and depression; avoidance of emotional stress; and desire to take things as they come. There is reason to believe this difference reflects a major change in the emotional appraisal of major life events (i.e., as people get older, particularly as they turn 65 and over, they increasingly expect physical life crises and are less angry, ashamed, and distressed by their occurrence). Thus, older persons may feel that controlling their emotional reactions is an effective way to regulate or prevent disease because they have less emotion with which to cope. This possibility was strongly supported in a study conducted by our group, in which over 160 respondents (40 at each age level—20 to 35, 35 to 55, 55 to 75, 75 and over) rated how they would feel if they contracted each of 22 different illnesses (E. Leventhal, in press). The participants indicated they would feel substantially less anger and shame if the diseases occurred late in life, particularly for many of the most severe illnesses such as lung and colon-rectal cancer and senility, as well as for illnesses that might be stigmatized such as alcoholism. Moreover, older respondents reported they would feel less fear at the thought of

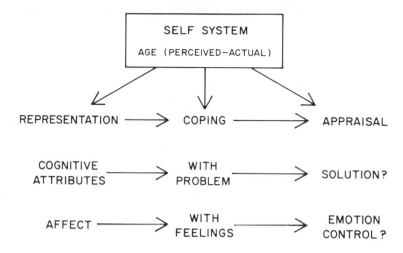

Figure 8.3. How Does Self-Regulation Change Over the Life Span?

contracting these diseases, the only exception to this latter trend being one of the cancers. The age differences in expected emotional response to these diseases were rather substantial, the oldest subjects (over 75) often reported about half the level of anger and shame on the 7-point rating scales than did the younger age groups. A major shift in affective appraisal appears to take place with age, seemingly an important finding for initiating and sustaining various preventive and curative behaviors in older persons.

Data relevant to age differences in affective appraisal are reported in Folkman and Lazarus's (1980) study of coping patterns of middle-aged (ages 45 to 64) adults in response to stressful events of daily living. They found that the use of problem-focused or emotion-focused coping strategies depended on the context and nature of the stressor rather than on the respondent's age. But they also found that older persons reported more health-related episodes with age, and that these episodes may stimulate cognitive change in emotion-focused coping. This discovery is consistent with other findings regarding increased use of cognitive-controlled strategies with age as a function of changes in health (McCrae, 1982; Quayhagen & Quayhagen, 1982).

We have begun to reanalyze a substantial body of data on patient reactions to chemotherapy treatment for cancer and to treatment for hypertension. Our work in cancer includes two cross-sectional interview studies, one with 59 breast cancer cases and the other with 60 lymphoma patients, and a longitudinal study, with approximately 240 subjects interviewed five times over a 7-month period. Data from each of the three studies show substantial age differences in response to treatment. One critical distinction between older and younger patients is that older patients show substantially less emotional distress in response to treatment-induced side effects, such as tiredness and weakness, when treatment has progressed in a normal or expected manner—for example, when patients did not have disseminated disease and when cancerous nodes disappeared gradually (rather than suddenly) with treatment. Older patients also showed far lower levels of conditioned or anticipatory nausea, a phenomenon clearly linked to anxiety during drug injections. These data strongly support the earlier findings of less reported anger and shame in response to cancer by older, healthy individuals.

An initial examination of our data on the response to treatment of 250 hypertensives over a 9-month period also shows changes in the types of factors controlling both medication taking and other risk-reducing (smoke cessation, reducing salt intake) health behaviors (Steele et al., 1983). As mentioned before, subjects who monitored bodily sensations were more likely to miss medications for relatively long periods of time, presumably because they felt well and saw no need for tight adherence to treatment. These subjects were also more likely to try, and succeed in, quitting smoking. The effects of symptom monitoring were strongest, however, for younger patients! Older patients were less likely to monitor symptoms to guide medication taking or risk reduction, and those who did monitor symptoms were not as likely to quit smoking as were the younger persons who monitored themselves.

These findings suggest that, though older people notice as many, if not more, bodily symptoms than do younger people, they make less use of them to guide health-promotive and risk-reducing actions. This difference may in part be due to the difficulty they experience in distinguishing signs of illness from signs of aging. In support of this hypothesis, Prohaska et al. (1983) found significant age trends ($p < .01$) in specific illness-symptoms associations, with older individuals (ages 50+) being less likely to use headache, weakness, and aches and pains as warning signs of illness. Yet, clearly this decreased use of symptoms to guide health actions has not resulted in a decrease in health-promotive actions. Therefore, these health actions must be controlled by alternative mechanisms such as a belief in increased vulnerability to illness or increased acceptance of the idea that chronic illness develops slowly, is caused by poor health habits, and is potentially reversible.

We can see changes both in type and frequency of health and risk behaviors over the life span and alterations in the mechanisms controlling these behaviors. The key periods for change appear to be the adolescent years (12 to 18), when health behavior deteriorates, and the later years (65 and up), when health-promotive behaviors increase and individuals become less affectively aroused both by illness threats and by the use of substances. The decrease in substance use affect is evidenced by the "burning out" of addictive behaviors such as smoking and alcoholism (Caplan et al., 1975). Furthermore, older people are more likely to believe that control of affect is effective in preventing disease, since they experience more symptoms and therefore have more difficulty using symptom-based representations to decide whether illness threats are present and need to be coped with. Additional research is needed to describe these patterns more fully.

Age-Related and Nonaging-Related Change

We have described differences in the levels of reported health behavior for people of different ages and have inferred that they reflect a developmental or aging process. We have noted also that the changes in behavior are apparently related to changes in specific, underlying mechanisms. For example, older subjects were less likely to experience distress due to tiredness and fatigue in cancer chemotherapy, and were also less likely to miss medications or to adopt favorable changes in health actions (quitting smoking, diet, salt reduction, etc.) due to symptom monitoring. The inference that these changes were due to age and not simply to a decrease in symptoms to monitor is based on the knowledge that older people actually experience more bodily symptoms than do younger people (NCHS, 1970) and may ignore the specific, illness implications of symptoms because they are so much a part of the daily experience of aging.

The above interpretation is plausible and appears to eliminate alternatives, such as attributing age group differences to cohort effects. The cohort interpretation seems particularly implausible given that subjects in our different age groups do not differ in their specific nonsymptom beliefs about illnesses (E. Leventhal, in press). There are, however, other alternatives. Possibly, any person, young or old, may ignore symptoms if he or she has a history of frequent symptom experience. Thus, a young person with a history of minor chronic ailments may come to ignore symptoms in much the same way as do our older subjects. The question becomes, therefore, whether the age differences are due to the age of the individual or to the presence of a history of symptom experience (i.e., the age of the symptom control system).

In an exciting interpretation of aging from a life-span perspective, Featherman (1983) has suggested that aging changes can be defined as state changes (changes in frequency of health behaviors or shifts from smoking to nonsmoking status) that can be systematically related to the duration of a prior state (how long one has experienced a symptom or has been a smoker). Although this suggestion is an intriguing heuristic, we would disagree in labelling all such duration-dependent effects as aging. From the perspective of our control systems model, an aging change would involve a state change (health behavior change) that is related to the amount of time a relevant control mechanism (symptom monitoring, anxiety) is activated, only if different durations of activation are required to produce the change at different ages in life. Alterations in both biological and psychological control mechanisms may cause this difference in activation durations to occur. A biological mechanism may change with chronological age and, therefore, produce differential outcomes for a given behavior of a given duration (e.g., more fatigue after running for 20 minutes at age 20 versus at age 60). A psychological mechanism such as attributions according to age stereotypes may also change with chronological age. This belief can lead to an inference that a given state change is due to aging rather than to disease, thereby resulting in different decisions about whether behavioral change is necessary or appropriate, even when the duration in the given state is held constant.

The following example illustrates these concepts. If I experience 4 days fatigue at 20 years of age, attribute the fatigue to illness, rest for a week, and return to a normal routine, and if I repeat this sequence when I become ill at the age of 25, I have developed a type of control system for coping with the fatigue induced by illness. Although this wisdom may come with age, it is not in itself aging. But, if I experience 4 days of fatigue at 50 years of age, attribute the fatigue to illness and the inability to tolerate illness because of my age, rest for a week, and reduce my level of activity subsequent to recovery, the change is an aging change, even though "objective" biological measurement may indicate no greater "need" for minimizing activity at 50 years of age! This difference is precisely what we would expect, however, given the age-related perceptions of the appropriateness of emotional control for preventing illness.

In the next section, we turn to the issue of whether our knowledge of the nature and consistency of health behaviors and life-span changes in behavior can generate ideas for intervention research and intervention programs. To address this issue we must examine both the goals of intervention and the current state of the art from a life-span perspective.

Goals for Intervention Research

Viewing preventive health behavior as a developmental process occurring across the life span suggests that interventions to change health behaviors consider the following issues. If different risk behaviors are initiated and maintained in different ways, it seems logical to match interventions to the specific behavior. If the same behavior is controlled by different factors for different people, it seems reasonable to match interventions to relevant personal variables (e.g., Best, 1975). If the same behavior is controlled by different factors for the same person at different ages, it seems reasonable to attempt to match interventions to the age and age-relevant concerns of the individuals.

The suggestion that different interventions are needed for different steps of the development of health behaviors corresponding to primary, secondary, and tertiary prevention (Kirscht, 1983) is consistent with this life-span approach. For example, if we believe that the onset of smoking is due to social pressures, primary prevention should focus on social skills training (Flay, d'Avernas, Best, Kersell, & Ryan, 1982). For tertiary prevention, modifying well-established behaviors such as smoking, we must take into account feedback in the biological system, since the individual's bodily responses to the withdrawal of substances are now conditioned to affective responses (see Leventhal & Cleary, 1980).

Interventions must not only consider the factors controlling the behavior, they must also take into account the individual's perception and evaluation of the intervention itself. Are people ready to consider change? Are they prepared to try, ready to act to stop or initiate a response, or are they in the maintenance phase (DiClemente & Prochaska, 1982)? Do individuals' conceptions of an effective intervention match the professional's? Finally, the types of factors that support an intervention may also change with age. At different points in the life span, different factors may determine willingness to consider change, decisions in favor of change, the way change is executed, and how it is maintained. We now turn to the current status of intervention research to see how adequately these concerns have been addressed.

Current Status of Intervention Research

The following 11 points outline the current status of intervention research, findings, and possibilities for incorporating these findings into a life-span perspective.

1. A wide range of intervention strategies, including behavioral modification and mass media programs, have been used to promote health-protective behaviors and to discourage risk behaviors. With few exceptions (Prochaska, Crimi, Lapsanski, Martel, & Reid, 1982), little attention has been given to developmental influences on intervention outcomes. We do not know whether the chronological age, the duration of the poor health habit, the time spent not engaging in positive behaviors, or the stage of the behavior relates to the success of the intervention. Furthermore, some investigators have failed to distinguish two components of success: (a) effecting behavior change, and (b) reducing morbidity and mortality as a function of behavior change.

2. The intensive behavioral strategies appear to achieve reductions in risk behaviors in a very substantial percentage of persons completing these programs (e.g., 50 to 70% or more) (Leventhal & Cleary, 1980;

Lichtenstein & Danaher, 1975; Stunkard, 1977). Little is known about differences between developmental groups (e.g., young vs. old) in successfully completing these programs, or whether these behavioral strategies work best for particular subgroups.

3. Less intense communication strategies appear most effective in changing knowledge and attitudes, but have less impact on behavior (Leventhal, 1968; Leventhal & Cleary, in press; Leventhal, Zimmerman, & Gutmann, in press; Thompson, 1978). Given that affective response to stressors differs by age, there is reason to believe that intensity of communication would not produce the same effect across the life span. We need to examine the role of affect in the relationships between intensity of communication, change in knowledge and attitudes, and health behaviors.

4. No matter what the initial success rate, no program has been able to maintain behavioral changes over long periods of time for most people (Hunt & Matarazzo, 1973; Kirschenbaum & Tomarkin, 1983; Leventhal & Cleary, 1980, in press). The relapse rate for the elimination of risk behaviors such as smoking, excessive alcohol use, and drug use rises steadily during the first 6 to 9 months after program termination, and levels off thereafter with varying percentages (15 to 50%) of long-term success. There are no intervention studies we know of on age differences in relapse rates.

5. Very few treatment strategies have been consistently effective in dealing with the problem of maintaining behavioral change. One possible exception is maintenance skills training (Erickson, Tiffany, Martin, & Baker, 1983; Marlatt & Gordon, 1980). Possibly, behavioral skills training works better for the young, while cognitive skills training works better for adults or for more deeply ingrained health practices.

6. There is evidence suggesting that a far greater percentage of people successfully initiate, complete, and *maintain* risk reduction (e.g., quitting smoking and losing weight) if they do so on their own; long-term success rates of 68% have been reported (Schachter, 1982). The difference between self-directed change and formal intervention programs could reflect differences in sampling, with users whose habit is more ingrained selecting treatment. Another difference might be in the way participants evaluate their competence in controlling their behavior, since intervention programs may reduce individuals' sense of personal control over their own behavior. It is possible that older individuals are particularly prone to lose the sense of competence in maintaining optimal health and to increase their belief that behaviors do not affect health outcomes. This attitude can lead older individuals to adopt the sick role more frequently and to develop an increasing sense of learned helplessness in health matters (Solomon, 1982).

7. Far less is known about interventions to implement health-promotive behaviors (e.g., exercising [Dishman, 1982], eating three meals a day, and achieving normal sleep patterns) than about interventions to foster risk-reducing behaviors (see Leventhal & Hirschman, 1982). If our preliminary findings of increased positive health behaviors with age are supported, it would be worthwhile to use this information to develop and investigate health-promotive interventions targeted for specific age groups.

8. Community-oriented public health programs show far less success than do studies that are "treatment"-oriented (Leventhal, 1968; Thompson, 1978).

9. Recent public health prevention programs have apparently achieved a higher level of success than has been seen in the past. This success is particularly true in the case of smoking prevention programs for schoolchildren (see Flay et al., 1982), but is also valid for a number of community-oriented programs where people are encouraged to persevere in trying different techniques for behavioral change (see Leventhal & Cleary, in press). However, there may be recent historical conditions, such as the availability of more consistent health-promotive information, that have produced a positive change in attitudes and, in turn, account for the better success rates in recent intervention programs. An example might be the improvement in the success rates of antismoking programs following the 1964 Surgeon General's report (see Leventhal & Cleary, 1980; Warner, 1977). The use of sequential strategies in evaluation research and in studies assessing the development of health and risk behaviors in different cohorts would help us separate the sources of variance in behavioral change due to treatment from those due to historical factors.

10. Recent public intervention trials tend to combine every possible known intervention strategy. The obvious limitation to this approach is the failure to ascertain the necessary and sufficient components of a successful intervention (Judd & Kenny, 1981).

11. There has been far less attention in recent research on preparing and motivating people to decide to adopt risk-reduction and health-promotion regimens (e.g., Hirschman & Leventhal, 1983) than on teaching skills for the execution of these regimens. Personal, historical, and developmental influences all play a role in motivating and preparing for change.

These 11 points clearly identify the major problems and current directions of intervention activities: we know how to help people change when they want to change, but are poor at helping them sustain it. We are also less well informed about preparing and motivating people to undertake change, and know less about health promotion than we do about risk reduction. In addition, we are not very certain how people succeed on their own. Also apparent, the current trend in community-wide interventions is toward multicomponent approaches. Finally, the question remains as to whether any of the changes we observe are evidence that our programs are really working, that the culture is changing, or both (i.e., that the programs can trigger change in the currently favorable cultural climate). These life-course issues will be increasingly difficult to investigate without recording changing health attitudes and health behaviors in successive cohorts as one attempts to evaluate each program component. However, we hope that the model described in this chapter provides useful guidelines in the search for life-span trends in health practices and control mechanisms, and, thereby, permits the development of theory and the accumulation of the practical skills so lacking in the 19th-century health reform movement.

Outline of a Strategy for Intervention Programs

We are now ready to describe more fully a strategy for meaningful, life-span-oriented investigations of health behavior interventions. Programs can be carefully designed to target the full range of subgroups and control systems for specific risk and health behaviors. We can identify the causes of success and failure if we are careful to conceptualize each component and to identify and assess its likely effects on thought, feeling, and the process of self-regulation, in addition to assessing outcomes. Understanding can also be enhanced if we include in our studies more than single control conditions. If we cannot control for single variable, we can at least control for sets of variables, for example, for symptom monitoring mechanisms, emotion mechanisms, or mechanisms to enhance the individual's sense of self-control.

As we progress, we can adopt the bootstrapping procedure used in biomedical clinical trials, where current treatments are the base-line control against which new treatments are compared. Studies can also assess impact by chronological age, by stage of health behavior, and by the mechanisms involved to define the contributions of developmental factors. Finally, smaller-scale studies in special populations or in the laboratory can single out specific factors for yet more intensive investigation.

A systematic strategy such as the above can combine the well-understood advantages of experimentation with random assignment and newly developed multivariate techniques, that allow one to develop and test causal models within experimental conditions and to compare the models (i.e., the mediating factors) across experimental conditions. However, this strategy should be adopted in close coordination with both cross-sectional and longitudinal studies that attempt to identify the mechanisms controlling risk and health behavior. For example, there is little virtue in undertaking a large-scale, weight reduction program that targets millions of people if we fail to address psychobiological set-point mechanisms, thereby producing substantial emotional distress, irritability, and cravings for food leading to breakdowns in diet control. Such breakdowns are likely to injure the self-esteem of the individuals participating in such a program.

Components of an Intervention Program

Cognitive behavior therapists (Beck, 1976; Kanfer, 1977; Mahoney, 1974; Meichenbaum, 1975), planners of community intervention programs (Maccoby, Farquhar, Wood, & Alexander, 1977), and designers of smoking prevention programs for schoolchildren (Evans, Smith, & Raines, 1983; Flay et al., 1982) have written at length about the components necessary for successful behavioral interventions, and there is no need to repeat the many excellent suggestions contained in those papers. Instead, we will focus on those issues raised by our review of the findings and models of health and risk behaviors. By giving major attention to the life-span data, we can avoid elaborating on those suggestions that have already been presented in papers from our own laboratory (Leventhal & Hirschman, 1982; Leventhal & Nerenz, 1983; Leventhal, Safer & Panagis, 1983).

Identifying the Target Group and Its Needs.
Interventions must obviously consider the groups to be targeted. Attention must be given to a number of obvious factors, ranging from the risk status of the audience or the relevance of the intervention to the issue (e.g., in designing a dental program, one should determine if dental decay is a problem for the target group [Lund & Kegeles, 1982]), to things such as the intelligibility of the message (Ley, 1979), access to the communication media, and availability of resources for behavioral change.

It is not enough just to consider the demographics or risk status of the audience; one must also consider where individuals may be with respect to the developmental history of the behavior under consideration. For example, both Horn (1977) and Prochaska et al. (1982) have pointed to several phases or steps in the process of smoking cessation. Smokers may be totally unconcerned with the issues of contemplating change, effecting change, trying to maintain change, and coping with setbacks. Unconcerned individuals may need information to become aware of their vulnerability. Those contemplating change may need information to bolster their decisions, including material suggesting how to start the process of change. Individuals attempting to maintain change or to deal with setbacks may need information warning them about threats to abstinence, skills and practice in coping with identified threats, competence training in health behaviors, and preparation to interpret setbacks so as to avoid damage to their sense of self-control (e.g., Hirschman & Leventhal, 1983). The types of defenses and threats to successful movement may differ at each stage. Finally, both the chronological age of the subject and the duration of the behavior may play an interactive role in each of these stages.

Though it is convenient to think of these temporal phases as sequentially arranged, it is very likely that movement through them is bidirectional. It is also likely that the individual represents and deals with these situations differently on subsequent encounters. For example, the second try at quitting smoking may begin with less confidence of a successful outcome than the first. In this respect, the emotional predisposition and extent of past experiences of the individual across the life span affect the outcome of an intervention.

Phases or developmental stages of this sort apply equally to primary prevention. The child who has never smoked may have different reasons for resisting versus trying his or her first cigarette, depending upon age and social context. The decision to try a second, which as we have seen may be a more important decision, may involve factors different from those for the first. Developmental approaches to the initiation of risk and health behaviors are relatively unexplored (see Leventhal & Cleary, 1980; Flay et al., 1982).

Identifying Mechanisms.
Knowledge of the mechanisms involved in the initiation, establishment, maintenance, and elimination of health and risk behaviors is an important step toward successful intervention. Thinking about mechanisms rather than at-risk target groups, phases, or variables has the particular advantage of focusing attention on a complete set of the interacting factors comprising a behavioral control system: that is, how does the individual *represent* the problem, what *coping* resources are brought to bear on the representation, and how are coping and representations *evaluated?* In addition, we must be sensitive to age-related changes, either in the representations that guide behaviors or in the emotional reactions and emotional coping strategies adopted when threatened with illness.

It is important to assess whether interventions cover each of the components in the control system framework. We need to know whether they identify critical cues or threats to health, provide a coping tactic appropriate to the threat, and provide a way of evaluating and sustaining the control system.

The terms we have used to describe these mechanisms—representation, coping, and appraisal—are of special importance since they demand that we find out how individuals represent threat, what coping strategies they perceive or automatically enact to threat perceptions, and how people evaluate success. When filter cigarettes were first introduced, switching from a nonfilter cigarette may have seemed perfectly sensible to the smoker who observed the discoloration of the filter, since it looked as if it was collecting dirty and potentially dangerous material. When individuals dropped a nonfilter for a filter brand, a switch that occurred for virtually all smokers (and made the tobacco companies a fortune), they perceived themselves as *coping* with danger. The power of symptoms to stimulate health actions and the failure to take preventive measures when feeling good are testimonies to the importance of the individual's phenomenology, that is, of perceptual and conceptual constructions that define health dangers and direct health action (see Lazarus & Launier, 1978). The emphasis on the individual's representation of risk and the selection and appraisal of coping strategies contrast with the way health and risk behaviors are dealt with in the framework of the health belief model (Cummings, Becker, & Maile, 1980). The earliest studies from the health belief framework attempted to assess risk perception from the subject's perspective (Hochbaum, 1958; Leventhal et al., 1960), but newer studies are less likely to do so since they use closed scales to measure variables of concern to the experimenter (Cummings, et al., 1980).

Hierarchical Systems.
Our investigations of health and illness behavior have convinced us of the importance of viewing the system controlling health behavior as a set of hierarchically arranged control mechanisms. At the "top" of the system is the volitional regulatory mechanism in which information is represented and evaluated in relation to abstract goals, in which coping plans are formulated over the long term, and where appraisals are laid out for the future as well as the present. Lower in the hierarchy are more "automatic" systems that participate in regulating moment-by-moment behavior. At the very "lowest" levels one might think of physiological regulatory systems that are brought into play both by accidental stimulation and as a consequence of higher level decisions and actions. For example, autonomic activity will be provoked automatically by a near miss with a speeding car and by the decision to risk skydiving (Epstein, 1983). Though there is substantial interest in hierarchical systems (see Carver, 1979; Carver & Scheier, 1981; Powers, 1973; Schwartz, 1979), there are, as yet, relatively little theoretical elaboration and data describing communication between the levels, for example, the ways in which emotion alters decisions or self-monitoring alters emotion (see Leventhal & Mosbach, 1983; Pennebaker, 1982).

The interaction of control systems at different levels is clearly of great significance for altering addictive behaviors such as smoking and alcoholism and for changing behaviors heavily dependent upon internal clocks and set-point mechanisms (e.g., altering sleep patterns, food intake, and weight). Focusing attention on a behavior tends to bring it under the control of a higher order (i.e., under conscious regulative systems) (Cupchik & Leventhal, 1974; Leventhal & Avis, 1976). However, these alterations are typically only short-term. Specifying exactly what one attends to is critical if we are to produce longer-term effects. For example, we can focus on the representation or some component of it, such as its sensory properties (Leventhal & Johnson, 1983), on the coping responses, on the criteria for appraisal, and on the method by which one interprets and deals with the information. The key issue is how to alter the control systems that are currently regulating and sustaining risk behaviors to produce lasting changes that include health-promotive actions within a stable, self-regulatory system. This process will require consideration of the biological, historical, contextual, and developmental factors that may influence these control systems.

Age and the Response to Interventions.
Though there is growing interest in interventions designed to control disease-induced morbidity and to avoid institutionalization, there is little discussion of primary prevention in the elderly. Research on primary prevention of risk behaviors such as smoking and the use of alcohol and other drugs generally focuses on children. In our opinion, this emphasis reflects at least two biases: one, that children are more maleable (Leventhal, 1973) and, second, that it is too late for primary disease prevention in the elderly.

We believe that both these biases merit critical examination. First, the healthy elderly may prove no more difficult to influence than the young, although they may be deterred from primary prevention efforts if they believe it is too late to benefit from them. Older people may no longer be excited by or motivated to stimulate their affect by risk taking or drug use, hence the "burnout" phenomenon for older smokers (Caplan et al., 1975). The strength of emotional cravings sustaining risk behaviors and other internal set-point regulators may weaken with age, and there may be less disruptive feedback with attempts at behavior change. Therefore, changes in the regulatory system at one level (e.g., weakening of automatic emotional cravings) may enhance the possibility for voluntary control. In addition, older people may be less concerned with social pressures and more willing to adopt actions that would embarrass a younger person if they believe these acts would enhance the quality of their remaining years.

Our data strongly suggest, nevertheless, that many interventions will be ignored by older persons because they have come to accept daily aches, pains, and tiredness as signs of age rather than as signs of treatable and removable conditons. Indeed, many of the elderly persons we have interviewed claim they are no longer able to distinguish between the distress of daily life and illness! While many of the changes of aging are indeed irreversible, many of its physically distressing aspects are either treatable, controllable, or at least susceptible to coping. Correcting misperceptions and teaching skills to eliminate, reduce, control, or just live with age and its bodily changes can be of great significance in developing health-promotive behaviors in the elderly. The success of individually directed programs may be highly dependent, however, on the way age and aging are viewed in the culture. Current emphasis on youth may make aging appear depressing and minimize the potential for effective health promotion in both younger and older cohorts. This attitude may demand interventions regarding aging that are broader in scope but more specific in aim than those advocated by the 19th-century health reformers.

Of course, we do not now how many years of life will be gained by health-promotive and treatment activities, but evidence is accumulating in several areas that there are real gains in longevity for patients engaging in health-promotive action (Belloc & Breslow, 1972). Treatment of elderly cancer patients with chemotherapy suggests that treatment of patients over 65, 70, or even 75 may be as beneficial as treatment of younger persons (Carbone, 1982). The data clearly failed to confirm the expectations of many oncologists and other medical practitioners. Though advancing age may temper expectations regarding some activities, clearly we must avoid the pessimism that accepts all age-related illnesses as inevitable and untreatable.

Contextual Factors in Self-Regulation

The final lesson on intervention to be drawn from the life-course perspective is the overriding importance of context. Individuals reside in an environment of family and friends and view themselves in relation to reference groups; people and their social contexts are, in turn, embedded in an institutional and physical ecology. Within an individual, the inward self forms the context for regulatory systems for specific behaviors, and these are hierarchically structured with specific biochemical and cellular control systems at the most basic level. These systems are in active interplay with the higher order social and cultural systems and context.

The picture is more complex, however, for both the individual and the culture are to a greater or lesser degree aware of their past and able to project an image of a future. Actions seemingly as simple as quitting smoking, redesigning one's eating habits, changing work schedules, or returning from illness to health are regulated by, and elicit feedback from mechanisms at each of these levels. It is easier, for example, to quit smoking if the culture is on a health binge and has instituted no-smoking sections in aircraft and restaurants, and if the nonsmoking peer group rewards abstinence and shakes its fists at violations. It is also easier to struggle with exercise and diet when one is a valued member of an intact family that gives meaning to one's daily activities.

Although context is complex, it is part of the system and it is susceptible to assessment and study (Moos, 1974). We can chart the cultural rates of response to smoking over the years and decades. We have statistics on income, quality of housing, number of intact families and solitary persons at different ages, and we can examine the impact of these factors on the way people represent, cope, and appraise health and risk actions.

In sum, if we use a life-span, contextually oriented approach to studying health behaviors, their control mechanisms, and the processes of behavior change, and do so with attention to the biological, psychological, and social determinants of behavior, we can achieve two goals—a science of prevention and a practice of prevention that is powerful and valuable since it will be based on a cumulative wisdom for living long and well.

References

Ajzen, I., & Fishbein, M. Attitude-behavior relations: A theoretical analysis and review of empirical research. *Psychological Bulletin,* 1977, *84,* 888–918.

Bailey, M. D., Haberman, P. W., & Alksne, H. The epidemiology of alcoholism in an urban residential area. *Quarterly Journal of Studies on Alcohol,* 1965, *26,* 19–40.

Baltes, P. B., Reese, H. W., & Nesselroade, J. R. *Life span developmental psychology. Introduction to research methods.* Monterey, Calif.: Brooks/Cole, 1977.

Baumann, L. J. *Psychological and physiological correlates of blood pressure and blood pressure prediction.* Unpublished master's thesis, University of Wisconsin-Madison, 1982.

Beck, A. T. *Cognitive therapy and the emotional disorders.* New York: International Universities Press, 1976.

Becker, M. H., & Maiman, L. A. Sociobehavioral determinants of compliance with health and medical care recommendations. *Medical Care,* 1975, *13,* 10–24.

Belloc, N. B., & Breslow, L. Relationship of physical health status and family practices. *Preventive Medicine,* 1972, *1,* 409–421.

Bennett, I. J., Jr. Technology as a shaping force. In J. H. Knowles (Ed.), *Doing better and feeling worse: Health in the United States.* New York: W. E. Norton, 1977.

Berkanovic, E., Telesky, C., & Reeder, S. Structural and social psychological factors in the decision to seek medical care for symptoms. *Medical Care,* 1981, *19,* 693–709.

Best, J. A. Tailoring smoking withdrawal procedures to personality and motivational differences. *Journal of Consulting and Clinical Psychology,* 1975, *43,* 1–8.

Bewley, B. R., Bland, J. M., & Harris, R. Factors associated with the starting of cigarette smoking by primary school children. *British Journal of Preventive and Social Medicine,* 1974, *28,* 37–44.

Braudel, F. *The structures of everyday life: The limits of the possible.* New York: Harper & Row, 1979.

Bullough, B. Poverty, ethnic identity, and health care. *Journal of Health and Social Behavior,* 1972, *13,* 347–359.

Caplan, R. D., Cobb, S., & French, J. R. P., Jr. Relationships of cessation of smoking with job stress, personality, and social support. *Journal of Applied Psychology,* 1975, *60,* 211–219.

Carbone, P. The elderly cancer patient and cancer therapy—The Eastern Cooperative Group experience. In R. Yancik & E. Leventhal (Chairs), *The spectre of cancer.* Symposium conducted at the 35th annual meeting of the Gerontological Society of America, Boston, November, 1982.

Carver, C. S. A cybernetic model of self-attention processes. *Journal of Personality and Social Psychology,* 1979, *37, 1251–1281.*

Carver, C. S., & Scheier, M. F. *Attention and self-regulation: A control-theory approach to human behavior.* New York: Springer Verlag, 1981.

Coburn, D., & Pope, C. Socioeconomic status and preventive health behavior. *Journal of Health and Social Behavior,* 1974, *15,* 67–78.

Cockerham, W. C., Sharp, K., & Wilcox, J. A. Aging and perceived health status. *Journal of Gerontology,* 1983, *38,* 349–355.

Cummings, K. M., Becker, M. H., & Maile, M. C. Bring the models together: An empirical approach to combining variables used to explain health actions. *Journal of Behavioral Medicine,* 1980, *3,* 123–146.

Cupchik, G. C., & Leventhal, H. Consistency between expressive behavior and the evaluation of humorous stimuli: The role of sex and self-observation. *Journal of Personality and Social Psychology,* 1974, *30,*429–442.

Dawber, T. R., Meadors, G. F., & Moors, F. E. Epidemiological approaches to heart disease: The Framingham study. *American Journal of Public Health,* 1951, *41,* 279–286.

DiClemente, C. C., & Prochaska, J. O. Self-change and therapy change of smoking behavior: A comparison of processes of change in cessation and maintenance. *Addictive Behaviors* 1982, *7,* 133–142.

Dingle, J. H. The ills of man. *Scientific American,* 1973, *229,* 77–84.

Dishman, R. K. Compliance/adherence in health-related exercise. *Health Psychology,* 1982, *3,* 237–267.

Doll, R., & Peto, R. Mortality in relation to smoking: 20 years observation in male British doctors. *British Medical Journal,* 1976, *2,* 1525–1536.

Dubos, R. *Mirage of health: Utopias, progress, and biological change.* New York: Harper, 1959.

Epstein, S. Natural healing process of the mind: Graded stress inoculation as an inherent coping mechanism. In D. Meichenbaum & M. E. Jaremko (Eds.), *Stress reduction and prevention.* New York: Plenum Press, 1983.

Erickson, L. M., Tiffany, S. T., Martin, E., & Baker, T. B. Aversive smoking therapies: A conditioning analysis of therapeutic effectiveness. *Behaviour Research and Therapy,* 1983, *21,* 595–611.

Evans, R. E., Smith, C. K., & Raines, B. E. Deterring cigarette smoking in adolescents: A psycho-socio-behavioral analysis of an intervention strategy. In A. Baum, J. Singer, & S. Taylor (Eds.), *Social psychological aspects of health.* Hillsdale, N.J.: Erlbaum, 1983.

Featherman, D. L. *Aging and development as population process.* Paper presented at the 36th annual meeting of the Gerontological Society of America, San Francisco, November, 1983.

Featherman, D. L. Biograpy, society and history: Individual development as a population process. In A. B. Sorensen, F. Weinert, & L. Sherrod (Eds.), *Human development: Interdisciplinary perspectives,* in press.

Fielding, J. Successes of prevention. *Milbank Memorial Fund Quarterly,* 1978, *56,* 274–302.

Flay, B. R., d'Avernas, J. R., Best, J. A., Kersell, M. W., & Ryan, K. B. Cigarette smoking: Why young people do it and ways of preventing it. In P. Firestone & P. McGrath (Eds.), *Pediatric behavioral medicine.* New York: Springer Verlag, 1982.

Folkman, S., & Lazarus, R. S. An analysis of coping in a middle-aged community sample. *Journal of Health and Social Behavior,* 1980, *21,* 219–239.

Fries, J. F. Aging, natural death, and the compression of morbidity. *The New England Journal of Medicine,* 1980, *303,* 130–135.

Glynn, K. *Juvenile illness behavior: Effect of age, sex, personalty, and distress* Unpublished doctoral dissertation, in progress, University of Wisconsin-Madison, 1983.

Hammond, E. C. Smoking in relation to death rates of one million men and women. In W. Haenszel (Ed.), *Epidemiological approaches to the study of cancer and other chronic diseases* (National Cancer Institute Monograph, no. 19). Washington, D.C.: U.S. Department of Health and Social Services, 1966.

Harris, D. M., & Guten, S. Health-protective behavior: An exploratory study. *Journal of Health and Social Behavior,* 1979, *20,* 17–29.

Hirschman, R. S., & Leventhal, H. The behavioral science of cancer. In S. Kahn, R. Love, C. Sherman, & R. Chakravorty (Eds.), *Concepts in cancer medicine.* New York: Grune and Stratton, 1983.

Hirschman, R., Leventhal, H., & Glynn, K. The development of smoking behavior: Conceptualization and supportive cross-sectional data. Manuscript submitted for publication, 1983.

Hochbaum, G. *Public participation in medical screening programs: A sociopsychological study* (Public Health Service Publication No. 572). Washington, D.C.: Government Printing Office, 1958.

Horn, D. A model for the study of personal choice behavior. *International Journal of Health Education,* 1977, *19,* 3–12.

Hunt, W., & Matarazzo, J. D. Three years later: Recent developments in the experimental modification of smoking behavior. *Journal of Abnormal Psychology,* 1973, *81,* 107–114.

Ikard, F. F., Green, D. E., & Horn, D. A. A scale to differentiate between types of smoking as related to management of affect. *International Journal of the Addictions,* 1969, *4,* 649–659.

Ikard, F. F., & Tomkins, S. The experience of affect as a determinant of smoking behavior: A series of validity studies. *Journal of Abnormal Psychology,* 1973, *81,* 172–181.

Jessor, R., & Jessor, S. C. *Problem behavior and psychosocial development: A longitudinal study of youth.* New York: Academic Press, 1977.

Judd, C. G., & Kenny, D. A. Process analysis: Estimating mediation in treatment evaluations. *Evaluation Review,* 1981, *5,* 602–619.

Kanfer, F. H. The many faces of self-control, or behavior modification changes its focus. In R. B. Stuart (Ed.), *Behavioral self-management: Strategies, techniques, and outcomes.* New York: Brunner-Mazel, 1977.

Kiesler, S. B. The aging population, social trends, and changes of behavior and belief. In S. B. Kiesler, J. N. Morgan, & Y. K. Oppenheimer (Eds.), *Aging: Social change.* New York: Academic Press, 1981.

Kirschenbaum, D. S., & Tomarkin, A. J. On facing the generalization problem: The study of self-regulatory failure. In P. C. Kendall (Ed.), *Advances in cognitive-behavioral research and theory* (Vol. 1). New York: Academic Press, 1983.

Kirscht, J. P. Preventive health behavior: A review of research and issues. *Health Psychology*, 1983, *2*, 277–301.

Kornitzer, M., DeBacker, G., Dramaix, M., & Thilly, C. The Belgian heart disease prevention project. *Circulation*, 1980, *61*, 18–25.

Langlie, J. Social networks, health beliefs, and preventive health behavior. *Journal of Health and Social Behavior*, 1977, *18*, 244–260.

Langlie, J. K. Interrelationships among preventive health behaviors: A test of competing hypotheses. *Public Health Reports*, 1979, *94*, 216–225.

Lau, R. R., & Hartman, K. A. Common sense representations of common illnesses. *Health Psychology*, 1983, *2*, 167–185.

Lazarus, R., & Launier, R. Stress-related transactions between person and environment. In L. A. Pervin & M. Lewis (Eds.), *Perspectives in interactional psychology*. New York: Plenum Press, 1978.

Leventhal, E. Aging and the perception of illness. *Research on Aging*, 1984, *6*, 119–135.

Leventhal, H. Experimental studies of anti-smoking communications. In E. F. Borgatta & R. R. Evans (Eds.), *Smoking, health, and behavior*. Chicago: Aldine, 1968.

Leventhal, H. Findings and theory in the study of fear communications. In L. Berkowitz (Ed.), *Advances in experimental social psychology*. New York: Academic Press, 1970.

Leventhal, H. Changing attitudes and habits to reduce chronic risk factors. *American Journal of Cardiology*, 1973, *31*, 571–580.

Leventhal, H. The integration of emotion and cognition: A view from the perceptual motor theory of emotion. In M. Clarke & S. Fiske (Eds.), *The Seventeenth Annual Carnegie Symposium on Cognition*. Hillsdale, N.J.: Erlbaum, 1982.

Leventhal, H. Behavioral medicine: Psychology in health care. In D. Mechanic (Ed.), *Handbook of health, health care, and health professions*. New York: Free Press, 1982.

Leventhal, H., & Avis, N. Pleasure, addiction, and habit: Factors in verbal report on factors in smoking behavior. *Journal of Abnormal Psychology*, 1976, *85*, 478–488.

Leventhal, H., & Cleary, P. Behavioral modification of risk factors: Technology or science? In M. L. Pollock & D. H. Schmidt (Eds.), *Heart disease and rehabilitation: State of the art*. Boston: Houghton-Mifflin, 1979.

Leventhal, H., & Cleary, P. D. The smoking problem: A review of the research and theory in behavioral risk reduction. *Psychological Bulletin*, 1980, *88*, 370–405.

Leventhal, H., & Cleary, P. Behavioral modification of risk factors: A problem for a bio-socio-psychological science. In M. L. Pollock (Ed.), *Heart disease and rehabilitation*. Boston: Houghton, Mifflin, in press.

Leventhal, H., & Hirschman, R. Social psychology and prevention. In G. S. Sanders & J. Suls (Eds.), *Social psychology of health and illness*. Hillsdale, N.J.: Erlbaum, 1982.

Leventhal, H., & Johnson, J. E. Laboratory and field experimentation: Development of a theory of self-regulation. In R. Leonard & P. Wooldridge (Eds.), *Behavioral science and nursing theory*. St. Louis: Mosby, 1983.

Leventhal, H., Meyer, D., & Nerenz, D. The common-sense representation of illness danger. In S. Rachman (Ed.), *Medical psychology* (Vol. 2). New York: Pergamon, 1980.

Leventhal, H., & Mosbach, P. The perceptual-motor theory of emotion. In J. T. Cacioppo & R. E. Petty (Eds.), *Social psychophysiology*. New York: Guilford Press, 1983.

Leventhal, H., & Nerenz, D. Implications of stress research for the treatment of stress disorders. In D. Meichenbaum & M. Jaremko (Eds.), *Stress reduction and prevention*. New York: Plenum Press, 1983.

Leventhal, H., Rosenstock, I., & Hochbaum, G. Epidemic impact on the general population in two cities. In I. M. Rosenstock, G. M. Hochbaum, H. Leventhal, et al. (Eds.), *The impact of Asian influenza on community life: A study in five cities* (U.S. Public Service Publication No. 766). Washington, D.C.: U.S. Government Printing Office, 1960.

Leventhal, H., Safer, M. A., Cleary, P. D., & Gutmann, M. Cardiovascular risk modification by community-based programs for life-style change: Comments on the Stanford study. *Journal of Consulting and Clinical Psychology*, 1980, *48*, 150–158.

Leventhal, H., Safer, M., & Panagis, F. D. The impact of communications on the self-regulation of health beliefs, decisions, and behaviors. *Health Education Quarterly*, 1983, *10*, 3–29.

Leventhal, H., Zimmerman, R., & Gutmann, M. Compliance: A self-regulation perspective. In D. Gentry (Ed.), *Handbook of behavioral medicine*. New York: Guilford Press, 1984.

Ley, P. The psychology of compliance. In D. J. Oborne, M. M. Gruneberg, & J. R. Eiser (Eds.), *Research in psychology and medicine*. London: Academic Press, 1979.

Lichtenstein, E., & Danaher, B. G. Modification of smoking behavior: A critical analysis of theory, research and practice. In M. Hersen, R. M. Eisler, & P. M. Miller (Eds.), *Progress in behavior modification* (Vol. 3). New York: Academic Press, 1975.

Lilienfeld, A. M., & Lilienfeld, D. E. *Foundations of epidemiology* (2nd ed.). New York: Oxford University Press, 1980.

Lund, A. K., & Kegeles, S. S. Increasing adolescents' acceptance of long-term personal health behavior. *Health Psychology*, 1982, *1*, 27–43.

Maccoby, N., Farquhar, J. W., Wood, P. D., & Alexander, J. Reducing the risk of cardiovascular disease: Effects of a community-based campaign on knowledge and behavior. *Journal of Community Health*, 1977, *3*, 100–114.

Mahoney, M. J. *Cognition and behavior modification*. Cambridge, Mass.: Ballinger, 1974.

Marlatt, G. A., & Gordon, J. R. Determinants of relapse: Implications for the maintenance of behavior change. In P. O. Davidson & S. M. Davidson (Eds.), *Behavioral medicine: Changing health lifestyles*. New York: Brunner-Mazel, 1980.

Matthews, K. A. Psychological perspectives on the Type A behavior pattern. *Psychological Bulletin*, 1982, *91*, 293–323.

McCrae, R. Age differences in the use of coping mechanisms. *Journal of Gerontology*, 1982, *37*, 454–460.

McKennell, A. C. British research into smoking behavior. In E. F. Borgatta & R. R. Evans (Eds.), *Smoking, health, and behavior*. Chicago: Aldine, 1968.

McKeown, T. *The role of medicine: Dream, mirage or nemesis*. London: Nuffield Provincial Hospitals Trust, 1976.

McKeown, T., Record, R. G., & Turner, R. D. An interpretation of the decline of mortality in England and Wales during the twentieth century. *Population Studies*, 1975, *29*, 391–422.

McKinlay, J. B., & McKinlay, S. M. Medical measures and the decline of mortality. In P. Conrad & R. Kern (Eds.), *The sociology of health and illness: Critical perspectives*. New York: St. Martins Press, 1981.

Mechanic, D. The stability of health and illness behavior: Results from a 16-year follow-up. *American Journal of Public Health*, 1979, *69*, 1142–1145.

Meichenbaum, D. Self-instructional methods. In F. H. Kanfer & A. P. Goldstein (Eds.), *Helping people change*. New York: Pergamon, 1975.

Meyer, D. *The effects of patients' representation of high blood pressure on behavior in treatment*. Unpublished doctoral dissertation, University of Wisconsin-Madison, 1981.

Moos, R. H. *Evaluating treatment environments*. New York: John Wiley & Sons, 1974.

Mortimer, E. A. Immunization against infectious diseases. *Science*, 1978, *200*, 902–907.

Mosbach, P. *Peer group influence, smoking behavior, and progression in the use of substances*. Unpublished doctoral dissertation, in progress, University of Wisconsin-Madison, 1983.

Mullen, B., & Suls, J. Know thyself. Stressful life events and the ameliorative effects of private self-consciousness. *Journal of Experimental Social Psychology*, 1982, *18*, 43–55.

Multiple Risk Factor Intervention Trial Research Group. Multiple risk factor intervention trial. Risk factor changes and mortality results. *Journal of the American Medical Association*, 1982, *248*, 1465–1477.

National Center for Health Statistics. *Selected symptoms of psychological distress* (Series 11, no. 37). Washington, D.C.: U.S. Government Printing Office, 1970.

Nerenz, D. R., Leventhal, H., & Love, R. Factors contributing to emotional distress during cancer chemotherapy. *Cancer*, 1982, *5*, 1020–1027.

Palmore, E. Health practices and illness among the aged. *The Gerontologist*, 1970, *1*, 313–316.

Pennebaker, J. *The psychology of physical symptoms*. New York: Springer Verlag, 1982.

Powers, W. T. Feedback: Beyond behaviorism. *Science*, 1973, *170*, 351–356.

Prochaska, J. O., Crimi, P., Lapsanski, D., Martel, L., & Reid, P. Self-change processes, self-efficacy, and self-concept in relapse and maintenance of cessation of smoking. *Psychological Reports*, 1982, *51*, 990–993.

Prohaska, T., Leventhal, E., Leventhal, H., & Keller, M. Health practices and illness cognition in young, middle-aged and elderly adults. *Journal of Gerontology*, in press.

Puska, P., Tuomilehto, J., Salonen, J., Neittaanmaki, L., Maki, C., Virtamo, J., Nissinen, A., Koskela, K., & Takalo, T. Changes in coronary risk factors during comprehensive five-year community programme to control cardiovascular disease (North Karelia Project). *British Medical Journal*, 1979, *2*, 1173–1178.

Quayhagen, M. P., & Quayhagen, M. Coping with conflict. *Research on Aging*, 1982, *4*, 364–377.

Richmond, J. B. *Healthy people: The Surgeon General's report on health promotion and disease prevention*. Washington, D.C.: U.S. Government Printing Office, 1979.

Riley, M. W. *Aging from birth to death*. Washington, D.C.: American Association for the Advancement of Science, 1979.

Rosenstock, I. M., & Kirscht, J. P. Why sick people seek health care. In G. C. Stone, F. Cohen, & N. E. Adler (Eds.), *Health psychology: A handbook*. San Francisco: Jossey-Bass, 1979.

Saward, E., & Sorenson, A. The current emphasis on preventive medicine. *Science*, 1978, *200*, 889–894.

Schachter, S. Recidivism and self-cure of smoking and obesity. *American Psychologist*, 1982, *37*, 436–444.

Schaie, K. W. A general model for the study of developmental problems. *Psychological Bulletin*, 1965, *64*, 92–107.

Schaie, K. W., & Baltes, P. B. On sequential strategies in developmental research and the Schaie-Baltes controversy: Description or explanation? *Human Development*, 1975, *18*, 384–390.

Schwartz, G. The brain as a health system. In G. C. Stone, F. Cohen, & N. E. Adler (Eds.), *Health psychology: A handbook*. San Francisco: Jossey-Bass, 1979.

Slesinger, D. The utilization of preventive medical services by urban black mothers. In D. Mechanic (Ed.), *The growth of bureaucratic medicine: An inquiry into the dynamics of patient behavior and the organization of medical care*. New York: Wiley-Interscience, 1976.

Solomon, K. Social antecedents of learned helplessness in the health care setting. *The Gerontologist*, 1982, *22*, 282–287.

Steele, D. J., Gutmann, M., Leventhal, H., & Easterling, D. *Symptoms and attributions as determinants of health behavior*. Unpublished manuscript, University of Wisconsin-Madison, 1983.

Steele, J. L., & McBroom, W. H. Conceptual and empirical behavior. *Journal of Health and Social Behavior*, 1972, *13*, 382–392.

Stunkard, A. J. Behavioral treatment for obesity: Failure to maintain weight loss. In R. B. Stuart (Ed.), *Behavioral self-control*. New York: Plenum Press, 1977.

Thomas, L. On the science and technology of medicine. In J. H. Knowles (Ed.), *Doing better and feeling worse: Health in the United States*. New York: Norton, 1977.

Thompson, E. L. Smoking education programs, 1960–1976. *American Journal of Public Health*, 1978, *68*, 250–257.

Truett, J., Cornfield, J., & Kannel, W. A multivariate analysis of the risk of coronary heart disease in Framingham. *Journal of Chronic Disorders*, 1967, *20*, 511–524.

U.S. Department of Health, Education, and Welfare, U.S. Public Health Service, Center for Disease Control. *Smoking and health: Report of the advisory committee to the Surgeon General of the Public Health Service* (Publication no. PHS 1103). Washington, D.C.: U.S. Government Printing Office, 1964.

Veterans Administration Cooperative Study Group on Antihypertensive Agents. Effects of treatment on morbidity in hypertension: Results in patients with diastolic blood pressures averaging 115 through 129 mmHg. *Journal of the American Medical Association*, 1967, *202*, 116–122.

Veterans Administration Cooperative Study Group on Antihypertensive Agents. Effects of treatment on morbidity in hypertension: II. Results in patients with diastolic blood pressure averaging 90 through 114 mmHg. *Journal of the American Medical Association*, 1970, *213*, 1143–1152.

Vogt, T. M. Cigarette smoking: History, risks, and behavior change. *International Journal of Mental Health*, 1982, *11*, 6–43.

Wallack, L. M. Mass media campaigns: The odds against finding behavior change. *Health Education Quarterly*, 1981, *8*, 209–260.

Wallston, K., & Wallston, B. Who is responsible for your health? The construct of health locus of control. In G. Sanders & J. Suls (Eds.), *Social psychology of health and illness*. Hillsdale, N.J.: Erlbaum, 1982.

Warner, K. E. The effects of the antismoking campaign on cigarette consumption. *American Journal of Public Health*, 1977, *67*, 645–650.

Whorton, J. C. *Crusaders for fitness: A history of American health reformers*. New York: Consumers Union, 1982.

Williams, A. F., & Wechsler, H. Interrelationships of preventive actions in health and other areas. *Health Service Reports*, 1972, *87*, 969–972.

Wilson, R. W., & Elinson, J. National survey of personal health practices and consequences: Background, conceptual issues, and selected findings. *Public Health Reports*, 1981, *96*, 213–225.

Winnick, C. Maturing out of narcotics addiction. *Bulletin of Narcotics*, 1962, *14*, 1–7.

Zimmerman, R. *Preventive Health attitudes and behaviors: A test of three models*. Unpublished doctoral dissertation, University of Wisconsin-Madison, 1983.

9
Economic Incentives and Health Behavior

Kenneth E. Warner and Hillary A. Murt

Health, or its absence, is a function of five classes of variables: (1) individual behaviors, (2) the physical environment, (3) the social environment, (4) personal health services, and (5) genetics. A large array of diverse tools can be employed to manipulate these variables with the intention of improving health. One important class of tools is incentives, the carrots and sticks that encourage both individuals and organizations to follow certain courses of action believed to influence health. In this paper we examine a venerable subclass of incentives: economic inducements. Through an array of economic mechanisms—taxes, insurance premium differentials, income supplements, and so on—employers, policymakers, and others have striven to alter behaviors and environmental conditions perceived to be deleterious to health.

Interest in economic incentives and health behavior is reflected in both the academic and trade literature on the subject. The latter provides much of the available information on the nature of health behavior incentive programs, particularly in business and industry, while the academic literature is the principal source of assessments of such programs. Some incentive-behavior links have been the subject of both policy and scholarly attention for decades, such as the effect of cigarette price increases on cigarette consumption (Harris, 1982; Laughhunn & Lyon, 1971; Lewit & Coate, 1982; Sackrin, 1962; Warner, 1981a). But some linkages are new and truly experimental, such as a handful of income-enhancement programs tied to specific healthful behaviors (discussed below).

The purpose of this paper is to discuss the results of an exploration of a wide range of economic incentives, reviewing the relevant literature in the context of a systematic consideration of incentives and their intended audience. Toward that end, the next section presents a conceptual discussion of economic health incentives, identifying the various kinds of in-

This paper was originally prepared under the title "Economic Incentives for Health." Portions of this paper are reproduced, with permission, from the *Annual Review of Public Health*, volume 5. © 1984 by Annual Reviews Inc.

centives and examining half a dozen characteristics that define how they work. To structure the ensuing discussion of the literature, we develop a matrix of four types of economic incentives and two loci for their application: within and outside the employment setting. The reason for the latter dimension is that the literature on work place health promotion programs is substantial and growing, with economic incentives playing a role in many programs; however, the literature on health promotion efforts outside the work place is not substantial, although the opportunities for incentives seem roughly similar in number, if not always in kind. The separation of work place and non-work place (which we call "individual") economic health incentives also serves to highlight certain principles underlying the working of incentives.

Following the next section's conceptual treatment of the subject, we review the literature in four sections of the paper, each focusing on one of the four major types of economic incentives. In each case, where possible, we consider several different specific examples of the type of incentive, illustrating diversity within a category, and examine applications of the incentives in both work place and individual settings, with examples related to a wide variety of health behaviors.

Types and Characteristics of Economic Incentives

Table 9.1 presents our matrix of economic incentives for health. Across the top are the four major types or categories of economic incentives: (1) enhancement or reduction of income, (2) changes in the prices of goods or services, (3) changes in other opportunity costs, and (4) regulatory policies that relate to health or health behaviors. The vertical dimension of the matrix is the locus, or intended audience of the incentive,

TABLE 9.1.
Types of Loci of Health-Related Incentives

	Types			
	Direct		Indirect	
Loci	Income enhancement or reduction	Price changes	Changes in other opportunity costs	Regulatory policies
Employment-based: Employer				
Employee				
Nonemployment-based				
(individual)				

divided into employment-based incentive programs and incentives directed at individuals outside the work place. The work place category is divided into two subcategories, employee and employer, reflecting the focal point of the incentive. (Note that it is possible for a single incentive program to have ramifications for both.) In the next four sections we will explain and illustrate each category in detail.

The horizontal dimension of the matrix suggests a few of the characteristics of economic incentives that warrant attention. A first, suggested by the label "Income Enhancement or Reduction," is that incentives can be positive or negative. The literature suggests that rewards work more effectively than punishments (Shepard, 1977). In some cases, the reward-punishment distinction is substantive. For example, an excise tax on cigarettes or alcohol is clearly a disincentive to consumption, while a state's exemption of food from the general sales tax is intended to encourage consumption (or at least not to discourage it). In other instances, the distinction between positive and negative incentives appears to be principally a matter of semantics, though the resultant perception can have important behavioral implications. An example is calling the premium differential for life insurance for the smoker and nonsmoker either a "nonsmoker discount" from the base rate or a "smoker penalty."

A second characteristic of economic incentives is that they can be direct or indirect. Direct incentives are those that directly relate to basic economic variables, such as income, profit, and price, while indirect incentives affect people's economic well-being in a less direct, perhaps less economically "palpable," manner. An employer offering employees a weekly bonus in their paychecks if they do not smoke on the job (Speedcall) is clearly using a direct economic incentive. By contrast, an employer providing employees with exercise facilities and time during the workday to use them is employing an indirect incentive (Barrett & Greene, 1983; Parkinson & Associates, 1982): the ready availability of time and facilities reduces the employees' opportunity costs of getting exercise. Free provision of the facilities also means employees do not have to pay for memberships in commercial health clubs.

A third characteristic, itself a dimension of the matrix, is whether the incentive works through or outside a work setting. The potential of a health promotion program to increase the productivity of the work force and, hence, profitability is an incentive restricted to the work setting (Berry, 1981; Fielding, 1979; Jacobs & Chovil, 1983; Kristein, 1982, 1983). By contrast, an excise tax on cigarettes, established by a governmental unit, is by definition a non-work place incentive. Some incentives can be employed both within and outside the work place. Insurance premium differentials can be tied to the health behaviors of individuals through individual policies, or to collective behaviors through group policies (Chadwick, 1982; Fielding, 1979; Kotz & Fielding, 1980).

A fourth characteristic is the level of coercion associated with the incentive. A small excise tax on alcohol leaves the consumption decision to the individual; in essence, response to the incentive is purely voluntary. The prohibition of selling alcohol to youths under the age of 18, however, combined with strict enforcement and serious penalties, takes compliance from the voluntary to the mandatory realm. (Obviously, an element of choice always remains.) The elements of coercion include the magnitude of the incentive (a substantial excise tax on alcohol might appear to be coercive) and whether response is legally voluntary or required.

The time frame of the incentive constitutes a fifth characteristic. Some positive economic incentives are offered on a once-and-for-all (lump-sum) basis, while others are provided on a periodic basis (Shepard & Pearlman, 1982).

Finally, a sixth characteristic is the level of intention or inadvertence of the incentive-behavior link. An employer's paying for employees' participation in a weight loss program represents a clear case of intending the incentive to affect behavior (Foreyt, Scott, & Gotto, 1980; Jeffery, Wing, & Stunkard, 1976; Shepard & Pearlman, 1982). Insurers' offering premium discounts to preferred risks, by contrast, is commonly motivated by the desire to reflect experience in order to improve the marketing of policies. Whether the discount affects the behavior of prospective clients is unknown, and may not even be of direct concern to the insurers (Kotz & Fielding, 1980). Historically, cigarette excise taxes have not been levied primarily to discourage smoking; rather, these taxes have been viewed as a convenient and effective revenue-raising device. Nevertheless, there is abundant evidence that cigarette price has a significant impact on consumption (Warner, 1981a).

There are undoubtedly several other characteristics that differentiate economic incentives for health. This section has addressed half a dozen characteristics that we believe are important in understanding the nature and workings of incentives. Now we turn to explicit consideration of the literature pertaining to each of the four major categories of incentives identified in Table 9.1.

Income Enhancement or Reduction

Employment-Based

Employer
The literature on work site health promotion programs has burgeoned in recent years (Alderman, Green, & Flynn, 1980; Danaher, 1980; DuPont & Basin, 1980; Fielding, 1979, 1982; Fielding & Breslow, 1983; Foreyt et al., 1980; Jacobs & Chovil, 1983; Kristein, 1982, 1983; Parkinson &

Associates, 1982). Some observers view this growth of interest and activity as suggesting that health promotion programs will be the "benefit of the 1980s"; but surveys indicate that the amount of existant programming at the outset of the decade was not substantial (Fielding & Breslow, 1983; Karson, 1982; NICSH, 1981). Chadwick (1982) observes that most of the publicized activity in health promotion has occurred in the 500 largest manufacturing companies. Even here, he estimates that only 10 to 15% of the companies are involved in health promotion programming (other than routine occupational safety and medical care). Across the spectrum of American companies, Chadwick places the percentage of employees covered by health promotion programming at 2.5 to 5%.

A theme of much of the literature on work place health promotion is that such programming constitutes a sound business investment. Sharply rising payroll costs for health benefits often have been cited in company proposals to increase emphasis on health promotion at the works site (Beck, 1982; Parkinson & Associates, 1982; Wright, 1982). Further, there is a widespread recognition that employees' poor health habits increase corporate costs (Berry, 1981; Berry & Boland, 1977; Brennan, 1982; Cron, 1981; DuPont & Basin, 1980; Fielding, 1979, 1982; Fielding & Breslow, 1983; Kristein, 1983; Walsh, 1982).

Considerations of employee preferences and morale seem to rule out most direct assaults on the cost problem, such as reducing health insurance benefits (Sapolsky, Altman, Greene, & Moore, 1981). Health promotion programs, by contrast, are viewed as a means of concurrently providing an appreciated benefit and potentially reducing health-related costs through improved health. Articles on the subject invariably refer to savings that can be realized in one or more of the following areas: (1) health care, disability, and other insurance; (2) workmen's compensation; (3) absenteeism; (4) productivity; and (5) employee turnover (Barrett & Greene, 1983; Berry, 1981; Conference Board Inc., 1974; Fielding, 1979; Kaplan, 1980, Kotz & Fielding, 1980; Parkinson & Associates, 1982; Shepard, Foster, Stason, Solomon, & McArdle, 1979; Wright, 1982).

In several instances, authors have concluded, or strongly implied, that health promotion programs return a clear net economic benefit to the employer in areas such as smoking cessation (Kristein, 1982; Weis, 1981), treatment and prevention of alcohol and drug abuse (Berry & Boland, 1977; Brennan, 1982; DuPont & Basin, 1980; OTA, U.S. Congress, 1983; Walsh, 1982), hypertension control (Fielding, 1979; Hannon & Graham, 1978; Kristein, 1982), and exercise (Shepard, Corey, Renzland, & Cox, 1982; Shepard, Cox, & Corey, 1981). Implicit in these analyses is the notion that since health promotion can enhance a firm's profitability, it can be sold to firms solely on its inherent, self-interested, economic merits.

A message emerging in the most recent literature, however, is that the profitability of work place health promotion programs is not certain. Indeed, while much lip service is devoted to the claim of productivity gains, for example, the literature offers few explicit discussions of the nature of productivity gains and few attempts actually to measure them. Even if all the relevant data could be collected, analytical complications would arise from phenomena such as the loss of long-term benefits through employee turnover: if health and associated economic benefits occur to a significant degree years after initiation of a health promotion activity, the employer may end up subsidizing other employers who hire "graduates" of the first company's health promotion program (Monheit, 1977). For example, Kristein (1982, 1983), an advocate of the cost-effectiveness of work place smoking cessation, has estimated that a long-term employee turnover rate of less than 10% would be necessary for companies to capture the long-term health cost savings associated with smoking cessation.

To date, attempted studies of the potential of work place health promotion often present such a wide range of estimates as to invite skepticism. For example, on the question of the annual costs of smoking to business, Kristein (1982, 1983) has estimated the figure at $336 to $601 per smoking employee (in 1980 dollars), while Weis (1981) has placed it at $4611 (in 1981 dollars). The superficiality of many of the analyses is illustrated by the fact that Weis entirely overlooked the pension implications of premature deaths associated with smoking.

The implications of positive health behaviors, or their absence, for pension plans are a source of much current debate regarding the profitability question, at least as regards behaviors highly associated with mortality (or its avoidance). More often than not, the pension implications of health promotion activities are ignored in analyses of costs and benefits (Hannon & Graham, 1978; Weis, 1981). The importance of the pension question is emphasized by a debate between Gori (1983) and Gori's critics (e.g., Kristein, 1983). In an analysis of the economic implications through the year 2000 of disease prevention efforts by the Ford Motor Company, Gori concluded that savings in the areas of life and disability insurance and utilization of medical care would be dwarfed by the increased demands on the company's pension fund: precisely because the prevention programs would work, they would prolong lives in their economically nonproductive retirement phase. The implication would be a net outlay of funds as a result of achieving health promotion objectives. Gori and Richter (1978) have previously assessed the nationwide implications of effective health promotion, again concluding that we will have to pay a considerable sum for the desired health benefits. In a recent study of a health promotion effort at the offices of Michigan Blue Cross Blue Shield, Faust (personal communication, 1983) derived a similar conclusion. Each of these studies emphasizes an important consideration—that we should be willing, as a society and as individual employers, to pay something for longer and better lives for our workers (Russell, 1983).

The importance of the pension question is not yet resolved. There are technical flaws in the work by Gori (1983), and Kristein (1983) points to the "Malthusian assumptions" employed in analyses such as that of Gori: the analyses assume that nothing else changes, while, Kristein argues, common sense suggests that work patterns will change, including retirement ages. Recent legislation postponing the Social Security retirement age supports this view. Regardless of the outcome of the debate, as the issue gains increasing prominence in the literature it may become progressively more difficult to "sell" health promotion to employers on its inherent economic merits.

It would be easy to overestimate the importance of this debate. Recent studies cast doubt on the belief that profitability has been an important consideration in businesses' adoption of health programs. In a survey of 69 major firms, Sapolsky, Altman, Greene, and Moore (1981) found that employers view health benefits as highly appreciated by employees and offer them primarily to recruit and retain employees. Newer health benefits—such as prevention programs—were also viewed as popular benefits, especially among professional and middle-class employees who hold values consistent with the promotion of exercise, proper nutrition, and the like (Celarier, 1983).

Clement and Gibbs (1983) support this view in a thoughtful examination of employers' evaluations of health costs and programs intended to address them. Though the authors document the substantial burden of health costs on firms, they conclude that health promotion programs are unlikely to be motivated substantially by expectation of cost savings. The three variables Clement and Gibbs identify as influencing business programming decisions are (1) the visibility of costs (i.e., whether costs are readily found in the firm's accounting information system); (2) the relevance of costs (i.e., whether a decision will have significant cost implications); and (3) the controllability of costs (i.e., whether managerial action is likely to have a significant effect on costs within a defined period of time). For a variety of reasons, including the lagged benefits of many prevention efforts and the inability of business accounting systems to capture productivity and absenteeism effects, Clement and Gibbs do not perceive health promotion programs as being of central economic interest to employers. Like Sapolsky et al. (1981), however, they note the other beneficial implications of health promotion programming: it is perceived as good for employee morale and can enhance corporate image.

In summary, the impression conveyed by the majority of contributions to the work place health promotion literature is that company "income enhancement," in the form of reduced costs and increased profit potential, dominates much of the contemplation of health promotion programming. Several thoughtful investigations of the subject, however, downplay the importance of the economic incentive as a motivator. Appreciation of the true economic potential of work place health promotion remains a goal for the future. Evidence accrued to date is largely conceptual and anecdotal. In the area of employee fitness programs, for example, both Fielding (1982) and Haskell and Blair (1980) have found claims of associated increased productivity and decreased absenteeism to be based more on conjecture than existing data; and, documented changes may result from a "halo" effect or Hawthorne effect as much as from improvements in physical health status (Barrett & Greene, 1983; Fielding, 1982; Haskell & Blair, 1980; Shepard, 1980; Shephard, et al., 1981).

Employee
In the present section, we concentrate on a relatively small subset of work place programs in which employees face direct income incentives for altering some health-related practice. While the literature reveals relatively few such programs, and only a handful of evaluations of them, the existent efforts warrant attention as the most innovative employment-based use of economic incentives to influence health behaviors.

The basic principle behind employee income incentives is simple and straightforward: employees are rewarded or punished economically for defined health-related actions. Incentives can involve cash or in-kind income (e.g., prizes such as vacations or consumer goods). Rewards can be paid periodically or in a single lump sum. Obviously, the size of an incentive can vary dramatically. Finally, realization of a reward (or punishment) can depend on the behavior of an individual employee or a group. Below we will illustrate each of these dimensions.

With the exception of the immediately following and concluding discussion, this section will examine only positive income incentive (reward) programs, which constitute by far the dominant form of incentive programming. The principal exception is the strong income disincentive that adheres to a few specific behaviors in specific occupational settings. The ultimate income sanction is the loss of a job or prohibition from securing a job. In recent years, several fire departments around the country have begun to refuse to employ smokers, based on the greatly increased risk of disability that smoking firefighters experience. Similarly, some employers have made continuing employment of alcohol abusers contingent on their accepting treatment (Kane, 1975).

In the realm of positive cash income incentives, Shepard and Pearlman (1982) have identified 15 smoking cessation, income incentive programs in businesses, with the precise structure of the incentive being unique to each program. Incentive amounts varied from $50 to $1000, with some paid as lump sums at a particular point in the program (e.g., six months after initiation of the program), while others were paid periodically. Illustrative of the latter is one of the few employee incentive programs whose effectiveness has been evaluated: employees at the Speedcall Corporation receive an extra $7 per week if they do not smoke on the job. Within a month of the program's initiation, the percentage of employees smoking on the job fell from 67% to 43%. During a four-year follow-up, the smoking percentage fell as low as 13% and on last assessment rested at 20% (Shepard, 1980). There are, however, serious flaws in the design of the evaluation of this program. For example, it tracks current employees, ignoring changes in the composition of the work force, and it does not adjust for external factors influencing smoking rates. Nevertheless, the study provides suggestive evidence that a periodic cash bonus can alter behavior, and do so in a sustained manner. Danaher (1980), however, has criticized the profusion of income incentive, smoking cessation programs for their failure to concentrate on the formal development of nonsmoking skills.

The apparently continuing success of the Speedcall program is consistent with Shepard and Pearlman's observation that on-going, periodic cash bonuses are more effective than one-time, lump-sum bonuses. In their sample of 15 smoking cessation incentive programs, they found a success rate of 63% for the periodic-payment minority versus a 45% success rate for the lump-sum programs. The difference was not statistically significant, but it was consistent with observations in the psychology literature that repeated reinforcement is superior to one-time reinforcement in sustaining behavior change.

Shepard and Pearlman's review also identified exercise and weight control programs that offered employees financial inducements. Two companies paid employees for exercise according to a predetermined formula (e.g., a given dollar amount per mile run). Three companies rewarded employees financially for weight control, either paying from $4 to $30 per pound lost, with additional bonuses for weight loss maintenance, or rewarding reduced caloric intake and attendance at exercise and weight control programs.

Two income incentive experiments offer insight into the potential of employee health behavior incentive programs. Jeffery, Wing, and Stunkard (1976) compared the effectiveness of three different-sized bonuses

($30, $150, and $300) in inducing weight loss in an overweight popula-
tion. The researchers observed a direct correlation between the size of the
incentive and the amount of weight loss immediately at the end of the
program. Within a year, however, the differences had evaporated, with
all three groups relapsing toward overweight. Maintenance of weight
loss was not rewarded. Fielding (1982) has discussed the use of financial
incentives to sustain weight loss.

Shepard et al. (1979) compared the results of five protocols for treating
high blood pressure (standard care, nurse counseling, home blood pressure checks, peer group meetings, and financial incentives). They found
that payments of $4 to $16 per visit for keeping clinic appointments and
achieving blood pressure goals, supplemented by sweepstakes prizes of
up to $500, proved to be more effective than the nonincentive alterna-
tives. This relatively costly approach to behavior change, however, contributed to the finding that other alternatives were more cost-effective.

Income incentives have also been offered by companies to encourage
employees to reduce their utilization of medical care services. Mobil
Corporation developed a program in which it divided its United States
employees into 10 experience groups and paid an annual bonus to the
groups realizing below average medical expenses. In 1977, the bonuses
totaled $1.4 million, averaging $55 for each employee who benefited
(Fielding, 1979).

Blue Shield of California offers prospective employers a program,
called Health Incentive Plan, through which employees can gain income
if they keep their annual medical expenses below a sum ranging from
$200 to $500. That amount is deposited into an account for each employee, who can draw against it to pay medical bills. At the end of the
year, the employee is entitled to keep whatever has not been spent. The
idea behind the program is that utilization will drop by inducing cost
consciousness in the employees. An evaluation of the impact of the program on service utilization is currently underway (Rodgers, 1983).

In-kind income incentive programs represent an alternative to cash
bonus programs. Of 25 incentive programs reviewed by Shepard and
Pearlman (1982), five distributed prizes and merchandise to employees
who met defined goals in exercise and weight control programs.

Management staff at the General Motors Proving Grounds has introduced an innovative in-kind incentive program to encourage seat belt
use by employees. Employees are encouraged to sign pledge cards on
which they promise to use their belts for a year. Actual usage rates are
monitored on the entrance road to the facility. If the group meets a
prespecified usage goal, a sweepstakes is held with the winners drawn
from among the pledge signers. Initiated in the fall of 1982, belt usage
increased from 45% prior to introduction of the program to 70% over a

period of six weeks, exceeding the group goal of 60%. Sweepstake prizes awarded were a weekend in Toronto, use of a company car for a week, and 15 watches. A second sweepstakes was initiated shortly thereafter, with a goal of 75% usage and a 10-day vacation in Hawaii as the major prize. Pledge cards were signed by 85% of the employees, and over 12 weeks 82% of signers used their seat belts. GM's intention is to monitor usage rates periodically, with no new sweepstakes planned if usage remains high, but a monthly $100 drawing for 80% use is being considered if postprogram rates drop considerably (Wingblad, 1983).

The GM program illustrates the application of a principle that could be applied in more work place incentive programs: when rewards are dependent on attainment of group goals, as opposed to individual ones, success rates may be higher. Though this principle is based on limited evidence in the health promotion field (Fielding, 1982; Jeffery, et al. 1976) the logic is that peer pressure to contribute to the group's success serves as an additional inducement for the individual. Of course, one can question whether that pressure may be unduly intense (Celarier, 1983).

Provision of free medical services can be an in-kind income incentive if the employees' alternative is to pay for the services themselves outside the work place. A common example of on-site care is the detection and treatment of hypertension (Alderman et al., 1980; Berry, 1981; Fielding & Breslow, 1983; Parkinson & Associates, 1982).

As this brief review may suggest, employee incentive programming is too novel for much evaluation to have occurred to date. Evaluations that have been undertaken are far from definitive: the number accomplished is small, they are program-specific and thus subject to the associated idiosyncracies, and evelution methodology has not always been optimal. Nevertheless, the preliminary evidence is supportive of the notion that income incentives can induce behavior change in the work setting. Issues such as the degree of effectiveness relative to alternative approaches and cost-effectiveness remain to be addressed.

In concluding this examination of employee income incentives, we must take note of two significant incentives that do not relate to health promotion programming. One is that the nature of workers' disability programs is such that employees have a major income incentive to establish disability claims: the prospect of early retirement on a pension and/or Social Security. The limited evidence currently available suggests that this incentive has contributed to some dramatic increases in certain categories of disabilities, particularly those apparently most subjective in nature (e.g., chronic back pain). The costs, to both business and governmental units, are substantial (Clement & Gibbs, 1983; Fordyce 1984; Parkinson & Associates, 1982). Disability programs are illustrative of the "moral hazard" problem in insurance, in which the existence of the coverage alters the extent of the behavior covered (Pauly, 1968).

The second income incentive unrelated to health promotion programming, but related to employee health, is the risk premium paid to workers who assume jobs exposing them to health risks. For example, construction workers laboring on a bridge or at the top of a building under construction may receive higher pay than workers performing identical tasks with feet planted firmly on the ground. The income differential is needed to attract workers to the riskier job (or to compensate them for the assumption of risk). Issues surrounding job risks and public policy toward them are discussed by Bailey (1980) and Viscusi (1983).

Individual

Our review of the literature failed to produce any significant examples of income enhancement or reduction incentives for individuals outside the work place. Certain tax policies can be viewed as falling in this category, such as the tax deductibility of a portion of out-of-pocket medical insurance premiums (being eliminated in 1983). However, we prefer to treat this incentive in the next section, as a price change for the consumer. Logically, income incentives are provided through the supplier of incomes, namely employers.

Price Changes

Our individual and collective health consumption and production decisions are affected, often substantially, by the prices of relevant goods and services. In this section of the paper, we explore how prices have been used, both intentionally and inadvertently, to affect health behaviors. Our review will focus on insurance-related prices and tax policy. Because most price incentives act on the individual (outside the work place), we open the section with an examination of the impact of price changes on the health behavior of individuals.

Individual

Insurance
Insurance-related price changes are of two major types: the price of insurance per se (i.e., premiums) and the effect of insurance coverages on the prices consumers pay for health-relevant goods and services. We shall examine in turn the effects of each of these as they pertain to the health behaviors of individuals. At the end of this discussion, we will briefly consider a new social approach to health insurance—hospital reimbursement based on diagnosis-related groups—a major national incentive program to alter the utilization of health care resources.

Risk rating of premiums. Risk rating of insurance policies—tying premiums to actuarially determined risks—is a well-established practice with certain health-related variables. The best example of the phenomenon is the risk rating of life insurance premiums by age and sex categories, a near-universal practice in the issuance of individual life insurance policies. Other factors, such as hypertension, have also been applied to the determination of health and life insurance premiums, increasing them for untreated hypertension and, in some cases, decreasing them for bringing high blood pressure under control (Fielding, 1982).

In recent years, considerable interest has developed in the notion of extending further the principle of risk rating of health and life insurance to include consideration of self-imposed, or modifiable, health risk factors. Notable among these are smoking, alcohol consumption, lack of exercise, untreated hypertension, obesity, and elevated blood cholesterol. Persons judged to be particularly good risks might qualify for "preferred risk" rates 10 to 30% below standard premiums. Several investigators have proposed such risk rating as a method of rewarding individuals leading healthy lifestyles and of encouraging high-risk individuals to alter their deleterious behaviors (Fielding, 1977; Greenwald, 1981; Haggarty, 1977; Stokes, 1983).

Some such risk rating is rapidly becoming the norm. In individual life insurance policies, for example, nonsmoker discounts are commonplace (Fielding, 1979; Kotz & Fielding, 1980). The State Mutual Life Assurance Company of America first introduced a nonsmoker's life insurance policy in 1964 and has monitored claims experience closely since then. They have found that the mortality experience of their smoking policyholders exceeded the standard table rates of 30%, while that of nonsmoking policyholders was close to half the standard table rates (Cowell & Hirst, 1980).

In 1979, State Mutual further differentiated its smoker and nonsmoker policies by increasing the dividends for nonsmoker policies. The combination of pricing and dividend policies results in nonsmoker life insurance averaging 30% less in net cost than that of smokers (Kotz & Fielding, 1980).

The motivation behind nonsmoker discounts appears to be primarily a marketing consideration, a recognition that price discrimination is sound in this area and is desired by a substantial proportion of the population of potential customers. Whether premium differentials affect smoking behavior is unknown. Greenwald (1981) suspects that the financial incentive in such differentials is insufficient in and of itself to motivate people to quit. Nevertheless, he suggests that the symbolic nature of the differential, linking smoking to illness, is potentially quite important.

Several other risk factors are used by individual insurance companies in establishing premium policies. Manhattan Life Insurance Company, for example, offers discounts of 10 to 15% for people who engage in regular physical fitness activities (MLOPDRE, 1979). Unity Mutual Life Insurance Company also discounts its whole life insurance policies, by 8 to 25%, for people who engage in "strenuous activity" (Attention joggers, 1981).

The purported determinants of driving safety are associated with many automobile insurance premium discounts. New York and Arkansas require insurers to offer discounts on liability premiums to individuals who complete an approved drivers training course; in New York, drivers are eligible for a 10% discount (Sullivan, 1981). A few companies offer a premium reduction for medical or personal injury protection coverage for cars equipped with passive restraints (air bags or passive seat belts) (Arnould & Grabowski, 1981). Cigarette smoking is a factor in a handful of automobile insurance premium determinants, since smokers have higher accident rates.

A number of insurance companies are currently considering substantial expansion of risk rating to incorporate modifiable risk factors (Kotz & Fielding, 1980). In the academic health literature, Stokes (1983) has called for such risk rating, arguing that medical care copayment levels could be adjusted in addition to premiums to reflect self-imposed risks. The potential for the individual to decrease premiums and copayments over time by modifying behaviors might serve as a significant inducement in encouraging health promotion.

The notion of categorical risk rating of modifiable risks is not without its drawbacks, however. For one thing, risk rating is the antithesis of risk sharing, a principle in many insurance policies that has an ethical value as well (Donabedian, 1976). Secondly, determination of what constitutes a modifiable risk is not invariably straightforward. Blood pressure is affected by behavior, but much high blood pressure is genetic in origin or, at least, beyond the control of the individual. Serum lipid level also falls into this category. For some people, alteration of smoking or obesity is arguably beyond the ability of the individual. In short, risk rating by modifiable risk factors can have a distinct blame-the-victim flavor (Greenwald, 1981; Pellegrino, 1980; Wikler, 1978a, 1978b). Finally, allowance for periodic (e.g., annual) changes in premiums to reflect changes in risk behaviors might entail an administrative cost that would exceed the actuarial value of reducing risk.

A reading of the trade literature leaves the impression that risk rating is likely to increase, principally as the result of the insurance industry's perception of marketing potential (Kotz & Fielding, 1980). There is also the possibility that risk rating will serve as a force to promote health by affecting behavior either directly, through responses to the financial incentive, or indirectly, through the symbolism created by risk rating. The potential for behavior change will grow as the practice of risk rating grows, for both the financial incentive and symbolism will increase as more behaviors are used in the determination of premiums for more kinds of insurance. Today, however, the potential of risk rating to improve health behavior is only a logical construct. The literature offers virtually no insights based on empirical study of the phenomenon.

Coverage and price: copayments and deductibles. The second way insurance can relate to behavior is in the depth and breadth of coverage. Interest in the economic impacts of coverage extends far beyond the desk of the insurance executive and the blackboard of the academic economist: the major national health policy problem of the day is the high and rising cost of health care. The nature and extent of health coverage are seen as both cause of and potential solution to this problem.

Unlike the poorly understood relationship between risk rating and health behavior, there is a wealth of empirical studies on the impacts of insurance on the utilization of a wide variety of medical services, including ambulatory care (Pauly, 1971; Phelps & Newhouse, 1972; Scitovsky & Snyder, 1972), hospital care (Berki, 1972; Feldstein, 1980; Feldstein, 1979; Weisbrod & Feisler, 1961), dental services (Feldstein, 1973), and mental health services (Goldberg, Krantz, & Locke, 1970; Wells, Manning, Duan, Ware, & Newhouse, 1982). Concern with the utilization-encouraging effect of early-dollar coverage has produced several proposals, dating back well over a decade, for catastrophic coverage national health insurance (Davis, 1975; Feldstein, 1971; Pauly, 1971). The search for an optimal mix of quality care and cost containment through insurance has included one of the largest social science experiments in this country's history: the Rand Health Insurance Study (Newhouse, Manning, Morris, Orr, & Duan, 1981).

A major issue, unresolved to date, is how different patterns of primary care utilization affect health and the later utilization of secondary and tertiary care. Subject to this rather critical limitation in our knowledge, we have learned the following:

1. The predominant form of health insurance coverage, providing substantial in-patient insurance and little coverage of ambulatory care, induces excessive hospitalization relative to outpatient care (Berki, 1972; Feldstein, 1980; Feldstein, 1979; Phelps, 1975). This pattern is evidenced both in direct studies and in the experience of health maintenance organizations (HMOs), which cover both ambulatory and in-patient care fairly completely: HMO patients experience less hospitalization and more ambulatory care than do patients in the conventional, fee-for-service, third-party payment system (Luft, 1981).

2. Changes in ambulatory coverage have a substantial impact on the utilization of ambulatory services. In the Rand Health Insurance Study, researchers found that free care (i.e., no deductibles or copayments)

resulted in 50% greater utilization than care paid for largely out-of-pocket (Newhouse et al., 1981). A similar pattern emerged for ambulatory mental health service utilization (Wells, et al., 1982).

3. In general, we observe greater utilization of preventive care services in HMOs than in the fee-for-service system (Luft, 1981). Some advocates of HMOs argue that this pattern reflects the prevention orientation and ethic of the HMO (Williams, 1971). Luft (1981), however, suggests that coverage is the operative factor: in the HMO, the patient often does not have to pay anything out-of-pocket to receive care, while few conventional insurance plans cover visits for preventive care. Logically, he argues, the system that ought to result in the greatest utilization of preventive services is the fee-for-service system, in which the insured have first-dollar coverage. In such a setting, the patient has no direct economic barrier to seeking services—as in the HMO—and the physician has a positive economic incentive (the fee) to provide the service. The latter is not characteristic of HMOs. Luft's emphasis on effective price to the consumer, rather than the HMO's prevention "ethic," is supported by Scitovsky and Snyder's (1972) finding that the introduction of coinsurance in a prepaid program significantly affected the utilization of preventive services, more than therapeutic care. The more elective, or discretionary, a service is perceived to be (e.g., asymptomatic physical exams are quite discretionary), the more responsive demand will be to price changes.

Interest in using findings such as these to develop high-quality, cost-containing health care packages extends from national and state health policymakers down to insurance companies themselves (Bailey, 1976; Havighurst, 1977), major corporations and unions (Zink, 1978), and small businesses (DiPrete, 1977; Schnert & Tillotson, 1978; Tillotson & Rosala, 1978). Reversing the historic trend toward broader and deeper coverage will not be easy, however. People are generally satisfied, even pleased, with their health insurance coverage and are reluctant to part with any of it (Havighurst, 1977; Sapolsky et al., 1981; Weber, 1979). This attitude is reinforced by tax policies (discussed below), which effectively reduce the price of health insurance coverage and make it a good buy.

Specific insurance coverages may have effects on specific health behaviors, as opposed to general utilization patterns. For example, coverage of treatment for alcoholism seems likely to encourage receipt of professional help, and, to the extent that such assistance can modify behavior, distinct health benefits could be realized (Beauchamp, 1976; Mosher, 1982; Walsh, 1982). Clearly, Stokes' (1983) notion of linking depth of coverage of hospitalization to health behaviors is another illustration. Outside the realm of conventional health insurance, a similar approach has been adopted by State Farm in the area of automobile insurance. State Farm will double the amount payable for certain injuries or death for accident victims who were wearing their seat belts at the time of the accident (SFDBFBU, 1983). Similarly, Fielding (1977) has suggested a reduction in benefits for a driver who had an elevated blood alcohol level at the time of an accident.

Conclusion. The effect of varying payment and coverage mechanisms on health care utilization can be considerable and is well understood, at least qualitatively. Less well understood are the implications for health of varying utilization patterns. Ironically, this situation is reversed in the case of risk rating of certain health behaviors. In that case, we have reasonable knowledge of the health consequences of behavior change, but little appreciation of the behavioral response to the economic incentive.

Diagnosis-related groups. In 1983, the federal government introduced a new method of reimbursing hospitals for care provided to Medicare patients. Known as diagnosis-related groups (DRGs), the method involves reimbursing hospitals a fixed lump sum for a given diagnosis, instead of reimbursing them for their experienced costs. Under DRGs, hospitals will profit if they can manage a case with fewer resources than the average (for which they are reimbursed); by contrast, they will lose money if they consistently provide more intensive care than average. The intent is to encourage hospitals and hospital-based physicians to become more efficient and to conserve on resource consumption (Berki, 1983; Reiss, 1980).

DRGs are directed at the behavior of professionals and institutions, not at individuals as we have defined the term for purposes of this paper. Nevertheless, DRGs are an excellent contemporary example of the use of economic incentives to affect health-related behavior, and decisions made in response to DRGs will directly affect millions of individuals. Both the policy and potential health implications of DRGs are of sufficient importance to warrant this digression from the basic substantive flow of this paper. There seems little doubt that DRGs will alter medical practice; the incentives are simply too strong to be ignored. The two major questions, unanswerable at this time, are how will medical practice be changed and what impact will these changes have on health. One predominant concern is that DRGs will encourage providers to "cut corners" and that the quality of health care will suffer (Iglehart, 1983).

Tax Policy

A variety of tax policies work to encourage or discourage certain consumption behaviors relevant to health. Prominent among these, and the focus of this discussion, are excise taxes and subsidies and tax treatment of health care costs. Because the preceding section examined the price effects of insurance, we open the present section with consideration of how federal income taxation influences the purchase of insurance and out-of-pocket health care expenditures.

Income tax policy. The federal tax system includes several inducements to purchase both health insurance and health care services. Altogether, these inducements have been estimated as costing the federal government $28 billion in lost tax revenues in 1982 (CBOUSC, 1982). An important set of these incentives works through employers' provision of health insurance as a fringe benefit, a subject addressed below under the heading employment-based price changes. Here we are concerned only with the incentives affecting individuals outside the work setting, operating through the personal income tax. These incentives have been the allowance of an itemized deduction of half of out-of-pocket health insurance premiums (up to $150) and the deductibility of medical expenses in excess of a certain percentage of adjusted gross income (AGI). Recent tax law changes have altered both these provisions. The deduction of half of premiums, eliminated effective in 1983, amounted to a reduction in the price of insurance of up to 25% (a maximum 50% tax bracket times 50% of premiums). Out-of-pocket health care expenditures over 3% of AGI were allowed as itemized deductions; the floor is being increased to 5%. This tax subsidy policy has the effect of reducing the effective consumer price by up to 50% for those expenditures exceeding the AGI percentage. In both cases, the effect of the tax provisions has been to reduce substantially the cost of health care to the individual. To the extent that health care utilization is responsive to price, these policies have increased the demand for and utilization of health care beyond what would result in a subsidy-free market. The recent tax law changes should diminish, though not eliminate, the economic incentive to utilize medical care.

One irony of these tax policies is that they have made certain kinds of health care and health insurance less expensive for the affluent, who receive large tax subsidies, than for the poor. In this context, labeling these provisions as "welfare for the rich" does not seem inappropriate (Mosher, 1983). Mosher (1983) points out that the tax provisions subsidize some attempts to improve health behaviors in a regressive fashion. For example, the affluent person will find the cost of a given alcoholism treatment program less expensive than will the poorer alcoholic. In effect, the personal income tax provides more encouragement for the rich taxpayer to seek professional assistance than it does for the poor.

On the other side of this coin, the *absence* of the tax deductibility of certain health-related expenses makes them less attractive than those that are allowed. For example, current tax policy generally does not permit deduction of expenses associated with smoking cessation, weight reduction, or fitness programs. It can be argued, therefore, that tax policy encourages the expensive treatment of illness once it has developed, rather than the inexpensive prevention of illness through health-promoting behavior changes (Brandon, 1982; Davis, 1975).

Excise taxes and subsidies. Excise taxes are imposed on specific goods. Most often, excise taxes have been viewed as revenue-raising devices, though, undoubtedly, many a state legislator has voted for cigarette or alcohol taxes on "moral" grounds, viewing them either as a deterrent to engaging in a specific behavior or as punishment for doing so.

Regardless of the underlying motivation, excise taxes do affect consumption patterns. The most thoroughly studied, health-relevant case is that of cigarette excise taxes. The overall price elasticity of demand for cigarettes—a measure of the responsiveness of demand to price changes—is −0.4 (Lewit & Coate, 1982), meaning that a 10% increase in cigarette price will decrease total cigarette consumption by 4%. Most of this decrease appears to reflect decisions to quit smoking or not to start, rather than decreases in daily consumption by continuing smokers (Lewit & Coate, 1982). For teenagers, the price elasticity of demand has been estimated at −1.4—a 10% price increase implying a 14% quantity decrease—again with the vast majority reflecting smoking participation decisions (Lewit, Coate, & Grossman, 1981).

The implications of these elasticities are indicated in Harris' (1982) estimate that the recent doubling of the federal excise tax, from 8¢ to 16¢ per pack, should result in a 3% decline in the number of adult smokers—or some 1.5 million people—and a 15% decline among teenagers—700,000 teens. Warner (1981) has estimated that a substantial tax hike, of 30¢ over the 1982 rate of 8¢, could decrease adult consumption by 15% and teenage consumption by more than 50%. Though a federal tax increase of this magnitude seems politically unlikely at this time, combinations of the recent federal increase of 8¢ and substantial state tax hikes can come close. In Michigan, for example, a 1982 increase of 10¢ in the state tax (from 11¢) combined with the federal increase should decrease adult consumption by 9% or more and teen consumption by close to a third (authors' calculations).

Figures such as these suggest the tremendous potential of cigarette excise taxes as an incentive to improve health behavior. While excise taxes have their opponents, supporters of taxes on commodities like cigarettes and alcohol argue that excise taxes should exist to offset, or compensate for, the high social costs of these behaviors. In the case of cigarette smoking and alcohol abuse, Luce and Schweitzer (1978) have placed the social costs of these behaviors at $27.5 billion and $44.2 billion, respectively (in 1976 dollars). The medical costs alone accounted, respectively, for 7.8% and 11.3% of the nation's health care bill in 1976.

Kramer (1979) argues that excise taxes should reflect the morbidity costs of modifiable behaviors. At minimum, one could argue for tax coverage of the shared social component of these costs—most notably, the federal and state tax dollars devoted to care of related illness and other costs among government dependents, including veterans and the poor and elderly (the VA hospital system, Medicaid, and Medicare). However such costs are counted, they will amount to billions of dollars. Kramer points out that this notion can only be applied to health behaviors involving a market transaction. There is no directly taxable activity for cases like obesity or lack of exercise.

In the early and mid-1980s, the climate for increased excise taxation seems attractive: governments are struggling to find revenue sources. The (relative) inelasticity of demand for cigarettes and possibly alcohol means that tax increases will generate substantial additional revenues (i.e., consumption decreases will not be large enough to outweigh price increases). Furthermore, in the case of cigarette smoking, the behavior is a minority habit, with only a third of adults claiming to be smokers in 1980 (Harris, 1982). Thus, for cigarettes, it can be expected that new tax activity will accelerate, following the lulls of the 1970s (Warner, 1982). Preliminary data indicate that this activity has been happening (Tobacco Institute, 1982).

A problem with excise taxation is that nominal increases in taxes erode in value as general price inflation occurs throughout the economy. Thus, the initial 8¢ federal tax imposed on cigarettes in 1952 dropped in real value (i.e., in constant 1952 dollars) to 2.5¢. The federal tax's share of retail price dropped from 35% in 1954 to 13% in 1980 (Warner, 1981). Also, although the nominal burden of all cigarette excise taxation (federal, state, and local combined) rose 34% from 1970 to 1980, the real value of the tax burden per smoker dropped by 37% (Harris, 1982). For this reason, Harris (1982) has called for ad valorem taxation of cigarettes, setting the tax at a fixed percentage of wholesale price.

Alcohol taxation poses a more complex problem for three reasons: (1) the possibilities of substitution are greater than for cigarettes (i.e., a drinker can switch from an expensive brand of liquor to a much cheaper one, or from liquor to wine, etc.), which increases price response for certain kinds of alcoholic beverages but may decrease the net effect on alcohol consumption; (2) unlike smoking, moderate drinking may not be harmful for the majority of alcohol consumers; and (3) it seems likely at an intuitive level (we are unaware of data satisfactorily addressing this issue) that the most price-responsive consumers of alcohol would not be problem drinkers, thus, a general alcohol excise tax might reduce alcohol consumption in toto but have relatively small effects on the population most adversely affected by drinking.

Studies of the price elasticity of demand for alcohol are few in number and often conflicting (DeLint, 1980); this area is certainly in need of further study. It is clear, nevertheless, that the federal government's failure to have increased its tax since the early 1950s has had the same effect as in the case of cigarettes: the real price of alcohol has fallen relative to other goods and services. Other things held constant, this price reduction must have led to a consumption increase. As a consequence, several public health analysts have called for increased excise taxation of alcohol and possibly ad valorem taxation (Beauchamp, 1976; DeLint, 1980; Jacobson, 1981, 1982; Mosher, 1982, 1983).

Excise taxation is an economic disincentive to consumption. The opposite strategy—positive price incentive—is a goods- or service-specific subsidy. Wikler (1978a) gives the example of a subsidy on nutritious snacks to encourage their consumption rather than "junk food." Subsidized hot school lunch programs have this quality. The free provision of childhood immunization by many state and local agencies is another important example. The principle in each case is the same: lowering the out-of-pocket price to the consumer will encourage consumption of a health-promoting good or service. The net result in each case is, again, a function of the price elasticity of demand. With some significant exceptions (e.g., food and housing), we lack good evidence as to the magnitude of consumers' responses to relevant price reductions.

Employment-Based

Employer
Employers confront several price incentives quite similar in nature to those confronted by individuals outside the work place. Due to this similarity, in this section and the following one on employees, we will note examples but keep discussion limited. The preceding discussion should suffice to explain principles.

Insurance. Risk rating is difficult to apply in group policies such as those purchased by employers. In very large firms that are experience rated or that self-insure, a successful health promotion program (i.e., one that reduces medical utilization) will directly reduce the employer's medical care costs. For smaller companies, however, successful utilization-reducing health promotion will rarely be rewarded by a reduction in health insurance costs. In this context, smaller firms lack the cost-savings incentive from which larger firms can benefit.

To encourage health promotion activities within smaller firms, Chadwick (1982) has proposed that insurance companies offer preferred rates to companies with better *aggregate* ratings on key risk factors (e.g., percentage of employees who smoke, percentage of employees with hypertension, etc.). An alternative or complementary approach would be for insurers to offer premium reductions to firms engaging in specified health promotion activities (e.g., smoking cessation clinics or blood pressure control programs). Fielding (1979) argues that companies that can demonstrate they are substantially reducing the risk levels of employees stand a better chance of negotiating lower premiums. He points to the example of the Speedcall Corporation, which received offers of 5% premium reductions from three insurance companies due to Speedcall's successful antismoking initiative.

Tax policy. A significant federal tax incentive for employers to provide health insurance benefits as a fringe is that such benefits are not included in the wage base for purposes of FICA taxation. Perhaps the greatest incentive for providing extensive health insurance, however, is that employees strongly prefer it (Sapolsky et al., 1981). This incentive is discussed further below.

In the area of excise taxes, all consumption-based taxes affect individuals outside the employment relationship. There is, however, one form of "excise taxation" directly relevant to producers: pollution taxes. Though not a widespread practice in this country, taxing effluents is a theoretically appealing means of encouraging pollution control in an efficient manner (Kneese & Schultz, 1975). The principle is a simple one: pollution imposes costs on the community *external* to the firm; that is, it is costless (or low cost) to the firm to dump waste into the air or water, but these acts impose costs, including health costs, on the community. Taxing the dumping of waste has the effect of *internalizing* the cost of polluting. Responding to the newly perceived price of polluting, the firm seeks nonpollution means of disposal that are less costly than the tax. In theory, the tax should equal the marginal social cost of the pollution. There are a few examples of application of pollution taxation (Kneese, 1964), and evidence of increased interest in the use of economic price incentives to control pollution (Selig, 1973).

Employee

Like employers, employees experience many price incentives similar in nature to those confronted by individuals outside the work setting. At least one important category of employee price incentives, however, has not been directly illustrated previously: effective price changes in employee health promotion programs. We comment on this category following brief mention of insurance and tax policy incentives affecting employees.

Insurance. All the relevant parameters of insurance price incentives have been disussed above. Employees can be expected to respond to employer-provided health insurance coverages in a manner identical to that of individuals outside the work place.

An innovative incentive scheme to reduce health care utilization—the Health Incentive Plan—was discussed above under income incentives, since employees can increase their incomes by reducing medical care utilization. An alternative way to characterize this incentive program is as a price incentive plan, since its net effect is to increase the price of primary care from near zero to essentially 100% of the provider's charge. Certainly a wealth of evidence suggests that this price change should reduce substantially utilization of primary services (Donabedian, 1976; Newhouse et al. 1981).

Tax policy. For employees, the principal tax system inducement to purchase health insurance is the treatment of fringe benefits as nonincome for purposes of individual income taxation. This tax break substantially increases the amount of health care coverage the employee can acquire for a given compensation by the employer. A dollar paid the employee in health insurance buys a dollar's worth of coverage. By contrast, were that dollar paid in direct wages, and were the employee in the 30% tax bracket (for example), the employee would net only 70¢. If this money were used to buy health care coverage, for the same dollar in compensation the employee would be able to acquire only 70% of the coverage available through the fringe benefit.

The theoretical impact of this incentive is clear. A recent study concludes that requiring employees to pay income tax on half of company-paid premiums could reduce national health expenditures by $13 billion, a full 5% of the nation's health care bill. The study estimates that the tax also would reduce premiums paid to health insurers by close to $30 billion, or 50%, while it would generate some $17 billion in revenues for the U.S. Treasury (Phelps, 1982).

A less economically dramatic, but potentially important, health behavior price incentive has been discussed by Mosher (1982), Beauchamp (1976), and others (DeLint, 1980; Jacobson, 1981, 1982). This incentive would be a change in the current tax policy of including business-related consumption of alcoholic beverages as allowable deductible business expenses. Mosher (Mosher, 1982) notes that, in 1979, business entertainment with alcohol exceeded $8 billion, some 12% of total consumer expenditures on alcohol. He estimates that this expenditure cost the government some $3 billion in foregone revenues. Adding in individual tax deductions for business entertaining would bring the total to $4 to $5 billion per year.

So far, this discussion has centered on the economic side of the picture. On the health behavior side, Mosher (1983) argues that current policy encourages drinking and contributes to alcohol problems, particularly in the upper income, managerial classes most directly affected by the policy. It is Mosher's conclusion, supported by others (Beauchamp, 1976; DeLint, 1980; Jacobson, 1981), that elimination of the tax deductibility of alcohol would significantly reduce both drinking and its associated health and social problems. Lacking hard evidence based on experience in this country, one can only "guesstimate" the magnitude of the potential impact.

Price changes in health promotion programs. A variety of price incentives has been adopted by employers to encourage employee participation in health promotion programs, including both positive and negative incentives. In the area of smoking cessation, for example, rebates have been offered for successful program completion (Fielding, 1979), amounting to a price reduction for the successful program graduate. Some employers, by contrast, have required employees to share in the price of a program that might otherwise have been provided by the employer for free (Fielding, 1982). In this case, the logic is that the employee will feel a deeper personal commitment to success by virtue of having invested his or her own money. As a final example, the Travelers Insurance Company has offered sports equipment to its employees at cost (Karson, 1982). This act is a direct price subsidy intended to encourage acquisition of equipment and, through use of it, physical fitness.

Conclusion

As this discussion should have suggested, the field of price incentives is a broad one, including such venerable subjects as excise taxes and such novel ones as price incentives to encourage employee participation in health promotion programs. Unlike the area of income incentives, we do possess well-developed understanding of the effects of certain price incentives. Good examples are excise taxes, especially on cigarettes, and copayments and deductibles in health insurance. Our knowledge of other price incentives is more limited. In this category we would point to the risk rating of insurance, an actuarially based practice that seems to make good marketing sense and holds some appeal as a health promotion incentive; but, the latter is today merely conceptual, with little empirical evidence available to help us explore whether risk rating ultimately can contribute much to the betterment of health. The demonstrated impacts of prices on smoking and health care utilization should, however, whet our appetites to learn more about using prices to encourage berhavior change.

Other Opportunity Costs

The opportunity cost of an activity (or good or service) is the value of alternative activities foregone as a result of undertaking the activity in question. For many activities, goods, and services, market prices and transactions provide a fair representation of opportunity costs. For a small but significant subset of activities, however, the market's cues as to value are indirect at best. These kinds of values will be of concern in the present section.

This category of "other opportunity costs" is necessarily less well defined or discrete than the other three in the matrix in Table 9.1. In some respects, it is a transitional category between the direct economic incentives (income and price) and the one well-defined indirect category (regulation, discussed below). In this sense, some examples cited here will fit one of the other categories as well; hence, our discussion here will be brief.

Employment-Based

Employer
Under the subject of income enhancement, we discussed the popular notion that employers establish health promotion programs as a means of increasing profitability or (what is the same, if more direct) reducing costs. That discussion concluded with examination of an alternative hypothesis to explain the growth in health promotion programming: namely, that it is a valued fringe benefit, building employee morale and loyalty (Barrett & Greene, 1983; Clement & Gibbs, 1983; Sapolsky et al., 1981). These two positions are not necessarily polar extremes. The notion making them compatible is that of opportunity cost. Improving employee morale and loyalty can have desired benefits for the employer, such as reducing absenteeism and turnover and possibly increasing productivity. Though these benefits may be difficult to gauge, in effect, health promotion activities may be reducing opportunity costs associated with other means of insuring employee retention and recruiting new workers. To the extent that productivity rises as the result of health promotion, employers may realize benefits, however subtle, on both the positive and negative sides of the business ledger (i.e., increased productivity and reduced costs, respectively). Perhaps this gain is a latter-day, corporate example of "doing well by doing good."

Explicit estimates of opportunity cost savings are relatively rare in the literature, but examples can be found. Fielding (1979) cites the calculation of the Gillette Company that its decision to provide medical services for employees on-site saved the firm $250,000 in 1976 by avoiding loss of work time. The costs experienced by the program included the staffing and administration of the on-site effort. The benefit was the difference between this realized cost and the opportunity cost of not offering the on-site services.

Employee
Employee opportunity cost incentives can be both positive and negative. Under the former category, the just-mentioned Gillette program had a distinct advantage for employees: it increased the convenience of seeking

and receiving services. One obvious opportunity cost avoided was the cost of travel time necessitated by off-site services. Some of these travel costs have direct economic measures—for example, the cost of gasoline to drive to off-site care—while others have only "shadow prices," indirect measures of cost. A notable example of the latter is the value of the employee's time consumed in getting to and from the off-site location.

Kotz and Fielding (1980) discuss a program of the Campbell Soup company in which the company dispensed free hypertension medications to employees. The on-site effort proved to be significantly less expensive than hypertensive employees' utilizing the private sector, and the ready availability and inexpensiveness of care increased incentives to maintain blood pressure control.

In the area of employee fitness and exercise programs, the availability of company facilities and equipment is a perfectly analogous example. The employee benefits from a reduced cost of travel to noncompany facilities. If use of facilities is free to employees, another benefit of an opportunity cost nature is realized, as personal expenditures on noncompany facilities are not necessary. Together, such inducements amount to a lowering of the opportunity cost of being involved in an exercise program. Economic logic argues that this savings should increase participation; Fielding (1982) has found that on-site programs have higher participation rates (from 20 to 40% of employees) than do employer-sponsored, off-site programs (10 to 25%). Fielding (1979) cites General Foods, Pepsico, Northern Natural Gas of Omaha, and Xerox as being among the companies that offer high-quality, on-site exercise facilities. Karson (1982) notes that Central States Health and Life Company constructed a $50,000 par course for its employees and had provided exercise facilities 15 years earlier.

The opportunity cost of exercise for the employee could be still lower if employees were granted work time to engage in exercise. Haskell and Blair (1980) recommend that both the employer and employee contribute time to exercise, thus enhancing the commitment of both parties to a serious exercise program.

An example of a negative opportunity cost incentive arises for smoking employees when a company introduces restrictions on smoking in the work place. In effect, the cost of smoking rises by requiring the employee to move to specific smoking-permitted locations at particular times.

Individual

The principal category of opportunity cost incentives experienced by individuals outside the work place relates to perceptions of convenience and risk associated with engaging in specific behaviors. As for employees, opportunity cost incentives can be positive or negative. The location of a commercial fitness center in a town not previously so served may decrease substantially the opportunity cost of staying fit by reducing travel costs, increasing access to equipment, and so on. To the extent the new establishment manages to extract the opportunity cost savings in fees for use of the facilities, the net benefit to users will diminish. But the fact that enrollment occurs testifies that users perceive benefits as exceeding costs.

Many opportunity cost incentives confronted by individuals are negative ones relating to regulation of the sale or use of products having deleterious health effects. Because this category overlaps so substantially with the next section's treatment of regulation, we introduce the concept only briefly by way of a few examples.

Legal restrictions on the availability or use of cigarettes or alcohol, for example, effectively increase search costs to acquire these products (Wagenaar, 1981). Search costs include costs of transportation, time, and the risk of being caught attempting to acquire the products illegally. Examples include licensing fewer retail outlets to sell cigarettes or alcohol and raising the minimum legal age of consumption. Some smoking-and-health activists concerned about the problem of children and teens initiating smoking habits have proposed the elimination of vending machine sale of cigarettes. Vending machines not only increase the geographic access of cigarettes, but they increase the potential for underage sales by avoiding a face-to-face confrontation between vender and consumer. The proposal is a clear example of increasing opportunity costs to reduce unhealthy behavior, an approach considered further in the next section.

Regulatory Policies

Governmental regulation is a pervasive phenomenon throughout our society, particularly in the areas of health and safety. In the present section, we will focus on a few examples of regulations and their associated economic incentives affecting health behavior, specifically concentrating on indirect or opportunity cost incentives; our feeling is that direct incentives (e.g., excise taxes) have been covered adequately above.

Individual

A common regulatory approach affecting several health behaviors involves restriction of access to a product or activity. This regulation can take a number of forms, including restriction by geographic location (e.g., liquor licenses), by functional location (e.g., ban on smoking in health facilities), by age (e.g., minimum age to be a licensed driver), and by hour of the day (e.g., blue laws). Whatever their form, restrictions raise the opportunity costs of consuming the product or engaging in the behavior. The opportunity costs will be affected by three aspects of a restriction: (1) the letter of the law, (2) its enforcement, and (3) the social norms surrounding it (Maisto & Rachal, 1980).

Through increases in opportunity costs, legal restrictions can have substantial effects on behavior, which in turn can translate into significant impacts on health. For example, Wagenaar (1981) has estimated that Michigan's increase in the minimum legal drinking age from 18 to 21 at the end of 1978 resulted in an 18% decline in motor vehicle crash involvements (1650 fewer crashes) among 18- to 20-year olds in 1979. Certainly, the basic premise—that increased opportunity costs affect behavior and thereby health—lies at the heart of general calls for more restrictive public policy on alcohol. Beauchamp (1976), DeLint (1980), and Mosher (1982, 1983) see the ready availability of alcohol as a major contributor to alcoholism and other forms of alcohol abuse. They argue for restrictions as public policy on point of sale, price (i.e., much higher taxation), and so on.

In the area of smoking and health, a spate of smoking restriction laws in the 1970s brought the number of states restricting smoking in certain public places from under half a dozen to over two-thirds in just 6 years. Though the restrictiveness of the laws varies markedly from one state to the next, each does limit smokers' ability to consume cigarettes in certain everyday locations (e.g., food stores, health care facilities, public transportation). Analysis to date has failed to demonstrate a statistically significant impact of such laws on aggregate cigarette consumption (Warner, 1981b; Bloom, 1979), though a thorough study of this question is now underway (Lewit, 1983). Ironically, there is evidence that "clean indoor air" or "nonsmokers' rights" laws—developed with the explicit intention of restricting smoking—have had less impact on smoking behavior than a public policy originally motivated only slightly by that objective, namely cigarette excise taxation (Warner, 1981b).

A second health-relevant regulatory approach is to require the use of safety equipment to use a product or engage in an activity. Motorcycle helmet laws stand out as an example of regulation that clearly saves lives yet for which the perceived opportunity costs were too high. In 1976, the federal government ended its policy of withholding highway funds from states that did not require helmet use by motorcyclists. Within a few years, over half the states had repealed their helmet-use laws. Watson, Zador, and Wilks (1981) have estimated that repeal was typically followed by nearly a 40% increase in the number of motorcycle accident deaths. According to simple economics, helmet laws appear to be cost-beneficial regulation (Muller, 1980); but, the standard cost-benefit calculus fails to take into account the opportunity costs perceived by motorcyclists—the discomfort of helmets, the loss of individual freedom inherent in a use law, and so on.

In contrast to the helmet law story, in recent years many states have jumped on the bandwagon in favor of mandatory child automobile restraint laws. From January through May of 1983 alone, 20 states adopted child restraint use laws, bringing to 40 the number of jurisdictions having such laws (IIHS, 1983). The relative novelty of these laws has precluded significant evaluation of their effects on behavior, though one of the early laws has been examined. Williams and Wells (1981) found that the Tennessee law could be credited with roughly a doubling of restraint use rates, with some 34% of children in that state wearing belts.

Use of restraints for children in Tennessee and other states represents a social response to the law. The fine for noncompliance in that state, $2 to $10, does not seem sufficiently high to have a significant impact on restraint use in and of itself. Likewise, the tentative approach in several state legislatures toward universal mandatory belt use laws is caught in something of a Catch-22: opposition to belt laws, on individual freedom grounds, is so great that legislative proponents have to water down the "less essential" elements of their bills. Thus, to establish the principle of belt use as law, legislators have sacrificed the stick that apparently contributed to compliance in other countries. Bills in such states as Michigan and Rhode Island (Paul, 1983) have proposed $10 to $15 fines for noncompliance, tantamount to admission of limited intent to enforce the law. In Australia, by contrast, where a mandatory belt use law is backed up by a larger fine, compliance is substantial and significant decreases in mortality have been documented (Arnould & Grabowski, 1981).

Conybeare (1980) and Peltzman (1975) offer an intriguing view of drivers' responses to automobile safety devices. Safety measures, they argue, reduce the level of risk drivers have elected to assume. Consequently, drivers increase their driving "intensity" (i.e., speed) to compensate, returning to their "optimal" level of risk. In both Australia (Conybeare's study) and the United States (Peltzman's), total death rates did not fall as much as introduction of safety measures had promised and nonoccupant death rates actually rose, suggesting riskier (i.e., faster) driving. Peltzman's study has been the subject of much critical analysis (Nelson, 1976; Robertson, 1977). The basic point of these analyses, however, is consistent with the opportunity cost concept we have been considering.

In addition to use of safety equipment, safety rules can be applied to govern many health-related behaviors. Perhaps most obvious in the area of highway safety is the speed limit. According to an estimate by the National Safety Council (NSC, 1980), the national 55 mile-per-hour speed limit has resulted in some 5500 fewer motor vehicle deaths annually than would have occurred in its absence. Of course, the law is not without its costs, since it increases travel time, which has an opportunity cost associated with it. The fear of apprehension and conviction, as well as simply respect for the law, have apparently outweighted the travel time cost in the aggregate.

Fear of penalty is a clear motivator, though precisely how such fear translates into perception of opportunity costs is not well understood. Ross (1982) points to the British Road Safety Act of 1967 to illustrate the complexity and nonpermanence of response. The act required imposition of a minimum one-year suspension of driving privileges for driving under the influence of alcohol. Ross estimated that the immediate impact of the law was a decrease of 25% in serious injuries and deaths. By 1970, however, the accident and casualty rates had returned to their pre-law levels, in part reflecting a general awareness that enforcement of the new law was no more active than what preceded it.

In concluding this introduction to some regulatory economic incentives, we turn to a different approach, one addressed briefly above. Regulation can impose requirements on institutions which, in turn, can produce incentives for individuals. As of 1976, some 13 states mandated that health insurance carriers provide coverage for treatment of alcoholism. Similarly, the federal Health Maintenance Organization Act of 1973 required federally funded HMOs to include alcoholism treatment coverage (DuPont & Basin, 1980). Such regulations can be expected to have a substantial effect on the utilization of health care services, because they significantly reduce the cost of obtaining such services.

Employment-Based

Employer
One major class of health-relevant regulatory policies has escaped attention to this point: the regulation of safety and health in the work place. Both the federal government and many state governments have formal bureaucracies charged with establishing regulations and monitoring and ensuring compliance by firms. The enormity of the problem is suggested by the large number of known and suspected safety and health risks and the paucity of regulatory resources. Cohen, Smith, and Anger (1982) suggest that the magnitude of the occupational disease problem is only beginning to surface as a result of expanded surveillance and epidemiological studies pertaining to work place health hazards. The burden of the regulatory problem is illustrated by experience under the California Occupational Carcinogens Act of 1977, under which only 23 inspections were performed in the first year and a total of 190 inspections by the end of the second year. This activity had to be measured against an inventory of more than 4000 users of carcinogens (Agran, 1980).

Occupational safety and health regulation is an economic incentive issue because firms' compliance with the law costs money, thereby eating into profits, yet the economic inducements to comply with the law are minimal. Viscusi (1983) notes that the chance of an Occupational Safety and Health Administration (OSHA) inspection in a given year is about 1 in 100 (excluding follow-up inspections). Furtheremore, the penalties assessed by OSHA are commonly the slightest of tokens. Standard procedure often gives a firm a chance to comply with an inspection-produced citation prior to being subjected to a fine or criminal sanction. When fines are assessed, their economic burden is minimal compared with the cost of complying with the regulation. Viscusi observes that each OSHA inspection yields a mean of 2.1 violations, for which the average penalty is $193. Viscusi estimates that this penalty translates into an average financial incentive of $7.08 for a firm to comply with OSHA regulations, or some 34¢ per covered worker.

In short, the regulatory financial stick is much shorter than the free enterprise profit carrot. From the industry data he has analyzed, Viscusi can find no significant impact of OSHA inspections and penalties on worker injuries and illness. The trick, of course, is to legislate sufficient penalties, and the resources to impose them, to make the expected value of the cost of noncompliance greater than the cost of compliance. The political will to accomplish this change seems unlikely to occur at present.

If occupational safety and health continues to grow as a public policy issue, as some observers clearly expect (Agran, 1980; Cohen et al., 1982), policymakers and society as a whole will have to confront the problem of creating adequate inducements to encourage firms to address identifiable risks in the work place. To date, safety and health regulation has functioned as a set of highly inadequate economic incentives, cloaked in the language of legal sanctions.

Employee

In several sections above we have addressed the incentives confronting employees as a result of regulatory policies. Certainly all the governmental safety and health policies directed at employers also affect employees; the tax treatment of business-related alcohol consumption is another example of a combined employer-employee incentive relating to the employee's health (Beauchamp, 1976; Mosher, 1982, 1983). In addition to governmental regulation, however, employees face employer-defined regulations. A prominent health-relevant example is restrictions on smoking in the work place (Danaher, 1980; Fielding, 1979). A regulation such as this imposes opportunity costs on the smoking employee. Earlier discussion addressed the implications.

Conclusion

Concurrent with the increase in health promotion activity has come a growth of interest in the use of economic incentives to encourage positive health behaviors. In part, this interest reflects the age-old recognition that people respond to economic inducements; in part, it represents the present era's concern with cost containment and with nonregulatory approaches to the achievement of goals. Economic incentives are perceived by proponents as having several desirable characteristics: they are efficacious and efficient and they do not impinge on personal freedom (Shepard & Pearlman, 1982). This assessment is not unanimous, however. To critics, incentives can be coercive, lose their effectiveness once they are withdrawn (i.e., behavior reverts to its pre-incentive phase), and decrease intrinsic motivation to change behavior (Shepard, 1977).

Early in this paper we identified several dimensions of incentives. Our review of the literature permits us to draw several highly tentative conclusions about the relative effectiveness of incentives along these dimensions. The words highly tentative must be emphasized in recognition of the fact that, in large part, the effectiveness of the incentives we have explored has not been studied. Even for those incentive programs for which effectiveness has been analyzed, studies must be characterized as program-specific and, often, analytically inadequate.

Subject to this important qualification, we note that certain "time-honored" incentives are among the few to have demonstrated a clear impact on health behaviors. Ironically, several of these were not established as incentives; that is, their existence is largely attributable to other motivations. Prominent examples are excise taxes on illness-associated products (e.g., cigarettes) and the federal tax treatment of health insurance and expenditures on medical services. In recent years, lessons from experiences with these policies have been applied with a more conscious orientation toward behavior change. Public health analysts have called for the use of excise taxes to reduce the health problems posed by cigarettes and alcohol (Beauchamp, 1976; DeLint, 1980; Harris, 1982; Mosher, 1982, 1983; Warner, 1981b). Additionally, health policy officials have inaugurated reimbursement by diagnosis-related groups with the explicit intention of affecting medical care utilization by powerful economic incentives.

Basic economic variables, such as income and price, have become the centerpieces of innovative economic incentive programs. In several cases, the economic factor has been established with the intent of changing a health-related behavior, as in the case of Speedcall's income supplementation for nonsmokers (Shepard, 1977). Preliminary evidence on a few such programs shows that they work. In other cases, notably the risk rating of insurance policies by modifiable risks, the principal motivation has not been behavior change, and evidence of impact on behavior is virtually nonexistant.

The literature offers tentative support for some basic psychological principles: periodic reinforcement appears to be more effective than once-and-for-all reward; maintenance reinforcement is often helpful and perhaps necessary; larger rewards have more impact than smaller ones; and peer pressure (through group incentives) is an effective inducement. Other basic principles do not receive support from the health behavior economic incentive literature. They are not refuted, but the evidence to support them is simply unavailable. A good example is the principle that positive incentives (rewards) work better than negative ones (sanctions or punishments).

A major theme to emerge from our review is the dominance of the work place as the locus of innovative efforts to use economic incentives to influence health. In part, this finding reflects the private sector's knowledge of and interest in economic incentives and their relationship to productivity. On the other hand, the literature's concentration on work place incentive programs reflects a research bias toward the occupational setting. This bias results from the large "captive audience" available at the work place, as well as derivative characteristics: employment-based programs potentially produce sizable bodies of data, relatively easy to collect and centrally available. In addition, good information on the design and application of such programs should be available.

Assuming that work place health promotion remains of interest for some years to come, the early explorations using economic incentives will surely be followed by more and better ideas. Hopefully, those responsible for health promotion programming will devote increasing attention to the design and evaluation of incentive programs. At the same time, we wish to emphasize the potential for achieving significant changes in health behaviors through the use of economic incentives in public policy. A governmental jurisdiction may lack the homogeneity and "captivity" of employees at work, but in its sheer size the public arena holds the potential for translating proportionately small impacts into numerically large ones. Creativity is called for, both on the job and in the realm of public policy.

References

Agran, L. Occupational cancer control policy. *Journal of Public Health*, 1980, *1*, 342–352.
Alderman, M., Green, L. W., & Flynn, B. S. Hypertension control programs in occupational settings. *Public Health Reports*, 1980, *95*, 158–163.

Arnould, R., & Grabowski, H. Auto safety regulation: An analysis of market failure. *Bell Journal of Economics*, 1981, *12*, 27–48.

Attention joggers. *Changing Times*, February 1981, 82.

Bailey, M. J. *Reducing risks to life: Measurement of the benefits.* Washington, D.C.: American Enterprise Institute, 1980.

Bailey, W. Rising health care costs—A challenge to insurers. *National Journal*, 1976, *8*, 608.

Barrett, K., & Greene, R. Sharing the profits of corporate fitness programs. *United*, May 1983, 74.

Beauchamp, D. E. Exploring new ethics for public policy: Developing a fair alcohol policy. *Journal of Health, Politics, Policy, and Law*, 1976, *1*, 338–354.

Beck, R. N. IBM's plan for life: Toward a comprehensive health care strategy. *Health Education Quarterly*, 1982, *9* (Suppl.), 55–60.

Berki, S. E. *Hospital economics.* Lexington, Mass.: Lexington Books, 1972.

Berki, S. E. The design of case-based hospital payment systems. *Medical Care*, 1983, *21*, 1–13.

Berry, C. A. *An approach to good health for employees & reduced health care costs for industry.* Washington, D.C.: Health Insurance Association of America, 1981.

Berry, R. E., Jr., & Boland, J. P. *The economic cost of alcohol abuse.* New York: Free Press, 1977.

Bloom, M. *Restrictions on smoking: Observations on their impact.* Paper presented at the 28th Tobacco Worker's Conference, Orlando, Fla., 1979.

Brandon, W. P. Health-related tax subsidies. *New England Journal of Medicine*, 1982, *307*, 947–950.

Brennan, A. J. J. Health promotion: What's in it for business and industry. *Health Education Quarterly*, 1982, *9* (Suppl.), 27–36.

Brevetti, F. Non-smoker rates gaining popularity. *The Journal of Commerce*, February 5, 1981.

Celarier, M. Big bucks in the wellness biz. *MS*, 1983, 127–28.

Chadwick, J. H. Cost-effective health promotion at the worksite? In R. S. Parkinson & Associates (Eds.), *Managing health promotion in the workplace.* Palo Alto, Calif.: Mayfield Pub. Co., 1982, pp. 288–299.

Clement, J., & Gibbs, D. A. Employer considerations of health promotion programs: Financial variables. *Journal of Public Health Policy*, 1983, *4*, 45–55.

Cohen, A., Smith, M. J., & Anger, W. K. Self-protective measures against workplace hazards. In R. S. Parkinson & Associates (Eds.), *Managing health promotion in the workplace.* Palo Alto, Calif.: Mayfield Pub. Co., 1982, pp. 272–287.

Conference Board Inc. *Industry roles in health care—A research report from the conference board.* 1974, 49–52.

Congressional Budget Office United States Congress. *Containing medical care costs through market forces.* Washington, D.C.: Government Printing Office, May 1982.

Conybeare, J. A. C. Evaluation of automobile safety regulations: The case of compulsory seat belt legislation in Australia. *Political Science*, 1980, *12*, 27–40.

Cowell, M. J., & Hirst, B. L. Mortality differences between smokers and non-smokers. *Society of Actuaries Transactions*, 1980, *32*, 185–213.

Cron, T. O. The nature of consumer health as a public health concept. *Public Health Reports*, 1981, *96*, 274–278.

Danaher, B. G. Smoking cessation programs in occupational settings. *Public Health Reports*, 1980, *95*, 149–157.

Davis, K. *National health insurance: Benefits, costs, and consequences.* Washington, D.C.: The Brookings Institution, 1975.

DeLint, J. E. E. Alcohol control policy as a strategy of prevention. *Journal of Public Health Policy,* 1980, *1,* 41–49.

DiPrete, H. A. Cost containment through benefit plan design. In R. H. Egdahl (Ed.), *Background papers on industry's changing role in health care delivery.* New York: Springer-Verlag, 1977, 117–133.

Donabedian, A. *Benefits in medical care.* Cambridge, Mass.: Harvard University Press, 1976.

DuPont, R. L., & Basin, M. M. Control of alcohol and drug abuse in industry— A literature review. *Public Health Reports,* 1980, *95,* 137–148.

Faust, H. Personal communication, 1983.

Feldstein, M. S. A new approach to national health insurance. *Public Interest,* Spring 1971, 93–105.

Feldstein, M. S. *Hospital costs and health insurance,* Cambridge, Mass.: Harvard University Press, 1980.

Feldstein, P. J. *Financing dental care: An economic analysis,* Lexington, Mass.: Lexington Books, 1973.

Feldstein, P. *Health care economics.* New York: John Wiley & Sons, 1979.

Fielding, J. E. Health promotions—Some notions in search of a constituency. *American Journal of Public Health,* 1977, *67,* 1082–1086.

Fielding, J. E. Preventive medicine and the bottom line. *Journal of Occupational Medicine,* 1979, *21,* 79–88.

Fielding, J. E. Effectiveness of employee health improvement programs. *Journal of Occupational Medicine,* 1982, *24,* 907–916.

Fielding, J. E., & Breslow, L. Health promotion programs sponsored by California employers. *American Journal of Public Health,* 1983, *73,* 538–542. (a)

Fielding, J. E., & Breslow, L. Worksite hypertension programs: Results of a survey of 424 California employers. *Public Health Reports,* 1983, *98,* 127–132. (b)

Foote, A., & Erfurt, J. C. Hypertension control at the worksite. *New England Journal of Medicine,* 1983, *308,* 809–813.

Fordyce, W. Pain, compensation, and public policy. In J. C. Rosen & L. J. Solomon (Eds.), *Prevention in health psychology.* Hanover, N.H.: University Press of New England, 1985.

Foreyt, J. P., Scott, L. W., & Gotto, A. M. Weight control and nutrition education programs in occupational settings. *Public Health Reports,* 1980, *95,* 127–136.

Golberg, E. D., Krantz, G., & Locke, B. Z. Effect of a short term outpatient psychiatric therapy benefit on the utilization of medical services in a prepaid group practice medical program. *Medical Care,* 1970, *8,* 419–438.

Gori, G. Unpublished manuscript, 1983.

Gori, G. B., & Richter, D. J. Macroeconomics of disease prevention in the United States. *Science,* 1978, *200,* 1124–1130.

Greenwald, M. Health promotion and health insurance. In L. K. Y. Ng & D. L. Davis (Eds.), *Strategies for public health.* New York: Van Nostrand Reinhold, 1981.

Haggerty, R. J. Changing life styles to improve health. *Preventive Medicine,* 1977, *6,* 275–288.

Hannon, E. L., & Graham, J. K. A cost-benefit study of a hypertension screening and treatment program at the work setting. *Inquiry,* 1978, *15,* 345–358.

Harris, J. E. Increasing the federal excise tax on cigarettes. *Journal of Health Economics*, 1982, *1*, 117–120.

Haskell, W. L., & Blair, S. N. The physical activity component of health promotion in occupational settings. *Public Health Reports*, 1980, *95*, 109–116.

Havighurst, C. C. Controlling health care costs. *Journal of Health, Politics, Policy, and Law*, 1977, *1*, 471–498.

Iglehart, J. K. Medicare begins prospective payment of hospitals. *New England Journal of Medicine*, 1983, *308*, 1428–1432.

Insurance Institute for Highway Safety. *The highway loss reduction status report.* Washington, D.C., June 1983.

Jacobs, P., & Chovil, A. Economic evaluation of corporate medical programs. *Journal of Occupational Medicine*, 1983, *25*, 273–278.

Jacobson, M. F. Taxes, information and warnings needed to fight alcohol abuse. *Miami Herald*, November 24, 1981.

Jacobson, M. F. Raise the taxes on alcohol and tobacco. *The Christian Science Monitor*, February 16, 1982.

Jeffery, R. W., Wing, R. R., & Stunkard, A. J. Behavioral treatment of obesity: The state of the art. *Behavior Therapy*, 1976, *9*, 189–199.

Kane, K. W. The corporate responsibility in the area of alcoholism. *Personnel Journal*, July 1975, *54*, 380–384.

Kaplan, J. Wellness epidemic sweeps companies. *Business Insurance*, September 1, 1980, 2–3.

Karson, S. G. A new emphasis on health promotion: The insurance business. *Health Education Quarterly*, 1982, *9* (Suppl.), 42–48.

Kneese, A. V. *The economics of regional water quality management.* Baltimore, Md.: Johns Hopkins Press, 1964.

Kneese, A. V., & Schultze, C. E. *Pollution, prices, and public policy.* Washington, D.C.: The Brookings Institution, 1975.

Kotz, H. J., & Fielding, J. E. (Eds.). *Health, education and promotion: Agenda for the eighties.* Summary report of Conference on Health Education and Promotion, Atlanta, Georgia, March 16–19, 1980 (sponsored by the Health Insurance Association of America).

Kramer, M. J. Self-inflicted disease: Who should pay for care? *Journal of Health, Politics, Policy, and Law*, 1979, *4*, 138–141.

Kristein, M. The economics of health promotion at the worksite. *Health Education Quarterly*, 1982, *9* (Suppl.), 27–36.

Kristein, M. M. How much can business expect to profit from smoking cessation. *Preventive Medicine*, 1983, *12*, 358–381.

Laughhunn, D .J., & Lyon, H. L. The feasibility of tax induced price increases as a deterrent to cigarette consumption. *Journal of Business Administration*, 1971, *3*, 27–35.

Lewit, E. Personal communication, 1983.

Lewit, E. M., & Coate, D. The potential for using excise taxes to reduce smoking. *Journal of Health Economics*, 1982, *1*, 121–145.

Lewit, E. M., Coate, D., & Grossman, M. The effects of government regulation on teenage smoking. *Journal of Law and Economics*, 1981, *24*.

Logan, A. G., Milne, B. J., Achber, C., Campbell, W. P., & Haynes, R. B. Cost-effectiveness of a worksite hypertension treatment program. *Hypertension*, 1981, *3*, 211–218.

Luce, B., & Schweitzer, S. Smoking and alcohol abuse: A comparison of their economic consequences. *New England Journal of Medicine*, 1978, *298*, 569–571.

Luft, H. S. *Health maintenance organizations: Dimensions of performance.* New York: John Wiley & Sons, 1981.
MacAvoy, P. The regulation of accidents. In H. G. Manne, & R. L. Miller (Eds.), *Auto safety regulation: The cure or the problem?* Glenridge, N.J.: Thos. Horton & Daughters, 1976.
Maisto, S. A., & Rachal, J. V. Indications of the relationship among adolescent drinking practices, related behaviors, and drinking age laws. In H. Wechsler (Ed.), *Minimum-drinking-age laws.* Lexington, Mass.: D.C. Heath & Co., 1980.
Manhattan Life Offering Premium Discount to Regular Exercisers. *Insurance Advocate,* May 5, 1979, 34–35.
Monheit, A. C. Economic implications of employer-provided health care delivery. In R. H. Egdahl (Ed.), *Industry's changing role in health care delivery.* New York: Springer-Verlag, 1977.
Mosher, J. F. Federal tax law and public health policy: The case of alcohol-related tax expenditures. *Journal of Public Health Policy,* 1982, *3,* 260–263.
Mosher, J. Tax-deductible alcohol: An issue of public health policy and prevention strategy. *Journal of Health, Politics, Policy, and Law,* 1983, *7,* 855–887.
Muller, A. Evaluation of the costs and benefits of motorcycle helmet laws. *American Journal of Public Health,* 1980, *70,* 586.
National Interagency Council on Smoking and Health. *Smoking and the workplace—Business survey.* Washington, D.C.: U.S. Government Printing Office, Spring 1981.
National Safety Council. *Accident facts.* Chicago: NSC, 1980.
Nelson, R. R. Comments on Peltzman's paper on auto safety regulation. In H. G. Manne & R. L. Miller (Eds.), *Auto safety regulation: The cure or the problem?* Glenridge, N.J.: Thos. Horton & Daughters, 1976.
Newhouse, J. P., Manning, W. G., Morris, C. N., Orr, L. L., & Duan, N. Some interim results from a controlled trial of cost-sharing in health insurance. *New England Journal of Medicine,* 1981, *305,* 1501–1507.
Office of Technology Assessment, U.S. Congress. *The effectiveness and costs of alcoholism treatment* (NTIS No. OTA-HCS-22). Washington, D.C.: U.S. Government Printing Office, March 1983.
Parkinson, R. S., & Associates (Eds.). *Managing health promotion in the workplace.* Palo Alto, Calif.: Mayfield Pub. Co., 1982.
Paul, B. Rhode Island seen close to passing care safety-belt law. *Wall Street Journal,* May 10, 1983.
Pauly, M. V. The economics of moral hazard. *American Economic Review,* 1968, *58,* 231–237.
Pauly, M. V. *Medical care at public expense: A study of applied welfare economics.* New York: Praeger Publishers, 1971.
Pauly, M. V. Economic aspects of consumer use. In S. Muskin (Ed.), *Consumer incentives for health care.* New York: Prodist, 1974.
Pellegrino, E. D. Health promotion as public policy: The need for moral grounding. In W. J. McNerney (Ed.), *In working for a healthier America.* Cambridge, Mass.: Ballinger Publishing Company, 1980.
Peltzman, S. The effects of automobile safety regulation. *Journal of Political Economy,* 1975, *83,* 677.
Phelps, C. E., & Newhouse, J. P. Effect of coinsurance: A multivariate analysis. *Social Security Bulletin,* 1972, *35,* 20–29.
Phelps, C. E. Effects of insurance on demand for medical care. In R. Anderson (Ed.), *Equity in health services.* Cambridge, Mass.: Ballinger Publishing Company, 1975.

Phelps, E. *Health care costs: The consequences of increased cost sharing.* Santa Monica, Calif.: Rand Corporation, 1982.

Reiss, J. B. A conceptual model of the case mix payment scheme for New Jersey hospitals. *Health Services Research,* 1980, *15,* 161–175.

Robertson, L. A critical analysis of Peltzman's "The effect of automobile safety regulation." *Journal of Economic Issues,* 1977, *3,* 587.

Rodgers, J. Personal communication, 1983.

Ross, L. H. *Deterring the drinking driver.* Lexington, Mass.: Lexington Books, 1982.

Ruchlin, H. S., & Alderman, M. H. Cost of hypertension control at the workplace. *Journal of Occupational Medicine,* 1980, *22,* 795–800.

Russell, L. Unpublished manuscript, 1983.

Sackrin, S. Factors affecting the demand for cigarettes. *Agriculture Economics Research,* 1962, *14,* 81–88.

Sapolsky, H. M., Altman, D., Greene, R., & Moore, J. D. Corporate attitudes towards health care costs. *Milbank Memorial Fund Quarterly,* 1981, *59,* 561–585.

Schnert, K. W., & Tillotson, J. K. *How business can promote good health for employees and their families.* Washington, D.C.: National Chamber Foundation, 1978.

Scitovsky, A. A., & Snyder, N. M. Effect of coinsurance on the use of physician services. *Social Security Bulletin,* 1972, *35,* 3–19.

Selig, E. *Effluent charges on air and water pollution: A conference report.* Washington, D.C.: Environmental Law Institute, 1973.

Shepard, D. S. Prediction and incentives in health care policy (Doctoral Dissertation, Harvard University, 1977). (University Microfilms)

Shepard, D. S. *Incentives for not smoking: Experience at the Speedcall Corporation.* Paper presented at the First Executive Conference of the Corporate Commitment to Health, Washington, D.C., 1980.

Shepard, D. S., Foster, S. B., Stason, W. B., Solomon, H. S., & McArdle, P. J. *Cost-effectiveness of interventions to improve compliance with anti-hypertensive therapy.* Paper presented at the National Conference on High Blood Pressure Control, Washington, D.C., 1979.

Shepard, D. S., & Pearlman, L. A. Unpublished manuscript, 1982.

Shephard, R. J., Corey, P., Renzland, P., & Cox, M. H. Fitness program reduces health care costs. *Dimensions,* 1982, *59,* 14–15.

Shephard, R. J., Cox, M. H., & Corey, P. Fitness program participation: Its effect on worker performance. *Journal of Occupational Medicine,* 1981, *23,* 359–363.

State Farm doubles benefit for belt users. *Underwriter's Report,* February 24, 1983, 6.

Stokes, J. Why not rate health and life insurance premiums by risk. *New England Journal of Medicine,* 1983, *308,* 393–395.

Sullivan, B. P. New York state plans to publicize discount for drivers who pass course. *Journal of Commerce,* June 13, 1981.

Tillotson, J. K., & Rosala, J. C. *How business can use specific techniques to control health care costs.* Washington, D.C.: National Chamber Foundation, 1978.

Tobacco Institute. *The tax burden on tobacco—Historical compilation.* Washington, D.C.: Tobacco Institute, 1982.

Toffany, V. Life is best at 55. *Traffic Quarterly,* 1981, *35,* 5.

Viscusi, W. K. *Risk by choice.* Cambridge, Mass.: Harvard University Press, 1983.

Wagenaar, A. C. Effects of an increase in the legal minimum drinking age. *Journal of Public Health Policy*, 1981, *2*, 206–225.

Walsh, D. C. Employee assistance programs. *Milbank Memorial Fund Quarterly*, 1982, *60*, 492–517.

Warner, K. E. The federal cigarette excise tax. In *Proceedings of the national conference on smoking or health*. New York. New York, N.Y.: American Cancer Society, Inc., 1981. (a)

Warner, K. E. State legislation on smoking and health: A comparison of two polices. *Policy Sciences*, 1981, *13*, 139–152. (b)

Warner, K. E. Cigarette excise taxation and interstate smuggling: An assessment of recent activity. *National Tax Journal*, 1982, *35*, 483–490.

Warner, K. E., & Luce, B. R. *Cost-benefit and cost-effectiveness analysis in health care*. Ann Arbor, Mich.: Health Administration Press, 1982.

Watson, G. S., Zador, P. L., & Wilks, A. Helmet use, helmet use laws and motorcyclist fatalities. *American Journal of Public Health*, 1981, *71*, 297–300.

Weber, A. Labor relations in transition. *New York Times*, December 21, 1979.

Weis, W. L. Can you afford to hire smokers? *Personnel Administrator*, 1981, *26*, 71–78.

Weisbrod, B., & Fiesler, R. J. Hospitalization insurance and hospital utilization. *American Economic Review*, 1961, *51*, 126–132

Wells, K. B., Manning, W. G., Jr., Duan, N., Ware, J. E., Jr., & Newhouse, J. P. *Cost sharing and the demand for ambulatory mental health services*. Santa Monica, Calif.: Rand Corporation, 1982.

Wikler, D. I. Coercive measures in health promotion: Can they be justified? *Health Education Monographs*, 1978, *6*, 223–241. (a)

Wikler, D. I. Persuasion and coercion for health: Ethical issues in government efforts to change life-styles. *Milbank Memorial Fund Quarterly*, 1978, *56*, 303–338. (b)

Williams, A. F., & Wells, J. K. The Tennessee child restraint law in its third year. *American Journal of Public Health*, 1981, *71*, 163–165.

Williams, G. *Kaiser-Permanente health plan: Why it works*. Oakland, Calif.: Henry J. Kaiser Foundation, 1971.

Wingblad, T. Personal communication, 1983.

Wright, C. C. Cost containment through health promotion programs. *Journal of Occupational Medicine*, 1982, *24*, 965–968.

Zink, V. Cost control strategies. In D. A. Weeks (Ed.), *Rethinking employee benefit assumptions*. New York: The Conference Board, 1978.

Promoting Coping with Illness

Introductory Notes

Efforts to prevent psychopathology fall into two basic categories: (1) interventions designed to enhance the competence of the individual at risk for psychopathology, and (2) interventions directed at the environment and designed to reduce stress. The first three chapters in Part II of this book, by Lazarus, Levy, and Koocher, are concerned with facilitating positive coping in individuals. Rather than review specific interventions, these authors step back to reexamine the coping process in illness situations. Prevention of psychopathology by health psychologists will be greatly aided by answers to the questions: What psychological sequalae of illness should be prevented? What individual differences sensitize patients to the stresses of illness? The next three chapters by DiMatteo, Moos, and Fordyce focus on different environments, including the medical setting, the family and other social networks, and the greater disability "system" in society, that can influence the psychological outcomes of illness.

Richard Lazarus is professor of psychology at the University of California, Berkeley. In his paper titled "The Trivialization of Distress," Lazarus reviews empirical data and presents a clinical perspective on how emotional distress in physically ill patients is handled by the social milieu and by professionals in the medical care system. He argues there is a general tendency for people to downplay or ignore emotional distress in medical patients and to interpret emotional distress as pathological and the result of a failure of the coping process. In addition, physically ill patients are often under pressure to exhibit positive psychological responses which, in Lazarus' view, are more "pathological" than the responses the environment seeks to suppress. The motivation for this social pressure is self-serving and not for the patient's benefit. Consequently, the patient may indeed exhibit more favorable social reactions, but underlying distress will not be alleviated. Another problem is that psychological treatments for physically ill individuals are mechanically applied without sufficient assessment of the patient's total functioning and needs. Further, psychological treatments have become too special-ized and too disease oriented. More attention should be given to the process of coping across disease categories.

Sandra Levy, a psychologist, is associate professor of psychiatry and medicine, University of Pittsburgh, and the program director of behav-ioral medicine in oncology at Western Psychiatric Institute. Psychosocial symptoms associated with physical disease are traditionally evaluated as adaptive or maladaptive according to some criteria of mental health. In her paper, Levy shows how psychological sequelae can feed back to the biological disease process, and she argues that the "healthiness" of such symptoms should be judged for their physical effects in addition to the impact on psychosocial adjustment. When mental health and physical health outcomes are evaluated simultaneously, some surprising contrasts can emerge. For example, psychological distress in cancer patients might have survival value, while the better adjusted patient might be less well off physically. Although it may be possible to change or to prevent these apparently risky behavioral responses to illness, the potential value of such interventions for physical disease is unknown at this time.

Gerald Koocher is the director of training and senior associate psy-chologist at Children's Hospital Medical Center, Boston. He also is as-sistant professor of psychology at Harvard Medical School. In his paper on promoting coping with illness in childhood, Koocher argues for a noncategorical, generic model for coping with illness in children that cuts across disease entities. This advocacy contrasts with the current trend toward disease-focused research. Further, he proposes a de-velopmental model of coping that deals with three major dimensions of development and their relation to coping with illness: (1) cognitive de-velopment—how do children conceptualize what their illness is; (2) emo-tional development—emotional effects of illness are determined by developmental tasks at hand (e.g., separation from parents); and (3) so-cial contexts—psychological sequelae are influenced by communication and stress in the social environment. Prevention of psychological disor-der involves three steps: (1) helping children anticipate the course of the disease and its treatment; (2) intervening with support at key points (e.g., at the diagnosis, treatment, re-entry into school); and (3) educating chil-dren so that they have greater control over the treatment process and are free to communicate about the disease.

Robin DiMatteo is associate professor of psychology at the University of California, Riverside. DiMatteo argues that physician behavior has a profound influence on the psychological/behavioral responses of the ill patient. She presents an analysis of the doctor-patient relationship from the standpoint of information exchange and physician communication skills that reveals that patients often gain little information in their visits to the doctor and that they exhibit a low rate of understanding and retention of the health information they are given. The cause of this problem is rooted in the fact that patients are socialized to be passive and physicians exert control over the interaction without regard to the patient's needs. Psychological responses to illness and treatment, such as satisfaction, compliance with medical regimens, and coping with stressful treatments, can be improved by education and by specific positive physician behaviors including positive affect and empathy.

Rudolf H. Moos, psychologist, is professor, director of the Social Ecology Laboratory, and director of Post-doctoral Research Training in the Department of Psychiatry and Behavioral Sciences at Stanford University. In his paper on "human contexts," Moos presents a model of the relationship of social networks, coping resources, and stress to psychological and physical dysfunction. Longitudinal studies show, in general, that poorer psychological and physical outcomes are predicted by stress, by few social resources, and by avoidance coping modes as opposed to active coping modes. Interventions can be directed at all three of these domains. While preventive interventions usually focus on coping in individuals, there is good reason to believe that interventions directed at the environment to enhance social supports would also be effective in preventing psychopathology. Moos calls for more emphasis on environmental assessment in order to determine the risk for poor psychological outcomes. He outlines specific social setting characteristics that predict greater illness and psychological dysfunction.

Wilbert E. Fordyce is professor of clinical psychology, Department of Rehabilitation Medicine, University of Washington. Fordyce presents an anlysis of trends in wage replacement compensation for physical disability and the effect of compensation on illness behavior. Beginning with a behavioral conceptualization of pain as a set of operants under the control of environmental contingencies, he points to money as being a powerful maintainer of illness behavior and a promotor of the sick and disabled role in society. In general, people who have compensation coverage on the job miss more work than people who do not. There has been a dramatic increase in awarding wage replacement compensation for certain disabilities, especially for musculoskeletal disabilities. The trend is greatest in female and young workers. Prevention of chronic, intractable, and maladaptive illness behavior necessitates a re-evaluation of the public policy for compensation.

The last chapter in this volume is by Charles A. Kiesler, professor of psychology and dean of the College of Humanities and Social Sciences at Carnegie-Mellon University. The purpose of his paper is to delineate the implications for public health policy of the prevention themes presented in both parts of the book, that is, preventing health risk behaviors and

278 JAMES C. ROSEN AND LAURA J. SOLOMON

promoting coping with illness. Health promotion holds great interest for the behavioral scientist because so many of the causes and consequences of physical illness are subject to behavioral analysis and control. Health promotion also represents a public policy issue because such a significant portion of national resources is allocated to this problem and because presently increasing resource allocation is not necessarily associated with a greater benefit in terms of health outcomes. The theme of Kiesler's paper is that the separate interests of scientific inquiry and public policy should be brought together. Some of his caveats are: (1) Many cause and effect relationships in health and behavior may not be translatable into specific public policy changes. (2) The current manpower in health professions is inadequate for individual efforts to promote behavior change, and programs that rely on individual caregivers will never keep pace with the demand. (3) Although it is important to demonstrate the effectiveness of interventions for the sake of determining cause and effect in health and behavior, such interventions should be evaluated for their potential impact on the national need.

10
The Trivialization of Distress

Richard S. Lazarus

No human problem is potentially more poignant than the distress caused by physical illness. Illness can incapacitate people, damage life-long values and commitments, destroy social relationships, produce role losses, generate discomfort and pain, result in repeated or continual loss of dignity, force a person to live with debilitating uncertainties, and threaten life itself.

There have been a number of excellent reviews and analyses of the problem of coping with physical illness, sometimes directed at particular illnesses such as cancer (e.g., Barofsky, 1981; Cohen & Lazarus, 1979, 1983; Dunkel-Schetter & Wortman, 1982; Leventhal & Nerenz, 1983; Mages & Mendelsohn, 1979; Taylor, Wood, & Lichtman, in press) and burn injuries in children (Wisely, Masur, & Morgan, 1983), and sometimes directed at very broad targets, as in Silver and Wortman's (1980) treatment of coping with undesirable life events, Coyne and Holroyd's (1982) discussion of illness, Kendall's (1983) review of the stresses of hospitalization and medical procedures, Sobel's (1981) account of behavior therapy in the care of the terminally ill, and a review by Anderson and Masur (1983) of research on psychological preparation of patients for invasive medical and dental procedures.

However, there seems to be a blind spot, a mind set if you will, which, if left unaddressed, will prevent us from getting full value from our research efforts on coping with illness. This impediment has to do with the way we treat distress itself. I will argue below that distress is trivialized by the social milieu and by the professionals who work in the medical care system.

The societal and professional tendency to downplay the negative and accentuate the positive trivializes distress by undermining its legitimacy and challenging the reality of the circumstances that generate it. It is as if

I want to express appreciation to a number of students and colleagues who carefully read and commented on early versions of this paper; they include James C. Coyne, Gayle Dakof, Anita DeLongis, Paul Ekman, and Rand Gruen. In addition, warm thanks are in order for the thoughtful editing and advice throughout all stages of the manuscript by Carol Carr, and my research colleague, Susan Folkman.

one were saying to the victims of tragedy that they have no right to feel bad about having lost what they regard as the most precious of life's possessions. Implicit in such trivialization, too, is that distress is unworthy and even pathological. Distressed persons are seen as failing to cope as they should; they have failed through weakness to remain cheerful and optimistic in the face of misfortune. Thus, they are not only victims of illness but also of the attitudes and judgments of the very people who present themselves as wanting to help.

What are the dimensions of this problem of trivialization? We are besieged by seemingly well-intentioned efforts to get the ill to think positively, to overcome any adversity, to root out negative feelings that display unhappiness or despair, to be upbeat about the tragic aspects of living—even of dying—and, at a more superficial level, to "have a nice day," a triumph of style over substance. Aside from the implication of push-button automatization of feelings in the latter remark, rarely, if ever, do we truly feel good if we think we have reasons for feeling bad. The recent passion for helping people cope with the adversities of illness by thinking positively is, in effect, part of a broader societal mandate to accentuate the positive and smilingly accept our lot, negative though it may be. The tyranny of this attitude is that one cannot refuse to comply without appearing to be a misanthrope and ingrate.

In her stage theory of dying, Kübler-Ross (1969) tells us that acceptance will be our terminal emotional state. As Rosenbaum (1982) sardonically suggests, this belief may lead to irresistible social pressure on the patient to race through the more painful stages of dying, such as anger and grief, in order to keep the nuisance of dying to a minimum, and may cause the caregiver to encourage a way of dying that is rationalized as a science-based, healthy norm. One should not, as Dylan Thomas urged his father, "rage against the dying of the light."

In the television program "Over Easy," devoted to aging and old people, we are treated to a succession of role models who demonstrate that being old (is) can be wonderful. What might be the reaction of ailing old people who watch such unremittingly upbeat portrayals of the extremely favored or heroic elderly? Inspiration? Envy? Or despair?

We trivialize the distress involved in aging when we hold up as models people who look like exceptions to the aging process, such as the 70-year-old man who plunges into ice water, suggesting we are physically the same at that age as we were at 30 or 40. Wouldn't it be better to value the things that *can* improve with age, for example, wisdom, perspective, a sense of history, and perhaps the weakening of social constraints that inhibit self-expression?

And what of the culture and ideology of the professional health care specialist? In behavioral medicine we are led to believe that almost any form of illness or disability can be—read this *should be*—transcended, that to feel unhappy, depressed, or upset with the realities of personal disaster or unsatisfying existence for more than a brief interval is a failure of coping. Would we want to say that getting sick is to be prized because it is an opportunity to demonstrate our ability to endure or to turn adversity into challenge? The media are dangerously close to this view in presenting people grateful for an illness-based "death sentence" because it gave them an appreciation of life. I recently read a little pamphlet for cancer patients called *The Sky Is Bluer Now: Thoughts on Living and Cancer* (Siegel, 1981), based on the inspirational experience of a 47-year-old woman, Anita Siegel, who had an 8-year bout with lung cancer. She comments as follows:

This may sound strange to you, but I'm sort of happy I got cancer. It changed my whole concept of what life is all about. My goals became different. My interests changed. . . . The last eight years of my life have been much different from what they could have ever been if I hadn't been faced with the fact that my life might be coming to an end. I've accomplished more and I've experienced more than I could possibly have imagined in an entire lifetime. (p. 3)

The pamphlet goes on to say that, remarkable as it might sound, the reader, too, can find a way to wrest challenge and growth and inner peace from illness instead of fear, isolation, and hopelessness. I have no reason to doubt that Anita Siegel and many others have had this experience. But for most, the point of view expressed here is a half-truth used for the purpose of swallowing a very bitter pill; and for still others, the statement is an implicit chastisement against experiencing their understandable anger, depression, and pain.

Consider further the popularization of a pathetically simplified interpretation of social support. Social relationships are among the most important and complex of human activities and can simultaneously be a source of stress *and* satisfaction. Recently, the state of California distributed an expensive-looking pamphlet with the title *Friends Can Be Good Medicine* (California Department of Mental Health, 1981), which trivializes the multiple and often contradictory functions of social support. The introduction says that "This book is designed to help you see the vital role that friendship plays in your life and to help you find out when, how and why loving, caring relationships with others can enhance your physical and mental health (p. 3)." The message is presented as a new idea based on the findings of medical research. About this pamphlet's exposure, Fischer (1982) recently observed:

Early last year Californians heard the message that friends can be good medicine on the radio, saw it on television, read it on bumper stickers and shopping bags, and discussed it in 2,000 workshops and special meetings. . . . In California, close to six million people probably got the message. . . . Other Americans may soon hear the same slogan, since the National Mental Health Association is now adapting the material for nationwide use. (pp. 74, 78)

Fischer raises many questions about the reasoning behind the argument, pointing to socioeconomic as well as cause-and-effect issues that could vitiate it. People in behavioral medicine, and in state departments of health, must develop more appreciation of the complexities involved in the psychology and health aspects of social support.

Surely it is desirable to have friends. No one wants bad relationships with others or to be lonely. However, inspirational messages like these do not tell people already feeling lonely and deprived of warm, supportive human relationships how to correct the deficiency. So, the dictum that friends are good medicine must only make the friendless feel even more alone and inadequate, even more deprived. Neither is there any mention of the fact that friendship is not a one-way street, that in order to have friends one must be a friend in return, and that friendship often takes its psychological toll both on the giving and receiving ends. Here we have a trivialization of the complex problem of social support, and, at the same time, a denigration of those who, for one reason or another, are functioning in the world without friends.

Consequences of the Trivialization of Distress

If the trivialization of distress had only a positive effect on victims of illness and other misfortune, it would be well justified or, at the very least, could be viewed with benign amusement rather than as a dangerous half-truth. We could, moreover, frown at the self-destructive emotionality of the characters in Greek tragedy and the despair of Tolstoy's Ivan Ilyich over not having lived fully, or regard as inane the existential crises faced by the contemporary protagonists in novels by Dideon, Styron, and Heller. But, as things now stand, the characters in fiction provide us with a fuller view of the complex, human struggle and basic dialectics of life than we are willing to grant our patients, loved ones, and fellow human beings. Do we as professionals want to put our stamp of approval on any one, simplistic doctrine of living when history shows there is no simple, one-sided solution?

Further, is it possible that the well-meaning banalities used to generate positive thinking might increase rather than decrease human misery? Most of us experience anger, depression, pain, and demoralization at one time or another. The ideal social image demanding that negative feelings be mastered is probably an added source of a sense of failure. The culturally prescribed veneration of self-control, dignity, and cheerfulness in adversity is not the only source of damaging pressure on many people; similar internal standards can also impose a heavy burden. Writing about Ernest Hemingway's depression and suicide, Yalom and Yalom (1971) state:

The individual cannot in real life approximate the superhuman scope of the idealized image. Reality eventually intrudes, and he realizes the discrepancy between what he wants to be and what he is in actuality. At this point, he is flooded with self-hatred, which is expressed through a myriad of self-destructive mechanisms. (p. 488)

An observational report by Hackett and Weisman (1964) is marvelously insightful about the plight of the hospitalized dying patient, facing the inability of friends, loved ones, and professional workers to face the problem honestly. Visitors conveyed a denial-centered, upbeat atmosphere that the patients dared not assault lest, in addition to having to cope with dying, they endanger the few social relationships yet remaining to them by driving people away with their distress. Coates and Wortman (1980) have speculated about the cover-up of feelings in depressed persons, reacting to the negative sanctions of others to any display of distress. They write:

The depressed person's attempts to conceal his or her symptoms may well prompt more favorable reactions from others, but these are not likely to prove very helpful in alleviating the depression. Because the depressed are concealing their problems and feelings, they will probably doubt that others really understand them. Consequently, the depressed are likely to feel that others' kindness is not meant for them as they are, but rather is meant for the most positive image they are presenting. The depressed may well conclude that others would not be so kind if they knew what the depressed know about themselves. . . . Therefore, despite others' positive responses to the reduced symptoms, depressed people are likely to feel hopeless, isolated, and lonely as ever, because they realize that they receive support only by concealing how they actually feel. (p. 172)

This theme has also been stated nicely by Weakland, Fisch, Watzlawick, and Bodin (1974), based on their work with depressed patients:

Consider . . . a common pattern between a depressed patient and his family. The more they try to cheer him up and make him see the positive sides of life, the more depressed the patient is likely to get: "They don't even understand me." The actions meant to *alleviate* the behavior of the other party *aggravate* it; the "cure" becomes worse than the original "disease." Unfortunately, this usually remains unnoted by those involved and even is disbelieved if anyone else tries to point it out. (p. 149)

Watzlawick and Coyne (1980) describe just such a family process in the following passage:

. . . the most remarkable, recurrent pattern of interaction consisted of their combined efforts to encourage Mr. B. [after a second stroke] to pull himself together, try harder, and to see his situation more optimistically—whereupon he invariably responded with increased helplessness, pointing out to them how little they understood the severity of his physical handicaps and of his dejection, to which they then responded with increased, obviously well-meant optimism and encouragement. The family thus seemed to be caught in a typical Game Without End—an interactional impasse in which more of a problem-perpetuating "solution" by one party is countered by more of the same reaction by the other. Although this pattern was obvious to the observers, the family was unaware of it and only conceded that they had not dealt well with his predicament. (p. 14)

Without abandoning the main thesis altogether, one could argue, too, that there are some circumstances in which negative sanctions against distress could be justified. General pronouncements without concern for the conditions under which they do not apply—including individual differences—are usually dangerous. This kind of qualification seems particularly appropriate for the above analyses of depression, too. For example, negative sanctions, in the form of evidence that others have begun to be fed up, or punishing the melancholy person's continued manifestations of affective distress with its implicit plea for sympathy (see also Coyne, 1976a, 1976b), might ultimately jar depressed people into deciding that they have had enough of self-pity and into taking steps to bring their downward emotional spiral to an end.

Moreover, we must somehow also come to terms with observations such as those provided in a recent report by Redd (1982), who described the behavioral treatment of a terminal cancer patient who wanted to die and who had been crying and moaning 48%—sometimes 60%—of his waking hours. The treatment consisted of depriving him of social stimulation contingent upon his crying behavior. By the tenth day of this operant reinforcement-centered treatment, the patient's crying had ceased and he was again able to engage in conversation with others. Here we have neither the trivialization nor denigration of distress, but a direct assault to expunge it, at least, in behavior.

We are not told anything in this study about the patient's subjective emotional state after treatment, and any inference about it from his behavior is hazardous. There may also be reason for uncertainty about whether it was the treatment program that resulted in the behavior change, since the evidence is based on a single case and the behavior change seems to have come about shortly before the patient's death; perhaps it was this nearness to dying that resulted in the dramatic change. However, in all fairness, the question must also be posed whether we can truly claim in this case that the superficially harsh sanction against the distressed and distressing behavior was damaging when it, at least, appeared to result for the first time not only in cessation of crying but also in successful interaction with others.

Although no one would argue that moaning and crying most of the time is a desirable behavioral pattern, indicative as it is of emotional misery, we cannot assume that calm and accepting people are necessarily better off than those who are distressed. Research evidence exists that some forms of emotional distress may actually facilitate survival. Janoff-Bulman and Marshall (1982) have found, for example, that institutionalized, aged subjects, who reported feeling positive about their lives, showed a higher mortality rate roughly three years later than those who had earlier complained and reported strong negative feelings. Presumably, the former accepted their lot comfortably, whereas the complainers were aggressively fighting to preserve control over their lives and make things better. The idea that the aged who fight to stay alive or complain might live longer than those who give up and accept their losses and impending death is also suggested by findings by Turner, Tobin, and Lieberman (1972) and Aldrich and Mendkoff (1963). Similar findings have been reported in a new study by Lieberman and Tobin (in press). To this evidence, we must also add findings cited by Levy (this volume) that cancer survival may be facilitated by aggressive, complaining, fighting emotional reactions and impaired by reactions of helplessness, passivity, and depression. Depending on how we define a positive adaptational outcome, we should be wary about slavishly assuming that aged or sick people are necessarily better off if they peacefully accept losses rather than display a pattern of struggle, with its accompanying distress.

Motives for the Trivialization of Distress

There appear to be a number of major social and personal pressures to trivialize distress. The first is the well-meaning intention to help ameliorate suffering. We want to encourage hope, and we know that people such as Anita Siegel in her struggle with cancer can sometimes be greatly benefited psychologically by achieving a positive outlook (Lazarus, 1983).

In this connection, we must not overlook the remarkable accomplishments of people who, severely handicapped by illness or accident or worn and deprived of strength as a result of illness, make heroic and sometimes remarkably successful efforts to overcome or compensate for their handicap. These instances can be a source of great inspiration, and just as it would be wrong to overvalue positive thinking and regard it as suitable for everyone or every condition, it would also be wrong to undervalue compensatory efforts against overwhelmingly negative

physical odds. Friends and loved ones often contribute to the infantilization of the ill and handicapped by assuming they are more helpless than
they really are. The issue is one of achieving a constructive balance, and
of not applying the same prescriptions and proscriptions across the
board.

Second, putting pressure on people to think positively and inhibit
manifestations of their distress is self-serving on the part of professionals
who deal with suffering, as well as on the part of close friends and loved
ones who must share the distress. Such sharing is a tremendous, loving
gift. Whatever it does for the recipient, facing the distress as a caring
friend or loved one exacts a price from the caregiver, and the more
caring, the higher the price. It is much easier to spare oneself pain by
encouraging the patient to curtail expressions of distress. To confront
distress is to take on a great human burden and to make major personal
sacrifices, supposedly what real friendship and affection are all about.
The emotional cost is lower for the more detached professional, but it
grows in proportion to the extent distancing is abandoned and professionals allow themselves to experience what the patient is experiencing.

Third, innocent suffering can be a major indictment of ourselves and
the justice of the world in which we live, a state of affairs that is highly
threatening. Lerner's (1980; Lerner & Miller, 1978) "just world" theory
suggests that when people become aware that someone else has experienced undeserved suffering or failed to get what he or she deserved, they
may doubt they can trust their own environment. To manage the threat
to ourselves, we tend to turn away from such people or blame them for
having brought the disaster on themselves. This action makes it possible
to continue to believe the myth that disaster cannot happen to us. We are
reassured, moreover, if the victim can transcend the tragedy through
heroic efforts, acceptance, or positive thinking. Negative moods and
despair are in general contagious, increasing the threat and cost to ourselves (Coyne, 1976a, 1976b; Strack & Coyne, 1983).

Fourth, there is a growing movement toward the mechanization of
intervention in the medical care system, based in part on the high-tech
features of modern medicine and, partly, on strong economic pressures
and the rapid increase in the size of institutions. This mechanization is
displayed in the tendency to treat diseases rather than people, and to be
more concerned with techniques of intervention than with processes. At
a time when people feel more dehumanized by society than ever before,
the medical profession is also in greater danger of losing sight of the
person in favor of the person's ailments and symptoms.

The first three motives for trivialization are part of the general human
condition and reflect the natural conflicts and tendencies of all people,
including those in the health professions. However, the outlook of health

professionals is a powerful force that trickles down to the popular culture through the media. The increasing tendency toward the mechanization of intervention seems so important and ominous that I will expand upon it further below.

The Mechanization of Intervention

The mechanization of intervention is, I think, well illustrated by the recent special issue (December 1982, Vol. 50) of the *Journal of Consulting and Clinical Psychology* on behavioral medicine. The chapter headings for this journal issue comprise the following ailments and problems that I will list verbatim: smoking, obesity, hypertension, headache, insomnia, chronic pain, asthma, Raynaud's Syndrome, Type A behaviors, adherence to medical regimens, gastrointestinal disorders, arthritis, diabetes, and aversive reactions to cancer treatment. The discussions, by and large able and scholarly treatments, center on the specific features of the disorder.

There are, of course, some good reasons for organizing etiological research and treatment by illnesses. For one thing, illness and illness behavior may, to some extent, reflect particular personality constellations whose role in the etiology of and reactions to the illness could greatly affect the course of intervention. Because causation, processes, and effects differ, one must deal with asthma differently in certain respects than with hypertension or cancer, and it is important to know the characteristics and course of the ailment. What is missing, however, is any overall concern with what might be common to these illnesses with respect to associated problems of living or with underlying processes, and with attempts to understand conceptually how the tactics or technology of behavioral interventions relate to each other or to common psychological processes. Since I assume the editor (Blanchard, 1982) must have sought and obtained what he was after, it was surprising and a bit reassuring to find him writing:

> As I read the articles in this issue, I was struck by one point in particular: The same intervention procedures (most commonly, relaxation and biofeedback) apply across a wide range of problems. What has been lacking in this field is a wide-ranging integration focusing on general behavioral-change procedures, such as stimulus control, and how they can be applied across a variety of problem areas. The compartmentalization of the field by problem areas rather than by change process is also apparent in this issue, but it is hoped that this situation will soon be redressed. (p. 796)

Blanchard is correct in noting this overreliance on rather mechanical intervention procedures, such as relaxation and biofeedback, which address symptoms rather than the problems generating distress. I am reminded here, too, of Andrasik and Holroyd's (1980; see also Holroyd & Andrasik, 1982) splendid research on biofeedback, in which it was found that regardless of whether subjects were learning to increase, decrease, or maintain constant levels of frontalis muscle tension, they showed similar reductions in headache symptoms, and that these positive effects were maintained in a follow-up evaluation 6 weeks after treatment ended. In other words, when biofeedback works, it does so not because of its peripheral, mechanical effects, but through some central processes, probably cognitive and coping related, that center on the person's ongoing relationship with the environment, including, perhaps, the difficulties underlying distress.

What is missing in the more mechanical approaches to intervention, with its major emphasis on the illness and its management, is an appreciation of the whole person in the context of his or her environment, including goals, obligations and commitments, wishes and fears, social ties, meanings, and sense of future—in short, all the factors in living that carry heavy emotional loadings when a person is harmed or threatened by illness. By only superficially addressing focal issues or symptoms by means of mechanical treatments, we ignore distress and its function as an indicator of how patients think they are faring in their lives.

Indeed, emotional distress is a major, common feature of illnesses such as cancer. In a study of many hundreds of cancer patients after their hospitalization for treatment, patient records revealed that mood disturbances, particularly anxiety, depression, suicidal thoughts, and guilt, constituted the second most frequently noted patient problem, with somatic side effects such as pain first, and impairment of family relationships—itself a highly emotional problem category—third (Wellisch, Landsverk, Guidera, Pasnau, & Fawzy, 1983; see also Plumb & Holland, 1981). Given the tendency to inhibit expressions of distress except to close others, my guess is that the actual number of patients struggling with distress is far higher. In any case, the authors write:

> Quality assessment of medical care should include wider evaluation than purely technical aspects of medical care. However, in a large-scale review of medical audits, 70% included no evaluation of psychosocial variables whatever. (p. 11)

In a recent, brief comment in *Psychology Today,* Thompson (as reported by Jean Stratton, 1983) notes that medical internists commonly fail to recognize that their patients are worried or unhappy about anything besides their physical health. Of 87 patients who regularly visited the clinic, more than 48 were seriously distressed about at least one matter other than the illness itself; 29% were very much worried about finances, 19% about work, 15% about sex, and 10% revealed suicidal tendencies. Nevertheless, except in the most obvious instances, internists repeatedly underestimated patients' distress—even after long experience with them—despite the fact that the patients were not at all reluctant to reveal such feelings when asked.

The National Institutes of Health also defines its research purview by separate divisions dealing with disorders such as heart disease, cancer, mental health, alcoholism, drug abuse, and so on, making it difficult, if not impossible, to determine to what extent and in what ways these illnesses have overlapping causes and consequences, engage common psychological, social, and physiological processes, and require common approaches to treatment and prevention. Thus, to this day we cannot say whether the Type A behavior pattern, for example, might contribute to mortality from diverse causes or only from cardiovascular disease.

The emphasis on specific illnesses in the special issue of the *Journal of Consulting and Clinical Psychology* has an added dehumanizing effect; little is ever said about individuals, and virtually nothing about emotion. Here are psychologists, not physicians, precisely epitomizing the dehumanization of modern medical care (see also Burnham, 1982).

In the December 1982 edition of the *APA Monitor,* medical doctors in training and in later practice are described as rigidly centered on the scientific technology of their field and resistant to developing the interpersonal skills whereby the patient can be listened to and feel heard. As one health professional concerned with children put it, "You could teach moral developmental stages, but doctors have five minutes with a patient and they want to know what to tell the child's parents." Another psychologist reports, ". . . all physicians want to know was, 'What are five signs of the syndrome? Just give me five signs.'" Still another comments, more sympathetically, "Medical students are required to learn such a huge amount of information dealing with life or death issues, and the cost of not getting it all down is so very high, that they almost have to create a distance from patients as human beings" (p. 31). We know, of course, from Sarason's (1977) rich account of physicians' declining morale at midlife that they have become trapped by these destructive dehumanizing values that now inhere in the medical care system and by which their early enthusiasm and sense of dedication have been co-opted. For a doctor's own account of his unhappy experiences as a patient with cancer, see *Vital Signs* by Fitzhugh Mullan (1982).

Lewis Thomas (1983) expresses the dilemma very well when he points out how medical treatment since the 1930s has improved the survival rate through its remarkable control of once deadly infections and its surgical tours de force, but, at the same time, has distanced itself from the patient. He writes:

The mechanization of scientific medicine is here to stay. The new medicine works. . . . It [treatment] looks to the patient like a different experience from what his parents told him about, with something important left out. The doctor seems less like the close friend and confidant, less interested in him as a person, wholly concerned with treating the disease. And there is no changing this, no going back; nor, when you think about it, is there really any reason for wanting to go back. If I develop the signs and symptoms of malignant hypertension, or cancer of the colon, or subacute bacterial endocarditis, I want as much comfort and friendship as I can find at hand, but mostly I want to be treated quickly and effectively so as to survive, if that is possible. If I am in bed in a modern hospital, worrying about the cost of that bed as well, I want to get out as fast as possible, whole if possible. (pp. 58–59)

Yet, the cost paid for this major and important improvement in the efficacy of modern medicine in the form of psychological distress and feelings of abandonment is also grave. In this connection, a comment by George Engel (1977), a prominent figure in biomedicine, is instructive:

. . . the behavior of the physician and the relationship between patient and physician powerfully influence therapeutic outcome for better or for worse. These constitute psychological effects which may directly modify the illness experience or indirectly affect underlying biochemical processes, the latter by virtue of interactions between psychophysiological reactions and biochemical processes implicated in the disease. . . . Thus, insulin requirements of a diabetic patient may fluctuate significantly depending on how the patient perceives his relationship with the doctor. Furthermore, the successful application of rational therapies is limited by the physician's ability to influence and modify the patient's behavior in directions concordant with health needs. Contrary to what . . . [many] would have us believe, the physician's role is, and always has been, very much that of educator and psychotherapist. To know how to induce peace of mind in the patient and enhance his faith in the healing powers of his physician requires psychological knowledge and skills, not merely charisma. These too are outside the biomedical framework. (p. 134)

It is often difficult to understand the multiple (sometimes disguised), emotionally significant meanings in what a patient is saying under even optimal circumstances. Sociolinguistic analyses of conversations between people of different backgrounds and experience suggest (cf. Gumperz, 1982) that if one does not know the discourse rules and strategies of the other person, it is easy to misunderstand what is really being said and respond literally and inappropriately. As DiMatteo (this volume) demonstrates in her review of extensive research on doctor-patient communication, doctors often fail to grasp the real message of their patients, which can include expressions of fear, brittle defenses against the fear, requests for reassurance, the need for more information, a sense of hopelessness, and lack of will to cope. Who among us in our role as patients has not dealt with physicians who, in their haste, fatigue from overload, boredom, or just plain insensitivity, distort or fail to hear what we are saying about our real and imagined ailments, and demonstrate this misunderstanding at every juncture of a pressured, 15-minute examination conversation? It takes both commitment and skill on the part of professionals—expressed minimally in the willingness to take the time to listen—to catch the cognitive-affective messages most patients and their families send.

Wanted: More Attention to the Emotional Life

My use of the theoretical concept of *cognitive appraisal* (e.g., Lazarus, 1981; Lazarus & Launier, 1978) expresses the need to understand individual differences in emotional response to similar conditions of life. Cognitive appraisal theory states that the intensity and quality of each experienced emotion flow from the way people evaluate the significance of what is happening for their well-being (see also Lazarus, 1982). Because illnesses are usually complex experiences, as well as being pervasive and sustained, they can involve all the distressing emotions in the human repertoire, as well as the positive emotions. These emotions can occur in the same time frame because each is an evaluative response to some particular facet or stage of the encounter. The kinds of emotions experienced and their intensity can tell us much about how a person interprets what is happening with respect to the fate of cherished values, commitments, and other sources of meaning in life.

Personal background agendas also help us understand why some people react with great distress, even when the harms or dangers of an illness seem, consensually speaking, minor, while others respond with equanimity or only moderate distress to harms and dangers that are consensually severe. If we do not consider the individual meaning or significance of an illness and the person characteristics that underlie it, we are at a loss to understand the emotional response, how it is managed, and how to manage it. Throughout this paper, my criticism has been directed against the assumption that a positive attitude on the part of the patient can be injected as easily as an antibiotic and, moreover, *should* be. It is as if the medical profession, although imbued with a concern for the psychological well-being of the ill, can express its concern only in those ways that are expedient and in tune with high technology. If we choose to ignore the fact of individual differences in appraisal and the emotional experience of our patients, we severely impair our ability to help them cope successfully.

In addition to the concept of cognitive appraisal and its role in emotion, it is also important to recognize that *coping* also affects emotion. There are at least two functions of coping: problem-focused coping is directed at changing the troubled person-environment relationship causing distress, and emotion-focused coping is directed at the management of the distressing emotions themselves (Folkman & Lazarus, 1980). Problem-focused coping is the target of most interventions for people facing the diagnostic, preventive, and treatment problems associated with major physical illness.

The function of emotion-focused coping, however, is equally important, especially in transactions in which there are limits to the control people have over harms and their sources (Folkman, in press). In these situations, feelings must be regulated so that physiological resources do not become depleted unnecessarily, thereby increasing the probability of inadequate problem-solving, exacerbating the existing illness, or inducing other illnesses through the debilitating effects of emotional distress on immune competency or the unwillingness to do what is necessary to manage the illness. In addition, emotion-focused coping includes maintaining a sense of hope, self-esteem, and the value of life on which continued problem-focused efforts to survive and flourish also depend.

The reader would misunderstand me by concluding that I do not value help in the control of pain, anxiety, and other forms of distress connected with diagnostic and treatment procedures even though it leaves untouched larger-order, long-range, existential sources of distress related to illness. There is every reason to admire and draw upon the splendid series of studies conducted over many years by Leventhal and his colleagues (cited in full in Leventhal & Nerenz, 1983), as well as research by many others (e.g., Kaplan, Atkins, & Lenhard, 1982, on interventions to help people cope with sigmoidoscopy). Nor does there seem to be much doubt that physical exercise (see Blumenthal, Wallace, Williams, & Needels, 1982; Blumenthal, Williams, Needels, & Wallace, 1982) and other superficial intervention procedures, such as relaxation and meditation (e.g., Benson, 1976; Boswell & Murray, 1979; Carrington, 1977; Davidson, Goleman, & Schwartz, 1976; DeGood & Redgate, 1982; Goldman, Domitor, & Murray, 1979; Goleman & Schwartz, 1976; Lyles, Burish, Korzely, & Oldham, 1982), can have physiological and psychological value.

What I have been saying is that too much of our efforts at intervention offer rather mechanical procedures for facilitating problem-focused coping with relatively minor, surface aspects of the problem of illness. Such approaches will be most useful for problems and distress that arise from lack of knowledge, skill, or experience at a procedure, uncomplicated by personal agendas. When the problems are uncomplicated or not severe, the task of intervention is to fill in knowledge and skill gaps. However, when we view people more holistically, in the context of their overall life situation—in the psychological sense intended by Lewin—we must be exceedingly humble about the contribution we have been making in the medical care setting.

The dismal record of adherence to medical regimens, for example, should alert us that we have been failing to convince most patients that the appropriate preventive or therapeutic problem-focused acts of self-care require their sustained attention and effort. Sackett and Snow (1979) suggest, for example, that the average rate of adherence for short-term medical regimens is only 65%, for long-term preventive regimens it is 57%, and for long-term treatment regimens, 54%. I believe this lack of success in convincing patients to act in their own best interests is, again, the result of ignoring the background life agendas that are the crucial underpinnings of the desired conduct.

So, to return to the place where we started, the trivialization of distress, what can we do for people who are distressed because of personal agendas—whether neurotic or a result of the universal plight of human existence—that make them vulnerable to distress? One thing we can do is to acknowledge individual differences in the ways people appraise and cope. The formula that works for some does not work for others. A major research task remains to establish the conditional variables on which cognitive appraisals and patterns of coping depend, so that people can be grouped on the basis of similarities and differences for purposes of intervention.

Secondly, the plight of the patient should be appreciated and not patronized by "a pastiche of gimmicks and pat statements," as Timnick (1982) phrases it. In some, perhaps most, instances, genuine acknowledgment and appreciation of the frightening or destructive situation being faced would go a long way toward gaining the trust of the patient and offering surcease. Although it is often useful to point to reasons for hope where they exist, there is nothing worse than pressing the point that the patient has inadequate grounds for distress, that is, to trivialize it. We must do what Vivian Cadden suggests in Caplan (1974), "*Help* [the sufferer] *to confront the crisis.* Help him to talk about and realize the danger, the pain, the trouble, the real element of the crisis. Help him to speak of unspoken fears, to grieve, and even to cry" (p. 293, emphasis added).

These recommendations do not constitute an argument for depth therapy. To recognize that there is distress, even when it lurks below the surface of a cheerful face, is not necessarily to advocate one kind of intervention over another, but to acknowledge the difficult task of managing emotional distress and to give emotion-focused coping the importance it deserves. Professionals are not likely to deal with distress if the only course of intervention is mechanical, symptom-centered, or militantly behavioral. In addition to concentrating on the immediate, problem-focused tasks created by illness, people must always be viewed in the broadest possible context of their personal agendas and life situations. Despite long-standing repetition and the more recent sloganeering of holistic medicine, this theme continues to be ignored, all the more so as medical care becomes increasingly technical and cost conscious.

So that intervention might become more differentiated with respect to types of patients and life circumstances, and therefore more effective in the aggregate, we must continue to search for ways of assessing stress and emotion and the coping processes that people use in illness and other life crises. We must use such measurement to identify patterns of coping that produce either positive or negative outcomes. There is already much evidence (see Cohen & Lazarus, 1983) that the same coping process may have positive effects in one context, say while the person is in the hospital, and negative effects after the person has returned home; positive effects before a heart attack and negative after; positive for one illness and negative for another; and positive at one stage of a crisis and negative at another stage. Given the widespread conviction that coping is important, it is somewhat shocking to realize that, except for the Cannon-Selye theme that stress produces neurohumoral changes affecting tissue function, few systematic speculations or analyses exist about the many ways coping might influence feelings of well-being, social functioning, and somatic health (see Holroyd & Lazarus, 1982; Lazarus & Folkman, in press), and there is still less programmatic research.

With patience, modesty, persistence, thoughtfulness, skill, humanity, and a search for the necessary knowledge, there is much reason to hope that we will be able to offer meaningful help to the victims of serious physical illness. However, it would be well for professionals, of all people, not to fall into the trap of popularization that now plagues media treatments of stress, coping and adaptation, and programs of stress management. When professionals take their simplistic formulas for intervention too seriously and oversell their product, thereby encouraging the public to think in terms of mechanical solutions that fail to address the most important sources of distress, they help create a culture in which distress is trivialized, or, at the least, encourage public acceptance of an already existing pattern of trivialization. The goal of realizing effective intervention requires more sophisticated thought than presently exists, and a deep respect for the person receiving our help.

References

Aldrich, C. K., & Mendkoff, E. Relocation of the aged and disabled: A mortality study. In B. L. Neugarten (Ed.), *Middle age and aging: A reader in social psychology*. Chicago: University of Chicago Press, 1963.
Anderson, K. O., & Masur, F. T., III. Psychological preparation for invasive medical and dental procedures. *Journal of Behavioral Medicine*, 1983, 6, 1–40.
Andrasik, F., & Holroyd, K. A. A test of specific and nonspecific effects in the

biofeedback treatment of tension headache. *Journal of Consulting and Clinical Psychology*, 1980, *48*, 575–586.

American Psychological Association Monitor, December 1982, p. 31.

Barofsky, I. Issues and approaches to the psychosocial assessment of the cancer patient. In C. K. Prokof & L. A. Bradley (Eds.), *Medical psychology contributions to behavioral medicine.* New York: Academic Press, 1981.

Benson, H. *The relaxation response.* New York: Avon (paperback), 1976.

Blanchard, E. B. Behavioral medicine: Past, present, and future. *Journal of Consulting and Clinical Psychology*, 1982, *50*, 795–796.

Blumenthal, J. A., Wallace, A. G., Williams, R. S., & Needels, T. L. Physiological and psychological variables predict compliance to prescribed exercise therapy in patients recovering from myocardial infarction. *Psychosomatic Medicine*, 1982, *44*, 519–527.

Blumenthal, J. A., Williams, R. S., Needels, T. L., & Wallace, A. G. Psychological changes accompany aerobic exercise in healthy middle-aged adults. *Psychosomatic Medicine*, 1982, *44*, 529–536.

Boswell, P. C., & Murray, E. J. Effects of meditation on psychological and physiological measures of anxiety. *Journal of Consulting and Clinical Psychology*, 1979, *47*, 606–607.

Burnham, J. C. American medicine's golden age: What happened to it? *Science*, 1982, *215*, 1474–1479.

California Department of Mental Health. *Friends can be good medicine.* San Francisco: Pacificon Productions, 1981.

Caplan, G. *Support systems in community mental health.* New York: Behavioral Publications, 1974.

Carrington, P. *Freedom in meditation.* Garden City, N.Y.: Anchor/Doubleday, 1977.

Coates, D., & Wortman, C. B. Depression maintenance and interpersonal control. In A. Baum & J. Singer (Eds.), *Advances in environmental psychology* (Vol. 1). Hillsdale, N.J.: Erlbaum, 1980.

Cohen, F., & Lazarus, R. S. Coping with the stresses of illness. In G. C. Stone & N. E. Adler (Eds.), *Health psychology: A handbook.* San Francisco: Jossey-Bass, 1979.

Cohen, F., & Lazarus, R. S. Coping and adaptation in health and illness. In D. Mechanic (Ed.), *Handbook of health, health care, and the health professions.* New York: The Free Press, 1983.

Coyne, J. C. Depression and the response of others. *Journal of Abnormal Psychology*, 1976, *85*, 186–193. (a)

Coyne, J. C. Toward an interactional description of depression. *Psychiatry*, 1976, *39*, 28–40. (b)

Coyne, J. C., & Holroyd, K. A. Stress, coping, and illness: A transactional perspective. In T. Millon, C. Green, & R. Meagher (Eds.), *Handbook of clinical health psychology.* New York: Plenum, 1982.

Davidson, R. J., Goleman, D. J., & Schwartz, G. E. Attentional and affective concomitants of meditation: A cross-sectional study. *Journal of Abnormal Psychology*, 1976, *85*, 235–238.

DeGood, D. E., & Redgate, E. S. Interrelationship of plasma cortisol and other activation indices during EMG biofeedback training. *Journal of Behavioral Medicine*, 1982, *5*, 213–223.

Dunkel-Schetter, C., & Wortman, C. B. The interpersonal dynamics of cancer: Problems in social relationships and their impact on the patient. In H. S.

Friedman & M. R. DiMatteo (Eds.), *Interpersonal issues in health care.* New York: Academic Press, 1982.

Engel, G. L. The need for a new medical model: A challenge for biomedicine. *Science,* 1977, *196,* 129–136.

Fischer, C. The friendship cure-all. *Psychology Today,* January 1982, pp. 74, 78.

Folkman, S. Personal control and stress and coping processes: A theoretical analysis. *Journal of Personality and Social Psychology,* in press.

Folkman, S., & Lazarus, R. S. An analysis of coping in a middle-aged community sample. *Journal of Health and Social Behavior,* 1980, *21,* 219–239.

Goldman, B. L., Domitor, P. J., & Murray, E. J. Effects of Zen meditation on anxiety reduction and perceptual functioning. *Journal of Consulting and Clinical Psychology,* 1979, *47,* 551–556.

Goleman, D. J., & Schwartz, G. E. Meditation as an intervention in stress reactivity. *Journal of Consulting and Clinical Psychology,* 1976, *44,* 456–466.

Gumperz, J. J. *Discourse strategies: Studies in interactional sociolinguistics.* Cambridge, England: Cambridge University Press, 1982.

Hackett, T. P., & Weisman, A. D. Reactions to the imminence of death. In G. H. Grosser, H. Wechsler, & M. Greenblatt (Eds.), *The threat of impending disaster.* Cambridge, Mass.: MIT Press, 1964.

Holroyd, K. A., & Andrasik, F. Do the effects of cognitive therapy endure? A two-year follow-up of tension headache sufferers treated with cognitive therapy or biofeedback. *Cognitive Therapy and Research,* 1982, *6,* 325–333.

Holroyd, K. A., & Lazarus, R. S. Stress, coping, and somatic adaptation. In L. Goldberger & S. Breznitz (Eds.), *Handbook of stress: Theoretical and clinical aspects.* New York: The Free Press, 1982.

Janoff-Bulman, R., & Marshall, G. Mortality, well-being, and control: A study of a population of institutionalized aged. *Personality and Social Psychology Bulletin,* 1982, *8,* 691–698.

Kaplan, R. M., Atkins, C. J., & Lenhard, L. Coping with a stressful sigmoidoscopy: Evaluation of cognitive and relaxation preparations. *Journal of Behavioral Medicine,* 1982, *5,* 67–82.

Kendall, P. C. Stressful medical procedures: Cognitive-behavioral strategies for stress management and its prevention. In D. Meichenbaum & M. E. Jaremko (Eds.), *Stress reduction and prevention.* New York: Plenum, 1983.

Kübler-Ross, E. *On death and dying.* New York: Macmillan, 1969.

Lazarus, R. S. The stress and coping paradigm. In C. Eisdorfer, D. Cohen, A. Kleinman, & P. Maxim (Eds.), *Models for clinical psychopathology.* New York: Spectrum, 1981.

Lazarus, R. S. Thoughts on the relations between emotion and cognition. *American Psychologist,* 1982, *37,* 1019–1024.

Lazarus, R. S. The costs and benefits of denial. In S. Breznitz (Ed.), *The denial of stress.* New York: International Universities Press, 1983.

Lazarus, R. S., & Folkman, S. Coping and adaptation. In W. D. Gentry (Ed.), *The handbook of behavioral medicine.* New York: Guilford, in press.

Lazarus, R. S., & Launier, R. Stress-related transactions between person and environment. In L. A. Pervin & M. Lewis (Eds.), *Perspectives in interactional psychology.* New York: Plenum, 1978.

Lerner, M. J. *The belief in a just world: A fundamental delusion.* New York: Plenum, 1980.

Lerner, M. J., & Miller, D. J. Just world research and the attribution process: Looking back and ahead. *Psychological Bulletin,* 1978, *81,* 1030–1051.

Leventhal, H., & Nerenz, D. R. A model for stress research and some implications for the control of stress disorders. In D. Meichenbaum & M. Jaremko (Eds.), *Stress reduction and prevention.* New York: Plenum, 1983.

Lieberman, M. A., & Tobin, S. S. *The experience of old age: Stress, coping and survival.* New York: Basic Books, in press.

Lyles, J. N., Burish, T. G., Korzely, M. G., & Oldham, R. K. Efficacy of relaxation training and guided imagery in reducing the aversiveness of cancer chemotherapy. *Journal of Consulting and Clinical Psychology,* 1982, *50,* 509–524.

Mages, N. L., & Mendelsohn, G. A. Effects of cancer on patients' lives: A personological approach. In G. C. Stone, F. Cohen, & N. E. Adler (Eds.), *Health psychology: A handbook.* San Francisco: Jossey-Bass, 1979.

Millman, M. *The unkindest cut: Life in the backrooms of medicine.* New York: William Morrow, 1977.

Mullan, F. *Vital signs: A young doctor's struggle with cancer.* New York: Farrar, Straus, & Giroux, 1982.

Plumb, M., & Holland, J. Comparative studies of psychological function in patients with advanced cancer: II. Interviewer-rated current and past psychological symptoms. *Psychosomatic Medicine,* 1981, *43,* 243–253.

Redd, W. H. Treatment of excessive crying in a terminal cancer patient: A time-series analysis. *Journal of Behavioral Medicine,* 1982, *5,* 225–235.

Rosenbaum, R. *Harper's,* July 1982, pp. 32–42.

Sackett, E. L., & Snow, J. C. The magnitude of compliance and noncompliance. In R. B. Haynes, D. W. Taylor, & D. L. Sackett (Eds.), *Compliance in health care.* Baltimore, Md.: Johns Hopkins Press, 1979.

Sarason, S. B. *Work, aging, and social change.* New York: The Free Press, 1977.

Siegel, A. *The sky is bluer now: Thoughts about cancer and living from Anita Siegel.* 1981. (Available from the Self Help Center, 1600 Dodge Avenue, Suite 5122, Evanston, IL 60201).

Silver, R. L., & Wortman, C. B. Coping with undesirable life events. In J. Garber & M. E. P. Seligman (Eds.), *Human helplessness: Theory and applications.* New York: Academic Press, 1980.

Sobel, H. J. *Behavior therapy in terminal care: A humanistic approach.* Cambridge, Mass.: Ballinger, 1981.

Strack, S., & Coyne, J. C. Social confirmation of dysphoria: Shared and private reactions. *Journal of Personality and Social Psychology,* 1983, *44,* 798–806.

Stratton, J. Unhappy patients, unseeing doctors. *Psychology Today,* June 1983, p. 83.

Sutherland, A. M. Psychological observations in cancer patients. *International Psychiatry Clinics,* 1967, *4,* 75–92.

Taylor, S. E., Wood, J. V., & Lichtman, R. R. It could be worse: Selective evaluation as a response to victimization. In R. Janoff-Bulman & I. H. Frieze (Eds.), *Reactions to victimization. Journal of Social Issues,* in press.

Thomas, L. *The youngest science: Notes of a medicine-watcher.* New York: Viking, 1983.

Timnick, L. Now you can learn to be likeable, confident, socially successful for only the cost of your present education. *Psychology Today,* August 1982, pp. 42–49.

Turner, B. F., Tobin, S. S., & Lieberman, M. A. Personality traits as predictors of institutional adaptation among the aged. *Journal of Gerontology,* 1972, *27,* 61–68.

Wachtel, P. L. *Psychoanalysis and behavior therapy: Toward an integration.* New York: Basic Books, 1977.

Watzlawick, P., & Coyne, J. C. Depression following stroke: Brief, problem-focused family treatment. *Family Process*, 1980, *19*, 13–18.

Weakland, J. H., Fisch, R., Watzlawick, P., & Bodin, A. M. Brief therapy: Focused problem resolution. *Family Process*, 1974, *13*, 141–168.

Wellisch, D., Landsverk, J., Guidera, K., Pasnau, R. O., & Fawzy, F. Evaluation of psychosocial problems of the homebound cancer patient: I. Methodology and problem frequences. *Psychosomatic Medicine*, 1983, *45*, 11–21.

Wisely, D. W., Masur, F. I., & Morgan, S. B. Psychological aspects of severe burn injuries in children. *Health Psychology*, 1983, *2*, 45–72.

Yalom, I. D., & Yalom, M. Ernest Hemingway: A psychiatric view. *Archives of General Psychiatry*, 1971, *24*, 485–490.

11
Emotional Response to Disease and Its Treatment

Sandra M. Levy

A common way of looking at psychosocial symptoms related to disease is in mental health terms, that is, as dependent variables or as functions of the illness or treatment. Examples of common symptoms in cancer populations include insomnia, pain, neuropsychological dysfunction, and distress. Such symptoms become targets for intervention in order to ameliorate them and to restore quality of life to the patient as it is commonly understood. One would certainly wish to relieve a cancer patient of extreme distress or depression if one had the intervention means to do so.

On the other hand, we could view behavioral factors associated with disease as independent contributors to the disease process in some way, either as increasing primary risk or contributing to disease progression and mortality. We could then examine the behavioral patterns associated with biological outcome, without making any a priori assumptions about the psychological "healthiness" of such behaviors. In fact, it could be the case that some of these behaviors—perhaps associated with *better* disease outcome—would be considered pathological by common psychiatric definition. In such a case, the implication might be that we have to redefine what we mean by psychopathology in clinically ill subgroups. At the very least, we may have to suspend our a priori assumptions about what is behaviorally "healthy"—and what is not.

Taking this second perspective, that is, considering behaviors as potentially independent contributors to disease, the following schema could be developed. Table 11.1 displays these potential associations between behavior and cancer.

As shown in this table, behavioral factors could have both an indirect or a direct effect on disease initiation, as well as disease progression. For example, behavioral noncompliance (Cell D) with optimal therapeutic regimens as a consequence of giving up, or as a consequence of actively seeking alternative, unorthodox treatments, could conceivably have an indirect effect on the course of treatment outcome. Opting for coffee

TABLE II.I.
*The Relationship Between Behaviors as
"Independent Variables" and Cancer*

EFFECT

	Direct	Indirect
Initiation	**A** *Examples:* Tobacco Occupational carcinogens UV Exposure	**B** *Examples:* Fatty Diet "Stress"
Progression	**C** *Examples:* Emotional Response "Fight"	**D** *Examples:* Noncompliance Screening/Detection Behaviors Other Host Factors

STAGE OF DISEASE (row label at left)

Reprinted from Levy, S. Host differences in neoplasia risk, *Health Psychology*, 1983, 2, 21–44, by permission of the publisher.

enemas instead of curative resection to treat early stage colon cancer would probably have a deleterious effect on tumor course.

On the other hand, depression and behavioral helplessness (Cell C) are potentially mediated by sympathetic-adrenal medullary release of catecholamine. Epinepherine, in turn, has been found to increase a type of immunological effector cell (T suppressor cells), potentially suppressing immune control over the growth of micrometastasis. This latter pathway is an example of a more direct effect of emotions on disease course.

Although the balance of this chapter will be devoted to an examination of evidence related to this more direct effect of emotions on cancer progression, there is perhaps a grey area related to disease in the disadvantaged (in the cancer literature, studies of cancer risk in black and poor populations) where all these factors (indirect ones, such as delay in diagnosis, and direct ones, such as nutritional and immunological defects) may play a role.

Cancer Risk in the Disadvantaged

Delay in Diagnosis of Disease

Cultural factors are significant in determining whether individuals are apt to participate in early disease detection activities. Communication patterns differ by population subgroups (thereby affecting what is heard and attended to by different cultural subgroups), and beliefs and values likely to shape willingness to comply with detection and diagnostic activities may also differ by cultural groupings. Evidence bearing on this issue may be found in a recent survey (Warnecke, 1980) that suggests that whites are more likely to get regular checkups from physicians than blacks, even holding socioeconomic status constant.

It is not only the patient's behavior that is important to consider. The health care provider's behavior is also an important source of health care variance. The general compliance literature (Haynes, Taylor, & Sackett, 1979) indicates the importance of the patient–physician relationship as a major variable influencing patient response in the health care process. Apparently, in many cases, the community physician does not accurately know the patient's risk status.

Continuity of patient care is also linked with system and patient characteristics, with the disadvantaged least likely to have a stable relationship with a health care provider. Survey data reported by Warnecke (1980) showed that the variable accounting for the most variance in having a pap test, prostate palpation, etc., was whether or not patients reported regular checkups with their own physicians. Even within a clinic setting, some consideration could be given to developing continuous links between patients and particular providers associated with that system.

Relevant to early diagnosis of cancer in the disadvantaged, barriers to symptom diagnosis and early treatment tend to be built into clinics and emergency rooms where the poor generally come for their health care. Emergency waiting areas are not set up for "in-reach" opportunities for cancer screening (Howard, 1982), and the long waits and discontinuous care-giver involvement found in clinics minimize the possibility of early detection for the disadvantaged, who are too poor to give up a half day's work for either asymptomatic screening or symptomatic diagnosis. Poor cancer prognosis in this population may not be solely a function of late diagnosis and inferior patterns of treatment, and I will return to the question of other "host" factors below. But whatever the proportion of variance attributable to health care system factors, this source of variance should be amenable to change.

Disease Outcome as a Function of Host Differences

Blacks and other disadvantaged population subgroups tend to be seen, diagnosed, and treated when the disease is already well established and, hence, when the prognosis is much poorer. Linden (1969) showed that one out of every two cancer patients in private hospitals had localized disease at the time of diagnosis, compared with only one in four among public hospital patients. This finding favored private hospital patients even after stratifying for site of cancer, sex, and age. Huguley and Brown (1981) found a strong association between race, socioeconomic status (SES), and stage of disease at diagnosis (blacks and low SES groups were in the less favorable diagnostic groups). Recent work by Howard, Lund, and Bell (1980) also showed that metastatic rate for black breast cancer patients was much higher than the rate for whites.

In a sense, the issue of class survival difference represents a transition to consideration of behavioral factors as *direct* contributors to physical status. It is not entirely clear why differential survival rates occur for the disadvantaged—particularly for blacks. In a study by Berg, Ross, and Latourette (1977), the association between economic status and survival was examined for various kinds of cancer for which indigent patients were seen during the years 1940 to 1969. For every form of cancer, mortality rates were worse for indigent clinic patients than for nonindigent clinic patients. Berg et al. argued that medical care was not an issue in their work because nonindigent and indigent "clinic pay" patients received essentially the same treatment. Though survival outcome was significantly different between these two groups, little difference in outcome was found between clinic pay and "private" patients—the latter in the same hospital but receiving different treatment. Factors associated with poor outcome were higher mortality from various other causes, and "excess cancer mortality not accounted for by stage differences, particularly among patients who should have had five-year survival rates between 40% and 70%" (p. 467). In these latter groups, cancer recurred earlier and more often among the indigent clinic patients.

These researchers speculated that host differences associated with indigence accounted for much of the obtained black-white and poverty level differences. The authors presented a number of competing explanations for differential cancer mortality between cases, including the possibility that blacks have more aggressive histological forms of neoplasia, that they are immunologically less resistant to the spread of the disease, and that there were host differences that caused differential biological response to the same treatment. They suggested that alterations in host characteristics among the very poor could be linked to nutritional deficits or alcoholism. They suggested that ". . . there is a tendency for cancer cells to implant themselves where tissue is abnormal and perhaps the connective tissue of the malnourished, like a bowel anastomosis, is a favorable site for cancer growth" (p. 476). Conceivably, such host differences could be reversible, increasing the possibility for survival among the socially disadvantaged.

Again, this increased risk in disadvantaged populations could be partially a function of indirect factors such as noncompliance or late detection. But other, more direct host factors—ranging from differential cell histopathology to biologically mediated distress or helplessness—should also be considered.

Direct Behavioral Contributors to Cancer Outcome

Historically, there have been several retrospective human studies that have addressed the possibility of a "cancer prone personality," but most of these have been methodologically flawed in one way or another. Currently, there are more carefully designed retrospective and prospective studies (Breslow, 1983; Glickman, 1983) that may shed light on this question. For example, in one study (Glickman, 1983), excess relative risk of lung cancer incidence as a function of life distress and consequent lymphocyte suppression is being studied in a cohort of asbestos-exposed workers. The outcome of this prospective study should increase our understanding of mediating biological pathways between coping behavior and incidence of disease. But, for the present, the evidence linking psychological variables with initiation of neoplasia is sparse.

The evidence is already more convincing, however, that a link can be made between behavior and cancer progression. Cox and MacKay (1982), in their recent review of studies linking psychosocial factors in cancer risk, concluded that the evidence was strongest for a relationship between inability to express emotion—particularly in relation to hostility—and cancer.

For example, findings from an early study by Blumberg, West, and Ellis (1954) showed that patients who died less than two years following primary treatment were characterized as overly cooperative and behaviorally inhibited persons when compared with longer survivors. Other, more recent researchers (Derogatis, Abeloff, and Melisaratos, 1979; Greer, Morris, and Pettingale, 1979) have reported similar findings, suggesting an association between blandness of affect in the face of stress and bad outcome (or conversely, negative reactivity and better outcome).

In the light of this literature, a study currently underway hypothesizes that negatively reactive, metastatic breast cancer patients live significantly longer than passive patients (Levy, Lippman, & Herberman, 1983). It is important to emphasize here that the major determiner of cancer outcome is the biology of the tumor—the histopathology of the cell and the genetic control of cell behavior by the probable function of oncogenes. What we are considering here, at least for some subclasses of patients, is that emotional/behavioral response may play some role in the rate of tumor development. If this hypothesis is the case, then the possibility exists of altering these emotional/behavioral factors associated with disease outcome. Whether such an alteration would affect disease endpoints is a fundamental issue to which we will return.

Advanced and Early Stage Breast Cancer Studies

In our study, first recurrent breast cancer patients at three major medical centers in a metropolitan area were given structured interviews. We elected to study breast cancer since it is an obvious, hormonally dependent tumor, and because we know that hormonal release is regulated by the central nervous system (CNS) through feedback loops. Though the pathways linking emotions, central nervous system, hormones, and tumor response are complex and, in many cases, poorly understood, *that* they are there is not disputable. Thus, breast cancer seemed like an obvious choice for studying the potential effects of certain CNS-mediated behaviors on tumor progression.

The patient's psychological status was rated by independent observers using a standardized rating instrument (Global Adjustment Illness Scale; Derogatis, Abeloff, & McBeth, 1976), and patients also filled out a psychiatric self-report form (Symptom Checklist-90; Derogatis, 1977) at initial and follow-up visits. Biological prognostic factors might also be associated with length of survival (such as direness of metastatic site and disease-free interval) were recorded from patient charts. Patients were assessed at base line (before beginning treatment for recurrence) and at 4 weeks into chemotherapy treatment. Survival status was recorded 1 year after the initial interview.

At the time of this analysis, 22 patients have been followed for 1 year. Reported here are preliminary findings comparing outcome groups on average base-line responses. The only base-line biological variable significantly differentiating those still alive versus those dead at 1 year was disease-free interval: patients still alive a 1 year had a significantly longer disease-free period from primary treatment. There was also an interesting association between 1-year survival and marital status at base line: patients clustering in the alive group at 1 year tended also to be married. This finding supports recent suggestions in the literature (Berkman & Syme, 1979) that intact social networks may have some survival value. There were no other demographic or biological variables differentiating the outcome groups at base-line testing.

Interesting and significant differences emerged when the outcome groups were trichotomized into stable ($N = 7$) versus progressing ($N = 9$) versus dead ($N = 6$) at 1 year and were compared on the base-line, psychiatric self-report measure. Those in the stable group reported significantly more psychiatric symptomatology at base line, while those in the bad outcome groups (i.e., progressing or dead) expressed *less* distress at base line. It also did not seem that those who were more ill simply did not have the energy to express or report distress, since there was no difference between groups on the Kornofsky scale, a measure of physical functional status. Finally, it should also be noted that there was no significant correlation between the psychological variables and the disease-free interval, suggesting an independent contribution to outcome by the emotional response variables rather than a mere confounding with biological status.

Clearly, these findings are preliminary and correlational. However, the most interesting fact at this point is that the psychological findings are consistent with an emerging body of literature suggesting that longer survival is associated with negative reactivity. Whether this reactivity is best conceived of as "fight" or coping in some sense versus apathy, helplessness, or giving up is not clear at this point.

In a study by this author of psychological response patterns in primary breast cancer patients (Levy et al., 1983), an immunological factor potentially associated with emotional response, the Natural Killer (NK) cell, is being measured. Many different immunological components have been identified that can interact with tumor cells, such as T lymphocytes, macrophages, humoral antibody, and K cells, as well as various combinations of these immunocompetent cells. Some of the components—such as NK cells—occur in hosts who have not been intentionally immunized by foreign, antigenic "invasion." These effector cells, which are cytotoxic for many types of tumor cells in vitro, have been implicated in host surveillance against tumors.

Specifically, NK cells were discovered as a result of studies showing that peripheral blood lymphocytes from normal individuals (who could not be expected to be previously exposed to tumor-associated antigen) were highly cytotoxic in vitro for cultured tumor cells. Although the evidence is fairly persuasive that NK cells play a role in tumor growth inhibition, there is *suggestive* evidence that these cells also play a role in surveillance against newly developing primary tumors. For example, if mice are experimentally given a tumorigenic substance, in the latent period after treatment—long before they develop tumors—there occurs a depression of NK activity. At the time of this depression, if these mice are given bone marrow or spleen cells that then reconstitute their NK activity, a decrease in tumor incidence has been observed (Herberman, 1982). In addition, there is recent in vivo clinical evidence that NK levels at the time of primary treatment may play a role in controlling distant spread of cancer cells (Levy, 1982).

As is true with other types of immunocompetent cells, clear lines of evidence suggest regulation by neuroendocrine function. For example, animals transported from one lab to another—or who are exposed to "normal" lab trauma—show a decrease in NK activity for 1 to 7 days post-stress, and immunosuppressive agents—including corticosteroids (under control of the hypothalamic-pituitary-adrenal axis)—decrease NK activity (Herberman, 1982). In sum, then, NK cells appear to be a very cancer-relevant cell to study as a potential mediator in our primary patient population.

The biological end point in this second study is time to recurrence (rather than death). Although it is too early to answer the major question concerning the association of affect with outcome when natural killer cell lytic activity was correlated with emotional response, a significant linear relationship was found. That is, patients rated as being more disturbed and less "well adjusted" by an observer tended to have higher levels of NK activity ($r = .67$). The patients rated as relatively undisturbed had lower NK activity. Of course, even if this relationship holds over time (these were base-line data) and emotional distress or lack of it continues to be significantly related to NK level, the prognostic significance of this finding will only be important if NK activity itself plays a role in stemming the growth of micrometastases. However, there is some recent evidence (Levy, 1982) that high NK level may deter spread of distant, in contrast with local, cancer. Also, in our preliminary analysis of these data, NK level was significantly associated with a powerful predictor of cancer recurrence, nodes positive at diagnosis. Patients with higher levels of NK lytic activity had significantly fewer positive nodes at time of initial treatment ($F = 6.0$, $p < .01$). Therefore, in this study population, Nk cells appear to be very relevant.

Animal Analogue of Human Passivity

In recent years, there have been a number of animal studies related to tumor genesis mediated by endocrine and immune factors. (This extensive literature will not be reviewed here. The interested reader is referred to Anisman and Sklar [1982]; Cochran [1978]; and Levy [1982].) But the situation is far from clear at this point. The aggregate experimental data suggests strongly that neuroendocrine and immunological responses to stress—both social and physical—are capable of modifying tumor initiation, growth, and even metastasis. Occasionally, however, the modulation is in the direction of inhibition of growth. There are clearly more puzzles than answers currently in this complex area of investigation.

Although there is a long leap from the animal laboratory to the human clinic, one animal analogue of the human helplessness or passivity we have been addressing in this chapter has been developed in the labs of J. Weiss and his colleagues at Rockefeller University, Hymie Anisman and colleagues at Carlton University in Canada, and Seligman and co-workers at the University of Pennsylvania. In general, these animal studies have shown that in the absence of behavioral control of stress, increased utilization of catecholamine will ensue, ultimately resulting in depletion of neurotransmitter levels.

Although the initial mobilization may be adaptive in dealing with environmental stress, the resulting depletion of the transmitter may leave the organism vulnerable to the effects of further stress. For example, ACTH release as a function of catecholamine changes will result in increased secretion of corticosterone from the adrenal gland. The corticosterone, in turn, may act as an immunosuppressant and may thus increase the incidence of disease states, including multiplication of neoplastic cells. It is just such a relationship between uncontrolled stress, animal helplessness, and increased tumor growth that has been reported from these various laboratories.

Visintainer, Volpicelli, and Seligman (1982) have measured tumor rejection as a function of controllability of shock by using a dose of Walker 256 sarcoma cells designed to induce tumors in 50% of the unshocked (normal) rats. Sprague-Dawley adult male rats received inescapable, escapable, or no shock 1 day after being implanted with tumor cells. Only 27% of rats receiving inescapable shock rejected the tumor, whereas 63% of rats receiving escapable shock and 54% of no shock rats rejected the tumors. These authors concluded that obviously it was not stress, per se, but a lack of control over stressors that reduces tumor rejection and decreases survival in these animals.

Although Visintainer et al. did not examine potential biological mechanisms mediating their observed effects, Anisman and Sklar (1982) have also reported significantly slower tumor growth (as well as less norepinephrine depletion) in animals that behaviorally cope by fighting their cage mates. This latter research examined behavioral control of environmental impingement (social impingement), in this case mediated by neuroendocrine response. Although Anisman and Sklar examined a neuroendocrine mediator of behavioral control and tumor response, more recent work (Greenberg, Dyck, & Sandler, 1983) has specifically linked behavioral helplessness, suppression of lymphocyte function—including NK function—and reduced clearance of NK sensitive tumor cells using this same behavioral model.

Apparently, then, behavioral helplessness in a situation of acute, stressful impingement plays an important role in tumor development. The analogy with our clinical findings is striking, and this line of investigation will be important in further analyses of our clinical data.

Behavioral Interventions in Patient Populations: Would it Make a Difference?

Two questions can be addressed at this point: (1) Can perceived helplessness and behavioral noncoping be altered? and (2) If one alters this perception and behavior, would it make any difference in either disease incidence or outcome?

The answer to the first question is undoubtably yes. That is, we know from the clinical intervention literature that techniques such as "mood elevation" (Velten, 1968), as well as other forms of cognitive-behavioral interventions, can alter depressive or helpless behavior (Seligman, 1978).

In a recent article (Peterson, 1982), it was suggested that behavioral strategies used to dispel helplessness in animals (e.g., forced exposure to contingencies between behaviors and outcome) might be utilized by medical practitioners to enhance feelings of controllability in patients. Peterson suggested that physicians consider highlighting patients' progress to them in understandable terms making such progress perceptually contingent on actual participation by patients, and enlisting patients as collaborators in their treatment. "You took this pill and your blood pressure was controlled." "You chose that type of catheter to be used and your symptoms were controlled."

Of course, one could utilize more direct means of intervention that more immediately effect the biological substrate. In Benson and colleagues' work (Hoffman, Benson, Arns et al., 1982), investigations have shown that the relaxation response in the face of physical stress reduced end-organ uptake of norepinephrine, resulting in increased levels of plasma catecholamine. Basically, the organism was less responsive to the stressful condition. Though one could stretch the significance of this response pattern to imply some kind of perceived control over the situation by the subject, this intervention may, in fact, short-circuit the cognitive apparatus and directly affect relevant biological systems. (Although, it is hard to imagine that the laboratory subjects would not perceive their situation and make sense out of it, as humans are wont to do; still, a kind of short-circuiting could be present with such an intervention.)

An even more direct control over biological responsivity would be a direct infusion of neurotransmitter enhancers during stress episodes, such as Weiss, Bailey, Goodman et al. (1982) suggested. One has, then, completely by-passed the cognitive apparatus of the responding human.

So, the answer to the first question—can one change helplessness into coping response—is most likely yes. However, the answer to the second question—does this change make a difference in terms of disease risk—is uncertain. What has been discussed here has been related to two categories of behavior. For the first category—behavior indirectly linked with disease incidence and outcome (such as noncompliance or late detection in the disadvantaged)—alterations of such behaviors clearly would have a major impact on decreasing disease risk.

For the second category we have been considering—those emotions, cognitions, and behaviors associated with coping, depression, and helplessness—the efficacy of such nontoxic behavioral interventions is unclear. Certainly we could enhance the psychosocial quality of patients' lives, improving their mental health as commonly defined and perhaps preventing psychopathology in such patient subgroups. But whether such interventions could affect disease status remains part of the puzzle to be answered through future investigation.

References

Anisman, H., & Sklar, L. Stress provoked neurochemical changes in relation to neoplasia. In S. Levy (Ed.), *Biological mediators of behavior and disease: Neoplasia.* New York: Elsevier/North Holland, 1982.

Berg, J., Ross, R., & Latourette, H. Economic status and survival of cancer patients. *Cancer,* 1977, *39,* 467–477.

Berkman, L., & Syme, S. Social networks, host resistence, and mortality: A nine-year follow-up study of Alameda County residents. *American Journal of Epidemiology,* 1979, *109,* 186–204.

Blumberg, E., West, P., & Ellis, F. A possible relationship between psychological factors and human cancer. *Psychosomatic Medicine,* 1954, *16,* 277–286.

Breslow, L. *Behavioral aspects in cancer incidence and mortality* (NIH-NCI Grant No. R18 CA33457-01). Rockville, Md.: National Institute of Health, 1983.

Cochran, A. *Man, cancer and immunity.* New York: Academic Press, 1978.

Cox, T., & MacKay, C. Psychosocial factors and psychophysiological mechanisms in the aetiology and development of cancers. *Social Science and Medicine,* 1982, *16,* 381–396.

Derogatis, L. *Scoring and Procedures Manual for the PAIS.* Clinical Psychometric Research, Baltimore, Maryland, 1977.

Derogatis. L., Abeloff, M., & Melisaratos, N. Psychological coping mechanisms and survival time in metastatic breast cancer. *Journal of the American Medical Association,* 1979, *242,* 1504–1508.

Derogatis, L., Abeloff, M., & McBeth, D. Cancer patients and their physicians in the perception of psychological symptoms. *Psychosomatics,* 1976, *17,* 197–201.

Glickman, L. *Psychosocial stress and cancer risk: prospective study* (NIH-NCI Grant No. R01 CA34618-01). Rockville, Md.: National Institute of Health, 1983.

Greenberg, A., Dyck, D., & Sandler, L. Opponent processes, neurohormones, and natural resistance. In B. Fox & B. Newberry (Eds.), *Impact of psychoneuroendocrine systems in cancer and immunity.* Toronto: Hogrefe Press, 1983.

Greer, S., Morris, T., & Pettingale, K. Psychological response to breast cancer: Effect on outcome. *Lancet,* 1979, *13,* 785–787.

Haynes, B., Taylor, D., & Sackett, D. (Eds.). *Compliance in health care.* Baltimore: The Johns Hopkins University Press, 1979.

Herberman, R. Possible effects of central nervous system on natural killer (NK) cell activity. In S. Levy (Ed.), *Biological mediators of behavior and disease: Neoplasia.* New York: Elsevier/North Holland, 1982.

Hoffman, J., Benson, H., Arns, P., et al. Reduced sympathetic nervous system responsivity associated with the relaxation response. *Science,* 1982, *215,* 190–192.

Howard, J. In-reach: An approach to the secondary prevention of cancer. In D. Parron, F. Solomon, & C. Jenkins (Eds.), *Behavior, health risks, and social disadvantage.* Washington, D.C.: National Academy Press, 1982.

Howard, J., Lund, P., & Bell, G. Hospital variations in metastatic breast cancer. *Medical Care, 1980,* 18, 442–455.

Huguley, C., & Brown, R. The value of BSE. *Cancer,* 1981, *47,* 989–995.

Levy, S. *Biological mediators of behavior and disease: Neoplasia.* New York: Elsevier/North Holland, 1982.

Levy, S., Lippman, M., & Herberman, R. *Emotional response to breast cancer and its treatment* (NIH-NCI Protocol No. 80-C-49). Rockville, Md.: National Institute of Health, 1983.

Linden, G. The influence of social class on the survival of cancer patients. *American Journal of Public Health,* 1969, *59,* 267–274.

Peterson, C. Learned helplessness and health psychology. *Journal of Health Psychology,* 1982, *1,* 153–169.

Seligman, M. Learned helplessness: Comment and integration. *Journal of Abnormal Psychology,* 1978, *87,* 165–179.

Velten, E. A laboratory test for the induction of mood states. *Behavior Research and Therapy,* 1968, *6,* 473–482.

Visintainer, M., Volpicelli, J., & Seligman, M. Tumor rejection in rats after inescapable or escapable shock. *Science,* 1982, *216,* 437–439.

Warnecke, R. *Knowledge and prevention of cancer among blacks.* Paper presented at the Fourth Annual Meeting of the American Association of Preventive Oncology, Chicago, 1980.

Weiss, J., Bailey, N., Goodman, P., et al. A model for neurochemical study of depression. In A. Levy & M. Spiegelstein (Eds.), *Behavioral models and the analysis of drug action.* New York: Elsevier/North Holland, 1982.

12
Promoting Coping with Illness in Childhood

Gerald P. Koocher

The range of human coping behavior is extensive. When one also considers the variety of adaptational demands inherent in accommodating different illness conditions and the complications introduced by developmental differences between infancy and adulthood, the behavior possibilities increase exponentially. In order to provide a rapid sampling of issues as a context for this presentation, I want to share three vignettes with you. For the sake of relative simplicity, I have drawn from a single illness category: childhood cancer.

Jennifer was just 5 years old when her malignant schwanoma was diagnosed. When the psychologist and nurse met with her following surgery to discuss the operation she had recently undergone and the treatments that lay ahead, Jennifer had several important questions: "After they cut me open, how did they put me back together?" and "Did they take out any parts I need?" Later she compared her surgery to ". . . being in a fight" because "they cut you with knives and stuff like that."

Mike's bone tumor, an osteogenic sarcoma, was diagnosed following an athletic injury at age 14. An attempt was made to avoid an amputation by replacing a bone segment with a steel prosthesis. The steel rod became infected and, after several months of painful treatment, the leg was amputated anyway. Mike, who had remained stoic and uncomplaining up to this point, subsequently presented his oncologist with a gift of homemade art. It depicted surgeons cutting on a patient's leg with an electric chain saw as Charles Manson looked on approvingly.

Jack, another osteogenic sarcoma patient, had his left leg amputated above the knee at age 14. When he returned for a follow-up visit at age 19, he was wearing a "peg leg" on his stump, rather than his state-of-the-art hydraulic prosthesis. Jack was now an amputee ski instructor and was about to depart for a weekend on the slopes. He observed that the "peg" was especially useful for him because it is "more obvious" than the prosthesis. He noted he could prop it up on a chair in the lounge après-ski and "use it as a lure to attract motherly women."

The attempts to cope with serious illness illustrated by Jennifer's inquiries, Mike's sublimated anger, and Jack's innovative conversation piece begin to reflect the range of possible diversity. We also get a sense of how magical thinking or childhood fantasy might complicate Jennifer's coping ability. We wonder whether there is some way to help Mike with his justifiable anger about the amputation. Perhaps we are unsure whether Jack's use of his handicap as bait in a social context is adaptive or pathological. This very complex set of response styles makes a simple characterization of the coping process in childhood a difficult task.

In the following pages, I shall attempt to address the psychological response of children to physical illness from four separate aspects. To begin, I shall attempt to highlight the ways in which the adaptation process in children differs from that of adults. Next, I shall point out the primary factors bearing on a child's ability to cope with the stress of illness. This discussion will lead to an examination of an approach for assessing the individual as a responder to stress in the course of childhood illness. Finally, I shall attempt to summarize what we know about the sorts of interventions that seemingly promote or facilitate coping with childhood illness.

There are two significant areas I shall not be addressing in this paper, chiefly to avoid producing a whole book rather than a single chapter. One of these areas is the substantial body of literature on the prevention of illness in childhood, health-promoting behaviors, and compliance with prescribed treatment regimens (see, for example, Haynes, Taylor, & Sackett, 1979; Rapoff & Christophersen, 1982; Stuart, 1982). Also, I shall not attempt to provide a scholarly definition of the coping process or theory of adaptation, since this area too has been the focus of much scholarly attention (Haan, 1977; Lazarus, 1966; Singer, 1983).

As I discuss coping in the following pages, I shall simply note that it is something all children and adults do every day. Coping is simply the process of accommodating to stress and disruptive events in one's life. Our real goal is to facilitate normal functioning as much as possible during such periods of stress.

Illness in childhood is certainly a disruptive life event with the potential to impede both normal functioning and adequate developmental growth. Onset may be acute or gradual, while being genetically or environmentally triggered. The duration of the illness may be transitory (e.g., a "24 hour virus"), lifelong (e.g., juvenile diabetes), or characterized by unpredictable, intermittent exacerbations (e.g., lupus or sickle cell disease). The symptoms may be massively debilitating or simply inconvenient, easily concealable or blatantly public, socially acceptable or repugnant to others. The prognosis may be uniformly favorable (e.g., an uncomplicated fracture), invariably terminal (e.g., cystic fibrosis), or life threatening with a core of realistic hope for recovery (e.g., acute lymphoblastic leukemia). These are but a few of the continua or dimensions along which important variability bearing on coping may occur.

The two types of published research one is likely to find relative to illness in childhood might best be termed *categorical* and *generic*. The *categorial research* focuses on a single disease entity, such as cancer, diabetes, asthma, or hemophilia, and discusses psychological problems and adjustment within that category or in relation to some other category of illness. Such research is helpful to clinicians working with these specific patient populations and tends to avoid the complications of comparing disease entities, as suggested by the sample continua listed above. Unfortunately, such research is complicated by the low incidence of some illness categories and the question of whether generalizable adaptation patterns can be identified and facilitated across illness groups.

What I have termed *generic* or *noncategorial research* is an emerging interest area among pediatric psychologists and health psychologists in general. Such investigations focus on the physical, emotional, and social burdens associated with the illness in question (Stein & Jones, 1982). Adjustment and coping may then be studied in relation to the quantifiable burdens that are the more precise disrupters in the patient's environment and social ecology. Quantifying, comparing, and equating such burdens is a difficult task, but one which is extremely promising. I shall attempt to illustrate the specificity of certain types of illness–related burdens in childhood by linking typical ones to important developmental issues.

Setting the Stage

This year has seen the publication of two important handbooks dealing with clinical child (Walker & Roberts, 1983) and pediatric psychology (Tuma, 1983). Both include detailed chapters on the psychological impact of physical illness in childhood (Siegel, 1983; Willis, Elliott, & Jay, 1983). Importantly, this material integrates considerable noncategorical, illness response research with developmental stage concepts.

The interface of such material is important for three psychological factors: the cognitive, affective, and social aspects of a child's response to illness. What children are capable of understanding and reasoning will govern the effectiveness of interventions designed to enable better coping. The emotional issues children must confront are also developmentally variable and dictate the specific needs that must be addressed relative to adaptation. The interpersonal ecology of the child is also a key factor, since children must generally rely on others for day-to-day care in a manner not necessarily true of adults.

Cognitive Development

A number of investigators have used developmental theory to formulate and test hypotheses about the types of and differences in illness concepts among children of different ages (Campbell, 1975; Neuhauser, Amsterdam, Hines, & Steward, 1978; Simeonsson, Buckley, & Monson, 1979; Whitt, Dykstra, & Taylor, 1979). Such studies have generally related some aspects of cognitive development, such as magical thinking or concrete-logical thinking, to the understanding of illness concepts. Bibace and Walsh (1980, 1981) have carried such work a step further by spelling out six qualitatively different stages of children's explanations of illness.

They begin by describing the prelogical child (or preoperational child if one prefers Piagetian terms) as moving through two categories for explaining illness: *phenomenism* and *contagion*. Phenomenism is the most immature type of explanation of illness. In this category, the child interprets the cause of the illness as an external, concrete phenomenon that may be quite distant in space or time from the illness itself.

Example:
How do people get colds? "From trees."
How do people get measles? "From God." How does God give people measles? "God does it in the sky."

Contagion is the more frequent type of explanation given by the prelogical child. In this category, the cause of illness is located in objects or people nearby but not touching the child. Magic provides the cognitive link.

Example:
How do people get colds? "From outside." How do they get them from outside? "They just do . . . they come when someone gets near you." How? "I don't know—by magic, I think."

When concrete-operational thought begins at about age 7, the child becomes able to differentiate between self and other in a new way. For the first time, children can distinguish between their own and others' experiences. The two types of explanations now possible are termed *contamination* and *internalization* by Bibace and Walsh. The younger child at this concrete-logical stage tends to think in terms of contamination.

That is to say, the cause is viewed as an external person, object, or action that has a harmful aspect to it and causes the illness through physical contact or through some harmful action of the child.

Example:
How do people get colds? "If you're outside without a hat in the wintertime and you start sneezing. Your head would get cold and it would go all over your body."

The older children in this group, ages 9 to 10, might be expected to use more internalization types of explanations. That is to say, although the ultimate cause of illness may be external, the illness itself is now located inside the body. The external cause is linked to the illness in the child's thinking by some process of internalization such as inhaling or swallowing.

Example:
How do people get colds? "In winter they breathe in too much air up their nose . . . germs get in by breathing." How does it get better? "Hot fresh air gets in the nose and pushes the cold air back."

Beginning with the formal-operational period at about age 11 or 12, the child becomes capable of hypothetical reasoning for the first time. In both *physiological* and *psychophysiological* explanations given by children at this stage, illness is located within the body, even though an external agent may be described as the ultimate cause. In the physiological approach used by the younger children at the formal-logical stage, the cause is often described as the malfunction of an internal organ or process, generally including a step-by-step sequence of events.

Example:
How do people get colds? "They come from viruses I guess. Other people have the virus and it gets into your blood stream and causes the cold. Your sinuses get all filled up with mucus and then you get a cough too."

According to Bibace and Walsh (1981), psychophysiological explanations represent the most mature understanding of illness. The child at this stage can give both physiological explanations of illness and show an awareness that thoughts and feelings affect the way a person's body functions.

Example:
What's a heart attack? "It's when your heart stops working right . . . it can be pumping too slow or too fast . . . it can come from being all nerve-racked . . . tension can affect your heart."

These examples were drawn from Bibace and Walsh (1981, pp. 36–38), along with the six types of explanations illustrating cognitive progress in understanding and interpreting the cause of illness. In addition, certain medical terms are sometimes misheard or misunderstood in ways that are at once anxiety provoking and humorous. One 5-year old understood she had "sick-sick fibrosis," while another was certain his hospitalization was for the treatment of "sick-as-hell anemia." Try to keep these developmental stages in mind as we consider the affective and social domains of childhood illness. Remember, however, that developmental stages are not necessarily unidirectional. During periods of crisis, individuals are prone to regress socially and emotionally. Intellectual regressions of a sort are also possible, and magical thinking (at least on a transitory basis) is not uncommon among older pediatric patients or their parents during certain critical periods.

Emotional Development

It is somewhat artificial to discuss emotional and cognitive development separately with respect to the impact of illness. On the other hand, we know that certain aspects of personality development are more vulnerable to influence at specific ages, whether we choose to use the system laid out by Freud, Erickson, or Allport. Willis and her colleagues (1983) point out that discussing illness in general is too diffuse a concept. They suggest focusing on the components of the specific illness, such as pain, immobility, isolation, and disfigurement. In that sense, they are arguing the same burden assessment model proposed by Stein and Jones (1982).

It is most appropriate to begin such an analysis by considering the primary developmental issues for each age group and by examining the ways in which development might be disrupted by specific illness burdens. In early childhood, for example, separation is a primary concern. The attachment of infants and toddlers to specific adults has been well documented as having critical importance. If the illness in question requires hospitalization, one can envision a whole subset of coping issues.

In an historical review of general hospital policy in the 1950s, Shore and Goldston (1978) noted that only 28 of 5500 facilities permitted parents to remain overnight with their sick children. In the past decade there have been major shifts toward preventing separations as stress issues, accompanied by a substantial body of research on means of helping children adjust to the hospital experience (Carey, 1983; Johnson, 1979; Siegel, 1983; Willis et al., 1983). Hospitals have become more accepting of parents rooming-in with their sick children and even participating in delivery of care to their children (Hardgrove & Rutledge, 1975). Many hospitals have taken steps to modify the ecology of patient care in order to facilitate such participation. In many cases, special arrangements are possible so that seriously ill or terminally ill children may be cared for at home (Martinson, 1980).

Although the research literature does not support the belief that hospitalization uniformly affects all sick children adversely (Siegel, 1983), the nature of the hospital experience can be varied to enhance adaptation, as will be discussed toward the end of this paper. One immediate example, however, is the issue of separation (or, to use the term adults use when speaking of themselves: loneliness). Adults often act as if young children are most vulnerable to separation problems, but this statement is a deceptive misconception. Loneliness can affect people of any age, although "big boys and girls" are often given a variety of social cues not to exhibit such feelings. The degree to which these feelings are addressed, for example, can have a major impact on reducing the incidence of behavior problems in the hospital, especially social withdrawal and noncompliance. Note that I did not say pediatric hospital.

Having focused on young children, let us consider adolescents for a moment. The onset of adolescence brings the capacity to think about the future and plan what might be in ways conceptually unavailable to the younger child. The adolescent moves away from a family focus toward a peer group focus. Being part of the group, attractive, active, and independent, are all very important. What happens when an illness highlights one's differentness and makes this difference obvious? What about a condition that keeps the teenager from attending school or socializing with peers for an extended period? What is it like to have no ability to care for your own needs or to salvage a degree of privacy during this period? Worst of all, what is it like when your future itself is uncertain or most likely nonexistent?

One adolescent with cystic fibrosis drew a rather telling self-portrait at age 17, depicting himself dressed in punk rock gear and seated on a chair in the desert. The figure has no face. An intravenous line leads from the arm to the ground and the face is visible at the bottom in a pool of blood. This example is a rather stark illustration of how some illnesses can erase one's identity and future-orientation, even when there is substantial life left to life.

It is not really possible to provide a template for assessing emotional coping out of context from the reality of the child's illness and the tasks of emotional development for that child's age and abilities (Zeltzer, Kellerman, Ellenberg, Dash, & Rigler, 1980). Still, we do have some ideas on what helps build coping resources, and these are summarized below.

Social Contexts

I have certainly mentioned the importance of social relationships earlier, including separation, loneliness, and peer contact issues. Most children, however, function in a family context, and the family can be either a major risk or benefit in the adaptational process. Communication problems, sibling conflicts, parental stress, and the hidden costs of treatment can combine to impair the sick child's social support network.

A prime example occurs when there is a known genetic link to the child's illness. The reverberations through the extended family of such a link can be enormous. Siblings may worry about their own risk or carrier status. Parents may feel especially guilty, and this guilt is certainly magnified when children with the disease are born after the risk was known.

Even under more routine illness circumstances, it may not occur to all parents to share information with the siblings or other family members. Closed communication patterns can lead to guilt, anger, jealousy, and other such feelings as a result of misunderstandings. In our studies of childhood cancer survivors (Koocher & O'Malley, 1981), the siblings of the cancer patients often told us they were intensely jealous of the special treatment the patient received, until they were informed about the nature of the disease, the risks, and the treatment protocols.

In other families, siblings may have to make extensive personal sacrifices because of the drain on financial resources the sick child's care demands. Perhaps a talented sibling gives up a dream to go to college or to buy a car because of family finances in light of the patient's needs. Perhaps the family cannot take a vacation together because an ill sibling must always be near a dialysis center.

The same cognitive and affective issues that may cause difficulties for the child patient may also adversely stress the siblings. The angry brothers or sisters who do not adequately comprehend the etiology and course of an illness may, for example, assume by magical thinking that they are to blame for what has happened. Perhaps the two most common questions on the minds of patients' siblings I have known are: "Did I do that?" and "Will it happen to me?" They may not always be directly articulated, but the idea and worry is nearly always present to some degree.

Another major hazard in the social context is the congruence of coping styles among family members. When family members' coping patterns have substantial similarities they tend to fare better as individuals than when each person copes in a different manner or in a manner that does not permit a substantial degree of mutual support. Two vignettes might help illustrate the point:

The Williams family's youngest son was diagnosed with an inoperable brain tumor and the prognosis was terminal, although clearly many months away. Mr. Williams approached the physician managing the case and offered to sign an autopsy authorization form in an inappropriately premature context several days after the diagnosis was made. He began to talk about his 7-year-old son in the third person while standing in the hospital room, and accused his wife of being "too emotional." Mrs. Williams accused her husband of giving up on the child and of not caring. She planned to move into the hospital 100 miles from the family home to care for the child, even though it was possible to transfer his care close to their home. In a family meeting organized by the unit's psychologist and social workers, Mr. Williams listened to his wife's complaints and noted, "You're overreacting again. I remember when my mother died. You took it harder than I did."

The Harris family's daughter was critically ill with a brain infection that seemed to defy diagnosis. Neither parent seemed to want to be around the other, although both spent long hours by their child's bed in the intensive care unit. They seemed to plan silently to trade off different shifts by the bedside. When Mrs. Harris complained that she felt unsupported by her spouse, the couple was encouraged to meet with the psychologist on the unit. When he heard his wife's complaint, Mr. Harris began to cry. He explained that he, too, was very worried about their daughter and had been walking in the woods near the family home crying to himself so as not to burden others who seemed (to him) to be coping much better.

Following the efforts at intervention with these two families, both youngsters died. Mr. and Mrs. Williams separated and were divorced within a few months. The Harrises are still married and report feeling well supported by each other. They were able to recognize each other's emotional needs and respond in a mutually supportive fashion. Mr. and Mrs. Williams were so incongruent in their coping styles that no shifts toward mutual support were possible. Perhaps as individuals they are coping as well with the loss of their child as the Harrises, but the family did not survive.

Risk Assessment Model

Having set the stage with some theory and examples, I would like to propose an assessment paradigm to explore the vulnerability of any given ill child. The a priori assumption is that one cannot assess the child outside the context of the family, the child's own developmental level, and the specific burdens or pressures the illness in question places on the child. First, consider the following three sets of questions.

The Child

What does the child understand about the illness, its etiology, treatment, and prognosis? What was the child's level of adaptation prior to the illness? What are the immediate and foreseeable disruptions in the child's life as a result of the illness?

The Family

Were there pre-existing, major adaptational problems in the family's life prior to the child's illness? We know that families that have a member with pre-existing psychopathology, that are intellectually limited, that have nonsupportive marital relationships, or that have minimal economic resources are at substantial risk for adjustment problems. Families that are linguistically or culturally dis-synchronous with the physicians and nurses will be at special risk, as will single parents and families with other physically or mentally ill members. The degree to which family members are able to communicate with each other and offer mutual support is also a critical factor.

The Setting

To what degree does the ecology of the care setting and the nature of the child's illness permit an individualized degree of integrated support planning? Obviously a hospital may be limited by its physical plant, staffing pattern, and ability to respond to special client needs (e.g., fee reductions, meals for family members away from home, interpreters, etc.). When the sick child is at home, what support is available from members of the community, social agencies, or extended family members? To what degree will a school system reach out to provide books and tutoring when needed and to help reintegrate the child in school when the time comes.

The Equation

In primary prevention work we are chiefly interested in group-oriented interventions, yet, the equation I have hinted at suggests quite clearly that some highly individualized assessment is needed to successfully reduce the disruption and stress burdens on sick children and their families. I believe that the study of individual cases tells us much about how to plan broader population initiatives. The questions presented above, however, are intended for two specific purposes.

First, they indicate some of the special risk factors and vulnerabilities, the knowledge of which could be useful when focusing on specific, high-risk populations. That is to say, when the circumstances reveal less than optimal coping potential because of special individual, familial, or setting factors, the child and family have an extra burden to address. One can reliably predict that such patients and their families have a higher marginal risk of psychopathology than those without such problems to face (Christ & Greenly, 1983).

In addition, the method of case analysis cited here also suggests ways of designing group-based, preventive intervention programs targeted to the special needs of specific age groups, illness categories, or treatment settings (Koocher, 1980; Koocher, Sourkes, & Keane, 1979). The questions raised suggest a beginning for those adapting a functional burden model for designing or assessing preventive interventions for sick children and their families (Stein & Jones, 1982; Stewart, Ware, & Brook, 1982).

What Works

Having highlighted some of the stresses and developmental issues complicating children's adaptation to illness, and having suggested a strategy for analyzing specific risk situations, it is time to consider interventions. That is, what do we know works effectively in reducing stress and disruption for children and their families, thereby facilitating better adaptive functioning? I have clustered my summary of effective interventions under five headings: anticipation, strategic interventions, patient education, enhanced internal control, and open communication patterns.

Anticipation

Anticipating future stressful events has long been known as a means of better preparing to deal with them. Knowing about future events that may or will happen permits a number of coping strategies, such as rehearsal, desensitization, or stress inoculation, to operate. In the case of children, where mastery drives can be important motivators or where unfamiliarity with the context may precipitate extreme anxiety, anticipatory interventions are especially important.

When a hospital admission is planned, pre-admissions programs designed to familiarize the child with the facility, staff, and procedures can be quite helpful (see, for example, the work of Melamed, 1977; Melamed & Siegel, 1975; Peterson & Ridley-Johnson, 1980). Such pre-admission programs also help reduce parents' anxiety (Visintainer & Wolfer, 1975) and have been applied to broad, general-use circumstances, such as classroom presentations to well children not necessarily facing hospitalization (Peterson & Ridley-Johnson, in press; Roberts, Wurtele, Boone, Ginther, & Elkins, 1981).

Similar preparation programs can also be effective in dealing with situation-specific, stressful disruptions related to illness, such as painful, time-consuming, or otherwise noxious medical procedures (McCue,

1980; Peterson & Shigetomi, 1981). Some of the preparations can be very simple and effective, but are occasionally ignored in the quest for rapid diagnosis or treatment. Here is a brief illustration:

> *Jack* was a 7-year-old cancer patient being treated with Adriamycin, a powerful antitumor drug that turns the urine red while it is being metabolized. No one had bothered to warn Jack about this benign, but anxiety-provoking side effect. He went to urinate and panicked when he thought he was bleeding in the urine. Later, the physician warned him that the medicine might make his "blood count drop" in 8 to 10 days. He explained to Jack that a fever might occur and that he may need to be admitted to the hospital for intravenous antibiotics, but that this situation was routine and expected. When Jack came down with a fever and needed such an admission, he told his mother, "I'm not worried, the doctor knew this would happen and he can take care of it."

As you might expect, Jack was relatively calm about the need for the hospital admission and treatment when an adequate warning had been given.

Strategic Intervention

For any illness there are known or predictable stress points, and strategic intervention around these crises can be especially valuable. Practitioners should recognize such stress points and provide any necessary supports or interventions to assist their patients during these particularly disruptive times. In the care of a cancer patient, for example, the following points might be noted as special times of emotional vulnerability:

1. Getting the diagnosis
2. Onset of treatment
3. Adverse side effects of treatment
4. Reaching the end of the prescribed treatment phase (elective cessation of treatment)
5. Re-entry into school, family, and social life
6. Recurrence or relapse of the disease
7. Terminal phase of illness and death
8. Anniversary phenomena or life marker events for the survivor (e.g., high school graduations or weddings)

When such crises are known, the practitioner can forewarn the family of potential stress and offer reassurance or timely interventions as needed.

Clearly, many families with a sick child will cope quite well much of the time. Most will not need psychotherapy, and those that do need help will not generally need treatment in the traditional, exploratory-interpretive model of psychodynamic psychotherapy. Rather, families will be struggling to deal with acute disruptive events that may often be dealt with as known potential risks, even if the temporal sequence remains unknown.

Patient Education

Providing educational materials targeted to the children themselves is a special need and has proven effective. Such books as *You and Leukemia* (Baker, Roland, & Gilchrist, 1976), *A Hospital Story* (Stein, 1974), and *Sidney Kidney* (Pamplin, Light, & Hyman, 1974), a book about renal dialysis and transplantation, all intended to be read together by parents and children, are examples of excellent work of this sort.

Attempts to provide explanations in the child's own language and addressing the child's unique viewpoint are also important in routine patient care situations. Recall from my initial case materials the little girl who wondered how the surgeons "put her back together" after the operation. Imagine the preteen who is embarrassed and cannot understand why he/she is asked to urinate while being x-rayed for a voiding cystoscopy. Consider the somewhat humorous example of the 14-year-old boy interested in his future reproductive capacity following cancer chemotherapy. When invited to leave a specimen for a sperm count, he left a urine sample.

These situations all illustrate the need for those treating children's illnesses to be able to address children at their own level. This communication is not done with a patronizing attitude, but with a willingness to offer information in simple terms and create a climate suggesting that questions will be answered. I always make one extra suggestion on this point as well. Ask the child to explain back to you what you have just communicated: "Pretend that I am your brother (sister, classmate, etc.) and you are going to tell me about the (procedure). What will you say?" This tactic permits the early detection and correction of misconceptions or special concerns.

Enhanced Internal Control

One interesting study (Tennen, Affleck, McGrade, & Ratzan, 1981) suggests that children who believed their diabetes was due to their own behavior coped better and controlled their disease better than children who had external attribution beliefs. The study grew out of Seligman's work (1975) on learned helplessness and depression. If we consider that children are relatively helpless to begin with, it seems to follow logically that the more control one is able to offer them the less depression and related symptomatology will be present.

There are many ways to effect such enhanced internal controls without placing the patient at additional risk. Providing a nurse's call button at the bedside for an immobilized child, offering a menu choice in the hospital, permitting the child to choose which arm will receive an injection, and other such interventions tend to enhance feelings of self-control. One youngster could tolerate painful bone marrow aspirations much more easily when the physician followed the child's instruction to "Count to ten first."

Involving the child patient in the consent-getting process for treatment, as well as in the selection of necessary home care items or medical appliances can also be important. Children are much more likely to comply with treatment regimens and undertake them with cooperation and initiative when they have been invited to play a role in planning them. I have heard children as young as 5 talk of "helping the doctors to fight (my) tumor" in the course of cancer treatment.

Open Communication Patterns

As implied earlier in this paper, I shall conclude with a strong call for enhanced communications within the family (and between health care professionals and the family) as a means of facilitating adaptation and promoting coping. This phenomenon is perhaps best illustrated by the reports of work with cancer patients, where there were strong disincentives to share fears openly in the family (Slavin, O'Malley, Koocher, & Foster, 1982; Spinetta & Spinetta, 1981). Childhood cancer patients who had been lied to about their diagnosis were more likely to show psychological adjustment problems years later than were peers whose families had openly shared this information with them (Slavin et al., 1982).

This data does not imply that giving information makes better copers in and of itself. Rather, the implication is that families communicating openly and, therefore, supporting their members more effectively are more likely to produce good copers than are families where communication inhibitions are present. Traditionally, those treating childhood illnesses have not concerned themselves with considerations related to family communication patterns. This lack of concern clearly overlooks a major avenue of potential assistance for these families.

In Closing

There is a considerable body of knowledge to guide those wishing to design pediatric care systems in ways that offer the greatest support and least stress to the families moving through them. By viewing such stress as a function of the disruption of normal life events and by attempting to make sure disruptions more tolerable, we can substantially reduce the emotional sequelae of childhood illness. There is an increasing recognition through initiatives such as this conference that programs designed to accomplish these ends are not only more humane, but also cost-effective in the long run. I look forward to the day when routine consideration of these issues is the rule rather than the promising exception.

References

Baker, L. S., Roland, C. G., & Gilchrist, G. S. *You and me.* Rochester, Minnesota: Mayo Comprehensive Cancer Center, 1976.

Bibace, R., & Walsh, M. E. Development of children's conceptions of illness. *Pediatrics,* 1980, *66,* 912–917.

Bibace, R., & Walsh, M. E. (Eds.). *Children's conceptions of health, illness and bodily functions.* San Francisco: Jossey-Bass, 1981.

Campbell, J. Illness is a point of view: The development of children's conceptions of illness. *Child Develoment,* 1975, *46,* 92–100.

Carey, W. B. Hospitalization. In M. D. Levine, W. B. Carey, A. C. Crocker, & R. T. Gross (Eds.), *Developmental-behavioral pediatrics.* Philadelphia: W.B. Saunders, 1983.

Christ, G., & Greenly, M. A. *Therapeutic strategies at psychosocial crisis points in the treatment of childhood cancer.* Manuscript submitted for publication, 1983 (Available from the Department of Social Work, Memorial Sloan-Kettering Cancer Center, 1275 York Avenue, New York, New York).

Haan, N. *Coping and defending: Progress of self-environment organization.* New York: Academic Press, 1977.

Hardgrove, C., & Rutledge, A. Parenting during hospitalization. *American Journal of Nursing,* 1975, *75,* 836–838.

Haynes, R. B., Taylor, D. W., & Sackett, D. L. (Eds.). *Compliance in health care.* Baltimore: Johns Hopkins University Press, 1979.

Johnson, M. Mental health interventions with medically ill children: A review of the literature, 1970–1977. *Journal of Pediatric Psychology,* 1979, *4,* 147–164.

Koocher, G. P. Initial consultations with pediatric cancer patients. In J. Kellerman (Ed.), *Psychological aspects of cancer.* Springfield, Ill.: C. C. Thomas, 1980.

Koocher, G. P., & O'Malley, J. E. *The Damocles Syndrome: Psychosocial consequences of surviving childhood cancer.* New York: McGraw-Hill, 1981.

Koocher, G. P., Sourkes, B. M., & Keane, M. W. Pediatric oncology consultations: A generalizable model for medical settings. *Professional Psychology,* 1979, *10,* 467–474.

Lazarus, R. S. *Psychological stress and the coping process.* New York: McGraw-Hill, 1966.

Martinson, I. M. *Home care for the child with cancer.* Minneapolis: University of Minnesota, 1980.

McCue, K. Preparing children for medical procedures. In J. Kellerman (Ed.), *Psychological aspects of childhood cancer.* Springfield, Ill.: Thomas, 1980.

Melamed, B. G. Psychological preparation for hospitalization. In S. Rachman (Ed.), *Contributions to medical psychology* (Vol. 1). New York: Pergamon, 1977.

Melamed, B. G., & Siegel, L. J. Reduction of anxiety in children facing hospitalization and surgery by use of filmed modeling. *Journal of Consulting and Clinical Psychology,* 1975, *43,* 511–521.

Neuhauser, C., Amsterdam, B., Hines, P., & Steward, M. Children's concepts

326   GERALD P. KOOCHER

of healing: Cognitive development and locus of control factors. *American Journal of Orthopsychiatry*, 1978, *48*, 334–341.

Pamplin, H. H., Light, J. A., & Hyman, L. R. *Sidney Kidney*. Washington, D.C.: Walter Reed Army Medical Center, 1974.

Peterson, L., & Ridley-Johnson, R. Pediatric hospital response to survey on prehospital preparation for children. *Journal of Pediatric Psychology*, 1980, *5*, 1–7.

Peterson, L., & Ridley-Johnson, R. Preparation of well children in the classroom: An unexpected contrast between the academic lecture and filmed-modeling methods. *Journal of Pediatric Psychology*, in press.

Peterson, L., & Shigetomi, C. The use of coping techniques to minimize anxiety in hospitalized children. *Behavior Therapy*, 1981, *12*, 1–14.

Rapoff, M. A., & Christophersen, E. R. Improving compliance in pediatric practice. *Pediatric Clinics of North America*, 1982, *29*, 339–357.

Roberts, M. C., Wurtele, S. K., Boone, R. R., Ginther, L., & Elkins, P. D. Reduction of medical and psychological fears by use of modeling: A preventive application in a general population of children. *Journal of Pediatric Psychology*, 1981, *6*, 293–300.

Seligman, M. E. P. *Helplessness: On depression, development, and death*. San Francisco: Freeman, 1975.

Shore, M. F., Goldston, S. E. Mental health aspects of pediatric care: Historical review and current status. In P. R. Magrab (Ed.), *Psychological management of pediatric problems* (Vol. 1). Baltimore: University Park Press, 1978.

Siegel, L. J. Hospitalization and medical care of children. In C. E. Wacker & M. C. Roberts (Eds.), *Handbook of clinical child psychology*. New York: Wiley, 1983.

Simeonsson, R. J., Buckley, L., & Monson, L. Conceptions of illness causality in hospitalized children. *Journal of Pediatric Psychology*, 1979, *4*, 77–84.

Singer, J. E. *Some issues in the study of coping*. Paper presented at the American Cancer Society's Conference on Methodology in Behavioral and Psychosocial Cancer Research, St. Petersburg, Florida, April 1983.

Slavin, L. A., O'Malley, J. E., Koocher, G. P., & Foster, D. J. Communication of the cancer diagnosis to pediatric patients: Impact on long-term adjustment. *American Journal of Psychiatry*, 1982, *139*, 179–183.

Spinetta, J. J., & Spinetta, P. D. (Eds.). *Living with childhood cancer*. St. Louis: C. V. Mosby, 1981.

Stein, R. E. K., & Jones, D. J. A noncategorical approach to chronic childhood illness. *Public Health Reports*, 1982, *97*, 354–362.

Stein, S. B. *A hospital story*. New York: Walker and Co., 1974.

Stewart, A. L., Ware, J. E., & Brook, R. H. *Construction and scoring of aggregate functional status measures*. Santa Monica, Calif.: The Rand Corporation, 1982.

Stuart, R. B. *Adherence, compliance, and generalization in behavioral medicine*. New York: Brunner-Mazel, 1982.

Tennen, H., Affleck, G., McGrade, B. J., & Ratzan, S. *Causal attributions and coping in juvenile diabetes*. Paper presented at the meeting of the American Psychological Association, 1981, and manuscript submitted for publication. (Available from the senior author at the University of Connecticut Health Sciences Center, Farmington, Connecticut).

Tuma, J. M. *Handbook for the practice of pediatric psychology*. New York: Wiley, 1983.

Visintainer, M. A., & Wolfer, J. A. Psychological preparation for surgical pediatric patients: The effects of children's and parents' stress responses and adjustment. *Pediatrics*, 1975, *56*, 187–202.

Walker, C. E., & Roberts, M. C. *Handbook of clinical child psychology*. New York: Wiley, 1983.

Whitt, K., Dykstra, W., & Taylor, C. A. Children's conceptions of illness and cognitive development. *Clinical Pediatrics*, 1979, *18*, 327–334.

Willis, D. J., Elliott, C. H., & Jay, S. M. Psychological effects of physical illness and its concomitants. In J. M. Tuma (Ed.), *Handbook for the practice of pediatric psychology*. New York: Wiley, 1983.

Zeltzer, L., Kellerman, J., Ellenberg, L., Dash, J., & Rigler, D. Psychological effects of illness in adolescence. II. Impact of illness in adolescents—Crucial issues and coping styles. *Journal of Pediatrics*, 1980, *97*, 132–138.

13
Physician–Patient Communication
Promoting a Positive Health Care Setting

M. Robin DiMatteo

"You have essential hypertension," said the physician to his patient. "Here is a prescription for hydrochlorothiazide b.i.d. for fluid retention. I also want you to reduce your sodium intake." "Thank you," said the patient. Although he had little idea what the physician was talking about, the patient was very impressed. The patient decided not to ask questions. He surely could figure out the recommendation on his own. That very night, before bed, the patient was satisfied to have made his first decision in taking care of his new medical condition. "I think nighttime is the best time to take my medication that causes fluid retention," he said to his wife. "That way, I won't have to get up in the middle of the night to go to the bathroom."

This small incident is not at all unusual. It illustrates a multitude of communication problems occuring every day in medical practice and suggests why patients and practitioners may, at times, become very frustrated with medical care. Whether the treatment situation involves care for a long-term chronic illness or surgery for a life-threatening condition, difficulties in communication can surface and wreak havoc on the participants.

Sick patients visit physicians to be cared for. Young medical students say they want to care for people. Health maintenance organizations boast "We Care." Yet, the actual experience of receiving medical care may appear totally unrelated to caring. Patients and physicians are too often frustrated, hostile, confused, fearful, and angry. The caring they expect to give or receive typically takes a back seat to less noble feelings. The problems typically stem not from poor intentions or goals, however, but from inadequate means. Faulty communication between physician and patient is often at the heart of the problem. In fact, it will be argued

This chapter is based, in part, on material presented and elaborated in M. R. DiMatteo & D. D. DiNicola, *Achieving Patient Compliance*, Elmsford, N.Y.: Pergamon Press, 1982. The author wishes to acknowledge the James McKeen Cattell Fund, which provided sabbatical support during the 1982–1983 academic year.

throughout this chapter that physician-patient communication plays a *central* role in medical care—particularly in the caring that is an integral part of all medical treatment.

Communication in Medicine

For many reasons, communication is a particularly formidable problem in the medical care setting. Physician and patient often do not seem to share the same language. Since illness and pain are subjective conditions (indeed, dependent not so much upon measurable physical states as upon the interpretation of them [Mechanic, 1968]), language symbols used by practitioner and patient are likely to have different meanings. Communication is also likely to be impeded when one party (or both) is anxious or emotionally upset, or when there are differences between them in knowledge, power, education, and/or social status. Similarly, differences in priorities and purpose of information exchange, as well as the use of professional "in-group" jargon, severely complicate the process of communication. In sum, "the factors that complicate the process of shared meaning are nearly all present in doctor-patient encounters" (Barnlund, 1976, p. 721).

Physicians seldom seek clarification of a patient's level of understanding, yet patients often do not comprehend the words their practitioners are wont to use (Samora, Saunders, & Larson, 1961). When practitioners use such words, most patients do not ask what they mean, preferring instead to attempt to decipher them within a given context. Thus, it is inappropriate to assign "blame" to one or the other party. Furthermore, their interaction is imbedded in a social context that imparts (or has imparted) behavioral expectations to the role each one plays. Patients are expected to be cooperative and submissive (Parsons, 1958), while physicians are expected to be dominant and in control (Parsons, 1951). Such expectations, of course, influence physician-patient interaction and the information communicated. Further, while motivation and commitment of practitioner and patient are necessary conditions for the development of effective communication, only skills can give these interactants the capacity to communicate effectively with one another.

A major aim of this section is to delineate carefully the specific behavioral skills necessary for the physician's effective communication with patients. The number and complexity of factors relating to practitioner-patient communication are emphasized, and "the temptation to search for demons" is avoided (Barnlund, 1976, p. 722). It is important to recognize throughout this analysis that no one party is to blame. Physicians as well as patients must cope every day with anxieties, fears, and uncertainties surrounding medical treatment. Each must find "some compromise between private impulse and social expectation" (Barnlund, 1976, p. 722). What can be done to improve communication toward the goal of a more positive health setting will be discussed.

Early theories of medical sociologists such as Talcott Parsons (1951) delineated the "proper" role of physician and patient in modern Western society. According to Parsons, the professional role of the physician demands technical competence, emotional neutrality, and a commitment to serving people. In this role as emotionally neutral healer, the physician is expected to remain detached and in control. The physician legitimizes the patient's entry into the sick role—a role exempting patients from many of their day-to-day responsibilities. In return, the patient is expected to seek competent medical help, to profess a desire to become well again, and to demonstrate this desire by cooperating completely with and deferring to the physician's authority.

Inherent in this relationship is a disparity of power based primarily upon the physician's expert command of an esoteric body of knowledge and, of course, upon his or her resources and skills in applying that knowledge. Parsons (1975) labeled this information differential the "competence gap."

Medical sociologist Eliot Freidson (1970) has persuasively argued that, in the physician-patient relationship, there is tremendous conflict. In fact, Freidson argued that we cannot ignore the *necessity* of conflict in the practitioner-patient encounter: "The professional expects patients to accept what he recommends on his terms; patients seek services on their own terms. In that each seeks to gain his own terms, there is conflict" (Freidson, 1961, p. 171). The conflict very often involves the exchange of information.

Information exchange, in Freidson's approach, is a complicated process. Patients cannot be considered lowly or childlike in their perspective, adhering to a strict pattern of expectations because of limitations in knowledge and expertise. Patients often have expectations quite different from those of the physician. In contrast to Parsons, Freidson argued that, for many patients, the authority of the physician is far from absolute and that the conflict that inevitably arises between the physician and patient in medical interaction can be resolved by *negotiation*.

Interaction in treatment should be seen as a kind of negotiation as well as a kind of conflict. The patient is likely to want more information than the doctor is willing to give him—more precise prognoses, for example, and more precise instructions. As Roth's study indicated, just as the doctor struggles to find ways of withholding some kinds of information, so will the patient be struggling to find ways of gaining access to, or inferring, such information (Roth, 1963). (Freidson, 1970, p. 322)

Empirical studies of the physician-patient communication and the negotiation that takes place have dealt with the specific details of social interaction. From these studies we can learn to identify communication problems and attempt to correct them. The specific behaviors involve finishing a thought, getting a word in edgewise, ascertaining that the other person is listening, asking questions, and getting questions answered. We must work on this detailed level in order to understand information sharing (and negotiations regarding it) in medical encounters. As a result, questions like the following become important: Who talks most in the practitioner (physician)-patient relationship? Who interrupts whom? Who listens, how often, and how well? Is information actually communicated? and, Does the transmission of information result in any demonstrable effects? Although there still exist some major unanswered questions, the empirical research to date clearly describes the physician-patient relationship and the problems that must be surmounted to achieve therapeutic goals.

Limitations in Practitioners' Communication to Patients

A surprising number of patients leave their doctor's office with little idea of what they are supposed to do to follow their treatment regimen. Many important empirical studies have demonstrated this point clearly, using methodologies that range from interviews, to clinic and pharmacy records, to observations of actual practitioner-patient encounters. In one classic study Svarstad (1974, 1976) found that 50% of patients did not know how long they were supposed to continue taking their medication; 17% of patients could not correctly report how often they were supposed to take their medication; and 23% could not identify the purpose of the drugs they were taking. Other research has identified similar problems. Brant and Kutner (1957), in interviews with 50 hospitalized surgical patients, found nearly all experiencing anxious uncertainty. The authors found that patients rarely knew in advance about the normal, predictable postoperative events they would experience, and many patients did not know why they were having surgery. In yet another study, Kane and Deuschle (1967) conducted interviews with medical patients who had been discharged (up to 13 months previously) from a University Medical Center in Kentucky. Among patients taking medication, 72% could not accurately identify their medicines, 26% had no idea why they were taking the medicines, and 37% "could not be counted upon to know when or how much of a prescribed medicine to take" (p. 263).

Teaching Patients.
When patients initially seem poorly informed, physicians often avoid taking the time necessary to translate medical explanations into terms the

patient can understand (Pratt, Seligmann & Reader, 1957). Physicians
tend significantly to underestimate the comprehension level of their patients (Segall & Roberts, 1980), however. Thus, patients often remain
unnecessarily confused and uninformed. These findings were also revealed in research by Duff and Hollingshead (1968), Cartwright (1964),
and Taylor (1979). In the hospital, explanations are particularly difficult
to obtain. Physicians rarely meet with their patients in unhurried conference to stay to talk with them after explaining something to be sure they
understand it (Brant & Kutner, 1957; and Golden & Johnston, 1970). In
one study, a significant number of physicians did not introduce themselves to the hospitalized patient (Cartwright, 1964).

A few empirical studies give us a fairly detailed look at practitioner-
patient communication. Waitzkin and Stoeckle (1976), for example, reported the results of a pilot study involving the direct recording and
analysis of physician-patient communications. During the medical visit
(lasting, on the average, 20 minutes), physicians spent on the average less
than 1 minute communicating information to each patient or informing
them about some aspect of their illness or treatment. Waitzkin and
Stoeckle reported that those same physicians estimated they spent 10 to
15 minutes (that is, 50 to 75% of their interaction time) giving information to their patients. Freemon, Negrete, Davis, and Korsch (1971) demonstrated that physicians gave information or instructions to mothers of
pediatric patients during only about 8% of their interaction time, and
Davis (1971) found that physicians "gave suggestions" to patients during
only about 10% of their interaction time. Bain (1976) reported that "giving instructions" occurred somewhat more frequently—16% of the interaction time.

An important study by Svarstad (1976) demonstrated that the amount
of time spent by physicians giving information to their patients may be
irrelevant, because physicians tend to be ineffective communicators.
Svarstad recorded the specific verbal instructions given to patients during
their medical visits and compared these instructions to those attached to
the patients' medication containers. She found that frequently physicians
did not discuss with patients their intentions to prescribe medication. Of
the 347 drugs prescribed to the patients in this study, 60 were never
discussed during the observed visit. In 90% of the drug-prescribing inci-
dents, physicians gave their patients no specific verbal advice on how to
use the medication. The observer concluded the physicians usually inferred their patients could easily figure out the dosage required and when
and how the medication was to be taken. (Remember the hypertensive
patient at the beginning of this chapter.) Often, physicians verbally
changed the dosage of a drug the patient had at home, but gave the
patient no written record of the change. Physicians assumed their pa-

tients understood the change and would remember it. In addition, instructions to be written on prescription drug containers almost never included the length of time the drug should be taken. Of the 347 drugs dispensed, 97 were to be used for symptomatic relief, but only 42 of these were dispensed with labels indicating this intended use. Finally, in 29% of the cases of drug prescription, the physician gave the patient neither the name of the drug nor any information about its purpose.

Listening to the Patient.

Listening to patients can be a critically important aspect of patient care. Patients have the opportunity to gather many clues about their conditions, such as details about the character and timing of symptoms. Much valuable information may be lost by insisting patients respond to questions with one-word answers. Listening fully to all the patient has to say may help the physician avoid the tendency of many in medical diagnosis of formulating a hypothesis too quickly and then fitting the empirical evidence to that hypothesis (Elstein, 1976). Listening also reflects physicians' respect for the patient and their willingness to share power in the relationship (Stone, 1979). Listening to patients tell their stories in their own words is a lesson emphasized again and again in medical training (Engel & Morgan, 1973).

In four major empirical studies, the various forms of verbal communication emitted by patient and by physician were tallied from tape recordings of the actual medical visit (Bain, 1976; Davis, 1971; Freemon et al., 1971; Stiles, Putnam, Wolf, & James, 1979b). In all four studies, similar patterns of verbal interaction were found, despite differences in population and setting. In short, the physician talked significantly more than did the patient. Physicians tended to verbalize quite extensively, and their utterances typically were *not* explanations or communications of information. Rather, about two-thirds of what physicians said are acknowledgements, questions, reflections, and clarifications. Freemon et al. (1971), however, noted that physicians do not typically realize this aspect of their communications, for many physicians believe they spend much more time listening to their patients than talking to them.

Medical Jargon.

Many patients are impressed by incomprehensible medical jargon (Korsch, Gozzi, & Francis, 1968). The physician's use of medical terminology is sometimes taken by patients as a compliment to their intelligence, or as a signal that the patient can relax into the submissive, safe, sick role. Using jargon, the practitioner remains in control (Shapiro, 1978).

The use of medical jargon may impress some patients, but it communicates very little useful information to them. Effective communication cannot be maintained if the patient does not know the relevant medical vocabulary (Becker & Maiman, 1980). Korsch et al. (1968), for example, found that pediatricians in a clinic used many vocabulary words that mothers simply did not understand. Words such as "incubation period" and "workup"—common terms in medical settings—confused and perplexed the mothers. After the visit, many mothers were left with no better idea of what was wrong with their babies than they had before it. The chance of noncompliance in the care of their children was, as a result, quite high.

A major, systematic study of patients' knowledge of medical vocabulary was carried out by Samora et al. (1961). A list of 50 words, judged by medical practitioners as appropriate for use in conversation with patients, was constructed. Each word was then embedded in a context sentence, and 125 patients (largely lower class) were asked to define each word. That definition was then scored according to the patient's apparent degree of understanding. The least number of words any patient could define adequately was 11. The most any patient knew was 47. The average number of words defined was 29 (the median was also 29).

Limitation: Patient Fallibility

Patients' lack of knowledge about their therapeutic regimen is by no means the sole responsibility of the practitioner. Patients forget what they have been told, they make interpretive errors, and, when they do not understand what they have been told, they neglect to say so. They are often unassertive and passive.

Failures of memory.
For effective communication to take place, recipients of messages obviously must remember what they have been told. An investigation by Ley and Spelman (1965) demonstrated, however, that, shortly after their consultation with the practitioner, clinic outpatients forgot about a third of what they had been told. Patients forgot 20% of the prognoses of a condition, as well as 56% of the instructions and 48% of the statements about treatment. Other research has shown that patients make interpretive errors. In one study, Mazullo, Lasagna, and Griner (1974) examined patients' responses to typed instructions for 10 commonly prescribed medications. Sixty-seven patients were interviewed and asked to read the label on each of 10 pill bottles and then asked to describe how they would take the drug. There was not one instance in which a label was interpreted the same way by all patients. The responses indicated marked variability in patients' interpretations of what most physicians would consider to be straightforward instructions. Even when the instructions were not at all ambiguous, the frequency of interpretive errors ranged from 9 to 64%.

Passive, unassertive patients.
A few studies have demonstrated that patients typically know more about medical issues (conceptual issues, *not* medical jargon) than their physicians anticipate (Kane & Deuschle, 1967; Pratt et al., 1957). The physician's underestimation of patient knowledge is likely to be detrimental to their communication, for, as Pratt et al. (1957) found, when physicians underestimated the patient's knowledge, they were less likely to discuss illness at length with the patient (perhaps because discussion was assumed to require a prohibitive amount of time). This problem is compounded, of course, when patients, knowing relatively little, are afraid to ask for more information. They may then simply let the physician decide what information to convey. Patients rarely attempt to inform their physicians when they do not understand or when they would like further explanation. Instead, they nod their heads knowingly at explanations they do not comprehend and decline to ask questions when given the opportunity. Objective analyses of verbal communication in physician-patient encounters support this hypothesis overwhelmingly (Bain, 1976; Freemon et al., 1971; Stiles et al., 1979b). As Coe (1970) has noted, patients are reluctant to ask the physician any questions during the interview for fear of demonstrating ignorance or incomplete trust in the physician.

It is important always to keep in mind that problems in practitioner-patient communication stem from both patient and practitioner variables—from practitioners' "failure" to explain as well as from patients' "failure" to comprehend. These variables have heretofore been examined separately—a practice significantly limiting research to date. Precisely how practitioners' behaviors affect patients' behaviors and vice versa (for example, what behaviors in one party trigger or reinforce behaviors in the other) has yet to be carefully examined. The nature of practitioner-patient *interaction* has yet to be explored.

The Positive Effects of Communicating Information

Effective communication between practitioners and their patients produces measurable, positive results—particularly, patient compliance with treatment, patient satisfaction, and enhanced outcome of treatment.

Improved Patient Cooperation with Treatment

Patient noncompliance with medical regimens is a major unsolved problem in medical practice today. The average noncompliance rate is around 40%, with higher rates for long-term regimens for chronic diseases and lower rates among short-term treatments for acute conditions. Although noncompliance appears to be a complex phenomenon with many contributing factors, the quality of communication in the practitioner-patient relationship (broadly defined) has been posited by many as the most important determinant (c.f. DiMatteo and DiNicola, 1982a). Patients must know specifically what to do in order to fulfill their required treatment regimens. Thus, information is central to patient compliance.

An excellent review of factors affecting "dropout" from treatment (both medical and psychotherapeutic) has been presented by Baekeland and Lundwall (1975). Their review documents dropout from treatment as a very troublesome feature of long-term medical care for chronic conditions. Patient dropout from treatment for such chronic conditions as hypertension and diabetes has been found to result from poor instruction concerning the problematic consequences of avoiding adequate treatment. Patients were more likely to discontinue treatment if they were unaware of the potential health dangers of their medical problems and the necessity of remaining under close medical supervision. Francis, Korsch, and Morris (1969) found a key factor in noncompliance was the mother's failure to receive an explanation of the diagnosis and cause of her child's illness. In a similar study using tape recordings, Freemon et al. (1971) found a trend toward high compliance in cases where the pediatrician focused discussion with the mother specifically on the diagnosis of the child's problem. Simple explanations, lacking jargon, were particularly important in helping mothers understand the medical problem and, hence, the importance of cooperation with the treatment. Compliance with long-term regimens for chronic illness depends heavily upon clear explanations as well. Hulka, Cassel, Kupper, and Burdette (1976) found, in a study of 357 chronically ill patients, that rarely (less than 3%) did patients fail to follow a treatment they fully understood.

Regarding the general issue of information and its relationship to compliance, Davis (1968) noted that "while there is not complete agreement on exactly how the doctor-patient relationship affects compliance, most investigators do recognize the importance of communication and explanation" (p. 287). Davis reviewed 20 studies in which this relationship was demonstrated.

An experimental study by Roter (1977) has provided some compelling evidence for the role of information in patients' commitment to treatment. This study is especially important because it employed random assignment of subjects to treatment groups and involved an experimental intervention designed to increase the information obtained by patients by motivating them to ask questions of their physicians. Experimental group patients, prior to their visit with a physician, were assisted by a health counselor to formulate questions they would like to ask their physicians. These questions (about diagnosis, etiology, treatment, and prognosis) were written down to facilitate recall. Control group patients were given some general information but no special help or encouragement to ask questions of their physicians. The results showed that experimental group patients (given the special intervention) asked more direct questions of their physicians than did control group patients. This finding was determined through analysis of tape recordings of the medical visit. Experimental group patients also demonstrated significantly higher appointment-keeping rates than did control patients.

Enhanced Patient Satisfaction with Treatment

Popular notions that patients who are informed by their practitioners are more satisfied with the medical care they receive are supported by empirical research. A strong positive relationship is typically found between patient satisfaction and the practitioner's provision of information about diagnosis, treatment, and prognosis. Korsch et al. (1968) studied the expectations of mothers bringing their children to an emergency clinic. Tape recordings of the physician–mother interaction were made and later analyzed in conjunction with the results of a chart review, postvisit interview, and follow-up interview with the mother. A striking finding of the research was each mother's intense concern with and need for information and explanation of her child's disease and what caused it. Mothers especially wanted to be reassured that they were not to blame for their children's illnesses. Failure to fulfill a mother's need for an explanation of the diagnosis and etiology often resulted in significant dissatisfaction on the part of the mother. Relatedly, Houston and Pasanen (1972) and Liptak, Hulka, and Cassel (1977) found that patients' satisfaction with care was directly related to the amount of information they received.

In objective analyses of patterns of interaction exchange in the physician–patient relationship, Stiles, Putnam, Wolf, and James (1979a) found that patient satisfaction, as expressed in a postvisit questionnaire, was related to the physician's transmission of information in "feedback" exchanges during the concluding segment of the visit. In another study, behaviors of physicians and patients were coded from videotaped interviews (Smith, Polis, & Hadac, 1981). The importance of information to patient satisfaction was again supported. Not surprisingly, significant negative correlations were found between the proportion of time the physician spent during the visit reading the patient's chart and both patient satisfaction and patient understanding.

Finally, Bertakis (1977) tape recorded physician-patient visits to determine the amount of information conveyed by the physician regarding diagnosis and etiology of the illness, further investigations such as laboratory tests, and treatment regimen required. Patients were, overall, more satisfied with physicians who gave them information. In addition, patients who retained more of all forms of information about their illness were more satisfied.

Information and the Outcome of Treatment

Outpatient Treatment.

In the care of both acute and chronic illness, the treatment of patients as passive recipients of care may not be in their best interest. Particularly when regimens require long-term medical involvement, an active patient orientation may be necessary to improve patient cooperation and to enhance the physical and psychological well-being of the patient. In a study by Schulman (1979), a systematic attempt was made to change patients' view of medical care toward an active orientation—an orientation that enhanced their knowledge of the regimen and their participation in it. In the study, 99 hypertension patients' direct involvement in their own care was considered in relation to their treatment outcomes. Patients' active orientation was induced by various methods of treatment and was measured as a quantitative variable using a self-report scale. Various cognitive, behavioral, and physical measures were also collected and blood pressures were recorded. Patients with a highly active orientation to their care were significantly more likely to have their blood pressure under control and were less likely to report side effects from their medications. They also adhered more closely to their treatment recommendations and were more likely to engage in health-enhancing behaviors (such as stopping smoking, relaxing more, reducing their salt intake, and having no alcohol). Patients with a highly active orientation also expressed greater feelings of self-efficacy, greater confidence in their professionals' expertise, and a greater belief in the benefit of treatment over the cost.

Stressful Medical Examinations and Procedures.

Research has revealed an overwhelming amount of evidence that pain is subject to cognitive and emotional factors (Melzack, 1972). Pain experiences are modified by thoughts regarding the "meaning" of the situation to the patient, by the person's anxiety about the source of pain, and by attentional factors (to what extent the person is focusing thoughts on the pain) (Beecher, 1959). Studies of various experimental interventions (cf., Kaplan, 1982) have shown that providing information to patients can have a significant impact on their abilities to cope with unpleasant or painful medical examinations or treatment procedures.

Folklore suggests that when facing a stressful event likely to cause pain, it may be best to "not think about it." Studies of avoidant thinking, however, show that this strategy is not an effective coping mechanism for most people facing medical procedures (Houston & Holmes, 1973). In the face of expected pain or discomfort, the opportunity to think about the details of what one is about to experience actually reduces the distress of experiencing it. Information is one of the best treatments for the stress of facing a difficult medical procedure.

Numerous intervention studies have examined this issue in the medical setting with patients facing these stressful procedures. For example, Johnson and Leventhal (1974) studied 48 patients about to undergo an endoscopy examination (requiring passage of a tube the thickness of a thumb down the throat and into the gastrointestinal tract, with the patient fully awake). Patients were given one of two types of preparatory information, both types of information, or no information at all. One type of information concerned the sensations that would be experienced (what would be seen, heard, felt, tasted), while the other instructions told patients what they would be asked to do during the examination (e.g., make swallowing motions). The results showed that the instructions giving a complete description of the sensory experiences best reduced patients' emotional distress. The information concerning what the patient was expected to do was only effective when it was used in combination with the sensory information.

Similar findings have come from studies of other medical procedures, such as pelvic examinations (Fuller, Endress, & Johnson, 1978), blood donation (Mills & Krantz, 1979), and sigmoidoscopy (Kaplan, 1982). The provision of sensory information (what will be experienced by the patient, the specific sensations, feelings, sounds, tastes, smells, etc.) had a profound effect on reducing self-reported anxiety and its behavioral concomitants (such as agitation, tenseness of muscles, amount of analgesic or tranquilizer required, etc.), many of which might interfere with the medical procedure itself. Shipley, Butt, Horwitz, and Farby (1978) found that the repetition of explicit information about the process of an endoscopy examination was most effective in reducing distress during the examination.

Surgery.
Studies of the effects of providing surgical patients with preliminary information about their surgical experience have been carried out over the past two decades, stimulated initially by the work of the psychologist Irving Janis (1958). Janis examined the phenomenon of the "work of worrying" on patients' adaptation to the stressful events surrounding surgery. Studies that grew out of Janis' work used as their outcome criteria various physical and psychological variables, including patients' anxiety level before surgery, their calmness, their need for painkilling medication, and their postoperative course (including the total number of days of hospitalization). Egbert, Battit, Turndorf, and Beecher (1963) found that information provided to patients in a supportive visit by the anesthetist prior to surgery had a more positive effect upon their drow-

siness and calmness before surgery than did the tranquilizing drug pento-
barbitol. When the drug was combined with the informative visit, the
most positive effect was achieved. A further investigation of this
phenomenon (Egbert, Battit, Welch, & Bartlett, 1964) showed a positive
effect from a supportive visit by the anesthetist, a visit in which sensory
information and instruction (in relaxing spasmodic abdominal muscles
after surgery) was provided. Patients in the experimental group required
less pain medication for the five postoperative days than did control
group patients. They were judged to be more comfortable and in better
physical and emotional condition, and were discharged from the hospital
an average of 2.7 days earlier than control group patients.

It has not yet been determined whether sensory information alone is
enough to ease the difficulties of surgery. Instructing patients in cognitive coping devices, including calming self-talk, a reappraisal of anxiety-
provoking events, and cognitive control, has been successful in some
studies (see Langer, Janis, & Wolfer, 1975). Reading (1979) and Schmitt
and Wooldridge (1973) have reported that the most positive effects for
surgical and nonsurgical preparation of patients result from a combination of information and coping techniques, with an emphasis on coping
techniques. In addition, some research has shown that information and
support presented to a person significant to the patient (such as a family
member) may improve the patient's reaction to surgery. Skipper and
Leonard (1968) presented experimental data indicating that social interaction with hospital personnel who provided information and emotional
support reduced a mother's stress and reduced the threatening aspects of
her child's hospitalization and surgery improved.

Mediating Mechanisms.
Precisely how information (and suggestions for specific coping) operates
to enhance the outcomes of patient care is still not completely clear.
Reading (1979) suggested the following explanations: (1) information
reduces patient anxiety; (2) personal control is increased; (3) attitude
toward the procedure is improved; and (4) instructions are provided for
utilizing established techniques for coping with pain. The importance of
information to the outcome of treatment is rather well established, but
the precise mechanisms that bring about the beneficial effects are not yet
understood.

Factors that Hinder Physician–Patient Communication

The Patient's Role

A sick person occupies a social role, the entry to which is governed by
physicians. Physicians are the "gatekeepers" of the sick role in American

society (Parsons, 1958). They take charge of the person who is ill, dispensing (for the society as a whole) privileges (e.g., absence from work) in exchange for obligations (e.g., cooperation and the expression of a desire to get well). Because of the importance typically placed on hospital and health care center routine, the patient faces another obligation as well—the obligation to be unswervingly cooperative and compliant with every detail of care and to submit totally to the authority of the practitioners. Many have noted that patients are often quite willing to accept the role of passive participants in their care (King, 1962; Lederer, 1952; Skipper & Leonard, 1965). Patients are often found anxious and fearful, and, when they are sick, many wish simply to be cared for.

One important reason patients do not ask questions of their practitioners may be that they have relinquished responsibility for their medical care. The source of this abandonment of self-control is still being debated. Patients' passive acceptance of all that is dealt them (and all that is hidden from them) has been attributed to their regression to a childlike state in response to illness (Lederer, 1952). Others (Lorber, 1975; Taylor, 1979), however, have argued that a passive role is *forced* on patients, because those who ask questions and demand answers are labeled "bad patients" by practitioners and hospital staff. Bad patients are often ignored, prematurely medicated, or referred to psychiatrists (Katz, Weiner, Gallagher, & Hellman, 1970; Lorber, 1975). For whatever reasons, illness is usually accompanied by a degree of dependency likely to interfere with practitioner-patient communication.

The anxiety and ego-involvement that tend to accompany physical incapacity, illness, and disease can easily interfere with effective communication (Barnlund, 1976). People rarely comprehend information clearly when they are emotionally upset. Learning and information processing take place most effectively when the individual is experiencing an intermediate level of anxiety. High anxiety that may accompany illness and dealings with the medical care system might also trigger defense mechanisms such as denial and repression. For many reasons, the patient may become distracted from what he is being told. Thus, explanations given to patients might do little to change their state of knowledge about their condition or their treatment *unless* their anxiety level is also reduced.

Poor communication between patients and physicians might be a reflection of patient resistance to influence. Patients' reluctance to ask questions and to provide clarifying information may represent their attempts to keep the practitioner uncertain of their beliefs, feelings, and behaviors. Patients may be able to "resist" without openly asserting their desires or confronting the practitioner with opposition to the treatment or regimen prescribed. For example, patients can resist the influence of the physician by not trying to understand the instructions. If patients do not comprehend the instructions, they cannot be held responsible for not complying with them. This method of engineering noncompliance may be appealing to the patient who wishes to gain control in the therapeutic relationship (Hayes-Bautista, 1976a, 1976b).

That patients may sabotage communication with their practitioners to gain control through noncompliance is not new (Haley, 1963, 1973) and suggests that patients value control (although they may use inappropriate means to achieve it). Patients' control and responsibility in the development and maintenance of their commitment to their treatment is a desirable outcome because it is linked positively to many aspects of their care. Effective communication enhances the constructive means available to patients for expressing their desire for control.

The Physician's Role

The formulation of effective explanations and the communication of clear and unambiguous information may require a great deal of effort (Martin, 1978). Some physicians are likely to dispense with the goal of patient education simply because they are unwilling or unable to spend the necessary time and energy. Indeed, some practitioners may wish to maintain a high degree of emotional detachment from their patients as a means of self-protection (Daniels, 1960; Lief & Fox, 1963). Practitioners may keep their patients unaware of their condition or of relevant information to prevent patients from arguing from a knowledgeable position. They may simply want to prevent their patients from causing them "trouble" (Lorber, 1975; McIntosh, 1974), bringing malpractice litigation against them (Thurlow, 1969), or exhibiting unmanageable emotional reactions (Skipper, Tagliacozzo, & Mauksch, 1964).

To understand fully practitioners' motives and behaviors, one must look at the broader societal context. Parsons' (1951) analysis of the role of the physician characterizes it as one of high status and control vis-à-vis the patient. Control and power are assumed by the physician in the patient's best interest. They are necessary for the practitioner to perform his/her healing function. As noted earlier, however, Freidson (1970) and Waitzkin (Waitzkin & Stoeckle, 1972; Waitzkin & Waterman, 1974) advocate a different viewpoint. The physician maintains control *not* because it promotes the interests of the patient, but because it maintains the institutional authority of the physician and the dependency of the patient. The practitioner's competence, expertise, and status as a healer bring with them social and political power; the maintenance of institutional authority and dominance is emphasized and reinforced throughout medical training (Shapiro, 1978). This dominance may be manifested in the practitioner–patient interaction by such obvious behaviors as withholding information and such subtle behaviors as interrupting the patient's speech (West, 1981).

Differing Backgrounds and Perspectives of Practitioner and Patient

Most patients have had less formal education and enjoy lower occupational status than the practitioners treating them. Health professionals are experts. Their status derives from their special knowledge as well as from their income and education. For many patients, medical practitioners also represent authority. As Barnlund (1976) has noted, the presence of higher status individuals often provokes fear and tension in patients, potentially interfering with their information processing. As demonstrated by White (1953) and by Seeman and Evans (1962), any emphasis on status distinctions between practitioner and patient will affect their personal interchange. Status hierarchies are likely to promote patient avoidance of contact with the professional, the withholding of information, and even the distortion of the information conveyed.

Differences in social status, in family background, in education, and in income represent other discrepancies between physicans and their patients. The value of health and the willingness to engage in preventive health practices are likely to be at variance for the two groups (Larson & Sutker, 1966) and may easily cause problems in communication. Health practitioners also tend to have a stronger focus on the future than do their patients (Mumford, 1977). Every day practitioners encounter disease statistics and care for patients who have not beaten the odds. Further, their long postponement of immediate goals in favor of education tends to reflect their belief in and commitment to the future. Few patients have as strong a commitment, even where their own future health is concerned.

Finally, miscommunication and misunderstanding may result from physicians' and patients' differing perceptions of medical care and their differing concerns regarding it. To a physician, the sick person represents a job. No matter how concerned and caring practitioners may be in their approach, each patient is one of many who must be cared for. To the patient, the illness is a very significant life event and may be accompanied by pain, discomfort, and anxiety. The physician–patient interaction actually involves a process of negotiation about how the medical problem will be perceived (Anderson & Helm, 1977). In fact, if concordance in perceptions is not achieved, difficulties in the interaction are likely to ensue, and the patient is likely to be unsatisfied and uncooperative (Jellinek, 1978; Taylor, Burdette, Camp, & Edwards, 1980).

344 M. ROBIN DIMATTEO

The Issue of Time

Time is a critically important issue in practioner-patient interaction. Physicians often claim they are limited by time in how well they can care for and educate each patient in their practice (Seligmann, McGrath, & Pratt, 1957). Patients cite the physician's apparent lack of time for them as one of the most important factors in their decision to change doctors (Gray & Cartwright, 1953). Patients who take up too much time (usually asking for information) are often labeled by hospital staff as "bad patients" (Lorber, 1975). Hospital patients often refrain from asking questions precisely because they expect the staff have no time to answer them (Skipper & Leonard, 1965). Thus, increased interaction time should seemingly improve practitioner-patient communication.

Research does not support this contention, however. Studies of the effects of time (measured objectively) on patient satisfaction and patient cooperation with treatment show that the length of the physician-patient interaction is *not* correlated with patient satisfaction (Freemon et al., 1971; Korsch et al., 1968). Although the length of the interaction does correlate with patient compliance with treatment, surprisingly, it was the shorter interactions that were associated with higher compliance (Freemon et al., 1971). The longer interactions were associated with *lower* compliance. Qualitative analyses of these longer interactions between pediatricians and mothers demonstrated that the physicians often wasted time, particularly by letting themselves be trapped into petty quarrels with the mother. Korsch et al. (1968) offered an example. A mother described what she called "vomiting" by her baby. The physician corrected her, referring to the baby's reaction as "regurgitation." Each countered the other's statement with insistence on the term they had chosen. The physician never acknowledged the mother's use of her own language to describe what she thought was wrong with her child. The physician continually repeated the information he wanted to convey but never sought to reassure her or demonstrate that he understood what she was trying to say. The mother felt the physician never understood that the child was vomiting, and as a result she ignored his prescription for treatment.

The National Ambulatory Medical Care Survey (Feller, 1979) indicated that the average time spent in face-to-face contact between office-based internists and their patients (in the late 1970s) was 18 minutes. The average time across all specialities was 15 minutes. If no time is wasted in unproductive miscommunication, practitioner-patient encounters can be satisfactory and effective in as little as 5 minutes (Korsch et al., 1968).

Nonspecific Factors in Effective Practitioner-Patient Communication

Difficulties in medical communication can be seen as the clear result of specific facets of interchange gone awry. The physician interrupts the patient, employs medical jargon, or neglects to write down instructions for the patient. Certainly, the elimination of these inappropriate and erroneous behaviors with substitution of more appropriate ones could probably do much to improve the quality of practitioner-patient communication and bring about many positive outcomes.

Unfortunately, things are not quite so easy. A simple endeavor such as writing down information for the patient may not, in fact, increase patient satisfaction, understanding, and compliance as expected. Patients might somehow perceive such an action as an attempt to put them off or to avoid giving a detailed explanation; or, the patient might be so emotionally distraught and anxious during the interaction (because of "something" about the practitioner) that nothing the practitioner says is understood and retained. It is not unreasonable to suggest, therefore, that there are some "emotional" components to practitioner-patient communication in addition to the purely "rational." Certainly, as we have seen, how well the practitioner and patient get along depends on how well they communicate. It may be frustrating, however, to realize that how well they communicate may depend on how well they "get along."

In the following sections, the emotional aspects of physician-patient communication are examined, and an attempt is made to "demystify" them. Interpersonal factors in the therapeutic relationship, such as trust and rapport, will be examined in light of recent research attempts to define and identify what it means for practitioner and patient to "get along."

Practitioner, Patient, and Illness

Although the relationships between patients and their medical practitioners are limited in time compared with most other relationships in the patients' lives, this relationship often takes on paramount personal importance. People usually remember much about the emotional and interpersonal tone of their encounters with health professionals (Francis et al., 1969; Korsch et al., 1968). In general, people tend to view their medical practitioners as very important figures (King, 1962). Physicians and other health practitioners are present at many emotionally momentous occasions in people's lives (for example, the births of their children and the deaths of their parents) and are typically approached under conditions of high anxiety and deep concern. Patients tend to be very sensitive to the interpersonal treatment they receive from their medical practitioners because of the emotional uncertainty they feel when faced with unfamiliar jargon and procedures, novel surroundings, and separation from the comfort and support of loved ones (Friedman, 1979b). Patients are often completely at the mercy of their practitioners, and very few physical or emotional boundaries separate practitioners from their patients. Health professionals are privy to all parts of the patient's body and to the most intimate details of the patient's life. When people are sick and highly anxious, they tend to "regress"—that is, to revert to a more childlike, dependent role characteristic of an earlier stage in their development (Lederer, 1952; Nemiah, 1961). Regression is a common phenomenon in the hospital, where it tends to be supported by a certain degree of infantilization imposed on the patient by the medical care process (Lorber, 1975; Taylor, 1979). Health professionals care for patients when the latter are most vulnerable emotionally as well as physically (Lederer, 1952). Because of this state of affairs, patients are highly sensitive both to their practitioners' demonstrations of protection and caring for them and to their practitioners' negative behaviors.

Emotions run deep in the medical encounter. The stakes are high and the issues weighty. Patients are highly sensitized to the subtleties of the situation and to the behavior of the practitioner. This sensitivity invariably affects their perceptions of the medical care rendered them. As Doyle and Ware (1977) have noted, the physician's conduct is the most important factor in patients' evaluations of their health services. Thus, the practitioner's interpersonal behavior toward the patient is an important part of the patient's care.

The Art of Medicine

During the fourth century, B.C., the Hippocratic writings put forth critical arguments in support of the art of medicine—the *manner* in which a practitioner provides care to a patient. In the *Corpus Hippocraticum,* the power of the art of medicine was described: "The patient, though conscious that his condition is perilous, may recover his health simply through his contentment with the goodness of the physician." The art of medicine has figured prominently throughout the history of medicine, and the practitioner's manner of caring for the patient has even been posited as the explanation for medicine's success as a healing profession (Frank, 1977; Shapiro, 1960). Prior to the 20th century, most medical remedies had absolutely no demonstrated therapeutic effects. Often, they were rather dangerous (such as the widely prescribed strichnine and arsenic tonics) (Houston, 1938; Shapiro, 1960). Until the advent of technological medicine, the art of medicine was by far the most critical aspect of patient care.

During the early part of the 20th century, effective medical treatments began to be developed. Antibiotics became available, and their therapeutic effects began to be understood. The developments of many scientific fields were applied to the care of patients, and medicine became a composite of many academic scientific disciplines. In 1910, the Flexner report to the Carnegie Commission argued for an end to the purely clinical teaching of the proprietary (privately owned, profit-motivated) medical schools of the day. Mere clinical instruction was deemed inadequate by Flexner. Instead, only university-based, basic science-oriented medical schools were allowed to grant medical degrees. New, stringent licensing laws led to the closure of the proprietary schools, giving rise to a model of medical education firmly grounded in the basic sciences such as anatomy, physiology, microbiology, pathology, pharmacology, and neurology. These sciences were taught as separate disciplines, and instruction in medicine centered around a definition of disease as negatively altered biology instead of as signs and symptoms present in a human being (Ebert, 1977). Particularly during the 1940s and 1950s, more and more discoveries in the basic sciences were applied to medical practice. The sheer volume of relevant scientific material forced a significant rift between the technological aspects of medicine and patient care. The new technology of medicine was seen as powerful and effective, while the art of medicine lost its prominent place and was typically viewed as superfluous and even a waste of time.

Of course, while medicine's scientific side was growing in importance, some physician-educators recognized the potential seriousness of the gap between the science of medicine and its actual practice. Shattuck (1907), for example, warned that the disease is one thing, but the diseased person is quite another. He proposed that the gap between the science of medicine and the care of the patient be bridged by the art of medicine. Shattuck warned that the scientific aspects of medicine should not replace compassion, sympathy, cheerfulness, and gentleness. The *care of the patient,* not basic science research, should remain the ultimate goal of medicine. Similarly, in 1904, another prominent medical educator and physician, Sir William Osler, told medical students, "The practice of medicine is an art, not a trade; a calling, not a business; a calling in which your heart will be exercised equally with your head" (Osler, 1904). Despite the emphasis on traditional scientific medicine, however, a few notable medical educators throughout the 20th century kept alive an interest in the art of medicine and stressed its importance. Among them were Henderson (1935), Engel (1977a, 1977b), and Eichna (1980).

The practitioner's interpersonal treatment of the patient (the art of medicine) and its antecedents and consequences have received some theoretical and empirical attention, particularly from the social science and public health perspectives. Recent reviews of this literature are available (c.f., DiMatteo & DiNicola, 1982b; DiMatteo & Friedman, 1982). The following is a short review of the most important issues related to interpersonal aspects of treatment.

The Interpersonal Aspects of Treatment: Empirical Findings

The Practitioner's Affective Communication

The interpersonal behavior of medical practitioners is typically scrutinized rather closely and with great care by their patients. Particularly when verbal communications toward the patient are limited and information is dispensed sparingly (as is often true in the medical care setting), patients attempt to gain information about their care and clues to the assessment of their own and their practitioners' performance by means of affective or emotional cues. For example, patients often focus on their practitioners' distressed expressions (which may be brought about by fatigue or confusion), as evidence for their practitioners' dislike of them, disapproval of their behavior, or grave concern about their threatening medical condition (Friedman, 1979b). As noted earlier, patients rarely try to clarify their perceptions by asking questions. Since they usually know relatively little about the purely technical aspects of the medical care they receive, they often judge the quality of their care on the basis of their own responses to the affective behavior of their practitioners (Ben-Sira, 1976, 1980; Freidson, 1970; Mechanic, 1968).

The importance of the practitioner's affective behavior has been noted by Ben-Sira (1976), who argued that the communication of positive affect from physician to patient is essential for developing a patient's confidence in the physician. This idea is not new. In the fourth century, B.C., the Hippocratic writings suggest the physician must ". . . bear in mind [his] manner of sitting, reserve, arrangement of dress, decisive utterance, brevity of speech, composure, bedside manners, care, replies to objections, calm self-control . . . his manner must be serious and humane; without stooping to be jocular or failing to be just, he must avoid excessive austerity; he must always be in control of himself."

Research has shown that nonverbal cues (such as facial expressions, body movements, and voice-tone expressions of emotion) are extremely important in communicating empathy, warmth, and caring. These cues may be even more important than verbal cues in many cases (Haase & Tepper, 1972). A number of aspects of nonverbal communication between health professionals and patients are relevant and have important implications for patient care.

Touch.

One extremely important component of nonverbal communication as it affects the establishment of rapport with patients is touch. Tactile stimulation can be extremely soothing to ill patients, as well as to human beings in general, and can communicate reassurance, comfort, value, and caring. Social scientists have found that touch may serve a tension-reducing function and that it is central to healthy social development (Montagu, 1978). Touch often enhances the therapeutic abilities of the health professional (Blondis & Jackson, 1977).

The effects of touch are likely to depend, of course, upon both the emotional context in which the touching takes place and the interpersonal meaning attached to it. A gentle touch on the patient's head may be seen by the patient to reflect the health practitioner's caring, understanding, and concern. This touch might just as easily signify the practitioner's control, however, because touch denotes power (Henley, 1977). Health professionals regularly touch patients, but patients rarely touch their health professionals. Thus, the practitioner's touch on the patient's head might be interpreted as condescending and as representing the health professional's power and complete access to the patient's body. Thus, the meaning of the nonverbal cue is best clarified with a verbal communication.

Gaze.

Gaze is another significant nonverbal cue that researchers have found to be extremely powerful (c.f., Ellsworth, 1975). People are usually aware of being stared at, and staring is likely to evoke a noticeable response. Eye contact, for example, intensifies the emotion (positive or negative) in a particular situation. A pleasant situation (such as a counselor or health professional communicating positive feedback and exhibiting warmth and understanding) may be experienced as even more positive in the presence of eye contact (LaCrosse, 1975). An arousing, upsetting, or threatening situation, on the other hand, may become even more negative when accompanied by eye contact (Ellsworth, Friedman, Perlick, & Hoyt, 1978). Thus, eye contact may be used judiciously by a sympathetic, encouraging, supportive health professional to enhance rapport and trust in the therapeutic relationship. Failure to maintain eye contact, on the other hand, might arouse feelings of suspicion in the patient or suggest the practitioner's interpersonal deviance or secretiveness.

Friedman (1979b) has pointed out that excessive staring at a patient will most likely have a negative interpersonal effect. Indeed, Larsen and Smith (1981), in a videotape study of first-time family practice clinic visits, found that greater use of "observation" (consisting of the physician looking directly at the face of the patient) was associated with lower patient satisfaction. Possibly (following Ellsworth et al., 1978), the anxiety felt by patients during their first visit with the physician was intensified by the physician's (possibly excessive) eye contact, producing an overall negative evaluation of the physician.

Facial expressions and voice tone.

Psychologists studying nonverbal communication have found that much detailed information about emotional states can be determined from facial expressions (Izard, 1977). Fatigue, confusion, or distress are usually easy to determine from individuals' facial expressions. Facial expressions are important in the communication of pain and related negative emotions, such as fear, sadness, distress, disgust, and anger. A health professional's feelings and reactions to a patient can be readily communicated through facial expressions (Friedman, 1979b, 1982).

Voice tone can likewise communicate emotion. Variations in pitch, loudness, emphasis, and the temporal spacing of words are independent of the verbal content of the message and can convey, usually quite clearly, emotions such as anger, sadness, and happiness. Health practitioners' anger can be perceived in their tone of voice as well and may have a significant effect on patients. For example, in a study by Milmoe, Rosenthal, Blane, Chafetz, and Wolf (1967), the amount of anger judged to be present in doctors' voices when they were talking about alcoholics was correlated significantly with the resistance demonstrated by their alcoholic patients to enrolling in a detoxification treatment program.

Research on the nonverbal expressiveness of medical practitioners has examined both facial expressions and voice tone cues in relation to practitioner–patient interaction. DiMatteo, Taranta, Friedman, and Prince (1980) reported two studies that measured directly the nonverbal expressiveness of medical house officers and examined the relationship of this communication ability to the satisfaction with care expressed by their patients. With audiotapes and films, 47 medical house officers were recorded as they attempted to express three different verbally neutral sentences in four different emotions or affects: happiness, sadness, anger, and surprise. The recordings were then displayed to college student judges who guessed which emotion was being communicated. The degree of accuracy of the college student judges at labeling the emotion served as a measure of the physician's ability to communicate messages of affect through facial expressions and voice tone. Patients' ratings of satisfaction with the interpersonal behavior of these physicians were also collected. Patient satisfaction was found to be positively and significantly correlated with the physicians' skills at sending (or purposely expressing) specific emotions.

Body postures and movements.

Finally, the enactment of certain bodily cues and gestures can cause a person to be perceived as either warm or cold, empathic or nonempathic.

Certain affiliative, nonverbal behaviors on the part of the practitioner, such as smiles, head nods, gestures with the hands, and a 20 degree forward lean, for example, have been found to increase perceptions by clients of their counselor's attractiveness and warmth (LaCrosse, 1975). Closed arm positions seem to indicate coldness, rejection, and inaccessibility, while moderately open arm positions tend to indicate warmth and acceptance (Smith-Hanen, 1977; Spiegel & Machotka, 1974). In the study of physician-patient interactions in a family practice center, higher patient satisfaction was associated with physicians' forward lean and bodily orientation toward the patient (Larsen & Smith, 1981). Backward lean and "neck relaxation" with chin elevated (possibly implying the communication of superiority) were correlated with patient dissatisfaction.

Nonverbal cues in context.

Nonverbal cues are, of course, only meaningful and interpretable within a situational context. This context may be the particular environment of the individual interaction and/or the verbal context of the communication. Nonverbal behaviors can be observed against the backdrop of the environmental context, or they can interact with the environment—particularly with verbal communication.

When used alone, nonverbal cues can serve a regulating function. For example, by nodding or by breaking eye contact individuals may signal that they are yielding to another person the turn to speak (Duncan, 1972). Nonverbal communication is also used to inform others whether or not their messages are being received. Feedback such as eye contact, facial expressions, and head movement indicates the listener is attending the speaker. Nodding may indicate understanding. Nonverbal communication might also function as a substitute for verbal behavior. The nonverbal message might actually replace the verbal one.

Nonverbal cues also interact with verbal ones. First, a nonverbal message may serve to accent or underline a verbal statement already made. For example, a health professional might nod his head while saying, "You really are doing well taking your medication. Your blood pressure is nearly under control." Nonverbal messages may complement verbal messages and add to them. For example, the physician might touch the patient's hand and say, "I understand how you must feel." Nonverbal communication enhances the verbal and vice versa. Voice tone, for example, may be used to emphasize particular points made to patients about their treatment regimen. Finally, nonverbal cues can contradict verbal cues (or at least *appear* to some persons to contradict them). If inconsistent verbal and nonverbal messages are conveyed to the patient, the likely result will be doubt concerning what is conveyed or diminished trust in the practitioner (Friedman, 1979a, 1982). It is, therefore, critically important to understand the role of verbal-nonverbal cue combinations.

The Practitioner's Sensitivity to Affective Cues

In the course of medical treatment, patients experience a wide range of emotions—from security and relief to profound fear and rage. As a result, a critical factor in the practitioner-patient relationship is likely to be the practitioner's sensitivity to patients' emotions. The value of this sensitivity will be dependent, of course, upon the practitioner's willingness to accept and deal effectively with the emotions patients communicate.

Words carry tremendous weight in the health care arena, for they usually symbolize issues of central concern to patient and practitioner. Issues of life and death, health and illness, can be very complex. The words used by patients in health care interactions normally reflect their understanding of these issues and the meaning each issue holds for them. Therefore, it can be very important for health practitioners to facilitate patients' expressions of their feelings through verbal communication. Linn and Wilson (1980) developed an instrument to measure a physician's ability to facilitate and clarify patients' communications and be responsive to patients' thoughts and feelings. This instrument, The Facilitating Response Inventory (FRI), was administered to 71 residents in internal medicine and proved very reliable. Among internal medicine residents whose specialty was primary care, the FRI was found to predict positively patients' appointment-keeping rates with the physicians in the general medical clinic. In this research, then, patients were more highly committed to physicians willing and able to facilitate patients' verbal communications. Interestingly, the FRI also correlated positively with ratings of the residents' clinical competence (ratings made by their attending physicians in the residency program). Although no causal inference can yet be made, physicians' open-ended, nonauthoritarian responsiveness may have played an important role in their technical care of patients as well.

The art of medicine and practitioner-patient rapport demand the practitioner's ability to receive, interpret, and accept patients' *nonverbal* communications. These nonverbal communications appear in all forms. They involve facial expressions, body movements, body postures, voice tone (e.g., frequency and pacing of speech), extralinguistic cues (e.g., groans, grunts), touch, and the distance between persons in the interaction. For many reasons, the practitioner's ability to "decode" these messages from patients may be critically important to the practitioner-patient relationship.

In the health care setting, patients typically experience a number of emotions that may be more easily recognized by attending to their nonverbal cues than to what they say. Since patients have little experience hiding or controlling emotions (such as fear and pain) in the medical setting, these emotions are often readily apparent in nonverbal behaviors. A health professional sensitive to patients' nonverbal communications will be provided with important insight into the patient's feelings and will be afforded a valuable opportunity to understand the patient. It is also important to note that many patients are hesitant to express their feelings regarding certain matters (for example, embarrassing disabilities, their discomfort in the medical setting, or dissatisfaction with treatment). By attending to the patient's facial expressions, body postures and movements, voice tone, and other nonverbal cues, the health professional may be alerted to the possibility that something is wrong or that a particular issue should be further explored.

Nonverbal sensitivity has been linked significantly to patient satisfaction with care from the physician. DiMatteo, Friedman, and Taranta (1979), for example, reported two studies involving 64 medical house officers and hundreds of patients at an urban community teaching hospital. The nonverbal sensitivity of the physicians was measured with the PONS test (Rosenthal, Hall, DiMatteo, Rogers, & Archer, 1979).

An average of six of each house officer's patients was interviewed about their satisfaction with the physician's interpersonal treatment of them. In both studies, ratings of the physicians by their patients were significantly correlated with the physicians' PONS-measured accuracy at decoding emotion expressed through body posture and movement. This finding is not surprising since, as noted earlier, studies by Ekman and Friesen (1969, 1974) implicated the body channel as the one from which unintended cues to emotion are most likely to leak. These studies, therefore, provide some important evidence that practitioners' abilities to decode nonverbal cues may be an important factor in their abilities to provide the understanding required for effective patient care.

By understanding the patient's nonverbal cues alone or as they accompany verbal cues, practitioners may enhance their abilities to identify important signs of confusion and discontent in patients (Friedman, 1979b). As an example, consider the physician's characteristic patient inquiry: "Do you have any questions?" Usually, the physician leaves the patient's presence promptly after hearing the patient's unconvincing "I don't think so." Yet, many times patients provide clues to their confusion or distress with their nonverbal behaviors, especially with their body movements and postures. They may sit down tensely, cast their gaze downward shyly, and/or writhe their hands nervously. Practitioners sensitive to these cues are likely to wait and to probe the issue a bit further. The manner in which this brief, exiting question is dealt with by the practitioner—whether patients' distress and confusion are recognized or ignored—may mean the difference between patients' understanding and implementing the medical regimen and their misunderstanding of or resistance to it.

Reassurance and Positive Expectations

Pictures, sketches, and descriptions often appear of the old-time family physician attending patients in their homes. He is portrayed as supportive and fatherly, worthy of enormous trust. He reassures patients and their families. He quells their anxiety.

Recently, researchers have begun to document empirically the profound effect of psychological factors on physical states (Pelletier, 1977, 1979). Anxiety, fear, and distress can jeopardize health and well-being and can significantly influence patients' responses to illness and pain. Psychological factors can mediate the outcomes of medical treatment such as surgery (Janis, 1958; Langer et al., 1975). In recent years, too, there has been an important recognition that social factors in the practitioner-patient relationship and aspects of the therapeutic interaction can affect patients' psychological, and hence their physical, states (DiMatteo & Friedman, 1982; Friedman & DiMatteo, 1979). Consider, for example, the study by Jarvinen (1955) in which he found a significant increase in the sudden deaths of coronary patients during or shortly after ward rounds conducted by the medical staff. Ward rounds are typically rather formal procedures during which physicians "display" their patients, describing and discussing them in medical terms and generally ignoring them as people. Patients often report feeling anxious, depersonalized, and even dehumanized. This study demonstrated that such distressing interpersonal treatment may actually jeopardize the patient's health. Jarvinen found that ward rounds increased patients' fear and anxiety to dangerously high levels, thus significantly increasing the risk (and the incidence, as documented by the researchers) of another heart attack. This phenomenon was examined further by Lynch, Thomas, Mills, Malinow, and Katcher (1974), who found that human contact in frightening, upsetting, or negative emotional situations has major effects on the cardiac rhythms and electrical impulses of the hearts of cardiac patients. This research suggests that upsetting circumstances in the physician-patient relationship may have a potentially detrimental effect on the patient. The research emphasizes the importance of reassurance and "bedside manner" in the care of patients, for the sake of their physical condition.

Reassurance "consists of a general optimistic and hopeful attitude and specific statements based on data and/or experience designed to allay exaggerated or unfounded fears of the patient. For reassurance to be effective, the physician should know the sources of the patient's fears. They often are based on an incorrect understanding of the disease or proposed procedure" (Leigh & Reiser, 1980, p. 295).

Perhaps the best known medical phenomenon reflecting the association between physiological and psychological variables is the "placebo effect." Beecher (1955) has defined the placebo as an inert substance that may have both physiological and psychological effects on the patient. Of course, these effects can be positive or negative. That is, the practitioner's expectation for both the good and bad sequelae (e.g., side effects) of a treatment can be effectively transmitted to patients and can influence their reactions.[1] The placebo effect results partly from the character of the practitioner–patient relationship. The practitioner, imparting confidence and being supportive and reassuring, is likely to bring about the positive therapeutic effect of the substance administered, and may even have the interpersonal power to reduce or eliminate completely problems such as patients' negative side effects.

As the technological aspects of modern medical care have blossomed, physicians, nurses, and other health professionals have relied less and less upon interpersonal behavior as a therapeutic medium. Health professionals even today underestimate their own potential impact on their patient's condition. Goodwin, Goodwin, and Vogel (1979), for example, found that practitioners use the placebo effect inappropriately. They reported they usually gave placebo medications to patients they disliked, or to those whose pain was believed to be of psychogenic origin. When the placebo effect did occur, it was misunderstood by the practitioners. Instead of viewing the placebo as a positive adjunct to therapy and as an indication of a potentially successful form of treatment, the practitioners noted the placebo effect as evidence that their patients' pain had no physiological basis. Unfortunately, practitioners often fail to recognize that the administration of "something" may help reduce their patient's anxiety and, in doing so, reduces pain and discomfort. This success is as legitimate an aspect of "healing" as any drug or surgery.

The incorporation of the positive therapeutic effect of the practitioner's reassurance and interpersonal behavior along with the techniques of modern medicine is likely to enhance greatly the efficacy of treatment and patients' cooperation with it. Technical medical care might even be ineffective unless reassurance and trust in the therapeutic relationship are strong (Cousins, 1979; DiMatteo & Friedman, 1982).

Conclusion: Merging the Art and the Science of Medicine

Throughout this chapter, the emphasis has been on performing detailed examinations of numerous aspects of both verbal and nonverbal communication as they relate to important outcomes in medical treatment. It

---

[1] On the average, a therapeutic outcome is 35% more positive (or negative) in a placebo control group than in a no-treatment control group, as reported in reviews by Beecher (1959) and Shapiro (1960).

has been argued that a significant degree of attention must be paid to issues of communication if the technical advances of modern medicine are to be translated into better patient care. As Saloman Neumann (cited in Rosen, 1972) noted in 1874: "Medical science is intrinsically and essentially a *social* science, and as long as this is not recognized in practice we shall not be able to enjoy its benefits and shall have to be satisfied with an empty shell and a sham."

Traditional medicine has been dominated by a dualism that separates body and mind (Engel, 1977b; Friedman & DiMatteo, 1979). Diseases of the body have been thought to reside in the purely physical realm, treated exclusively with the scientific principles pertaining to physical matter. Problems of the mind, including psychopathologies, addictive behaviors, and noncompliance with medical treatments have been thought, instead, to reflect distorted or uncooperative personalities. That physical and psychological factors might influence one another, or that both might be influenced by yet another realm—social factors—is an idea that has typically met with resistance.

A related dichotomy is that between the science and the art of medicine. Art is typically viewed as dependent upon the personal qualities of the caregiver rather than upon principles that can be taught and examined. Such a viewpoint relegates the art of medicine to an attitude (such as "samaritanism" [McDermott, 1977]) or even to a semimystical realm, while pointing to the disciplines of biology, chemistry, pathology, and so on as science. The science and the art of medicine are often presented as phenomena of entirely different character.

Empirical research on these two aspects of medicine presents quite a different picture, however. Early research (reviewed by Ware, Davies-Avery, & Stewart, 1978) on patient satisfaction found consistently high correlations between patients' evaluations of physicians on technical factors and their evaluations of the interpersonal aspects of the care physicians delivered. Although the argument is sometimes made that patients were unable to judge the technical quality of their care and so judged both dimensions equally, such an interpretation has been refuted. DiMatteo and DiNicola (1981) replicated these high correlations among patients' ratings and found similar ones among ratings made by supervising and peer physicians certainly capable of distinguishing between the two aspects of care. Since supervising and peer physicians can distinguish between the art and the science of medicine, *if* such a distinction actually exists, these high correlations likely reflect the strong association between these two dimensions of medical care. Interestingly, research has shown that patients *can*, in fact, make the distinction between these dimensions *if* the medical care encounters they evaluate actually portray such a distinction. The fact that, in their evaluations of medical care, physicians and patients make little distinction between technical and interpersonal skills suggests the existence of a substantial correlation between the two abilities in the actual practice of medicine (Barnlund, 1976; Barro, 1973; Ware, Kane, Davies, & Brook, 1980).

Many skills are required for successfully formulating an accurate diagnosis and effective treatment regimen when caring for a patient. Not the least of these skills involves the interpersonal factors of respect, genuineness, and empathy that establish the trustworthiness and expertness of practitioners and enhance their capacities to influence patient compliance with the treatment regimen. Thus, practitioner competency is likely to involve scientific technical knowledge translated into practice through interpersonal skills and the art of medicine (DiMatteo & DiNicola, 1982b).

Patients' thoughts and feelings are inextricably intertwined with their physical conditions. It is estimated that about 35% of visits to primary care physicians in this country are primarily for psychosocial care. At least that many more are for illnesses to which psychosocial factors are relevant (Baker & Cassata, 1978). Thus, clinical medicine depends upon the ability of the practitioner to understand and help thinking, feeling human beings.

A pair of kidneys will never come to the physician for diagnosis and treatment. They will be contained within an anxious, fearful, wondering person, asking puzzled questions about an obscure future, weighed down by the responsibilities of a loved family, a job to be held, and bills to be paid. . . . The clinician must learn the facts about it all, comprehend it all, and develop a plan of management for all of it. Otherwise, his approach is superficial. (Tumulty, 1970, p. 21)

How do practitioners develop the interpersonal aspects of patient care? The answer is suggested in Tumulty's quotation above and in the following one by communication specialist Barnlund (1976):

Commitment to humane values is rarely enough, any more than the simple desire to relieve suffering automatically confers diagnostic or surgical talent. Skill must be acquired to translate respect for patients as persons and the capacity to engage them communicatively as equals. Communication skills must be cultivated that respect patients' intelligence, acknowledge their needs, accept their feelings, value their opinions and promote collaboration in decision-making. (p. 723)

The interpersonal aspects of patient care comprise a set of communication skills that can be developed. Studies of the relationship between practitioner personality and components of the art of medicine have characteristically produced very weak and equivocal results. Likewise, in the same studies, attempts to link intellectual variables (such as scores on the Medical College Admissions Test, as well as premedical and medical grades) to the art of medicine have produced near zero correlations, or findings that are inconsistent across studies (Flom, 1971; Gough, Hall, & Harris, 1963, 1964; Richards, Taylor & Price, 1962). On the other hand, the research reviewed in this chapter suggests strongly that the broadly defined "art of medicine" consists of a set of definable skills, all of which can be learned by practitioners and incorporated into their care of patients.

Attention to a scientific approach to feelings has special pertinence for clinical medicine, the practice of which so much depends on the ability of the physician to understand and to help thinking, feeling human beings. . . . the ultimate goal of a scientific approach to patient care is to render rational and accessible to conscious awareness and reporting the basis for the decisions and the means of their implementation. . . . They must be predicated on reliable data correctly interpreted and on principles amenable to scientific study and validation. Such standards must apply as much to minute-to-minute microdecisions as to more major decisions, whether to linger a moment longer at the bedside as well as when and how to propose open heart surgery. (Engel, 1977a, pp. 222, 223)

References

Anderson, W. T., & Helm, D. T. *The physician-patient encounter: A process of reality negotiation.* Paper presented at the meeting of the American Sociological Association, September 1977.

Baekeland, F., & Lundwall, L. Dropping out of treatment: A critical review. *Psychological Bulletin,* 1975, *82*(5), 738–783.

Bain, D. J. G. Doctor-patient communication in general practice consultations. *Medical Education,* 1976, *10*, 125–131.

Baker, R. M., & Cassata, D. M. The physician-patient relationship. In R. B. Taylor (Ed.), *Family medicine: Principles and practice.* New York: Springer-Verlag, 1978, pp. 143–148.

Barnlund, D. C. The mystification of meaning: Doctor-patient encounters. *Journal of Medical Education,* 1976, *51*, 716–725.

Barro, A. R. Survey and evaluation of approaches to physician performance measurement. *Journal of Medical Education,* 1973, *48*, 1051–1093.

Becker, M. H., & Maiman, L. A. Strategies for enhancing patient compliance. *Journal of Community Health,* 1980, *6* (2), 113–135.

Beecher, H. K. The powerful placebo. *Journal of the American Medical Association,* 1955, *159*, 1602–1606.

Beecher, H. K. *Measurement of subjective responses.* New York: Oxford University Press, 1959.

Ben-Sira, Z. The function of the professional's affective behavior in client satisfaction: A revised approach to social interaction theory. *Journal of Health and Social Behavior,* 1976, *17*, 3–11.

Ben-Sira, Z. Affective and instrumental components in the physician-patient relationship: An additional dimension of interaction theory. *Journal of Health and Social Behavior,* 1980, *21*, 170–180.

Bertakis, K. D. A method for increasing patient retention and satisfaction. *The Journal of Family Practice,* 1977, *5*(2), 217–222.

Blondis, M. N., & Jackson, B. E. *Nonverbal communication with patients*. New York: John Wiley & Sons, 1977.

Brant, C. S., & Kutner, B. Physician-patient relations in a teaching hospital. *Journal of Medical Education*, 1957, *32*(10), 703–707.

Cartwright, A. *Human relations and hospital care*. London: Routledge, Kegan Paul, 1964.

Coe, R. M. *Sociology of medicine* (1st ed.). New York: McGraw-Hill, 1970.

Cousins, N. *Anatomy of an illness as perceived by the patient*. New York: W. W. Norton, 1979.

Daniels, M. J. Affect and its control in the medical intern. *American Journal of Sociology*, 1960, *66*, 259–267.

Davis, M. S. Variations in patients' compliance with doctors' advice. An empirical analysis of patterns of communication. *American Journal of Public Health*, 1968, *58*(2), 274–288.

Davis, M. S. Variations in patient's compliance with doctors' orders: Medical practice and doctor-patient interaction. *Psychiatry in Medicine*, 1971, *2*, 31–54.

DiMatteo, M. R., & DiNicola, D. D. Sources of assessment of physician performance: A study of comparative reliability and patterns of intercorrelation. *Medical Care*, 1981, *19*, 829–842.

DiMatteo, M. R., & DiNicola, D. D. *Achieving patient compliance: The psychology of the medical practitioner's role*. Elmsford, New York: Pergamon Press, 1982. (a)

DiMatteo, M. R., & DiNicola, D. D. Social science and the art of medicine: From Hippocrates to holism. In H. S. Friedman & M. R. DiMatteo (Eds.), *Interpersonal issues in health care*. New York: Academic Press, 1982. (b)

DiMatteo, M. R., & Friedman, H. S. *Social psychology and medicine*. Cambridge, Mass. Oelgeschlager, Gunn, & Hain, 1982.

DiMatteo, M. R., Friedman, H. S., & Taranta, A. Sensitivity to bodily nonverbal communication as a factor in practitioner-patient rapport. *Journal of Nonverbal Behavior*, 1979, *4*, 18–26.

DiMatteo, M. R., Taranta, A., Friedman, H. S., & Prince, L. M. Predicting patient satisfaction from physicians' nonverbal communication skills. *Medical Care*, 1980, *18*, 376–387.

Doyle, B. J., & Ware, J. E. Physician conduct and other factors that affect consumer satisfaction with medical care. *Journal of Medical Education*, 1977, *52*, 793–801.

Duff, R. S., & Hollingshead, A. B. *Sickness and society*. New York: Harper & Row, 1968.

Duncan, S. Some signals and rules for taking speaking turns in conversations. *Journal of Personality and Social Psychology*, 1972, *23*(2), 283–292.

Ebert, R. H. Medical education in the United States. *Daedalus*, 1977, *106*(1), 171–184.

Egbert, L. D., Battit, G. E., Turndorf, H., & Beecher, H. K. Value of preoperative visit by anesthetist: Study of doctor-patient rapport. *Journal of the American Medical Association*, 1963, *185*, 553–555.

Egbert, L. D., Battit, G. E., Welch, C. E., & Bartlett, M. K. Reduction of postoperative pain by encouragement and instruction of patients: A study of doctor-patient rapport. *New England Journal of Medicine*, 1964, *270*, 825–827.

Eichna, L. W. Medical education, 1975–1979: A student's perspective. *New England Journal of Medicine*, 1980, *303*, 727–734.

Ekman, P., & Friesen, W. V. Nonverbal leakage and clues to deception. *Psychiatry*, 1969, *32*, 88–106.

Ekman, P., & Friesen, W. V. Detecting deception from the body or face. *Journal of Personality and Social Psychology*, 1974, *29*, 288–298.

Ellsworth, P. Direct gaze as a social stimulus: The example of aggression. In P. Pliner, L. Krames, & T. Alloway (Eds.), *Nonverbal communication of aggression*. New York: Plenum Publishing, 1975.

Ellsworth, P., Friedman, H., Perlick, D., & Hoyt, M. Some effects of gaze on subjects motivated to seek or to avoid social comparison. *Journal of Experimental Social Psychology*, 1978, *14*, 69–87.

Elstein, A. S. Clinical judgment: Psychological research and medical practice. *Science*, 1976, *194*, 696–700.

Engel, G. L. The care of the patient: Art or science? *The Johns Hopkins Medical Journal*, 1977, *140*, 222–232. (a)

Engel, G. L. The need for a new medical model: A challenge for biomedicine. *Science*, 1977, *196*, 129–136. (b)

Engel, G. L., & Morgan, W. L. *Interviewing the patient*. Philadelphia, Pa.: Saunders, 1973.

Feller, B. A. *Characteristics of general internists and the content of care of their patients* (USDHEW, HRA-79-652). Washington, D.C.: U.S. Government Printing Office, 1979.

Flexner, A. *Medical education in the United States and Canada. Bulletin #4.* New York: Carnegie Foundation for the Advancement of Teaching, 1910.

Flom, P. Performance in the medical internship (Doctoral dissertation, University of California at Berkeley, 1970). *Dissertation Abstracts International*, 1971, *32*(2-B), 1188.

Francis, V., Korsch, B., & Morris, M. Gaps in doctor-patient communication: Patients' response to medical advice. *New England Journal of Medicine*, 1969, *280*(10), 535–540.

Frank, J. D. Mind-body relationships in illness and healing. *Journal of the International Academy of Preventive Medicine*, 1977, *2*, 3.

Freemon, B., Negrete, V. F., Davis, M., & Korsch, B. M. Gaps in doctor-patient communication: Doctor-patient interaction analysis. *Pediatric Research*, 1971, *5*, 298–311.

Freidson, E. *Patients views of medical practice*. New York: Russell Sage Foundation, 1961, pp. 171–191.

Freidson, E. *Profession of medicine*. New York: Dodd, Mead & Co., 1970.

Friedman, H. S. The interactive effects of facial expressions of emotion and verbal messages on perceptions of affective meaning. *Journal of Experimental Social Psychology*, 1979, *15*, 453–469. (a)

Friedman, H. S. Nonverbal communication between patients and medical practitioners. *Journal of Social Issues*, 1979, *35*, 82–99. (b)

Friedman, H. S. Nonverbal communication in medical interaction. In H. S. Friedman & M. R. DiMatteo (Eds.), *Interpersonal issues in health care*. New York: Academic Press, 1982.

Friedman, H. S., & DiMatteo, M. R. Health Care as an interpersonal process. *Journal of Social Issues*, 1979, *35*(11), 1–11.

Fuller, S. S., Endress, M. P., & Johnson, J. E. The effects of cognitive and behavioral control on coping with an aversive health examination. *Journal of Human Stress*, 1978, *4*(4), 18–25.

Golden, J. S., & Johnston, G. D. Problems of distortion in doctor-patient communications. *Psychiatry in Medicine*, 1970, *1*, 127–149.

Goodwin, J. S., Goodwin, J. M., & Vogel, A. V. Knowledge and use of placebos by house officers and nurses. *Annals of Internal Medicine*, 1979, *91*, 106–110.

Gough, H., Hall, W., & Harris, R. Admissions procedures as forecasters of performance in medical training. *Journal of Medical Education*, 1963, *38*, 983–998.

Gough, H., Hall, W., & Harris, R. Evaluation of performance in medical training. *Journal of Medical Education*, 1964, *39*, 679–692.

Gray, P. G., & Cartwright, A. Choosing and changing doctors. *Lancet*, December 19, 1953, 1308–1309.

Haase, R. F., & Tepper, D. T. Nonverbal components of empathic communication. *Journal of Counseling Psychology*, 1972, *19*, 417–424.

Haley, J. *Strategies of psychotherapy.* New York: Grune & Stratton, 1963.

Haley, J. *Uncommon therapy: The psychiatric techniques of Milton H. Erickson, M.D.* New York: W. W. Norton, 1973.

Hayes-Bautista, D. E. Modifying the treatment: Patient compliance, patient control, and medical care. *Social Science and Medicine*, 1976, *10*, 233–238. (a)

Hayes-Bautista, D. E. Termination of the patient-practitioner relationship: Divorce, patient style. *Journal of Health and Social Behavior*, 1976, *17*, 12–21. (b)

Henderson, L. Physician and patient as a social system. *New England Journal of Medicine*, 1935, *212*, 819–823.

Henley, N. M. *Body politics.* Englewood Cliffs, N.J.: Prentice-Hall, Inc., 1977.

Houston, B. K., & Holmes, D. S. Effect on avoidant thinking and reappraisal for coping with threat of involving temporal uncertainty. *Journal of Personality and Social Psychology*, 1973, *27*, 261–275.

Houston, C. S., & Pasanen, W. E. Patients' perceptions of hospital care. *Hospitals*, 1972, *46*, 70–74.

Houston, W. The doctor himself as therapeutic agent. *Annals of Internal Medicine*, 1938, *11*, 1416–1425.

Hulka, B. S., Cassel, J. C., Kupper, L. L., & Burdette, J. A. Communication, compliance, and concordance between physicians and patients with prescribed medications. *American Journal of Public Health*, 1976, *66*(9), 847–853.

Izard, C. E. *Human emotions.* New York: Plenum Press, 1977.

Janis, I. L. *Psychological stress: Psychoanalytic and behavioral studies of surgical patients.* New York: Wiley, 1958.

Jarvinen, K. A. J. Can ward round be a danger to patients with myocardial infarction? *British Medical Journal*, 1955, *1*, 318–320.

Jellinek, M. Referrals from a psychiatric emergency room: Relationship of compliance to demographic and interview variables. *American Journal of Psychiatry*, 1978, *135*(2), 209–213.

Johnson, J. E., & Leventhal, H. Effects of accurate expectations and behavioral instructions on reactions during a noxious medical examination. *Journal of Personality and Social Psychology*, 1974, *29*(5), 710–718.

Kane, R. L., & Deuschle, K. W. Problems in patient-doctor communications. *Medical Care*, 967, *5*(4), 260–271.

Kaplan, R. M. Coping with stressful medical exams. In H. S. Friedman & M. R. DiMatteo (Eds.), *Interpersonal issues in health care.* New York: Academic Press, 1982.

Katz, J. L., Weiner, H., Gallagher, T. F., & Hellman, L. Stress, distress, and ego defenses. Psychoendocrine response to impending breast tumor biopsy. *Archives of General Psychiatry*, 1970, *23*, 131–142.

King, S. H. *Perceptions of illness and medical practice.* New York: Russell-Sage, 1962.

Korsch, B. M., Gozzi, E. K., & Francis, V. Gaps in doctor-patient communication. I. Doctor-patient interaction and patient satisfaction. *Pediatrics,* 1968, *42,* 855–871.

LaCrosse, M. B. Nonverbal behavior and perceived counselor attractiveness and persuasiveness. *Journal of Counseling Psychology,* 1975, *22,* 563–566.

Langer, E. J., Janis, I. L., & Wolfer, J. A. Reduction of psychological stress in surgical patients. *Journal of Experimental Social Psychology,* 1975, *11,* 155–165.

Larsen, K. M., & Smith, C. K. Assessment of nonverbal communication in the patient-physician interview. *Journal of Family Practice,* 1981, *12*(3), 481–488.

Larson, R., & Sutker, S. Value differences and value consensus by socioeconomic levels. *Social Forces,* 1966, *44,* 563–569.

Lederer, H. D. How the sick view their world. *Journal of Social Issues,* 1952, *8,* 4–16.

Leigh, H., & Reiser, M. F. *The patient: Biological, psychological, and social dimensions of medical practice.* New York: Plenum, 1980.

Ley, P., & Spelman, M. S. Communication in an outpatient setting. *British Journal of Social and Clinical Psychology,* 1965, *4,* 114–116.

Lief, H. I., & Fox, R. C. Training for "detached concern" in medical students. In H. I. Lief, V. F. Lief, & N. L. Lief (Eds.), *The psychological basis of medical practice.* New York: Harper & Row, Hoeber Medical Books, 1963, 12–35.

Linn, L. S., & Wilson, R. M. Factors related to a communication style among medical house staff. *Medical Care,* 1980, *18,* 1013–1019.

Liptak, G. S., Hulka, B. S., & Cassel, J. C. Effectiveness of physician-mother interactions during infancy. *Pediatrics,* 1977, *60*(2), 186–192.

Lorber, J. Good patients and problem patients: Conformity and deviance in a general hospital. *Journal of Health and Social Behavior,* 1975, *16,* 213–225.

Lynch, J. J., Thomas, S. A., Mills, M. E., Malinow, K., & Katcher, A. H. The effects of human contact on cardiac arrhythmia in coronary care patients. *The Journal of Nervous and Mental Disease,* 1974, *158,* 88–99.

Martin, M. Healthy respect for the word. *Journal of the American Medical Association,* 1978, *239*(26), 2776–2777.

Mazullo, J. M., Lasagna, L., & Griner, P. F. Variations in interpretation of prescription instructions. *Journal of the American Medical Association,* 1974, *227*(8), 929–930.

McDermott, W. Evaluating the physician and his technology. *Daedalus,* 1977, *106*(1), 135–158.

McIntosh, J. Processes of communication, information seeking, and control associated with cancer: A selective review of the literature. *Social Science and Medicine,* 1974, *8,* 167–187.

Mechanic, D. *Medical sociology: A selective view.* New York: The Free Press, 1968.

Melzack, R. Psychological concept and methods for the control of pain. In J. Bonica (Ed.), *Advances in neurology, 4.* New York: Raven Press, 1974.

Mills, R. T., & Krantz, D. S. Information, choice, and reactions to stress: A field experiment in a blood bank with laboratory analogue. *Journal of Personality and Social Psychology,* 1979, *34*(4), 608–620.

Milmoe, S., Rosenthal, R., Blane, H. T., Chafetz, M. L., & Wolf, I. The doctor's voice: Postdictor of successful referral of alcoholic patients. *Journal of Abnormal Psychology,* 1967, *72,* 78–84.

Montagu, A. *Touching.* New York: Harper & Row, 1978.

Mumford, E. The responses of patients to medical advice. In R. C. Simons & H. Pardes (Eds.), *Understanding human behavior in health and illness.* Baltimore, Md.: Williams & Wilkins Co., 1977.

Nemiah, J. C. *Foundations of psychopathology.* New York: Oxford University Press, 1961.

Osler, Sir W. The master-word in medicine. In *Aequanimitas with other addresses to medical students, nurses, and practitioners of medicine.* Philadelphia, Pa.: Blakiston Co., 1904, pp. 369–371.

Parsons, T. *The social system.* Glencoe, Ill.: The Free Press, 1951, 428–479.

Parsons, T. Definitions of health and illness in the light of American values and social structure. In E. G. Jaco (Ed.), *Patients, physicians, and illness.* New York: The Free Press, 1958, 165–187.

Parsons, T. The sick role and the role of the physician reconsidered. *Milbank Memorial Fund Quarterly/Health and Society,* 1975, *53,* 257–278.

Pelletier, K. R. *Mind as healer, mind as slayer.* New York: Dell, 1977.

Pelletier, K. R. *Holistic medicine.* New York: Delacorte Press, 1979.

Pratt, L., Seligmann, A., & Reader, G. Physicians' views on the level of medical information among patients. *American Journal of Public Health,* 1957, *47,* 1277–1283.

Reading, A. E. The short term effects of psychological preparation for surgery. *Social Science and Medicine,* 1979, *13A,* 641–654.

Richards, J., Taylor, C., & Price, P. The prediction of medical intern performance. *Journal of Applied Psychology,* 1962, *46,* 142–146.

Rosen, G. The evolution of social medicine. In H. E. Freeman, S. Levine, & L. G. Reeder (Eds.), *Handbook of medical sociology,* (2nd ed.). Englewood Cliffs, N.J.: Prentice-Hall, 1972, pp. 30–60.

Rosenthal, R., Hall, J. A., DiMatteo, M. R., Rogers, P. L., & Archer, D. *Sensitivity to nonverbal communication: The PONS Test.* Baltimore, Md.: Johns Hopkins University Press, 1979.

Roter, D. L. Patient participation in the patient-provider interaction: The effects of patient question asking on the quality of interaction satisfaction and compliance. *Health Education Monographs,* Winter 1977, 281–315.

Roth, J. A. *Timetables.* Indianapolis: Bobbs-Merrill Co., 1963.

Samora, L., Saunders, L., & Larson, R. F. Medical vocabulary knowledge among hospital patients. *Journal of Health and Human Behavior,* 1961, *2,* 83–89.

Schmitt, F. E., & Wooldridge, P. J. Psychological preparation of surgical patients. *Nursing Research,* 1973, *22,* 108–111.

Schulman, B. A. Active patient orientation and outcomes in hypertensive treatment: Application of a socio-organizational perspective. *Medical Care,* 1979, *17*(3), 267–280.

Seeman, M., & Evans, J. Alienation and learning in a hospital setting. *American Sociological Review,* 1962, *27,*–782.

Segall, A., & Roberts, L. W. A comparative analysis of physician estimates and levels of a medical knowledge among patients. *Sociology of Health and Illness,* 1980, *2*(3), 317–334.

Seligmann, A. W., McGrath, N. E., & Pratt, L. Level of medical information among clinic patients. *Journal of Chronic Diseases,* 1957, *6,* 497.

Shapiro, A. K. A contribution to a history of the placebo effect. *Behavioral Science,* 1960, *5,* 109–135.

Shapiro, M. *Getting doctored: Critical reflections on becoming a physician.* Ontario, Canada: Between the Lines, 1978.

Shattuck, F. The science and art of medicine in some of their aspects. *Boston Medical and Surgical Journal,* 1907, *157,* 63–67.

Shipley, R. H., Butt, J. H., Horwitz, B., & Farby, J. E. Preparation for a stressful medical procedure: Effect of amount of stimulus pre-exposure and coping style. *Journal of Consulting and Clinical Psychology*, 1978, *46*(3), 499–507.

Skipper, J., & Leonard, R. (Eds.). *Social interaction and patient care*. Philadelphia and Toronto: J. B. Lippincott, 1965.

Skipper, J. K., & Leonard, R. D. Children, stress, and hospitalization: A field experiment. *Journal of Health and Social Behavior*, 1968, *9*, 275–287.

Skipper, J. K., Tagliacozzo, D., & Mauksch, H. Some possible consequences of limited communication between patients and hospital functionaries. *Journal of Health and Human Behavior*, 1964, *5*, 34–39.

Smith, C. K., Polis, E., & Hadac, R. R. Characteristics of the initial medical review associated with patient satisfaction and understanding. *The Journal of Family Practice*, 1981, *12*(2), 283–288.

Smith-Hanen, S. Effects of nonverbal behaviors on judged levels of counselor warmth and empathy. *Journal of Counseling Psychology*, 1977, *24*, 87–91.

Spiegel, P., & Machotka, P. *Messages of the body*. New York: The Free Press, 1974.

Stiles, W. B., Putnam, S. M., Wolf, M. H., & James, S. A. Interaction exchange structure and patient satisfaction with medical interviews. *Medical Care*, 1979, *17*(6), 667–679. (a)

Stiles, W. B., Putnam, S. M., Wolf, M. H., & James, S. A. Verbal response mode profiles of patients and physicians in medical screening interviews. *Journal of Medical Education*, 1979, *54*, 81–89. (b)

Stone, G. C. Patient compliance and the role of the expert. *Journal of Social Issues*, 1979, *35*, 34–59.

Svarstad, B. *The doctor-patient encounter: An observational study of communication and outcome*. Unpublished doctoral dissertation, University of Wisconsin, 1974.

Svarstad, B. Physician-patient communication and patient conformity with medical advice. In D. Mechanic (Ed.), *The growth of bureaucratic medicine*. New York: John Wiley & Sons, 1976.

Taylor, R. B., Burdette, J. A., Camp, L., & Edwards, J. Purpose of the medical encounter: Identification and influence on process and outcome in 200 encounters in a model family practice center. *The Journal of Family Practice*, 1980, *10*(3), 495–500.

Taylor, S. E. Hospital patient behavior: Reactance, helplessness, or control? *Journal of Social Issues*, 1979, *35*, 156–184.

Thurlow, R. M. Malpractice: A growing threat to doctor-patient relations. *Medical Economics*, 1969, *46*, 212.

Tumulty, P. A. What is a clinician and what does he do? *New England Journal of Medicine*, 1970, *283*, 20–24.

Waitzkin, H., & Stoeckle, J. D. The communication of information about illness: Clinical, sociological and methodological considerations. *Advances in Psychosomatic Medicine*, 1972, *8*, 180–215.

Waitzkin, H., & Stoeckle, J. D. Information control and the micropolitics of health care: Summary of an ongoing research project. *Social Science and Medicine*, 1976, *10*, 263–276.

Waitzkin, H., & Waterman, B. *The exploitation of illness in capitalist society*. Indianapolis, Ind.: Bobbs-Merrill, 1974.

Ware, J. E., Davies-Avery, A., & Stewart, A. L. The measurement and meaning of patient satisfaction. *Health and Medical Care Services Review*, 1978, *1*(1), 1–14.

Ware, J. E., Kane, R. L., Davies, A., & Brook, R. H. *An experimental approach to the validation of patient quality of care assessment.* Santa Monica, Calif.: The Rand Corporation, 1980.

West, C. When the doctor is a "lady": Power, status, and gender in physician-patient conversations. In A. Stromber (Ed.), *Women, health, and medicine.* Palo Alto, Calif.: Mayfield, 1981.

White, A. The patient sits down. *Psychosomatic Medicine,* 1953, *15,* 256–257.

14
Creating Healthy Human Contexts
Environmental and Individual Strategies

Rudolf H. Moos

For some 20 years my colleagues and I have been examining five basic questions. What are the fundamental characteristics of social environments and how can they be measured? How can we identify the most salient environmental stressors and resources in social settings and assess their impact on health? What factors determine the balance of stressors and resources in an environment and why are some individuals located in more stressful or less supportive contexts than others? What are the major coping and social resources that help individuals avoid and alleviate stress and through what processes do these resources fulfill their function? Finally, how can new knowledge about these issues be used to create more adaptive human contexts? This paper provides a progress report on our work in these areas.

Health-Related Effects of Social Environments

We began our work by developing a set of Social Climate Scales that focus on several different types of social settings (Moos, 1974b). The scales measure three underlying domains of variables characterizing these settings. Relationship dimensions assess the extent to which people are involved with and supportive of one another. Personal growth or goal orientation dimensions assess the underlying goals toward which a particular setting is oriented; for instance, autonomy in psychiatric treatment settings and task orientation in work groups. System maintenance and change dimensions deal with the degree of structure, clarity, and

This paper has evolved from invited addresses to the American Psychological Association Convention, Los Angeles, California, August 1981; The Department of Psychology and School of Social Work, Tel Aviv University, Tel Aviv, Israel, March 1982; and the Department of Psychology, University of Washington, Seattle, Washington, May 1983. Preparation of the manuscript was supported in part by NIMH Grant MH28177, NIAAA Grant AA02863, Veterans Administration Medical *and Health Services* Research funds, *NIAMD Grant AM20610,* and the John D. and Catherine T. MacArthur Foundation. John Finney and Josh Holahan made valuable comments on an earlier draft.

openness to change that characterize the setting. Dimensions drawn from these three categories have been related to such factors as complaints of depressed mood and physical symptoms, rates of illness and use of health services, and indices of treatment outcome.

The Social Climate of Health Care Settings

In an initial set of studies, the Ward Atmosphere Scale (WAS) and the Community-Oriented Programs Environment Scale (COPES) were used to relate the treatment environments of psychiatric and substance abuse programs to indices of treatment outcome. We found that psychiatric patients are more likely to drop out of treatment programs that lack peer and staff support and that are disorganized and unclear about rules and procedures. Certain aspects of the treatment setting may affect such patients differentially, depending upon their level of disturbance. Specifically, less disturbed patients do better in programs emphasizing involvement and spontaneity, while more disturbed patients need a well-structured setting that insulates them from too much interpersonal stimulation (Cronkite, Moos, & Finney, in press; Moos, 1974a). These assessment procedures have also been used to describe the quality of the social environment of medical settings such as hemodialysis (Rhodes, 1981) and oncology (Alexy, 1981–1982) units.

Living Group Social Climate and Student Health

In a subsequent project, we examined some of the stressors related to the high prevalence of physical and emotional symptoms among college students and to their use of campus health services. Living groups in which students complained of more physical symptoms than expected were seen as academically and socially competitive.[1] Students reported a lack of involvement in group activities, as well as strained relationships among peers and between students and administrators. Students in such competitively oriented residence units visited the health center more often than expected for relatively minor symptoms (such as respiratory and gastrointestinal complaints) and showed higher than expected utilization rates of psychiatric and personal counseling services (Moos, 1979a; Moos & Van Dort, 1979). In contrast, students in living groups characterized by supportive interpersonal relationships complained of fewer physical symptoms than expected, even when there was a strong emphasis on academic achievement. We have also found sharply elevated student absenteeism rates (for medical as well as nonmedical reasons) in high school classes characterized by competition and teacher control but

[1] Expected scores for symptoms and health center use were derived from a student's sex, physical symptom score on entrance to college, and propensity to use health services as indexed by the use of such services during the preceding year.

lacking a moderating emphasis on student involvement and teacher support (Moos & Moos, 1978).

Burnout and Illness in the Work Place

A third line of research has explored stressful social-environmental factors in the work place. One study of human services counselors identified more dysfunctional reactions and staff burnout in clinical settings characterized by high work pressure, disorganization, and unclear expectations, and that lacked cohesive relationships among employees and between employees and their supervisors (Berkeley Planning Associates, 1977). Another set of projects examined job milieu factors contributing to outbreaks of mass "psychogenic" illness in several industrial plants. More physical symptoms were reported in job settings characterized by high work pressure, lack of clarity and organization, and less support from peers and supervisors (Schmitt & Fitzgerald, 1982). These work environment factors also differentiated affected and nonaffected employees in the plants (Colligan, Urtis, Wisseman, Rosensteel, Anani, & Hornung, 1979; Murphy & Colligan, 1979).

Formulating an Integrative Conceptual Framework

In conjunction with a considerable body of other research (Kiritz & Moos, 1979; Moos, 1979c), the foregoing studies clarify some of the health-related effects of social-environmental stressors and resources. Indices of illness and dysfunction are higher in settings characterized by strong, competitive orientations and time pressure, by restrictive organization and control, by a lack of emphasis on personal choice and autonomy, and by ambiguity about the rules and policies governing the environment. Not surprisingly, supportive interpersonal relationships among individuals and between individuals and their "supervisors" (such as teachers and managers) seem to provide some protection against dysfunctional health outcomes. However, too much interpersonal stimulation can have problematic effects on some individuals. In addition, many individuals are not adversely affected by stressful environments, while others seem to suffer even though they are located in relatively benign settings.

These findings raise two questions. First, why do social environments develop in such disparate ways; that is, what factors affect the emergence of an emphasis on competition, on autonomy, or on cohesion? Second, why do environmental stressors affect some people more than others? More specifically, can factors such as social resources and coping processes prevent the development of stressful life circumstances and moderate their effects on adaptation when they do develop? My colleagues and I have formulated a general conceptual framework to guide us in addressing these issues.

The model shown in Figure 14.1 considers the link between stressful life circumstances and health to be affected by an environmental system (Panel I) and a personal system (Panel II), as well as by social network resources[2] and appraisal and coping responses (Panels III and IV). The environmental system includes physical and architectural features, policy and program factors, suprapersonal factors (that is, the aggregate characteristics of the individuals in a setting), and social climate factors such as competition and cohesion. The personal system includes an individual's sociodemographic characteristics and such personal resources as health status and functional ability, and self-esteem and general problem-solving skills. Stressful life circumstances include relatively discrete events of short-term duration (such as an argument with the boss at work), as well as sequential combinations of such events (separation, divorce, child having problems at school) and chronic life strains (being trapped in a highly pressured job or being relocated to a residential care facility that lacks cohesion and autonomy).

The conceptual model suggests that life stressors (Panel III) and the environmental and personal factors related to such stressors (Panels I and II) can shape social network resources and appraisal and coping responses (Panels III and IV), as well as their effectiveness (Panel V). In addition, factors in the environmental system (a high neighborhood crime rate)

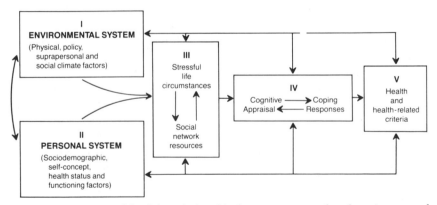

Figure 14.1. A model of the relationship between personal and environmental factors and health

[2]The term "social network resources" is used here to refer to indices developed from network analysis techniques, as well as to measures of social connectedness based on factors such as membership in social and community groups and the quality of contacts with friends and relatives. This usage is employed as a convenient way of referring to a diverse set of measures, all of which attempt to assess the characteristics of social relationships (see Moos & Mitchell, 1982).

and personal system (a vigilant perceptual style) can lead to cognitive appraisal (the perception of danger to personal safety) and coping responses (placing safety locks on windows and doors) that change the environmental system and reduce the probability of experiencing a stressful event (being robbed or burglarized). The fully nonrecursive nature of the model (that is, the bidirectional paths) reflects the fact that these processes are transactional and that reciprocal feedback can occur at each stage.

Elaborating the Environmental System

In one phase of our working we explored the relationships among the sets of factors comprising the environmental system (Panel I in the overall framework). As previously noted, we have found it useful to view this system in terms of four domains: physical and architectural factors, policy and program factors, suprapersonal factors, and social-environmental factors. A growing body of literature has indicated that these four domains can be used to characterize social settings and to explore their impacts.

Measuring the Environmental Domains

My colleagues and I used these four environmental domains to guide us in developing a Multiphasic Environmental Assessment Procedure (MEAP) to assess residential environments for older people. The MEAP consists of four main instruments, the content of which follows the conceptual organization of the four environmental domains (see Table 14.1).[3] For example, the Physical and Architectural Features Checklist (PAF) assesses such dimensions as physical amenities, safety features, and space availability, while the Policy and Program Information Form (POLIF) measures dimensions such as policy clarity, resident choice and control, and provisions for privacy. The Resident and Staff Information Form (RESIF) covers the residents' social backgrounds, degree of diversity, and functional abilities. The Sheltered Care Environment Scale (SCES) assesses residents' and staff members' perceptions of the facility's social environment for dimensions such as cohesion, independence, and organization (Moos & Lemke, in press).

Exploring the Determinants of Social Environments

Drawing on the MEAP and our prior research, we formulated some hypotheses about how these four domains of the environmental system are related to each other. Our ideas are based on the assumption that

---

[3] In addition to the four parts described here, the MEAP includes a Rating Scale that covers evaluation judgments by outside observers on four dimensions: two tap physical and architectural resources and two tap resident and staff resources.

physical, policy, and suprapersonal factors affect the stress and resource characteristics of the social environment. In turn, these social-environmental factors can mediate the influence of the other three environmental domains on health and adaptation. I illustrate these ideas here by drawing on our research on residential care settings for older persons, but we have also used them to probe the interrelationships of the four domains in educational and other settings (Moos, 1979a).

We identified orientations toward cohesion and independence as two of the most important social-environmental resources in sheltered care settings. Conversely, we believe that lack of emphasis on these factors is a significant source of stress. We hypothesized that more cohesive climates would develop in settings with comfortable, well-situated lounges and seating grouped for easy conversation. We also thought that physical features could affect resident cohesion through their impact on program functioning and on the types of people deciding to enter a setting. Settings with more available space tend to facilitate resident activities and, thereby, increase resident cohesion, while settings with better physical features attract more socially competent residents who promote a sense of autonomy. Policy and suprapersonal factors were thought to influence the social environment through similar processes.

From data from the MEAP gathered on 90 residential care settings to explore these ideas, we found that cohesion among residents, in fact, was more likely to develop in settings with more physical amenities (such as

TABLE 14.1.
Selected Variables in the Environmental System

(1) Physical and Architectural Features
Physical Amenities
Safety Features
Space Availability

(2) Policy and Program Factors
Policy Clarity
Resident Choice and Control
Provisions for Privacy

(3) Suprapersonal Factors
Resident Social Resources
Resident Heterogeneity
Resident Functional Abilities

(4) Social-Environmental Factors
Cohesion
Independence
Organization

attractive decorations in the halls), better social-recreational aids (such as lounges furnished for casual conversation), and more available personal space. Such settings also tended to have more socially competent and functionally able residents (suprapersonal factors), as well as policies providing these residents with broader personal choice and more opportunity to participate in making decisions about how the setting should be run.

Our findings showed that a climate of independence was more likely to emerge in facilities that allowed their residents more flexibility in organizing their daily lives and more control over certain aspects of facility policies. Physical features such as social-recreational aids and the degree of choice allowed by architectural factors contributed to resident independence by enabling facilities to select and recruit more socially competent residents and, thereby, to foster more flexible, autonomous policies.

Residents in settings emphasizing cohesion and autonomy participated more actively in facility-based and community-based activities and showed lower rates of utilization of health and daily living assistance services, as well as lower 3-month turnover rates. These findings indicate that architectural, policy, and suprapersonal factors enhance the development of certain types of social environments. In turn, these social environments can have important consequences for aspects of health-related functioning among older persons (David, Moos, & Kahn, 1981; Moos, 1981a; Moos & Igra, 1980). Recent studies in nursing homes have supported these findings by showing that increases in resident autonomy are linked to decreases in morbidity and mortality rates (Rodin, 1980; Schulz & Hanusa, 1979). With respect to intervention programs, it is important to recognize that the four environmental domains are interrelated and should be considered together in formulating plans to increase social environmental resources.

Coping Resources and Stressful Life Circumstances

In another phase of our research, we are using the conceptual framework to explore the role of social network and coping resources in preventing stressful life circumstances and in moderating their effects. This work involves a set of related projects on families randomly selected within specfied census tracts in the San Francisco Bay Area. The sample was drawn to explore the health and adaptation of an adult community group, as well as to serve as a sociodemographically matched comparison group for a sample of families of treated alcoholic patients. The patient and community families were assessed twice at approximately 12- to 15-month intervals with respect to variables included in four of the five sets of domains encompassed by the framework. The longitudinal results are based on over 100 alcoholic patients and their spouses and a community sample of over 240 husbands and wives (for a description of the sampling procedures and measurement methods involved, see Holahan & Moos [1981] and Moos, Finney, & Chan [1981]).

Measuring the Stress and Resource Domains

To facilitate our work, we constructed new indices of stressful life circumstances, of the quality of social network resources, and of coping responses (Moos, Cronkite, Billings, & Finney, 1983). Stressful circumstances were measured by the occurrence of negative life change events, as well as by indices of ongoing strain in family and work settings. Family strain was tapped by the degree of dysfunction shown by the individual's spouse, as indexed by factors such as the spouse's depressed mood, physical symptoms, and medical illnesses. A second index of family strain involved a measure of the physical and emotional problems of children currently living in the family. With respect to work strain, the Work Environment Scale (WES) was used to develop a composite index that assessed high work pressure, supervisor control, and lack of autonomy and clarity (Billings & Moos, 1982c). Our use of these measures reflects the belief that stressful circumstances encompass both acute events and ongoing problems in central life spheres (see Pearlin & Lieberman, 1979).

We constructed indices of social network resources by measuring not only the respondents' "connectedness" to family, friends, and community groups, but also the perceived quality of the social relationships in families and work settings. For example, the Family Environment Scale (FES) covers the supportiveness of family relationships on such dimensions as cohesion, expressiveness, and conflict, as well as for aspects of social connectedness or integration such as intellectual and recreational orientation and religious concern (Moos & Moos, 1981). Aside from tapping the major sources of work strain mentioned earlier, we used the Work Environment Scale to tap the work-related social rsources (such as involvement, peer cohesion, and supervisor support) that may prevent the development of work stress or buffer its effects (Moos, 1981b).

To assess coping responses, we divided active attempts to resolve stressful circumstances into cognitive (intrapsychic) and behavioral strategies, while separately clustering attempts to avoid the problem or reduce the emotional tension associated with the stressor (Lazarus, 1980). Active cognitive coping includes attempts to manage one's appraisal of the stressfulness of an event, such as trying to see the positive side of a situation and drawing on one's past experiences in similar situations. Active behavioral coping refers to overt attempts to deal directly with a problem and its effects, such as trying to find out more about the situation and taking some positive action. Avoidance coping refers to attempts to avoid confronting the problem (for instance, by preparing for the worst and keeping one's feelings to oneself), or to attempt to reduce emotional tension by behavior such as increased eating or smoking. We measured these coping responses by asking respondents to describe how they dealt with a recent personal crisis or stressful life circumstance. The items were classified into the three coping categories on the basis of conceptual and empirical criteria (for details, see Billings & Moos, 1981).

Exploring the Conceptual Framework

We used these stress and resource measures to explore three issues related to the overall conceptual framework (see Figure 14.1).

First, what are the direct or simple relationships between stressful life circumstances, social network, coping factors, and health-related criteria (that is, between variables in Panels III, IV, and V)?

Second, are life stressors, social network, and coping resources predictively associated with health-related criteria? Can resources attentuate the influence of life stressors on health? Moreover, are these processes affected by cross-situational influences; for example, can work stressors be moderated by family resources? To address these issues, we controlled for initial levels of personal resources and functioning (that is, variables in Panel II) and then examined relationships among variables in Panels III, IV, and V.

Third, what are the determinants of stressors and social network resouces, that is, what factors are related to the balance of stressors and resources experienced by an individual? Conversely, do personal and social resources play a preventive role; for example, do persons with more social network and coping resources subsequently experience fewer life events or strains? The analyses used to explore these issues also involved variables in four of the five panels of the framework.

These issues were examined in a number of separate projects of which only the most relevant highlights are presented here. In general, analyses were conducted separately for men and women (or alcoholic patients and their spouses). Some studies used panel analyses or multiple regression procedures, while others employed path analyses and decomposition of the predicted variance to identify the unique and shared effects of different sets of variables. A range of criteria were employed, but the results of measures of physical symptoms and depressed mood are emphasized here.

Stress and Resource Correlates of Adaptation.
We first identified some simple relationships between stressors and resources and our criteria. As expected, persons in the community sample

experiencing more stressful life circumstances (life events and family and work strains) reported more depression and physical symptoms. High levels of social network resources (both social connectedness and the perceived quality of relationships) and the use of active cognitive coping responses were associated with better health and adjustment, whereas avoidance coping was related to more complaints of depressed mood and physical symptoms. In general, we obtained similar findings among alcoholic patients and their spouses. Moreover, the severity of dysfunction among the patients was strongly associated with depression and physical symptoms among their spouses (Finney, Moos, & Mewborn, 1980; Moos, Finney, & Gamble, 1982). The importance of the source of network support was shown in the community group by the finding that the quality of personal relationships in the work environment was more closely related to the criteria among men than among women, while the quality of the family environment was especially important among unemployed women (Billings & Moos, in press; Holahan & Moos, 1982).

Stress and Resource Predictors of Adaptation.

Among the alcoholic patients, stressful events experienced during the 6 months after residential treatment were associated with more depression 18 months later, even with sociodemographic variables and initial levels of depression controlled. Conversely, the quality of family relationships (high cohesion and lack of conflict) and the extent of family social integration (intellectual-cultural and active-recreational orientation) were predictively related to less depression (Finney et al., 1980). Lack of family and work support at follow-up were still linked to the severity of depression after both initial depression and initial levels of support were considered (Billings & Moos, in press). Among spouses of alcoholic patients, the most salient stressor was the degree of dysfunction shown by their partners, which predicted depression independently of initial spouse depression, stressful events, and family resources. The use of avoidance coping also exacerbated depression among both alcoholic patients and their spouses (Cronkite & Moos, 1980; Finney, Moos, Cronkite, & Gamble, 1983).

The results for the community group showed that stressful life events and decreases in the quality of social network resources were related to increases in depressed mood and symptoms over the 12- to 15-month period of study (Billings & Moos, 1982b; Holahan & Moos, 1981). There were also some important gender differences. Though the use of avoidance coping was associated with depression among both men and women, stressful events and family social resources were more closely related to depression among women than among men (Cronkite & Moos, 1982). In fact, lack of family and work resources was linked to depression among women after initial levels of depression and resources were considered (Billings & Moos, in press). Finally, there was some evidence for a mastery or coping effect among men, in that a high initial level of stressful events was predictive of less depression than expected given the initial level of depressive complaints and subsequent life events (Billings & Moos, 1982b).

In exploring these issues, we found that salient features or work and family environments influenced each other. Men experiencing more work stress also experienced less family support, while high stress in a married woman's job setting was associated with her husband's reports of less positive family relationships and complaints of more physical symptoms. Moreover, work pressure experienced by the spouses of married alcoholics was related to higher conflict and lower cohesion in their families. Stress in the work place may adversely affect spouse and family functioning by reducing the adaptive energy necessary to manage effectively conflicts and maintain a cohesive and supportive family (Billings & Moos, 1982c; Moos & Moos, in press).

Correlates and Predictors of Stressors and Resources.
Our findings indicate that life stressors and resources are associated with changes in depression and physical symptoms. We are now considering the factors related to the occurrence of stressors, the development and maintenance of personal and social network resources, and the extent to which such resources may prevent stress. Consistent with the work of other investigators, we have found that individuals of higher social status tend to function better, to be exposed to fewer stressors, to enjoy more social resources, and to use active-cognitive and active-behavioral rather than avoidance-oriented coping strategies (Billings & Moos, 1981; Cronkite & Moos, 1980, 1982; Finney et al., 1983). In terms of levels of functioning, alcoholic patients who were less depressed subsequently experienced fewer stressful events, while spouses who complained of fewer physical symptoms subsequently experienced less dysfunction with their alcoholic partners (Cronkite & Moos, 1980; Finney et al., 1983). Conversely, more severe dysfunction among the partner and spouse, as well as negative life events and work stress, were associated with less family cohesion and expressiveness (Moos & Moos, in press).

The men in our community group who were initially more depressed also experienced more stressors than expected (on the basis of their initial level of stress) in the subsequent 12- to 15-month interval (Billings & Moos, 1982b). In turn, more stressors were associated with fewer family resources (Cronkite & Moos, 1982). Married women who were initially more depressed subsequently experienced less family support and (for those employed) less interpersonal support at work (Billings & Moos, in press; Cronkite & Moos, 1982). Moreover, the stressful circumstances experienced by a wife contributed to her use of avoidance coping strategies, related to a lack of family social resources (Cronkite & Moos, 1982). These findings begin to clarify the mutual interconnections between the sets of domains involved in the stress and coping process.

Applications to Patients with Medical Conditions

The general thrust of these findings is consistent with recent studies among patients with serious medical illnesses (Moos, in press). For example, Bloom (1982) interviewed women after surgery for breast cancer and related measures of social contact and family cohesion (FES) to three indices of psychosocial outcome. Both the lack of availability and perceived adequacy of support were linked to greater reliance on accommodative or emotion-focused coping (such as more smoking, eating, and drinking), which, in turn, was related to poorer adaptation. In a longitudinal study, Spiegel, Bloom, and Gottheil (in press) found that high family expressiveness and low conflict were predictive of better adjustment among women with metastatic breast cancer. Family cohesion and expressiveness has also been linked to "self-care agency" (motivation and reported behavior involved in self-care) among diabetic adults (Brugge, 1981), as well as to successful long-term rehabilitation among hemodialysis patients (Dimond, 1979).

Family social resources seem to foreshadow better adaptation for families of children with such chronic illnesses as anorexia, diabetes, autism, and cerebral palsy (for example, see Bristol, in press; McCubbin, Nevin, Cauble, Larsen, Comeau, & Patterson, 1982). One study compared two matched groups of juvenile anorexia patients, one with and one without the syndrome of bulimia. The family environment of bulimics was characterized by more conflict and less cohesion and organization than the nonbulimic anorectic families. These findings were consistent with evidence of greater affective instability and behavioral deviance among the bulimic patients (Strober, 1981). Family interpersonal resources have also been related to the degree of metabolic control among diabetic youth. Adolescents in poor metabolic control saw their families as high in conflict and low in cohesion compared to the families of adolescents in good and fair metabolic control. The mothers of the adolescents in poor control saw the family as less expressive and less encouraging of independent behavior (Anderson, Miller, Auslauder, & Santiago, 1981).

Family social relationships may reflect the results of an illness as well as contribute to it. In this regard, Breslau (1983) compared over 300 families of children with a serious disability (such as cystic fibrosis or cerebral palsy) with a representative group of control families in which the children were not disabled. The presence of a disabled child was related to lower family cohesion (as indexed by FES cohesion and conflict) and less family social connectedness (as indexed by FES intellectual-cultural and active-recreational orientation). The two family process factors (lack of cohesion and external stimulation) reduced the mother's feelings of mastery and increased her personal distress. These connections were stronger for black than for white families, probably because black families had fewer economic resources to deal concomitantly with child disability.

The Generality of Stress and Coping Processes

The foregoing studies constitute first steps toward an understanding of the factors involved in the development and process of adaptation to stressful life circumstances. The findings on the role of social network resources are especially robust, since they have been replicated across measurement procedures, patient and community groups, and diverse functioning and outcome criteria. Moreover, a preponderance of evidence indicates that such methodological problems as perceptual bias and retrospective falsification cannot explain the connections between social network resources and adaptation. Indices of social resources based on data other than the ill individual's perception have been related to physical illness, and some studies have shown that a relative lack of social resources can predict physical and psychological dysfunction as far as 20 years in the future (Moos, in press).

From a conceptual perspective, the framework we have used may be helpful in clarifying stress and coping processes among a variety of populations. The model seems to apply to alcohol abusers and their spouses, representative groups of "normal" men and women, and persons with serious medical conditions. Most recently, we have found the framework useful in integrating the diverse literature on psychosocial perspectives of depression (Billings & Moos, 1982a). In this regard, we believe that the salient variables and processes related to depressed mood and behavior (or other indices of functioning such as level of alcohol consumption) are analogous (albeit accentuated) to those involved in the development of "diagnosable" depression (or alcohol abuse). Since there are underlying commonalities in the development and impact of stressful life circumstances, a general conceptual framework should lead to a more comprehensive understanding of stress and coping processes.

Implications for Intervention

My colleagues and I have used a conceptual framework to explore the "determinants" of social stressors and of health-related indices of adaptation. Since each path in the framework identifies a process potentially alterable, the model is rich with implications for intervention at both the environmental and the individual level. At the environmental level, each of the four domains provides a different perspective on an environment, and each highlights specific techniques and strategies for implementing change. At the individual level, programs can be developed to enable people to use their personal resources and coping skills more effectively to avoid potential stressors and to create and sustain supportive social networks.

Environmental Assessment and Evaluation Research

Environmental assessment procedures can play a valuable role in implementing a process-oriented framework for evaluating health care programs. Until recently, most evaluation researchers were guided by an idealized paradigm in which individuals were assessed, assigned to treatment (or control) conditions, and then reevaluated at follow-up to identify treatment-related changes in their behavior and adaptation. Current trends in health psychology and evaluation research have led to a two-pronged expansion of this "summative" paradigm.

Since intervention programs typically are neither implemented as planned nor delivered to recipients in a fixed, standard manner, one area of development involves monitoring the adequacy of treatment implementation. Measures of the social environments of health care settings provide an index of the viability of new methods for delivering health services (Greenwood, Marr, Roessler, & Rowland, 1980). In one relevant study with the WAS, some patients with multiple disabilities were provided an integrated, team-oriented rehabilitation program, while others were given standard treatment. The fact that patients exposed to the enriched program reported more support from staff and other patients, more concern with their personal problems and feelings, and less staff effort to maintain control suggested that the program was implemented as intended (Crisler & Settles, 1979). A similar line of reasoning was used by Steiner (1982) to show that a therapeutic community milieu could be developed on an adolescent psychosomatic unit that combined a medical and psychiatric treatment orientation. When the treatment is being delivered as intended, the relationship between specific treatment components (including the quality of the social environment) and treatment outcome can be explored. At this point, the evaluator can help clinicians reorient the program and concentrate its resources on those components associated with better outcome.

Evaluators are also realizing that powerful extratreatment or life context factors can affect the relative benefits of health care programs. Specifically, factors such as stressful life events and characteristics of patients' families and work settings are implicated in health maintenance behavior, in the initiation and duration of treatment, and in treatment compliance and outcome. In an evaluation of alcoholism programs, for example, we found that patients' life stressors and coping resources had as strong an influence on their posttreatment adaptation as did the treatment itself. Knowledge of these life context factors can help to understand how health care programs (especially the psychosocial components) exert their effects, to monitor the process of relapse and recovery, and to guide the reformulation of treatment approaches (for further discussion, see Moos & Finney [in press]).

Changing and Improving Environments

Information derived from measures of people's actual and preferred social environments can be used to facilitate and monitor change (Moos, 1979b). For example, we have used the Work Environment Scale (WES) to help ameliorate work stress in an intensive care unit for treatment of serious burns. Unit staff were showing dysfunctional reactions (such as mild depression and physical and emotional withdrawal from patients) that seemed attributable to work pressure, confusion about unit policies, and lack of personal autonomy and support from supervisors.

Staff were assessed and provided with feedback on the WES results and on the discrepancies between their actual and preferred work milieu (Koran, Moos, Moos, & Zaslow, in press). Target areas for change were identified and a liaison psychiatrist worked with unit staff to formulate and implement changes. Staff felt that the actual work setting was closer to their preferred work setting after the intervention period. Dayshift staff were most affected by the changes in the unit and reported greater involvement and staff cohesion, as well as increases in program clarity and staff autonomy and decreases in work pressure. Improving the work environments of health care and other human services professionals is an effective first step toward improving the quality of the programs they provide for their clients (for reviews of related studies, see Moos [1979a, 1979b]). In this regard, there is evidence that the supportiveness of health care work settings may be enhanced by a well-managed, quality assurance program (Sinclair & Frankel, 1982).

Individuals can use information about the four domains of variables included in the environmental system to understand better their settings, to clarify their goals, to formulate and implement needed changes, and to monitor the results of a program of change. For instance, our findings on the factors related to the development of cohesion and independence in residential care settings can provide facility administrators and staff with guidelines by which to understand and change the social milieu. Knowledge about the "determinants" of social stressors and resources can identify directions in which change is likely to occur and indicate the types of settings most amenable to change. A focus on all four domains can help ensure that changes in one domain are compatible with system functioning, and can help develop integrated strategies involving related dimensions from different domains, such as adding physical features and instituting new social-recreational activities, both of which foster resident interaction.

Enhancing Clinical Formulations and Interventions

With respect to individual applications, the use of the conceptual framework can enhance the completeness and accuracy of clinical case descriptions. For example, we (Moos & Fuhr, 1982) have used semi-structured interviews and structured questionnaires to conceptualize the influences of the social-ecological environment on a 15-year-old adolescent girl. The girl was being counseled for school-related difficulties, but information about her classroom and family settings indicated her problems were primarily interpersonal and social rather than academic. She experienced considerable stress due to her parents' demands for academic achievement in conjunction with their inability to provide a supportive family climate. These problems stemmed in part from her parents' over-involvement in very responsible but highly stressful jobs. Our examination of social-ecological factors clarified that stressors in her parents' work settings indirectly influenced the girl's adaptation by their negative impact on the family milieu. We have recently begun to explore how such information about family and job settings can be used to facilitate the therapeutic process and enhance social resources (Fuhr, Moos, & Dishotsky, 1981).

More generally, a social ecological perspective can sensitize clinicians to the personal and environmental factors involved in the development of health problems and to the need to consider the role of coping and social resources in planning interventions. In this connection, my colleagues and I have used our framework to describe the recovery and relapse process among psychiatric patients and to examine why conceptually different interventions appear to be equally effective in alleviating psychiatric problems (Billings & Moos, 1982a; Cronkite & Moos, 1980). Since there are complex linkages between the domains shown in the framework, changes in a domain targeted by a specific treatment procedure may affect, or be affected by, changes in the other domains. With respect to depression, for example, although cognitive treatment is oriented toward modifying maladaptive cognitive schemas, it may also alleviate depression by affecting appraisal and preferred coping responses and by changing the orientation toward the development and use of social resources. Similarly, behaviorally oriented interventions, designed to improve social skills, may also affect depression by reducing stress, increasing supportive social resources, and providing new coping alternatives. By depicting the interconnections between the sets of factors involved in adaptive functioning, the framework can help health psychologists design more effective assessment and intervention procedures.

Future Directions

Although it is just a beginning, the framework we have described can help guide and integrate research in what typically are separate lines of empirical work. For instance, the model can identify commonalities and gaps in our knowledge about the influence of the weather or morbidity and mortality, of population density and crowding on illness, and of air and noise pollution on physical symptoms and mood states (Moos, 1979c). However, several methodological and conceptual issues must be addressed to make fundamental progress in these areas.

Identifying Common Dimensions of Stressful Life Circumstances

First, we must broaden our thinking about stressful life circumstances. In conjunction with the work of other investigators (Brown & Harris, 1978; Pearlin & Schooler, 1978), our research has clarified the need to consider the chronic strains and difficulties associated with various social roles (such as parent, spouse, employee) as well as acute stressful episodes in assessing stressful life circumstances. For example, we have found that negative events and chronic strains are independently related to the severity of depression reported by clinically depressed patients and their spouses, as well as to depressed mood among "normal" controls and their spouses (Mitchell, Cronkite, & Moos, in press). The conceptual and methodological overlap between acute stress and chronic strain highlights the need to develop common dimensions by which stressful circumstances can be compared. Potential dimensions include the duration, desirability, and severity of stressors, as well as the degree to which they are anticipated and controllable. It is also important to formulate ways of evaluating the degree of readjustment required by an event, for example, by estimating the extent and duration of resulting changes in an individual's daily routine.

Measuring Social Resources and Coping Processes

Secondly, to explore the context of stress and the role of preventive and moderating factors more deeply, we need to develop new procedures to assess coping and social resources. Although the complexity of stress and coping phenomena has been generally recognized, empirical work has not adequately reflected the multicausal, interrelated nature of the processes involved (for reviews of these issues, see Antonovsky [1979],

Dohrenwend & Dohrenwend [1981], and Liem & Liem [1978]). Our work emphasizes the interdependence of environmental stressors and resources, as well as of appraisal and coping responses. For example, a change in the level of stressors (such as the death of a spouse, sudden unemployment, moving to a new residence) often involves concomitant changes in social resources and in outlets for channeling coping efforts (Mueller, 1980). Furthermore, negative aspects of an interpersonal relationship can be conceptualized both as a stressful life event (increased conflict with spouse) and as lack of social network resources (feeling that one's spouse is not supportive or understanding). In addition, such life events as change of residence and job promotion may simultaneously have both stress and resource features.

A related point involves the value of tapping the problematic aspects of social ties (such as competition and conflict), as well as the potential negative concomitants of what are typically seen as social "resources." For example, cohesive relationships can place undue pressure on individuals to conform to normative expectations and can foster collective rejection and scapegoating. Network members can increase stress by precipitating crises, by convincing an individual that a crisis is more threatening than originally perceived, or by exacerbating an already severe crisis. Another issue is that the effects of qualities such as cohesion depend in part on the overall context in which a relationship is embedded. Thus, for example, family cohesion is likely to have different effects on health compliance among adolescents, depending upon whether it occurs in a context of high or low independence.

The conceptual problems in this area may be clarified by considering life stress and resource factors in conjunction with one another, and by describing some of the effects of life events in terms of changes in these factors. We are currently pursuing this issue by attempting to develop a semistructured interview to focus on stressors and resources in three health and material domains (physical status, housing and neighborhood factors, finances), and five interpersonal domains (occupational, marital, parental, extended family, and friendships and social groups). We hope to construct an Environmental Resources and Stressors Profile to summarize the data obtained in each of these areas (for reviews of existing measures in these areas, see Moos & Billings [1982], and Moos & Mitchell [1982]).

Person–Environment Transaction and Congruence

Most prior research has examined the role of coping resources without considering the personal characteristics or preferences of the individuals involved. However, the conceptual framework suggests that the impact of environmental and coping factors can depend on personal factors such as sociodemographic or personality characteristics. In this regard, Chesney and her colleagues (1981) have shown that peer cohesion may have more positive effects on individuals with a Type A than on those with a Type B behavior pattern. Since Type A's tend to be more extroverted than Type B's, it is possible that a Type A individual is congruent in a cohesive work setting, while a more introverted Type B individual may experience such a setting as aversive.

Another set of studies has focused on stressful life events, personal "hardiness" (as assessed by indices of commitment, control, and challenge), and perceived family and work support among male business executives. As expected, high perceived support from supervisors was related to less physical illness among men experiencing more stressful events (most of which were job related). With family support, however, the findings varied according to the level of hardiness of the individual. Executives low in hardiness and located in cohesive families showed higher illness scores, particularly when experiencing more stress. The authors suggest that high family support during stressful periods may contribute to a vulnerable man's alienation from his job and thus to his illness (Kobasa & Puccetti, in press). More detailed examination of such interactions is likely to prove fruitful in understanding stress and coping phenomena, especially if personal and environmental factors are conceptually linked (such as personal hardiness and environmental stress).

Understanding the Positive Aspects of Coping with Stress

Finally, although there is an association between stress and mental and physical dysfunction, most people are able to adapt successfully to problematic circumstances and many show increased morale and life satisfaction when challenged by such circumstances (Antonovsky, 1979; Chiriboga & Cutler, 1980; Lowenthal & Chiriboga, 1973). Stress is often associated with long-term growth, the development of self-esteem, and a more mature personality (Elder, 1979; Selye, 1974). Moreover, an overly "supportive" environment that lacks stimulation and challenge can lead to boredom as well as to mental and physical decline (Lawton, 1982).

In this regard, Haan (1977) reported that men and women who experienced more changes during adolescence and the early adult years were more empathic and tolerant of ambiguity in middle age. Moral development in the preadult period was fostered by ego processes that permitted stress to be experienced and resolved rather than simply negated. In addition, some persons report enhanced personal growth and integration, and a "transcendental redirection" of their lives in the aftermath of an acute health crisis (White & Liddon, 1972). Survivors of serious illness often show greater concern for and sense of community with others, a change in focus of energy from the constant pressure of work to family relationships, more realism and acceptance of life, and heightened awareness of religious and humanitarian values. We need a fundamental shift in our research designs and assessment methods to incorporate the recognition that stressful life circumstances are an inherent part of the human condition and that they can lead to greater personal effectiveness, as well as to illness and dysfunction.

Conclusion

In addition to identifying psychosocial mechanisms by which social network and coping resources can prevent and moderate stress, collaborative research is needed to explore the links between such resources and physiological and biochemical indicators that can affect disease directly. For example, social network factors (such as marital and job strain) can influence disease processes by affecting endogenous psychological factors such as depression, which may predict increased cancer risk and affect the immune system directly. Alternatively, social factors can affect illness indirectly by changing health risk behaviors such as smoking and drinking patterns (Fox, 1982; see also Holroyd & Lazarus, 1982). With improved measurement procedures and an integrated conceptual framework to guide our efforts, we can develop a deeper understanding of the environmental contexts and coping strategies related to adaptive functioning. Such an understanding can help health psychologists design more effective interventions at both the environmental and the individual level and, thereby, contribute to primary as well as to secondary and tertiary prevention.

References

Alexy, W. Perceptions of ward atmosphere on an oncology unit. *International Journal of Psychiatry in Medicine*, 1981–1982, *11*, 331–340.

Anderson, B., Miller, J. P., Auslander, W., & Santiago, J. Family characteristics of diabetic adolescents: Relationship to metabolic control. *Diabetes Care*, 1981, *4*, 586–594.

Antonovsky, A. *Health, stress and coping*. San Francisco: Jossey-Bass, 1979.

Berkeley Planning Associates. *Evaluation of child abuse and neglect demonstration projects, Vol. IX, Project management and worker burnout*. Springfield, Va., 1977. (NTIS No. PB278 466)

Billings, A., & Moos, R. The role of coping responses and social resources in attenuating the stress of life events. *Journal of Behavioral Medicine*, 1981, *4*, 157–189.

Billings, A., & Moos, R. Psychosocial theory and research on depression: An integrative framework and review. *Clinical Psychology Review*, 1982, *2*, 213–237 (a)

Billings, A., & Moos, R. Stressful life events and symptoms: A longitudinal model. *Journal of Health Psychology*, 1982, *1*, 99–117. (b)

Billings, A., & Moos, R. Work stress and the stress-buffering role of work and family resources. *Journal of Occupational Behavior,* 1982, *3,* 215–232. (c)

Billings, A., & Moos, R. Social support and functioning among community and clinical groups: A panel model. *Journal of Behavioral Medicine,* in press.

Bloom, J. Social support, accommodation to stress, and adjustment to breast cancer. *Social Science and Medicine,* 1982, *16A,* 1329–1338.

Breslau, N. Family care of disabled children: Effects on siblings and mothers. In L. Rubin, G. Thompson, & R. Bilenker (Eds.), *Comprehensive management of cerebral palsy.* New York: Grune & Stratton, 1983.

Bristol, M. Family resources and successful adaptation to autistic children. In E. Schopler & G. Mesibov (Eds.), *The effects of autism on the family.* New York: Plenum Press, in press.

Brown, G., & Harris, T. *Social origins of depression: A study of psychiatric disorder in women.* New York: Free Press, 1978.

Brugge, P. The relationship between family as a social support system, health status, and exercise of self-care agency in the adult with a chronic illness (Doctoral dissertation, School of Nursing, Wayne State University). *Dissertation Abstracts International,* 1981, *42*(11–B), 4361.

Chesney, M., Sevelius, G., Black, G., Ward, M., Swan, G., & Rosenman, R. Work environment, Type A behavior and coronary heart disease risk factors. *Journal of Occupational Medicine,* 1981, *23,* 551–555.

Chiriboga, D., & Cutler, L. Stress and adaptation: Life span perspectives. In L. W. Poon (Ed.), *Aging in the 1980s.* Washington, D.C.: American Psychological Association, 1980.

Colligan, M., Urtis, M., Wisseman, C., Rosensteel, R., Anani, T., & Hornung, T. An investigation of apparent mass psychogenic illness in an electronics plant. *Journal of Behavioral Medicine,* 1979, *2,* 297–309.

Crisler, J., & Settles, R. An integrated rehabilitation team effort in providing services for multiple disability clients. *Journal of Rehabilitation,* 1979, *45,* 34–38.

Cronkite, R., & Moos, R. The determinants of posttreatment functioning of alcoholic patients: A conceptual framework. *Journal of Consulting and Clinical Psychology,* 1980, *48,* 305–316.

Cronkite, R., & Moos, R. The role of predisposing and mediating factors in the stress–illness relationship. Social Ecology Laboratory, Stanford University and Veterans Administration Medical Center, Palo Alto, Calif., 1982.

Cronkite, R., Moos, R., & Finney, J. The context of adaptation: An integrative perspective on community and treatment environments. In W. A. O'Connor & B. Lubin (Eds.), *Ecological models in clinical and community mental health.* New York: Wiley, in press.

David, T., Moos, R., & Kahn, J. Community integration among elderly residents of sheltered care settings. *American Journal of Community Psychology,* 1981, *9,* 513–526.

Dimond, M. Social support and adaptation to chronic illness: The case of maintenance hemodialysis. *Research in Nursing and Health,* 1979, *2,* 101–108.

Dohrenwend, B. S., & Dohrenwend, B. P. (Eds.). *Stressful life events and their contexts.* New York: Neale Watson, 1981.

Elder, G. Historical change in life patterns and personality. In P. B. Baltes & O. G. Brim (Eds.), *Life span development and behavior* (Vol. 2). New York: Academic Press, 1979.

Finney, J., Moos, R., Cronkite, R., & Gamble, W. A conceptual model of the functioning of married persons with impaired partners: Spouses of alcoholic patients. *Journal of Marriage and the Family,* 1983, *45,* 23–34.

Finney, J., Moos, R., & Mewborn, R. Posttreatment experiences and treatment outcome of alcoholic patients six months and two years after hospitalization. *Journal of Consulting and Clinical Psychology*, 1980, *48*, 17–29.

Fox, B. Endogenous psychosocial factors in cross-national cancer incidence. In J. R. Eiser (Ed.), *Social psychology and behavioral medicine*. New York: Wiley, 1982.

Fuhr, R., Moos, R., & Dishotsky, N. The use of family assessment and feedback in ongoing family therapy. *American Journal of Family Therapy*, 1981, *9*, 24–36.

Greenwood, R., Marr, J., Roessler, R., & Rowland, P. The social climate of a rehabilitation center: Implications for organizational development. *Journal of Rehabilitation Administration*, 1980, *4*, 20–24.

Haan, N. *Coping and defending: Processes of self-environment organization*. New York: Academic Press, 1977.

Holahan, C. J., & Moos, R. Social support and psychological distress: A longitudinal analysis. *Journal of Abnormal Psychology*, 1981, *90*, 365–370.

Holahan, C. J., & Moos, R. Social support and adjustment: Predictive benefits of social climate indices. *American Journal of Community Psychology*, 1982, *10*, 403–415.

Holroyd, K., & Lazarus, R. Stress, coping, and somatic adaptation. In L. Goldberger & S. Breznitz (Eds.), *Handbook of stress: Theoretical and clinical aspects*. New York: Macmillan, 1982.

Kiritz, S., & Moos, R. Physiological effects of social environments. *Psychosomatic Medicine*, 1974, *36*, 96–114.

Kobasa, S. C., & Puccetti, M. C. Personality and social resources in stress-resistance. *Journal of Personality and Social Psychology*, in press.

Koran, L., Moos, R., Moos, B., & Zaslow, M. Changing hospital work environments: An example of a burn unit. *General Hospital Psychiatry*, in press.

Lawton, M. P. Competence, environmental press, and the adaptation of older people. In M. P. Lawton, P. G. Windley, & T. O. Byerts (Eds.), *Aging and the environment: Theoretical approaches*. New York: Springer, 1982.

Lazarus, R. The stress and coping paradigm. In C. Eisdorfer, D. Cohen, A. Kleinman, & P. Maxim (Eds.), *Theoretical bases in psychopathology*. New York: Spectrum, 1980.

Liem, R., & Liem, J. Social class and mental illness reconsidered: The role of economic stress and social support. *Journal of Health and Social Behavior*, 1978, *19*, 139–156.

Lowenthal, M. F., & Chiriboga, D. Social stress and adaptation: Toward a life course perspective. In C. Eisdorfer & M. P. Lawton (Eds.), *The psychology of adult development and aging*. Washington, D.C.: American Psychological Association, 1973.

McCubbin, H., Nevin, R., Cauble, A., Larsen, A., Comeau, J., & Patterson, J. Family coping with chronic illness: The case of cerebral palsy. In H. McCubbin, A. Cauble, & J. Patterson (Eds.), *Family stress, coping, and social support*. Springfield, Ill.: C. C. Thomas, 1982.

Mitchell, R., Cronkite, R., & Moos, R. Stress, coping and depression among married couples. *Journal of Abnormal Psychology*, in press.

Moos, R. *Evaluating treatment environments*. New York: John Wiley, 1974.(a)

Moos, R. *The Social Climate Scales: An overview*. Palo Alto, Calif.: Consulting Psychologists Press, 1974. (b)

Moos, R. *Evaluating educational environments: Procedures, measures, findings and policy implications*. San Francisco: Jossey-Bass, 1979. (a)

Moos, R. Improving social settings by social climate measurement and feedback.

In R. Munoz, L. Snowden, & J. Kelley (Eds.), *Social and psychological research in community settings.* San Francisco: Jossey-Bass, 1979. (b)

Moos, R. Social-ecological perspectives on health. In G. Stone, F. Cohen, & N. Adler (Eds.), *Health psychology: A handbook.* San Francisco: Jossey-Bass, 1979. (c)

Moos, R. Environmental choice and control in community care settings for older people. *Journal of Applied Social Psychology,* 1981, *11,* 23–43. (a)

Moos, R. *Group Environment Scale manual.* Palo Alto, Calif.: Consulting Psychologists Press, 1981. (b)

Moos, R. Evaluating social resources in community and health care contexts. In P. Karoly (Ed.), *Measurement strategies in health psychology.* New York: Wiley, in press.

Moos, R. & Billings, A. Conceptualizing and measuring coping resources and processes. In L. Goldberger & S. Breznitz (Eds.), *Handbook of stress: Theoretical and clinical aspects.* New York: Macmillan, 1982.

Moos, R., Cronkite, R., Billings, A., & Finney, J. *The Health and Daily Living Form manual.* Social Ecology Laboratory, Stanford University and Veterans Administration Medical Center, Palo Alto, Calif., 1983.

Moos, R., & Finney, J. The expanding scope of alcoholism treatment evaluation. *American Psychologist,* in press.

Moos, R., Finney, J., & Chan, D. The process of recovery from alcoholism: I. Comparing alcoholic patients and matched community controls. *Journal of Studies on Alcohol,* 1981, *42,* 383–402.

Moos, R., Finney, J., & Gamble, W. The process of recovery from alcoholism: II. Comparing spouses of alcoholic patients and spouses of matched community controls. *Journal of Studies on Alcohol,* 1982, *43,* 888–909.

Moos, R., & Fuhr, R. The clinical use of social-environmental concepts: The case of an adolescent girl. *American Journal of Orthopsychiatry,* 1982, *52,* 111–122.

Moos, R., & Igra, A. Determinants of the social environment of sheltered care settings. *Journal of Health and Social Behavior,* 1980, *21,* 88–98.

Moos, R., & Lemke, S. Supportive residential settings for older people. In I. Altman, J. Wohlwill, & P. Lawton (Eds.), *Human behavior and the environment: The elderly and the physical environment.* New York: Plenum Press, in press.

Moos, R., & Mitchell, R. Social network resources and adaptation: A conceptual framework. In T. A. Wills (Ed.), *Basic processes in helping relationships.* New York: Academic Press, 1982.

Moos, R., & Moos, B. Classroom social climate and student absences and grades. *Journal of Educational Psychology,* 1978, *70,* 263–269.

Moos, R., & Moos, B. *Family Environment Scale manual.* Palo Alto, Calif.: Consulting Psychologists Press, 1981.

Moos, R., & Moos, B. The process of recovery from alcoholism: III. Comparing family functioning among alcoholic and matched control families. *Journal of Studies on Alcohol,* in press.

Moos, R., & Van Dort, B. *Student physical symptoms and the social climate of college living groups. American Journal of Community Psychology,* 1979, *7,* 31–43.

Mueller, D. Social networks: A promising direction for research on the relationship of the social environment to psychiatric disorder. *Social Science and Medicine,* 1980, *14a,* 147–161.

Murphy, L., & Colligan, M. Mass psychogenic illness in a shoe factory: A case report. *International Archives of Occupational and Environmental Health,* 1979, *44,* 133–138.

Pearlin, L., & Lieberman, M. Social sources of emotional distress. In R. Simmons (Ed.), *Research in community and mental health* (Vol. 1). Greenwich, Conn.: JAI Press, 1979.

Pearlin, L., & Schooler, L. The structure of coping. *Journal of Health and Social Behavior,* 1978, *19,* 1–21.

Rhodes, L. Social climate perception and depression of patients and staff in a chronic hemodialysis unit. *Journal of Nervous and Mental Disease,* 1981, *169,* 169–175.

Rodin, J. Managing the stress of aging: The role of control and coping. In S. Levine & H. Ursin (Eds.), *Coping and health.* New York: Plenum Press, 1980.

Schmitt, N., & Fitzgerald, M. Mass psychogenic illness: Individual and aggregate data. In M. Colligan, J. Pennebaker, & L. Murphy (Eds.), *Mass psychogenic illness: A social psychological analysis.* Hillsdale, N.J.: Lawrence Erlbaum, 1982.

Schulz, R., & Hanusa, B. Environmental influences on the effectiveness of control and competence enhancing interventions. In L. C. Perlmuter & R. A. Monty (Eds.), *Choice and perceived control.* Hillsdale, N.J.: Lawrence Erlbaum, 1979.

Selye, H. *Stress without distress.* Philadelphia, Pa.: Lippincott, 1974.

Sinclair, C., & Frankel, M. The effect of quality assurance activities on the quality of mental health services. *Quality Review Bulletin,* 1982, *8,* 7–15.

Spiegel, D., Bloom, J., & Gottheil, E. Family environment as a predictor of adjustment to metastatic carcinoma. *Journal of Psychosocial Oncology,* in press.

Steiner, H. The sociotherapeutic environment of a child psychosomatic ward. *Child Psychiatry and Human Development,* 1982, *13,* 71–78.

Strober, M. The significance of bulimia in juvenile anorexia nervosa: An exploration of possible etiologic factors. *International Journal of Eating Disorders,* 1981, *1,* 28–43.

White, R., & Liddon, S. Ten survivors of cardiac arrest. *Psychiatry and Medicine,* 1972, *3,* 219–225.

15
Back Pain, Compensation, and Public Policy

Wilbert E. Fordyce

Introduction

An aspect of prevention not often recognized concerns events that turn otherwise short-term problems into long-term ones. The case of clinical pain is an example. The problem of clinical pain usually should be short-term. In some instances, however, as will be illustrated, both health care strategies and public policy operate to make the problem persist longer than need be the case. This situation becomes a problem of prevention: of preventing the occurrence of events that unduly prolong a problem.

The impact of pain-contingent compensation on the persistence of pain has long been recognized (e.g., Beals & Hickman, 1972; McGill, 1968). If it can be shown that compensation-related factors exert influence on the persistence of the pain problem, a number of important conceptual and public policy issues must be reconsidered. The present paper will describe data bearing on the relationship between the persistence of disability and compensation issues and will consider some of the implications.

The disability category for which compensation issues apparently assume their greatest importance is chronic low back pain. The magnitude of that problem in virtually all the societies of the so-called developed world can hardly be overstated. Chronic back pain originates with injury to soft tissue or bony structures. The frequency of occurrence is high. Svensson and Andersson (1982) estimate 50 to 80% of a population will have back complaints. Most back pain problems resolve themselves in a matter of days or a few weeks; however, many do not. Hult (1954) observed that approximately 20% of a population he studied were incapacitated for periods ranging from 3 weeks to 6 months; and 4% were incapacitated for more than 6 months. Johnson (1978) reports similar data from a workmen's compensation sample. Many studies have addressed the scope of the problem (e.g., Block, 1982; Nachemson, 1976; Svensson & Andersson, 1982); however, perhaps the most graphic illustration is found in the data from the Social Security Disability Insurance (SSDI) records (Social Security Statistical Supplement, 1979).

Social Security Disability Insurance came into being in the mid-1950s. SSDI is awarded if an injured worker covered by Social Security has been disabled continuously for 6 months and is medically and, subsequently, legally adjudicated as totally disabled. These benefits are not intended automatically to continue indefinitely, however, until very recent years, once awarded, benefits have not often been terminated (Miller, 1976). Figure 15.1 compares the mean number of SSDI awards for selected categories of disability for the first 3 years of the SSDI program (1957–1959) with corresponding data for the 3 most recent years for which data are available (1973, 1975–1976). Figure 15.1 also reports the percentage increase of the population of the United States from the two most closely associated figures, 1960 and 1980, as a reference for assessing the values shown. As Figure 15.1 portrays, the percentage increase of SSDI awards for lung cancer, the second most rapidly increasing diagnostic category, was 458% in the 1970s when compared to the 1950s. The corresponding figure for back pain is 2680%. No evidence has been found indicating any even remotely corresponding increase in the incidence of back pain during that interval.

Before proceeding, a conceptual point should be made. Traditionally, pain has been viewed within the context of a Disease Model frame of reference. The assumption has been that pain is a symptom or observable manifestation of some underlying tissue, nerve, or bony structure defect. The symptoms themselves are behaviors the person displays, which cause others to conclude the person is suffering from pain. These are pain

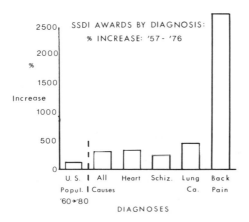

Figure 15.1. Increases in SSDI Awards in Selected Disability Categories. Source: *Social Security Statistical Supplement,* 1977–79, p. 197, Table 129.

392   WILBERT E. FORDYCE

behaviors (Fordyce, 1976b). If evaluation of the patient reporting pain fails to reveal supporting evidence for the observable pain behaviors in the form of physical findings, except for a few conditions recognized as central pain states, the inference has usually been that the expression of pain behaviors reflects some form of mental, emotional, or motivational state (e.g., psychogenic, psychosomatic, hysterical, or perhaps malingering). Since the focus here is on low back pain, the central pain states will be put aside, except to note the pain problems included in the central pain state category—phantom limb pain, trigeminal neuralgia, sympathetic reflex dystrophy, deafferentation syndromes relating to paraplegia or quadriplegia, and a few others. Chronic back pain is not implicated.

The traditional Disease Model view of pain can be seen as a closed system. The assumption is that the events of interest, the manifestations of pain via symptoms or pain behaviors, are causally related to events within the body and not without; hence, the term closed system.

In recent years, pain has also been viewed from the perspective of behavioral science (e.g., Fordyce, 1976b. Fordyce, Fowler, Lehmann, & DeLateur, 1968; Roberts & Reinhardt, 1980). The behavioral perspective of pain can be characterized briefly as based on the observation that pain behaviors are behavior. As such, they are subject to the factors that influence all behavior. Chief among these factors are conditioned stimuli and contingent consequences or reinforcement. Those events—conditioned stimuli and contingent consequences—may, and typically do, reside outside the organism. If these factors have the capacity to elicit or maintain pain behaviors, and it has been shown that they do (e.g., Block, 1982; Follick, Zitter, & Ahern, 1982; Fordyce, Fowler, Lehmann, DeLateur, Sand, & Trieschmann, 1973; Roberts & Reinhardt, 1980), it becomes necessary to recognize that pain is an open system. Events critical to the occurrence/nonoccurrence of pain behaviors exist outside the organism. They must be taken into account to understand the nature of pain problems.

The implications of viewing pain as an open system clearly are of considerable importance. The data described below help document this importance.

The necessity of distinguishing acute or recent onset from chronic pain has often been stated (e.g., Fordyce, 1976b; Sternbach, 1974). Learning or conditioning effects on the occurrence and persistence of pain behaviors could play a more important role in chronic pain because greater opportunity for conditioning exists. However, experience prior to an injury and the awareness of pain behavior contingent consequences could play a role in acute pain as well. In one study with acute back pain patients, Fordyce, Brockway, Bergman, Spengler, and Rock (1984) collected data indicating that a group of persons employed at the time of back injury, but subdivided into those eligible for wage replacement funding and those ineligible, differed markedly in the amount of time lost from work following onset of the pain problem. Figure 15.2 examines days not worked in the 6 weeks between onset and first follow-up. Those injured on the job and therefore eligible for wage replacement funding (WRF) were compared with those who, though employed, were injured in off-the-job events for which compensation was not a contingency. The WRF group averaged almost three times as many days off work because of the pain problem. Comparison of the back examinations carried out at time of onset for the two subgroups indicated no differences in severity of injury. Thus, even soon after onset, contingencies external to the person appear to have had major impact on persistence of disability.

Efforts to amend the Social Security laws pertaining to the definition of compensable, pain-related disability (Grossman, 1979) led to testimony before the federal Congress on the effects of compensation on persistence of disability. The following data were prepared by John Miller (1976) in support of the congressional testimony.

The first question addressed is the impact of duration of benefits on persistence of disability. Miller (1976) studied samples of persons covered by private insurance with a 2-year limit on benefits and persons with benefits terminating upon resolution of the disability. A comparison of the percentage of health care costs during the second year of coverage to costs during the first (100%) showed that those who knew benefits would end after the second year accrued only 64% of first-year costs, whereas the indefinite benefit group continued at 100%. Clearly, antici-

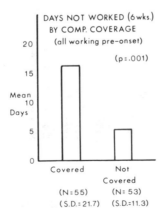

Figure 15.2. Effect of Compensation on Persistence of Disability in Recent Onset Back Pain.

pation of the end of benefits was associated with the beginning of withdrawal from disability status and reduced health care utilization.

The next question to be considered concerns persistence of disability as
a function of percentage of wage replacement funding. If wage replacement funding is higher, will there be greater persistence of disability?
Miller's data (1976), as shown in Figure 15.3, indicate that this result is
the case. At the time the data were prepared (1975–1976), the average
WRF in this country was approximately 57% for the various programs
studied. Figure 15.3 shows that those below the national average of 57%
made up a disproportionately smaller percentage of the pool of people in
disability status. The proportions remained at approximately those for
the national average until examination of those receiving more than 70%
of what was being earned before. That group made up a disproportionately high percentage of the total pool of WRF recipients (i.e., they
showed the greatest persistence of disability).

The questions of duration of benefits and percentage of WRF can be
merged by comparing, as Miller (1976) did, figures for the United States
and Holland. Miller compared data for selected diagnostic categories in
the two countries. He calculated the ratio of disability awards for 1972 to
those for 1967. The 1972 data are in the numerator; hence, the greater the
increase from 1967 to 1972, the greater the value shown. It should be
noted that in Holland in that era there was a guaranteed 82% WRF, and

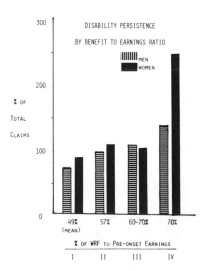

Figure 15.3. Persistence of Disability According to Wage Replacement Fund-
ing Ratio.
From Miller, J. H., "Preliminary Report on Disability Insurance," *Ways and
Means Com., 94th Congress,* May–June 1976.

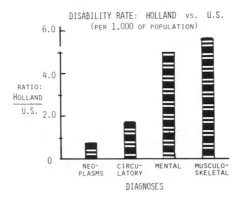

Figure 15.4. Persistence of Disability in Holland vs United States: Selected Categories.
From Miller, J. H., "Preliminary Report on Disability Insurance," *Ways and Means Com., 94th Congress,* May–June, 1976.

duration of benefits was virtually indefinite, with little reported surveillance or rechecking of function as to persistence of disability. The values shown in Figure 15.4 show clearly that for two of the conditions shown, back pain and "mental disorders," Holland showed a markedly greater increase from 1967 to 1972 than did the United States. The combination of probably greater duration of benefits and higher WRF ratios is associated with increasing numbers of awards of disability status for back pain and mental disorders, but markedly less so for other categories.

The next question to be considered concerns the impact of compensation on selected diagnostic categories. Is it equivalent? The data from Holland suggest it may not be. The data from Figure 15.5 indicate yet further that the growing problem of persistence of disability, as pertains to compensation, is found mainly in back pain and mental disorders. Miller (1976) calculated the ratio of the 1972 SSDI awards in this country to those of 1967. He limited this comparison to disability categories showing above average increases from 1967 to 1972. Figure 15.5 shows that the greater increments are clearly in back pain and mental disorders.

Implications

To recapitulate briefly, the data reported suggest that the rate of award of SSDI for back pain is increasing at a rate more than 10 times the growth of our population. The data also indicate that eligibility for wage replacement funding (WRF), duration of benefits, and percentage of WRF all may influence persistence of disability. Finally, these effects are much greater for two disability categories: back pain and mental disorders.

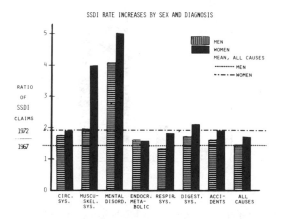

Figure 15.5. SSDI Award Trend by Selected Disability Categories: 1967 to 1972.
From Miller, J. H., "Preliminary Report on Disability Insurance," *Ways and Means Com., 94th Congress,* May–June, 1976.

What distinguishes back pain and mental disorders from other categories? When that question is viewed from a behavioral perspective, one possibility immediately arises. The criterion for determining that a condition or disability exists in both back pain and mental disorders uses assessment procedures based, in part, on verbal or nonverbal behavior expressed by the patient. Such expressions, like all behavior, are subject to influence from exogenous factors such as conditioned stimuli and contingent consequences.

Since the concern here is with back pain and not mental disorders, no further consideration will be given the latter category. It is an important problem which, hopefully, will be dealt with elsewhere.

The distinction between respondents and operants needs to be drawn before proceeding. Respondents are actions that occur reflexively in response to an antecedant stimulus. They can be characterized as under control of the antecedant stimulus, as distinguished from voluntary control by the person. Respondents generally are responses mediated by the autonomic nervous system (Miller, 1969). Operants are actions that, involving striated or voluntary musculature, are subject to control by the person. They may be initiated by an antecedant stimulus, but their occurrence is theoretically capable of being determined by decision of the person. Operants have, beyond question, been shown to be sensitive to the influence of contingent reinforcement. Their occurrence can be shown to be influenced by the consequences they meet or have met in the past. It should be noted that work in recent years with biofeedback, pioneered by Miller and coworkers (1969) and subsequently studied by many others, has shown that even autonomically mediated responses may become influenced systematically by contingent reinforcement.

Determination of a compensable back injury is based on a mixture of nonbehavioral parameters such as x-ray findings, CT scans, myelograms, electromyographic studies, and both the verbal report of the patient and the back examination. The back examination, in turn, is itself a mixture of elements. Data obtained from palpation of a spasming muscle or testing for lower extremity reflexes probably represent, for the most part, respondents (i.e., actions occurring reflexively in response to antecedant stimuli). In addition, some data represent operations (e.g., heel to toe walking, flexing of the trunk, straight leg raising). The latter are patient behaviors subject to voluntary control. Because they are operants, they are sensitive to the effects of contingent reinforcement. Additional data, of course, include all the verbal report behavior, grimacing, limping, or grasping the involved body part, the gasping or modification of breathing rate, all of which are operants. These pain behaviors undoubtedly influence the examiner's judgment about the data from the back examination, from which clinical judgments will be made (Lankhorst, van de Stadt, Vogelaar, van der Korst, & Prevo, 1982; Nelson, Allen, Clamp, & DeDombal, 1979).

In the absence of physical findings, or when findings are deemed questionable (e.g., marginal L5-S1 disc space narrowing, possible bulging of a disc) but patients report by word and deed that they are, indeed, suffering significant back pain, sometimes the physician, nonetheless, concludes there is a compensable pain problem. Such a conclusion may be based on inferences that the questionable physical findings are sufficient to warrant determination of disability. If there has been a prior surgery for the pain problem, the assumption may be that scar tissue accounts for the pain behaviors. Sometimes, without recourse to a reassessment of the physical findings data, a conclusion is made that the presence of pain behaviors in the absence of physical findings is presumptive evidence either that the workup missed a significant source of nociception or that physical findings are not essential to a determination that a persisting and disabling pain problem exists for which compensation is appropriate.

Decisions that there is a compensable pain problem in the absence of physical findings, or where their presence is either questionable or only inferential, are based on a Disease Model or closed system concept of pain. That view ignores the evidence that pain behaviors may persist for reasons unrelated to physical findings from the originating injury. Inevitably, this error results in persons being medically determined as having compensable pain problems when there may no longer be a basis for it consistent with the intent of disability law.

There is, as yet, no empirical basis for determining the extent to which the virtual explosion of rates of SSDI awards for back pain is a result of a flawed conceptual basis for medical determinations as to pain status. Apparently, there is, however, ample conceptual basis for questioning the award of compensation or disability status in the absence of physical findings for such categories as low back pain.

The physician asked to determine whether there is a compensable pain problem is placed in a virtually impossible situation. The available diagnostic tools include a back examination that confounds operants with respondents. The conceptual model of pain the physician has learned fails to consider highly relevant variables influencing the pain problem. As a caring person who must cope with a patient continuing to display suffering behaviors when no physical basis can be found, that physician may feel great pressure to conclude compensation is indicated; for, after all, that suffering person gives every indication of being unable to work because of "pain."

The physician's conclusion may be that the physical data are too limited in scope to permit the conclusion that there is no physical basis for the persisting pain behaviors. Alternatively, the conclusion may be that, even if there are no or only questionable physical findings, this suffering person cannot be expected to resume employment and that, therefore, the award of disability status is warranted. In weighing the matter, the physician is confronted with a suffering patient looking to that physician for a solution to his or her dilemma. Under those conditions, the physician's conclusion is perhaps better described as a form of social engineering, not medical judgment.

Waddell, McCulloch, Kummel, and Verner (1980) have approached this problem by developing a special set of diagnostic maneuvers, "The Waddell Tests." These tests could be characterized mainly as eliciting operants from patients for which they have little or no experience from which to anticipate consequences. The patient has little or no basis for anticipating that emitting a particular response to a Waddell test is indicative of physical findings. Waddell's data are promising for assisting in distinguishing patients whose pain behaviors are influenced by nonorganic factors. Much more study is needed, however, before The Waddell Tests should be accepted as the definitive criterion.

One implication of the foregoing apparently is that the medical and legal determination of the persistence of pain should be based on both Disease Model and behavioral science considerations. The Waddell Tests are a useful beginning. More is needed. The examining physician should be insulated from having to confound medical judgment with social engineering. Physicians should be permitted to do what they are equipped to do—namely, evaluate the Disease Model aspects of chronic pain problems. Medical judgment should be restricted to concluding the presence or absence of demonstrable physical findings.

A second implication is that the evaluation of chronic pain should be based on the concurrent assessment of physical/medical (i.e., respondent) and behavioral (i.e., operant) factors. The standard medical evaluation of a chronic pain problem can do little to assess the role of contingent reinforcement and prior conditioning on the pain behaviors of the person. The result is that a potentially significant part of the data spectrum is ignored or only casually estimated. Conversely, a behavioral analysis (Fordyce, 1976a; Heaton, Getto, Lehmann, Fordyce, Brauer, & Groban, 1982) of a chronic pain problem has nothing to say about the presence or absence of physical findings. It can only address the viability of alternative explanations for the persistence of pain behaviors beyond expected healing time.

A third implication is that the legal or adjudication process, by which compensation, disability status, or, in tort actions, the presence and extent of damages from pain, needs to take into account the implications of pain viewed in behavioral terms.

There is much work to be done to clarify further what factors influence what persons in what ways, so that pain behaviors may come under systematic control or the influence of learning or conditioning. As has been amply shown by various reviews of outcome data for treatment program based on behavioral methods (e.g., Block, 1982; Lassiter, 1982; Linton, 1982; Turner & Chapman, 1982), it is not yet possible to specify which behaviorally based interventions will influence which persons and which pain problems. There can be little question, however, that the behavioral perspective on chronic pain has demonstrated a powerful influence on our understanding of the nature of pain and what to do about it. Our legal, compensation, insurance, and health care delivery institutions have seemingly not yet caught up with that fact.

Bibliography

Beals, R. K., & Hickman, N. W. Industrial injuries of the back and extremities. *Journal of Bone and Joint Surgery*, 1972, 54-A, 1593–1611.

Block, A. R. Multidisciplinary treatment of chronic pain: A review. *Rehabilitation Psychology*, 1982, *27*, 51–63.

Follick, M., Zitter, R., & Ahern, D. Failures in the operant treatment of chronic pain. In E. B. Foa & P. Emmelkamp (Eds.), *Failures in behavioral therapy*. New York: Wiley & Sons, 1982.

Fordyce, W. E. Behavioral concepts in chronic pain and illness. In P. O. Davidson (Ed.), *The behavioral management of anxiety, depression and pain*. New York: Brunner/Mazel, 1976. (a)

Fordyce, W. E. *Behavioral methods for chronic pain and illness*. St. Louis: Mosby & Co., 1976. (b)

Fordyce, W., Brockway, J. A., Bergman, J., Spengler, D., & Rock, D. *Prevention of chronicity in acute back pain.* Manuscript in preparation, 1984.

Fordyce, W., Fowler, R., Lehmann, J., & DeLateur, B. Some implications of learning in problems of chronic pain. *Journal of Chronic Disability,* 1968, *21,* 179–190.

Fordyce, W., Fowler, R., Lehmann, J., DeLateur, B., Sand, P., & Tricschmann, R. Operant conditioning in the treatment of chronic clinical pain. *Archives of Physical and Medical Rehabilitation,* 1973, *54,* 399–408.

Grossman, H. I. Personal communication, May 3, 1979.

Heaton, R., Getto, C., Lehmann, R., Fordyce, W., Brauer, E., & Groban, S. A standardized evaluation of psychosocial factors in chronic pain. *Pain,* 1982, *12,* 165–174.

Hult, L. The Munkfors investigation. *Acta Orthopedica Scandinavica,* 1954 *42* (Suppl. 16), 174–175.

Johnson, A. D. *The problem claim. An approach to early identification.* Dept. of Labor and Industries, State of Washington, 1978. (Mimeo)

Lankhorst, G., van de Stadt, R., Vogelaar, T., van der Korst, J., & Prevo, A. Objectivity and repeatability of measurements in low back pain. *Scandinavian Journal of Rehabilitation Medicine,* 1982 *14,* 21–26.

Lassiter, P. External contingency management for chronic pain: A critical review of the evidence. *American Journal of Psychiatry,* 1982, *189,* 1308–1312.

Linton, S. A critical review of behavioral treatments for chronic benign pain other than headache. *British Journal of Clinical Psychology,* 1982, *21,* 321–337.

McGill, C. M. Industrial back problems: A control program. *Journal of Occupational Medicine,* 1968, *10,* 174–178.

Miller, J. H. *Disability insurance program* Written statement submitted to public hearings, Subcommittee on Social Security of the Committee on Ways and Means, House of Representatives, 94th Congress, second session, May 17, 21, 24; June 4, 11, 1976. Washington, D.C.: U.S. Government Printing Office 72-831-0, 1976.

Miller, N. E. Learning of visceral and glandular responses. *Science,* 1969, *163,* 434–445.

Nachemson, A. The lumbar spine: An orthopedic challenge. *Spine,* 1976, *1,* 59–71.

Nelson, M., Allen, F., Clamp, S., and De Dombal, F. Reliability and reproducability of clinical findings in low back pain. *Spine,* 1979, *4,* 97–101.

Roberts, A., & Reinhardt, L. The behavioral management of chronic pain: Long-term followup with comparison groups. *Pain,* 1980, *5,* 151–162.

Social Security Administration. *Social Security Statistical Supplement, 1977–79.* Washington, D.C.: U.S. Government Printing Office, 1979.

Sternbach, R. *Pain patients: Traits and treatment.* New York: Academic Press, 1974.

Svensson, H., & Andersson, G. Low back pain in 40–47 year old men. I. Frequency of occurrence and impact on medical services. *Scandinavian Journal of Rehabilitation Medicine,* 1982, *14,* 47–53.

Turner, J., & Chapman, R. Psychological interventions for chronic pain: A critical review (I, II). *Pain,* 1982, *12,* 1–46.

Waddell, G., McCulloch, J., Kummel, E., & Verner, R. Non-organic physical signs in low back pain. *Spine,* 1980, *5,* 117–125.

16
Prevention and Public Policy

Charles A. Kiesler

I have been asked to comment on these various papers and relate them to public policy in general, and mental health policy in particular. The two major threads here are: (1) research related to prevention or change of behavioral factors that can cause or lead to physical illness; and (2) research related to the prevention of psychiatric symptomatology after or during illness, particularly that which could fuel further illness.

These are critical issues, and one could note some premises on which to rest the discussion. First, there is rapidly increasing evidence related to bilateral linkages between health and mental health (cf., Broskowski, Marks, & Budman, 1981). This evidence suggests that to study health and mental health in isolation could be seriously misleading, particularly if one is trying to develop a national statistical base and national policy alternatives. Second, we now spend between two and three hundred billion dollars a year on health and approximately one-tenth of that on mental health. The national bill—both monetary and psychological—for physical and mental health disorders is very substantial, and anything that could prevent or lessen their impact is certainly in the national interest. Third, in spite of advances in medical technology, one could argue—and economists such as Fuchs (1974) have—that the overall quality of health in the United States is not increasing. Thus, the cost of health is increasing rapidly, but there is little evidence that the quality of the health of the nation as a whole is increasing accordingly. Further, there is recent evidence that specific habits or behaviors underlie most of the major causes of death in the United States. One can see why there has been and should be a great seriousness of purpose of the individuals presenting papers here.

My approach here will be to look at this set of problems in their policy context, interweave some themes from the particular papers presented, and then point in some detail to certain methodological issues and empirical needs that have contact with the several substantive areas already discussed.

The approach I stress is top–down policy analysis. In this approach for mental health, for example, we could ask: What is the total array of things we now do in the name of mental health, whether de facto or de jure; to whom do we do them, with what effect, and at what cost? I note that much of what has been discussed in this conference has dealt with the de facto health system, rather than the de jure.

To phrase it more generally, we could ask what are the national problems to which we should apply policy analysis? What do we already know scientifically that can be applied to a specific problem? Can we apply what we know? That is, are there specific legislative, regulatory, or value consensus actions that could be taken? What are the current policy options? What otherwise attractive policy alternatives need more research before implementation?

The top-down policy approach is to look at the overall national problem as best one can and consider potential alternative solutions. The approach can lead to some startling conclusions. For example, take mental health services: As I have noted elsewhere (Kiesler, 1980), the overall epidemiological estimates for the United States are that 15% of the population is in need of mental health services in any given year (Regier, Goldberg, & Taube, 1978). This estimate is conservative, with other epidemiological estimates running as high as 35% (Dohrenwend, Dohrenwend, Gould, Link, Neugebaur, & Wunsch-Hitzig, 1980). Fifteen percent of the population means that we have approximately 33,000,000 people in need of some mental health service or another. To tackle this problem, the nation has approximately 45,000 psychiatrists and licensed/certified psychologists potentially available to provide services. What services could they provide? Traditional psychotherapy is one option: if they provided traditional psychotherapy three times a week for a year, how would that fit with the national problem? Suppose this traditional approach were applied and all the psychiatrists and psychologists worked at it full time. The implication of this policy assumption is that they would meet approximately 2% of the national need. Indeed, other data suggest that percentage is the number of cases in need that are actually receiving specialized mental health care (Regier et al., 1978). Phrased a different way, the nation has available approximately two hours a year per person in need, given the number of doctoral level service providers available.

A bottom-up analysis can be sketched out as well. Bottom-up is the approach typically implied in NIMH testimony, textbooks, talks at the two APA's, and the like. A bottom-up analysis looks at changes at the margin. That is, one assumes as a given the status and outcome of service delivery and inspects changes since that, in this instance, time. Thus, the bottom-up analysis emphasizes improvements over previous practices or times. Top-down analysis starts with the definition of the national problem and works down to inspect the degree to which current practices are solving the problem. Bottom-up analysis suggests that we have made substantial progress in the last 20 years in mental health. That is, we have improved the training of professionals, we have increased the number of professionals available, and we have developed various more sophisticated diagnostic systems; we certainly can point to new advances in research and practice, and have a number of new insurance programs. All these statements are true and could lead one to have a very positive view of what has been happening in mental health recently.

On the other hand, from the top-down one gets quite a different view. A top-down analysis leads us to assert that the approach of traditional psychotherapy will never solve the national problem, and hence we should look more extensively at things that possibly could. Of course, I am not suggesting that we need one type of policy analysis more than the other. Clearly, both bottom-up and top-down analyses are needed, but they represent quite different perspectives on the problem and consequently inform us independently.

Psychologists and mental health professionals are rather unaccustomed to a top-down analysis of policy. For example, I recently presented an invited paper at the American Psychopathological Association on the evaluation of the effectiveness of psychotherapy for policy (Kiesler, in press [a]). I said, in essence, the following: (1) I believe the data on effectiveness of psychotherapy (e.g., Smith, Glass, & Miller, 1980). These data clearly show that psychotherapy is effective and suggests that it is cost-effective, as well. Further, meta-analysis demonstrates that psychotherapy is about as effective as psychotropic drugs for even the most serious cases. (2) However important the effectiveness of psychotherapy is as a scientific issue, it is a much less important policy issue since the technology, if we can call it that, would never satisfy the national need. (3) Therefore, we need to spend more time on policy-relevant areas, such as research regarding systems of care (e.g., HMOs versus private practice), expanding the network of care through volunteers and paraprofessionals, prevention, and behavioral treatment of related disorders. These latter issues are critical and central from a top-down analysis; they could easily be seen as more peripheral via a bottom-up analysis.

Beliefs about Science

One of the issues that bedevils us in policy analysis in health and mental health is the beliefs that even scientists develop about what is scientifically known, knowable, or feasible. The general *zeitgeist* inhibiting the study of prevention in mental health is based more on beliefs about science than on scientific findings. Many of the papers presented at this conference have clear-cut data directly relevant to national policy in health and mental health. However, I predict there will be considerable resistance to general acceptance of many of these findings, perhaps particularly among professionals. There are certain quasi-scientific myths we all develop about what is true and what is false that seem to inhibit our acceptance of new scientific information. Let me give a couple of examples.

Mental Hospitalization

Over the past few years, I have been reviewing and reanalyzing the national data base related to mental hospitalization. In writing papers and presenting them at various conferences, I noticed that people's reactions to the data were often based more on myth than on fact. Indeed, over the course of some months I came to the conclusion there was an interrelated set of such myths about mental hospitalization that professionals held rather unquestioningly. These beliefs include the following (see Kiesler, 1982a):

1. We are putting fewer people into mental hospitals.

2. Mental hospital stays are much shorter than they used to be and continue to decrease.

3. A "revolving door" exists, such that people are staying in mental hospitals for shorter periods of time but are more likely to return.

4. Mental hospitalization is effective treatment for the people utilizing the service. That is, the few people we are hospitalizing are correctly placed becaused no alternative exists to treat them more effectively.

5. Because of the small numbers involved, mental hospitalization is a fairly trivial part of overall national policy on hospitals.

I have seen these generalizations presented implicitly or explicitly in textbooks, articles, and congressional testimony. However, all these generalizations are either demonstrably false, true for only a small part of the national picture, or essentially uninvestigated. The following represents a more correct set of general statements regarding mental hospitalization.

1. Mental hospitalization is increasing well in excess of the population rate. Primary data escaping national notice were inpatient episodes in general hospitals without specialized psychiatric units. When one includes them, and there is no reason why one should not, the rate of mental hospitalization has been increasing in a linear fashion over the last 15 years or so. If one excludes inpatient episodes or general hospitals

without psychiatric units, the more typical approach, then the rate of mental hospitalization has been stable over that time period.

2. The site of hospitalization has changed dramatically, however. The public image of mental hospitalization, probably the state mental hospital and the private mental hospital, now accounts for only about 25% of the total incidence of mental hospitalization.

3. Hospital stays for mental disorders have decreased recently only in state mental hospitals and in VA psychiatric hospitals, which together account for only about 20% of total episodes and still average stays of 6 and 5 months, respectively. Other sites of hospitalization, accounting for the other 80% of national episodes, have had fairly stable lengths of stay over the last decade or so.

4. The evidence does not indicate that mental hospitalization is more effective than alternative care outside a mental hospital. In a recent review (Kiesler, 1982b), I found 10 studies where seriously disturbed patients were randomly assigned either to a mental hospital or some alternative mode of care. In all 10 cases, the alternative mode of care (the specifics of which varied from study to study) was more effective. Further, in these studies, mental hospitalization appeared to be self-perpetuating. That is, patients randomly assigned to a mental hospital were more likely after discharge to be later readmitted than patients randomly assigned to alternative care were likely ever to be hospitalized.

5. There is very little evidence, pro or con, on the notion of the revolving door phenomenon. Rehospitalization rates may be increasing for state mental hospitals, but since those hospitals are taking an increasingly smaller proportion of national inpatient episodes, the type of patient may well have changed. A recent 5-year investigation in one eastern county did not show any general increase in mental rehospitalization over that time period.

6. Mental hospitalization days is an important national phenomenon. Approximately 25% of the total hospital days in the United States are for mental disorder (as defined by diagnoses in the medical records).

Here we have a case where professionals have developed strongly held beliefs about their own field that are quite inconsistent with the data. Further, it is not simple ignorance. I even find active resistance to accepting this information. I once gave a talk describing some of these data as dispassionately as I could. After the talk, a psychiatrist came up to me, obviously agitated, and told me it was one of the most biased talks he had ever heard. I asked him how it could be considered biased since I had only described scientific data and made a special effort to be dispassionate about it. He replied that my data were "wrong." How do you know they are wrong? I asked. He replied, "My 25 years of clinical experience tell me they are wrong." Clearly, his desire to see the world in a certain way is dominating his interpretation and acceptance of scientific data.

This case is not the only one of personal beliefs pretending to be science. Sometimes what we feel is also what we think is right. Assessing what we know is a critical part of policy analysis. For example, take meta-analysis. Meta-analysis is one way of aggregating data across studies in terms of the power and reliability of a manipulation or a policy alternative. I note parenthetically that it is very important in policy analysis to assess what we know relevant to policy. There are problems with meta-analysis, to be sure, but it has its uses. The principal ingredient in a meta-analysis is the effect size. We can assess both a positive or negative effect size and ask the question, does A have a more positive effect size than B has a negative one?

I have done a little experiment recently, with highly significant findings. I asked some of my own faculty at Carnegie-Mellon University, and a half dozen individuals at this conference the same questions.

I asked two questions (not necessarily at the same time): Does psychotherapy have any positive effects? and Does smoking cause lung cancer? Uniformly, the conference individuals and my faculty responded that psychotherapy does not have a positive effect, and smoking does cause lung cancer. The data actually are that the positive effect size of psychotherapy is five or six times the negative effect size of cigarette smoking. In a sense, people are more critical of research they do not want to accept on personal and nonscientific grounds than they are of research they do want to accept on such grounds. These distortion effects are not a new issue in science but are often critical for policy analysis.

The critical ingredient here is that we must accept these cognitive flaws in our ability to think scientifically and try to develop ways of assessing scientific data for policy analysis that are not dominated by our a priori values. There is a place for values in policy analysis, of course, but that place comes after the data analysis and not before or during.

How to Begin Thinking About Policy Issues

A major question is how we begin to ask top-down policy questions in a rapidly emerging area. I suggest that the first line of questioning should include the following: What is the national problem being addressed? What specific policy alternatives are suggested by the data? What effects would they have? How confident are we of the reliability and power of the public actions to be taken? How much would they cost? Are these the only ways to accomplish these goals? Are there unintended negative consequences or side effects of the recommended actions?

Let me give a fairly detailed example of the kinds of questions one might ask. I have recently been reviewing the literature on the relationship between social support and physical and mental health. In a chapter I am still working on, I outline the kinds of questions one might ask of the data base on social support, specifically from a policy perspective. Let me go over some of these questions in this context, because one could as well plug in exercise, stress reduction techniques, or smoking cessation programs and ask very similar kinds of policy-related questions. I am suggesting that many of these questions are generalizable over several of the substantive areas discussed in the papers presented here.

Policy Issues: An Example

One popular hypothesis in the social support literature is that social support buffers or reduces the effect of subsequent stress. Consequently,

1. The first policy question might be, does social support buffer the effects of stress so as to reduce its negative impact in ways that can be measured and are socially desired? For example, does social support lead to fewer physical symptoms, less use of physical health resources (thereby decreasing the national medical bill), less incidence of specific, costly national problems such as alcoholism and absenteeism, increased productivity in the work place, less frequent mental hospitalization, or longer life?

2. If the answer to question number one is yes, is the effect causal? That is, can we decrease these undesirable outcomes? A subsidiary part of this question is, are the methods of increasing social support cost-effective?

3. How does social support, and its related guises such as self-help groups, relate to the effects now produced by professionals? That is, does social support through, say, a self-help group have an ameliorative effect on health and mental health problems similar to that of professionals? If it does have an effect, is the effect independent of professional services, or do social support and professional services interact in their impact?

4. Can social support or self-help groups substitute for professional services? Can their effects be enhanced in some way by a more active involvement by professions?

5. If social support reduces risk, what are the ways open to the public to increase social support? For example, could reduced health and mental health insurance premiums for a group less at risk (presumably those high in social support) produce an effective incentive for individuals to increase their social support?

6. What are the demographic differences (e.g., race, age, and sex) in the amount and type of social support available and used? Are some of

these groups more at risk than others? Does a specific type and amount of social support vary in its availability, attractiveness, and effect for different groups? If so, which public policy alternatives would be fair and equitable across groups?

7. Does the current style of service provision facilitate or interfere with increasing social support and its impact on physical and mental health? That is, most health and mental health services are now delivered through private practice with third-party payment, where professionals wait in a central place for a patient with a problem to come to them. Do some of the potential effects of social support relate to this essentially reactive style of service provision? If so, would more direct effects come through changing the method of service provision? A different way of phrasing this question is to ask if any effects of social support are direct, or whether they *depend* on a cold, reactive form of service provision. If the latter, would they still be observed in less reactive forms of delivery, such as holistic health?

8. Does the effect of social support work in similar ways in health and mental health? What are the potential savings to be realized by enhancing social support?

I think most of the topics discussed at this conference could beneficially be analyzed by the type of top-down approach I have detailed here for social support. I stress that, typically, when we build or generalize upward from applied or scientific psychology to public policy we are engaging in a form of bottom-up policy analysis. This type of analysis, if taken in isolation, can be quite misleading in its presumed policy implications. To counterbalance this tendency, we need also to carry out the sort of top-down analyses I have just outlined. I stress that neither type of analysis is preferred. Since they independently inform us, they should be used in conjunction with one another.

In the remainder of this chapter I want to discuss issues related to causality and some methodological issues for translating the data discussed at this conference into public policy.

Causality and Other Methodological Issues

Cause

There is an uneasy linkage between perceived causality and public policy. The question of causality runs throughout the subfields described in this conference. I am specifically referring to issues concerning extrapolating from research to public policy.

Consider policy alternatives as possible experimental treatments. To be seriously considered for public policy they must produce some necessary outcome very reliably. However, what we, as scientists, consider a deep level of causal explanation may or may not be necessary to extrapolate to public policy. Conversely, a satisfyingly deep theoretical explanation may or may not be amenable to a reliable effect in an uncontrolled setting (for instance, applying some technique to 240,000,000 people).

In a sense, we are taking Mechanic's notion mentioned earlier in this volume of precise versus imprecise knowledge and extrapolating it to a question of "precise for what?" For example, we may know exactly why, in Robin DiMatteo's paper in this book shorter physician visits lead to greater compliance to medical regimens. On the other hand, we may not know enough about other variables to translate that knowledge into policy changes. We certainly should not draw the inference that artificially shortening physician visits would lead to greater medical compliance. Similarly, we may also know exactly why a high rate of churchgoing leads to fewer health problems, but we still may not infer public policy from that conclusion. In these cases, we presumably know why an effect occurs, but that knowledge does not help us describe specific policy alternatives. On the other hand, we may not know exactly why parents staying in the child's hospital room, as described by Koocher in this volume, has a positive effect on a child's recovery from surgery. There is a host of possibilities. On the other hand, perhaps this effect is sufficiently positive and reliable to implement as a public policy.

The point is that scientific knowledge generally and knowledge about cause specifically does not necessarily lead to responsible public policy. I argue here that one can most easily and reliably detect when it does and does not through top-down policy analysis.

Pretest Score and Change

In many of these research areas there is a methodological problem regarding change, specifically, whether it occurs across the continuum. This question is basic and runs through a number of papers. Suppose we find that variable A is correlated with variable B. For example, Margaret Chesney in her paper published here found that a composite Jenkins Activity Survey score was related to heart risk. Others have found that social support is related to health. Peter Nathan discussed whether increased knowledge could lead to change in drinking habits. The basic question in these cases for public policy is, if we changed A, would B also change?

Some would say this question restates the old correlation–causality cliché. However, I mean it much more deeply than that. Let us suppose we have an experimental treatment (or some prospective study) on which we want to base public policy. If the experimental treatment reliably produces the effect (a change in A leads to a change in B), we still do not necessarily have the basis for a reasonable public policy. The critical question here depends on the degree of change along the continuum of the independent variable. For example, Haskell showed that, for some individuals (the elderly), exercise produces a main effect. However, he found the main effect was really due to a change at one part of the continuum: that is, when one went from essentially zero exercise to some exercise. For this set of data, no further positive effect of exercise was obtained for people already getting some exercise. If one based public policy on these data and tried to entice all the (elderly) population to get more exercise, it would be relatively fruitless. Any effect that occurred would be limited to a small subpart of the population. The more general case would be experiments with a positive statistical overall main effect, but in which the main effect is limited to one small segment of subjects (on the independent variable side).

As another example, there are several excellent prospective studies (Berkman & Syme, 1979; House, Robbins, & Metzner, 1982) in which people (correcting for age and risk factors) reporting a higher level of social relations and activities in 1967–1969 were significantly less likely to die during the subsequent decade. Are there policy implications to be derived from such studies? The answer is, not necessarily. The issues are complicated. For example, the empirical outcome from House et al. seems to have been determined by people with essentially no social relationships or activities. Those people have a substantially greater mortality rate. As I read the House et al. data, increases beyond that zero level had little or no effect. Thus, public policy that attempted to increase social relationships across the continuum of existing social relationships could be expected to have an effect for only a very small segment of the population. That small segment, people presumably socially incompetent, might well be totally unaffected by the sorts of experimental variations or incentives to develop more or better social relationships that would occur to a potential policy person. The general point here is that, even with excellent experimental or prospective studies, we must be careful before directly exrapolating to policy alternatives. In particular, we must have evidence of change along the whole continuum of the independent variable before attempting to design a public policy based on even otherwise impeccable experimental or prospective epidemiological data. This general methodological issue is relevant to a number of topics that have been disucssed here.

There is a great methodological need as well for specific types of outcome research. We need to look at outcomes of value to Congress and society. Such outcomes might include increases in productivity or decreases in absenteeism, fewer divorces, a greater probability of finishing school, less job turnover, fewer days in a hospital, etc. The more general issue here is that, if we are to design a public policy, it is presumably to benefit the public. What exactly are the benefits to be obtained, and how reliable are they? Does the public value them as much as the investigator? Do the benefits save us money in some way?

Further, in looking at outcome research, we must cast a very broad net. Leventhal in his paper has educated us to look for greater complexity in both the independent and dependent variables. He demonstrated some rather interesting complex interactions between types of independent and dependent variables in which A effects A' but not B, and B affects B' but not A, and A and B fit together imperfectly. These kinds of interactions will become very important as researchers more often move into the interaction between health and mental health.

We need the same kind of attention to potential complexities on the dependent variable as well. For example, in the Kaiser-Permanente studies on the effects of psychotherapy, they found that psychotherapy led to significant reduction in the cost of physical health services and a significant reduction in absenteeism (Cummings & Follette, 1968). Of the hudnreds of studies on the effects of psychotherapy, only a very small number has assessed such variables as potential outcomes. However, these two outcomes are seen to be very valuable by the public. The public's perception of psychotherapy and its usefulness would be dramatically affected if these two effects were reliably produced as an outcome variable. It is wise, in the sorts of research described in this conference, to think broadly about potential positive outcomes (or a reduction in negative ones) that might come about as a function of the implied public policy change and that could be assessed in further research.

It is also important, when considering some of the potential "technologies" explored here, that we compare the technology to other alternatives. That we need a control group or a nontreatment group is obvious to us. However, less obvious is the desirability of comparing a particular technique with other techniques. One possible comparison might be with less expensive alternatives (Kiesler, 1973) or perhaps with only part of a more complex independent variable. This type of research assesses not only whether a particular public action is desirable in absolute terms, but also whether it is the most desirable public action to accomplish the same goal.

Risks and Unintended Consequences

One must be very careful in this kind of research to assess certain risks and consequences that may not be intended. For example, Nathan in this volume has mentioned a public law allowing police officers to stop random motorists to assess whether they had been drinking. He has mentioned that this law does indeed have a clear effect on drinking behavior and is a reliable public policy. On the other hand, it seems to me there are serious risks regarding the civil rights of the populace. Stopping a motorist to check for drinking is, in my opinion, no different regarding civil liberties than searching the trunk of one's car, strip searches, and the like. They are all instances of interrupting someone's life to check for law violations when there is no evidence that one has occurred. Of course, there are tradeoffs in almost any public law; however, the drinking law would have to be incredibly successful for me to be other than utterly opposed to it—just as I would be opposed to the analogue laws. The principle is very similar. Almost regardless of the effectiveness of the law, I am unwilling to accept the unintended negative consequence of a threat to civil liberties.

In conclusion, I have found this set of papers and talks excellent. These are important areas for public policy, and there is clear promise that future policies might well be based on the data described here. However, there is much important research work to be done in trying to make the giant step from scientific and applied research to public policy. I look forward to seeing some of this work carried out in the future.

References

Berkman, L. F., & Syme, S. L. Special network host resistance and mortality: A nine year follow-up study of Alamada County residents. *American Journal of Epidemiology*, 1979, *109*, 186–204.

Broskowski, A., Marks, E., & Budman, S. H. *Linking health and mental health.* Beverly Hills, Calif.: Sage Publications, 1981.

Cummings, N. A., & Follette, W. T. Psychiatric services and medical utilization in a prepaid health plan setting: Part II. *Medical Care,* 1968, *6*, 31–41.

Dohrenwend, B. P., Dohrenwend, B. S., Gould, M. S., Link. B., Neugebaur, R., & Wunsch-Hitzig, R. *Mental illness in the United States: Epidemiological estimates.* New York: Praeger Publishers, 1980.

Fuchs, V. R. *Who shall live? Health economics and social choice.* New York: Basic Books, 1974.

House, J. S., Robbins, C., & Metzner, H. The association of social relationships and activities with mortality: Prospective evidence from the Tecumseh community health study. *American Journal of Epidemiology*, 1982, *116*, 123–140.

Kiesler, C. A. Evaluating social change programs. In G. Zaltman (Ed.), *Process and phenomenon of social change.* New York: Wiley, 1973.

Kiesler, C. A. Mental health policy as a field of inquiry for psychology. *American Psychologist*, 1980, *35*, 1066–1080.

Kiesler, C. A. Public and professional myths about mental hospitalization: An empirical reassessment of policy-related beliefs. *American Psychologist*, 1982, *37*, 1323–1339. (a)

Kiesler, C. A. Mental hospitals and alternative care: Noninstitutionalization as potential public policy for mental patients. *American Psychologist*, 1982, *37*, 349–360. (b)

Kiesler, C. A. Policy implications of research on social support and health. In S. Cohen & L. Syme (Eds.), *Support and health*. New York: Academic Press, in press. (a)

Kiesler, C. A. Psychotherapy research and top-down policy analysis. In R. L. Spitzer & J. B. Williams (Eds.), *Psychotherapy research: Where are we and where should we go?* New York: Guilford Publications, Inc., in press. (b)

Regier, D. A., Goldberg, I. D., & Taube, C. A. The de facto U.S. mental health service system. A public health perspective. *Archives of General Psychiatry,* 1978, *35,* 685–693.

Smith, M. L., Glass, G. V. & Miller, T. I. *The benefits of psychotherapy.* Baltimore, Md.: Johns Hopkins University Press, 1980.

Contributors

Margaret A. Chesney, Ph.D. Program Director and Senior Health Psychologist, Department of Behavioral Medicine, SRI International; Clinical Faculty, Department of Psychiatry, Stanford University Medical Center.

Rita Yopp Cohen, Ph.D. Assistant Professor, Department of Psychiatry, University of Pennsylvania.

Robin DiMatteo, Ph.D. Associate Professor, Department of Psychology, University of California, Riverside.

Richard I. Evans, Ph.D. Professor and Director of the Social Psychology/Behavioral Medicine Research and Graduate Training Group, Department of Psychology, University of Houston.

Michael R. J. Felix, M.A. Executive Director, County Health Improvement Program, Lycoming College, Williamsport, Pa.

Wilbert E. Fordyce, Ph.D. Professor, Department of Rehabilitation Medicine, University of Washington.

Nanette M. Frautschi, Ph.D. Coordinator of Health Psychology, West Los Angeles VA Medical Center.

William L. Haskell, Ph.D. Clinical Associate Professor of Medicine, Stanford University School of Medicine; Co-Director of the Stanford Cardiac Rehabilitation Program.

Robert S. Hirschman, M.A. Department of Psychology, University of Wisconsin—Madison.

Charles A. Kiesler, Ph.D. Professor and Dean, College of Humanities and Social Sciences, Carnegie-Mellon University.

Gerald P. Koocher, Ph.D. Senior Associate Psychologist, Children's Hospital Medical Center, Boston; Assistant Professor, Harvard Medical School.

Richard S. Lazarus, Ph.D. Professor, Department of Psychology, University of California, Berkeley.

Howard Leventhal, Ph.D. Professor, Departments of Psychology and Sociology, University of Wisconsin—Madison.

Sandra M. Levy, Ph.D. Associate Professor of Psychiatry and Medicine, University of Pittsburgh.

David Mechanic, Ph.D. Professor and Dean, Faculty of Arts and Sciences, Rutgers University.

Ruth Striegel-Moore, Dipl. Psych. Associate in Research, Department of Psychology, Yale University.

Rudolf H. Moos, Ph.D. Professor, Department of Psychiatry and Behavioral Sciences, Stanford University.

Hillary A. Murt, M.P.H. Senior Social Psychology Research Associate, Medical Care Organization, School of Public Health, University of Michigan.

Peter E. Nathan, Ph.D. Professor, Director of Clinical Training, and Director of the Alcohol Behavior Research Laboratory, Department of Psychology, Rutgers University.

Thomas R. Prohaska, Ph.D. Postdoctoral Research Associate, Department of Psychology, University of Wisconsin—Madison.

Judith Rodin, Ph.D. Professor, Department of Psychology, Yale University.

James C. Rosen, Ph.D. Associate Professor and Director of the Clinical Psychology Program, Department of Psychology, University of Vermont.

Ray H. Rosenman, M.D. Senior Research Physician, Department of Behavioral Medicine, SRI International.

Laura J. Solomon, Ph.D. Assistant Professor, Department of Psychology, University of Vermont.

Albert J. Stunkard, M.D. Professor, Departments of Psychiatry and Psychology, University of Pennsylvania.

Kenneth E. Warner, Ph.D. Associate Professor and Chairperson, Department of Health Planning and Administration, School of Public Health, University of Michigan.

Name Index

Subject Index